Can't Stop
Won't Stop

Can't Stop Won't Stop

A History of the Hip-Hop Generation

Jeff Chang

Introduction by **DJ Kool Herc**

St. Martin's Press ≈ New York

www.stmartins.com

www.cantstopwontstop.com

Design by James Sinclair

ISBN 0-312-30143-X
EAN 978-0312-30143-9

First Edition: February 2005

10 9 8 7 6 5 4 3 2 1

To Lourdes, who walks with me

To Eugene and Eleanor and Nestor and Melinda,
who haven't always understood where we were going
but packed lunch and warm clothes anyway

To Jonathan and Solomon, who will soon be leading us

Special Livication to
Rita Fecher, Benjamin Davis, Richie Perez and the Ancestors

Longing on a large scale is what makes history.

—Don DeLillo

Contents

Contents

Introduction

by DJ Kool Herc

When I started DJing back in the early '70s, it was just something that we were doing for fun. I came from "the people's choice," from the street. If the people like you, they will support you and your work will speak for itself. The parties I gave happened to catch on. They became a rite of passage for young people in the Bronx. Then the younger generation came in and started putting their spin on what I had started. I set down the blueprint, and all the architects started adding on this level and that level. Pretty soon, before we even knew it, it had started to evolve.

Most people know me as DJ Kool Herc. But sometimes when I introduce myself to people. I just tell them that my friends call me Herc. Later on, they might ask, "Are you *that* Herc?" My thing is: come and meet me as who I am. My head is not swollen, I don't try to front on people. If you like what I do, if you like me playing music or giving parties, hey, that's what I do for my friends and people. It's what I've always done.

To me, hip-hop says, "Come as you are." We are a family. It ain't about security. It ain't about bling-bling. It ain't about how much your gun can shoot. It ain't about $200 sneakers. It is not about me being better than you or you being better than me. It's about you and me, connecting one to one. That's why it has universal appeal. It has given young people a way to understand their world, whether they are from the suburbs or the city or wherever.

Hip-hop has also created a lot of jobs that otherwise wouldn't exist. But even more important, I think hip-hop has bridged the culture gap. It brings white kids together with Black kids, brown kids with yellow kids. They all have something in common that they love. It gets past the stereotypes and people hating each other because of those stereotypes.

People talk about the four hip-hop elements: DJing, B-Boying, MCing, and Graffiti. I think that there are far more than those: the way you walk, the way you talk, the way you look, the way you communicate. Back in my era, we had James Brown and civil rights and Black power; you did not have people calling themselves hip-hop activists. But these people today are talking about their era.

They have a right to speak on it the way they see it coming up.

Hip-hop is the voice of this generation. Even if you didn't grow up in the Bronx in the '70s, hip-hop is there for you. It has become a powerful force. Hip-hop binds all of these people, all of these nationalities, all over the world together.

But the hip-hop generation is not making the best use of the recognition and the position that it has. Do we realize how much power hip-hop has? The hip-hop generation can take a stand collectively and make a statement. There are lot of people who are doing something positive, who are doing hip-hop the way it was meant to be done. They are reaching young people, showing them what the world could be—people living together and having fun.

But too often, the ones that get the most recognition are those emphasizing the negative. And I think a lot of people are scared to speak on issues. "Keeping it real" has become just another fad word. It sounds cute. But it has been pimped and perverted. It ain't about keeping it real. It's got to be about keeping it right.

For example, rappers want to be so "bling-bling." Are you really living a luxurious life? Don't you have other issues? What things touch you? That's what we'd like to hear rappers speak about. Start a dialogue with people. Talk about things going on in the neighborhood.

Music is sometimes a medication from reality, and the only time you get a dialogue is when tragedy happens. When Tupac or Biggie or Jam Master Jay died, that's when people wanted to have a dialogue. It was too late. Not enough people are taking advantage of using hip-hop as a way to deal with serious issues, as a way to try to change things before tragedy strikes.

We have the power to do that. If Jay-Z comes out one day with his shirt hanging this way or LL Cool J comes out with one leg of his pants rolled up, the next day everyone is doing the same thing. If we decide one day to say that we're not gonna kill somebody senselessly, everyone will follow.

I don't want to hear people saying that they don't want to be role models. You might already have my son's attention. Let's get that clear. When I'm telling him, "Don't walk that way, don't talk that way," you're walking that way and talking that way. Don't just be like a drug dealer, like another pusher. Cut the crap. That's escape. That's the easy way out. You have the kid's attention. I'm asking you to help me raise him up.

You might be living lovely. But if you came out of the neighborhood, there was somebody who was there to guide you when you needed it, someone that said, "Son, here's two dollars." You might have beat up on the ghetto to get out of it, but what have you done for the ghetto lately? How can you come from nothing to get something, but yet the same time, still do dirt to tear it all down?

Hip-hop has always been about having fun, but it's also about taking responsibility. And now we have a platform to speak our minds. Millions of people are watching us. Let's hear something powerful. Tell people what they need to hear. How will we help the community? What do we stand for? What would happen if we got the hip-hop generation to vote, or to form organizations to change things? That would be powerful.

Hip-hop is a family, so everybody has got to pitch in. East, west, north, or south—we come from one coast and that coast was Africa. This culture was born in the ghetto. We were born here to die. We're surviving now, but we're not yet rising up. If we've got a problem, we've got to correct it. We can't be hypocrites. That's what I hope the hip-hop generation can do, to take us all to the next level by always reminding us: It ain't about keeping real, it's about keeping it right.

Prelude

Generations are fictions.

The act of determining a group of people by imposing a beginning and ending date around them is a way to impose a narrative. They are interesting and necessary fictions because they allow claims to be staked around ideas. But generations are fictions nonetheless, often created simply to suit the needs of demographers, journalists, futurists, and marketers.

In 1990, Neil Howe and William Strauss—both baby boomers and self-described social forecasters—set forth a neatly parsed theory of American generations in their book, *Generations: The History of America's Future, 1584 to 2069*. They named their own generation "Prophets," idealists who came of age during a period of "Awakening," and their children's generation "Heroes," who, nurtured by their spiritually attuned parents, would restore America to a "High" era. In between were "Nomads" inhabiting a present they described as an "Unraveling." What Howe and Strauss's self-flattering theory lacked in explanatory power, it made up for with the luck of good timing. The release of *Generations* intersected with the media's discovery of "Generation X," a name taken from the title of a book by Douglas Coupland that seemed to sum up for boomers the mystery of the emerging cohort.

Howe and Strauss's book was pitched as a peek into the future. Cycles of history, they argued, proceed from generational cycles, giving them the power to prophesize the future. Certainly history loops. But generations are fictions used in larger struggles over power.

There is nothing more ancient than telling stories about generational difference. A generation is usually named and framed first by the one immediately preceding it. The story is written in the words of shock and outrage that accompany two revelations: "Whoa, I'm getting old," and, "Damn, who are these kids?"

Boomers seem to have had great difficulty imagining what could come after themselves. It was a boomer who invented that unfortunate formulation: "the end of history." By comparison, everything that came after would appear as a decline, a simplification, a corruption.

Up until recently, our generation has mainly been defined by the prefix "post-." We have been post–civil rights, postmodern, poststructural, postfeminist, post-Black, post-soul. We're the poster children of "post-," the leftovers in the dirty kitchen of yesterday's feast. We have been the Baby Boom Echo. (Is Baby Boom Narcissus in the house?) We have been Generation X. Now they even talk about Generation Y. And why? Probably because Y comes after X.

And so, by the mid-1990s, many young writers—sick of what Howe and Strauss and their peers had wrought—took to calling themselves "the Hip-Hop Generation." In 2002, in an important book, *The Hip-Hop Generation: Young Blacks and The Crisis in African American Culture,* Bakari Kitwana forged a narrow definition—African Americans born between 1965 and 1984—a period bracketed by the passage of the Civil Rights Act and the assassination of Malcolm X on one end and hip-hop's global takeover during the peak of the Reagan/Bush era at the other.

Kitwana grappled with the implications of the gap between Blacks who came of age during the Civil Rights and Black Power movements and those who came of age with hip-hop. His point was simple: a community cannot have a useful discussion about racial progress without first taking account of the facts of change.

Folks got bogged down once again in the details. How could one accept a definition of a Hip-Hop Generation which excluded the culture's pioneers, like Kool Herc and Afrika Bambaataa, for being born too early? Or one that excluded those who had come to claim and transform hip-hop culture, but were not Black or born in America? Exactly when a Hip-Hop Generation began and whom it includes remains, quite appropriately, a contested question.

My own feeling is that the idea of the Hip-Hop Generation brings together time and race, place and polyculturalism, hot beats and hybridity. It describes the turn from politics to culture, the process of entropy and reconstruction. It captures the collective hopes and nightmares, ambitions and failures of those who would otherwise be described as "post-this" or "post-that."

So, you ask, when does the Hip-Hop Generation begin? After DJ Kool Herc and Afrika Bambaataa. Whom does it include? Anyone who is down. When does it end? When the next generation tells us it's over.

This is a nonfiction history of a fiction—a history, some mystery and certainly no prophecy. It's but one version, this dub history—a gift from those who have illuminated and inspired, all defects of which are my own.

There are many more versions to be heard. May they all be.

Jeff Chang
Brooklyn and Berkeley
January 1998 to March 2004

And if I don't get my desire

Then I'll set the spaceships on fire

—Gregory Isaacs

Babylon Is Burning
1968–1977

"Ladies and gentlemen, there it is."
Photo © Matt Daly/Code Red/911 Pictures

The St. Athanasius school baseball team, South Bronx

Photo © Mel Rosenthal

1.

Necropolis

The Bronx and the Politics
of Abandonment

When you come to the ballpark, you're walking into a place that is all deception and lies. . . . There's nothing truthful at the ballpark. Except the game.

—Barry Bonds

It was a bad night for baseball in the South Bronx—an angry arctic wind, an ominous new moon.

The largest crowd of the year filled Yankee Stadium for the second game of the 1977 World Series, the New York Yankees versus the Los Angeles Dodgers, east coast versus west.

The Yankees were the best team money could buy. When Major League Baseball raised the curtain on free agency before the 1977 season, owner George Steinbrenner opened his checkbook and with a $3 million offer landed the biggest prize in the game, home-run slugger Reggie Jackson, the son of a Negro Leaguer who had received seven dollars a game. For the Yankees—who did not sign their first Black player until nine years after Jackie Robinson broke the color line—Jackson was their most expensive signing in history.

Manager Billy Martin seethed. He had opposed signing Jackson. He refused to attend the press conference introducing Jackson in pinstripes. As the season began, he cold-shouldered the star, sometimes benched him. When he was upset, he called Jackson "boy."

Jackson got along no better with his new teammates. Some resented his salary, even though white players like Catfish Hunter had million-dollar contracts as well. They thought Jackson too flamboyant, flaunting his blonde girlfriends in the Rolls-Royce Corniche that Steinbrenner had bought him. But it was his arrogance that finally turned them. In a magazine article, Jackson dissed captain Thurman Munson, saying, "This team, it all flows from me. I've got to keep it all going. I'm the straw that stirs the drink." Maybe he had not meant to say it that way. Maybe he was just telling the truth. Jackson's teammates stopped talking to him.

During a June game against the Red Sox, the tension finally exploded. After Jackson missed a flyball in right field, Martin angrily pulled him off the field. Jackson trotted slowly and angrily for the dugout. "What did I do?" he asked Martin.

"What did you do?" Martin barked. "You know what the fuck you did."

"I wasn't loafing, Billy," Jackson protested. "Nothing I could ever do would please you. You never wanted me on this team. You don't want me now. Why don't you just admit it?"

"I ought to kick your fucking ass!" Martin screamed.

Jackson lost it. "Who the fuck do you think you're talking to, *old man*?"[1] The Yankee coaches leaped up to restrain Martin from punching Jackson, while TV cameras rolled.

That night in his hotel room, Jackson came to tears in front of a small group of news reporters. "It makes me cry, the way they treat me on this team. The Yankee pinstripes are Ruth and Gehrig and DiMaggio and Mantle and I'm a nigger to them," he moaned. "I don't know how to be subservient."[2]

It had been thirty seasons since Jackie Robinson, playing one game, had changed another, by taking Ebbets Field in Dodger blue. The postwar thrust away from racial segregation began with the pivotal cultural moment when Robinson stepped out of that formerly whites-only dugout.

After Robinson retired, he brought his commitment to integration into politics. The 1960s had begun, the Dodgers were in Los Angeles, and Ebbets Field was sprouting boxy brick and concrete beanstalks, honoring Jackie with towering public housing projects. American politics was lurching to catch up with the changes already felt in the culture and Robinson's legacy was being openly questioned.

In 1963, one of those inquisitors was Congressman Adam Clayton Powell, who made a point of appearing at a massive Harlem rally with a firebrand named Malcolm X. A contemporary of Robinson, Malcolm had been in jail while Jackie was on the field. Both had seen the worst of America. Both wanted the best for their children. But their lives had not brought them to the same conclusions. At the heart of the issue was the age-old African-American question: Shall we fight for the nation or build our own? Shall we save America or ourselves?

Robinson denounced the congressman for aligning with the Black Muslim. "You have grievously set back the cause of the Negro," Robinson wrote in an open letter to Powell on the pages of the *New York Amsterdam News*. "For you are aware—and have preached for many years—that the answer for the Negro is to be found, not in segregation or in separation, but by his insistence upon moving into his rightful place—the same place as that of any other American—within our society."

On the same pages, Malcolm X himself responded to Robinson: "You have never shown appreciation for the support given you by the Negro masses, but you have a record of being very faithful to your White Benefactors."[3]

Later that year, in Washington, D.C., Martin Luther King Jr. gave his "I Have a Dream" speech. In Harlem, days of street protests over education and poverty gave way to nights of clashes between white police and Black youths, the start of the long, hot summers that gripped America the rest of that turbulent decade.

As the '60s drew into the '70s, King and X were gone, the well of faith and idealism that had sustained the movements against the forces of rationalization and violence drained, and a lot of Black dreams—integrationist or nationalist—simply burned. For the next generation, there would be no more water for the fires. Robinson would approvingly quote his former adversary: "Jackie, in days to come, your son and my son will not be willing to settle for the things we are willing to settle for."[4]

So there was Reggie Jackson in a finely appointed hotel room in the summer of 1977, slugging behind both civil rights and Black power, playing one game and the other. "I'm a big, Black man with an IQ of 160, making $700,000 a year, and they treat me like dirt," Jackson said. "They've never had anyone like me on their team before."[5]

Four months later, when baseball fans filed into Yankee Stadium for the World Series on that cold hungry October night, many debts of history were waiting to be redeemed. New Yorkers had never forgotten Jackie Robinson's Dodgers or forgiven owner Walter O'Malley for pushing Robinson out and stealing the team from Brooklyn. To them, the very existence of the Los Angeles Dodgers represented the triumph of greed and betrayal. But the Dodgers were like a red Corvette in a Malibu morning, a team perpetually speeding into the future. Home runs came easily to them; four of their hitters had topped thirty homers that year. Two of them were Black, two were white.

The Yanks had already taken Game One. But in this game, by the third inning, three Dodgers had already hit Catfish Hunter's pitches to the beer-drenched bleachers. In four at-bats, Jackson never even got on base. It was useless. Down by four runs, the Yankees would never catch up. The crowd turned ugly. Smoke bombs traced slow arcs in the air and firecrackers crackled off the concrete. Drunks tossed their cups over the top deck rails. Fans hurdled the retaining walls and dashed across the outfield, stopping play. Fights erupted in the stands. The winds picked up, howling in from the west.

Outside the stadium, over the right field stands, past the most secure parking lot in the South Bronx, just a mile to the east, wisps and curls of grey smoke drifted into the sky. Then the gusts caught and ashen clouds billowed. A small crowd gathered at Melrose and 158th Street for a five-alarm show, a passing distraction as ordinary as a World Series. Beyond the game, the abandoned Public School 3 was aflame and imploding.

"Ladies and gentlemen, there it is," Howard Cosell told 60 million viewers as the helicopter cameras zoomed in on PS 3. "The Bronx is burning."

Mass Movements

In 1953, the future of the Bronx could be seen along the seven-mile man-made trench cutting through it. Once an unbroken continuum of cohesive, diverse communities, the trench was now the clearing for the Cross-Bronx Expressway, a modernist catastrophe of massive proportions.

As the gray concrete slab plowed from the east into the South Bronx toward Manhattan, it left behind a wake of environmental violence. "(W)here once apartment buildings or private homes had stood were now hills of rubble, decorated with ripped-open bags of rotting garbage that had been flung atop them," the historian Robert Caro wrote. "Over the rumble of the bulldozers came the staccato, machine-gun-like banging of jackhammers and, occasionally, the dull concussion of an exploding dynamite charge."[6] These were the sounds of progress.

Forward in the Expressway's path, the Irish and Jewish families that had once occupied well-appointed, if not plush, lower-middle-class apartments had been given months to relocate, with a paltry $200-per-room as compensation. In the meantime, as they struggled to find new quarters in a city with few vacancies, they huddled in heatless, condemned buildings. The man responsible for all of this was named Moses. Robert Moses, the most powerful modern urban builder of all time, led the white exodus out of the Bronx.

It began with a master plan designed in 1929 by the New York Regional Plan Association. The business interests behind the master plan wanted to transform Manhattan into a center of wealth, connected directly to the suburbs through an encircling network of highways carved through the heart of neighborhoods in the outer boroughs. Buoyed by a post–World War II surge of government investment, Moses rose to unparalleled power. He saw his immortality fixed in the roads; they were monuments to a brutal kind of efficiency. The Cross-Bronx Expressway would allow people to traverse the Bronx from the suburbs of New Jersey through upper Manhattan to the suburbs of Queens in fifteen minutes.

In engineering terms, it was the most difficult road ever built. Caro wrote, "The path of the great road lay across 113 streets, avenues, and boulevards; sewers and water and utility mains numbering in the hundreds; one subway and three railroads; five elevated rapid transit lines, and seven other expressways or parkways, some of which were being built by Moses simultaneously."[7] More important, 60,000 Bronx residents were caught in the crosshairs of the Expressway. Moses would bulldoze right over them. "There are more people in the way—that's all", he would say, as if lives were just another mathematical problem to be solved. "There's very little real hardship in the thing."

In Manhattan's ghettos, using "urban renewal" rights of clearance to condemn entire neighborhoods, he scared off thriving businesses and uprooted poor African-American, Puerto Rican, and Jewish families. Many had no choice but to come to the places like east Brooklyn and the South Bronx, where public housing was booming but jobs had already fled. Moses's point, one of his associates said, was that "if you cannot do something that is really substantial, it is not worth doing."[8]

In his grand ambitions, high modernism met maximum density. Vast housing complexes were designed on the idyllic-sounding "tower-in-a-park" model, a concept that had been advanced by the modernist architect Le Corbusier as part of his vision of a "Radiant City." Bronx River Houses and Millbrook Houses opened with 1,200 units each, Bronxdale Houses with over 1,500 units and Patterson Houses with over 1,700 units.

To Moses, the "tower-in-a-park" model was a blackboard equation that neatly solved thorny problems—open space in the urban grid, housing for the displaced poor—with a tidy cost-efficiency. It also happened to support the goals of "slum clearance," business redevelopment, and the decimation of the tenants' union movement.[9] So in the New York area's construction explosion of the 1950s and '60s, middle-class whites got sprawling, prefab, white picket-fence, whites-only Levittown suburbs, while working-class strugglers and strivers got nine or more monotonous slabs of housing rising out of isolating, desolate, soon-to-be crime-ridden "parks."

By the end of the decade, half of the whites were gone from the South Bronx. They moved north to the wide-open spaces of Westchester County or the north-eastern reaches of Bronx County. They followed Moses's Cross-Bronx and Bruckner Expressways to the promise of ownership in one of the 15,000 new apartments in Moses's Co-op City. They moved out to the cookie-cutter suburbs that sprouted along the highways in New Jersey and Queens and Long Island. Traversing the Cross-Bronx Expressway, Marshall Berman would write, "We fight back the tears and step on the gas."[10]

White élite retrenchment found a violent counterpart in the browning streets. When African-American, Afro-Caribbean, and Latino families moved into formerly Jewish, Irish, and Italian neighborhoods, white youth gangs preyed on the new arrivals in schoolyard beatdowns and running street battles.[11] The Black and brown youths formed gangs, first in self-defense, then sometimes for power, sometimes for kicks.

Political organizations like the Black Panther Party and the Young Lords competed with these neighborhood gangs for the hearts and minds of those youths for a time, but they soon invited constant, sometimes fatal pressure from the authorities. The optimism of the civil rights movement and the conviction of the Black and Brown Power movements gave way to a defocused rage and a long exhaustion. Militants turned their guns on themselves. Curtis Mayfield, who had once sung "Keep on Pushing" for Martin Luther King Jr. and other freedom marchers, now warned of the "Pusherman." Heroin dealers, junky thieves and contract arsonists filled the streets like vultures. One Bronx cop waxed philosophical: "We are creating here what the Romans created in Rome."[12]

One official told author Jill Jonnes, "The idea always was to bypass Manhattan with the ugliness as much as possible. You had public housing and highways in the South Bronx, and then, on top of both of those, which were destabilizing enough, you added a deliberate program of slum clearance to displace the worst. You were then at the point that it all started to go downhill."[13]

Bad Numbers

Here was the new math: the South Bronx had lost 600,000 manufacturing jobs; 40 percent of the sector disappeared. By the mid-seventies, average per capita income dropped to $2,430, just half of the New York City average and 40 percent of the nationwide average. The official youth unemployment rate hit 60 percent. Youth advocates said that in some neighborhoods the true number was closer to 80 percent.[14] If blues culture had developed under the conditions of oppressive, forced labor, hip-hop culture would arise from the conditions of no work.

When the sound of automobiles replaced the sound of jackhammers on the length of the Cross-Bronx Expressway, the fuel was in place for the Bronx to burn.

Apartment buildings passed into the hands of slumlords, who soon figured out that they could make more money by refusing to provide heat and water to the tenants, withholding property taxes from the city, and finally destroying the buildings for insurance money. As one fireman described the cycle: "It starts with fires in the vacant apartments. Before you know it, it's the whole wing in the building."

The downward spiral created its own economy. Slumlords hired rent-a-thugs to burn the buildings down for as little as fifty dollars a job, collecting up to $150,000 on insurance policies.[15] Insurance companies profited from the arrangement by selling more policies. Even on vacant buildings, fire paid. Groups of organized thieves, some of them strung out on heroin, plundered the burned buildings for valuable copper pipes, fixtures, and hardware.

A fireman said, "Every fire in a vacant building had to be arson. No one lives there, and yet when we pull up, the fire's out thirty windows." He continued, "People move out. The landlord starts to cut back on his maintenance. When he stops making the profit, more and more apartments become vacant . . . and, before you know it, you have a block with no one living there."[16]

Journalists Joe Conason and Jack Newfield investigated arson patterns in New York City for two-and-a-half years and found that insurance agents made commissions based on the number and dollar amount of policies they sold. "There is simply no incentive for banks, insurance companies, or anyone else with money to invest in building or rebuilding dwellings at reasonable rents," they wrote. "In housing, the final stage of capitalism is arson."[17]

But some argued that the South Bronx presented indisputable proof that poor Blacks and Latinos were not interested in improving their lives. Daniel Patrick Moynihan, New York's Democratic senator, was heard to say, "People in the South Bronx don't want housing or they wouldn't burn it down."[18] In 1970, he had written an influential memo to President Richard Nixon, citing Rand Corporation data on fires in the South Bronx and bemoaning the rise of radicals like the Black Panthers. "The time may have come," he famously wrote, "when the issue of race could benefit from a period of 'benign neglect.' "

Moynihan would later complain that he was misunderstood, that the memo should never have been leaked to the press, that he never meant to suggest services should be withdrawn from Black communities. But whatever his intention, President Nixon had pencilled "I agree!" on the memo and forwarded it to his Cabinet.[19] When it became public, "benign neglect" became a rallying cry to justify reductions in social services to the inner cities, further fuel for the backlash against racial justice and social equality.

When "benign neglect" was inflated into pseudo-science, the results were literally explosive. Armed with unsound data and models from the Rand Corporation, city politicians applied a mathematics of destruction to justify the *removal* of no less than seven fire companies from the Bronx after 1968.[20] During the mid-1970s budget crisis, thousands more firefighters and fire marshals were laid off. As the ecologists Deborah and Rodrick Wallace would put it, the result was a "contagion" of fires.

Less than a decade later, the South Bronx had lost 43,000 housing units, the equivalent of four square blocks a week. Thousands of vacant lots and abandoned buildings littered the borough. Between 1973 and 1977, 30,000 fires were set in the South Bronx alone. In 1975, on one long hot day in June, forty fires were set in a three-hour period. These were not the fires of purifying rage that had ignited Watts or a half dozen other cities after the assassination of Martin Luther King Jr. These were the fires of abandonment.

1977

Not just another summer. The bottom point of the loop between the Malcolm X's assassination and Public Enemy's call to arms. The year of the snake. A time of intrigue and uprisings, coups and riots.

After dark on July 13, as if an invisible hand was snuffing them, the streetlights blew out. The city had plunged into a blackout. Looters took to the streets in the ghettos of Crown Heights, Bedford-Stuyvesant, East New York, Harlem and the Bronx. At Ace Pontiac on Jerome Avenue, fifty brand new cars were driven out of showroom. On the Grand Concourse, shopkeepers armed themselves with guns and rifles, but for the next thirty-six hours most would be helpless against the rushing tide of retribution and redistribution.

"That particular night, one thing I noticed," a resident would later say, "they were not hurting each other. They weren't fighting with each other. They weren't killing each other."[21]

"It was an opportunity for us to rid our community of all the people who were exploiting us," graffiti writer James TOP told historian Ivor Miller. "The things that were done that day and a half were telling the government that you have a real problem with the people in the inner cities."[22]

A thousand fires were set. Prisoners at the Bronx House of Detention blazed up three dormitories. Hundreds of stores were cleaned out.

Smoke and glass, police and thieves even got into sitcom character George Jefferson's clothes, perplexing the laugh track. In the made-for-TV version of the blackout, George left his Upper East Side deluxe apartment in the sky to protect his uninsured dry cleaning business in the South Bronx, the one where he had begun his road to the riches. "I ain't gon' clean it up," he vowed. "I'm gon' close it up." There, he confronted looters until he was mistaken for one and nearly arrested by Black cops. In the end, a Bronx resident convinced George to keep his

Black business open. It was the kind of tale of reversal that the hip-hop generation would grow up to love: what moves on up must be brought right back
down, 360 degrees.

Under Mayor Abraham Beame, mighty New York City was heading toward
massive financial ruin. In mourning the city's fallen glory, columnists had prattled
on about the broken subway system and the prostitution in Times Square. But
these were mere totems next to the magnificent destruction of the South Bronx. In
the words of one Dr. Wise, a neighborhood clinic director, the South Bronx was
nothing less than "a Necropolis—a city of death."[23]

For his CBS report *The Fire Next Door*, reporter Bill Moyers led his crew
across the East River to follow a Bronx fire company. They plunged into scenes
of chaos: burning apartment buildings emptying families into the night streets;
anxious firemen cutting away a roof to save an occupied building; neighborhood kids—many of them laughing, happy to be on television, no longer invisible—gathering on a rooftop to help firemen aim a hose at the threatening flames
of the building next door.

Moyers also returned to capture the grim aftermath: an elderly Mrs. Sullivan
waiting for a moving truck that would never come, her few remaining belong-
ings ransacked by youths as she stood on the stoop being interviewed by Moyers; a young Black mother in a Panther-styled leather jacket and bright orange
headwrap describing life with her two children in a burned building, her cold
room's only decoration a magic-markered list of the Five Percenters' Supreme
Mathematics written on the blank white wall ("7: God; 8: Build or Destroy; 9:
Born; 0: Cipher").

"Somehow our failures at home paralyze our will and we don't approach a
disaster like the death of the Bronx with the same urgency and commitment we
carry to problems abroad," Moyers concluded as he stepped out of a building
scorched black against brown brick, blue sky visible through the topmost windows. The shot pulled back to reveal a block of 100-foot ghost-shell structures
casting long afternoon shadows against each other on the desolate street.

"So the Vice President travels to Europe and Japan, the Secretary of State to
the Middle East and Russia, the UN ambassador to Africa," Moyers solemnly in-
toned. "No one of comparable stature comes here."[24]

Then, a week before Catfish Hunter's first pitch in the World Series, President

Carter emerged from a state motorcade at Charlotte Street in the heart of the South Bronx—three helicopters overhead, a passel of Secret Service agents at his side—to gaze silently upon four square blocks of dead city.

Even the gangs who had once claimed this turf—the vicious Turbans and the fearsome Reapers—were now gone, as if they had been blown to dust by the forces of history. The president stood amidst the smashed brick and concrete, stripped cars, rotting vermin, shit and garbage—his secretary of housing and urban development Patricia Harris, Mayor Beame and a small army of reporters, photographers, and cameramen wagging behind.

The president took in the devastation. Then he turned to Secretary Harris. "See which areas can still be salvaged," he said softly.

The Wasteland

Here was the unreconstructed *South*—the South Bronx, a spectacular set of ruins, a mythical wasteland, an infectious disease, and, as Robert Jensen observed, "a condition of poverty and social collapse, more than a geographical place."[25] Through the 1960s, the Bronx's prefix was merely descriptive of the borough's southernmost neighborhoods, like Mott Haven and Longwood. But now most of New York City north of 110th Street was reimagined as a new kind of "South," a global south just a subway ride away. Even Mother Teresa, patron saint of the world's poor, made an unannounced pilgrimage.

The mayor's office rushed out a report entitled *The South Bronx: A Plan For Revitalization*. "The most damaging indicators cannot be measured in numbers," the report concluded. "They include the fear that prevails among many business people in the South Bronx over the future of the neighborhood, concern over the security and safety of investments; the waning faith and sense of hopelessness that induces many of them to give up and flee to other areas."[26]

Edward Logue, an urban renewal official recruited to work in New York City after leveling some of Boston's historic neighborhoods, spun it differently for a reporter: "In a marvelous, sad way, the South Bronx is an enormous success story. Over 750,000 people have left in the past twenty years for middle-class success in the suburbs."[27]

But other wonks were less disingenuous. Professor George Sternlieb, the director of the Center of Urban Policy at Rutgers University, said, "The world can operate very well without the South Bronx. There's very little in it that anyone cares for, that can't be replicated elsewhere. I have a science-fiction vision of coming into the central city in an armored car."[28]

One mayoral official, Roger Starr, following the Rand Corporation and Senator Moynihan, articulated an end-game policy of "planned shrinkage" in which health, fire, police, sanitation, and transit services would be removed from the inner-cities until all the people that remained had to leave, too—or be left behind.[29] Already, schools had been closed and abandoned, after first being starved of arts and music programs, then of basic educational necessities.

Moses himself imagined a capstone befitting his career. In 1973, in retirement, at the age of eighty-four, he declared, "You must concede that this Bronx slum and others in Brooklyn and Manhattan are unreparable. They are beyond rebuilding, tinkering and restoring. They must be leveled to the ground." He proposed moving 60,000 South Bronx residents into cheap, high-rise towers to be erected on the grounds of Ferry Point Park. The best apartments there could have a fine vista of the sparkling, trash-filled East River, the gleaming suburbs of Queens to the east, the barbed wire and brutal towers of Rikers Island to the west, and the jets leaving LaGuardia Airport for distant cities.

Just a Friendly Game of Baseball

During the sixth game of the 1977 World Series, Reggie Jackson stepped up to the plate in Yankee Stadium. He had homered in the two previous games, bringing the Yankees to the brink of a championship, three games to two. Tonight history would call. Against three pitchers and three pitches, Jackson slammed three home runs. In dramatic fashion, the Yankees won 8 to 4.

As Yankee pitcher Mike Torrez secured the last out, thousands of fans rushed the field. They ran after Jackson, who mowed some of them down as he dashed for the dugout. They tore the seats off their moorings. They grabbed handfuls of sod and second base. They tossed flying bottles at the mounted police. Near third base, cops gave a man a concussion. Above the chaos and confusion of the mob, three words cohered: "We're number one!"[30]

In the locker room, the triumphant Jackson and Martin grinned ear-to-ear, wet with champagne. They gave each other a bear-hug. Jackson waved a gold medallion of Jackie Robinson at reporters, and said "What do you think this man would think of me tonight?"[31]

Columnist Dave Anderson caught Thurman Munson and Jackson as the celebration wound down:

"Hey coon," called the catcher, grinning. "Nice goin', coon."

Reggie Jackson laughed and hurried over and hugged the captain.

"I'm goin' down to the party here in the ballpark," Thurman Munson said, grinning again. "Just white people, but they'll let you in. Come on down."

"I'll be there," Reggie Jackson said. "Wait for me."

. . .

Thurman Munson reappeared. "Hey, nigger, you're too slow, that party's over but I'll see you next year," the captain said, sticking out his hand. "I'll see you next year wherever I might be."

"You'll be back,' Reggie Jackson said.

"Not me," said Thurman Munson. "But you know who stuck up for you, nigger, you know who stuck up for you when you needed it."

"I know," Reggie Jackson said.[32]

It was 1977. A new arrow of history was taking flight.

In Kingston, Jamaica, the reggae group Culture sang a vision of Babylon beset by lightning, earthquake and thunder. The two sevens had clashed, they warned. The apocalypse was upon Babylon.

But in their own way, the new generation—to whom so much had been given, from whom so much was being stolen, for whom so little would be promised—would not settle for the things previous generations had been willing to settle for. Concede them a demand and they would demand more. Give them an apocalypse, and they would dance.

Trenchtown youths, 1976 and 1995.
Photo 1976 © Alex Webb/Magnum Photos
Photo 1995 © Brian Jahn

2

Sipple Out Deh

Jamaica's Roots Generation and the Cultural Turn

*You know how a thing and the shadow of that thing could be in almost the
same place together? You know the way a shadow is a dark version of the
real thing, the dub side?*

—Nalo Hopkinson

In Jamaica, you drive from the wrong side of the car on the wrong side of the
road. Rounding the hill down into Montego Bay, you hug the curves on two-lane
roads. Even at rush hour, you slow for cows and goats chewing grass along the
gutter side, because apparently all the animals in Jamaica are free-range.

It's dusk on Thursday, a school night, but the youths have taken over
Mobay's narrow streets. Traffic is backed up along all of the roads into and out
of the seaside town. Even transactions at the turnaround in Sam Sharpe Square—
where unmetered taxis swoop in to drop off and pick up customers in a bewil-
dering free-for-all—are slowed by the weight of teenage bodies.

They stream through the streets like tributaries toward the ocean, where, in a
waterfront spit of dirt called Urban Development Park, ten-foot high columns of
speakers rise in a half-circle around a small stage. The pouting, Tupac-shirted
boys and the spandexed, braided girls ripple through the 6:30 P.M. commute—
concrete mixers, oil trucks, and family vans caught bumper to bumper on the
Bottom Road—and in through a small gap in a low barbed-wire fence. On the
field, they pass dice games played by kerosene lamp, higglers selling Red
Stripe and Ting. The air smells faintly of ash from mountain fires. Smoke from
dozens of portable roast-peanut and jerk-chicken carts hazes the half moon
rising.

The rest of the countryside follows. Uniformed schoolchildren swinging their book bags, young denim-skirted mothers with toddlers on arm, the barmaids and working boys stride off their shift and into the dance. The elder locksmen and the gray-haired grannys sway to the music. In the front of an earbleed-inducing bassbin tower, a turbaned Boboshanti gives an inscrutable grin, his fingers touching finger-to-finger, thumb-to-thumb in the sign of the Trinity.

Through modern Jamaican history, much more than musical vibes could be at stake in settings like these. In the dance, political fortunes might rise or fall, society made or undone. If political parties controlled jobs and turf, wealth and despair, they rarely exerted much control here. This was the people's space, an autonomous zone presided over by music men and women, a shelter of collective memory.

Tonight, while the band sets up onstage for a star-studded bill of twenty-first-century dancehall stars, the sound-system operators, housed in a series of special tents that enclose the circle of speakers, drink up and play music. Candle Sound System, the local "foundation sound," is spinning the classics. An old Bob Marley song, "Chances Are," inspires a resounding wheel-up and cries of "Big tune!" It is a thirty-year-old ballad, not danceable, but something more—a sweet echo of the post-independence years, before Marley was an international star, when his was a voice of a young nation bursting with hope and pride. Everyone, no matter their age, seems to know all the words. They sing, "Though my days are filled with sorrow, I see it—a bright tomorrow."

From his turntables, Candle's selector shifts time forward, cueing a Dennis Brown bassline. Another roar of recognition goes up, and a blast of approving airhorns. This time, hundreds of lighters raise, flickering lights over a black sea. As Brown sings the opening lines—"Do you know what it takes to have a revolution?"—the country youths release their aerosol cans into the butane. At the start of a new century, they recreate an elemental, biblical sight. Against the purple sunset, bolts of flames shoot up, tongues of fire licking up the night sky like history and prophecy.

The blues had Mississippi, jazz had New Orleans. Hip-hop has Jamaica. Pioneer DJ Kool Herc spent his earliest childhood years in the same Second Street yard that had produced Bob Marley. "Them said nothing good ever come outta Trenchtown," Herc says. "Well, hip-hop came out of Trenchtown!"

Reggae, it has often been said, is rap music's elder kin. Yet the story runs much deeper than just music. During the 1970s, Marley and the roots genera- tion—the first to come of age after the island nation received independence from Great Britain in 1962—reacted to Jamaica's national crisis, global restructuring and imperialist posturing, and intensified street violence. Seeing politics ex- hausted, they channeled their energies into culture, and let it flow around the world. They pulled global popular culture into the Third World. Their story is the prelude to the hip-hop generation, felt as a portentous shudder from the dub side. "Some are leaves, some are branches," Bob Marley had sung. "I and I a di roots."

So Long Rastafari Call You

When the 1970s opened in Jamaica, national pride was surging.

A song contest had played a major role. In 1966, Edward Seaga, a ranking conservative in the leading Jamaican Labour Party (JLP), who had been one of the first music executives to record indigenous music, instituted the annual Ja- maica Festival Song Competition. The contest supported the young island indus- try and fostered national identity by introducing and making stars of patwa-singing, ghetto-identifying artists like Toots and the Maytals and Eric Don- aldson. Long before many of his contemporaries, Seaga understood that Ja- maica was the kind of place where it was hard to tell where the politics ended and the music began.

But the economy, still dependent on the former colonial arrangements, sput- tered. Banana farming needed price supports and protection. The bauxite and tourist industries—the kind of businesses that extracted more than they put in—were growing, but had little effect on an island where more than one in three was un- employed. Here was where the optimism of official nationalism broke down.

The gospel of Rastafari offered faith, history, prophecy and redemption, a people's nationalism that countered the official nationalism. Rastafarians fol- lowed in the tradition of the Black nationalist Marcus Mosiah Garvey. Born in 1887 in the northern town of St. Ann's Bay, Garvey's mother had wanted to name him Moses. His followers in the Black diaspora of the Caribbean, North and Central America, and Africa—which, at the peak of his powers, likely num- bered in the millions—called him the Black Moses.

Inspired by Booker T. Washington's *Up From Slavery*, and moved by the debased condition of Black farmers and canal workers he met on a visit to Panama, Garvey returned to the streets of Kingston to preach Black redemption and repatriation to a united Africa. He founded the United Negro Improvement Association in 1914 to formally spread the message. "Wake up Ethiopia! Wake up Africa!" he told his followers. "Let us work towards the one glorious end of a free, redeemed, and mighty nation. Let Africa be a bright star among the constellation of nations."

Two years later, Garvey left for Harlem after followers discovered he had used organization funds to pay for his living expenses. In the United States, Garvey's fiscal weaknesses were further exploited when he became the political target of a young Justice Department official named J. Edgar Hoover. But while his reputation had been sullied, his words remained the stuff of prophecy. He had said, "We Negroes believe in the God of Ethiopia, the everlasting God—God the Son, God the Holy Ghost, the one God of all ages." And by the mid-1930s, former Garveyites found that God in the figure of Ethiopia's newly crowned emperor, born Ras Tafari—"Ras" meaning "Duke" in Amharic and "Tafari" the surname of the royal family—and renamed Haile Selassie, "The Might of The Trinity."

To the followers of Rastafari, Selassie was god made flesh, the King of Kings, the conquering lion of Judah, the redeemer and the deliverer of the Black masses who had come in accordance with Garvey's prophecy. Rastafarianism was an indigenous fusion of messianism and millenarianism, anticolonialism and Black nationalism, and it gave the cause of "Black supremacy" spiritual, political, and social dimensions. The religion found a fast following in the impoverished western Kingston ghettos, especially in the yard called Back-O-Wall, where Rastas constructed a camp of wood and tin. Through the mid-1960s, amidst frequent and constant run-ins with the colonial authorities, their influence over the tenement yards grew.

Under a musician named Count Ossie, Rastafarians learned Burru drumming, an African art that had survived from the days of slavery and had come to the Kingston ghettos after slavery was abolished. Burru centered on the interplay of three drums—the bass drum, the alto *fundeh*, and the repeater. The repeater was reserved for the best drummer, who imbued it, in the scholar Verena Reckford's words, with color and tension, protest and defiance.[1] DJs, the Jamaican term for rappers, would later mimic the play of the Burru repeaters over reggae instrumentals, echoes across time.

Count Ossie gave the Rastas a medium for their message, and the drumming spread with Rastafarianism across Kingston from camp to camp. Ossie would receive and mentor many of the most important Jamaican ska, rock steady and reggae musicians at his haven on Wareika Hill. Due in no small part to his efforts, Jamaican musicians began to blend the popular New Orleans rhythm-and-blues with elements of folk mento, jonkanoo, kumina and Revival Zion styles into a new sound.

But while Rasta thought—first in coded forms, then gradually more explicitly—spread through popular music, the authorities portrayed Rastas as bizarre cultists. Many of Jamaica's Black and brown strivers held the same opinion. As a child in Kingston, DJ Kool Herc recalls, he was told that anyone who had their hair twisted up was, in local parlance, a badman. In 1966, Rastas began to move from the margins to the mainstream of Jamaican society. On April 21, Haile Selassie came to Jamaica and was greeted by a gathering of more than a hundred thousand followers. As the plane landed, the rain stopped, which all gathered took for a sign.

"I remember watching it on TV," DJ Kool Herc recalls. "They took buses and trucks and bicycles and any type of means of transportation, going to the airport for this man who they looked upon as a god. That's when Jamaica really found out there was a force on the island.

"When that the plane came down, they stormed the tarmac," he continues. "Haile Selassie came out and looked at the people and went back on the plane and cried. He didn't know he was worshiped that strongly." The Rastas were exuberant, and their ranks swelled with new converts.

But three months later, history took another sharp turn. Seaga—then the Minister of Community Development and Welfare—was in need of a new political base. The JLP leader, former music exec, and cultural patron was an ambitious man with dangerous connections. He once faced down some hecklers at a political rally by saying, "If they think they are bad, I can bring the crowds of West Kingston. We can deal with you in any way at any time. It will be fire for fire, and blood for blood."[2]

Now Seaga fingered the Back-O-Wall ghetto, the west Kingston yard where the camps of the Boboshanti and two other Rasta sects thrived. It was an area that had voted for the opposing political party, the democratic socialist People's National Party (PNP), and Seaga wanted it cleared. So on the morning of July 12, armed police filled the air with tear gas, and dispersed the residents with batons and rifles. Bulldozers rolled in behind the police, flattening the shanties. "When the first raided camp was demolished," Leonard Barrett reported, "a blazing fire of unknown origin consumed what remained to ashes while the fire company stood by."[3]

On the site, Seaga built a housing project named Tivoli Gardens and moved in a voting constituency of JLP supporters. He recruited and armed young badmen to protect the area and expand the JLP turf, a gang that called itself, appropriately enough, the Phoenix.[4] The lines were now drawn for generations to come.

"And I can see it with my own eyes," Culture sang a decade later on "Two Sevens Clash." "It's only a housing scheme that divides." Politics, apocalypse—some reasoned—was it a coincidence the two words sounded so similar?

Globalizing the Roots Rebel

In 1973, Jamaica's record industry was on the verge of a major international breakthrough. Up until then, the island had produced occasional novelty hits, like Millie Small's "My Boy Lollipop," that crossed over from Britain's growing West Indian immigrant community to the Top of the Pops and the American top 40. But with the twin vehicles of film and music, the Third World roots rebel made his global debut.

Debuting in Jamaica in 1972, with wider global release the following year, Perry Henzell's movie *The Harder They Come* was a portrait of the Jamaica few yankees would ever trod. The movie opened with a country bus navigating a narrow northern road, the coconut trees of the stormy coastline eerily headless, their fronds and fruits sheered off by plague. Singer Jimmy Cliff played Ivan O. Martin, a peasant making the well-worn trip from rural parish to concrete jungle, the metaphoric journey of a newly freed nation into modernity. But this was not to be a narrative of progress.

Vincent "Ivanhoe" Martin was a real-life fifties Kingston outlaw who renamed himself Rhygin and summoned Jamaica's Maroon pride. *The Harder They Come* updated his story for a nation defining its postcolonial identity in and through its homegrown popular music. Cliff's Ivan was to be exploited by a greedy music producer, reviled by a Christian pastor, and eventually tortured and hunted by corrupt police. A country *bwai* innocent remade into the urban renegade Rhygin, he shoots down a cop and goes underground. A picture of him posing with two pistols hits the papers and his song controls the airwaves. "As sure as the sun will shine, I'm gonna get my share now, what's mine," he sings, "and then the harder they come, the harder they'll fall, one and all." The new legend of Rhygin would frame the island's turbulent seventies.

In another landmark 1973 film, *Enter the Dragon*, Jim Kelly's African-American activist character Williams had gazed at Bruce Lee's Hong Kong home from a sampan and said, "Ghettos are the same all over the world. They stink." Like Bruce Lee, the Third World reggae heroes seemed to First World audiences an intriguing mix of the familiar and fresh. The soundtrack to Henzell's film, and the debut album by Bob Marley and the Wailers positioned reggae as a quintessential rebel music, steeped in a different kind of urban Black authenticity.

The Wailers' album, *Catch a Fire*, would be a product of the sometimes giddy, sometimes halting dialogue between Third World roots and First World pop. When Bob Marley delivered the rough master tapes to the Island Records offices in London in the dead winter of 1972, a lot was riding on the getting the mix right.

Just months earlier, the Wailers had been stranded in Britain, abandoned by their manager after a European tour failed to materialize. Island Records head Chris Blackwell, a prominent financier of Henzell's film, bailed them out by signing them, advancing them £4,000, and sending them home to Kingston to record the album. They took their opportunity seriously—it was a chance for the boys from Trenchtown to bring the message of Jamaican sufferers to the world.

Blackwell, a wealthy white descendant of Jamaican rum traders now living in London, was beginning to have success in the rock market, and knew he might be on a fool's mission in trying to cross reggae over. But, emboldened by the success of *The Harder They Come*, and embittered by Jimmy Cliff's snubbing to sign a deal with EMI, he was eager to see how far reggae could be taken into the mainstream. He gave the Wailers fancy album packaging and put them on tour with rock and funk bands. Most importantly, he sent the music back for overdubs by rock session musicians, keyboardist Rabbit Bundrick and guitarist Wayne Perkins.

The album's leadoff track, "Concrete Jungle," illustrated the perils and promise of translating Jamaican music for First World audiences. The opening notes drifted into a disorienting key, Robbie Shakespeare's bassline seemed to omit more notes than were played, Bunny Wailer and Peter Tosh's harmonies floated and attacked like rope-a-dope boxing. Marley's lyrics described the unrelenting bleakness of the west Kingston yard. "No chains around my feet," the Wailers sang, "but I'm not free." It was utterly brilliant, but the music, Blackwell decided, sounded far too Jamaican.

When he first played the music to Perkins, the Muscle Shoals guitarist couldn't understand the riptide of riddims. But as the song built to the break, Perkins cut loose with a bluesy torrent, culminating in a ringing sustain. Blackwell and engineer Tony Platt hit the echo machine and the note fed back, soaring up two octaves. "It gave me goosebumps, it was one of those magical moments," Perkins says.[5] Marley, who had spent long, cold, destitute years in America pursuing his pop dream, thought so, too.

Their album would only sell 14,000 copies in its first year, but the Wailers had taken the first step in turning their local music into an international phenomenon. *Catch a Fire* was a landmark moment in the globalization of Third World culture. Fulfilling the destiny the elder Rastas in Trenchtown had long seen for him, Marley was on his way to becoming a worldwide icon of freedom struggle and Black liberation—the small axe becoming the first trumpet.

Sounds and Versions

The pop audience demanded heroes and icons, but reggae, perhaps more than any other music in the world, also privileged the invisible music men, the sonic architects—the studio producer and the sound system selector. Together, during the seventies, these two secretive orders emerged as sources of power in Jamaica.

One center, though it may not have seemed so at the time, was an odd backyard studio in the Kingston suburb of Washington Gardens. Lee "Scratch" Perry, its eccentric owner, was a diminutive man with a feverishly large imagination. Beginning in December of 1973, and continuing night and day for five years, Perry recorded an unceasing parade of harmony groups, singers, and DJs in the tiny, stuffy, concrete structure that he called the Black Ark. The music emerging from the Ark—including Junior Murvin's "Police and Thieves," The Heptones' "Mr. President," and The Congos' "Children Crying"—was mesmerizing and shocking, and would soon reverberate across the globe.

It was a gloriously weird place, this Black Ark, another autonomous zone. Its exterior walls sported a blue, red, and white image of Emperor Haile Selassie and the Lion of Judah, surrounded by purple handprints and footprints like a child's finger paintings. The interior walls were painted red and green, and were crammed with Rasta imagery, Bruce Lee posters, Upsetters album jackets, Teac equipment brochures, Polaroid shots, record stampers, horseshoes, and other ephemera, all covered over by a dense layer of Perry's obscure, signifying graffiti.

Behind a cheap four-track mixing desk, which by the standards of the time was hopelessly outdated, Perry whirled and bopped and twiddled the knobs, imbuing the recordings with wild crashes of echo, gravity-defying phasing, and frequency-shredding equalization. Influenced by his work with Osborne "King Tubby" Ruddock, Perry used aging analog machines like the Echoplex to turn sounds over and back into themselves like Möbius loops. Melodies became fragments, fragments became signs, and the whole thing swirled like a hurricane.

Upon his arrival in Kingston from his native northern countryside in 1960, Perry had headed straight for the powerful sound systems to try to find work, eventually becoming a songwriter for Duke Reid, then moving on to become a scout and operator for Reid's competitor, Coxsone Dodd. According to dancehall historian Norman Stolzoff, sound system culture had evolved in Kingston after World War II when the ranks of live musicians dramatically thinned due to immigration to the United Kingdom and the United States and the rise of the North Coast tourist industry.[6] By the time Perry came to Kingston, sound systems had largely replaced live bands.

Outfitted with powerful amplifiers and blasting stacks of homemade speakers, one only needed a selector and records to transform any yard. The sound systems democratized pleasure and leisure by making dance entertainment available to the downtown sufferers and strivers. The sound systems championed the people's choice long before commercial radio, and as independence approached, they moved from playing mostly American rhythm-and-blues to homegrown ska, rock steady, and finally, reggae.

The fiercely competitive sound systems—including Duke Reid's Trojan, Coxsone Dodd's Downbeat the Ruler, Prince Buster's Voice of the People, King Edwards the Giant, and Tom the Great Sebastian—fought for audiences; some of them even sent thugs to shoot up their rivals' dances and destroy their equipment in fits of anger or desperation.[7] More usually, they distinguished themselves from each other with "specials," records that no other sound system had, songs that mashed up their competitors and drew away their audiences. They even sometimes "clashed" live in the same hall or yard, song for song, "dub fi dub."

Early on, selectors made frequent trips to America to secure obscure exclusives. As the Jamaican music industry expanded during the sixties, sound systems began to record local artists' songs onto exclusive acetates or "dubplates."[8] In 1967, a sound system head affiliated with Duke Reid named Ruddy Redwood stumbled onto Jamaican music's next great innovation.

One afternoon Redwood was cutting dubplates when engineer Byron Smith forgot to pan up the vocals on The Paragons' hit, "On the Beach." Redwood took the uncorrected acetate to the dance that night anyway, and mixing between the vocal and the dub, sent the crowd into a frenzy during his midnight set. Rather than apologize for his mistake the next day, Redwood emphasized to Reid that the vocal-less riddim could be used as a B-side on the commercial release of the singles. Reid, for his part, realized he could cut his costs by half or more. One studio session could now produce multiple "versions."[9] A single band session with a harmony trio could be recycled as a DJ version for a rapper to rock *patwa* rhymes over, and a dub version in which the mixing engineer himself became the central performer—experimenting with levels, equalization and effects to alter the feel of the riddim, and break free of the constraints of the standard song.

Dub's birth was accidental, its spread was fueled by economics, and it would become a diagram for hip-hop music. A space had been pried open for the break, for possibility. And, quickly, noise came up from the streets to fill the space—yard-centric toasts, sufferer moans, analog echoes—the sounds of people's histories, *dub histories*, versions not represented in the official version. As musical competition was overshadowed by violent political competition, dub became the sound of a rapidly fragmenting nation—troubling, strange, tragic, wise slow-motion portraits of social collapse.

Roots and Culture

Every Jamaican politician knew what every Jamaican musician knew—the sound systems were crucial to their success. During the seventies, the fight for political dominance between the conservative Jamaica Labour Party (JLP) and leftist People's National Party (PNP) seemed inevitably to turn on the mood of the people in the dance. All any prime minister had to do to gauge the winds was to listen closely to the week's 45 rpm single releases; they were like political polls set to melody and riddim.

The message was becoming decidedly roots and radical. In the fall of 1968, the JLP-led government had banned Black-power literature and icons like the pan-Africanist leader Walter Rodney from the University of the West Indies campus, then violently crushed the political riots that ensued across the city. But this did not stop the electorate from moving hard left. Intellectuals high on Malcolm X, socialists stricken by Castro, middle-class strivers impatient for price stability, poor strugglers facing dim prospects, even Rastas traditionally reluctant to participate in what Peter Tosh called the Babylon *shitstem* all clamored for change. Sufferer anthems took over the sound systems. The resistance to roots reggae finally gave way on JBC radio, as listeners came home from the yard dances to demand that tunes like Delroy Wilson's "Better Must Come" and the Wailers' "Small Axe" (cut with Perry) be played during daytime hours. Burning Spear summed up the mood of the time: "The people know what it is they want, so they themselves go about getting it."[10]

Compared to Seaga, who had worked the nexus of culture and politics for years, Michael Manley, the democratic socialist PNP candidate, was a latecomer. But as Manley geared up for the 1972 elections, he began appearing at political rallies with his "rod of correction," a staff that he said had been handed to him by Haile Selassie, in explicit recognition of the influence Rastafarianism held among the poor. The rod, he said, would lead him to redressing injustice. Befitting his new image, he spoke of reggae as "the people's language," and selected Wilson's "Better Must Come" as his campaign theme. The following year, the PNP swept the JLP out of office. In Laurie Gunst's worlds, Jamaica in the '70s was "a fever-dream of raised consciousness and high hopes."[11]

But better never came. The twin downpressing forces of Cold War positioning and global economic pressures ripped Jamaica apart.

Manley's democatic socialist government pushed through key social reforms, including lowering the voting age to eighteen, making secondary and university education free, and establishing a national minimum wage. But when Manley moved to reestablish relations with Cuba and build solidarity with leftist leaders in the Caribbean and Africa, CIA surveillance sharply intensified, and First World leaders withdrew aid and investments. In 1971, Jamaica received $23 million in aid from the United States. By 1975, that amount was down to $4 million.[12]

The worldwide oil crisis-fueled recession hit the Jamaican dollar hard, unleashing economic chaos. Prices tripled while wages declined by half; a paycheck suddenly bought one-sixth of what it used to. Labor unions unleashed an unprecedented number of walkouts. Between 1972 and 1979, there were more than three hundred strikes.

North American banks refused to renew aid loans. Jamaica's debt doubled between 1975 and 1980 to $2 billion U.S., the equivalent of 90 percent of the country's gross domestic product.[13] After a bitter internal fight, the PNP reversed course and finally agreed to accept emergency loans for Jamaica from the International Monetary Fund (IMF), who imposed severe austerity measures that caused goods shortages and massive layoffs. The IMF's plan wreaked long-term havoc on the island's economy, wiping out entire industries. To pay off the skyrocketing debt, the PNP raised taxes, causing other businesses to flee the island.

In 1973, gun violence broke out between rival gangs in the Kingston yards. Manley first placed the island "under heavy manners," expanding police powers to search and raid, and stepping up joint police-military operations. He then established a special Gun Court, where gunmen and illegal firearms traffickers faced mandatory indefinite sentences for their crimes.

By the end of 1976, when Manley declared a State of Emergency—the Jamaican equivalent of martial law—it was becoming clear that much of the violence was politically motivated. In the Kingston yards, gangs had divided and mapped their turf. As Seaga had long understood, gang leaders were useful to party machinery—they delivered a yard's votes in election years, fought the ground war during the off years. In turn, politicians granted jobs, favors, and programs to the area dons, who organized the youths into work-groups or militias.

Bounty Killer, the dancehall DJ who grew up in the Riverton neighborhood during the 1970s and '80s, says, "We used to love politics. When time de MP (Member of Parliament) come an' say, 'Bwoy, we a go gi' weh dis an we a go gi' weh dat'—we interested.

"A poor people—weh a look a likkle help an' a look a hope inna Jamaica—a listen when de Govament a talk," he added. "But no hope no deh deh. Dem haffi hold *oonu* (everyone) inna dat position so dem can get *oonu* attention."[14] In 1974, singer Little Roy went into the Black Ark to record an anguished plea for peace, "Tribal War," a tune whose cyclical revival over the next three decades spoke to the permanence of political gang violence.

While Seaga and the JLP officials turned up the rhetorical heat on the Manley government in Parliament, the JLP gangs lit up PNP yards with Molotov cocktails and gunfire. PNP gangs retaliated in kind, fire for fire, blood for blood. When firefighters arrived in Rema, a JLP community, in January 1976, they confronted youths tossing stones from behind roadblocks of blazing tires. The shanties were left to burn.[15] Manley felt he saw a design to the violence—a devil's bargain between the CIA and the pro-U.S. JLP, Washington bullets in the Kingston streets. He wrote in his memoirs, "I have no doubt that the CIA was active in Jamaica that year and was working through its own agents to destabilise us."[16]

With guns and money flowing to the opposition party, the tribal wars rose to a new pitch. Smoke thickened the heavy air in the zinc yards, and Rhygins in JLP green or PNP red raged through the ghetto. In May, the warfare peaked when gangsters surrounded a tenement yard in West Kingston at Orange Lane and set it ablaze, trapping five hundred residents inside. Gunmen blasted away at the police and firemen who arrived at the scene, and eleven perished in the conflagration. As debate raged in Parliament over which party was responsible for the carnage, and the elections neared, hundreds more were gunned down.

During the tribal wars of the mid-sixties, the Wailers had cut "Simmer Down," a tune encouraging rudies to "control your temper." Now Bob Marley met Lee "Scratch" Perry at the Black Ark to record another track that might cool down the ghetto, "Smile Jamaica," and agreed to do a free concert bearing the same name on December 5. Hearing this news, the PNP scheduled elections for December 20, and made a show of sending armed guards to watch Marley's uptown compound at 56 Hope Road. Marley was enraged. Like many Rastas, he had supported Manley and the PNP in 1972, but now he was disgusted with where *politricks* had led the country.

Two nights before the show, the armed guard mysteriously disappeared. Minutes later, six assassins entered the mansion. Rita Marley was shot in the head, and manager Don Taylor took five bullets destined for Bob, whose chest was grazed as the last bullet entered his left arm. But on the night of the show, Bob was wheeled into National Heroes Park, where a crowd of 80,000, including Manley and a large PNP entourage, had gathered. Marley played a triumphant concert, then left for the Bahamas in a self-imposed exile.

Rumors spread that the JLP, perhaps even the CIA, was behind the hit. The point had been made: violence was striking dangerously near the heart of the people.

The Dub Side

And so they sang of clashes, of war. From imagining distant and free African skies in songs like The Abyssinians' "Satta Massa Gana," The Mighty Diamonds' "Africa," Junior Byles's "A Place Called Africa," or Bunny Wailer's "Dreamland," they moved to plead for relief from the violence borne of "isms and schisms."

Leroy Smart's "Ballistic Affair" was a tragic dispatch from the fire-scarred danger zone of Seventh Street, the militarized border between Rema and Concrete Jungle, a PNP yard whose Junglist gang was thought to be behind much of the violence:

> We used to lick chalice, cook ital stew together
> Play football and cricket as one brother
> Now through you rest a Jungle
> A you might block a Rema
> You a go fight 'gainst your brother.

Max Romeo and Lee "Scratch" Perry captured the moment's treacherous flux. As Romeo told David Katz: "I had this song 'War In A Babylon' where me say, 'It wicked out there, it dread out there.' I took it to [Perry], said, 'You like it?' He said 'Yeah!' with excitement, 'but no dread and no wicked, it *sipple* out deh!' So I said, 'Yeah that have a ring to it', because sipple mean slippery, it's slidey out there."[17] In his new chorus, Romeo asked "So wha fi do?" and the answer came, "Mek we *slide* out deh." As the song climaxed, Romeo retreated high up to the Rasta hills as Kingston exploded under the burning sun:

I man satta on the mountaintop
Watching Babylon burning red hot
Red hot!

Here was *The Harder They Come*'s Ivan, a reef fish battling the ocean current, a flash of color in the tidal surge, pursued by police and enemies, making a last run through the ghetto, leaving graffiti tags on the concrete walls that mocked, "I was here but I disapear (sic)"—laughing mightily, knowing that he'd already become indelible in the public imagination, that even politics could not erase him—and, like a premonitory smoke above the shanty roofs: "I AM EVERYWHERE." Celebrating survival itself was the point.

While singers and DJs offered words of mourning or escape for the sufferers, dub reggae—the mostly wordless music of dread—ran directly into the heart of the darkness. In Perry's "Revelation Dub," time was creakily kept by a distended, phasing hi-hat and Romeo's vocal was either reduced to the low hum of some distant street protest or chopped into sudden nonsensical stabs—"Warinna!" "Balwarin!"—as if all words, even warnings, could not be trusted. The riddim—which Marley would later version for "Three Little Birds," with its bright chorus, "Don't worry about a thing, 'cause every little thing's gonna be alright"—was swung off its moorings, the textual integrity and authority was undermined. Perry's sound was the epitome of *sipple*. Dub answered the question: what kind of mirror is it that reflects everything but the person looking into it?

Dub had a compelling circularity. It exploded in the dancehall at the moment the tenement yards exploded in violence. Dub was the "B-side" to the soaring visions of the democratic socialist dreamers or the apocalyptic warnings of the Rasta prophets. As reggae historian Steve Barrow says, "The music of dub represents literally and figuratively *'the other side.'* There's an up and a down, there's an A-side and a B-side. It's a dialectical world."

As the two sevens clashed, dub peaked with album sets from Perry (*Super Ape*), Keith Hudson (*Brand*), Niney the Observer (*Sledgehammer Dub*), the Mighty Two—Joe Gibbs and Errol Thompson (Prince Far I's *Under Heavy Manners*, Joe Gibbs' *State of Emergency*, *African Dub All-Mighty* series), Philip Smart (Tapper Zukie's *Tapper Zukie In Dub*), Harry Mudie (the *Dub Conference* series), and the most influential dubmaster of all, King Tubby.

Born Osborne Ruddock in 1941, Tubby had collaborated with Perry to demonstrate the possibilities of dub on the 1973 album, *Blackboard Jungle Dub*. With *King Tubbys Meets Rockers Uptown*, an album-length collection of sides with melodica player Augustus Pablo dating to the beginning of Manley's first term, musical innovation and political disintegration seemed to stoke each other.

On the title track, a version of Jacob Miller's "Baby I Love You So," Tubby left Pablo's melodica, Carly Barrett's drums, and Chinna Smith's guitar in shards. Miller had sung, "Night and day, I pray that love will come my way." But Tubby clipped his lines—"Baby I-I-I-I," "night and day," "that love," "And I-I-I-I"—transforming Miller's longing into a prison. On the original, Miller had scatted loosely, then chuckled, perhaps at having missed an essential cue. Tubby added a ghostly echo, leaving the laugh to hang like a haunting, the smoke of Rhygin's trail. At the end, Miller's cry dissolved in a barrage of oscillations, a plunge through a trapdoor.

The last track, inexplicably left unannounced on the original album sleeve and label, was a dub of the Abyssinians' 1969 single, "Satta Massa Gana," colloquially known as the Rastafarian national anthem. In mistranslated Amharic, its title meant to "give thanks and praise" to Haile Selassie, while its harmonies yearned for "a land far far away."[18] Tubby gutted the song to a bass pulse and drum accent. The song's basic chords were twisted out of shape and pitch. Drums dropped like thunderclaps. Tubby's mirror world was the sound of the dreamland alliance of Rastas and democratic socialists disintegrating, its utopia looted by thugs and left to the whipping hurricane winds of global change.

It was music of the crossfire lifted out of the progression of time, politics, and meaning. Dub embraced contingency. Everything was up for grabs. Dub declaimed, distorted, or dropped out at the razor's edge of a moment. It gave a clipped, fragmented voice to horrors the nation could not yet adequately articulate.

One Love Peace Music

When 1978 arrived, another round of election-year violence seemed imminent. But then the unexpected happened. Somehow in early January, Bucky Marshall, a gunman from the PNP-backed Spanglers Posse, ended up in the same General Penitentiary cell as some JLP gangsters and they got to talking.

They spoke of the event that had ended 1977. Renegade soldiers from the Jamaican Defense Force had set up and ambushed an unarmed posse of JLP roughnecks, killing five. But five more got away, and they told the story of the extra-legal set-up to *The Gleaner*. The resulting scandal potentially incriminated both PNP and JLP politicians, and many felt that a coup or a civil war was imminent. Certainly, the rival gunmen in that jail-cell reasoned, no political affiliations could save anyone from the army if something that serious was afoot.

When Marshall stepped out of jail, he went to meet with Claudie Massop, Seaga's man in Tivoli Gardens, who had come up through The Phoenix and was now the area don. The next morning, at a spot straddling the border of JLP and PNP territories in central Kingston, they announced a peace treaty. Marshall and Massop took photos together, and spoke to the press. "This is not political," said Marshall. "This is from we who have felt the pangs of jail."[19] Massop added, "The youths have been fighting among themselves for too long and is only them get dead. Everybody I grow up with is dead."[20] Amidst the spreading truce, elated youths left their yards and began to gather in parks and dances that had formerly been in enemy territory.

With the help of the Rasta sect, the Twelve Tribes of Israel, Marshall, Massop, and the ranking PNP don from Concrete Jungle, "Red Tony" Welch, went to London to see the man who had first brought them together, Bob Marley. Welch and Massop had been frequent guests when Marley was holding court on Hope Road. Now they asked him to return to Jamaica and headline a "One Love Peace Concert." The benefit would raise money for the most suffering PNP and JLP ghettos, to be distributed by the newly formed Central Peace Council, but more importantly, it could curtail the possibility of civil war or a military coup. Marley agreed, and flew home. In the days leading to the concert, Marley toured through the yards to talk up the peace treaty. At the Black Ark, he and Perry recorded "Blackman Redemption" and "Rastaman Live Up" as Massop and Marshall vibed together in the listening room.[21]

On April 22, thousands packed Kingston's National Stadium to hear the island's top musicians, including Dennis Brown, Culture, the Mighty Diamonds, Big Youth, Beres Hammond, Ras Michael and the Sons of Negus, Dillinger and Jacob Miller, who, with his band Inner Circle, had the most popular tune in the country in "Peace Treaty Special," a rockers-style tribute to Marshall, Massop and the tribes set to a version of the American Civil War–era song, "When

Johnny Comes Marching Home Again."[22] "Man can walk the street again, hurrah-ah-e-ah hurrah," Miller sang joyously. "From Tivoli to Jungle, Lizard Town to Rema—hurrah!" Peter Tosh played a scorching set, laced with withering criticisms of the politicians in attendance. Then Marley took the stage, and the crowd swelled to a roar.

As the Wailers gave an inspired performance of "Jamming," Marley called the political leaders onstage. His long dreads cut arcs through the night air, and he danced as if possessed, singing, "Show the people that you love 'em right, show the people you gonna unite." Manley stood to the left of Marley, Seaga to the right, and they tentatively gave each other a handshake. Marley clasped their hands, put them in a power grip and lifted them over his head, holding them high for all to see. The crowd was stunned. "Love, prosperity be with us all," Marley said. "Jah Rastafari. Selassie I."

Through music, Marley had brought together a trinity of power, and restored unity to the young nation. Culture, it seemed, had transcended politics.

The Pressure Drop

But there were other signs as well. Five days before the concert, army soldiers fired on a peaceful ghetto march for better sanitation, killing three demonstrators. The leader of the Central Peace Council, who had called for an end to police corruption, fled the island in fear for his life. Police stopped and searched a taxi Claudie Massop was riding in, then coldly executed him in a hail of fifty bullets.[23] The peace treaty was over. So was Manley's democratic socialist experiment. In 1980, Seaga and the JLP would be overwhelmingly victorious at the polls, stepping up just in time to be courted by the new Reagan administration in Washington. Almost nine hundred people would die in election-year violence.

The reggae industry, too, felt the pressure drop. During the heady independence years of the sixties, Coxsone Dodd's Studio One and Duke Reid's Treasure Isle had been built from local sound system profits. But the Black Ark studio had been financed by the globalization of the reggae industry. Perry's dubs had been partly an answer to the growing international demand for reggae. Reggae music was not only a socially stabilizing force, it had become an important commodity.

The pressures fell disproportionately on the slender shoulders of musicians.

Uptown, Bob Marley's Hope Road residence had become a magnet for Twelve Tribes Rastas, a sect that openly and controversially courted the wealthy, whites and browns. But many more displaced sufferers also frequented the Hope Road yard. Marley archivist Roger Steffens believes that by the late '70s, Marley was directly responsible for the economic fortunes of six thousand people. By 1979, the Marley camp had also become aware of CIA operatives tailing them. And yet, despite being diagnosed with cancer, Marley maintained a hectic touring schedule through the end of 1980, perhaps because of such obligations. "It took its toll," Steffens says. "He really wanted out." On May 11, 1981, he was dead.

At the beginning of 1978, Perry's Black Ark had become a center for the Boboshanti, an orthodox Rasta sect led by Prince Emmanuel Edwards that adhered to the ideal of Black Supremacy. Perry biographer David Katz notes that the Bobos hoped Perry and his Ark could help disseminate their message, much the same way Marley did for the Twelve Tribes, and that hundreds of people materially depended upon Perry's riddim factory. By the end of the year, Perry had ejected the Bobos, shaved his budding dreads, and turned away Rasta groups and visitors. He began dismantling the studio. He covered the Ark with brown paint and graffiti tags, crossing out words and pictures with Xs. In the summer of 1983, the Black Ark burned to the ground. Perry said he did it himself.

Years later, Perry dictated an extraordinary statement to Katz, a peripatetic freestyle. He began, "The First World and the Second World live, but the Third World is finished because I, Lee 'Scratch' Perry, knows the head of the IMF—the IMF big boss, the Bank of England big boss, the Midland big boss, the International Giro Bank big boss . . .

"The Third World drawn in," he continued. "The game blocked; the road block, the lane block, and the street block, so who can't see good better see them eye specialist and take a good look upon the road. The road blocked; all the roads are blocked . . .

"Reggae music is a curse, the ultimate destruction", he said. "Logical Fox, solid-state logic."[24]

Fevered dreams of progress had brought fires to the Bronx and Kingston. The hip-hop generation, it might be said, was born in these fires.

On the block in the South Bronx with the Ghetto Brothers and the Roman Kings.
Benjy Melendez (center), Victor Melendez (right, on drums).

Photo © Librado Romero/New York Times Agency

3

Blood and Fire, with Occasional Music

The Gangs of the Bronx

Ay, cuando llegará la justicia
Justicia para los boricuas y los
niches?

When will justice come
Justice for Puerto Ricans and
Blacks?

—Eddie Palmieri

We are tired of praying and marching and thinking and learning
Brothers want to start cutting and shooting and stealing and burning

—Gil Scott-Heron

At summer's twilight, the Bronx begins to shimmer.

Parents gather in chairs outside the multilingual bodega, sipping on beer and juice, bathing in fluorescent conversation on wide sidewalks. Teens carom around the corner, tall on gleaming bikes. Boys in squeaky new sneakers pound a basketball down the glassine asphalt. Salsa, dancehall and hip-hop pour into the air like the cool water out of an old, leaning corner hydrant.

The girl sitting there wipes her brow. Light sparkles off her curly brown ringlets. It glints off the cyclone fencing encircling the vacant lot, the discarded Snapple bottles and chip bags, the polished mirror of the NYPD car parked where a three-story-high staircase descends to a subway stop. Night is coming aglow in the urban canyons.

Halfway up the other hill, in this neighborhood that the maps call Morris Heights, the residents call the East Bronx, and the rest of the world calls the South Bronx—"everything south of Fordham Road," as the saying goes—stands a junior high school, PS 117.

"I live near here but I never come around," says Michael "Lucky Strike" Corral, as he walks into the unlit playground. Once a member of the Savage Skulls gang, he is now a Zulu King and a member of the Zulu Nation's World Council. He walks through these streets with respect, keeping an eager, wide-eyed pit bull pup pulling ahead of him on a short leash. Two days earlier, he had saved the pup from young Bloods who were about to pump a couple of slugs into it for fun.

A high concrete wall rises in the corner of the schoolyard, separating the handball court from the rest of the yard, only one way in and one way out. The court sits in the dark cast by the five-story school building. Behind it, two stories above, the sidewalks along the intersection of 176th Street and Morris Avenue offer a prime seat for the gladiator activities below—whether handball contests or gang initiations.

"Back in the seventies, this was the Apache line for the Javelins," Lucky says. "I used to come down here and watch."

Painted on the middle of the wall was a graffitied genie, the symbol of passage, the end of the Apache line. Two rows of twenty guys stood in the way. If a kid could make it past the swinging fists and boots and chains and baseball bats to touch the genie, they could don the Javelins' colors: a denim jacket with a hand-painting of the green genie on the back, ready to be customized with letters and patches, iron crosses and swastikas, emblems of war. They earned their stripes up to the crowning piece on the back: a large hand-painting of a bronze-skinned warrior wielding a spear. "They were put to the test to see if they more or less had the heart to do it," he says. "Most of the time they would get hurt." Some never passed the test.

Lucky could still picture himself, a sullen teen slung against the fence, watching the Javelin initiates run the line below. He was an outlaw in combat boots and Lee jeans and a decorated denim jacket with cutoff sleeves. At his nape, a black hoodie hung over his own colors: a grinning white skull under a steel German war helmet.

Born a Savage, To Die a Skull One Day

Other gangs kept Third Avenue hot—the Chingalings and the Savage Nomads to the west, the Black Falcons to the north. Below Crotona Park, in the heart of the burnt-out South Bronx, were the turfs of the Ghetto Brothers, the Turbans, the Peacemakers, the Mongols, the Roman Kings, the Seven Immortals and the Dirty Dozens. Most of these gangs were predominantly Puerto Rican. East of the Bronx River, the Black Spades consolidated the youths of the mostly African-American communities. Further east and north across Fordham Road, in the last white communities in the Bronx, gangs like the Arthur Avenue Boys, Golden Guineas, War Pigs and the Grateful Dead were foot soldiers for angry wiseguys who spent their days cursing the imminent loss of their neighborhood.

But the Savage Skulls were one of the most feared gangs in the Bronx. They were brazen and reckless. The First Division of the Skulls, the original set, had moved their base on Leggett Avenue and Kelly Street in the Longwood section to an abandoned apartment building just a block away from the infamous Forty-first police precinct—the one called Fort Apache, a "fort in hostile territory." If you were looking for protection or trouble, you quit your clique and joined the Skulls.

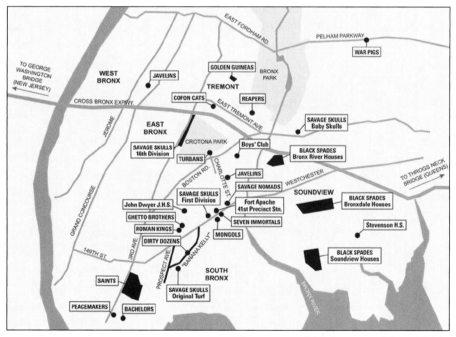

The gangs of the Bronx, 1970–1973.

Map layout by Sharon Mizota

By the time Lucky joined the Sixteenth Division, the Skulls were second in size only to the Black Spades. As many as fifty divisions of the Savage Skulls were flung across the borough and into Queens, New Jersey and Pennsylvania. Alongside the western edge of Crotona Park, on Third Avenue at the Cross-Bronx Expressway, at the very beginning of the mile that the women of East Tremont had fought and lost to Robert Moses in 1952, the Skulls' Sixteenth Division had taken over four blocks of abandoned buildings and transformed them into their clubhouses. Lucky was not the kind of kid that looked for trouble, but the Skulls ruled his neighborhood.

To Lucky's Puerto Rican father and Cuban mother—who arrived from Miami during the mid-1960s as part of a Latino wave that filled former Jewish communities along the Grand Concourse—he was simply Michael, a boy who loved birds. He cut school to be with his birds, dashing across the street past truancy officers and climbing several flights to a pigeon coop he had built on the roof of an abandoned building. He told a friend, "When you're on the roof, when the birds are actually flying and nobody's around you, it feels more free."

But things changed quickly. One day, he and some friends went up to Little Italy, north of Fordham Road near Bedford Park, looking for some pet stores to buy some birds. Twenty Italians swooped down on them, brandishing bats and chains and yelling slurs. Michael and his friends ran all the way back to the train station. They were learning you just didn't go *anywhere* without backup.

He met Carlos, a kid just a year older who called himself "Blue," the only one who seemed to know more about flying birds than he did. They became fast friends, and built a fortress coop of five hundred birds across the street from Michael's school. One day they took down some birds from a roof a block away. The owners came over to get them back—two big, scowling Savage Skulls in their early twenties named Cubby and Ruben.

As soon as he was asked to, Blue joined the Skulls. He came back and told Michael to do it, too. "They're just like a family," he said. In order to be down, he would have to be checked out by the Skull leaders. If they thought he could be a good Skull, he would go through the initiation. But there was no Apache Line here. To become a Savage Skull, you played a game of Russian Roulette.

It was a summer's twilight when Michael arrived at the main Skulls clubhouse. He was sweating, nervous as hell. In the initiation room, a few older Skulls, their faces masks of stone, told him to take a seat. One of them brought out a rusty .22. Michael was told to examine the long bullet. The Skull dropped it into the chamber of the six-shooter, spun the barrel, and passed it to Michael. It was the first gun he had ever held. He was told he could either put it to his chin or to his head.

He closed his eyes. He lifted the cocked gun to his head. He thought, this is it. He thought, this rusty old thing, maybe it'll get stuck. He thought, what if it's all gonna end right here. Sweat dripped from his chin. He pulled the trigger.

For a while—an eternity, perhaps—he kept his eyes closed. Then, he thought, I did it. He had heard the chamber click over—just like that, click, nothing else—and the enormity of what he had done began to fill him up. Damn, he thought, *I did it*. He took a deep breath and exhaled.

When the Skulls led him out of the room, they broke open a beer for him. It was the first one he had ever drank. That was how Michael got the name "Lucky Strike"—just plain Lucky, for short. He was thirteen years old.

Soon the Skulls would be spinning out of control and Blue would be dead, killed by rivals and left in the gang clubhouse. Lucky would quit the Skulls and meet Afrika Bambaataa, a former Black Spade who was uniting Blacks and Puerto Ricans in an organization called Zulu Nation. In so many accounts, the story begins there. But here is the half that comes before, the half less often told.

The Gangs and the Revolution

The lifespan of youth style in New York City parallels the life-cycle of a neighborhood. It's about five years, the time it takes for youths to come through their teens, long enough for them to imprint their own codes, styles, and desires on the block. Youth gangs returned to the Bronx around 1968.

Back then, new rebellions were exploding every week. The Black Panther Party for Self-Defense staged "Free Huey" rallies. Ten thousand Mexican-American high school students in Los Angeles marched against racism in the schools, launching the Chicano youth movement. Black power leaders Stokely Carmichael and H. Rap Brown joined antiwar protesters to shut down the Columbia University campus. Students of color hoisted the banner of the Third World Liberation Front, demanding a college of ethnic studies at San Francisco State. Onto the Paris streets striking students, workers and *les Enragés* poured, while the spraypainted walls cried, "Be Realistic, Demand the Impossible."

Young radicals thought they could smell revolution in the air. "We thought it would take five years, at most," says Gabriel Torres, a former member of the Young Lords Party. "Maybe by 1973."

But the urgent spring soon descended into a long hot summer. Martin Luther King, Jr. was shot dead on April 4. Bobby Hutton was shot dead on April 6. Bobby Kennedy was shot dead on June 6. The generations clashed at the Democratic Party Convention. By September, J. Edgar Hoover had announced war on the Panthers, "the greatest threat to the internal security of the country." Perhaps it was a bad season for the Black Panther Party for Self-Defense to set up their New York offices.

The Panthers' discipline and fearlessness drew in disaffected kids from the 'hood to their offices in Harlem, Brooklyn and the Bronx, and across the country. Many pushing the ten-point program—demanding freedom, jobs, justice, housing, education and an end to police brutality—had been former gang members. In Chicago, Panther leader Fred Hampton was forming alliances with the powerful Blackstone Rangers, Mau Maus, and the Black Disciples gangs.[1] He believed that the gangs collected the fearful and the forgotten. If gangs gave up robbing the poor, terrorizing the weak, hurting the innocent, they might become a powerful force for revolution.

In a March 1968 memo, J. Edgar Hoover had laid out the objectives of the FBI COINTELPRO operation against "Black Nationalist-Hate Groups," including the Nation of Islam and the Black Panthers. Hoover's last goal was to "prevent the long-range growth of militant Black nationalist organizations, especially among youth."[2] To that end, the FBI joined with local police agencies to sweep up the Panthers, netting 348 arrests. On April 2, 1969, twenty-one Panthers from the New York leadership of the Party were rounded up and arrested on charges of conspiring to set off Easter day bombs in the midtown shopping district.

One of the New York 21, a woman named Afeni Shakur, addressed her captors in a letter she composed in her cell. "We know that you are trying to break us up because you can't control us. We know that you always try to destroy what you can't control," she wrote. "History shows that wars against oppression are always successful. And there will be a war—a true revolutionary war—a bloody war. No one not you nor us nor anyone in this country can stop it from occurring now. And we will win."[3]

The charges did not stick and after two years behind bars, the Panther 21 walked free. But amidst constant internal and external harassment from authorities, the Panthers imploded in convulsions of bullets and bodies. Newton himself expelled the New York chapter, and the Party split into armed camps. The revolution that Afeni had fought for—full employment and decent housing—left her with nothing. She raised her son Tupac Amaru alone, often jobless, sometimes homeless.

When the Young Lords Party brought their purple berets from East Harlem across the river to the South Bronx in early 1970, local gang leaders were not impressed. The Savage Skulls' leader Felipe "Blackie" Mercado told his gang members, "Politics is only about bullshit."

Richie Perez was a South Bronx native who had grown up on Kelly Street, where the Skulls had taken over. He returned there with his cadres as the Young Lords' Minister of Information and got a rude welcome: "One night after we had finished our work for the day, we closed up the office, and were sitting out front on some chairs and just talking. We got hit with three firebombs, Molotov cocktails from across the street. The grapevine had it that it was done by some gang members."

But later that summer, Fort Apache cops intensified their stop-and-frisk operations in the neighborhood, with the pretext of stopping the Skulls. One afternoon cops were seen beating down residents on Longwood Avenue, including a Skull member. Members of the Young Lords joined angry residents to encircle the police and jeer. Mercado led his Skulls into the angry crowd. Since the Lords and the residents only wanted to yell, he says, "We started it off, threw the bottle, all hell broke loose."

Police cars were smashed and set afire. Besieged, the cops retreated for more support. When they returned, they were showered with rocks and Molotov cocktails from the tenement roofs. Perez says, "We told them, 'Get the fuck out of here! This is a liberated zone.' "

The battle raged back and forth through the week, along Longwood and down to Prospect, up to 163rd and down to 139th. At times, the police vehicles cruised slowly through the neighborhood, so that everyone could see their drawn guns. The Skulls and the Lords had found a common enemy.

"After we had battled the cops for about four or five nights, one day we were hanging out with the Savage Skulls," Perez continues. "And they said, 'You know? You guys ain't so bad after all. They told us you're a bunch of fucking communists and that you was here to hurt the community.' They told us straight up that some anti-poverty pimps in the neighborhood had paid for them to fire-bomb us. And it was funny. We said, 'We are communists!' "

The rapprochement between the Young Lords and the Savage Skulls reached its peak late in 1970 when the Young Lords began a health care campaign. First the Lords seized an X-ray truck from the Lincoln Hospital and placed it on Simpson and Southern Boulevard to provide free services for the community. Then they staged a full-scale takeover of the hospital. In both actions, the Savage Skulls and the Savage Nomads served as the first line of defense against the cops.

But the relationship was short-lived. By 1971, the Young Lords refocused on exporting their revolution to Puerto Rico. With the Lords in San Juan and the Panthers off the streets, the youth gangs were left to fill the void of the revolutionaries.

The Other Side of the Sixties

The story of the Bronx gangs is a dub history of 1968 through 1973, the other side of the revolution, the exception that became the rule.

At 162nd and Westchester, in the Hunt's Point section of the South Bronx, Benjamin Melendez and his friends formed the Ghetto Brothers. They spawned a number of other gangs—including the Roman Kings, the Savage Nomads and the Seven Immortals. The Savage Skulls had taken their name from Melendez as well. Across the Bronx River, a small band of hardrocks at the Bronxdale Houses called the Savage Seven grew and adopted a new name, the Black Spades. By 1968, the stage was set for a new generation of gangs to take over the Bronx. What should have been five years of revolution instead became five years of gang strife.

This generation was a different breed than the Wanderer generation, the silk-jacketed, doo-wop singing gangs of the late 1950s and early '60s. Nor were they the optimistic youth of the mid-'60s period of brown/Black crossover, the bugalú/boogaloo generation, who had danced their nights away with James Brown, Joe Cuba, and Pete Rodriguez. And most of them did not share the college-bred, high-flying idealism of their peers, the political radicals. Only one in four youths in the borough even graduated from high school.

The gangs were a vanguard of the rubble. They were rough, grimy, dirty-down, all cut sleeves and Nazi patches. They had no reason to sing sweet harmonies. They were the children of Moses's grand experiment, and the fires had already begun. They did not dance in integrated clubs. Those venues had closed, and the borough was resegregating, isolating Black and brown and white. They did not burn for a distant ideology. They idolized the Hell's Angels.

"You know that one percent that don't fit in and don't care? We were living our lifestyle," Mercado says. That lifestyle was distilled into the colors on their jacket. "Back in England every family had their coat of arms. This is our family coat of arms. We don't want to be dealing with society's bullshit. This is what we are, this is what we be. You give me respect I give you respect. Simple."

Gangs structured the chaos. For immigrant latchkey kids, foster children outside the system, girls running away from abusive environments, and thousands of others, the gangs provided shelter, comfort, and protection. They channeled energies and provided enemies. They warded off boredom and gave meaning to the hours. They turned the wasteland into a playground. They felt like a family. "We like to ride and we like to stay together so we all do the same things and we're happy that way," said Tata, a Savage Skull girl. "That's the only way we can survive out here, because if we all go our own ways, one by one, we're gone."[4]

The gangs preyed on the weak: the elderly, drug addicts, store-owners, unaffiliated youths, each other. But in time, some residents began to see them as the real law on the streets. Savage Skull Danny DeJesus says, "Before they would go to the local police, the people would come to us to solve their problems." Even *New York Post* columnist Pete Hamill wrote, "The best single thing that has happened on the streets of New York in the past ten years is the re-emergence of the teenage gangs . . . These young people are standing up for life, and if their courage lasts, they will help this city to survive."[5]

Hamill especially celebrated the gang's crusade to push to rid the streets of junkies and pushers. The gangs' reemergence had coincided with the sudden availability of Southeast Asian heroin. DeJesus says, "It got to the point where they were shooting up on the rooftops, in the hallways. And then what else came with drug addiction? Burglaries. So we get rid of them, we get rid of the problem that comes with being an addict, which is robbing, stealing, taking my mother's pocketbook. The cops weren't doing anything. We were doing their dirty work."

Gangs broke into shooting galleries to warn junkies and pushers that they had twenty-four hours to leave. Then things would get violent. When a member of the Seven Immortals was stabbed by a junkie, the gang retaliated by raping and murdering another. In the summer of 1971, the Savage Skulls declared war. "We took it out on any junkie we saw," says Mercado. "We did them in."

What happened next became known as the "Junkie Massacre." As soon as open season was declared, the Ghetto Brothers, Savage Nomads, Roman Kings, the Brothers and Sisters, and the Black Spades all came down for a piece of the action. From Prospect Avenue to Simpson Street, gangs roved down blocks, buildings, and alleys looking for heroin-addled buzzards to draw blood.

"It was a way of helping the community, but we wasn't thinking that. It was a spur-of-the-moment thing because they jumped two of our brothers," Mercado says. Instead, it was about pride and preservation and club rules and going all the way.

The Ghetto Brothers

In three years, the gangs colonized the borough. Gang colors transformed the bombed-out city grid into a spiraling matrix of beefs. "If you went through someone's neighborhood, you were a target. Or you had to take off your jacket," Carlos Suarez, the president of the Ghetto Brothers, recalls. "If you got caught, they beat the hell out of you."

The bigger gangs fragmented into many more, and when one neighborhood got organized into a gang, another sprang up in self-defense. The police and the media suddenly realized that gangs had divided up the Bronx from Morris Heights to Soundview. In time, they estimated that there were a hundred different gangs claiming 11,000 members, and that 70 percent were Puerto Rican, the rest Black. The gangs figured the member estimates were too low, and that the racial estimates revealed more about policing than reality.[6]

The Ghetto Brothers gang was one of the most powerful, with more than a thousand members in divisions as far away as New Jersey and Connecticut.[7] Suarez was their leader, a handsome twenty-one-year-old martial arts expert with dark curly locks and a coy, secretive smile. On the street, he was known as the short-tempered, street fighting "Karate Charlie," but to women and outsiders, he conveyed a boyish curiosity and a shy charm. He had joined a gang called the Egyptians at the age of twelve, but left as its members all became strung out on heroin, joining other gangs until he befriended Benjamin Melendez.

Melendez, the vice-president, was the skinny, whip-smart nineteen-year-old who had founded the gang. He was a teenage diplomat turned young revolutionary, a gifted organizer and orator. "Yellow Benjy," as he was called, was known to give impromptu speeches to his followers, often laced with blood-and-fire Old Testament scripture. They half-mockingly called him "The Preacher." He could fight as well as anyone, but his real love was music. As children, he and his brothers had won a talent contest singing Beatles songs for Tito Puente. Now he led the Ghetto Brothers' Latin-rock band and was at the center of any clubhouse party. When they broke out the guitars, he especially favored a Beatles tune called "This Boy," a song whose sweet, close harmonies masked menace and foreboding. It began: "That boy took my love away. He'll regret it someday . . ."

If other gangs spoke of themselves as "families," the Ghetto Brothers actually began as one. Benjy, Ulpiano, Victor, and Robert Melendez were brothers whose family was among thousands of Moses's lower Manhattan refugees. In 1961, Moses began an "urban renewal" project to clear the slums of Greenwich Village, Little Italy, Soho, and Chinatown to make room for office and highrise apartment buildings and the eight-lane Lower Manhattan Expressway. Although a citizen's campaign to stop the Expressway succeeded by the end of 1962, the Melendezes joined Moses's exodus into the Bronx.

Settling near the Cross-Bronx Expressway, Benjy followed two of his friends, Huey and Raymond, into a small Tremont gang on Marmion Avenue called the Cofon Cats. When Benjy tired of hanging out with the Cats and his family moved south of Crotona Park, he formed a new clique with his brothers and friends, including Huey, Raymond and Karate Charlie. Benjy came up with a number of names—including the Savage Skulls, the Seven Immortals and the Savage Nomads—and they settled on the Ghetto Brothers.

Suarez's grandmother kicked him out of the house when he was eighteen, so he enrolled in the Marines and ran with the gang before shipping out for boot-camp. On Christmas break in 1970, he went AWOL and came back to the gang. So he went by many names: Charles Kariem Lei, Charles Rivera, Charles Magdaleno. He told reporters his first name was Charlie and his surname was Melendez.

When Charlie returned, Benjy conspired to make him president. Suarez brought discipline and battle-readiness to the gang. He says, "I tried to teach them hand-to-hand combat. I tried to teach them how to throw a Molotov cocktail."

The two became a formidable core. Suarez says, "Benjy was my Yin and I was the Yang. Good cop, bad cop. I was the one that grabbed them by the throat and administered punishment. Benjy was the one that intervened."

Benjy had become a supporter of the Puerto Rican Socialist Party, and was pulling the group toward politics. "The guys were wearing black berets and red stars," says Suarez. "Everybody had grown their hair real long. They looked more militant."

In some ways, the Ghetto Brothers had begun to resemble a *lumpenteen* version of the Young Lords Party. They criticized the quality of health care at the Lincoln Hospital, a place they called the "Butcher Shop," questioned why youths had no jobs or recreation available to them, and decried heavy-handed policing. They forced slumlords to allow them in to clean the tenements, and set up a free-breakfast program and free-clothing drive. They became security for prominent Puerto Rican nationalists. They referred to themselves as "the people's army." By the summer of 1971, Melendez had come up with another name that described their new activities: The South Bronx Defensive Unit. He told Charlie, "Let's stop this gang stuff and form an organization for peace."

A charismatic twenty-five-year old, half-African-American, half–Puerto Rican ex-junkie named Cornell Benjamin had come into the fold. Known as "Black Benjie," he became the third staff leader of the Ghetto Brothers. Most gangs had "warlords," whose chief duties involved stockpiling the arsenal, training the members in fighting skills and military techniques, and negotiating times and places for rumbles. But at Melendez's suggestion, Black Benjie became Peace Counselor.

If there was a gang that could bring peace to the Bronx, perhaps it would be the Ghetto Brothers.

The Teachers

After three years of gang proliferation, Dwyer Junior High had become the central flashpoint for the Bronx gangs. Located at Stebbins Avenue near 165th, the school was at the center of a number of turfs, and its halls were crowded with rival gangbangers. In March, a boy at Dwyer harassed a Savage Nomad sister. She called on Suarez and Savage Nomad president Ben Buxton to back her up. It became an event. Hundreds gathered to see the perpetrator beat down, then they followed as the gangs marched triumphantly through the schoolyard.

From a safe distance teacher Manny Dominguez watched, awestruck. He was convinced that the gang leaders were the most promising young people in the area. They weren't sheep like the rest of the students; they were rebels with sharpened, anti-authoritarian reflexes, rappers possessed of mother-wit, renegades to whom the future should belong. With school principal Morton Weinberger's consent, Dominguez began meeting with the gangs.

Dominguez's wife, Rita Fecher, had separately gone down to the Ghetto Brothers clubhouse to demand that they leave her students alone. As they talked, Fecher became interested in their lives. Realizing no one was going to tell their stories, she picked up a Super 8 camera and began filming interviews with the teen leaders, which would be gathered years later for Fecher's and Henry Chalfant's classic Bronx gang documentary, *Flyin' Cut Sleeves*.

In these frames, Fecher captured the vitality and tragedy of the emerging gangs. Here was Melendez and the Ghetto Brothers band on a tar-beach rooftop, wailing out Grand Funk Railroad's epic of paranoia and disease, "I'm Your Captain": "Everybody listen to me and return me my ship, I'm your captain I'm your captain though I'm feeling mighty sick"; a teenaged Blackie Mercado under a straw hat, a relaxed, dimpled grin on his face, talking about uniting Blacks and Puerto Ricans for the purpose of attacking a rival gang—"They wanted to make it a racial problem, so we made it an *un*-racial problem"; Ben Buxton in the street proudly bragging about the murders he had committed, then later, behind closed doors, thoughtfully analyzing legal aspects of his upcoming gun-charge sentencing (his verdict: he'd be gone for a long time); and most tellingly, a group of angry Puerto Rican girls confronting Buxton and Mercado. "How would you like it," one of them asked, "if someone came along and took your kid's life, your wife's life, or maybe even *your* life?"

Together, Dominguez and Fecher took the Ghetto Brothers, the Savage Skulls, and the Savage Nomads under their wing. At their West Village flat, they held what Fecher described as "salons," where they discussed youth crises, Puerto Rican independence, the criminal justice system, global issues. The two teachers became advocates for the gang members, particularly Melendez and Suarez from the Ghetto Brothers, in whom they found an uncommon wisdom and a desire to move beyond the streets.

Melendez, in particular, was ready for a change. "You can't walk the streets peacefully these days," he said. "You could never tell what's gonna happen around the corner—where those drug addicts could jump you or another club could stop you, say 'Give me your money,' and right there they kill you."[8]

They secured the Ghetto Brothers a storefront clubhouse on 163rd and Stebbins, fully funded by the city's Youth Services Agency. Through contacts at New York University, they provided the gang with musical instruments. The media, attracted by the teachers, came to the Bronx to report on the gangs.

The photogenic, articulate Ghetto Brothers were ready. Photographers captured them relaxing at a Friday block party, looking more like playground kids than fearsome predators. Black Benjie, Yellow Benjy, and Charlie appeared on network talk shows—the hard-scarred, vulnerable faces of a forgotten revolutionary generation. Documentary producers flocked to the Ghetto Brothers' storefront to capture their transformation into "an organization." Through it all, the GBs delivered angry soundbites and played funky music.

The Bronx youths' invisibility was over. Indeed, the Ghetto Brothers cut a romantic profile of embattled, misunderstood youths struggling to do right. When that image reflected back to the forgotten youths of the Bronx, peace seemed to be an actual, viable alternative.

War in the Bronx

In 1971, the Bronx gangs were quickly burning down two tracks—one toward peace, the other toward more blood.

As the days grew hotter, the violence in the South Bronx escalated. Even as the Ghetto Brothers moved publicly toward the revolution, they became more embroiled in growing conflicts. In May, three Ghetto Brothers were shot in the clubhouse, leaving one paralyzed. Victor Melendez, Benjy's brother, the musical heart of the Ghetto Brothers band, and then-president of the Savage Nomads, was stabbed. The Ghetto Brothers and the Savage Nomads figured that the Mongols were behind the hits. For weeks, Suarez and Buxton handed out beatings to any with the bad luck to wander near them. Beefs opened up with the Javelins, the Dirty Dozens, and the Turbans.

In November, gang wars seemed to hit a new level across the resegregated borough. "It was catastrophe after catastrophe. If it wasn't Black against Hispanic, it was Black against white," says Suarez. "Just hate on hate on hate." The Black Spades and a white confederation of the Golden Guineas and the War Pigs called Ministers Bronx went to war at Stevenson High. The Spades and the Savage Skulls, the largest Black and the largest Puerto Rican gangs in the Bronx, erupted into a rumble at a South Bronx movie theater. There were reports that heavy artillery was pouring into the streets—handguns, machine guns, even grenades and bombs.[9]

Social workers urgently pressed for a peace treaty. Working with the gangs of East Tremont, a peace organizer for the Youth Services Agency, Eduardo Vincenty, secured truce commitments from dozens of gangs, including the Javelins, the Peacemakers, the Reapers, the Young Sinners and the Black Spades.[10]

Separately, Suarez and Melendez had been meeting with gang leadership. "I was getting tired of being called in the middle of the night and loading a pistol or bringing down the samurai sword and running down the street to take somebody's head off and don't know if I'm ever gonna see that street again," says Suarez. They hosted informal Friday gatherings at one of their apartments, sometimes extending invitations to leaders of gangs they were warring with. There would be women, music, spliffs, Suarez says. Then they would turn off the music and talk.

As the wars peaked in November, they convened an emergency summit meeting at Bethesda Fountain in Central Park with leaders from the Skulls, the Nomads, the Roman Kings, the Bachelors, and the Black Spades. *New York Post* columnist Jose Torres praised the gang's efforts, writing, "The 'Ghetto Brothers' gang is moving in the right direction. They don't believe in bloody confrontations, they don't think that violence is a substitute for persuasion."[11] But nothing concrete came of either Vincenty's treaty commitments or the Central Park summit. The streets remained tense.

And then, on December 2, word reached the Ghetto Brothers clubhouse that three gangs—the Mongols, the Seven Immortals, and the Black Spades—were in their neighborhood jumping local youths. Melendez sent Cornell Benjamin to mediate. With several Ghetto Brothers tailing him, Black Benjie headed up to Horseshoe Park on 165th and Rogers where the three gangs were massing.

Earlier that day, the Immortals and the Spades had beat down some Roman Kings at the handball courts at John Dwyer Junior High School, sending one to the hospital. The rumor was that the Mongols, the Seven Immortals, and the Spades were now returning down Southern Boulevard for a rumble with the Savage Skulls. As Black Benjie descended the Park's long staircase, the park was filling up with dozens of bangers, wire-taut and waiting for something to happen.

"Listen brothers," Black Benjie said as he walked into the park, holding up his hands to show he had no weapons, "we're here to talk peace." The Spades, the

Mongols and the Seven Immortals surrounded Benjie and the Ghetto Brothers. "Peace, shit," said one of the Immortals, taking out a pipe. Another pulled out a machete. In desperation, a Ghetto Brother whipped out his garrison belt and began swinging it. This was not going to be a day for peace.

"Tip, brothers, tip!" Black Benjie said, and most of the Ghetto Brothers scattered. Then the pipe came crushing down on Black Benjie's head, and he fell to the ground. The gangbangers closed the cipher around him, stomping, cutting and beating him to death.

Hours later, with Black Benjie's body lying in Lincoln Hospital, police patrols quietly circled Dwyer Junior High and reporters descended on the Ghetto Brothers' clubhouse. "What are you going to do?" they asked the gang members, as if they were sniffing blood. "Will you retaliate?"

The Daily News's headline would read, PEACEMAKER KILLED IN MELEE. BRONX TEEN WAR. Dwyer Junior High principal Weinberger told the reporters, "This was bound to come."

Crisis

Black Benjie's murder threatened to destabilize the borough, and the future lay in the Ghetto Brothers' hands. They could lead the Bronx into a bloodier war than had ever been imagined, or toward a peace the borough had never seen.

Suarez could not hide his dismay at Black Benjie's weakness. "He just couldn't do what I did, walk into the fire and not get burned," Suarez says. "He walked into the fire and was consumed immediately." Suarez called all the division leaders, some as far away as Queens and New Jersey. "We were going to find the presidents and we were going to destroy everybody," he says.

As the word spread across the borough the afternoon of December 2, many gangs came to the Ghetto Brothers clubhouse, hoping to avoid the GB's wrath. The Turbans came—Vietnam veterans in their throwback black-satin jackets, wearing their floppy berets topped by yellow yarn pom-pom ball, reminiscent of the early 1960s bopping gangs—to bury their beef and pledge their support. Bam Bam, the president of the Spades, personally came to the clubhouse to declare that the Spades had not been involved in the murder and would also join them in a war.

But Melendez was firm that the Ghetto Brothers needed to maintain peace. He recalls, "There were two or three Ghetto Brothers who actually told me, 'Regardless of what you say, if you don't declare war we're going to go out there.' I said, 'Listen brothers, you're not going to go. I'm telling you right now we're not going to lose any more of you guys. When Black Benjie died, he went for peace and if you go out there to declare war, it will make his mission in vain.'"

Melendez left for the hospital. Suarez prepared for war. In the clubhouse, the Ghetto Brothers stacked guns, knives, machetes, bow-and-arrows, and Molotovs. Then they went out looking for the Seven Immortals and the Mongols. "I was prepared to hurt the one who had hurt one of ours," Suarez says.

By dusk, the Bronx police had mobilized their special operations teams, and were at a state of high alert. They had arrested a teen Black Spade in connection with Black Benjie's murder. But word on the street had come back to the Ghetto Brothers that the killer was a guy named Julio, a leader of the Seven Immortals. They knew him well. He had once been a Ghetto Brother.

Suarez and the gang returned to the clubhouse empty-handed. But Melendez was there and the spot was crowded with GBs and Roman Kings. Julio and four others, all members of the Seven Immortals and Mongols, had their legs tied and their arms bound behind their backs.

Melendez watched as Suarez took a .45 and pressed the gun to Julio's head, and then put into Julio's mouth. "I'm gonna blow your brains out," Suarez said. Melendez stepped up and put his finger between the hammer and the bullet.

Suarez and Melendez argued. "You want to save this stupid son of a bitch who killed one of us?"

"We're all 'one of us.'"

Finally Suarez wheeled around and kicked Julio. The rest of the clubhouse descended on the Immortals and Mongols and beat them bloody. Then Suarez ended it, pulled the accused up and pushed them out into the winter night.

Later that evening, Suarez and Melendez went to Black Benjie's apartment to comfort Gwendolyn Benjamin, his mother. "Everyone loved Benjie. He was the man," Suarez told her. "If something's not done all hell is gonna break loose."

Mrs. Benjamin was clear: "No revenge. Benjie lived for peace."[12]

Suarez recalls, "Benjy Melendez and myself sat up that night. He was saying that war was totally crazy. 'They're still our brothers and sisters. We got to show them by example.' And I said, 'I don't think I can do that, man.' He said, 'Charlie, the only way you can beat them is by showing them.' We had to beat them by example and not retaliate and call a peace treaty. All the gangs."

The next morning, reporters gathered at the Ghetto Brothers clubhouse. Melendez was the designated spokesperson. "All the gangs are waiting for one word—'Fire'—but I'm not going to say it because that won't bring Benjie back," he said. "I notice you reporters look disappointed because you didn't want to hear that, right? You wanted to hear about these South Bronx savages. But I'm not going to give you the pleasure."

Suarez recalls that many Ghetto Brothers were angry. "They said we were pussies," he says. But after Black Benjie was buried in an emotional ceremony, the Ghetto Brothers issued a call for a truce meeting to be held on the evening of December 8 at the Bronx Boys Club, a sanctuary in the heart of the Fort Apache battleground.

Peace Brother Peace

And so they came, the Black and brown gangs of the Bronx. The smaller families—the Liberated Panthers, the King Cobras, the Majestic Warlocks, the Ghetto Warriors, the Flying Dutchmen. The hungry ones—the Young Sinners, the Young Cobras, the Young Saints, the Young Saigons, the Roman Kings. The established ones—the Turbans, the Brothers and Sisters, the Latin Aces, the Peacemakers, the Dirty Dozens, the Mongols. And the major families—the Javelins, the Bachelors, the Savage Nomads, the Savage Skulls, the Black Spades, and the Seven Immortals.[13]

The unprecedented gathering threatened to explode from the accumulated fuel of unresolved slights and unpaid blood debts. Sniper cops perched on the roofs of nearby buildings. Television cameras, photographers and reporters filed into the gym.

The presidents, vice presidents and warlords, including a young Black Spade named Afrika Bambaataa, filled the folding chairs set in a circle in the middle of the gym floor. Social workers, school teachers, and other gang members filled the bleachers. The girl gangs were locked outside in the December freeze.

Inside, the tension was thick. Charlie Suarez, wearing a black beret with a red star, black vest and denims instead of his Ghetto Brothers colors, opened the meeting with a command: "I would like for the police to leave or we got nothing to say." An undercover cop left to great applause, a momentary release.

Suarez reminded the gang leaders that they were there because Black Benjie had died for peace, and then opened the floor. Marvin "Hollywood" Harper, a Vietnam vet and a slim Black member of the Savage Skulls sporting a beret and a gray combat shirt under his colors, stepped up. He said, "When I heard about Benjie dying, I told Brother Charlie of the Ghetto Brothers that I would take a life for Benjie. Charlie told me no, so I won't. If the Ghetto Brothers want peace, then there will be peace."

Then he pointed at the Seven Immortals, the Mongols and the Black Spades, and accused them of attacking his fellow Skulls and taking their colors. He pointed at them and blamed them for the death of Black Benjie. One smirked, "I wasn't there man, I was in court."

Bam Bam, the leader of the Black Spades, accused the Skulls of invading Spades' turf with shotguns. The meeting was spinning out of control. Gang members stood up in the bleachers, as if they were ready to set something off. Suarez silenced them all with a word, "Peace."

Hollywood stepped back up to address the Spades. He gestured angrily with his cigarette: "All we did is ask you people for the colors and you people didn't give us our colors back. You don't see us stripping you people, man. You don't see us stripping the Turbans, you don't see us stripping the Ghetto Brothers. You don't see us stripping no other crowd. When we have static, we settle it among ourselves, man, because, like wow, we have to *live* in this district."

And here the meeting turned. "The whitey don't come down here and live in the fucked-up houses, man," Hollywood continued, his hands a blur of stabbing motion, his voice a newfound weapon. "The whitey don't come down here, man, and have all the, the fucked-up, fucking no heat in the wintertime. You understand? We do, *jack*, so therefore we got to make it a better place to live."

The crowd, even the Spades, rose enthusiastically in assent. Hollywood called for an end to rumors, for a step toward peace. "If we don't have peace now, whitey will come in and stomp us," he shouted.[14] The gangs roared in agreement, holding up peace signs and Black power salutes.

Bam Bam spoke about dealing with junkies and cops, and the talk turned to how to pressure politicians and change the Bronx. Then Benjy Melendez stepped forward. He looked Black Benjie's killer in the eye. "You took away one of our brothers' lives, man," Melendez said. "You don't want us to become a gang anymore, right? Because I *know* you. You was up in the meeting and you told me, 'Benjy I want to get out alive.'"

Melendez concluded, "The thing is, we're not a gang anymore. We're an *organization*. We want to help Blacks and Puerto Ricans to live in a better environment."

Suarez and Vincenty directed the gangs into smaller caucuses to discuss the fine points of the Peace Treaty. It read:

To All Brothers and Sisters:

We realize that we are all brothers living in the same neighborhoods and having the same problems. We also realize that fighting amongst ourselves will not solve out common problems. If we are to build up our community to be better place [sic] for our families and ourselves we must work together. We who have signed this treaty pledge peace and unity for all. All of us who have signed this peace will be known from now on as The Family. The terms of the Peace are as follows:

1. All groups are to respect each other—cliques, individual members and their women. Each member clique of the Family will be able to wear their colors in other member cliques' turf without being bothered. They are to remember in whose turf they are and respect that turf as if it were their own.

2. If any clique has a gripe against another clique the presidents of each are to meet together to talk it out.

    If one member of a clique has a beef with a member of another clique, the two are to talk it over. If that does not solve it then they will both fight it out between themselves, after that it is considered finished.

    If there is any rumors about cliques going down on each other the leaders of each of these groups shall meet to talk it out.

3. For those cliques outside of the Peace Treaty—the presidents of the Family will meet with the clique to explain the terms of the Peace. The clique will given [sic] the opportunity to

    a. join

    b. disband

    c. be disbanded.

4. The presidents of the Family will meet from time to time to discuss concerns of the groups.

This is the Peace we pledge to keep.

<u>PEACE BETWEEN ALL GANGS AND A POWERFUL UNITY.</u>

At the end, Suarez and the Boys Club director, a young priest named Mario Barbell, summoned the presidents into the center of the floor to have them put their hands together as if they were in a huddle. As the photographers and cameramen jockeyed for position, they said "Peace!" and strode out.

The social workers loved it; it seemed an unqualified victory to them. Mayor Lindsay's corrupt, ineffectual Youth Services Agency director Ted Gross—who had arrived in a pimp-style red-and-white brocade suit and admitted of the meeting, "I thought it was frightening as hell"—stood before the reporters and took full credit.[15] The media was electrified, news reports would be glowing.

In some respects, the meeting was a leap forward. The Ghetto Brothers had demonstrated a different kind of street justice, administered within the codes of the gangs. Black Benjie's alleged murderers were never snitched out to the police. Instead of meeting blood with more blood, the gangs had come to a consensus.

The meeting also left much to be desired. Although many of the girl gang-bangers had been alongside the boys in the street violence that inspired the meeting, they were not even represented in the room, while the media and the social workers got bleacher seats. In the end, the truce meeting mainly felt like a public trial, particularly for the Seven Immortals. But it had failed in its most basic purpose: to convince street gangs to maintain a borough-wide truce.

To this day, Blackie Mercado still scoffs, "We went because we had to go and represent. As soon as we walked out, it was back to the Skulls fighting the Galaxies and all these motherfuckers. How can all this shit be going on when we're walking out?"

Many other gang leaders left the meeting feeling it was some sort of an elaborate charade. That weekend, the Ghetto Brothers again gathered the presidents, this time in their clubhouse, away from the social workers and the media. The two-hour meeting at the Boys Club, Melendez told the gang leaders, "was a big show. It was just for the media to see, 'Oh see, the city got the gangs together.' But people went out of there feeling angry, feeling pissed off, and it wasn't genuine. Let's speak for real, because a lot of us here are still holding anger inside."

In the confines of the clubhouse, the presidents talked of the anger still roiling their ranks over the death of Black Benjie. They said that they were doing all they could to keep anyone from taking the matter into their own hands. Julio of the Seven Immortals admitted he knew the gang was marked and broke down as he apologized. Melendez jumped back in, pointing to Julio. "Attacking these guys is not gonna bring Black Benjie back again," he said. "It never should have happened, but it happened. Let it never, never happen again."

That night, the truce was sealed.

The Long Dissipation

But it was bound to end. The warning signs came quickly. Just days after the Boys Club meeting, NYPD's Bronx Youth Gang Task Force quietly opened for business. One officer bluntly outlined their *raison d'etre*: "We talk to the gangs. We tell 'em—'With some thirty thousand cops, we got the biggest gang in the city. You're going to lose.' "[16]

They tried to get operatives to join the gangs, but when the operatives balked at going through initiations, the cops tried a different tack. "There was a group that the police force made from ex-Marines called the Purple Mothers," says Afrika Bambaataa. "It was like a fake, secret type gang that was going around attacking people and assassinating them. And word was on the street that whoever catch these cats, they definitely gon' be dealt with, or if they catch you, you gon' be dealt with."

Through interrogations and sweep arrests, the Task Force compiled three thousand dossiers on gangs and gang members in just over a year.[17] Mercado says, "Police was fucking with us a lot. They see more than three of us walking, they would arrest us for unlawful assembly." In short order, the cops had enough to bring down many of the gang leaders. By early 1972, Mercado was in jail. Savage Nomad president Ben Buxton and Turbans president Manny Araujo were also hauled off to prison. "The enemy around the Bronx now at this very moment," said one of the gang members on a local TV show, "is the policemen."[18] With each succession in leadership, the truce eroded just a little bit more.

The post-truce experiences of the two men who had run the Bronx Boys Club meeting, Eduardo Vincenty and Charlie Suarez, were representative. Vincenty was shot in the face when he tried to stop a fight. While he recovered, the Youth Services Agency eliminated his job, along with the ten-person youth crisis-management team charged with mediating gang beefs. All the proposals the gangs were drawing up for jobs, service, and recreation programs were dead on arrival.

Just two days after the second truce meeting, FBI agents, alerted by the publicity over Black Benjie's murder, arrested Charlie Suarez on his AWOL charge. As soon as they legally could, the Marines moved him out of his Brooklyn Navy Yard holding pen, fearing the Ghetto Brothers were preparing a massive gang attack on the Yard. After Congressman Herman Badillo interceded to have Suarez receive an Undesirable Discharge from the Marines, Suarez slowly drifted away from the Ghetto Brothers, eventually departing for Philadelphia with a full-blown heroin addiction.

As resources dried up, so did the Ghetto Brothers' fervor. In a round of budget cuts, the Youth Services Agency closed the GB's storefront. Some drifted away, some into the armed services, others to family and jobs, still others to drugs and jail. Melendez took a youth-worker job with the community organization, United Bronx Parents, and stepped down from the gang's leadership. For his gang advocacy, Manny Dominguez was fired from his job at Dwyer Junior High.

In the streets, the romance with the gangs was over. On the part of Kelly Street called "Banana Kelly" for the way it curves, near where the Savage Skulls, the Young Lords and the block's residents had once battled cops side by side, vigilante groups were chasing out gang members with pool sticks, pool balls, chains, and knives.

The largest gangs, Black Spades and the Savage Skulls, were fragmenting. Some Spades were registering voters, some were embroiled in the long war with the white gangs of the North Bronx, others were elbowing into the drug market. Some Skulls had begun motorcycle clubs, others were running protection rackets.

For the young Afrika Bambaataa, now a leader in the Black Spades, the peace meetings had a profound effect. He had been with Bam Bam as they cleared the blocks of drug dealers. Now he and other Spades assisted with community health programs. Bam Bam was fighting in Vietnam, and Bambaataa was gravitating to the disco parties that former Spades were throwing.

Across town, someone finally made a movie of the Savage Nomads and the Savage Skulls, the gang documentary *80 Blocks from Tiffany's*. But they seemed to be going through the motions. Hollywood, the fiery soul of the Bronx Boys Club meeting, was still flying cut sleeves but his protean energy was gone. Blackie was raising two children with his wife, struggling to make it between prison bids, and feeling nostalgic. "In the old days, it was nice," he said, tentatively, "we just lived for *now*." The youthful confidence he displayed in Rita Fecher's reels had been replaced by adulthood and doubt. Only scenes of a block party—featuring a DJ spinning Chic records on Technics turntables as a teenage beauty named India chanted, "Yes yes y'all! Freak freak y'all!"—gave the movie any emotional lift.

If the Skulls and Nomads had dissipated, some Ghetto Brothers still spoiled for the great war. Amidst death threats to his wife and daughter from some of his Brothers, Benjy Melendez finally quit the group that had been his life, gathered up his family and disappeared. Bronx legend had it that Melendez died in prison and Suarez of a heroin overdose, GBs to the end. The only things that remained were the graffitied walls bearing the arrow-tipped tags of the gang and its members, and the music of the Ghetto Brothers' Latin-funk band.

Gonna Take You Higher

The peace treaty had been momentous. Change was sweeping through the Bronx. Youthful energies turned from nihilistic implosion to creative explosion. Typically, the Ghetto Brothers were at the vanguard of this development as well.

Sometime after they had become Bronx celebrities, the Ghetto Brothers were approached by Ismael Maisonave, the owner of a small Latin label called Salsa International/Mary Lou Records who had mostly recorded *descargas* and *guaguancos* by the likes of Charlie Palmieri, Cachao, and Chivirico Davila. Benjy and Victor Melendez jumped at the chance to record their original compositions in a real studio, and signed the five-hundred-dollar contract. No date is listed on their eight-song album, *Ghetto Brothers Power Fuerza,* but it was probably released in 1972.

"This album contains a message; a message to the world, from the Ghetto Brothers," the handwritten liner notes read. "If the Ghetto Brothers' dream comes true, the 'little people' will be 'little people' no more, and make their own mark in this world." But this wasn't the protest or counterculture music the notes seemed to promise.

The Melendezes had grown up listening to the Beatles, the Beach Boys, and doo-wop. Other Bronx Puerto Ricans—like Willie Colon, a former gangbanger who wrote anthems for the street kids and sufferers, or Ray Barretto and Eddie Palmieri, whose music reflected Brown Power ferment—were updating Cuban roots music into a uniquely Nuyorican sound. But the Ghetto Brothers' post-*bugalú* music seemed closer to the teen-themed Latin pop of California than the *salsa* of the Bronx, more Willie Bobo than Willie Colon.

Benjy and Victor brought back sweet melodies to the South Bronx, mostly writing closely harmonized pop with a wicked Latin backbeat, songs of love and betrayal with titles like "There Is Something in My Heart" or "You Say You Are My Friend." Only "Viva Puerto Rico Libre"—a composition that moved through *jibaro, bolero* and funk styles—revealed their politics. The album was recorded in one take—lo-fi, raw, brimming with enthusiasm, a feeling that all their pent-up creativity could finally be released.

The Ghetto Brothers' album never sold many copies or moved far beyond the Bronx, but it signaled an important shift. After the truce, the Ghetto Brothers band played Friday block parties, plugging their amps into the lampposts and inviting all the gangs to their turf. They were difficult, rowdy crowds, but songs like "Got This Happy Feeling," a nod to The Beginning of the End's "Funky Nassau," and "Mastica Chupa Y Jala," with its Santana guitar-hero aspirations, kept them dancing. The band's signature song, "Ghetto Brothers Power," was a funky Joe Bataan–meets–Sly Stone sure-shot. Benjy called out, "If you want to get your thing together, brothers and sisters, let's do it Ghetto Brother style." Then they launched into the kind of blazing drum-and-conga breakdown that drove the Bronx kids crazy. The song climaxed with a promise: "We are gonna take you higher with Ghetto Brother Power!"

Instead of the kind of power that came from ideology, collectivity, or the barrel of a gun, this was the kind of power that came from celebrating being young and free. The turf grid was disintegrating. Gangs were dissolving. The new kids coming up were obsessed with flash, style, *sabor*. For them, the block party—not the political party—was the space of possibility.

The gangs had risen out of the ash, rubble, and blood of 1968. Five years later, the circle was ready to turn again.

The Father.
Photo © Marlon Ajamu Myrie

4.

Making a Name

How DJ Kool Herc Lost His Accent and Started Hip-Hop

. . . the logic is an extension rather than a negation. Alias, a.k.a.; the names describe a process of loops. From A to B and back again.
                                                                    Paul D. Miller

It has become myth, a creation myth, this West Bronx party at the end of the summer in 1973. Not for its guests—a hundred kids and kin from around the way, nor for the setting—a modest recreation room in a new apartment complex; not even for its location—two miles north of Yankee Stadium, near where the Cross-Bronx Expressway spills into Manhattan. Time remembers it for the night DJ Kool Herc made his name.

The plan was simple enough, according to the party's host, Cindy Campbell. "I was saving my money, because what you want to do for back to school is go down to Delancey Street instead of going to Fordham Road, because you can get the newest things that a lot of people don't have. And when you go back to school, you want to go with things that nobody has so you could look nice and fresh," she says. "At the time my Neighborhood Youth Corps paycheck was like forty-five dollars a week—ha!—and they would pay you every two weeks. So how am I gonna turn over my money? I mean, this is not enough money!"

Cindy calculated it would cost a little more than half her paycheck to rent the rec room in their apartment building at 1520 Sedgwick Avenue. Her brother, whom she knew as Clive but everyone else knew as Kool Herc, was an aspiring DJ with access to a powerful sound system. All she had to do was bulk-buy some Olde English 800 malt liquor, Colt 45 beer, and soda, and advertise the party.

She, Clive and her friends hand-wrote the announcements on index cards, scribbling the info below a song title like "Get on the Good Foot" or "Fence-walk." If she filled the room, she could charge a quarter for the girls, two for the guys, and make back the overhead on the room. And with the profit—presto, instant wardrobe.

Clive had been DJing house parties for three years. Growing up in Kingston, Jamaica, he had seen the sound systems firsthand. The local sound was called Somerset Lane, and the selector's name was King George. Clive says, "I was too young to go in. All we could do is sneak out and see the preparation of the dance throughout the day. The guys would come with a big old handcart with the boxes in it. And then in the night time, I'm a little itchy headed, loving the vibrations on the zinc top 'cause them sound systems are powerful.

"We just stay outside like everybody else, you know, pointing at the gangsters as they come up, all the famous people. And at the time they had the little motorcycles, Triumphs and Hondas. Rudeboys used to have those souped up. They used to come up four and five six deep, with them *likkle* ratchet knife," Clive says. He still remembers the crowd's buzz when Claudie Massop arrived at a local dance one night. He wanted to be at the center of that kind of excitement, to be a King George.

Cindy and Clive's father, Keith Campbell, was a devoted record collector, buying not only reggae, but American jazz, gospel, and country. They heard Nina Simone and Louis Armstrong and Nat King Cole, even Nashville country crooner Jim Reeves. "I remember listening to Jim Reeves all the time," Clive says. "I was singing these songs and emulating them to the fullest. That really helped me out, changing my accent, is singing to the records."

In the Bronx, his mother, Nettie, would take him to house parties, which had the same ambrosial effect on him that the sound systems had. "I see the different guys dancing, guys rapping to girls, I'm wondering what the guy is whisperin' in the girl's ears about. I'm green, but I'm checking out the scene," he recalls. "And I noticed a lot of the girls was complaining, 'Why they not playing that record?' 'How come they don't have that record?' 'Why did they take it off right there?' " He began buying his own 45s, waiting for the day he could have his own sound system.

As luck would have it, Keith Campbell became a sponsor for a local rhythm and blues band, investing in a brand new Shure P.A. system for the group.

Clive's father was now their soundman, and the band wanted somebody to play records during intermission. Keith told them he could get his son. But Clive had started up his own house party business, and somehow his gigs always happened to fall at the same times as the band's, leaving Keith so angry he refused to let Clive touch the system. "So here go these big columns in my room, and my father says, 'Don't touch it. Go and borrow Mr. Dolphy's stuff,' " he says. "Mr. Dolphy said, 'Don't worry Clive, I'll let you borrow some of these.' In the back of my mind, Jesus Christ, I got these big Shure columns up in the room!"

At the same time, his father was no technician. They all knew the system was powerful, but no one could seem to make it peak. Another family in the same building had the same system and seemed to be getting more juice out of it, but they wouldn't let Keith or Clive see how they did it. "They used to put a lot of wires to distract me from chasing the wires," he says.

One afternoon, fiddling around on the system behind his father's back, Clive figured it out. "What I did was I took the speaker wire, put a jack onto it and jacked it into one of the channels, and I had extra power and reserve power. Now I could control it from the preamp. I got two Bogart amps, two Girard turntables, and then I just used the channel knobs as my mixer. No headphones. The system could take eight mics. I had an echo chamber in one, and a regular mic to another. So I could talk plain and, at the same time, I could wait halfway for the echo to come out.

"My father came home and it was so loud he snuck up behind me," he remembers. Clive's guilt was written all over his face. But his father couldn't believe it.

Keith yelled, "Where the noise come from?"

"This is the system!"

Keith said, "What! Weh you did?"

"This is what I did,' " Clive recalls telling his father, revealing the hookup. "And he said, *'Raas claat,* man! We 'ave sound!!!

"So now the tables turned. Now these other guys was trying to copy what I was doing, because our sound is coming out monster, monster!" Clive says. "Me and my father came to a mutual understanding that I would go with them and play between breaks and when I do my parties, I could use the set. I didn't have to borrow his friend's sound system anymore. I start making up business cards saying 'Father and Son.' And that's how it started, man! That's when Cindy asked me to do a back-to-school party. Now people would come to this party and see these big-ass boxes they never seen before."

It was the last week in August of 1973. Clive and his friends brought the equipment down from their second floor apartment and set up in the room adjacent to the rec room. "My system was on the dance floor, and I was in a little room watching, peeking out the door seeing how the party was going," he says.

It didn't start so well. Clive played some dancehall tunes, ones guaranteed to rock any yard dance. Like any proud DJ, he wanted to stamp his personality onto his playlist. But this was the Bronx. They wanted the breaks. So, like any good DJ, he gave the people what they wanted, and dropped some soul and funk bombs. Now they were packing the room. There was a new energy. DJ Kool Herc took the mic and carried the crowd higher.

"All people would hear is his voice coming out from the speakers," Cindy says. "And we didn't have no money for a strobe light. So what we had was this guy named Mike. When Herc would say, 'Okay, Mike! Mike with the lights!', Mike flicked the light switch. He got paid for that."

By this point in the night, they probably didn't need the atmospherics. The party people were moving to the shouts of James Brown, turning the place into a sweatbox. They were busy shaking off history, having the best night of their generation's lives.

Later, as Clive and Cindy counted their money, they were giddy. This party could be the start of something big, they surmised. They just couldn't know how big.

Sacrifices

Clive Campbell was born the first of six children to Keith and Nettie Campbell. Nettie had moved to the city from Port Maria on the northern coast. Keith, a city native, worked as the head foreman at the Kingston Wharf garage, a working-class job with status.

Keith was something of a community leader, he held the kind of job title that drew the attention of politicians. But he chose not to take sides when the JLP and PNP began their violent jockeying for position. The year before Clive left for the United States, Edward Seaga had unleashed the West Kingston War in Back-

O-Wall. Clive says, "I remember police riding around in big old trucks, tanks. And some people who were brothers or friends would turn on each other. It was like a civil war."

By then, the Campbells no longer lived in Trenchtown near the frontlines. They had moved east across the city to a house in Franklyn Town, a quieter urban neighborhood of strivers below Warieka Hill and the upper-class neighborhood called Beverly Hills. It was a modest but lush property near the famous Alpha Boys School.

"We had like seven different fruits growing in our yard. We had different types of peppers, flowers, you know, it was tight!" Clive recalls. "We wasn't too far away from the beach. So, as a matter of fact, it was a traditional thing with us for my father to take us to the beach on Sunday. Every Sunday we'd look forward to go out to the beach after church."

The Campbells were able to afford a housekeeper. Their grandfather, aunts and older cousins all pitched in to raise the children, a fact that would become significant when Nettie decided to supplement the family income by working and studying in the United States. Many other Jamaicans were already leaving for Miami, London, Toronto and New York City to escape the instability and seek their fortune. During the early 1960s, Nettie had departed for Manhattan to work as a dental technician and to study for a nursing degree. She saved money to send home and returned with a degree, convinced that the United States offered a better future for the family.

Cindy says, "She saw the opportunities. The public schools were free, because in Jamaica we went to private schools. So she told my father that when she finished with school that what she wanted was for the family to live here. And he didn't want to come."

But Keith could see Nettie's reasoning. Even his own friends and relatives were leaving the country. Before Nettie returned to New York City in 1966, they agreed to move to America. Clive would be the first to join her, then the rest of the family would follow. Cindy says, "A lot of immigrants have to do that. You have to make sacrifices. It breaks up the family for a small amount of time but eventually the family gets back together."

Clive and Cindy agree that Keith remained a Jamaican at heart. "He just said, 'America was a place for you to excel and do better for your kids.' But after a while you go back home, you go back to your country. And he believed in that. He loved his country," Cindy says. Years later, after raising his children with Nettie in New York City and becoming an American citizen, he returned to his beloved island for a visit. While swimming in strong currents off Bull Bay, he had a heart attack. The Campbells buried him in Jamaica.

Becoming American

From Kingston to the Bronx. Stones that the builders refused.

Clive Campbell came to New York City on a cold November night in 1967. A fresh snowfall lay on the ground, something the twelve-year-old had never seen before. He took a bus from Kennedy Airport into the gray, unwelcoming city. This wasn't the America he had seen on his neighbor's television, or imagined from his father's records. He had no idea how to begin again, he says, "All I could do was just look out the window."

His mother's apartment was at 611 East 178th Avenue, between the Bronx's Little Italy and Crotona Park, in what had been the Cross-Bronx Expressway's most contested mile. "Now I'm living in a tenement building. There's no yard. This is all boxed and closed in," Clive recalls. His mother feared Clive would fall prey to the heroin plague. She told Clive, "Don't let anybody tell you they're gonna stick something in your arm. Don't let them trick you by calling you chicken."

Clive looked and spoke and felt like a country boy. "Here I am all hicked out, got a corduroy coat on, with the snow hat with the flip-up-and-come-over-your-ears. I had that on with these cowboy boots," Herc recalls. "And this girl at school started teasing the hell out of me. She was calling my shoes 'roach killers.' She had the whole hall laughing, 'Ah roach killers, roach killers!'

"At that time, being Jamaican wasn't fashionable. Bob Marley didn't come through yet to make it more fashionable, to even give a chance for people to listen to our music," he says. "I remember one time a guy said, 'Clive, man, don't walk down that way cause they throwing Jamaicans in garbage cans.' The gangs was throwing Jamaicans in garbage cans!"

Herc was learning the ways of the Bronx. He found himself hanging out with young Five Percenters, absorbing their slang and science. For a time, he even rolled with the Cofon Cats, the same Tremont gang that Benjy Melendez had joined when he first moved to the Bronx a few years before. It wasn't much of an experience. The Cofon Cats spent one long afternoon getting chased out of Little Italy by the Golden Guineas.

At Junior High School 118, Clive began running cross-country and track and winning medals. His physicality won him American friends. After school, he began hanging out with a Jamaican American named Jerome Wallace, who was a unicyclist. Jerome had already been through the transition Clive was going through. He taught Clive how to ride on one wheel, and how to balance his Jamaican past and his Bronx present. Clive began to see the Cofon Cats as punks who were nothing without the security of the gang. "The gang members started asking us to be division leaders because they see we have respect. So we didn't need that anymore," Herc says. "And I had a few other things to worry about besides the gangs, like getting my ass whipped by my father."

Clive tuned into rock and soul disc jockeys like Cousin Brucie and Wolfman Jack as if he had caught religion, listening to these smooth men rap their silver-tongued rap. He began going to "First Fridays" youth dances at a local Catholic school and at Murphy Projects. His mother took him to house parties, where he heard music he had never heard on WBLS or WWRL. The Temptations, Aretha Franklin, Smokey Robinson, and, most important, James Brown became his tutors; they were teaching Clive how to lose his accent.

"I was more around Americans. And I was tired of hearing them say 'What did you say?' My accent really started to change," he recalls. By the time Clive began attending Alfred E. Smith High School, some of his Jamaican friends didn't even know he was Jamaican. He was in the process of reinventing himself, creating a new identity.

He wasn't alone. All across the city youths were customizing their names or giving themselves new ones and scrawling them across the naked city surfaces. The young graffiti writers were the advance guard of a new culture; they literally blazed trails out of the gang generation. Crossing demarcated turfs to leave their aliases in marker and spraypaint, they said "I'm here" and "Fuck all y'all" at the same time. Gang members, who had trapped themselves in their own neighborhoods, had to give them respect. Clive and the post-gang youths were a different breed, more interested in projecting individual flash than collective brawn, and they would soon render the gangs obsolete.

Graffiti expert Jack Stewart traces the emergence of the modern-day movement to Philadelphia's neighborhoods of color as early as 1965.[1] Aerosolist and activist Steve "Espo" Powers says that the Black teenager, CORNBREAD, who is credited with popularizing the tagging of the Philly subways, was only trying to attract the attention of a beauty named Cynthia. By 1968, the movement had spread to New York City. CORNBREAD's protégé, TOP CAT, moved to Harlem and brought with him the "gangster" style of lettering. A Puerto Rican youth calling himself JULIO 204—the number was the street he hailed from—began at about the same time. When a Greek American named TAKI 183 told the *New York Times* in the summer of 1971 why he tagged his name on ice cream trucks and subway cars—"I don't feel like a celebrity normally, but the guys make me feel like one when they introduce me to someone"—thousands of New York youngsters picked up fat markers and spray paint to make their own name.[2] Writers like LEE 163d!, EVIL ED, CLIFF 159, JUNIOR 161, CAY 161, CHE 159 and BARBARA and EVA 62 were saying their names loud all across buildings, bus stops, and subway station walls uptown.

Roaming through gang turfs, slipping through the long arms and high fences of authority, violating notions of property and propriety, graffiti writers found their own kind of freedom. Writing your name was like locating the edge of civil society and planting a flag there. In Greg Tate's words, it was "reverse colonization."[3] The 1960s, as the hip-hop generation would so often be reminded, were a great time to be young. The world seemed to shake under young feet so easily back then. The revolutionaries expected the whole world to be watching and when they were given the spotlight, they cast a long shadow. But these writers weren't like the revolutionaries, or even the philosopher-activist wall-writers in Lima, Mexico City, Paris, and Algiers. Theirs were not political statements. They were just what they were, a strike against their generation's invisibility and preparation for the coming darkness.

They held no illusions about power. No graffiti writer ever hoped to run for mayor. And unlike the gang bangers, none would submerge his or her name to the collective. They were doing it to be known amongst their peers, to be recognized for their originality, bravado, daring, and style. Norman Mailer, one of the first to write seriously about graffiti, got it instantly: the writers were composing advertisements for themselves.

In the summer of 1970, TAKI 183's tags seemed to explode across the city. Like thousands of other kids, Clive, Jerome and their friend Richard picked up markers and spraycans. Rich became UNCLE RICH, Jerome became YOGI and Clive became CLYDE AS KOOL.[4]

"They couldn't recall my name Clive," he says. "So the closest you could come was Clyde, from the Knicks basketball player. They'd be like, 'You mean like 'Clyde' Frazier?' 'Yeah. Clyde. Let's leave it like that.' So I started to write that. And where I picked 'Kool' from was this TV cigarette commercial. A guy was driving one of them Aston-Martins, like this James Bond car, and his cigarette was right there by the gear shift, white gloves, dark glasses and just driving through the countryside—whoooooo! The girl with him, she reached over to touch his cigarette; and he goes—rrrrrrrrnt! Stops the car, leans over, opens the door, points his finger, tells her, 'Get out!' And she got out. And the commercial said, 'Nobody touches my silver-thin.' I was like, wow, that's 'Kool'! So I picked KOOL.

"Wherever you see UNCLE RICH, you see CLYDE AS KOOL," he says. "I put a little smiling face in it, the eyes, the nose, and mouth and a little cigarette hanging out, and a little tam on it, like a little Apple Jack's hat."

Writing brought him into contact with the premier stylists, and he began hanging out with the EX-VANDALS, the legendary supercrew that had begun in Brooklyn and now included SUPER KOOL 223, EL MARKO, STAY HIGH 149 and PHASE 2. As graffiti moved off the walls and onto the subway steel, EL MARKO and SUPER KOOL revolutionized the name game by painting top-to-bottom masterpieces on the train-cars in late 1971 and early 1972. Just as city officials enacted the first in what would become decades of increasingly severe anti-graffiti laws, the great Bronx writer PHASE 2 launched a series of next evolutionary steps, introducing ever more imaginative refinements on the rolling steel canvases.

But Clive would finally make his name elsewhere. He was running track, pushing weights, playing rough schoolyard basketball. His classmates kidded him, dubbing him "Hercules" for his bullish power drives to the hoop. "I went back to the block and I said, 'Yo fellas, this guy at school, man, he's calling me Hercules. I know he means well, but I don't like it.' So I said, 'What's the shortening for Hercules?' They said 'Herc.' Aaaaaah—sounds unique! So I said, 'Yo man, just call me Herc, leave off the 'lees', just call me Herc.' Between high school and the block, I put the two names together and I dropped the CLYDE. I started calling myself Kool Herc, and that was it."

New Fires

A fire sent the Campbells out of their Tremont apartment. Their baby brother was striking matches, lighting pieces of paper and tossing them out the window. A breeze caught a burning paper and blew it back in, setting the window curtains aflame. Although the firemen were able to put it out without anyone getting hurt, Cindy remains angry at what happened afterward. "When the fire department came in there, they were looking for money. The fire was really in one room, but in the bedroom the drawers were pulled out. My father had a tin-pan of quarters that he was saving, and that tin-pan had at least three- or four-hundred dollars in quarters at the time. That was just missing," she says.

Populations were in flux. Whites were leaving for Co-op City and the suburbs. With government vouchers and assistance money, the Campbells joined the Black and brown exodus into the West Bronx. They moved into the Concourse Plaza Hotel on the Grand Concourse at 161st Street, where many burned-out families had been temporarily relocated.

After the family moved into a brand new apartment building at 1520 Sedgwick, Kool Herc would return to the hotel to frequent the disco downstairs, the Plaza Tunnel. A friend of his from high school named Shaft spun records there, as well as a DJ named John Brown. In gay and Black clubs at the time, DJs were pushing the emerging four-on-the-floor disco beat. But the Plaza Tunnel DJs had a rawer sound. John Brown "was the first to play records like 'Give it Up or Turn it Loose' by James Brown and 'Get Ready' by Rare Earth," pioneering hip-hop journalist Steven Hager wrote. "['Get Ready'] was a favorite in the Bronx because it lasted over twenty-one minutes, which was long enough for the serious dancers to get into the beat. They loved to wait for the song's two-minute drum solo to show their most spectacular moves."[5]

The dance styles began as elaborations of moves people had seen James Brown doing on TV. Zulu Nation DJ Jazzy Jay, who began as a b-boy says, "You could be dancing with your girl and spin away from her, hit the ground, come back up. It was all about 'smooth.' Like how James used to slide across the floor and the fancy footwork and all of that." They even called it—a hard-won irony—"burning."

James Brown's career had peaked in the late 1960s with the Black Power Movement. He performed "Say it Loud (I'm Black and I'm Proud)" without apology on national television, and his mere presence in town, it was said, prevented riots in racially tense Boston in the immediate aftermath of Martin Luther King, Jr.'s assassination.

But during the early 1970s, attitudes changed. Across the country, Black mayors took over in cities that had once burned, class gaps widened and Black radio shifted to the tastes of upwardly mobile listeners. Coleman Young became mayor of Motown, while Berry Gordy departed for Hollywood. James Brown's career went into steep decline.

Bronx-born hip-hop historian Davey D recalls, "If you listened to the Black radio station at the time, WBLS—Black-owned, Black-run, the station that everyone listened to—you did not hear James Brown. Not even at nighttime. So while James Brown was being tossed out, we were embracing him."[6] His music, dance and style now possessed outlaw appeal. At the climax of a Plaza Tunnel night, when DJ John Brown put on "Soul Power," Hager says Black Spades would overrun the floor, hollering "Spade Power!" The firecracker energy being generated at the Plaza Tunnel gave Herc the standard to aim for with his own parties.

The Man with the Master Plan

At the same time, discos were shutting down and house parties were declining, partly because gangs like the Spades were making them unsafe. But the West Bronx had not suffered the same kind of devastation as the South Bronx. And all these youths needed somewhere to party. These reasons may explain why Sedgwick Avenue was ripe for a fresh new party scene.

The crowds at the Campbells' early Sedgwick parties were mainly high school students who were too young or too clean or living too far west to fall under the waning influence of the gangs. In those days, Herc would tell the weed-smokers to head around the block, and he'd even play slow jams. "Now and then a mom or pop might come in to see what's going on," says Herc.

Cindy adds, "My father was always there. People knew him in the neighborhood and they respected him so we never had violence or anything like that.

We didn't have to hire security guards. We never searched people. When people came, they came out of respect. It was a recreation thing for them to meet people. A lot of people met their boyfriends or girlfriends there."

Buzz spread about the back-to-school party, and they found themselves throwing parties almost on a monthly basis at the rec room. "Herc actually took away a lot of house parties and basement parties," says Cindy. "At those house parties, after a while, the parents would come in, flick on the lights and tell you, 'You kids got to get out' or 'Too many people in here' or 'I don't know who this one is' and 'Who's this burning up my floor with the cigarettes?' People didn't want to go back to that anymore."

Herc's reputation spread along the Bronx high-school circuit as well, after Cindy, through her role in student body government at Dodge High School, secured a successful boat cruise dance. By the summer of 1974, when Herc was playing regular parties to a loyal following, he decided to play a free party on the block. "And after the block party," he says, "we couldn't come back to the rec room."

Outdoors, he knew he was putting the sound system at risk, and that fights could potentially break out. "So when I come out there, I said, 'Listen. The first discrepancy, I'm pulling the plug. Let's get that straight right now. There's kids out here, there's grown folks out here and we're gonna have a good time. So anybody start anything any disturbance or any discrepancy, any beef, I'm pulling the plug because I'm not gonna be here for the repercussions. All right?' So they said, 'All right, Herc, no problem.' And I start playing for the older heads, and then I go on for the younger heads and I'll go back and forth like that," he says. "We broke daylight. I played to the next morning."

Herc wanted to summon the same kind of excitement he felt as a *pickney* down yard. Along with his immigrant friend Coke La Rock, he distinguished their crew from the disco DJs by translating the Kingstonian vibe of sound system DJs like Count Machuki, King Stitt, U-Roy and Big Youth for the Bronxites. Herc hooked up his mics to a Space Echo box, yard dance style. They set off their dances by giving shout-outs and dropping little rhymes. They developed their own slang. At an after-hours spot Herc spun at, a drunken regular greeted his friends with the call: "To my mellow! My mellow is in the house!" With lines like these, the two created larger-than-life personas.

Herc carefully studied the dancers. "I was smoking cigarettes and I was waiting for the records to finish. And I noticed people was waiting for certain parts of the record," he says. It was an insight as profound as Ruddy Redwood's dub discovery. The moment when the dancers really got wild was in a song's short instrumental break, when the band would drop out and the rhythm section would get elemental. Forget melody, chorus, songs—it was all about the groove, building it, keeping it going. Like a string theorist, Herc zeroed in on the fundamental vibrating loop at the heart of the record, the break.

He started searching for songs by the sound of their break, songs that he would make into his signature tunes: the nonstop conga epics from The Incredible Bongo Band called "Apache" and "Bongo Rock," James Brown's "live" version of "Give It Up Turn It Loose" from the *Sex Machine* album, Johnny Pate's theme to *Shaft in Africa,* Dennis Coffey's "Scorpio"—Black soul and white rock records with an uptempo, often Afro-Latinized backbeat.[7] Then he soaked off the labels, Jamaican style. "My father said, 'Hide the name of your records because that's how you get your rep. That's how you get your clientele.' You don't want the same people to have your same record down the block," Herc says. Here was one source of hip-hop's competitive ethic and beat-this aesthetic.

In a technique he called "the Merry-Go-Round," Herc began to work two copies of the same record, back-cueing a record to the beginning of the break as the other reached the end, extending a five-second breakdown into a five-minute loop of fury, a makeshift *version* excursion. Before long he had tossed most of the songs, focusing on the breaks alone. His sets drove the dancers from climax to climax on waves of churning drums. "And once they heard that, that was it, wasn't no turning back," Herc says. "They always wanted to hear breaks after breaks after breaks after breaks."

To accommodate larger crowds, Herc moved his parties further up Sedgwick Avenue into Cedar Park. He had seen construction workers hooking up power by tapping the lightposts, and so he started doing the same. "I had a big Mackintosh amp. That thing cost a lot of money and it pumped a lot of juice. It was 300 watts per channel. As the juice start coming, man, the lights start dimming. And the turntables, I had the Technics 1100A, the big ones, so it wouldn't turn." Finally they found a tool shed in the park. They would send a young boy through the stone-broken window to plug into enough juice for the sound system.

The results shocked the borough, and brought in new audiences. Aaron

O'Bryant, who would later become DJ AJ, was a marijuana dealer living near St. Mary's Park. "Everyone was talking about this guy DJ Kool Herc. And I was really excited. I knew all the women was gonna be there. I was excited by Herc but I really wanted to see could I bag something!" he laughs. "I became a Kool Herc freak. Everywhere he played I was there."

A teen from Fox Street in the South Bronx named Joseph Saddler, who called himself Flash, also heard about Herc's exploits and went up to Cedar Park to see it for himself. "I seen this big six-foot-plus guy with this incredible sound system, heavily guarded. People just enjoying themselves from like four years to forty. I'm like, wow! He looked sort of like this superhero on this podium playing this music that wasn't being played on the radio. I liked what he was doing and what he was playing, and I wanted to do that, too."

The gangs were dissolving and Herc was popularizing a new hierarchy of cool. Turfs were still important but in a different way. Jazzy Jay says, "Instead of gangs, they started turning into little area crews where they would do a little bit of dirt. In every area, there would be a DJ crew or a breakdance crew. They would be like, 'Okay, we all about our music and we love our music but you come in this area wrong and we all about kicking your ass.' Competition fueled the whole thing."

Herc's parties drew in the crews, gave them a chance to strut their stuff and make their names. He kept the peace by taking a live-and-let-live policy and skillfully working the mic. "Everybody had to make money, even the stick-up kids. The guy selling weed would come to me, 'A-yo Herc, man, say I got weed.' I'd say, 'You know I can't say you got weed!' So I'd say it indirectly, 'Yo, Johnny, you know I can't say you got weed, right?' He'd take the heat."

"Or if I know there's a certain party up in there starting trouble, I never would say their name, I just say, 'Yo kill it, cut the bullshit out. You're my man, cut the dumb shit. *You* know and *they* know who I'm talking about. Okay? Alright.' They'd be like 'Oh shit, Herc gave me a little warning.' I might be playing music but I'm no sucker."

The real action was in the dance ciphers, with the kids who had come for Herc's "Merry-Go-Round," and were becoming personalities in their own right. They were too excitable and had too much flavor to conform to the precision group steps of dances like The Hustle. They would simply jump in one after another to go off, take each other out, just "break" wild on each other. Herc called them break boys, b-boys for short.[8]

There was Tricksy, Wallace Dee, the Amazing Bobo, Sau Sau, Charlie Rock, Norm Rockwell, Eldorado Mike, and Keith and Kevin, the Nigger Twins. They did dances like The Boyoing, where a b-boy sported a Turbans-like pom-pom topped hat, and stretched, wiggled, and shook back and forth to make the ball go "boyoing." "It was called that because that's basically what they see," says Jazzy Jay, "just bounce all over the place, hit the ground, go down. It wasn't like a lot of the acrobatics. It was more from style and finesse. You could do a whole routine standing up before you even hit the ground."

"Another kid uptown called it the cork-and-screw," says Jeffrey "DOZE" Green, a Rock Steady Crew member and second-generation b-boy who first saw The Boyoing in the North Bronx in 1975. "It's 'cause they used to spin down, pop up, do a split and then go whoop! Come up, and then go down again into a split into a few baby-rocks into a little baby freeze. People were spinning on their butts then, too."

"Tricksy had a huge afro," says Cindy. "And he had that soft hair because his hair grew. And he did a move where he would jump up and his afro would start to bounce also. There was also a move called the Frankenstein move, where he'd start moving like Frankenstein and his afro would start bouncing. It was like a show, you know?"

Herc assembled his own clique of DJs, dancers and rappers, and dubbed them the Herculords: Coke La Rock, DJ Timmy Tim with Little Tiny Feet, DJ Clark Kent the Rock Machine, the Imperial JC, Blackjack, LeBrew, Pebblee Poo, Sweet and Sour, Prince, and Whiz Kid. He refused to call them a crew. "That name 'crew' took the place of gang. When they said, 'crew', we knew it was a gang. So it was never the Herculord crew. That's what people start calling us. But we never had on our flier saying 'The Herculord crew.' It was billed with the sound system we called the Herculoids."

After reinvesting his money in a few different sound system sets, Herc was ready to take it to the next level. By 1975, he was doing all-ages dances at the Webster Avenue P.A.L. But he was turning twenty, and didn't only want the kiddie crowd anymore. He found a club called the Twilight Zone on Jerome Avenue near Tremont, and started hosting parties there with his clique and his sound system. He says he screened Muhammad Ali videos until they said, "Yo Herc, stop showing them Ali fights, you souping them motherfuckers up!"

At a hot spot called the Hevalo, he passed out flyers for his Twilight Zone shows until he was chased out. One day, he vowed, I'll play this spot. On a stormy night, Herc emptied the Hevalo by playing a party at the Zone. "Rain," he says, "was a good sign for me." The Hevalo owner quickly called him up to make a deal. Soon, Herc was playing there and at another club called the Executive Playhouse for a full-fledged adult crowd.

They came to hear Herc rap: "You never heard it like this before, and you're back for more and more and more of this here rock-ness. 'Cause you see, we rock with the rockers, we jam with the jammers, we party with the partyers. Young lady don't hurt nobody. It ain't no fun till we all get some. Don't hurt nobody, young lady!"

Coke and another crew member named Dickey let the crowds know: "There's no story can't be told, there's no horse can't be rode, a no bull can't be stopped and ain't a disco we can't rock. Herc! Herc! Who's the man with a master plan from the land of Gracie Grace? Herc Herc!"

By 1976, he was the number-one draw in the Bronx. No more roach killers. DJ Kool Herc dressed the role, sporting fabulous Lee or AJ Lester suits. All the high rollers, bank robbers, and hustlers from Harlem were coming up to see him. He says, "The reputation was, 'Who is making money up in the Bronx? Kool Herc and the guy Coke La Rock with the music.' "

Two Sevens Redub

1977 started off very well for Herc. But as it would be everywhere, trouble was ahead.

It was not, as many well-meaning journalists and academics would later erroneously write, that the block party or sound system showdown had replaced the rumble or the riot. That notion was as misguided as Robert Moses's contention that nothing good could ever again come from the Bronx. The truth was, in fact, much less dramatic and much more profound. In the Bronx's new hierarchy of cool, the man with the records had replaced the man with the colors. Violence did not suddenly end; how could it? But an enormous amount of creative energy was now ready to be released from the bottom of American society, and the staggering implications of this moment eventually would echo around the world.

By 1977, Herc and his competitors had divided the Bronx into a new kind of grid. In the South Bronx from 138th to 163rd streets, where the Bachelors, the Savage Nomads, the Savage Skulls and the Ghetto Brothers had once run, Grandmaster Flash, backed by the local Casanova Crew, was emerging as the area celebrity. In the Southeast, formerly the territory of the Black Spades, P.O.W.E.R. and the Javelins, Afrika Bambaataa held sway with his Zulu Nation. In the north, there was DJ Breakout and DJ Baron. And the West Bronx neighborhood and the East Bronx nightclubs were still Herc's. Herc remained the undisputed king of the borough by virtue of his records, his loyal crowd, and his sound system.

"It was ridiculous. He was god," says Zulu Nation DJ Jazzy Jay. At a legendary Webster P.A.L. contest, Herc drowned out Bambaataa's system with little effort. "Whenever Kool Herc played outside, shit was loud and crystal clean. When we'd play outside, we'd be hooking up a whole bunch of little wires, a bunch of four or five amps and—errnt! Zzzzt! Shit would be blowing up." And every time Grandmaster Flash came to a Herc party, Flash chuckles, "Herc always used to embarrass me."

After being threatened by some cops for his drug selling, Herc's fan Aaron O'Bryant moved on to promoting parties. He rented the Savoy Manor nightclub on 149th Street and the Grand Concourse. "I wanted to have Kool Herc versus Pete DJ Jones. Back then Pete DJ Jones was number one on the disco set and Kool Herc was just number one, period," he recalls. "So I had a commitment from Pete DJ Jones because he was a businessman, he took on all bookings. The first thing Kool Herc wanted to know was where did I get his telephone number from. And he was explaining to me that I was not a proven promoter. Plus, he also insinuated that he could go to the Savoy Manor and rent it himself and do that battle if he wanted. He didn't want to let me eat."

By the end of the spring, Herc noticed his audiences were declining. "People are getting older now, it wasn't all about me. All of a sudden now you're not eighteen no more, you're twenty-four and twenty-five. You can drink now. You ain't coming to no little seventeen-, eighteen-year-old party," he recalls. "And other people was coming up."

After the blackout and the looting, there were plenty of new crews with brand new sound systems in the streets, and Herc's main rivals were luring away his crowd. Flash had precision, sophistication and an entertainer's flair. Bambaataa had his records and the power of Bronx River behind him. O'Bryant himself had begun DJing. As DJ AJ, he teamed with a new turntable tutor, Lovebug Starski, and expanded into Harlem. Herc says, "I stayed behind, I didn't move with them to downtown. I stayed up in the Bronx."

Herc finally agreed to play with DJ AJ at a back-to-school party at the Executive Playhouse. It was sold out, AJ recalls, but Herc was no longer the main draw. "Flash was at my show. I let Flash get on and I let Melle Mel get on the mic," AJ says. "But it didn't help Herc's career at all because he was fading fast."

A few months later, Herc was preparing for another night at the Playhouse, now renamed The Sparkle, when he heard a scuffle breaking out. "Mike-With-The-Lights had a discrepancy with somebody at the door," Herc recalls. Mike was refusing to allow three men into the club and they had become increasingly agitated. When Herc went to mediate the situation, one of the men drew a knife. Herc felt it pierce him three times in the side. As he put his bloodied hand up to block his face, the attacker stabbed him once more in the palm before disappearing with the others up the stairs and into the night. "It made me draw back into a little shell," Herc says, exhaling for a long moment.

It was 1977.

Bob Marley was in a foreign studio, recovering from an assassin's ambush and singing: "Many more will have to suffer. Many more will have to die. Don't ask me why." Bantu Stephen Biko was shackled, naked and comatose in the back of a South African police Land Rover. The Baader-Meinhof gang lay in suicide pools in a German prison. The Khmer Rouge filled their killing fields. The Weather Underground and the Young Lords Party crawled toward the final stages of violent implosion. In London, as in New York City, capitalism's crisis left entire blocks and buildings abandoned, and the sudden appearance of pierced, mohawked, leather-jacketed punks on Kings Road set off paroxysms of hysteria. History behaved as if reset to year zero.

In the Bronx, Herc's time was passing. But the new culture that had arisen around him had captured the imagination of a new breed of youths in the Bronx.

Herc had stripped down and let go of everything, save the most powerful basic elements—the rhythm, the motion, the voice, the name. In doing so, he summoned up a spirit that had been there at Congo Square and in Harlem and on Wareika Hill. The new culture seemed to whirl backward and forward—a loop of history, history as loop—calling and responding, leaping, spinning, renewing.

In the loop, there is the alpha, the omega and the turning points in between. The seam disappears, slips into endless motion and reveals a new logic—the circumference of a worldview.

Fanga alafia ashé ashé

[Welcome, peace be unto you]

—Yoruban children's rhyme

LOOP 2

Planet Rock

1975–1986

DMC (right) and Run (center) rocking at record mogul Charles Koppelman's daughter's Sweet Sixteen party.

Photo © Josh Cheuse/WFN

Afrika Bambaataa flying his cut sleeves downtown.

Photo © Lisa Haun/Michael Ochs Archive.com

5

Soul Salvation

The Mystery and Faith of Afrika Bambaataa

I was born out of time.

—Napoleon Wilson, *Assault on Precinct 13*

Afrika Bambaataa was a teenager with a big rep. "When he walked through the projects," recalls Jayson "Jazzy Jay" Byas, "he was like The Godfather walking through Little Italy." Jay had moved into the Bronx River Houses in 1971 after his family's Harlem tenement was consumed by a fire. Like hundreds of other youths at Bronx River, Jay started following Bambaataa.

"Bam used to put his speakers out the window and play music all day. He used to live right outside what you'd call the Center. The center of Bronx River was like a big oval. The community center was right in the middle and Bam used to live to the left of it. He used to play his music, and I would ride my bike around all day popping wheelies, you know?" Jay says. "He was like the Pied Piper."

As the gang days were receding, Bambaataa saw the future before anyone else. Each of the housing projects had its own gangs, sometimes turning the two-block distance between them into a no-man's land. But he was ready to take people across borders that they didn't know they could cross, into projects they weren't sure they could be in. Bambaataa—he told them his name was Zulu for "affectionate leader"—would lead them where they didn't know they were ready to go.

Still astonished at the thought of it three decades later, Jay recalls, "Bam used to say, 'Hey, they throwing a block party in Bronxdale,' and he has his box and a bagful of tapes with all the music. He grabs the box and when he starts walking to Bronxdale, he'd have like forty people walking behind him.

"Bam was the leader. You'd roll up in—Bronx River is represented. We up in Bronxdale, we up in Soundview, we in Castle Hill—wherever they was throwing a block party, we was there. Here comes Bam, here comes the entourage, here comes *the army*. Wherever Bam was going, that's where some shit was gon' be, that's where you need to be. If you wasn't there even for the march up, you know the word got back real quick. 'Yo! Bam and them *moving*, there's a party going on over there.' "

Living Twice at Once

Of the three kings, the trinity of hip-hop music—DJ Kool Herc, Grandmaster Flash and Afrika Bambaataa—the most enigmatic is Bambaataa Kahim Aasim.

It is not because he is reclusive. In fact, unlike Herc and Flash, he has never retreated far from the public eye. Through his prolific recording career and his ongoing stewardship of the Universal Zulu Nation organization, Bambaataa has lived a very generous life. He regularly crisscrosses the world, graciously giving of himself to fans, journalists, Zulu members and hip-hop heads everywhere. And yet he also remains essentially a mystery. There are things that everyone seems to know about Bambaataa, and things that no one seems to know. The philosopher Claude Levi-Strauss might have called Bambaataa someone who lives twice simultaneously—once as a man in history, and separately as a myth above temporality.

His story seems well documented. He was the Black Spade warlord who became the Master of Records. The shaman who had hundreds of hard-rocks dancing to his global musical mash-up of Kraftwerk, Fela Anikulapo-Kuti, the "Pink Panther" theme, the Rolling Stones and the Magic Disco Machine. The founder of the Universal Zulu Nation, the first hip-hop institution, an organization that tried to raise consciousness like it raised the roof. The preacher of the gospel of the "four elements"—DJing, MCing, b-boying and Graffiti Writing. The missionary who took the hip-hop message to the four corners of the globe, and then beyond Planet Rock.

When hip-hop lost its way, he added a fifth element—"knowledge." Zulus, he explains, are about having "right knowledge, right wisdom, right 'overstanding' and right sound reasoning, meaning that we want our people to deal with factuality versus beliefs, factology versus beliefs." But some facts about his own life are slippery like quicksilver.

It is known, for example, that Bambaataa was born in Manhattan to parents of Jamaican and Barbadian descent. But he refuses to disclose when or under what name. Many biographies have incorrectly listed his birth name as Kevin Donovan, another man who happened to be the leader of record-label owner Paul Winley's house band, the Harlem Underground Band.[1] Perhaps he was in perpetual reinvention as a youth. He had multiple graffiti tags, including BAM-BAATAA, BAM 117 and BOM 117—the latter an acronym he once told German interviewers stood for Bambaataa Osisa Mubulu.[2]

Bios often list Bambaataa's birthdate as April 10, 1960. Other biographers have listed his birthdate as June 17, 1957. The month of April seems correct. Kool Herc, born in mid-April, has thrown joint birthday parties with Bam. But if Bambaataa was actually born in 1960, he would have joined the Black Spades at the age of nine, been a warlord before the age of ten, and started The Organization, the precursor to the Zulu Nation, at the age of thirteen. Most likely, Bambaataa was born in April of 1957. He won't say. "We never," he pointedly admonishes interviewers dumb enough to ask, "speak on my age."

He has good reasons for not revealing such personal information. Earlier in his career, revealing his true age might have hurt his credibility with young fans. And he has always been suspicious of surveillance from hostile authorities that have periodically—and wrongly—attacked the Universal Zulu Nation as a violent gang syndicate. So it seems as if Bambaataa is who he is because he's *always* been. He appears as a man outside of time and age.

For his part, Bambaataa conjures himself with good humor. The Zulu Nation's Infinity Lesson #2 explains that the original Bambaataa was a late-nineteenth-century Zululand leader who led an anti-tax revolt against the British colonial authority in South Africa. This Bambaataa was not above using mystical means to inspire his people. After calling on them to abandon the signs and objects of European culture—except for their guns—he told them a resurrected witch doctor had given him a potion that made him bulletproof. He drank it, then stood before a firing squad and commanded them to shoot. "But when the smoke cleared there stood Bambaataa, smiling and unhurt," the Infinity Lesson reads. "The explanation? Blank cartridges." Sometimes factualities and factologies matter less than the myths we want to believe. "Stopping bullets with two turntables isn't about sociology," Gary Jardim wrote in a famous 1984 *Village Voice* profile on Bambaataa, "it's about finding the spirit in the music and learning how to flash it."[3] No one ever debated whether Bambaataa could stop the bullets. He made you *believe* he did.

So Bambaataa is the generative figure, the Promethean firestarter of the hip-hop generation. He transformed his environment in sonic and social structure, and in doing so, he called forth the ideas that would shape generational rebellion. So many of the archetypes of the hip-hop generation seem to rise from the body of facts and myths that represent Bambaataa Aasim's life—godfather, yes, but also original gangster, post–civil rights peacemaker, Black riot rocker, breakbeat archaeologist, interplanetary mystic, conspiracy theorist, Afrofuturist, hip-hop activist, twenty-first-century griot.

But two dates help to place the man back into his time and place. In 1971, the year of the Bronx gang truce, a young Bambaataa was first bused to Stevenson High School at the eastern, white edge of Soundview as part of a court-ordered desegregation order. Within weeks the appearance of Black students, some of whom were Black Spades, caused white gang members to organize and a racial war broke out across the borough's borderlands. School grounds became stomping grounds, integration's bloody frontline, with the gangs as the shock troops.

But by 1981 Bambaataa was in the middle of a very different kind of desegregation, a wholly voluntary one. He was taking the music and culture of the Black and brown Bronx into the white art-crowd and punk-rock clubs of lower Manhattan. The iron doors of segregation that the previous generation had started to unlock were battered down by the pioneers of the hip-hop generation. Soon hip-hop was not merely all-city, it was global—a Planet Rock.

Most old school hip-hoppers look back on those heady days—the '70s turning into the '80s—with a sense of wonder that something they had been involved in as wide-eyed youths could have become so big, so powerful. Never Bambaataa. To him, it was always supposed to be this way. "Each step was a stepping stone, the gang era and all that, that helped to bring about this formation," he says, as if he had already been to the mountaintop long ago.

Sound Destiny

Afrika Bambaataa grew up on the ground floor of one of the fifteen-story towers of the Bronx River Projects, a complex of a dozen buildings in the vicinity of two other postwar superdevelopments, the Bronxdale Houses and the James Monroe Houses.

Bambaataa was raised by his mother, a nurse from a family immersed in international Black cultural and liberation movements. As he came of age during the turbulent late '60s, he experienced the fierce ideological debates over the Black freedom struggle—integration or separation, the ballot or the bullet—as close as the dinner table or the living room. His uncle, Bambaataa Bunchinji, was a prominent Black nationalist. Many in his family were devoted Black Muslims.

He seemed born with a sense of destiny. David Hershkovits, a journalist who came to know Bambaataa during the early '80s in the downtown club scene, says, "At some point early on, people had kind of spotted him as somebody to educate and talk to about what's going on in the rest of the world outside of the Bronx. I think he was somehow chosen."

The late '60s were a period of irreconcilable forces locked in struggle with each other. In the community, political positions on integration, violence, and revolution could harden into matters of life and death. But through his mother's record collection—an eclectic shelf that included Miriam Makeba, Mighty Sparrow, Joe Cuba, and Aretha Franklin—Bambaataa developed a different kind of perspective. In the rhythmic pull of James Brown's "I'll get it myself" black-power turn or Sly Stone's "everyday people" integrationist dance, these positions lost all their rigidity. James Brown could sing Black pride to all-white audiences. Sly Stone could get down with the Black Panthers. Music made ideologies shed their armature, move together, find a common point of release, a powerful unity.

Bambaataa was coming of age in an accelerated popular culture, a quantum explosion in sounds and images. He began imposing his own order on the chaos of representations. As a youth he became fascinated with the 1964 movie *Zulu*, a Michael Caine vehicle recounting the 1879 siege of Rorke's Drift in Natal, South Africa. The battle remains a celebrated moment in the military history of the British Empire, an unlikely triumph of a hundred redcoats defending a lonely colonial outpost against an overwhelming onslaught of four thousand Zulus. Indeed, Rorke's Drift is remembered as something like the Queen's Fort Apache, an Alamo where the whites actually won.

Zulu is told exclusively from their point of the view. There are hundreds of

African extras, but not a single Black role of any consequence. In the climactic scene, the red-suited soldiers stand with their bayonets arrayed silently before a pile of Black bodies, a dark tide stopped at the very lip of their boots. Had the movie been released two decades later, after civil rights and Black power, activists might have boycotted it.

But when the young Bambaataa saw it in the early '60s, he was captivated. The movie opens after the Zulus have routed the British camp at Isandhlwana, with a slow pan of hundreds of dead redcoats strewn across the African plain. It then detours to a majestic scene of a Zulu mass marriage ceremony and victory dance. The ragtag Brits are seen as individualists who tend to feud loudly amongst themselves. By contrast, the Zulus remain a primitive, undifferentiated mass. Here is the central tension of the movie: Can the divided, outnumbered defenders of white western democracy get their act together in time to prevail over the unceasing armies of ancient Dark Continent despotism?

But what Bambaataa saw in *Zulu* were powerful images of Black solidarity. Before the attack on Rorke's Drift, hundreds of Zulu warriors appear atop the ridge, leaving the imperial soldiers awestruck. They bang their spears to their shields, give a resounding war cry and storm the garrison. Although many of them fall before the British muskets, they just don't quit. Into the night, the Zulus continue their assaults and succeed in setting the outpost on fire.

"That just blew my mind," Bambaataa says. "Because at that time we was coons, coloreds, negroes, everything degrading. We was busy watching Heckyl and Jeckyl, Tarzan—a white guy who is king of the jungle. Then I see this movie come out showing Africans fighting for a land that was theirs against the British imperialists. To see these Black people fight for their freedom and their land just stuck in my mind. I said when I get older I'm gonna have me a group called the Zulu Nation."

Later he would give his followers a round Black face with white eyes and lips to wear around their necks—an emblem taken from one of New Orleans's oldest and most famous Black Mardi Gras groups, the Zulu Krewe. Civil rights groups had once pressured the Krewe to disband for what they took to be offensive blackface stereotypes. But Bambaataa approached *Zulu* and the Zulu Krewe the way he did political ideologies and his own records. He pulled out what was precious and tossed the rest. He created new mythologies.

On the Move

Outside the political ferment of Bambaataa's household the revolution was being pre-empted. In 1968, heroin made a sudden, dramatic return to the streets of the southeast Bronx. Richie Perez, later of the Young Lords Party, was then a teacher at Monroe High School across the street from Bronx River Houses. "It came fast and there was a lot of it. It was all over the place. Students I knew were getting strung out," he says. At the same time, white gangs joined together in a loose federation to prey upon on youths of color. Black and Puerto Rican gangs in the Soundview area surged in response to the junkies and the white gangs, and then they turned on each other.

Bambaataa was drawn into the gang life as inexorably as any young boy from Bronx River would have to be. The first gang that caught his attention was a group founded there called P.O.W.E.R., an acronym he says stood for "People's Organization for War and Energetic Revolutionaries." P.O.W.E.R. took up the Black Panthers' rhetoric but had the somewhat less lofty, if no less urgent, purpose of protecting Bronx River from being overrun by Bronxdale's Black Spades. Bambaataa enlisted, but when the group began a war with the white gangs, he says, escalating violence and police repression eventually drove their leaders underground. "That's when I decided to turn Spades and then flip Bronx River into Spades," he says. P.O.W.E.R.'s only remaining claim to history is to be the first gang named on the 1971 Peace Treaty.

As a Spade, Bambaataa made his rep by being unafraid to cross turfs to forge relationships with other gangs. He says, "I was a person who was always in other areas. So if I was a Spade, I still was with the Nomads. If I was with the Nomads, I was hanging with the Javelins. When I came into any group, I had the power, the backing of the other group I was with. Although I was a Spade, I still had power and control of some of the Nomads, some of the Javelins." Soon, Bambaataa's ability to move between gangs did not look like a weakness, but a strength. "I was the person that if you had problems, I could rally up three to four hundred at one time and move on you," he says.

The Spades' president, Bam Bam, made the whip-smart young Bambaataa a warlord. He was responsible for building the ranks and expanding the turf of the Spades. "I took my things of attacking areas from the history of Napoleon,

Shaka Zulu. I used things I was reading in school to attack areas and make them join up with us," Bambaataa says. He helped consolidate Bronx River's control of the Black Spades and enable their spread to the Soundview, Castle Hill and Monroe Houses, and as far west as Patterson Houses. The Spades soon moved into the projects of Harlem, Brooklyn, and Queens and became the city's biggest gang. "Everywhere there was a police precinct, there was a Spades chapter," Bambaataa says.

When racial tensions exploded at Stevenson High School, Bambaataa led Spades in confrontations with white gangs all across Soundview and West Farms. But he also showed signs of ambivalence. "For the first week things seemed to go okay," he wrote in a class assignment. Then, in the third person, he described the escalation of racial gang tensions to a climactic shopping center rumble. "After that day Stevenson was never the same peaceful high school again."[4]

As these battles were escalating, the 1971 truce brought together Black and brown gangs in the South Bronx. The peace treaty, particularly the Spades' president Bam Bam's personal commitment to it, had a profound impact on the young warlord. Bambaataa began to search for a way out, and he found his skills in mobilizing for war could just as easily be turned to peace. As his friend Jay McGluery told journalist Steven Hager, "There were so many gangs and he knew at least five members in every one. Any time there was a conflict, he would try and straighten it out. He was into communications."[5]

Herc's New Cool offered Bambaataa a way forward, and two former Black Spades had also become DJs—Kool DJ D at Bronx River and Disco King Mario at Bronxdale. Bambaataa apprenticed with both ex-Spade DJs, then began throwing his own parties in the community center just steps from his front door. "When I did become a DJ, I already had an army with me so I already knew that my parties would automatically be packed," he says.

That year, he began the Bronx River Organization as an alternative to the Spades. In some ways, the move resembled the Ghetto Brothers' transformation.[6] Bambaataa says, "We had a motto: 'This is an organization. We are not a gang. We are a family. Do not start trouble. Let trouble come to you, then fight like hell.'"

But some battle lines were dissolving. Partying was a new thing. Bambaataa formed a strategic alliance with Disco King Mario's Chuck Chuck City Crew at Bronxdale, and people from other housing projects came into his fold. The Organization eventually dropped the Bronx River prefix, and evolved into a vehicle for Bambaataa's expanding gatherings and parties.

While Kool DJ D, Disco King Mario, and other Bronx River DJs like DJ Tex played uptempo disco music popular on the radio, Bambaataa was taken more by DJ Kool Herc's break-centered—as opposed to song-centered—style. Bam's sound became a rhythmic analogue to his peace-making philosophy; his set-lists had the same kind of inclusiveness and broad-mindedness he was aspiring to build through The Organization. He mixed up breaks from Grand Funk Railroad and the Monkees with Sly and James and Malcolm X speeches. He played salsa, rock, and soca with the same enthusiasm as soul and funk. He was making himself open to the good in everything. He eclipsed the other DJs as the most renowned programmer in the borough.

Each weekend Bambaataa would preside over a ritual of motion and fun. Jazzy Jay says, "Block parties was a way to do your thing, plugging into the lamppost. Sometimes we used to play till two in the morning. And we had the support of the whole community. It's like, we'd rather see them doing that, doing something constructive than to be down the block beating each other upside the head like they used to do in the gang days."

Soulski

He had found something that was powerful, creative, something that signaled life. But it was a death that reversed Bambaataa's course for good. On January 6, 1975, police killed his cousin Soulski—he will not divulge Soulski's real name—in a bloody shootout.

Deep in Section B of the January 11 edition of the *Amsterdam News* was this police-blotter clip:

TWO SHOT DEAD IN BRONX DUEL

Two young men were shot to death during a gunfight with the Bronx police Monday night on Pelham Parkway off White Plains Road, and another was taken to the hospital suffering with injuries. The dead men were identified as Ronald Brown, 20, who lived at 2187 Washington Ave., and

Ronald Bethel, 17, who lived at 2100 Tiebout Ave. Taken into police custody was James Wilder, 20, of 2507 Washington Ave.

Disobey

Police said Officers Jeffrey Matlin and Robert Visconti were on patrol on Pelham Parkway when they observed three men in a car who were acting suspiciously.

The police motioned to the car to pull over. The car stopped and the three men got out but instead of walking toward the police car the three walked to the rear of the car.

Police said one of the men had a shotgun and the other two were also armed. The officers reportedly ordered the men to drop their guns but were fired on instead. The police returned the fire and the three ran into the wooded area of Pelham Park.

Shootout

The three suspects ran East on Pelham Parkway with the police chasing them. The two officers were later joined by Officers Charles Iacovone, Donald Powers and John B. Kelly who aided the two officers in the shootout.

Police said the 1968 Mercury, in which the three were riding, is owned by Brown's mother, Mrs. Sarah Williams. Det. Edward Heck of the Ninth Homicide zone is assigned to the case.[7]

Bambaataa, who still keeps a copy of Soulski's death certificate, does not speak much on the incident. But he clearly believes something else was going on. His voice lowers to a whisper as he says, "They shot him all in the lungs and the chest, a whole bunch of spots. They tore him up."

A month after Soulski's killing, Bronx cops shot dead a fourteen-year-old who had been joyriding in a stolen car. A police spokesperson claimed the officers fired after the boy had lunged at them with a knife, but autopsies showed he had been shot through the back. Both these incidents precipitated a different kind of crisis than Cornell Benjamin's had for the Ghetto Brothers; they directed the gangs' rage outward against the authorities.

Representatives from the *Amsterdam News* joined community leaders in a

grassroots effort to reduce tensions in the neighborhoods. They urged Bambaataa and the Spades not to retaliate, to let the justice system do its work. But
the Peacemakers gang had already declared open season on police and firefighters. Other gang leaders called Bambaataa to offer their support should he
choose to declare war on the cops.

Many years later, he would do a song that he called "Bambaataa's Theme," an
electro version of the score from John Carpenter's 1976 movie, *Assault on Precinct
13*. That movie had ushered in a new genre—the urban horror flick—which would
come to include films like Daniel Petrie's 1981 remake of the 1948 John Wayne
vehicle *Fort Apache*, called *Fort Apache: The Bronx*. Instead of Indian braves, Zulu
warriors or graveyard zombies, *Assault on Precinct 13*'s heroes defended themselves in a desolate police station against marauding waves of dark, heavily armed
gang members seeking revenge for their cop-killed brothers. Bambaataa's attach-
ment to the movie raises intriguing questions: Did he sympathize with the attackers
or the attacked? What kinds of emotions could that filmic assault have fired in him?

At the conclusion of *Zulu*, the South African warriors appeared on the mountaintop above Rorke's Drift once again. But instead of attacking, they raised
their *assegais* and their voices in praise-song and tribute to the bravery of the
British soldiers. Then they withdrew quietly back to KwaZululand. In 1964, a
year after Kenya gained its independence from Great Britain, it may have
seemed the perfect ending for the nostalgic audiences of the fading Empire—the
natives retreating, despite their overwhelming numbers, before the bloodied but
unbowed exemplars of imperial virtue. But in 1975, Bambaataa, thinking not of
the past but the future, may have seen that ending much differently.

At the request of community leaders, Bambaataa and his followers had
agreed to watch the white cops go to trial in both the police shooting incidents.
But the cops were acquitted and the Bronx gangs were ready to roll. Bambaataa had finally reached his turning point. The gangs never launched a final
do-or-die attack on the police precincts. Instead, like the chanting Zulu warriors,
Bambaataa and his followers withdrew, to live.

Closing the Loop

The alienated youth of the Bronx needed something to believe in. While Bambaataa had been in the Spades, he says, "a lot of the organizations came to

speak to us. You had some Christian groups that came around from different churches, radical reverends that came out and spoke to a lot of the street gangs. Some of us just pushed it aside."

After Malcolm X, who would hear of a heaven for the meek? Only controversial prophets of the Garveyite tradition like the Honorable Minister Louis Farrakhan of the Nation of Islam and Dr. Malachi Z. York (also called Imam Isa, or As Sayyid Issa Al Haadi Al Mahdi), the leader of the Ansaaru Allah community, could speak to alienated youth. Bambaataa says, "They held the teachings of 'You're not a 'nigga.' You're not colored. Wake up Black man and Black woman and love yourself. Respect your own. Turn back to Africa.' That started sticking with a lot of the brothers and sisters."

Racialized calls to redemption gave Bambaataa's anger a focus: "I wasn't agreeing with what white people was saying. You start questioning all that and you start traveling and meeting other people and seeing the struggles everybody had. Everybody is talking about what the white man did from country to country. You start believing strongly what the Honorable Elijah Muhammad was saying, that the white man is the devil. But as you get older and wiser, you see why he did that—to clear off Black people's thinking that they was inferior and whites are superior and start saying they are of gods.

"What the Nation was saying was, 'When you're ready to come, we'll be waiting for you.' And that always stuck in my mind and heart. I said I have to do some type of change to get the mindset of the masses that was following me to lead them to another way," he says.

Months before Soulski's passing, Bambaataa won a Housing Authority essay-writing contest. The prize was a trip to India. "You had to write an essay on why you would want to go to India. So I won, but when it was time for me to meet up with the people that send you off to go, I was outside giving out flyers for the next party I was giving and forgot all about it. So I lost the trip, which was great, because the following year I won the trip to go to Africa and Europe," he says.

For a youth who had known nothing but the streets of the Bronx, the trip was life-changing. "I saw all the Black people waking up in the early morning, opening their stores, doing the agriculture, doing whatever they have to do to keep the country happening," he says. "Compared to what you hear in America about, 'Black people can't do this and that,' that really just changed my mind."

His head bursting with ideas, Bambaataa came back to the Bronx ready to transform The Organization. "My vision was to try to organize as many as I could to stop the violence. So I went around different areas, telling them to join us and stop your fighting," Bambaataa says.

As the summer of 1975 drew closer, the word began getting out. Jazzy Jay says, "I remember my friend came up and said, 'Yeah you heard that cat Bambaataa? He's calling himself Afrika Bambaataa and the Zulu Nation now. He got some movement called the Zulu Nation."

Movement was literally at the heart of the organization, in the form of the Zulu King dancers. "The Zulu Kings started with five main guys: Zambu Lanier, Kusa Stokes, Ahmad Henderson, Shaka Reed, Aziz Jackson. Then came the Shaka Kings and Queens. And it was just as many women that could tear guys up on the dancefloor as there was men," Bambaataa says. Then the rappers came in. "We had Queen Lisa Lee and Sha-Rock, who was the first two females that was blowing it up, then Pebblee Poo."

Zulu Nation was returning the Bronx to an era of style, celebration and optimism. "It was no more where you had the Hell's Angels looking type jackets or you rolling around in dirt-stank shit just to show you were an outlaw and you could be the most dirtiest bastard out there," he says. "It almost flipped back to the fifties gangs where they was wearing the nice satin jackets and the nice names. As you got into the graffiti artists, then you had the aerosol paintings on the jackets. People was getting more cool. It just started switching the whole culture around into this whole 'party and get down' atmosphere."

At the same time, Bambaataa recast the Organization's credo. "What is the job of a Zulu?" his Infinity Lessons would later ask. "The job of a Zulu is to survive in life. To be open-minded dealing with all walks of life upon this planet Earth and to teach [each] other truth (Knowledge, Wisdom, and Understanding). To respect those who respect them, to never be the aggressor or oppressor. To be at peace with self and others, but if or when attacked by others who don't wish peace with the Zulus, then the Zulus are ordered in the name of AL-LAH, Jehovah to fight those who fight against you."

Gang Legacies

But Bambaataa's moves were not received well by all. "You had members who were like, 'What is this? Stop all this Zulu thing,'" Bambaataa says. "Some of The Organization didn't like what we was doing. They became known as the Gestapos. Other ones became the Casanova Crew and other crews that were out there."

Strands of Nazi symbolism, a remnant of the Hell's Angels influence, had run through the gangs of the early '70s. They kept private "Gestapos," inner-core cliques of their fiercest warriors who would act as elite intelligence and battle units. As the gang era gave way, early graf writers like BONANZA and SANTANA 204 were known to draw swastikas next to their names.[8] One writer even named himself HITLER II. Bambaataa describes the new Gestapos and other similar breakaway crews as "the stickup kid, gangsta style that caused a lot of havoc in the city."

Authorities had long abandoned large parts of the Bronx; renegade party-starters never had to worry about permits and police. But crowd control was always going to be an issue. There were still turfs, Bambaataa says, and "you still had violence."

So DJs backed themselves with area crews who kept the peace, and, often, other crews out. Grandmaster Flash, for instance, secured the Casanovas. As big as DJ Kool Herc was, he would not play Bronx River unless Bambaataa extended an invitation. On the other hand, only at Bambaataa's parties could the rawest rival crews come together, their tensions transmuted into raucous energy.

"Sometimes you'd be at parties and they'd start their chanting and we'd start our chanting," he chuckles. "It'd be like, 'Zulu! Gestapo!' And that became known as the 'War Chant.' Sometimes there might be other crews there that might get smart and they end up getting it from both sides!"

This adrenaline-pumping unpredictability held an allure—girls, music, dancing, guns, anything could happen. "Sometimes when DJs played against other DJs, you might have lost your whole system if you didn't win and you didn't have a large group backing you up," says Bambaataa. "But if somebody didn't do right and did wrong in our area, they had to really think, because it was a large percentage of areas that was down with Zulu.

"In the early seventies, there used to be a big thing for [angel] dust. And I started a big campaign on my flyers—'Stop smoking that dust y'all.' I had my little cliches, had my rappers doing it, and the dealers in Harlem didn't like that. They sent some Hitlers to come out and hammer us. But they made a mistake. They find out that at a Bambaataa party, everyone at the party is down with Afrika Bambaataa, so they must have ain't done research to find out what's up."

He laughs, "They were history, whatever."

Taking It to the Bridge

But if Bambaataa was to expand his vision beyond his sphere of influence, he would need to convince brown youths on the other side of the Bronx River that the peace was for real. During the early '70s, while white gangs had pressed the Black Spades from the east, the Puerto Rican gangs—especially the Savage Skulls and the Savage Nomads—were a buffer on the west. The Bronx River remained a dividing line between African-American and Puerto Rican youths.

Ray Abrahante—who would later become an original member of the Rock Steady Crew and gain fame as the graffiti writer named BOM 5—was then an eleven-year-old Baby Skull. He had followed his older cousin, a shot-caller, into the gang. Soon after he joined, two young Skulls ended up dead, and the fingers pointed to the Black Spades.

The Baby Skulls' hangout spot was in the East Tremont neighborhood near the west bank of the river, right where the Bronx River Parkway cut through a hook in the Cross-Bronx Expressway, under a high, rusting Amtrak train layup. There they scrambled up the lattice of steel girders into the high reaches under the layup to hang ten-foot ropes from the beams. They would mount the ropes, dangling three stories above the ground, and swing themselves at each other, trying to knock the other down just for kicks.

When the Baby Skulls came out from under the layup, dusting the dirt off their colors, maybe bloody and bruised from a nasty thirty-foot plunge, they could see the towers of the Bronx River Houses scraping the sky to the south. Everything that lay in between—the tagged-up bus yard, the train repair track and the commuter line, the furious Parkway and Expressway—might as well have been a DMZ. Traffic from everywhere rushed through there and over them, but never across. They'd go back under the layup and swing madly at each other again in a kind of metronome limbo.

A few blocks away, the 174th Street Bridge connected East Tremont with the Bronx River Houses, but this was no-man's land, a no-crossing zone. Abrahante was a reckless kid. One day he wandered onto the bridge on his bike. A burly Black tagger was spraypainting BAM 117, WRITERS INC. Abrahante, who was the Baby Skulls' tagger, took the spraycan, and wrote his own tag, SPIDER. He wasn't wearing his colors, and by the size of this guy, he knew not to write SKULLS next to his name. He handed the spraycan back to the tagger, and they gave each other an unspoken recognition. Then they went back their separate ways.

A few days later when Abrahante went across the bridge again, he had it in his head to try to tag the Skulls name deep in Spades territory. He headed across the Bridge in full colors, and cruised into the Bronx River Houses. A group of Spades came out from the basketball courts, hurled bottles at him and chased him back across the bridge. He noticed that the tagger he had met on the bridge was with them, simply watching.

By the time the summer ended, things had changed. The Savage Skulls were falling apart, turning on each other, snitching out each other to the cops. The leadership wasn't stable. Abrahante was ready to take on more responsibility in the gang. But his cousin had made up his mind and told him, "Fuck that, that shit ain't no good for you. That shit ain't good for me." Abrahante says, "He told the Skulls, 'I'll fight whoever to get me and my cousin out.' He pushed me out by beating me up."

In September, Abrahante received a flyer for a party in the Bronx River Houses. The promoters had been going through the neighborhoods, shouting, "Free jam! Come one come all, leave your colors at home! Come in peace and unity." His cousin didn't believe it. "Don't go," he said, "it's a set-up. The Spades will pound you."

It was a warm afternoon when he and some Skulls and Nomads walked across the bridge. They joined the crowd heading toward the Community Center. Abrahante noticed a lot of gang members, maybe even the ones who had bottled him, but he was surprised to see a lot of Puerto Ricans as well. At the door, they lined up to be searched by a pair of big bouncers. But the mood was one of anticipation, not tension as he had expected.

The music was blasting. Onstage, a DJ worked two turntables. He recognized the music and the dances from the gang parties and the park jams, but it was like he was experiencing it again for the first time. When the room filled, the DJ stopped the music. Then that guy from the bridge got on the microphone.

"Bambaataa talked," Abrahante recalls. "He was saying how happy he was that people came out. That this gang thing, the cops put us up to this stuff. Society put us all in here to fight against each other and kill us off, and we're not getting nowhere."

Abrahante was impressed. "A week later, I was meeting more and more kids, and he was trying to open Bronx River to everybody. I mean it was inspiring." With the Zulu Nation, Bambaataa was integrating a new generation in the Bronx.

The Lessons

Zulu chapters proliferated throughout the tri-state area as quickly as had the Black Spades. To be down with the Zulus conferred street power and respect, but perhaps just as important, the promise of good times. While gang legacies remained, Bambaataa steadfastly pushed the organization in the direction of his new motto: "Peace, Love, Unity and Having Fun." By the early '80s, he had largely succeeded. But without the military hierarchy of the gang structure, the Zulu name was still prone to being tarnished by knuckleheads.

Bambaataa says, "We had to come up with something to get the order back. That's when I started thinking, and it was coming back to me, all the teachings and everything I experienced. I started sitting down and writing things from my head. Other people started saying, 'Well this is a belief that I've had.' So then I started taking from all people of knowledge to make up our lessons. And it started catching on and keeping people in check."

In place of a set of beliefs or a ten-point platform, the Universal Zulu Nation offered Seven Infinity Lessons, which formed the basic foundation of principles for a member. The lessons established a fundamental code of conduct and gave broad directives to the Zulu "way of life."

Like a Bambaataa DJ set, the Infinity Lessons followed a ranging eclecticism, mixed a bit of the familiar with a lot of the arcane. They touched on the origins of Universal Zulu Nation and its South African antecedents, and offered a Bronx River view of the origins of hip-hop. They highlighted esoterica like Elijah Muhammad's dietary pronouncements and Dr. Malachi Z. York's racial interpretations of Biblical history. They were presented in the same question-and-answer studies and keyword glossary forms used by the Nation of Islam and the Nation of Gods and Earths, better known as the Five Percenters.

The Infinity Lessons drew on the Black Muslims' evocation of a glorious, original African past, but not their impulse to racial separation. And although the Lessons leaned hard on the language of the Nation of Islam, they disdained dogma and orthodoxy. "The religion of the Universal Zulu Nation is truth wherever it is," reads Infinity Lesson #4. "So our way of life is knowledge, wisdom and understanding of everything, freedom, justice and equality."

The Lessons picked up the Black Panthers' call for self-defense, but they dropped the programmatic demands for housing and employment. Formed at a time when the arc of Black Power was dropping precipitously, the Universal Zulu Nation was not about politics. As Elijah Muhammad had preached, Zulus first had to come to know themselves, attain knowledge of self. Consciousness did not come from the unmasking of social forces, but from having a true reckoning with one's god within. The revolution did not emanate from mass organizations struggling against systems and institutions, but in one's personal transformation. Only then could one "overstand," that is, comprehend and confront the injustice of the world by manifesting one's power.

Most important, the Lessons were an evolving document. They would expand and change as more members came into the fold. By definition, they were open-ended, infinite.

To the ministers and ideologues moving in the Bronx, the Zulus presented a question mark: they were agnostic devotees, skeptical true-believers, noncommittal revolutionaries. The Infinity Lessons seemed a quasi-theological mess, an autodidactic crazy-quilt, a political road map to a nowhere. But to Bambaataa the ideas were less important than the process.

If you are of gods, Bambaataa seemed to say, then it follows that you are just as capable as I am to make this new world. Zulus celebrated the instinct for survival and creation. Living young and free in the Bronx was a revolutionary act of art. To unleash on a social level these vital urges was the surest way to ward off mass death. Bambaataa's message was: *We're moving. There's room for you if you get yourself right.* Perhaps this is why, of all the utopias proffered to the teeming rabbles of outcast youth, Bambaataa's spread through the streets of the Bronx and then out into the world like a flaming wick.

So here they were, Bambaataa's army—the MCs, the DJs, the graffiti writers, the b-boys and b-girls, the crews they brought and the crowds they moved. They were elemental in their creative power—four, after all, was "the foundation number," representing air, water, earth and fire, and in another sense, the rhythm itself. What they were doing was yet to be named. But in the cooling sunlight of a park jam or the mercury-bursting intensity of an indoor one—from everywhere a crowd rising, the DJ excising and extending the groove, ciphers and crews burning, distinctions and discriminations dissolving, the lifeblood pulsing and spirit growing—Bambaataa took Herc's party and turned it into the ceremony of a new faith, like he knew that this was exactly how their world was supposed to look, sound and flow.

In the cipher at Patterson Projects, the South Bronx, 1982.

Photo © Henry Chalfant

6.

Furious Styles

The Evolution of Style in the Seven-Mile World

Style involves conflict, the strain of races, classes, ages and sexes pitted against each other in the arenas of clothing and music and slang.
—Richard Goldstein

It's funny, 'cause people say, "I practice style." It's either you got style or you don't!

—Richie "Crazy Legs" Colon

It may be hard to imagine now but during the mid-1970s, most of the youthful energy that became known as hip-hop could be contained in a tiny seven-mile circle.

Take a map of New York City and shift your gaze up from Manhattan to the Bronx. Place the point of your compass in the heart of Crotona Park and trace the circumference. Beginning in the east, there was the Zulu Nation empire; along the northern rim, Edenwald projects and the Valley, where the Brothers Disco and the Funky 4 + 1 More rocked the parties, and the 2 and 5 Train Yard, where thousands of masterpieces by BLADE and TRACY 168 and THE FABU-LOUS 5 began and ended their subversive circuits; to the west, across the river from Kool Herc's Sedgwick Avenue and Cedar Park cipher, the Ghost Yard, the misty, violent backdrop of graffiti lore, and Inwood and Washington Heights, where TAKI 183 first picked up his pen; further down through southern curve, Harlem, where disco DJs rapped on demand, and Spanish Harlem, where the Baby Kings chapter of the Spanish Kings gang did the outlaw dance on the hard concrete. There were eruptions happening in Brooklyn, Queens, Long

Island's Black Belt and the Lower East Side. But in 1977 this circle felt like a hot-house of style, the tropic zone of a new culture.

Richie "Crazy Legs" Colon, the leader of the Rock Steady Crew, tells this story. One night, when he was a wide-eyed ten-year old, his cousin Lenny Len and a neighborhood buddy Afrika Islam began practicing moves to a new dance in his living room. He had been learning to box, was picking up some martial arts, but this dance, he wanted to know everything there was to know about it. He had to wait until the following summer, the blackout summer, when Lenny took him to his first jam in a schoolyard on Crotona Avenue and 180th Street, near the heart of the seven-mile circle.

"Ah, I was just blown away," Crazy Legs recalls. "I just saw all these kids having fun, comparing the graf on the wall to their books, checking out the whole scene, and it was my first time watching the dance with the music being played, so it made more sense. I just immediately became a part of it. My cousin started teaching me how to get down, a few moves here and there, and I guess it just kept on going."

He had just been initiated into a secret Bronx kids' society. Later he would say that jam had made him a witness to the rise of hip-hop's "four elements"—b-boying, DJing, MCing, and graffiti. In time, the story would take on a patina of myth.

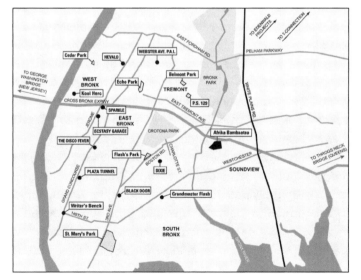

The heart of the Seven-Mile World, 1977–1980

Map layout by Sharon Mizota

In fact, old-schoolers still passionately debate how congruent these youth movements in music, dance, and art really were. Elder graffiti writers like Sandra "LADY PINK" Fabara object to their art being grouped with rap. "I don't think graffiti is hip-hop," she says. BLADE, SEEN and IZ THE WIZ say their musical tastes were closer to jazz, doo-wop, and rock. The Rolling Thunder Writers, says graf historian Andrew "ZEPHYR" Witten, were influenced by the prog-rock album covers and posters of Roger Dean and Rick Griffin, and the music of Hot Tuna and The Grateful Dead. "Frankly I grew up with disco music," says PINK. "There's a long background of graffiti as an entity unto itself."

Perhaps only within the seven-mile circle did all these youth movements come together the way Crazy Legs had experienced it. Regardless, they shared a revolutionary aesthetic. They were about unleashing youth style as an expression of the soul, unmediated by corporate money, unauthorized by the powerful, protected and enclosed by almost monastic rites, codes, and orders. They sprung from kids who had been born into the shadows of the baby boom generation, who never grew up expecting the whole world to be watching. What TV camera would ever capture their struggles and dreams? They were invisible.

But invisibility was its own kind of reward; it meant you had to answer to no one except the others who shared your condition. It meant you became obsessed with showing and proving, distinguishing yourself and your originality above the crowd. It put you on a relentless quest to prove to them that you were bigger, wilder, and bolder than circumstances dictated you should ever be, to try to generate something from nothing, something no one else had, until everyone around you had to admit that you had something they might never have, something that might even make other people—big, important people—stand up and take notice themselves, offer you money, give you power, or try to crush your very soul. That was the key to having style.

DJing: Style As Science

When Kool Herc first came on the scene, he stayed ahead of the other DJs with the power of his sound system. Bambaataa changed the game with his programming genius. Both men were titans in the streets, backed up by major crew. But in the beginning, Joseph Saddler didn't have expensive equipment, a deep record collection, or a posse of hardrocks. All he had was his style.

He was the fourth of five children of Barbadian immigrants, a boy in a house of girls, living on Fox and 163rd streets in the heart of Fort Apache amongst Skulls and Spades and Ghetto Brothers. He was less attracted to the street life than he was to the broken radios lying in the street. "I was a scientist looking for something. Going inside hair dryers, and going inside washing machines and stereos and radios, whatever you plugged into the wall," he recalls. As strung-out junkies plundered arson-devastated abandoned buildings for copper pipes to support their smack habit, Saddler scoured abandoned cars for their radios and speakers. He took them back to his bedroom to see if he could make them sing again.

"I wanted to know what's a resistor? What's a capacitor? What's a transformer? What's AC? What's DC? Why do these things do what they do?" he says. "Although there was crazy violent things happening around me on Fox Street, I was in my own world, in my own room."

Saddler wouldn't go to a Kool Herc or a Pete "DJ" Jones jam to get high, holler at the girls or be seen. He hung back in the cut and took it all in—the DJ, the crowd, the equipment, the music. Back in his room with his screwdriver, soldering iron and insatiable curiosity, the kid who would be named Grandmaster Flash was theorizing the turntable and mixer, pondering the presentation of the party, trying to figure out how to turn beat-making and crowd-rocking into a science.

The thing that both Herc and Jones did was release the music on the record from linear and temporal constraints. But Herc, Flash felt, was sloppy. The break went around, but it never came back on beat because Herc was dropping the needle all over the place. Flash saw Pete "DJ" Jones seamlessly extending disco records by mixing two copies of the same record, and realized he could apply the same technique to the music he really loved—the breaks Herc was spinning. Flash wanted to lift these slices of recorded time out of the progression of time, to re-enclose a song's break in a perfect new loop.

Apprenticing himself to Jones, he began to work toward the idea at weekend parties in an abandoned apartment in his building. Weekdays, he studied the mixer—jerry-rigging a headphone cue into his cheap set—and the turntable—trying to understand which model and what cartridges and styli were the most durable, which platters had the best torque. He considered Jones's simple circuit—begin break on record 1, cue record 2 on the headphone, end break 1, begin break 2, recue break 1. Then he understood that each record's rhythm had its own circumference to trace, that the break could be measured from point-to-point, and he developed a theory based on sectioning off the record like a clock. This was he breakthrough, he says. "I came up with the Quick Mix theory, which was like cutting, the backspin, and the double-back."

After months of study and refinement, Flash finally felt he had perfected the mix. In the summer of '75, it was time to take it to the waiting world. But the reaction was not what he had expected. "The first time I did it, the crowd just stood there, just watched me. I was hoping to get, 'Whoa yes, I love it!' But it was like, no reaction, no movement. Just hundreds of people standing there. They were just trying to understand.

"And I cried for like a week," Flash says. "Why did things go wrong?"

It was a lesson. You could be smart, you could be good, you could be scientific, but being smart and good and scientific wasn't going to rock a party all by itself. And Flash figured he got off easy that day—if a party wasn't being rocked, violence was always lurking right behind. He was going to have to win his crowds over to his new style. So Flash set his mind to theorizing the rest of his show. "I realized I needed vocal accompaniment to help spark this concept," he says.

Robert Keith "Cowboy" Wiggins was a former Bronx River Black Spade who had moved down to the South Bronx, and was already a feared street legend known to be nice with the hands. When he started hanging out with Flash, he became known to be nice with the mic. He would praise his DJ Flash, and command the crowd to "Say ho!" and "Throw your hands in the air and wave 'em like you just don't care!" He linked with two more regulars at Flash's jams, the Glover brothers, Melvin "Melle Mel" and Nathaniel "Kidd Creole," and together they rewrote Shirley Ellis, the Last Poets, "Hustler's Convention" and the dozens. They devised ever more intricate lines, finishing each other's rhymes, throwing in unexpected melodies and harmonies, exhorting the crowd higher and higher.

In 1976, they moved into a club called the Black Door, where they enlisted the Casanova Crew as their rough-and-ready backup, and then later on to the Dixie. The posse grew. Grandmaster Flash and the Three MCs became the Furious 4 and finally the Furious 5. They also continued to play the parks—St. Ann's, Mitchell, 23 Park, 63 Park. As the DJ scene expanded and the playlists became more standardized, crowds cared less about speaker size than showmanship and style. DJ AJ says, "Kool Herc couldn't draw a crowd after people saw Flash."

While the MCs kept the energy high, Flash unveiled eye-catching tricks—cutting while flipping around, scratching with his elbows, cross-fading with his backbone. Sometimes he would bring out thirteen-year-old Theodore, soon to be named Grandwizard Theodore, who had applied Flash's theories to invent the scratch, and who could drop a needle right onto the spinning breakbeat. With a complete show, Flash's DJ innovations—the scratch-and-mix techniques and the high-performance dazzle—finally took hold. "I got ridiculed for a couple of years. 'You're the guy that ruins records!' " laughs Flash. "But all the DJs had to change their style."

By 1977, DJs that weren't already rapping, like Lovebug Starski and Eddie Cheeba, were looking to line up rap crews as raw as the Furious. And one by one they did: the L Brothers, the Mighty Force (later known as the Cold Crush), the Funky 4 + 1 More. Soon, in an instant, the scene would change beyond their wildest dreams.

B-Boying: Style As Aggression

By 1975, the b-boy dance had been picked up by kids too young to get into the clubs. It used to be a private thing for them, something they taught each other in living rooms or building hallways, something to do at house parties, but the outdoor jams brought the dance out in the open. Now that the gangs no longer controlled the streets, the bedroom b-boys could travel across the borough to find other kids to battle.

Before he began DJing, Jazzy Jay says, "I used to be a b-boy myself. We used to just go from area to area. I'll never forget, one time it was me, my cousin Theodore, and a couple other cats, and we went over to Webster Avenue and they got a whole bunch of b-boys. So we went over to the other side of the Bronx, and they had a little project party up on some floor. Some guys was playing some music there. We went in there and took out the whole crew. At first they were jumping and everyone wanted to get in the circle. After we got done with our thing nobody wanted to get back in the circle. We went and scooped up all the girlies and we was out, you know?"

As in the ciphers at Herc's parties, there were rarely group routines, instead the spotlight was on each dancer's style. "Each individual cat got up and did his thing," Jay says. "Plus it wasn't like today where they come down and put down some nice linoleum so you don't get burnt up. I mean, we used to b-boy right in the middle of the park with broken glass everywhere! And you'd get up and you'd be all scratched and bruised and bleeding and you would be ready to go right back in the circle. You'd just wipe the glass off your elbows and go right back in."

"We used to get tore up," says BOM 5, the former Savage Skull who joined Zulu Nation, then became an original member of Rock Steady Crew. "It was called battle scars. You had to go through it. You didn't care. If you cared, it wouldn't be no breaking!"

Jorge "Popmaster Fabel" Pabon, a b-boy historian, first encountered the dance in his projects during the mid-'70s, the Jackie Robinson Houses in Spanish Harlem, watching a Puerto Rican gang called the Baby Kings. He says, "The style of a b-boy, I never saw nothing like it. I'd never seen a dance approached like that original b-boy flavor, that straightforward, aggressive sort of I'ma-tear-up-this-floor feeling. A lot of times in my neighborhood I didn't see smiles on their faces. They were on a mission to terrorize the dancefloor and to make a reputation, ghetto celebrity status."

The dance looked different from the floor-spinning form that would become popularized a decade later. Fabel says. "It was all strictly top-rocking, interesting drops to get down to the floor, incredible blitz-speed footwork. It was actually really unpredictable. Bouncing around, pivoting, turning, twists, front-sweeps, you know? And very aggressive, really aggressive, to the point that I thought it was a gang dance at first."

In fact, the line between dance and martial arts was thin. Black street-dance legend Rennie Harris came up in North Philadelphia during the early '70s, where the popular dance-style was steppin', something like tapdancing without taps. Steppin' was as competitive as b-boying but, Harris says, not nearly as militaristic. "If you really look at hip-hop dance, it's really a rites-of-passage thing. You never see the arms release down. They're always up in fighting position. *It's going to war*," he says. "What do we say? We say you're going to battle. You go out there to fight."

Many specific b-boy styles had their roots in the gangs, practiced from the Bronx and uptown Manhattan to the Brooklyn ghettos of Bushwick and Bedford-Stuyvesant, as a prelude to a rumble. According to Luis Angel "Trac 2" Matteo, "They would have a get-together between the rival gangs for specific turf and the two warlords would go at it, and the winner to that dance actually decides where the rumble's going to be held."[1] One of the wardances became known as "the Uprock," which gave a new meaning to the old Apache line. Rivals lined up across each other, and went head-to-head—making as if they were jigging, stabbing, battering each other.

In the 1930s, Zora Neale Hurston had written that African-American dance was "dynamic suggestion. No matter how violent it may appear to the beholder, every posture gives the impression that the dancer will do much more."[2] In the 1970s, Trac 2 says, b-boying was "a lot of motion and a lot of gestures, what one person was going to do to another, what one gang was going to do to another gang."[3] Sometimes a dance was enough to settle the beef, sometimes the dance set off more beef. This was style as aggression, a competitive bid for dominance.

The b-boys tapped into the same spirit that had given rise to New Orleans's Mardi Gras Indian gangs—segregated Blacks who, from the early 1900s, came out on Mardi Gras Day "masked Indian" in boldly colored, hand-sewn costumes to meet and confront other gangs, dancing rank by rank to the second-line street rhythms, climaxing in a great showdown between the two Big Chiefs—or Harlem's original Lindy Hoppers, the pioneering African-American jitterbuggers who emerged from pool-hall gangs like the Jolly Fellows in the late 1920s to galvanize uptown's integrated nightclubs and then, a decade later, the entirety of American popular dance with their floor steps, air steps and breakaways.

It is impossible to see b-boying now and not be impressed by its similarities to forms of Angolan and Brazilian capoeira, Cuban rumba, or Chinese gung fu—all of which by now have been incorporated into the dance. But, Crazy Legs emphasizes, the dance evolved in a very specific time and place. "We didn't know what the fuck no capoeira was, man. We were in the ghetto! There were no dance schools, nothing. If there was a dance school it was tap and jazz and ballet. I only saw one dance school in my life in the ghetto during that time, and it was on Van Nest Avenue in the Bronx and it was a ballet school," he says. "Our immediate influence in b-boying was James Brown, point blank."

By the mid-'70s, Puerto Ricans had begun adopting the b-boy dance. "There was 'a time when there was some racial tension," says Fabel. "Certain Black folks would look at us and say, 'Pssh, why you trying to do our thing?' And then there were times where we would dis ourselves, like 'Why you trying to do that cocolo thing?' And then we had our parents, the older generation, older sisters and brothers saying, 'Why you dressing like a *cocolo?* Why you want to be like them?' Man, it was hard."

Trac 2 told hip-hop journalist Cristina Verán, "See, the jams back then were still close to 90 percent African-American, as were most of the earliest b-boys, but they took breaking more like a phase, a fad. I say this because I had to see the reactions on their faces when we started doing it. They were like, 'Yo, breaking is played out' whenever the Hispanics would do it."[4]

Instead, they breathed new life into the dance. Between 1975 and 1979, crews proliferated, including mixed or dominantly Puerto Rican crews. Coming from Bronx River, Beaver and Robbie Rob led the Zulu Kings crew. Near Crotona Park, a number of mainly Puerto Rican crews were making their name—Salsoul with Vinnie and Off, Starchild La Rock with Trac-2, Rockwell Association with Willie Will and Lil Carlos, the Bronx Boys (also called The Disco Kings) with Batch. To the west on Burnside Avenue, there was the Crazy Commanders, with the infamous "man of a thousand moves," Spy. The dancers often formed new alliances under new names in the struggle to stay on top.

From top-rocking and up-rocking, the dance descended to the floor. "It got into elaborate footwork, into a freeze, and then you mixed up the top-rocking, then the floor-rocking, the spin into a freeze," says Rock Steady member "DOZE" Green. Crazy Legs says, "Ours was just a natural progression from standing up to going down. It's funny because a natural progression would be from down to up, but for b-boys, it's up to down." Styles evolved quickly, Legs says, because, "it was like, what you gonna have next week? What you gonna have when you go to Mom and Pop's Disco or the Crotona Avenue basement party? 'Cause all the dope b-boys are gonna be there. And that's what you strive for—you strive to take your move to the next level. It's about shock value, always shock value, but keeping it flavor and stylized and making it yours."

On the west side, Spy had unleashed new styles of flying footwork, propping his body with one hand to generate flurries of legs and feet. Then in the east, Zulu King Robbie Rob answered with the chair freeze—suspending motion to balance his body upside down on a single elbow and toe point, twisting the rest of his body away to taunt his opponent. Sometime later, someone did a baby freeze, propping both legs on his elbows, kicking up one of his sneakers in his opponent's face, looking like a snapshot of Pele in an overhead kick. From the freezes, dancers seeking to extend their routine discovered basic body spins like swipes, the backspin, and the headspin. Then they closed with another freeze, monumentalizing themselves into statues of middle-finger attitude. Now the story was complete.

Each time a b-boy or a b-girl stepped in the cipher, they wrote their own generational narrative. Starting upright in the top-rock, hands up and stabbing like a gang-member in motion, feet moving side to side like Ali in a rope-a-dope, dropping down like James Brown, turning hurricanes of Spy's *boricua* footwork, exploding into a Zulu freeze, tossing in a spin and punctuating it all with a Bruce Lee grin or a mocking Maori tongue—the entire history of the hip-hop body in a virtuoso display of style.

Graffiti: Style As Defiance

After TAKI 183 got his name in the *New York Times* in 1971, graffiti took off. "Every new school year was a new graffiti season," says IZ THE WIZ.

To Hugo Martinez, the sociology student and youth gang advocate who in 1972 organized the first graffiti association, United Graffiti Artists, "Graffiti writing is a way of gaining status in a society where to own property is to have identity." Your name was your currency, and you created value by making your mark in the niches or getting into mass production. Here was the logic of reverse colonization, a virus spread by the faceless fellow travelers of roaches and rats. "You started on your street, then you went to the buses. You take over your neighborhood, then you take over your home line, then you take over your division, then you take over all city," says Luke "SPAR ONE" Felisberto.

You wanted fame. To an invisible generation, fame itself was wealth, liability transformed into asset. Maybe you hung yourself off the side of a building or climbed the steel beams supporting an elevated subway station to rock a tag that would make cleaning men scream in frustration and the other writers shake in jealously. Or you were outrageous enough to hit the biggest, riskiest target you could find, as the pioneering female writer STONEY did in 1972 when she tagged the Statue of Liberty.[5] You tagged everywhere you went. Inside the cars, you and the other writers staked space as if it were a turf to claim with your names. The train riders would treat your tags as invasions of their daily anonymity.

Still only a few tags, like those of the spliff-star saint STAY HIGH 149, could really register much louder than the dull ad placards. The "pieces," on the other hand, were personal pageants of light, line, and color, rolling billboards for the self. And when writers added style to these, it was like they had begun printing million-dollar bills. Soon hundred of kids were scaling barbed wire fences, leaping instant death on electrified third rails, and running from police just to piece cars in the train yards and layups in ever bolder detail and wilder style.

The graffiti underground was an elite cloistered order. But it was also the first movement to break out of the seven-mile world. From this point forward, developments in the graffiti movement would anticipate the arcs of the other movements.

Centers of power outside of the Bronx and Uptown sprung up quickly. The Brooklyn crew, the EX-VANDALS, for instance, had spread back along the train lines to the Bronx. And because it had overrun sociogeographic cages, the graffiti movement was surprisingly desegregated. First practiced largely by inner-city youths of color, by the mid-'70s the second generation of writers was more integrated than the army.

Upper East Side whites apprenticed themselves to Bronx-based Blacks. Brooklyn Puerto Ricans learned from white working-class graf kings from Queens. They met up in the back cars of off-hour trains or in the afternoon at the Writer's Benches at 149th Street or Atlantic Avenue. Together they went on spray-paint stealing raids—they said they were "inventing" paint—and midnight bombing runs. They created an alternative world—in itself, quite an invention.

ZEPHYR was a self-described "hippie wanna-be" and "problem kid" who grew up in Yorkville section of Manhattan near the Mayor's Mansion, the land of Gracie Grace. He apprenticed with LSD OM and SHADOW (Spike Lee's younger brother) of The Rebels, lifted his name from the legendary Dogtown-based surf and skateboard team in Santa Monica, California, and finally got fame writing with the Rolling Thunder Writers in 1977.

"Everybody wrote," he says, "but no one was all that serious about it, it was just a rite-of-passage type thing. Like you fuckin' rob a marker, and you fuckin' mark shit up for six months, then you throw that shit away and get into some other shit." But for him and his peers, graffiti was a permanent outlet for their fizzy reckless energy, a legacy to maintain and a future to enter. He says, "We knew it wasn't starting with us and it wasn't ending with us, that it was already an eight-year-old tradition, that we were stepping to it, and that we were trying to bring some of our vibe to it."

There were rebel codes to follow, and as one of a tiny number of girl writers among the ten thousand boys getting up, LADY PINK had to break through all of them. In 1979, she had begun tagging her boyfriend's name, KOKE, after he was sent back to Puerto Rico by his parents, she chuckles, "for being naughty." After being accepted into the High School of Art and Design soon afterward, she found a core group of ambitious teens intent on making an impact on the graffiti scene. They were all well aware that famous writers like TRACY 168, DAZE and Lee Quiñones had already come through the very same halls.

"I was studying with guys like ERNI, SEEN TC5, DOZE TC5, FABEL, MARE 139, LADY HEART," she says. "We specifically had a Writer's Table. So for years and years whoever was the best automatically got the best table. Anyone who was worthy would sit, anyone else who wasn't worthy would just stand around. And that would go on for at least four periods of lunch! No one would go to class, we would just sit at the writer's table."

She wanted badly to be down, she says, but "I was getting sexism from ten-, twelve-year-olds saying that you can't do that, you're a girl. It took me months to convince my old homeboys from high school to take me to a train yard. They were not having it. They were not taking some silly little girl into danger like that. So I had to harp on them and convince them and finally they said, 'Fine. Okay. Meet us inside the Ghost Yard.' They left it to me to find my way in there and meet them inside."

The Ghost Yard was a vast train depot perched on the northern tip of Manhattan on the Harlem River at 207th Street, a servicing shop for cars from many different lines. It had been built on a graveyard, and at night a howling wind often rose from the River. Because of its wealth of cars, a number of graffiti crews turned the Ghost Yard into violently contested ground.

PINK recalls, "I walked around the entire yard, couldn't find my way in. So I just climbed the nearest ten-foot fence. They tell me it was in sight of the guard tower, but no one stopped me. So I was inside the train yard and I waited for them. I see my friends coming through the bushes, and then they just come up to the fence and they just peel back a whole section of it like a big doorway."

She was down, but the trials would not end. "I had to prove that I painted my own pieces. Because whenever a female enters the boy's club, the world of graffiti, immediately it's thought that she's just somebody's girlfriend and the guy is putting it up. But they're not gonna believe that some girl is strong enough and brave enough to stand there for that period of time and do something big and massive and colorful. They just think that she's on her knees and bending over for the guys. And that's the kind of word that went out about me and goes out about every single girl that starts to write," she says. "So you have to stand strong against that kind of adversity and that kind of prejudice or you're just a little bitch slut."

But PINK also knew that all toys had to prove themselves. Graffiti was not for the weak-hearted. "You've gotta be strong, carry your own point, have a lot of endurance, a lot of nerve. You can't go hysterical and run screaming. You also have to be strong in character that if you get grabbed and they put the squeeze on you and they're beating you silly and they have you upside down and they're painting your balls purple, will you stay shut or will you sing and tell them all your friends and phone numbers and everything that they want?" she says. " 'Cause this is a serious game. We might have been playing cops and robbers but it was some serious shit."

Graffiti is, PINK says, "an outlaw art. When we train other graffiti writers, we're not training fine artists to exhibit in a museum. We're training criminals. We're training kids how to take life in their own hands and go out there and hopelessly paint on some wall or some train that will do nothing for you except get you fame with other vandals and criminals."

In the spring of 1973, journalist Richard Goldstein famously made the case for graffiti in a *New York Magazine* cover story: "It just may be that the kids who write graffiti are the healthiest and most assertive people in their neighborhood. Each of these people has to 'invent' his life—his language, his culture are lifted, remodeled and transformed. In that ferocious application of energy to style lies the source of all flash . . ." To Goldstein, graffiti was "the first genuine teenage street culture since the fifties."[6]

New York's spraycan writers presented their own stunning defense. "If Art like this is a crime," they wrote, "may God forgive me."[7] Graffiti writers had claimed a modern symbol of efficiency and progress and made it into a moving violation. As their mini-riots spilled all-city all day every day, authorities took their work as a guerilla war on civility. They were right. Ivor Miller has written that northbound trains had once been a symbol of freedom, and in decaying postindustrial cities, subway trains were merely the beginning of the daily circuit of alienating labor. Quiñones told Miller, "Subways are corporate America's way of getting its people to work. It's used as an object of transporting corporate clones. And the trains were clones themselves, they were all supposed to be silver blue, a form of imperialism and control, and we took that and completely changed it."[8] The writers replaced the circular logic of trains with their own.

From the primacy of the name, subway graffiti evolved spectacularly under innovators like PHASE 2, RIFF, TRACY 168 and BLADE, and into another generation of stylists including DONDI, KASE 2 and SEEN. Homely letters grew outlines, colors, patterns, highlights, depth, shadows, arrows. Names were bubblized, gangsterized, mechanized. Letters dissected, bisected, cross-sected, fused, bulged, curved, dipped, clipped, chipped and disintegrated. They filled with shooting stars, blood drips, energy fields, polygons. They floated on clouds, zipped with motion lines, shot forward on flames. And they got bigger and bigger. Expanding from window-downs to top-to-bottom to end-to-ends, the pieces began appearing as dazzling thematic murals by 1974, covering entire sides of twelve-foot-high, sixty-foot-long cars. They were imposing themselves, to use Goldstein's words, in bigger, more unavoidable ways.[9] This was style as confrontation.

Politicians and bureaucrats played an unwitting role in the development of style. The first major anti-graffiti campaign began in 1972. But graffiti's inherent risk and its perpetual removal catalyzed innovation and ingenuity; its countless deaths generated countless, more magnificent rebirths. When the Metropolitan Transit Authority completed repainting its 6,800-car fleet in November of 1973, writers were temporarily relieved of the problem of having to cover another writer's existing piece when executing a new one, and they began a golden age of style.[10]

Space on the subway car exteriors was a resource made even more limited by their limited access, the exploding numbers of painters vying for them, and the risk entailed in their painting. So in these early years, graf writers refined the finer points of their hierarchy. You became the king of a subway line by being more inescapable than anyone else—either through sheer ubiquity or ferocious displays of style. Toy writers might have their pieces covered by a cloud or written over with a HOT 110 tag by an established writer. The masters did not have to respect wack writing; they were concerned with the advancement of style.

But by 1975, MTA efforts to stop graffiti were all but shackled by the city's impending bankruptcy, and tags and pieces covered virtually every imaginable space. Writers like IN, VAMM and AJAX began getting up with quick, easy "throw-ups"—essentially two-color tags on steroids, sometimes done side-by-side to cover a whole car, and mainly meant to cover over other writers' work. The advent of throw-ups shifted the kinging system from quality to quantity.

Graffiti historian Jack Stewart wrote, "The graffiti problem on the tracks became so bad in 1976 that many of the graffitiists even believed the whole thing was going to come to an end, a victim of its own excess. The only way a writer could hit the trains was to cross out someone else's work and this practice became so common that it began to demoralize many of the writers."[11]

At the bottom of its economic torpor, city officials rallied to attack the problem again, unleashing a new creative spirit among the writers. Subway graffiti's most influential period of style began. These writers dreamed and painted big, and this was the era of some of the most legendary cars. The biggest were two 10-car, whole-train productions—CAINE 1, MAD 103 and FLAME ONE's "Freedom Train" Bicentennial tribute and the FABULOUS FIVE's 1977 "Christmas Train." BLADE's 1980 nuclear blast whole-car sampled the expressionist ghost of Edvard Munch's "The Scream." FAB 5 FREDDY painted a 1979 whole-car tribute to Warhol's famous Campbell's soup cans, offering a "Pop Soup," "Da-Da Soup," and "Futurist Soup," next to a "Fred Soup." His writing partner, Lee Quiñones, seared feverish statements about war and violence into unsuspecting subway riders' heads. He called the 5 line, where they bombed, "a rolling MOMA."[12]

Graf developed a wide range of style. Although it represented only a small part of what they did, DONDI and SEEN were best known for their large, precise, readable words, and their bold, elegant designs. In particular, DONDI's

1980 "Children of the Grave" whole-car series, in which his name appeared in huge stylized letters against subtly shifting color fields and which photographer Martha Cooper shot during its execution, would become an artistic blueprint for the hundreds of youths jumping into the graffiti scene. PHASE 2 and one-armed KASE 2 moved toward deconstructing the word and the name in less readable forms, encoding their names and letters in theory, dimension, and abstraction. The word was now growing armaments, curling like vines, whipping like boomerangs, penetrating with arrowheads. This was the form that, after TRACY 168's groundbreaking crew, would come to be known as "wildstyle." Its energy seemed to shatter concrete, burst through steel. FUTURA's 1980 "Break" car exploded the bounds of the word completely, a crackling fission of orange-and-burgundy spilling across the exterior like visual dub music or an electro-Bronx encounter between Wassily Kandinsky and Jack Kirby.

The graffiti writers epitomized the extreme alienation of a generation coming of age under the long shadow of the baby boom. They were artists, individualists, stylists who had become comfortable in the cut, out of the glare of the media. In a time of diminishing returns and vaporizing expectations, they freed no one but themselves. They came out to make their word and stake their flags, then they slipped back into the darkness. Continual destruction only stoked their creative fires. Style was a way to defy a hostile world.

"I think graffiti writing is a way of defining what our generation is like," says LADY PINK. "Excuse the French, we're not a bunch of pussy artists. Traditionally artists have been considered soft and mellow people, a little bit kooky. Maybe we're a little bit more like pirates that way. We defend our territory, whatever space we steal to paint on, we defend it fiercely."

A 1981 piece by NOC 167 summed up the graffitiist's mission. On the left-hand side, between an ominous guard-tower and a gleaming new train lay the deadly third rail. A seething "STYLE WARS" rose out of mists of white, pink and blue. At the right, a cool, top-hatted cat rode an angry, blue-jacketed, fire-breathing dragon next to a portrait of the writer as a young rebel—staring nonchalant from behind his ski goggles like he'd already beaten the transit cops and the toys. *No matter how hard you try, you can't stop me now.*

Style absorbed technology, accepted method and technique, aspired to science. It spun self-defense into skill, skill into art. It invented itself, violently, enclosed itself in outlaw codes and attacked normality. Out of ruin, it pulled beauty.

Style would make you friends, inspire loyalty and devotion, spawn a hundred imitators. It would make you enemies, unleash jealousy and fear, bring down the brute force of authority. The one thing style would never leave you was neutral. As King KASE 2 would say in the movie *Style Wars*, "When they see you got a vicious style, they wanna get loose about it. And that's what keeps it going."[13]

In every generation, radicals nurture scorn for authority and the old. They tap into a desire to destroy convention and induce shock. They demand tribal commitment and discipline. They risk everything to bring the new into being.

By the beginning of 1979, this desire had matured and outgrown the seven-mile world. In each of these youth movements, there might be a sense of possibility, an inkling of many possible directions, many possible futures, like arrows jumping through and out of a PHASE 2 piece. Or the movements might simply decline. They were youth movements after all, and youth is a passing condition.

The next shocks came not from within, but from the outside.

DJ Kay Slay (far right), then famous as the graf writer DEZ, with his crew in front
of an abandoned public school in East Harlem, 1982.

© Henry Chalfant

7

The World Is Ours

The Survival and Transformation of Bronx Style

We had this as kind of a refuge. Otherwise you would not have pride about anything.

—DOZE

In the journey from the seven-mile world to Planet Rock, nothing was ever guaranteed.

B-boying might have gone back to the living rooms, a dance to be taken out like a fading picture album late on a Saturday night after a couple of forties. Rapping and scratching might have remained a Bronx novelty, a curious musicological artifact. Graffiti crews might have been crushed like the gangs, its chief practitioners systematically rounded up and herded into prison. The flamboyant kids of the postgang generation might have grown up and moved on or disappeared or died, another five-plus years in the street life of a small part of New York come and gone in a flicker of the city's eye.

Certainly that's how the future seemed in the Bronx in 1979. But by the beginning of the new decade, brought out by commercial interests, pressed down by the state, and saved by traditionalists, the Bronx-born culture jumped its borders forever.

The First Death of Hip-Hop

On the one hand, rap was becoming known outside the seven-mile cipher. Live bootleg cassette tapes of Kool Herc, Afrika Bambaataa, Flash and Furious 5, the L Brothers, the Cold Crush Brothers and others were the sound of the OJ Cabs that took folks across the city. The tapes passed hand-to-hand in the Black and Latino neighborhoods of Brooklyn, the Lower East Side, Queens and Long

Island's Black Belt. Kids in the boroughs were building sound systems and holding rap battles with the same fervor the Bronx once possessed all to itself.

But in the Bronx, hip-hop was a fad that was passing. "I called it the Great Hip-Hop Drought," says Jazzy Jay. "Everybody started fleeing away from hip-hop."

The kids raised on Herc and Bam and Flash and Lovebug Starski and DJ AJ had graduated from high school and were looking for the next thing. "People started growing up and calling that 'kiddie music,'" says Jay. "You ain't gonna go into no high school gymnasium to party no more."

He would peek over the balcony at the gym-sized T-Connection, and be shocked to find only forty people dancing in the whole room. He longed for the old days of battling at the Webster Avenue P.A.L. "It was a terrible time," Jay says. "I done got all my techniques down pat, I done got my belts, I done whipped Flash's ass, I done whipped Theodore's ass, I'm looking for whose ass can I whip next! I'm like, you mean I done went through all of these stepping stones just to *not* be the man? Hip-hop is gonna die like this?"

The audiences had moved on from Bronx sound-system battles and outdoor jams to the drinking-age uptown nightclubs, depriving b-boys and DJs of their competitive setting. At the same time, disco nightclub DJs in Harlem were finding success by adapting the Bronx rap styles and mixing techniques into their gigs, offering a more sophisticated version of the Bronx beat for a maturing crowd.

"I was wondering where my core audience was going," says Grandmaster Flash. "They were going to see people like DJ Hollywood, who would get a party going from twenty-three and older. When they moved on, they wanted to wear a dress or they wanted to wear a suit. They were just getting older and their taste changed in music."

He continues, "When I went to go see DJ Hollywood, I would say, 'Oh Regina, what are you doing here? I haven't seen you in a long time!' 'Yeah this is where I come now.' And there was this guy who was saying these incredible rhymes on the mic, he was about three, four hundred pounds and he had the crowd in an uproar the same way my Furious Five would have them. DJ Hollywood was quite incredible, he had the people singing his rhymes. So a lot of our audience was going to parties like that now, Eddie Cheeba parties, Hollywood parties, Pete "DJ" Jones parties. The bottom sort of dropped out. It was either you survive and you go with the changes or you get left back."

The DJs themselves wanted more. It was no longer about rocking the block party and establishing a rep. They wanted to make a living. But the economics of the music had changed. "If Friday was the 25th, you would see DJ Hollywood in five places on five different flyers. How was this possible? How could he be in Manhattan, the Bronx and Queens all in one night?" Flash says he asked himself. "Only to discover that he didn't carry a sound system. All he did was carry his records. He had a crew and a car. And he would do an hour here, get in the car, do an hour there an hour there and an hour there. After a while, people that had the huge sound systems became a dinosaur. Because now you could go and do five parties. And if you had a little record out, you could *really* make some money."

Flash learned this last point the hard way. By 1979, independent Black record producers like Harlem's Bobby Robinson and Paul Winley, and Englewood, New Jersey's Sylvia Robinson (no relation to Bobby) had all heard about the rap phenomenon and were scouring the clubs in the Bronx and Harlem and doing their math, trying to figure out if rap could be financially viable. Flash and the Furious Five were at the top of everyone's signing wish-list.

But Flash refused to meet with any record-label heads. To him, the idea was absurd. Who would want to buy a record of Bronx kids rapping over a record? He and the Furious Five were still a big draw in the clubs, and making a record wasn't guaranteed money in the bank, like getting onstage.

"I kinda kicked these guys to the side. I kinda like had my security keep them people away from me. I didn't want to talk deals. As bad as they wanted to talk to me, no is no. That was that," he says. As long as he had gigs to do all week, that was a sure bet, and he was content to play that game.

Then in October of 1979, the game changed.

The End Run

In retrospect, it makes perfect sense that a no-name group using partly stolen rhymes—the very definition of a crew with *no* style—would have been the first to tap hip-hop's platinum potential. When three anonymous rappers stepped into Black indie label owner Sylvia Robinson's studios to cut "Rapper's Delight," they had no local expectations to fulfill, no street reputations to keep, no regular audience to please, and absolutely no consequences if they failed.

Sylvia Robinson and her son, Joey, had been trying to sign a rap group but had been met with skepticism from Bronx luminaries like Flash and Lovebug Starski. Undoubtedly, the appearance of "King Tim III (Personality Jock)" on a B-side of a single by Brooklyn funkateers the Fatback Band in the summer of 1979 raised the pressure on the Robinsons to make a deal.

Henry "Big Bank Hank" Jackson was a Herc follower and a Bronx nightclub bouncer who somehow became a manager for Grandmaster Caz and the rappers who became the Cold Crush Brothers. He was making pizzas in New Jersey to pay for Caz's sound system, and rapping along to a Caz tape one afternoon at the parlor, when Joey Robinson heard him and asked him to come to Jersey for an audition. On the way back, two other rhymers jumped into Joey's car, Guy "Master Gee" O'Brien and Michael "Wonder Mike" Wright, and the three auditioned that evening. Sylvia Robinson immediately signed them to be the first group on her new imprint, Sugar Hill Records. Nobody knew who they were. They were the perfect people to vault hip-hop into the realm of pop.

" 'Rapper's Delight' was astonishing to me," says Bill Adler, then a music critic for the *Boston Herald* who would later become Def Jam's publicist, "not because the artists were rapping and not singing. What was remarkable about it was that it was fifteen minutes long. Boston had one Black music radio station and it was an AM station called WILD. Whenever they played "Rapper's Delight"—which was all the time—they played the entire fifteen-minute version, which was unheard of."

But at the far edge of the rap universe in the Black neighborhoods of Long Island, Chuck D, then a nineteen-year-old MC, remembers the impact of "Rapper's Delight"differently. "I did not think it was conceivable that there would be such thing as a hip-hop record," he says. "I could not see it." The famous DJ Eddie Cheeba had been out to Long Island and broken "Good Times" to Black audiences in May, promising as he played it that his own rap record would be out soon. "I'm like, record? Fuck, how you gon' put hip-hop onto a record? 'Cause it was a whole gig, you know? How you gon' put *three hours* on a record?" Chuck says. "Bam! They made 'Rapper's Delight.' And the ironic twist is not how long that record was, but how short it was. I'm thinking, 'Man, they cut that shit down to fifteen minutes?' It was a miracle."

Chuck first heard "Rapper's Delight" while he was on the mic. "Good Times" had been the record of the summer of '79, replacing MFSB's "Love Is the Message" as the beat that sent the dancers running to the floor and the MCs running to the microphone. One night in October, Chuck was rocking his Cheeba-styled party rhymes over "Good Times." "All of a sudden, the DJ I'm hearing he's cutting in this shit behind me. Right? And I'm rhyming over words," he laughs. "The crowd don't know. They're just thinking that I'm rhyming and I'm changing my voice or whatever. I held the mic in my hand, I heard words and I lip-synched that motherfucker. Folks thought that shit was me. I was a bad motherfucker after that, believe! The next day, Frankie Crocker broke that shit on BLS. By the next party, folks were looking at me like, 'Pshhhh. You a bad motherfucker, but you ain't that nice!' "

Three unknowns beating superstar Eddie Cheeba at his boast. A rap on a record trumping a live rap. In fifteen minutes, clearly, the whole world had changed.

"Rapper's Delight" crossed over from New York's insular hip-hop scene to Black radio, then charged up the American Top 40, and swept around the globe. Imitations popped up from Brazil to Jamaica. It became the best-selling twelve-inch single ever pressed. At one point, 75,000 copies were selling a week and the indie upstart from across the Hudson was straining to keep up with the demand. Tom Silverman, a DJ and journalist covering the dance music scene, had never seen anything like it. "I was there in Brooklyn on Fulton Street when they brought 'Rapper's Delight' in stores, in '79 right around Christmastime," he recalls. "Ten boxes came out of the truck, they went onto the floor and they opened the cardboard boxes and literally handed two copies to everybody in the store who went right to the cash register. They must've moved two million records in a month on twelve-inch vinyl just in New York. I said, 'I gotta be in this business, this is great!' "

The disco era had peaked. Major labels were at their creative and financial end. The biggest song on the charts was a collaboration between Donna Summer and Barbra Streisand that was as pricey as it was hokey, "No More Tears (Enough Is Enough)." By contrast, "Rapper's Delight" sounded fresh from its very first words—"I said uh hip-hop . . ." To the Bronx heads, the whole thing was a sham.

But the breakthrough may not have happened any other way. When the top Bronx acts made their recording debuts after "Rapper's Delight," they usually tried, and often failed, to be true to the experience of their shows. These live per-formances thrived on quick-witted improvisation and call-and-response audience participation. When they worked up routines, they gave their DJ and the neigh-borhood their props first and foremost. After all, they were onstage at the discre-tion of the DJ, the king of the party, and at the mercy of the audience, his subjects.

The rap amateurs of the Sugar Hill Gang never had a DJ. Assembled in a New Jersey afternoon, they were a studio creation that never stepped on a stage until after their single became a radio hit. They wrote with the ears of fans, and the enthusiasm of dilettantes. Their raps on "Rapper's Delight" were the stuff that sounded good not in the parties, but on the live bootleg cassettes playing in the OJ Cabs and on the boomboxes—the funny stories, the hookish slang, the same kind of stuff that would strike listeners around the world as both universal and new, not local and insular. "Rapper's Delight" was tailor-made to travel, to be perfectly accessible to folks who had never heard of rap or hip-hop or The Bronx.

The inexplicable success of the Sugar Hill Gang transformed the scene overnight. Artists and labels scrambled to cash in. The Funky Four + 1 More and the Treacherous Three signed on to do singles for Bobby Robinson's Enjoy Rec-ords. The Sequence signed with Sylvia Robinson. Afrika Bambaataa agreed to record for Paul Winley. Two Bronx-based reggae labels, Wackies and Joe Gibbs Music, put out rap singles. Kurtis Blow, managed by a young Queens native named Russell Simmons, became the first major-label rap artist when he signed to Mercury for the platinum-selling "Christmas Rappin'" and "The Breaks." And even Flash finally relented when he and the Furious Five struck a deal with Bobby Robinson, "Superappin'" was released a month after "Rapper's Delight." In Flash's mind, having a record out might increase their bookings.

Ironically, the Sugar Hill Gang helped revive the dying Bronx club scene. But club-going turned into a more passive experience than ever. The b-boys disap-peared and, Charlie Ahearn says, "Nobody was dancing. Period! Rap became the focal point. MCs were onstage and people were looking at them." DJs were no longer at the center of the music. The new indie rap industry—with its fear of music publishers—had no place for them, other than to advise the house-bands on how to emulate the spirit of their turntable routines. "This is 1980," Ahearn says. "In other words, hip-hop is dead by 1980. It's true."

If "Rapper's Delight" turned hip-hop into popular music, "Superappin'" shows how pop began to destroy what hip-hop was. The song begins with haunting silences. In unison, the Furious Five raps, "And it won't be long 'til everyone is knowing that Flash is on the beatbox going, that Flash is on the beat-box going . . . and . . . and . . . and . . . sha na na!"[1] In the original routine, the Furious Five would pause and point to Grandmaster Flash as he banged out fre-netic fills on his electronic drum-machine. But on the record, Flash is MIA. The Five shout out Flash as "the king of the Quickmix," but he never gets to demon-strate why. Instead the house band interpolates one of Flash's favorite platters, the Whole Darn Family's "Five Minutes of Funk," while Flash paces the studio like a coach. For the length of "Superappin'," the tension between what rap was—a live performance medium dominated by the DJ—and what it would be-come—a recorded medium dominated by the rappers—is suspended. When the Five shout, "Can't won't don't stop rockin' to the rhythm, 'cause I get down when Flash is on the beatbox," history seems to be held in place.

On the other hand, there was an overwhelming sense of release on many of these early records, especially the ones captured on Bobby Robinson's aptly named Enjoy label, the sound of rappers exuberantly pouring rhymes they had honed for years in front of skeptical Bronx crowds onto wax for the world and eternity. Robinson's nephew Spoonie Gee spun a story of fast girls and cheap sex on "Love Rap," backed only by a steaming, phased break by Pumpkin, the legendary drummer behind so many early hip-hop records. "So let's rock y'all! To the beat y'all!" he rapped in a heart-racing adrenaline rush, the tinge of echo making him seem ten-feet tall. On the Treacherous Three and Spoonie Gee's "New Rap Language," Kool Moe Dee, L.A. Sunshine, Special K, and Spoonie demonstrated their mastery of the Furious Five's group dynamics, and added quicksilver-tongued, metaphor-drunk skills. The crew turned its gaze "to the south, the west, to the east, to the north," brimming with the child's-eye self-importance that hip-hop music would need to jump out of the boroughs and go worldwide.

Record execs realized there were potentially many more millions of fans out there for the music. The number of rap crews exploded, living-room fantasies fu-eled by platinum dreams. For the next decade and a half, hip-hop music moved away from the parks and the community centers and the clubs and into the lab. Indie labels invested in researching and developing how to make hip-hop music, specifically rap, fit the standards of the music industry, how to rationalize and exploit the new product—how to find, capture, package, and sell its essence like a bottle of lightning. Six-man crews would drop to two. Fifteen-minute party-rocking raps would become three-minute ready-for-radio singles. Hip-Hop was refined like sugar.

The tension between culture and commerce would become one of the main storylines of the hip-hop generation.

Broken Windows

The other was the relationship between youth and authority. If rap presented an opportunity for hip-hop culture to be commodified, graffiti presented an opportunity for it to be demonized. The graffiti movement had been the effect of benign neglect, mass media, and youth rebellion. It would not be long before the most extreme demonstration of the generation's revolutionary new aesthetic provoked the most extreme backlash.

From the first surfacing of TAKI 183 in the *New York Times* in 1971, graffiti moved from being a neighborhood teenage curiosity to a municipal issue with national political implications. And that's where it would stay. In the summer of 1972, with his presidential campaign on the ropes, Mayor John Lindsay launched the first "War on Graffiti" with the exasperated cry: "For heaven's sake, New Yorkers, come to the aid of your great city—defend it, support and protect it!"[2] He called the graffiti writers "insecure cowards" and suggested they all had mental health problems. The mayor's anti-graffiti program called not only for restriction of markers and aerosol paints, increased security measures and use of chemicals, solvents and paints to deter graf, but the deployment of psychological measures.

To Lindsay, graffiti was the most infuriating crime. It had a "demoralizing visual impact," and he declared, "It's a dirty shame that we must spend money for this purpose in a time of austerity."[3] But the war would go on. Politicians had found a way to agree with their constituents that the city was going to hell, while doing little else to get it off that track. The War on Graffiti covered over municipal government's inability to deal with multiple real crises—of which bankruptcy was the most urgent. So-called "quality of life" campaigns were symbolic, and often expensive, appeasement to malaise-weary voters.

In 1976, as the city hurtled toward bankruptcy, it found $20 million to establish "the buff," a chemical washing of graffitied trains, to add to the usual $25 million in annual expenditures to wage its war. The buff not only left the cars an aesthetically dull color, it was harmful; hundreds of workers became sick and one man died of long-term exposure.[4]

The same year, the Transit Authority established a four-man Anti-Graffiti Squad, which quickly issued a misleading "Profile of a Common Offender":

Sex—Male
Race—Black, Puerto Rican, other (in that order)
Age—Variable, predominantly 13 to 16 years
Dress—Carries package or paper bag, long coat in cold weather
Occupation—Student (lower social economic background) . . . [5]

It is easy to scoff now at the profile's obvious inaccuracies, just as it is easy to dismiss the transit police efforts as largely bumbling and ineffective. But police also made thousands of arrests and stepped up intelligence of youths of color—monitoring their crews, confiscating writer's black books, interrogating graffiti perps and raiding writer's homes. These surveillance-and-sweep techniques generated their own kind of ideology. The profile became its own kind of sick truth, with bloody consequences.

In 1979, an astonishingly disingenuous *Public Interest* article by neoconservative Nathan Glazer provided justification—*theory* is all too strong a word—for increasingly hysterical policing and punishment efforts directed against youths of color. The central premise of the piece rested not on well-tested empirical data but, as Glazer himself admitted, raw fear of the Other. Musing on the graffiti problem, he wrote, "(W)hile I do not find myself consciously making the connection between the graffiti-makers and the criminals who occasionally rob, rape, assault, and murder passengers, the sense that all are a part of one world of uncontrollable predators seems inescapable."[6]

Harvard criminologist James Q. Wilson would further develop this incoherent argument into what would come to be called "the broken windows" theory. If one broken window was allowed to go unfixed, the "theory" said, a neighborhood's violent plunge into Fort Apache would soon follow. Broken windows theory paved the way for the brutal zero tolerance "quality of life" campaigns of surveillance, harassment and propaganda that a new generation of mayors perfected by the 1990s. Again, despite scant empirical evidence, the City Hall sound bite that graffiti was a gateway to violent crime necrotized into unimpeachable truth.

Glazer and Wilson had simply repackaged the same old there-goes-the-neighborhood racism that had driven the white flight of the '60s, albeit in a way that seemed prophetic. Two decades later, Malcolm Gladwell's influential book, *The Tipping Point,* would still be celebrating "broken windows" as a bleeding-edge idea, less proving the "theory" 's viability than showing the complete success these ideologues had in transforming urban policy. Glazer's and Wilson's articles, in fact, represented a different kind of tipping point: once named, the neocon reaction to graffiti would become one of the hinges on which the politics of abandonment would turn toward a politics of containment. Both these politics would profoundly shape the hip-hop generation.

In the media, racial profiling and the War on Graffiti converged. The subway epitomized New York's anarchic ruin, a city that had been given over to the rule of criminally undisciplined dark-skinned youths. In 1984, self-styled "subway vigilante" Bernhard Hugo Goetz shot four Black teenagers on a train at close range, paralyzing one, and became a national hero overnight. It was a climax that SKEME, a frustrated Black teenager with talent to burn, had foreseen a few years earlier, telling subway riders in a window-down burner: "All *you* see is . . . CRIME IN THE CITY."

Pre-Teen B-Boy Preservationists

By the end of 1979, rap and graffiti were being thoroughly transformed by capital and authority. As Flash had said, it was time to survive and change or get left behind, the turning of another five-year cycle of style.

But then there were the pre-teens, the ones who once could not wait to grow up so they could have their own battles and block parties, rock their own styles, make their own names. The stylistic explosions of the mid-'70s were over, and time, money, and power seemed to be conspiring to steal their chance to shine. If these youth movements were to survive with their traditions intact, they needed nostalgic shorties who remembered how it used to be back in the day.

Two years after the Crotona Avenue jam, Crazy Legs was living in far uptown Manhattan on 207th Street, near the Ghost Yard. He and his cousin Lenny had battled two leaders of the original Rock Steady Crew from Echo Park, Jimmy Dee and Jimmy Lee, and lost. Still they had shown much heart and now they were members. But it wasn't like it was. The legends had drifted away from the dance and the crews dissipated. Even worse, he says, "There weren't too many crews out there when I moved into Manhattan. Very few people were doing the dance." He was being cheated of his chance to prove himself. He was all of thirteen years old, and he ached for the past.

So Crazy Legs embarked on a mission. Like a character in one of the Times Square kung-fu flicks he loved, he traveled through the city to find and challenge every remaining b-boy. "I went and met this guy named Lil' Man, who eventually became Lil' Crazy Legs. I met Take One, this kid named Quiquito, we used to call him Little Kicks, and I battled them. When I would come across b-boys, I would start hanging out with them and one person would tell me, 'Yo, I know a b-boy from this area down here.' He might be fifty blocks away or whatever. I'd be like, 'Come on let's go there.' My little kung-fu flick mission continued. And eventually I recruited all of them," he says.

Down in the Upper West Side, Wayne "Frosty Freeze" Frost was part of a group formed by Zulu Kings called the Rock City Rockers. Jeffrey "DOZE" Green and Ken "Swift" Gabbert had a crew called the Young City Boys. There were others, too, like Buck 4 and Kuriaki. Crazy Legs met and battled them all. Then Jimmy Dee gave him the Rock Steady Crew name. He says, "Jimmy Dee had seen that I had so many people down and I kept it going and a lot of the other b-boys weren't still as active. It was a humble stance he took. He reduced his own rank and gave me everything and never got in my way of doing things, but was still there to give me guidance at being a crew leader." The new Rock Steady Crew became a magnet for isolated Bronx-styling youths across the city, a second-generation supergroup, the last b-boys standing.

DOZE says, "Every Saturday, me, Legs, Frosty and Kenny spent all day in the movies in Times Square. Three dollars for ten movies, some crazy shit! Just watch Shaw Brothers movies and just bug out. And so we started incorporating those moves into the dance. That's how we started getting our own style." When they practiced their moves in the park at 84th and Amsterdam, they may have made an odd sight, a lost school of b-boy monks. They had inherited the dance, and they took that legacy seriously.

DOZE had first seen the dance in the North Bronx in the early '70s, in the Edenwald Projects where the outlaws danced with radios on their shoulders. He and Ken honed in on the gangsters' up-rock and made that the core of their style. "The dance is actually very long. It's like a fifteen-minute dance. It has a lot of steps. It goes from a format of standing up and being still and kinda like out doing with the hand gestures, then it goes to a strut, like a skip, then to a strut, then a backwards step and then it goes into a forward step, and then it's like a hesitate, and then you drop. We took that part, the ending. We saw that, and said, 'That's the shit.' The thrust forward and drop—that's like the most powerful part of the dance, that's like the breakdown. Me and Kenny learned from the last folks, we learned a fraction of it, but what we did with that dance is took it to a whole 'nother level."

Frosty Freeze came up with new freezes, like the Suicide—where he did a flip and landed on his back. Crazy Legs and Ken Swift did the same for spins, injecting into the dance stunning new body mechanics, physics, and speed. Soon Rock Steady members had gone beyond the backspin and headspin into windmills and handspins. Crazy Legs says, "All these moves that we came about doing were by accident. I didn't set out to evolve the backspin. I was practicing a chair freeze and I over-rotated and I spun fast. And then I over-rotated again on another time, and went into a continuous backspin and kept on doing it."

Rock Steady Crew began rolling into skating rinks and parks and dances to shock teens with their style. Crews that tried to battle them found them unstoppable. DOZE says, "Frosty and I were like the goofs of the crew, we used to just mimic people and act like a clown and do like Drunken Monkey style, like fall all over the place and come out—Boom! It was like, 'Yo send DOZE in, clown him!' I would clown him. 'Alright now send in Buck and Kuri.' They were the secret weapons, boom baaaat! It was like *5 Deadly Venoms*."

They won audiences over, and their ranks swelled. They expanded their membership to include kids interested in any of the old Bronx arts. "SHY 147 was down with us. DONDI was down with us. We had people that were rollerskaters down with Rock Steady. We had girls, people that were Webo dancers. We had people that was just fly girls, people that just supported and hung out with us. We had a multifaceted crew," says Crazy Legs. "Rock Steady back then was at least five hundred deep."

Then one by one, members headed off to form their own crews. The Rock Steady members who remained derisively called them "expansion teams." But some of them, like the New York City Breakers and the Dynamic Rockers, would become Rock Steady's fiercest competitors.

By then Rock Steady had already done its job. They didn't know it then, but their vision of the Bronx old-school would indelibly shape the hip-hop generation. They had revived the dance, canonized old moves and invented bold new ones. Throbbing with uptempo post-*búgalu* Afro-Latin rhythms and good vibes, songs like Booker T & The MG's "Melting Pot," Herman Kelley and Life's "Let's Dance to the Drummer's Beat," and Lonnie Liston Smith's "Expansions" captured their optimism. One of their theme-songs said it all: "It's Just Begun."

Crazy Legs and the Rock Steady Crew at the Dyckman Street playground, uptown Manhattan, 1981. From left: Lil Crazy Legs, Kippy Dee, Lennie Len, unknown friend, Crazy Legs, Fast Break, Take One, Ken Swift.

© Henry Chalfant

8

Zulus on a Time Bomb

Hip-Hop Meets the Rockers Downtown

Pop artists made art out of pop culture. These tough kids are reversing the process, making pop culture out of art.

—Kim Levin

It wasn't about your little local neighborhood. It was always you were going all-city, that's what you were supposed to do. So why shouldn't art be all-city?

—Charlie Ahearn

To uptown kids like Crazy Legs and DOZE, their culture was simply what it was. It didn't need external validation. It even thrived with opposition. It needed nothing but its own codes, its own authority. But downtown, other people were beginning to see something big in it. "It was a high school youth culture," says Charlie Ahearn, an East Village filmmaker who was venturing to the Bronx to soak up the new energy. "And to me, it was a radical avant-garde culture."

The youth movements seemed to look like a single culture, just as Afrika Bambaataa had envisioned years before with Zulu Nation, an expression of a new generation of outcast youths whose worldview felt authentic, original, and liberating. This first wave of downtowners—white baby boomer outsiders, young white bohemian dropouts, white art rebels, Black post-jazzsters—were enthralled. They were the earliest adopters, the ones who placed themselves closest to the fire, and they would be central in bringing hip-hop to the world.

Boomer Outsiders

Soft-spoken sculptor named Henry Chalfant had come of age during the stifling fifties in Sewickley, Pennsylvania, a tiny white-picket fence town north of rusting Pittsburgh. His father ran the family's steel-pipe manufacturing firm. His mother had helped found a private-care institution for handicapped children. In the Allegheny Valley, Chalfant's very name evoked aristocracy and connection. His great-great grandfather, the area's pioneering Henry, was an inkeeper and proprietor so beloved that a town east of Pittsburgh had been named for him in 1914. But the younger Henry felt alienated in the land of his ancestors.

"We used to argue over whose family was poorer while being driven to school by the chauffeur," he says. "I was definitely unhappy where I grew up, which was very privileged, very white, very hide-bound, rule-bound, and rather empty.

"So you know," he chuckles, "I drove fast—hot rods, motorcycles. Generally I was a menace in that way." When he graduated, he sped toward the California sunset, where he enrolled at Stanford in 1958. He majored in classical Greek, immersed himself in art and became a sculptor, and when Berkeley students closed the McCarthy era with their Free Speech Movement and antiwar demonstrations, he was drawn into that as well.

In 1967, he left the Bay Area for Europe with his wife, the actress Kathleen Chalfant, to soak up art and sculpture in Barcelona and Rome. But on frequent visits back to New York City, he became intoxicated by the colorful, intricate graffiti on the sides of the subway cars. These weren't Pompeii scrawls in the dustbins of history. They were alive, mysterious, alluring, dangerous. In 1973, he and Kathleen moved to New York permanently, and he began to photograph the tags. "What immediately peaked my interest was seeing what seemed to be all these rebellious kids. What I ended up doing was living it to the hilt the second time through—not my own adolescence, but vicariously through these writers," he says.

From the summer of 1976 to 1979, Chalfant went out on weekends to document the train art. Writers began to notice the balding white man, standing for hours on subway platforms with an expensive camera, snapping furiously and sometimes futilely when the trains screeched into the stops, and figured he was either a cop or one of them, a die-hard junkie for aerosol art. One day he found himself staring at a writer named NAC, who was also taking pictures. They got to talking. When Chalfant let him know what he was doing, NAC told him to drop by the Writer's Bench at 149th Street after school one day. The writers befriended him and brought him into the fold, passing him through their crews, calling him to brag about their latest victories, which he then went out to capture on film. Chalfant's hobby became a daily obsession. In turn, he opened up his Greenwich Village studio to them.

Uptown, ZEPHYR and FUTURA were gathering writers at Sam Esses's studio to begin translating graffiti for the art gallery world. Chalfant's Grand Street studio, by contrast, was a library of subway style. The photos were the best the writers had ever seen. After 1978, Chalfant had begun using a motor-drive on his camera. While standing in one spot, he could shoot entire cars on a flat angle. The photos presented the cars as if they had just pulled up to the station in their full glory. Younger writers especially flocked to Chalfant's studio to study the photos and learn the styles.

Like the ambivalent anthropologist, Chalfant realized he had altered the scene. "In the old days before photography, you would get style from a king. He would grant you this style and then you could copy the outline if you were part of his crew," he says. "But when people from other parts of the city start rocking your style, you weren't happy. Someone like SKEME, he was getting a lot of fame and for about a year, he was taking over everything. And a lot of his style came from my photos of DONDI." But Chalfant's interest had never been merely academic. He wanted to be taken, he says, "by the daily surprise of it all."

In September 1980, Chalfant displayed his photos publicly for the first time in an exhibition at the O. K. Harris Gallery in Soho. He was astonished at the reception he got. The few print reviews he got were brief and lukewarm, but the streets spoke loudly. "They came to the gallery as if on a pilgrimmage," Chalfant says.[1]

From across the city, hundreds of graffiti writers arrived dressed in their flyest customized denims and sneakers, all color and swagger and joy. The writers took over the gallery, gazing at the twenty shots of whole-car murals in a rush of recognition and future shock. They spilled out of the tiny gallery back onto the street, tagging each other's books and the storefront walls. They formed new crews, secured affiliations and made plans. Chalfant, the quiet student of the youth culture, and all of his less worldly art-world peers were awestruck anew at how big the thing really was.

Dondi White brought Martha Cooper, a newsphotographer for the *New York Post* and an urban folklorist to meet Chalfant. Cooper and Chalfant were aware of each others' work and had privately nursed a professional jealousy, but in person the vibes melted away and they greeted each other as long-lost colleagues. Both understood that the writers' eye-zapping virtuosity and the art's butterfly ephemerality demanded documentation and advocacy.

Chalfant shot the trains as if they were already in the museums. Cooper contextualized them as they rushed through the grimy backdrop of the dying city—"Art vs. Transit," as her famous shot of a 1982 train by DURO, SHY 147 and KOS from CIA illustrated, a metaphor for bottom-up urban renewal. Together they began making a case for graffiti. Glazed to boredom by abstraction, "the art-world was ready for it," Chalfant says.

Events snowballed. Once the Esses Studio closed, the energy ZEPHYR and FUTURA had gathered moved into spaces like ALI's Soul Artists workshop, the center of "Zoo York," and the Fashion Moda storefront gallery in the South Bronx. In October, Fashion Moda's "Graffiti Art Success for America," put together by CRASH, opened in the South Bronx. In December, the New Museum brought many of the pieces down for an exhibition at its location in Greenwich Village. All of a sudden, there no longer seemed to be an expiration date on a graffiti lifestyle. Writers considered making a living at it. Major museum curators and gallery owners, eagerly sniffing out the new, began to venture out of their safe Manhattan turfs with their checkbooks.

The week after Christmas, *The Village Voice* announced the art-world's new alignment with street culture in a cover story by graf's public defender Richard Goldstein called "The Fire Down Below." There were fashionable black-and-white portraits of PINK, ZEPHYR, FAB 5 FREDDY and FUTURA 2000 and a full-color pullout section featuring Chalfant's iconic photos of classic trains by Lee Quiñones, BLADE, SEEN, DONDI, KELL and FUTURA. The sense of anticipation was palpable. Goldstein quoted FAB 5 FREDDY, on his way to a gallery opening of his works in Milan: "With a little time and paint, anything is possible."[2]

Young Bohemians

The walls of northern segregation could come down, for one thing.

As New York City staggered out of the 1970s—bloodied and broke—it was more separate and less equal than ever, the culmination of three decades of top-down urban renewal, Third World dislocation and white flight. During the decade, more than 1.2 million whites, fully a quarter of the white population—including almost a third of whites in Brooklyn and half of whites in the Bronx—had abandoned the city. Poverty rates soared, especially in those two boroughs.[3]

Pop culture mirrored the segregation. Movies like *Badge 373* and *Fort Apache: The Bronx* looked, especially to Blacks and Latinos, like exploitative tales that reinforced race and class hatred more often than they raised empathy. At the end of the '70s, Puerto Rican and Black activists, led by the former Young Lord Richie Perez and other veterans of the Black and Brown Power movements, organized to boycott such films and demand more faithful and truthful media representations. At one protest, two brown Bronx girls carried a picket saying, "Fort Apache—Indians are not savages. Neither are we."[4] Even pop music, with its long history of crossover and miscegenation, offered little hope. After disco, radio cleaved into ever more rigid rock (white) and urban (Black) formats.

Yet graffiti had infected the young post-hippies gathering in Central Park. Through the decades, the locus of the city's young bohemia had shifted northward, from Greenwich Village to Central Park's Bethesda Fountain, and then into the heart of the Park at the field behind the Naumberg Bandshell. The "parkie" scene embraced native and immigrant sons and daughters of philosophers and kings, hard-hat workers and maids.

To ZEPHYR, a Jewish kid from the Upper East Side who cut classes to hang out, the scene behind the bandshell was an opening into a different world. "You get out of school, fuckin' get your little bag of reefer, going to the park, meeting up with your homeboys, kids from Brooklyn, the Bronx," he says. "It was extremely mixed, like a freak scene of young kids. Some of the kids were really from wealthy families and then some were like more down and out, some were homeless. But it was really cool because that scene went on for, I'd say, the better half of a decade."

There, the "parkies" found a safe space to experiment with drugs (especially marijuana and psychedelics), sex and style. "The cops had a total hands-off policy. There was fucking clouds of pot smoke. It looked like the parking lot of a Grateful Dead concert. Imagine that every day, seven days a week." When he met writers like BILL ROCK, MIN ONE, REVOLT and others there, ZEPHYR's secret obsession with graffiti flowered. Through graffiti, the parkies' scene began to mix with the punk-era art-activists of the East Village.

Art Rebels

As soon as they were able—1973, to be precise—Charlie Ahearn and his twin brother, John, had moved from their upstate middle-class collegiate suburb of Binghamton to New York City to become contemporary artists. Charlie enrolled in the Whitney Museum's program and found an apartment in the middle of the heroin-bingeing East Village. He and John became part of an artists' movement there called Co-Lab—a collective determined to, he says, "get the hell out of the art world, get the hell out of art galleries and find a way to be creative in a larger sense."

"Coming from a middle-class background, I always wanted to be as adventurous as possible, to see a larger picture," Ahearn says. "The idea was people that are involved in any kind of struggle are interesting. It's not about going into a studio and making work and selling it in an art gallery. You go right out there. You're an activist. You're changing things by creating stuff."

Charlie went down to the Alfred E. Smith projects in the Lower East Side, at the Manhattan end of the Brooklyn Bridge, with a Super 8 camera. He filmed the kids practicing martial arts and then played the film back for them. He was as taken as they were with the all-day kung-fu festivals in Times Square, then a pre-redevelopment *Taxi Driver* carnival of red-bulb burlesque and Five Percenter ciphers. And so he collaborated with the kids to do their own kind of homage, which he called "The Deadly Art of Survival."

While filming, he had become captivated by Lee Quiñones's handball court murals—animals and spacemen floating and roaring off the walls in bright comic-book colors. "I would ask kids in the neighborhood, who painted these murals? And they'd go, 'Lee!' Like it was the most obvious thing cause he's so famous, one of the most up graffiti artists in New York City. And I'd say, 'Okay, where can I find him?' And everyone would go, 'I don't know, he's around but he's kinda secretive. He's hard to find.' "

When Lee ventured by the set one day, Ahearn cornered him. "He had this big afro and he was this skinny kid with a motorbike. And I'd say, 'I want to work with you on this movie.' And he said, 'Bet.' And I said, 'Well, how can I get to you? Do you have a phone number?' 'Nah, I'll just be around.' And then he'd never be around," laughs Ahearn. "He was mythical."

In June 1980, the Co-Lab collective took over an abandoned massage parlor in Times Square at 41st Street and Seventh Avenue for a massive exhibition. "Everyone just sort of rushed in, bumrushing the place and throwing artwork up," Ahearn says. "There was a lot of street art at the time, and there was a lot of homeless people making sort of weird things on the street, that all became part of the show. So graffiti slipped in there, it seemed like a very natural thing to include in the show."

The show would be widely reviewed, remembered as historic. A new crop of graffiti-inspired "street artists" were introduced in the show—Jean-Michel Basquiat, Kenny Scharf and Keith Haring. And Ahearn finally got to work with Lee Quiñones and his partner, FAB 5 FREDDY.

In Search of a Post-Jazz Cool

Frederick Brathwaite was a tall slim African American raised in the do-or-die Bed-Stuy. He looked out at the world from behind his ever-present Ray-Bans, as if he had just stepped out of Minton's Playhouse.

He had spent his childhood in casual proximity to Black genius. The bebop elite frequented his family's house, people like Bud Powell, Thelonious Monk, Clifford Brown, and Freddy's godfather Max Roach. His grandfather had been an associate of Marcus Garvey. His father, an accountant, was in the audience at the Audubon Ballroom when Malcolm X was shot. Freddy was born with an awareness of walking proudly through history.

Brathwaite wanted to become a serious artist. But he was also searching for an artform he could organize his own worldview around—the same way his father saw his world through jazz. He found fresh energy in the Brooklyn mobile DJ scene, at shows thrown by Grandmaster Flowers, Maboya, and Pete DJ Jones. On hooky trips he went to the Metropolitan Museum of Art to study its collections of art and armor. He immersed himself in Caravaggio, Duchamp, Boccioni and Warhol. And he tagged BULL 99 and SHOWDOWN 177.

Graffiti brought it all together. "I had looked at all the movements that were kind of radical, like Futurism, the Dadaists, the Impressionists, the Abstract Expressionists into the Pop Artists. To me, it was like, wait a minute, this shit is a lot like what graffiti is," he says. "So I was thinking about how to make moves into the art world, but still keep the integrity of what graffiti was."

He too was inspired by Lee Quiñones's work, and decided he needed to meet the artist. Sometime in 1978, he boldly strode into Lee's high-school classroom. Before being told to leave, Freddy whispered to Lee to meet him outside after school. Lee was suspicious, but when they spoke, they realized they had found the perfect foil in each other. Lee was shy and elusive, Freddy radiated confidence and cool. Lee kept his thoughts to himself, Freddy talked to anyone. Through Lee, Freddy met the rest of the Fabulous Five—all in various stages of retiring from the lines—and was brought into the crew. As FAB 5 FREDDY, he painted trains and walls and publicized graffiti in the downtown art scene. In early 1979, he appeared in a *Village Voice* article about graffiti, smoking a cigarette under Lee's GRAFFITI 1990 mural, and offering his contact info. By the end of the year, the two had landed the first graffiti art show in Italy, at the Galleria La Medusa.

FAB floated right into the burgeoning downtown scene. He hung out at *Interview* magazine editor Glen O'Brien's cable access show, a central hub of the New Wave/No Wave movement. He partied at the Mudd Club with Deborah Harry and Blondie, Jean-Michel Basquiat, Keith Haring and Andy Warhol. At the same time, he was checking out Grandmaster Flash and the Furious Four at the Smith Houses with Lee, and collecting bootleg cassettes of all the rap crews. The nineteen-year-old found himself moving through two very different worlds, and he had both the charisma and the desire to bring them together.

Four Movements to One Culture

Bambaataa's vision of a revolutionary youth culture was unfolding before FAB's eyes and he began to see what his role could be. "As a painter at the time, and having read a lot about art, I wanted to make sure that we weren't perceived as folk artists," he says.

"Not everybody doing graffiti had aesthetic intentions, but many did. Those that did were the ones that drove the development from just simple tags to elaborate window-down wildstyle. Those heads were on some creative shit. I wanted to make sure that the scene that I was coming from was actually seen in that light, basically that we were smart enough to understand that game as well," he says.

"I once read somewhere that for a culture to really be a complete culture, it should have a music, a dance and a visual art. And then I realized, wow, all these things are going on. You got the graffiti happening over here, you got the breakdancing, and you got the DJ and MCing thing. In my head, they were all one thing," he says. FAB understood the history of artistic movements, and he realized that he was right at the beginning of a big one. He had an idea to set it off.

At the Times Square Show, Mudd Club and Co-Lab co-conspirator Diego Cortez introduced Charlie Ahearn and FAB 5 FREDDY. FAB had seen "The Deadly Art of Survival" and knew Ahearn could be just the person to speak to. Ahearn recalls, "Fred told me that he wanted to make a movie with me. He said, 'We should make a movie about this graffiti thing', and he said he knew Lee Quiñones. So I said if you can bring Lee to me, come by tomorrow and I'll give you guys fifty dollars 'cause I wanted them to do a mural outside the building. They came by the next day. And I said, 'Okay, here we are, the three of us.' That became the beginnings of the idea of *Wild Style*."

Ahearn and FAB began a year of immersion in the culture, finding themselves one night in a far corner of the north Bronx, at a party presided over by Chief Rocker Busy Bee and DJ Breakout. "It was in a place called The Valley. It's in a large park and it was dark. I remember there was a dub reggae band playing and the other side was hip-hop music. And we wandered to the hip-hop music," Ahearn says. "I often wonder what would have happened had we ended up going toward the dub band.

"Fred and I were standing by the side of this little tiny stage," he recalls. "This guy next to me later told me he was sweating bullets because he thought I was a cop. Everyone *always* thought I was a cop. I don't blame them. For a year that I was hanging out there, I never saw anyone that was from downtown or that was white hanging out in any place I went to.

"So Busy Bee was there and he says, 'What are you doing here?' and I said, 'I'm Charlie Ahearn and I'm here to make a movie about the rap scene.' And he takes me by the hand and he leads me out on the stage where there's a microphone and there's an audience."

Ahearn's twin, John, had moved to the Bronx two years before, and was becoming something of an art-world star for his cast sculptures of his neighbors on Walton Avenue, an area where the Savage Skulls had once roamed. Another close associate, Co-Lab member Stefan Eins, had opened a gallery he called Fashion Moda on East 147th Street at Third Avenue in the heart of the South Bronx. "The Bronx was a hip place to go if you were an artist, everybody was going up there," Charlie says. "But *this* was not the same. It was a totally different scene—high school kids—and it was wild.

"It was dark and Busy Bee leads me out onto stage, to the microphone—and you gotta understand, everybody who is anybody in hip-hop is right *there*. The Funky 4 were there, Mercedes Ladies, all these people were all in the audience right there. So Busy Bee puts his arm around me and he says, 'This here is Charlie Ahearn and he's my movie producer. We're making a movie about the rap scene.' Boom! That's all it took."

Ahearn and FAB became regular guests of the biggest rap crews in the scene, frequenting clubs like the Ecstasy Garage, the T-Connection and the Disco Fever. As he had done at Smith Houses, Ahearn took pictures, made slides, and brought them back to project them on the walls of the clubs. He was practicing his activist art.

When he met graf writers CRASH and DAZE, he walked them the short distance from their residences to meet Eins at the Fashion Moda. "No graffiti artist had ever heard of Fashion Moda," Ahearn says, despite the fact that the gallery was only two blocks from the Writer's Bench. "CRASH organized the 'Graffiti Art Success for America' show. Fashion Moda became one of the capitals of graffiti in a month."

FAB 5 FREDDY was thrilled to be meeting all of his Bronx heroes, and he began opening doors for them downtown. Grandmaster Flash says, "FAB was like one of the town criers. He would come into the hood where whites wouldn't come and then go downtown to where whites would, and say, 'Listen there's some music these cats is playing, man, it's hot shit. You gotta book these guys.' So I got my first taste of playing for an audience that wasn't typically Black."

FAB invited Bambaataa down to play at Keith Haring's black-light art exhibition in a tiny church basement on St. Mark's Place called Club 57. It was exactly the kind of opportunity Bambaataa had been waiting for. The crowd loved it, and FAB brought Bam and his Zulu Nation DJs, Jazzy Jay and Afrika Islam, back to play at venues like the Jefferson Hotel and the Mudd Club.

In April 1981, FAB curated an art show at Mudd Club called "Beyond Words: Graffiti-Based, -Rooted and -Inspired Work." The line-up read like a who's-who of the punk, subway graf, and street art scenes. Photos by Cooper and Chalfant hung next to canvases and installations by Lee, PHASE 2, LADY PINK, ZEPHYR DONDI, John Sex, Jean-Michel Basquiat, Keith Haring, Alan Vega, Iggy Pop and FAB's notorious running partner, RAMMELLZEE, an eccentric painter and freestyler obsessed with military codes and alphabet armaments.

At the opening, FAB brought in the Cold Crush Brothers, the Fantastic Freaks, and Bambaataa's Jazzy Five MCs to perform. "That was the first official time when hip-hop really hit downtown," FAB says. "It was wildly received. All these cool new wave heads came down and loved it. I knew nobody had a sense or clue about anything because barely any real rap records had hit the market commercially, maybe 'Rapper's Delight,' but nobody really understood it as like a scene."

When the hip-hoppers met the rockers, parkies, and freaks downtown, a weird new nightclub elite emerged. "We used to go to Bowl-Mor and we would bowl," ZEPHYR laughs. The high-flying, Studio 54, velvet-rope, VIP-exclusive club era was over. People were going downtown where gutter-familiar scenesters mixed freely, the picture of a wild and fabulous new pluralism.

"We had this team called the Pinheads," ZEPHYR says. "It was a big mix of people from the Mudd Club. FAB 5 FREDDY was down with us, and Grace Jones used to come down and go bowling.[5] These very new-wave/punk type people from downtown, less eccentric folks, some of the old hippie dudes like me and my boys. And then of course, from the Bronx, you had a little more macho folks. Everything overlapped. It was really surreal."

On the season's shortlist, race and class segregation was out, cultural crossover was in. "There was this shifting and mixing that was very exciting to people," says Ahearn. "The racial thing was a big deal. Mixing a lot of Black,

Puerto Rican and white people downtown all together is very combustible, because people are coming from very different types of areas and they are getting used to the idea that they can hang out with each other."

Graffiti Success in America

Before long, the elite of the art-world came calling. Once cloaked in secrecy and code and executed under the constant threat of violence, graffiti suddenly became a very public performance, for the consumption of high society. The temporary and fleeting tried to fix itself as permanent.

Graffiti had flirted with the big-time in 1973, when Hugo Martinez secured for his elite graffiti union, the United Graffiti Artists, a Twyla Tharp commission and a downtown exhibition at the Razor Gallery. UGA got an avalanche of publicity, including a *Newsweek* article, and even sold some canvases for as much as $2,500. But by 1975, UGA had fizzled amidst slacking patronage and internal discord. Other similar community-based efforts to bridge graf and the art world, like Jack Pelzinger's NOGA and ALI's Soul Artists, also eventually faded.

As the 1980s arrived, Modernism was dead. Minimalism and Conceptualism had become increasingly cold, detached, cerebral, feeble. The art world thought it was ready for something authentic and passionate, something innocent and incandescent. It wanted to feel deeply again. After an era of self-referentiality and white-room obscurantism, the art world wanted a door-opening gust of the sights, smells and tastes of the real world.

Upper Manhattanites and Europeans who had supported the explosion of Pop Art during the 1960s rushed in to buy anything marketed as graffiti. In a year, Jean-Michel Basquiat—who had never painted on a train—went from homelessness to international art stardom, commanding as much as $10,000 a canvas. Teenage bombers found they could cut school and pocket $200 for a quick canvas on the way to the lay-up.

Many of the paintings were little more than tags, albeit with a buff-proof, overglowing impertinence that came with the "for sale" sign. And although collectors oohed and awed at the novelty of it all, dealers pushed the writers to give them more complex work, to make statements. Some of them did. As journalists and the media gathered to watch, ZEPHYR painted an unfurling American flag. Then he slammed a big, wildstyle "Z" across it, daring critics to embrace a new idea of "American graffiti."

PINK, the youngest of the gallery writers, displayed a feminist take on war, psychological repression and sex work. CRASH fostered the link between Pop and graffiti, sampling Lichtenstein, Warhol and Rauschenberg. Lee Quiñones moved toward an intense social realism, abandoning words and cartoons for harrowing scenes, such as the lonely, desparing junkie shooting up between the Statue of Liberty and an American flag in "Society's Child."

The most influential—DONDI, PHASE 2, RAMMELLZEE and FUTURA—developed new visual languages. PHASE 2, whose 1973 canvases had been widely recognized as defining the early genre, continued deconstructing the letter into hard lines, third eyes, horns, drills, spikes, arches, Egyptian pharoahs and dogs, pure geometrics. RAMMELLZEE's canvases swirled with forces locked in struggle, a visual analogue of his insurgent theories about the letter and word as armored vehicle in a militarized world. DONDI, the high priest of wildstyle, played with letters, arrows, often faceless head and bodies, constantly commenting on the various representations of himself in the world—names, diagrams, checking account numbers, currency.

The most visually accessible of the artists, FUTURA, provided critics with a target they could interpret. Some called him the Watteau or Kandinsky of graffiti; others used him to deride the entire movement as empty and directionless. He combined a militant, almost architecturally precise line and an understanding of industrial design and fonts with a nonpareil spatial sense of the abstract and the fantastic. He became the most famous in-house performance graffiti writer of the "Wheels of Steel" night at Negril and the Roxy, and his best work perfectly captured the atom-crashing, buzzsaw energy of the time, the rapture of the cipher, the cut, the light, the truss and the arc.

The graffitiists' work was remarkable for their outsiderness, the way in which they completely collided with the big-money gallery sensibility. Art critic Elizabeth Hess called the moment "a genuine disruption of form in the history of art."[6] In a *People Magazine* feature, Claudio Bruni, the man who had set off the frenzy by bringing FAB 5 FREDDY and Lee Quiñones to Italy in 1979, said, "To me, it was not just vandalism. It was the new expression of art, unsophisticated but very real. An art so strong it hurt people."[7]

Cynics thought the art world's embrace of graffiti represented the worst kind of white liberal guilt, a bizarre flirtation with the repressed Other. But the artists remained hopeful. ZEPHYR said, "People might say graffiti looks really out of place in a gallery. But I think it's good if graffiti is out of place. Sneaking into these places is just what graffiti is supposed to do."[8]

A Riot of Their Own

As the Reagan era commenced, hip-hop was a force that had begun reintegrating the downtown clubs, and vaulted society's outcasts into the rarified art world. But these places still represented the fringes of the avant-garde. On the streets, reality was still as color-coded and divided as ever.

FAB FIVE FREDDY says, "Things were relatively polarized. There was a term called 'bridge-and-tunnel,' which was the people that came from the outer boroughs that were really just dumb, ignorant white kids that were really racist. And they would cause problems for everybody. They would want to fight, you know what I mean? Like tough, kinda street white kids that was really not on some creative shit."

At the same time, across the Atlantic, punk's great idealists, The Clash, were so enchanted with rap that they recorded one in early 1980 called "The Magnificent Seven" for their epic *Sandinista!* album. When they arrived in New York the following summer, they were thrilled to find it had become an unlikely hit on the Black radio station, WBLS. With Don Letts, their partner and documentarian, they took a video camera to Times Square to film graf writers, b-boys, rappers and boombox renegades.

The Clash had come a long way, ideologically and musically, since they had issued "White Riot," a naive, revolutionary statement of solidarity with the West Indian immigrant rebels of the 1976 Nottinghill Carnival riots. That record had paradoxically left many wondering whether the record wasn't expressing neo-Nazi sentiments. "White riot!" they had shouted, "I wanna riot, a riot of my own!" In fact, they were searching for audiences who, as Strummer rapped on "This Is Radio Clash," recognized Sugar Minott's ghettology as Afrika Bambaataa's Lil' Vietnam.

They were set to play eight nights in June 1981 at an aging Times Square disco, the Bonds International, and they announced their stand with a dramatic unfurling of a magnificent banner painted by FUTURA. But on the eve of their opening, the fire department threatened to shut down the club for overselling the shows, and their fans finally had their white riot when mounted police stormed down Broadway to meet the punks in the streets.

The Clash compromised by agreeing to perform eleven additional gigs, and hurried to find opening acts. In yet another naive act of solidarity, they booked Grandmaster Flash and the Furious Five. But, as Michael Hill wrote in *The Village Voice*, "Rather than achieve a cultural crossover, it threatened to widen the gap."[9]

When Flash and the Furious Five stepped onstage on The Clash's opening night, the white punks stood bewildered as Flash began his "Adventures on the Wheels of Steel" routine on three turntables. Then the Furious Five, dressed in fly leather suits, jumped onstage and started rapping and dancing. Some in the crowd began shouting their disgust. They hadn't come to see no disco. When Flash paused so that the Five could try to regain the crowd, the crew found themselves ducking a hail of beer cups and spit. The next night, dressed down this time in street clothes, they suffered the same reception. They left the stage angrily, with Melle Mel admonishing, "Some of you—not all of you, but some of you—are *stupid*," never to return.[10]

The Clash responded by excoriating their own fans in interviews, and future Bronx-bred openers, The Treacherous Three and ESG, received marginally better treatment. But in 1981, the American punks clearly wanted the riot to remain exclusively their own.

Rocking and Fighting

While the British punks learned something about American racism, the downtowners found their own liberal assumptions being tested.

Henry Chalfant was managing the Rock Steady Crew. It had begun in an innocent, fortuitous way. A couple of months after the O. K. Harris show, Martha Cooper and he were in his studio and she showed him pictures of her next project. Cooper explained that a year before, she was called on assignment to a "riot-in-progress" at a Washington Heights subway station. When she got there, she encountered a group of kids in Pro-Keds and transit cops who were still scratching their heads. Whatever had happened was apparently over, so the cops told the kids to show her what they were doing. A kid stepped up, went down and spun on his head. Cooper was stunned. She said, "I called *The Post* and said, 'Well, this is more interesting than a riot—they were dancing!'"

For the better part of the following year, she and NYU dance professor Sally Banes had tried to track down b-boys and b-girls, frequenting high school dances and rap shows to see if they could find anyone who did it. "Everybody said, 'Ah, we don't do that anymore. It's finished, over,'" Cooper recalled. When they caught back up with the High Times Crew, the members said they were now into roller-skating.

With Cooper's story in mind, Chalfant later asked some graffiti writers at his studio if they had ever heard of folks who did a dance called "rocking." TAKE ONE said he knew the best in the city. He happened to be in a crew called Rock Steady. The next day, TAKE brought Crazy Legs and Frosty Freeze to Chalfant's studio. Chalfant saw them dance, and asked them if they would like to perform at a graffiti slide show he was doing at a Soho loft performance space near his studio called The Common Ground, a name which would later prove rich in irony.

Chalfant had been at FAB's "Beyond Words" show the month before, and he invited FAB FIVE FREDDY and RAMMELLZEE to come and rap. He, too, wanted to present graffiti, DJing, rapping, and b-boying together. The term "hip-hop" was not yet being popularly used to describe the youth movements, so Chalfant called the show "Graffiti Rock." On the Common Ground's promotional postcard, which also advertised a performance-painting event and a Chekhov reading, the event was described this way: "Using music, rapping, and dance, graffiti artists transform the static image into a unique performance dynamic. Scupltor/photographer Henry Chalfant coordinates graffiti artists in a multifaceted performance event."

Rock Steady decided to stage a battle. They split their crew into two, and he, Banes and Cooper bought them t-shirts customized with iron-on letters. They began energetic rehearsals. DOZE recalls being stunned by RAMMELLZEE's bizarre freestyling. "I was like, 'Who the fuck is this?' This fucking guy was like, 'Werrnnnnnt werrnnnnnt! Rock rock! Plop plop fizz fizz, oh what a relief it is! Bob! Jellybeans! Spam! Ham!'" he laughs. "I figured, this guy is off his wig."

More important, Banes and Cooper landed a cover story in *The Village*

Voice. Titled "To the Beat Y'all: Breaking Is Hard to Do," it was the first major story on b-boying. Cooper's photos from the Graffiti Rock practices were evocative: Frosty Freeze in a leftward feint, Ty Fly suspended in a back-flip. Banes, for the first time in print, speculated on b-boying's origins:

> For the current generation of B Boys, it doesn't really matter that the Breakdown is an old name in Afro-American dance for both rapid, complex footwork and a competitive format. Or that a break in jazz means a soloist's improvised bridge between melodies. For the B Boys, the history of breaking started six or seven years ago, maybe in the Bronx, maybe in Harlem. It started with the Zulus. Or with Charlie Rock. Or with Joe from the Casanovas, from the Bronx, who taught it to Charlie Rock. "Breaking means going crazy on the floor. It means making a style for yourself."[11]

The article was also perhaps the first to link graffiti, rapping and b-boying—which Banes called "forms of ghetto street culture" that were all "public arena(s) for the flamboyant triumph of virility, wit, and skill. In short, of style."[12]

The line that most captured the liberal imagination was this one:

> [B]reaking isn't just an urgent response to pulsating music. It is also a ritual combat that transmutes aggression into art. "In the summer of '78," Tee [of the High Times Crew] remembers, "when you got mad at someone, instead of saying, 'Hey man, you want to fight?' you'd say, 'Hey man, you want to rock?' "

Rocking instead of fighting—the idea would become one of the most enduring myths of hip-hop—but history would once again belie it.

Many around town seemed to be talking about the "Graffiti Rock" event, including Rock Steady's envious rivals. The afternoon before the show, Chalfant had gathered everyone for a dress rehearsal at the Common Ground. They were interrupted by a Dominican crew from Washington Heights. "We had a war with this crew called the Ball Busters back then 'cause we were Zulus," says DOZE. Afrika Bambaataa remembered the beef as one "between Puerto Ricans and Dominicans." Chalfant says that he later pieced together that the beef had begun in a violent dispute over graffiti turf between affiliates of the Rock Steady Crew and the Ball Busters, and that it had likely spilled over along ethnic lines. Whatever the case, this wasn't something that would be settled with a rhythm and a dance.

The Ball Busters walked into the Common Ground loft, and while a number of white downtowners looked on, the words began to fly. Someone shouted that there was a gun, RAMMELLZEE and his DJ crew pulled out machetes, Chalfant called the police, and the Ballbusters chased a Rock Steady–affiliated graffiti writer out of the loft toward the subway station.

The next day, one of Chalfant's graf-writing friends called him and said, "We've got it all worked out. We've got a lot of back. We've got shotguns in the car. We've got a nine millimeter for you. The Salsoul Brothers are gonna come and police it." But when large crowds, including many of the East Village art and nightclub elite, gathered to see the show that afternoon, Chalfant stood at the door to send them away. The violence had caused the Common Ground's owner to pull the plug.

The Folkies

Hip-hop's future was still unclear. It might be a folk art, a cultural expression whose authenticity needed to be preserved. Or it might be a youth uprising, a scream against invisibility that wanted nothing more than to be heard by the world.

One future offered a nicely trimmed path to folk art museums and cultural institutions that might nurture hip-hop in a small safe world. The other was a bumpy, twisting road, which might lead to cultural, economic and social significance, but also to co-optation, backlash and censure. Hip-hop's downtown advocates, especially the older ones, understood the tensions. They favored authenticity over exploitation, and they vacillated between being protective of the culture and championing it.

Cooper and Banes made presentations at folk-culture and academic conferences, met with corporate event planners and civic arts programmers, and pitched stories to magazines like *The Smithsonian* and *National Geographic World*. Cooper recalls that her folklorist peers were "genuinely excited and enthusiastic." But they also had their limits. Cooper and Banes attended one mind-numbing meeting with a city-funded arts group interested in doing a film series on forms of New York City street dance. After much struggle, the group accomplished nothing other than arrive at this yawner of a definition: "Street dance is nontheatrical participatory dance in environments available to the public."[13] Predictably, the project fizzled. Meanwhile, the file of rejection letters from magazine and book editors got fatter.

Cooper arranged for the Rock Steady to perform at the High Bridge Library. The librarians produced a crude stick-figured flyer for "BREAKING, RAPPING & GRAFFITI, an original blend of dancing, acrobatics and martial arts," and appended a special note at the bottom: "Young adults especially invited." Then Chalfant landed a summer show for the Rock Steady Crew in the plaza of the Lincoln Center. This time, DOZE drew a graf-style flyer depicting a ski-goggled, big afroed b-boy smirking and saying, "Breaking or otherwise known as (B-Boy) is a competitive warlike dance, making the opponent look bad." The news media, including ABC's 20/20 newsmagazine show, came out in droves.

Chalfant had coordinated and filmed a battle between Rock Steady and the Dynamic Breakers at the United States of America roller rink in Queens earlier in the year.[14] He wanted to restage that battle. "I thought that would really be authentic," he says. "What I hadn't banked on was that the crews would bring all their neighborhood."

The Rock Steady Crew rolled out thick, their people from all the boroughs representing fresh and bold in light grey jumpsuits. Their Queens rivals, the Dynamic Rockers, came out just as deep in beige and maroon athletic suits. The plaza was transformed into a massive cipher. A small raised stage was placed at the center and covered with kitchen floor linoleum. Hundreds of seats were set up around it. As the battle intensified, the circle enclosed and most of the audience could no longer see the action. The crowd drifted away.

But as the temperatures rose, so did a few tempers, and the battle deteriorated into small fights. Just as the USA battle had ended, so did this one—with a lot of riffing and posturing about who actually won. "And it ended in a kind of mini-wilding spree," Chalfant adds. "A few hot-dog stands were kicked over, and on the train that I got onto, the Broadway local, somebody punched out a window."

To say that Rock Steady's biggest shows had been a little rough around the edges was an understatement. But Chalfant possessed a sense of humor and no small feeling of responsibility for them. Despite his misgivings about his abilities, he gallantly labored on as their manager. "I was the only one who was kind of like an adult with connections," he says.

"I was a terrible manager in terms of finding gigs," he says, smiling and shaking his head. "I got things like the Clearwater Festival, a Pete Seeger thing on the Hudson River in Croton-on-Hudson, which was complete culture clash for everyone. I had a Volkswagen van and we all piled in and we went up. There were all these nice little people. There was somebody trying to do sign language for RAMMELLZEE's rap, Rock Steady looking at the vegetarian food and going, 'Eccccccch!' It was a big, big culture clash!"

He adds, "I know we tried to get something done with commercials—McDonald's and others. We'd put together a package, like, 'Here's this amazing dance group!' And—nothing."

Chalfant's business relationship with Rock Steady would not last much longer. Perhaps the artist in him objected to wringing commerce from the culture, or perhaps he was too old and settled to have the hunger for it. "Crazy Legs and I have often talked about it. 'Henry, you should have been our manager,' " Chalfant says with a twinge of sadness, "but I wasn't good enough, or really aggressive."

When hip-hop finally broke through two years later, its global demand blindsided Chalfant, Banes and Cooper. "Graffiti became huge internationally and I wasn't prepared for that. I never thought that would happen," Chalfant says. Within a year and a half, Banes and Cooper had to retool their pitches to discuss how b-boying "had drastically changed from a folk art form to the hottest entertainment of New York's nightlife . . . sparking world-wide interest in hip-hop style."[15] In their book proposal, they promised to discuss why graffiti, rapping, and b-boying is "not taken seriously because it diverges drastically from the 'proper' Euro-American high culture our educational system imposes."[16] So the rejection letters continued to pile up. The three were still struggling to try to present the youth movements as purely as they had first encountered them.

Separately, Chalfant and Cooper had been shopping graffiti books to no avail. They teamed together and suffered two more years of rejections from New York publishing houses. They were told that Norman Mailer's 1974 book

The Faith of Graffiti was the last word on the subject. Chalfant says, "The other reason, truly, was that they were scared, and they were afraid that they'd get hell."

Their book, *Subway Art*, was finally accepted and published in 1984 by a London-based house, Thames and Hudson. The book brought the energy of the Writer's Bench and Chalfant's studio into the world, and became a style canon and study-guide for the third, now global generation of aerosolists. *Subway Art* went on to sell more than 200,000 copies.

With American and British public television, foundation and government arts grants and even support from Nathan Glazer, though not a penny from the William Bennett–run National Endowment for the Humanities, Chalfant and documentary filmmaker Tony Silver put together the classic hip-hop movie *Style Wars*. Shot between 1981 and 1983, it captured the youth movements in a moment of high flux as they stood on the brink of becoming a generation's global culture.

The movie had begun as a short on b-boying, but when Chalfant and Silver ran out of money, Rock Steady blew up on the downtown scene and were no longer available. So after hearing Kathy Chalfant describe the drama Henry was living through with his graffiti-writing friends—it was an aria, he later said—Silver shifted the focus to graffiti. He was convinced that they had a Wagnerian opera on their hands: Here was a street art poised on becoming a legitimate artform; but first it would have to get through Mayor Koch, MTA chief Richard Ravitch and a snarling graf writer named CAP ONE. *Style Wars* stands as a landmark achievement for hip-hop film, the seminal documentary of graffiti and b-boying.

All these works now evoke an era of Apollonian innocence. But at the time, the downtowners felt they had backed into an ideological wasp's nest. The movie had a successful run on PBS stations across the country, proving especially popular in West Coast markets like Seattle and the San Francisco Bay Area. But after a single showing on the PBS outlet in New York, it never returned. The documentary's sympathetic portrayal of graf artists was deemed irresponsible.

When Silver and Chalfant began screening *Style Wars* for audiences around the country, many people their age thought the two should have known better.

Even some liberals who had survived the '60s with their long-hair values intact were upset. Chalfant wrote, "The audience at any showing of *Style Wars* attended by Tony or me always raises the same questions: in one, angry citizens berate us for encouraging vandalism everywhere, and in the other, the purists ask if we regret being part of a process that has destroyed urban folk culture."[17]

World's Famous

For Malcolm McLaren, all these earnest folkies were only worthy of being pranked. Authenticity was a bad word, exploitation was not.

McLaren was a carrot-topped London art student energized by the Parisian spirit of '68, who then embarked on a career of anarchic fun-making. By 1977, with an eye on the Big Idea and a gift for self-promotion, he had succeeded like no other Situationist before him, dropping the Sex Pistols on quaint old England like a blitz bomb. After the spectacular collapse of the Sex Pistols and the post-colonial pop candy of Bow Wow Wow, McLaren's first "serious" project was a sendup of global folk dances called *Duck Rock*.

For the project, McLaren positioned himself as a sort of arch-browed, postmodern Alan Lomax. He would go around the world collecting ethnic dance music on a little tape recorder and brand it all with his general dadaist nonsense. "I think it's gonna be the biggest thing that ever happened. I think it's gonna be the most truthful," he boasted to one journalist. "And I think it's gonna create an awareness that will bring together whatever they're doing in El Salvador or Peru with whatever they're doing in Zululand or Appalachia."[18]

McLaren had realized the future was in global rhythms, what marketers would later call "world beat." He owed this new worldview to Afrika Bambaataa. Arriving in New York City the same summer as The Clash, McLaren met Michael Holman, a downtown club promoter and one of Rock Steady Crew's new managers, who took him up to Bronx River Community Center for a Zulu Nation throwdown. Hip-hop was pastiche, bricolage. It was worldly wise and you could dance to it. Best of all, it was dangerous.

McLaren later admitted he was scared out of his wits. At the end of the night, when a fight broke out and the entourage was hustled to a back wall as the fists and knives flew, all of his stereotypes were confirmed, and, typically, he had come up with a plan for how to exploit them. He began by asking Bambaataa, the Soul Sonic Force and the Rock Steady Crew to open Bow Wow Wow's downtown show at the Ritz. Then, he made plans to visit the Zulu townships of South Africa.

Back in London, his partner, Vivienne Westwood, matched McLaren's musical ambition with a line of "ethnic hobo" clothing, a style that made its models look like raccoons wearing shopping bags. McLaren's young associate in New York, Ruza Blue, opened a nightclub called Negril in the East Village where she booked the Zulu Nation DJs and the Rock Steady Crew. McLaren returned to recruit a DJ crew to front the project, and after lots of heads turned him down, the World's Famous Supreme Team, a two-man crew of Five Percenters named Just Allah the Superstar and Cee Divine the Mastermind who had a rowdy, popular late-night show at WHBI, finally agreed.

In the fall of 1982, he unleashed a stunning little single called "Buffalo Gals." McLaren's collaborator Trevor Horn tried to replicate the feel of Bam's funky breaks, using brand-new sampling technology to add on Supreme Team show call-ins, township jive groans, Just Allah's rap, and McLaren's interpretation of the old "hilltopper" song. The video, shot in the middle of the freaky Greenwich Village Halloween parade, featured the Rock Steady Crew popping and breaking, Dondi White painting a graf piece and Westwood's models going round the outside and looking like hobos. With a video, a radio show, a nightclub, and a clothing line all ready for consumption, McLaren and his team had come up with hip-hop culture's first corporate synergy plan.

The album that followed, *Duck Rock*, was backwards brilliant. Using hip-hop's global vacuum signifier intake as their method, McLaren and Horn brought together popular and religious regional dance music—*merengue*, *mbaqanga*, mambo, sacred Lukumi drumming, the odd square dance and, of course, hip-hop. The Supreme Team's raucous, hilarious radio call-ins held the whole thing all together. In a sense, a hip-hop worldview allowed McLaren to sum up the "world music" genre a decade before its fixture in the First World pop marketplace, and deconstructed it at the same time. In the United States, the record was released by the pioneering "world music" label, Chris Blackwell's Island Records.

The *Duck Rock* video captured scintillating double dutch and township dance performances and gave many outside of New York their first glimpse of graffiti, b-boying, popping, and DJing. In an inspired signifier mashup, McLaren played a British redcoat mock-shocked, upside down, and bleeding to death on a battlefield—the opening scene of *Zulu* redux. As a *shebeen*-styled guitar beat unfurled, the scene cut to township dancers kicking up dust while wearing Rock Steady—style cotton tees emblazoned with iron-on letters that read, ZULUS ON A TIME BOMB.

McLaren told journalists that in darkest South Africa he had regaled the Zulus with tales of the Sex Pistols, which inspired them to pen some of *Duck Rock's* songs. But this was just his crude imperialist fantasy. In fact, far from being "folk" songs he'd discovered in a distant village, the township jive and merengue songs had been local pop hits in the '70s, replayed note-for-note by pick-up bands in Johannesburg and New York City. Their inspirations—such as the "Indestructible Beat" of South African guitarist and composer Marks Mankwane, his legendary Makgona Tsohle Band, and the groaner, Mahlathini, and vocal group, the Mahotella Queens—went unacknowledged and uncredited. A flood of lawsuits would follow. Perhaps it was perfectly hip-hop.

On the other hand, McLaren's self-serving pomo-imperialist-as-new-rock-star mythology was annoying. The longform video shredded context, running b-roll of Brazilian carnival over Dominican merengue, even as McLaren gave goofy, lyrical shouts to rock-n-roll, calypso, "m-m-m-mambo" and "discago"—*descarga*, that is. Brain-curdling bushman stereotypical images accompanied the sacred batá rhythms. In the same year *Duck Rock* was released, Robert Farris Thompson's book on the diasporic links between African and African-American art and philosophy, *Flash of the Spirit,* came out. Bambaataa had inducted McLaren into the same world of rhythm and soul that Thompson was describing, but McLaren had returned from his journey with less than half the story, and that portion was scrambled.

Duck Rock's liner notes mocked folkie earnestness and anthropological "discovery." Moreover, they seemed to anticipate an academic petrifaction of the hip-hop subject. But the liner notes also revealed McLaren's crassly exploitative desire, the dark underside of his ironic distancing:

The performance by the Supreme Team may require some explaining but suffice it to say, they are d.j.'s from New York City, who have developed a technique using record players like instruments, replacing the power chord of the guitar by the needle of the gramophone, moving it manually backwards and forwards across the surface of the record. We call it 'scratching.'

Despite McLaren's ambitions, *Duck Rock* never became "The Great Hip-Hop Swindle." Instead of McLaren swallowing hip-hop, hip-hop devoured him. He would not fully comprehend the lessons Bambaataa and his followers had taught him until long afterward. By then, he had become a parody of himself, remaking *Duck Rock* in myriad failed ways before finally giving up on a recording career. Years later Bambaataa himself would chuckle at the mention of McLaren's name and dismiss him with two words: "culture vulture."

Now that they were no longer invisible, the young rebels made it clear that they wanted more. FAB 5 FREDDY told a journalist, "I didn't want to be a folk artist, I wanted to be a fine artist. I wanted to be a *famous* artist."[19]

At the Graphiti International gallery, with paintings by CAINE and CRASH. From left:
TRACY 168, WASP 1, LADY PINK, IZ THE WIZ, ERNI. Standing: FREEDOM.

Photo © Martha Cooper

9.

1982

Rapture in Reagan's America

The room was hot, sweaty, highly charged and had the feel of destiny to it.

—Chi Chi Valenti

You just had the sense of the future, like you could do anything you wanted to.

—Ruza "Kool Lady" Blue

It was morning in Ronald Reagan's bright white America. Elected by a landslide in 1980, he rode into office like a celluloid cavalry colonel coming to the rescue of the beleaguered frontiersmen. When Reagan's campaign trail took him through the dead land of Fort Apache to Charlotte Street, it followed almost exactly the same route that Jimmy Carter had taken in 1977. There, Carter had given his soundbite: "I'm impressed by the spirit of hope and determination by the people to save what they have." Three years later, on the same empty block, the only things new were John Fekner's graffiti stencils on the blasted brick walls, which read: FALSAS PROMESAS and BROKEN PROMISES. Reagan stopped in front of one of these stencilled walls, to the eternal grief of his handlers and positioners, and told the media: "I'm impressed with the spirit of hope and determination by the people to save what they have."[1] The presidential campaign had become a nitrate film, looping in advanced decomposition.

In downtown's tiny art-crammed sweatboxes, whites were watching young brown and Black b-boys go off to throbbing Afro-Latinized versions of soundtrack music from the spaghetti westerns often played by mixed-race bands like the Incredible Bongo Band's "Apache" and Babe Ruth's "The Mexican," dramatic rewrites of Ennio Morricone themes that the b-boys favored for their head-bursting percussion, thundering basslines and Morricone's cascading, whooping melodies. In particular, "The Mexican," sung by Jenny Haan, captured the fall of the Alamo through the eyes of a Mexican *bandito* caught on the American side when the fighting commenced. It climaxed with a final battle cry: "Morning, sad morning, heaven will be there!"

Downtown Utopia

The nightclub had become a communal sacred space, a chance to escape the chafing oppression of time, to vault the restrictions of the social order, a place to watch the rules become liquid, and peer into possibility.

In the body heat and thumping beats, Ruza Blue, a true believer in the power of clubbing, was seeking a sensual utopia and a democratic alternative. "It was the Reagan era and there was talk of war and nuclear weapons," she says. "But then there was this whole thing going on in New York where it was the youth culture getting together in unity and peace and having fun. No segregation and everyone joining together. Just the opposite of what was going on politically."

And Crazy Legs, a true believer in the power of hip-hop, saw what many others saw—a bit of magic happening. "It was the beginning of the breaking down of racial barriers," he says, "'82 was the beginning of worldwide understanding." But there would be a price to pay, too. They were promised heavens—false heavens and heavens which never materialized. The nights of radiant children always came to an end.

When spring bloomed in 1981, the giddy affair between uptown and downtown topped the charts. Deborah Harry—who, by the number of canvases dedicated to her, seemed to be the object of every graffiti artist's desire—was sweetly sighing out of every radio in the country: "Wall to wall, people hypnotized, and they're stepping lightly, hang each night in rapture." Then she turned sly, and rapped: "FAB 5 FREDDY told me everybody's fly, DJ's spinning I said, 'My, my!' Flash is fast, Flash is cool. *Francois c'est pas flashe non deux.*" Not that anyone outside of New York—least of all Paris—knew what she was talking about. Not yet.

The rapture was still mainly in the minds of the believers, a small tribe moving to the edge of reshaping pop culture. Ruza Blue, a recent immigrant from London, was one of the believers. By day, she ran World's End, Vivienne Westwood and Malcolm McLaren's Soho boutique. In London, she had been a regular at a landmark new wave club run by Steve Strange called The Blitz. She recalls, "I used to go down there every Tuesday night to the club, sometimes not even getting in because sometimes Steve wouldn't let you in. I used to stand outside, 'Please let me in!' And I thought one day, I'm gonna do a club like this. I don't know what I'm going to put inside it, but I'm gonna do something like that." After she saw Bambaataa and the Rock Steady Crew open for Bow Wow Wow at the Ritz, she knew she had found religion. She began frequenting the Disco Fever with FAB 5 FREDDY, who dubbed her "Kool Lady Blue."

By November, Blue started hosting her own Thursday night "Wheels of Steel" parties at a tiny basement reggae club—capacity: 200—called Negril. Once frequented by Bob Marley, Negril had become the after-hours hangout for the Clash and other Brit punk expats. With Michael Holman, she brought in what seemed to have become the party-starting bill of the year: Bambaataa and the Zulu Nation DJs, FAB 5 FREDDY, RAMMELLZEE and the Rock Steady Crew. Then she promoted it to her punk peers, "People heard, 'Oh wow, the Clash are hanging out there.'" When they arrived, they encountered iconic Bronx b-boys hanging outside in kangols, ski goggles, and bubble jackets, and inside, a racially mixed crowd who had cleared a circle for the Rock Steady Crew and were moving to the sounds of Bambaataa, Jazzy Jay and Afrika Islam on the turntables and FAB 5 FREDDY on the microphone.

Blue's "Wheels of Steel" night at Negril was the next logical step from FAB's "Beyond Words" show at the Mudd Club, Henry Chalfant's abortive Common Ground show, and the revived "Graffiti Rock" shows with FAB and The Rock Steady Crew and a host of graf artists at the Kitchen. Jazzy Jay says, "First couple times we played at Negril, it was an a-ight crowd, not too many people was in there. By the time a couple of weeks went by, man, it was standing room only!"

The tiny club hummed with sensory overload. Jorge "Popmaster Fabel" Pabon, who was initiated into Rock Steady on the Negril dance floor, recalls, "Here we are looking at punk rockers and different types of bugged out people, you know, those Village type people. It was a whole new experience."

Negril had been a space for punks and Rastas and like-minded scenesters to meet on equal terms. Now, Blue handed the club over to the Bronx and uptown crew, and the exclusive crowd soaked up the vibe. Jazzy Jay says, "We'd school from the DJ booth, you know what I'm saying? That's what we was doing downtown. We was schooling them on our artform. Bam would put these breaks on and drive them wild and then I'd get on the turntables and start cutting shit up and they'd be losing their minds. MCs get on, that was it. B-boys take the floor, it was like, yo!"

Fabel recalls, "We fed off of the crowd a lot; to get them hyped was half of the reason we did it. Well, at least a quarter. Three-fourths were for more selfish reasons," he chuckles. "Like, there's some fine girls around here, yo!"

Jazzy Jay couldn't believe his luck either. "I'm a carpenter by trade," he says. "I'm making as much from this as I'm making from my union gig. You know what? The union gig can wait. My hobby is doing me alright." After four dazzling months, the crowds were bursting the club's walls. Fire department officials stepped in to shut Negril down. No matter. Negril would turn out to be merely a prelude.

By then, everyone was humming another downtown hit. Tom Tom Club, a lighthearted spinoff group of the heralded post-punk band Talking Heads, caught ears with "Genius of Love"—a girlish ode to the deepest, coolest guy in town that slipped, somehow appropriately, into a celebration of the Black rhythms of George Clinton, Bootsy Collins, Bohannon, Bob Marley and Sly and Robbie. The song captured the peculiarly downtown ecstasy: "There's no beginning and there is no end. Time isn't present in that dimension." By the last verse, however, it was clear that the affair—sweet as it was—was doomed.

Be What You Be

In April of 1982, Afrika Bambaataa unleashed a grand statement for what he was now calling the hip-hop movement. It was called "Planet Rock."

Bambaataa was the right man to do it. He walked through downtown the way he did in the Bronx, the warrior-king of a massive, expanding tribe. He shaved a mohawk into his head—a salute, it seemed, not only to the rebels of Kings Road and the Bowery but a young, shocking Sonny Rollins. His crew dressed like a wild cross between a band of New Orleans Mardi Gras Indians and interstellar Afrofuturist prophets. Downtowners were impressed. "This guy carries weight," Gary Jardim wrote in *The Village Voice*, "like the music stars in the '60s did."[2]

After cutting two singles with Paul Winley—different versions of "Zulu Nation Throwdown" (Bambaataa says "Death Mix" was unauthorized)—and being disappointed with the results, Bambaataa met Tom Silverman, a white music journalist who had started a record label for twelve-inch dance singles.

"Bambaataa was very, very different than anybody else was from the Bronx. He said, 'I don't want to be a star because stars fall,'" Silverman recalls. "When you're in the presence of a person like that you just feel a different kind of energy. I've seen this guy when he was DJing and a fight would break out. He'd stop the music and then he'd play like four bars of James Brown and stop the music again. And he goes, 'You like that? Stop fighting.' And everyone would stop fighting and he'd turn on the music again." Silverman knew he wanted to do business with this guy.

While publishing a popular tip-sheet called *Dance Music Report,* Silverman had first heard about hip-hop music from a friend at Downstairs Records. "I knew the store because I used to buy doo-wop music there. They'd opened a new room and it was called the 'B-boy Room' and it was like a closet the size of a small office. It had a high desk in the front and in the back they had the records. It was the specialty room where you have kids come in and buy these breakbeat records.

"They were buying things like cut-out records that were like a dollar each but they were being sold for ten dollars. Albums like The Eagles' *The Long Run* and Billy Squier's "Big Beat," all these weird records! Bob James, "Apache," "Dance to the Drummer's Beat"—a lot of them on 45s, a few off albums and a lot of people would buy them just for one break and the break would only be for seven seconds long or three seconds long so they have to buy two of them so they could mix it. The kids were fifteen and sixteen. They'd chip in money, then three or four of them would come in and buy records together. I asked them how they find out about which records had the breaks, where they find out about the breaks, and they say there's this guy in the Bronx called Afrika Bambaataa and he had this thing called the Zulu Nation. So I went up to check it out."

Bambaataa was spinning at the T-Connection at a Zulu Nation anniversary party. Red Alert and Jazzy Jay were standing sentry, handing him records. "It was the weirdest mix of music I ever heard in my life but it was amazing," says Silverman. After returning to Bam's parties a few more times, Silverman asked him if he'd like to make records. They talked for a minute, then before Silverman left Bambaataa handed him a business card that read, "Afrika Bambaataa Master of Records." Under Silverman's label, Tommy Boy, Bambaataa released "Jazzy Sensation" in November 1981.

Silverman had brought in a young dance producer named Arthur Baker to oversee "Jazzy Sensation." Baker had begun to learn how to use drum machines, synthesizers and early sampling technology. The record was a success, and the three wanted more.

By then Bambaataa had realized, "I could use my albums to send messages. And the record companies played their role of sending these messages to all these places." He told Silverman he had an idea for a song. He and Jazzy Jay had already drawn up a rough blueprint of the music, based on some of his favorite records: Babe Ruth's "The Mexican," Captain Sky's "Super Sperm," Kraftwerk's "Numbers" and "Trans-Europe Express," B.T. Express' "Do You Like It" and Rick James' "Give It to Me." Together, he and Silverman put together a rough eight-track demo on synthesizers. In the meantime, Bam went to his rapper MC GLOBE and gave him the concept to begin laying out the rap.

Bambaataa had hooked up with gearhead and keyboardist virtuoso John Robie, who had a dance single that Bam was playing. Silverman, seeing the obvious, blessed the project and sent the Bam, Baker and Robie to Vanguard Studios in the Village to assemble the record. The final version included only Kraftwerk and Babe Ruth.

This stripped-down result somehow perfectly captured Bambaataa's mystery. "Planet Rock" 's polycultural pastiche, framed by swooping, synthesized orchestral stabs, sucked the listener into another world—where dramatic melodies drifted across a barren landscape, "where the nights are hot, where nature's children dance inside a trance," where everyone could rock it, don't stop it. Not only did it sound unlike anything that had ever come out of the Bronx, it sounded unlike anything else anywhere. "Planet Rock" was hip-hop's universal invitation, a hypnotic vision of one world under a groove, beyond race, poverty, sociology and geography. The Soulsonic Force shouted, "No work or play, our world is free. Be what you be, just be!"

Bambaataa says, "I really made it for the Blacks, Latinos and the punk rockers, but I didn't know the next day that everybody was all into it and dancing. I said, 'Whoa! This is interesting.' " Silverman says that the record cost eight hundred dollars to make. It went on to sell 650,000 copies. But its importance would be felt far beyond the number of copies it sold.

" 'Planet Rock' had more impact than any record I've ever been involved in," Silverman says. "The only record I can think of in the hip-hop movement that maybe had more of an impact was 'Rapper's Delight' because that's the first one that opened the door.[3] But 'Planet Rock' took it in a whole 'nother way. That was the record that initiated that it wasn't just an urban thing, it was inclusive. It was okay for rockers, new wavers, uptown coming downtown. That's when they started pouring in from France and England to cover hip-hop. That's when hip-hop became global."

Street Culture's at the Roxy

When Kool Lady Blue finally found a new home for her "Wheels of Steel" night, her club became the steamy embodiment of the Planet Rock ethos. In Negril, Blue had seen the potential of a model that countered the elitism of the Blitz. To its ecstatic followers, the Roxy would become "a club that changed the world."[4]

After getting kicked out of Negril, Blue had done a couple of "Wheels of Steel" nights at Danceteria, another downtown new wave club. But convinced that she was on to something big and magnificent, she fell in love with a huge, nearly block-long roller rink in Chelsea on West 18th Street and Tenth Avenue. The Roxy's capacity was twenty times that of Negril. "I said the Roxy is mega-big, I can't see you packing that joint," says FAB 5 FREDDY. "She said, 'Well I think we have an idea, we can bring this curtain and cut off more than half of the club.' So she took me to show it to me and I gave her my thumbs up on some shit like that. Then from there it was like, boom!"

In June, Blue hung out a sign at the rink: COME IN PEACE THROUGH MUSIC. Her gamble was immaculately timed. She opened the club with all of the scene's leading lights at the beginning of a hot summer when graffiti and b-boying and hip-hop music was on everyone's minds.

For the first few nights, a curtain painted by FUTURA was set in the middle of the floor. Each week, the crowd grew and the curtain moved back toward the wall, until it was literally against the wall. Long lines snaked down West 18th toward the Hudson. After clearing the bouncers, clubbers stepped up into a long hallway that featured neon-colored graf murals and felt the tricky beats set their hearts to racing. They were stepping into another world.

"The regulars were Bam and Afrika Islam, and then Grandmixer DST, Jazzy Jay, Grand Wizard Theodore, Grandmaster Flash, and I'd rotate them," she says. "We had no booth. The DJ would be in the center of the floor on a podium. Everyone could see what he was doing, and he was kind of elevated to rock star status." On both sides of the DJ, large projection screens displayed Charlie Ahearn's slides of Bronx b-boys, rappers, and scenemakers. Nearby, the Rock Steady Crew convened all-night ciphers on the beautiful blonde wood floors. PHASE 2 designed the club's flyers and he, FUTURA, DOZE and others often did graf pieces live onstage. Here were the four elements, re-presented downtown as performance art on an epic and mythic scale.

FAB 5 FREDDY recalls the turning point as the July night Blue decided to book a screening of McLaren's Sex Pistols movie, *The Great Rock 'N' Roll Swindle* before the regular opening of the club. "The crowd initially was mostly heads from the scene. The night when it all really mixed I remember vividly," he says. "[The film] attracted all of these cool punks, white new wave heads, whatever. The film was shown kinda early like around nine. When it was over, a lot of that crowd stayed. And then the crowd for the hip-hop night started to come and I was wondering like, 'Yo what's gonna happen?' And everybody kinda bugged out looking at each other. You had these ill b-boys with the poses and shit, checking out these kids with the crazy haircuts and that whole vibe. And everybody kinda got into each other, so to speak. That's when it really kinda took off as the first really major downtown club that had like a legitimately mixed scene."

The East Village elite came west—all the Mudd Club regulars, the Co-Lab activists, bands like the Talking Heads and the B-52s, the come-ups known by a singular name: Basquiat, Haring, Madonna. Blue billed it as the anti–Studio 54. But the stars came anyway, blown in by the winds of change, the promise of something ineffably new and vibrant. David Bowie and Andy Warhol descended from the VIP booth to the join the masses on the dancefloor.

The scene also felt inviting for mainstream whites, like David Hershkovits, a music journalist who would go on to publish *PAPER* magazine. "It was cool, it wasn't rowdy. And I don't remember it smelling dangerous or anything like that, the way those things eventually turned into," he says. "What attracted me to it at first was it was a hip-hop thing coming downtown from the Bronx into my neighborhood and mingling with the artists and the writers and the people who were in Manhattan who didn't have any direct contact with hip-hop at the time. The doors were open.

"The crowds were very diverse. That was why I was so excited to be there. Suddenly this racially mixed group was having a good time partying in a room together, which was a very rare thing. On the level of music and art, people were able to bridge all these boundaries."

He adds, "The other thing that reminds me of those days is the style, because we were coming out of a sloppy era. Punk rock was about wearing torn clothes, T-shirts and just messy. Here you got these guys who would wear their jeans, but they'd be creased and they'd be perfect. And they'd have their sneakers but they'd be completely white. I remember one time I went into the bathroom and I said, 'What are you doing?' And it was FAB 5 FREDDY and another guy with toothbrushes cleaning their shoes. Here were these guys from the ghettos coming out and showing everyone how to dress, how to be fresh, how to be clean, how to have it together—whether it was the way you did your dance or your graffiti or your rapping or your DJing, it was all style."

Among the masses on the floor were a new generation of white kids, watching the future rush right up to their shelltoes. Dante Ross, who would become a key hip-hop A & R exec during the late '80s, remembers, "I used to go to the Roxy, me and my neighbor Adrock. Me and the Beastie Boys and the girls from Luscious Jackson, we were like the handful of people who got to experience shit while it was still open and ill, before New York was corny and everything was kind of co-opted. The word 'alternative' didn't exist. It was this great moment, man, the 'Graffiti Rock' moment. Everything was all mixed up, it was cool to be eclectic." The music was uptempo, bright—Malcolm McLaren's "Buffalo Gals," Chuck Brown's "Bustin' Loose," Manu Dibango's "Soul Makossa," the Rolling Stones' "Start Me Up," Aleem's "Release Yourself," new rap records by FAB 5 FREDDY and PHASE 2—a perfect showcase for the Rock Steady.

Crazy Legs, all of sixteen, was amazed at how far he and his crew had come in three short years. "We were the stars," he says. "When we had started performing, we were the people that were at the jams in the Bronx outside the ropes. Now we had become the people that were inside the ropes. Now we had the opportunity to perform with Cold Crush Brothers, Fantastic Five, Grandmaster Flash, Grandmixer D.ST., Funky Four + One, we became part of that elite clique in hip-hop. We thought about that a lot. We were just appreciating the fact that we were at a place where we could be recognized for our skills by all these people we wanted to be."

"We were just innocently having fun," he says, "not realizing that we were setting a foundation for what is a multibillion dollar a year industry."

Charlie Ahearn recalls, "You would go to a night at the Roxy and there would be eight b-boying circles. Girls would be getting laid in the back room by fourteen-year old graffiti artists that couldn't wait to do some blonde. It was all good. A lot of excitement, a lot of energy."

"Ah man, the Roxy," sighs DOZE. "Home! That's when the money was rolling and cocaine was flowing!

"I call them Dustland Memories. Fuck Stardust memories, it's Dustland memories!" he laughs. "Just everyone being on zoo-bang, walking around with cocaine wrapped up in newspaper, and just being in the VIP room with Madonna, and Shannon and fucking Jody Watley and fucking Shalamar and all them heads. It was just funny." He shakes his head at his teen mischief, halfway between pride and sadness.

"You go from the real new waver to the hardcore punk to the b-boy to the stick-up kid b-boy to the Dale Webo fashion boy to the Funhouse Jellybean Benitez look to the Madonna lace-fiend to the wannabe artist *nouveau* bohemian. It was just an eclectic bunch. But it was cool 'cause everybody got along and you got to meet some real cool chicks. Kinda weird chicks, too. Weird weird weird weird!"

Then he becomes animated. "Crazy shit went on in that place. My mom even went! Ken Swift's mom used to go. Crazy Legs's mom used to go. Yeah! We'd be embarrassed. Like—'Ah Ma! Get outta here, come on!' 'I'm so proud of you, come here!' We'd be like, 'Fuuuuck, get outta here!' So we'd hide 'til they leave, 'cause parents have to go home early." He's laughing hard now. "They'd leave, then we'd be like, 'Yeah! Aiiight! Wassup baby!' " he laughs, making a high-five, then bending his head as if over a mirror laced with white lines. "Snnnnnooooort! Ahhh. Aiiight!"

Chi Chi Valenti, a downtown personality and sometime host at the Roxy, wrote, "By late 1982, Fridays had become a required stop for visiting journalists and Eurotrash—to be in New York and miss the Roxy was unthinkable. More than anything the Roxy embodied a certain vision of what New York could be—a multiracial center of a world culture, running on a current of flaming, uncompromised youth."[5]

Blue tried to match all the artistic ambition with a booking policy that was just as eclectic and innovative. She brought an uptown who's-who to the downtown stage: Double Trouble, the Treacherous Three, the Fearless Four, the Disco Four, The Crash Crew, The Sequence, Masterdon and the Def Committee DJs. In the earliest stages of their careers, New Edition, Madonna and Run DMC stepped onto the Roxy stage. She brought in the Double Dutch girls, and featured a Harlem youth dance troupe and a Brazilian capoeira crew. She even hired Native Americans to perform a sundance.

But as high as the highs were, some of the hip-hop heads were beginning to wonder about what was really going on. Were they being paid fairly? Were they being exploited? Just how did this white downtown crowd really see them? Did being a part of the anti–Studio 54 only mean that the street kids got a chance to sniff coke, too?

Crazy Legs says, "The Roxy could have also been a zoo. People were able to hang out in the cage with us and feel safe from getting beat up or stuck up, as opposed to coming to the Bronx, coming to a jam. It's like they were allowed to hang out in the cage and party with the animals, you know? It was a safe haven for a lot of people. But on the flip side, it was also us getting into places that we never thought we could get into. So there was an exchange there."

He concludes, "I'm not gonna sit here and act like, 'Oh wow, it was so great back then!' There were things—that was also the beginning of us getting jerked. I'm not bitter about it. I'm over that. But that's a reality."

Close to the Edge

Outside the floating world of the Roxy, Reagan's recession had bloated unemployment levels to the highest levels since the Great Depression—30 million searching for work.[6] The official Black unemployment rate hit 22 percent.[7] Poverty rates were soaring too. Black poverty hit a twenty-five-year peak in 1983, with 36 percent of the population counted as living below the poverty level. It was much worse for young people. One estimate was that only one in five New York City teens had a job, only one in ten African Americans, the lowest ratios of youth employment in the country.[8]

After dark, DJs cut up Trouble Funk's "Pump Me Up," with its ironic command for people to dance their troubles away: "All we want to see is your body work!" But the Roxy night always opened into a Reagan morning that was much more than a comedown. "The Message," released just weeks after the Roxy opened, was a downtempo track that perfectly captured that after-dawn crash when the buzz wore off.

It was credited to Grandmaster Flash and the Furious Five, but the story behind that naming revealed other tensions as well. The song was a home-studio concoction of Sugar Hill songwriter and house band percussionist Ed "Duke Bootee" Fletcher, featuring a memorable synthesizer hook from Jiggs Chase, that seemed to bear the influence of Peter Tosh's "Stepping Razor" and Black Uhuru's *Red*. Bootee and Sugar Hill mogul Sylvia Robinson could not interest Flash in recording it. He and the rappers felt the song had no energy, that the lyrics would get them booed offstage by their hardcore fans. You went to a party to forget about shit like this.

But Robinson and Bootee recorded the track anyway, peeling off Furious Five rapper Melle Mel to add his last verse from a forgotten version of "Superappin'." Robinson decided "The Message" had to be released as a single. Flash saw where this was going, and he pushed the rest of the Five into the studio to try to rap Bootee's lines. It didn't work. Instead, Bootee and Robinson added them at the end of the record, in streetside arrest skit recalling Stevie Wonder's interlude in "Living for the City." But Pandora's Box had been opened. The ensuing tug-of-wars between the group and the label and between Mel and Flash resulted in Flash leaving Sugar Hill the following year. The video appeared, with Flash and the crew lip-synching along to a rap only Mel had helped compose.

Sugar Hill's second most important rap record had been as A&R–driven and market-driven as its first, and the consequences for hip-hop music were also far-reaching. Not only was "The Message" another boost for the rapper over the DJ, the crew itself became a dramatic casualty of rap's realignment towards copyrights, trademarks, executives, agents, lawyers and worldwide audiences. By the end of 1983, there were two groups called the Furious Five, competing in civil court for the rights to the name, and dousing their creative fires under thousands of dollars of cocaine. From this point, questions of ownership and authorship would become hip-hop generation obsessions.

But Robinson's instincts had been exactly right: the record became the fifth rap single to reach gold-selling status. The single certainly did not represent the first time post-'60s rappers had chosen to touch on themes of social dislocation and institutional racism—Kurtis Blow's "The Breaks," "Hard Times" and "Tough," Brother D and the Collective Effort's "How We Gonna Make the Black Nation Rise," and Tanya "Sweet Tee" Winley's "Vicious Rap" were just some of the recorded examples. But because it was set to a beat too slow to rock a crowd, "The Message" focused the listener on Bootee and Mel's vivid lyrics and their delivery—neither frenetic nor flamboyant, but instead, by turns, resigned and enraged. Flash's instincts had been correct, too: it was the grimmest, most downbeat rap ever heard.

And that vibe matched a rising disgust with Reaganomics, the culmination of fifteen years of benign neglect, and a sense of hopelessness that only seemed to be deepening. Liberal music critics who had been sitting on the fence about rap jumped off with both feet. "[I]t's been awfully easy to criticize mainstream, street-level rap for talking loud and saying nothing. No more," wrote Vince Aletti in *The Village Voice*, praising the song's chorus as "a slow chant seething with desperation and fury," and the track's "exhilarating, cinematic sprawl."[9]

It's among hip-hop history's greatest ironies that "The Message," so artificial and marginal by the standards of the culture then, would prove at once to be a song so truthful about the generation's present and, in its righteous retail math, so influential to that generation's future culture.

Fun and Guns

The visions of "Planet Rock"—universal communion and transcendence—and "The Message"—ghetto strife and specificity—could only be brought together on the dance floor. But in the graffiti movement, both a bellwether and a vanguard, the contradictions were intensifying. Mike "IZ THE WIZ" Martin, a king from Queens, says, "1982, in my opinion, was the beginning of the end for graffiti. That's why I did as many pieces as I could during that time period. I knew it was the last hurrah."

Dondi White, for instance, had made his legend during the blackout of 1977. When the next summer morning came, the sixteen-year old's name had been emblazoned over a staggering number of cars and he had begun his journey toward becoming the Stylemaster General.[10] Five years later, he was leaving the subway underworld for the light of the galleries—a carnival of openings, meetings, contracts, exhibitions. On Valentine's Day in 1982, he opened his first solo show at the dizzying, packed Fun Gallery.

The public face of the Fun Gallery was its magnetic co-director, Patti Astor, a '68er, sometime Warhol associate, and a former underground movie star, who had just finished a role in *Wild Style* playing a journalist who brings the hip-hop scene downtown. Her tiny storefront in the East Village became a more traditional gallery counterpart to the Bronx's freewheeling Fashion Moda. It was a downtown lodestar from which a shortlist of writers could catapult themselves into the art scene.

When it opened in August of 1981, it was a temporary space with no name. The artists would give it one when they showed there. "Kenny Scharf came up with 'Fun Gallery,' FAB FIVE FREDDY was next. He wanted to call it 'The Serious Gallery,'" Astor said. "We stayed with 'Fun.'"[11] FAB's show vaulted the gallery into the international spotlight. The East Village, once needle-stick somnambulant, was suddenly fun. At its peak, it featured over seventy galleries.[12]

There was a growing duality in the movement. Some writers called the galleries their new yard. But they would never master the art-world the way they had their world of yards and transit cops, toys and enemies. Years later, Elizabeth Hess would ask the question that was never answered at the time, "Was it their work or their class and racial exoticism that inspired patrons to support them and dealers to legitimize their unorthodox talents?"[13]

"Between '82 and '85 I created enough work to supply ten dealers in five galleries," Dondi told ZEPHYR. "The thing is, I felt if I wasn't painting then people would think I wasn't a real artist to begin with."[14] Collectors dabbling in graffiti as radical chic wrapped the artists in an unfamiliar, uncomfortable straitjacket of preconceptions and expectations.

It was becoming clear to the artists that while the biggest galleries were eager to make stars of Haring and Basquiat and Scharf, they saw the artists from the subways as a bunch of primitives. ZEPHYR says, "One thing that always comes back in my mind is that CRASH, FUTURA—totally different artists, completely different aesthetics visually—all were struggling with the fact that the people who were presenting this work were often unwilling or unable to present those artists as individuals with a very distinct vision. Every artist had their own thing visually. But it didn't come out because very few of the dealer/owners, with a few exceptions, had the willingness to avoid group shows."

In 1981, the group shows had been a way for the smaller galleries to make their name and for marginal artists to join together to administer the shock of the new. By 1983, group shows were another form of marginalization. And even as the slightly tipsy art-world toasted itself in opening itself to ghetto youths, the subway and street graf scene was undergoing an explosion of violence it had never seen before.

Mayor Ed Koch and the MTA's Richard Ravitch militarized the yards with $20 million worth of razor-wire fences and guard dogs. The cars were white-washed, turned into "The Great White Fleet," and the MTA shifted its strategy towards defending the clean cars. Suddenly the amount of painting space dropped.

This problem was exacerbated by all of the media attention. At the same time, Chalfant's and Cooper's photos, the anti-graffiti campaigns, the TV shows, the magazine articles and the gallery buzz swirled into a mega-TAKI effect. In the past when a young toy was seen in the yard, he would be carrying the paint-bag of a master. Now IZ was finding himself face to face in the yards with packs of thirty and forty little kids, descending in clouds of noise, hitting him up to tag their piece books, leaving empty cans all over the place, always setting off cop raids.

With the buff and the toy flood, a new breed of bombers took over. IZ says, "One of the cardinal rules of graffiti was you didn't go over somebody. And if you did, you made sure it was very clear it wasn't a dis. Like if somebody had a throw-up, you did a whole car and naturally you buried it, so it wasn't disrespectful." Now, as Chalfant and Silver would document in their brilliant documentary *Style Wars*, bombers like CAP ONE could overturn that rule. When the masterpieces were erased, the definition of fame changed, the underlying structure of respect collapsed and graffiti's code of conduct unraveled.

To CAP, the distinction between his throw-up and your piece was meaningless. If you went over him, he was going to go over you—everywhere, he emphasized. He began attacking on multiple fronts. These cross-outs weren't, like Basquiat's, for play, they were for blood.

There had always been beatdowns, but now crews mobilized to defend themselves and their spaces, and more consciously and viciously policed their layups and yards. The beefs sometimes spilled into block parties and neighborhood jams. There was, SPAR ONE says, "a whole war mentality. That's when I remember things started getting really violent."

At the High School of Art and Design, PINK curated a graffiti-art exhibit with twenty of the school's best writers. She recalls, "We had a wonderful exhibit with canvases and big eight-foot panels, free standing, and illustrations and black books and the works. We had everything in glass cases, hung up. All in all, it was a successful opening and I went home at three that afternoon, I was all exhausted. And I catch my exhibit on the six o'clock news.

"Apparently CAP and PJAY showed up, pulled out a .45 and shot my school full of holes. Shot one kid in the back. That was it. They closed the show the next day and the principal requested I just leave their school. I never graduated from the High School of Art and Design and the faculty really cracked down on graffiti writers after that."

Graffiti was caught between acceptance and rebellion, aspiration and motivation. IZ says, "It was getting to a point where beef was getting settled at gallery shows, because you couldn't find them anywhere else."

A World Tour

At the same time, the four elements were being packaged to tour for the first time outside of New York. As a measure of how big hip-hop was dreaming, the tour would bypass America and head straight for the Old World. In November, Kool Lady Blue sent the stars of the Roxy to tour England and France.

Organized by French journalist and indie record label owner Bernard Zekri, the bill was headlined by Afrika Bambaataa and the Soulsonic Force, and included the Rock Steady Crew, the World Champion Fantastic Four Double Dutch girls, FUTURA, DONDI, Grandmixer D.ST. and the Infinity Rappers, RAMMELLZEE and FAB 5 FREDDY.

FAB recalls, "Heads were like, 'Yo, what's our show gon' be, what we gon' do?' I thought about it, I said, 'Let me just tell you. Look, being that I got an art background I done seen some weird shit on the performance art tip. So no matter what we do onstage, we gon' always look cool. Just keep it real natural. Like if you just want to walk out onstage and give your man a pound or whatever, that's cool, that's how we gon' do it!' "

David Hershkovits hopped on the bus to cover the tour for the New York Daily News. They planned to play seven dates in France and England on the two-week tour. "They had this whole show," he remembers, "It wasn't just a band, it was the graffiti and the breakdancers and the DJs and the whole experience."

After long bus trips broken up only by full-scale tagging and pilfering attacks at the gas stops, the twenty-five-member entourage would head onstage to try to replicate the organic feel of the Roxy for the crowds. DST spun, and his rappers rapped. Bambaataa got up and played and the b-boys would get up and dance as the spirit moved them. The Double Dutch girls headed up for a few routines. FAB and RAMMELLZEE took turns on the mike, while FUTURA and DONDI painted live pieces.

Hershkovits recalls, "Not too many people showed up to these shows. Especially some of these little towns where they didn't have a critical mass audience anyway. They're not the hippest people out there. We'd play in some school gymnasium in some town, maybe fifty kids would show up. And the French are not demonstrative, even in Paris where there was a decent turnout. I remember looking at the people and they would just sort of be looking at each other trying to figure out if they should like it or not. They didn't know quite how to react. It was so new."

Legs laughs, "Typical European audiences, man. But that's just the way it is. We were asked like really stupid questions like, 'Yo, are there trees in the Bronx?' "

In Strasbourg, France, they got a taste of that old Bronx River unpredictability. Crazy Legs recalls, "We did a show and there was these drunk people, and the Double Dutch girls were onstage doing their thing. They threw bottles at them." The music stopped. D.ST armed himself with a broken bottle, PHASE 2 picked up a chair. "Next thing you know, people were backstage talking about, 'We gon' get them!' DONDI led the people out there. DONDI had his belt with his name buckle on and the dudes caught a beatdown. After they got beat down, everybody stepped back onstage, and then the people in the audience started clapping! It went from a show to a brawl to getting applause." Bambaataa went back to playing his records, and their legend was sealed. By the time they reached Paris, the media came out to meet them like they were the real thing.

When the hip-hop heroes returned to the Roxy, the innocence seemed to be fading. ZEPHYR says, "Everyone was trying to hustle something. Someone had an angle, someone was like, 'Can I take your picture?' 'Can I make a movie about you?' 'Can I do a series of shows at The Kitchen with you?' 'Can I write an article in *The Village Voice?*' "

Rolling Stone, People and *Life* came down with photographers and journalists. Fashion designers prepared their next year's lines by taking notes and trading numbers with the graffiti writers. Post-disco indie-label owners like Tom Silverman, Corey Robbins and Steve Plotnicki of Profile Records, Aaron Fuchs of Tuff City Records or Will Socolov of Sleeping Bag Records might be buying artists drinks at the bar. Soon these white-owned indies would eclipse the Black-owned ones; even the mighty Sugar Hill never recovered from the acrimonious collapse of its biggest act, Flash and the Five. Harry Belafonte had begun to soak up ideas for a multimillion dollar Hollywood movie that would be called *Beat Street*. A year later, the Roxy's owner ousted Kool Lady Blue. The dispute, she says, was over money.

A Little Story That Must Be Told

Perhaps the most lasting tribute to the spirit of '82 is the movie that Charlie Ahearn, Fab 5 Freddy, and Lee Quiñones gathered to talk about in the abandoned massage parlor in Times Square, *Wild Style*. The movie captured the sense of discovery, the new thing in all its raw, unpolished glory.

Perhaps much of its wonder had to do with its surrender to the culture. Ahearn—whose previous movie, *The Deadly Art of Survival*, had been shot on Super 8, with its main budget expense going to "buying pizza for the kids"—admits, "I'd never written a script. I really had no connection to the movie business whatsoever. I had never been to film school or been in the film business. But everyone accepted me as a Hollywood movie producer right off the bat. It was a matter of innocence on all sides."

Ahearn was out, he says, to make a "Bruce Lee movie. A simple hero, a simple story. Lee Quiñones was gonna be the hero. What is his problem? He's in love with this girl but she doesn't know he's the famous graffiti artist. That's it. That's all the movie is. And in a way, it reflected exactly how I saw things—in a comic book fashion."

The movie's principals were heads in the scene. There were no professional actors. PINK says, "There was a script that we all chuckled about. Picture that, a white guy just introduced to the scene and he's trying to write slang. That was funny!"

But Ahearn also truthfully described the scene's deepening schisms. ZEPHYR says, "The whole thing of the whole sensibilities of the downtown and the uptown, and the woman Neva who wants to seduce Lee—'Oh can I buy your painting? Oh sit down!' All that shit seems like it's laughable when you watch the movie, and yet it all happened. All those things were so real. Charlie didn't say, 'I'm gonna parody the scene.' "

By now he was deep in it, enough to understand the subtleties of off-screen realities like PINK and Lee's tortured relationship. Lee had refused to star in the movie until Ahearn made two things clear. If he did it, he would be paid. If he didn't, someone else would have to do the scripted love scenes with PINK. "When we shot the scene where Lee goes to the art collector, and he's supposed to be in bed with this woman, that could have been something else entirely," he says. "PINK found out that he was shooting this scene. She showed up at that apartment. She sat right between the camera and Lee the entire time. That's why he was so nervous. And like, you know, it was hard to direct!"

During Charlie and Fab's yearlong advanced seminar in the post–"Rapper's Delight" club scene, they walked into a marquee rivalry between Charlie Chase's Cold Crush Brothers and Grand Wizard Theodore's Fantastic Five Freaks, which became a major organizing theme for the movie. They caught the rappers on the stoop and in the limo, at the Dixie and the Amphitheatre, even on the basketball court. Over wickedly exciting dubplate special riddims—cut by

Blondie's Chris Stein with FAB and a downtown session band and recut Bronx-style by Theodore, Chase, DST and KK Rockwell—they captured three of the most electrifying, influential ensemble routines ever committed to tape.

Here was Fantastic's Prince Whipper Whip, channeling H. Rap Brown: "I am the New Yorker, the sweet walker, the woman stalker, the jive talker, the money maker"—bragging about being "the least conceited". And undefeated, at least until Cold Crush's JDL dispensed him with a shrug: "If you still got money and you wanna bet, well I bet a hundred dollars that I'm not whipped yet."

The movie's climax was a feverish reimagining of a Bronx park jam, another downtown presentation of the four elements, but with one crucial difference. Instead of taking hip-hop up-market, *Wild Style* went back to the people hip-hop came from. Ahearn had always been concerned about *where* he screened the work as much as *what* was being shown. That was why *The Deadly Art of Survival* and his hip-hop slides always looped back to be shown in their points of genesis: the Smith Houses, the Bronx clubs. His greatest ambition for *Wild Style* had been to screen it in Times Square for the b-boys and b-girls, the street rappers, the Five Percenters, all the folks from around the way. Here, once again, was representation as liberation, art as activism. So the show was staged at an abandoned amphitheater near the Williamsburg Bridge in East River Park.

The cast and crew cleaned it and fixed it up and Lee and others painted it into full hip-hop glory. Then they invited all the neighborhoods to the party. In a sense, it really was a park jam. No permits, no city fees, it was wholly a self-generated creation. The night of the shoot, thousands had gathered and the show was getting into full swing when the law finally showed up. As the police car pulled near the gate, Ahearn ran over, clipboard in hand, and said, "Oh man, I'm so glad you guys showed up. We thought you would never get here. We just need you to stand right here and help us keep this thing together." The cops took one look at the scene, got back in their car, and drove off, never to return.

Aside from such regular displays of improvisational genius from the producers and performers, the brilliance of *Wild Style* lay in the decision of Charlie and FAB never to cork the ferocious competitive energy, the feverish call-and-response, the phantasmic sense of possibility present in a hip-hop moment. *Wild*

Style remains the only hip-hop film and soundtrack that adequately conveys the communal thrill of merging with the tide, riding the lightning.

The timeless moment of *Wild Style* is the night before Reagan's morning, sad mourning, in America. Shockdell is talking homelessness like a prophet. Ikonoklast panzer RAMMELLZEE strides onstage waving a sawed-off shotgun in one hand, reaching down and pulling rhymes out his pocket with the other. One second he's stepping out at Cypress Hills, beating down a toy with his def graffiti, the next he's signing off with an apple-pie flourish, shouting out the Rock Steady on the linoleum and the cops in the crowd. That ricochet unpredictability, that badder-than-bold, bolder-than-bad chest-thumping, the volatile combo of sociology-shattering disbelief and Sunday-morning faith it inspired in anyone it touched—all this was *Wild Style*'s, and 1982's, gift to the world.

Waiting for something to happen: FUTURA 2000 (foreground), Anita Sarko (background), b-boy, and bobby-soxer at the Roxy.

Photo © Josh Cheuse/WFN

10.

End of Innocence

The Fall of the Old School

All the symbols of a new generation—its sense of style, scale and solidarity—are read as evidence of nascent terrorism.

—Richard Goldstein

When the *Wild Style* entourage stepped into the hot quickening buzz of Yoyogi Park in Tokyo's Harajuku shopping district in 1983, they were walking into a battlefield of pop style. In the heart of the crowded city, Japanese youths were deep into their own generational rebellion.

There was a circle of *Bosozoku* rockers, the Wild Drivers—guys with high-pomaded pompadours leaning on their motorcycles, the girls in pink party dresses dancing to Gene Vincent and Jerry Lee Lewis. There was the *Takenoko-zoku* circle, the Bamboo Shoots—boys and girls with teased-out hair, faces caked with makeup, swinging and posing in loose unisex silk clothing halfway between New Romantic and Kabuki to Yellow Magic Orchestra and Culture Club tapes.

The style tribes had taken over the park and established their turfs. They co-existed in a strange equilibrium with the passing crowds of the Harajuku and each other, a balance between projecting the menace they needed to preserve their space in the park and the flamboyance that attracted the attention they craved. So as they stared at these Bronx boys, they must have felt equally curious and threatened.

Here were the American b-boys in their *Wild Style* T-shirts, Chief Rocker Busy Bee, a white towel draped over his head, scanning the scene sagely from behind dark sunglasses. The crew was deep—FAB 5 FREDDY, DONDI, FUTURA, Double Trouble, the Cold Crush Brothers. Always up for battle, they grabbed their radio and set up their own circle.

"As a group we were so much more than what anyone could understand," recalls Charlie Ahearn. "We just blew these people out of the park.

"Within three days," he says, "there were people scratch-mixing. Graffiti was popping up in imitated fashions. And by the time we left, they were so excited." City by city, country by country, Bambaataa's Planet Rock was being born.

Renegades

Tom Silverman was a former college radio DJ who had abandoned a doctorate program in environmental geology to move to New York and leap headlong into the disco scene. After scoring three hits with Bambaataa on his Tommy Boy label, he understood exactly what he had to do and who he was doing it for. "My skill is marketing these things and understanding who you're selling records to," he said, "which in the case of Tommy Boy is [a] thirteen-year-old Black youth."[1]

When he started, Silverman had planned on releasing only twelve-inch singles. But Bambaataa's success demanded an album. Silverman and Bambaataa began to argue. "He likes rock and calypso and reggae. He wanted every song different. And people wanted more 'Planet Rock'," Silverman says. The album was delayed as Bambaataa's and Silverman's lawyers tangled. "The record companies would try to tell us what we should make, what we should do," Bambaataa says. "We said, 'Listen, we're the renegades, we sing what we want to sing, dress how we want to dress and say what we want to say."[2] Out of this tension, Afrika Bambaataa would create another manifesto.

"Renegades of Funk" began with a lyric from The Temptations' 1969 Black power anthem, "Message From A Black Man": "No matter how hard you try, you can't stop us now." Then, as Arthur Baker and John Robie set off an orchestra of electronic drums that pounded harder than anything they had yet done, the Soulsonic Force invoked the "renegades of their time and age"—Chief Sitting Bull, Tom Paine, Dr. Martin Luther King and Malcolm X—in a wildstyle view of history that connected the high period of the Italian Renaissance with the rise of the Bronx's "Big Street Beat," and affirmed the power of "everyday people like you and me" to "change the course of history."

Bam stepped into the studio bursting with ideas. For "Renegades Chant," producer Arthur Baker simply played the break and let Bam freestyle at the mic. Bam let loose with Afrodiasporic refrains and children's rhymes. He ran through Bronx bad boys Willie Colón and Hector Lavoe's salsa adaptation of a Ghanaian play song, "Ghana'E," Manu Dibango's makossa groove, "Weya," the Black New Orleans Mardi Gras standard, "Iko Iko." "Fanga alafia ashé ashé," he trilled, the big man from the Bronx offering a child's welcome in a singsong Yoruba. Pieced together by Baker into a stream-of-consciousness rap that built into ecstatic chants, Bam's performance had the same effect as one of his famous sets—effortlessly making connections, capturing a fresh worldview.

At the same time, Temple University professor Molefi Kete Asante was pressing his idea of Afrocentricity, pulling the field of African-American Studies out of the ebony tower toward the pyramids of Egypt. Asante advocated inspirational scholarship that bridged the Pan-Africanist historiography of Cheikh Anta Diop and the cultural nationalism of Maulana Karenga.[3] "Renegade Chant" was instead a kind of proto-Afrocentrism rising up from the streets—a new world heard through children's ears.

Tommy Boy packaged the single behind a comic-book-styled cover calculated to knock a thirteen-year-old's socks off. A mohawked Bam was depicted in a blue cape and gold genie pants, leading the Soulsonic Force—Pow Wow in full Mardi Gras Indian gear, Mr. Biggs in purple-and-leopard-skin tights, G.L.O.B.E. slicing an avenging sword—over a crumbling Bronx brick wall. Critics who had been enraptured by the Roxy and compelled by the intellectual implications of everything Bam did were confused: was this single meant to be a statement? Or a cartoon?

It was the fundamental question of the day: was hip-hop the latest surge of the freedom struggle, an Afrofuturist flash of the spirit? Or was it a kid's fad whose marketing possibilities had not yet been exhausted?

Hip-Hop Exploitation

As the 1970s gave way to the '80s, popular culture still largely depended on the decisions of a small, centralized few who dictated the seasonal tastes of the masses. For the tastemakers, Michael Jackson and Prince signified Black, urban, dangerous and not ready for MTV, much less any boombox-banging crew chilling on the corner in a b-boy stance.

Sometimes, rarely, ideas came from the bottom-up rather than the top-down. Just as Gordon Parks's *The Learning Tree* and Melvin Van Peebles's *Sweet Sweetback's Baadasssss Song* had set off an era of blaxploitation flicks, *Wild Style* and *Style Wars* clued Hollywood producers into a potential market for hip-hop themed movies.[4] Would they respond by taking the audience seriously or patronizing them? On the eve of *Wild Style's* New York opening, Richard Grabel wrote presciently: "*Wild Style* might be the first of a new genre, a *Beach Blanket Bingo*, a teen film for the '80s. Or its verisimilitude might help posterity see it as something more important, a *The Harder They Come* of hip hop."[5]

After the unexpected success of 1983's *Flashdance*—which featured Rock Steady Crew members b-boying to "It's Just Begun" and body-doubling in Jennifer Beals's climactic audition—Hollywood decided to cash in, and 1984 and 1985 saw a wave of teen-targeted hip-hop exploitation flicks. The two biggest movies—*Breakin'* and *Beat Street*—were the first out of the box, rushed to meet an early summer opening. *Body Rock, Fast Forward, Krush Groove, Delivery Boys, Turk 182, Rappin'*, even *Breakin' 2: Electric Boogaloo* followed—and failed—in short order.

Breakin' expanded Rock Steady's *Flashdance* cameo into a full-length feature: aspiring female dancer finds herself and love via a journey through the scary, streetwise—but not too scary or streetwise—postindustrial Los Angeles pop-locking scene. *Beat Street* had a more ambitious scope. Prowling the Roxy, the producers—Harry Belafonte and David Picker—gathered a DJ, rap and dance A-list: DJ Kool Herc, Afrika Bambaataa and the Soulsonic Force, Jazzy Jay, Zulu Queens Lisa Lee and Sha Rock (performing with Debbie D as Us Girls), Melle Mel, the Treacherous Three, Doug E. Fresh, Rock Steady Crew, New York City Breakers, the Magnificent Force. On paper, this was the historical equivalent of landing Louis Armstrong, Duke Ellington, Billie Holiday, the Nicholas Brothers, Honi Coles and Cholly Atkins and Whitey's International Hoppers for a feature film about jazz.

Beat Street's dramatic thrust was fed by the main themes of *Wild Style* and *Style Wars*—the competitive drive of the culture's devotees, the generational, racial and class tensions the culture fueled, the perilous negotiations between uptown and downtown. The original script had been written by the highly respected Steven Hager, one of the first journalists to cover the rap and graffiti scenes for the New York *Daily News* and alternative papers like *The Village Voice, East Village Eye* and the *Soho News.* Hager made explicit what most other journalists had not, that the subcultures of b-boying, rap and graffiti were related. He wrote a book called *Hip Hop: The Illustrated History of Break Dancing, Rap Music and Graffiti,* tying together the three. Hager's book and David Toop's more rap-oriented book, *The Rap Attack: African Jive to New York Hip Hop,* would together constitute the Old Testament of hip-hop, the foundational works of hip-hop journalism and scholarship.

Hager had approached Harry Belafonte with a concept for a script. He says, "I wanted to get the story told as accurately as possible, and I knew the influx of money was rapidly changing the scene." Belafonte, whose commitment to Afro-diasporic folk arts was unquestionable, loved the idea, and hired Stan Lathan, an African-American director with extensive experience in film musicals, to direct it. *Beat Street* hit the theaters in June, just weeks after *Breakin'* had already clocked an amazing $30 million. But Hager says his script had been completely rewritten. "Not a single word of anything I actually wrote made it into that unfortunate film," he says.

Despite some riveting scenes shot at the Roxy, including a classic battle between Rock Steady and New York City Breakers, *Beat Street* proceeded from form the assumption that hip-hop needed to be dumbed down for the kids. Most of the graffiti—including a lousy replica of the Fabulous Five's famous "MERRY CHRISTMAS" train—was painted by a theatrical union crew. Professional actors spoke like Shakespeareans stranded by their agents in the concrete jungle. Afrika Bambaataa's Zulu Nation saga became inconsequential backstory for the lead character, Kenny. Lee Quiñones's angst-ridden ZORO and Jean-Michel Basquiat's Magic Marker alter-ego SAMO were conflated in the Puerto Rican train writer RAMO. The main antagonist, based on CAP ONE, was renamed SPIT and, like Pam Grier's wordless character, Charlotte, in *Fort Apache: The Bronx,* stripped of a voice. Martha Cooper's Washington Heights b-boy encounter became a choreographed, klieg-lit uprock battle devoid of any tension. In *Beat Street,* stickup kids never came to the party and cops never swung their batons, they only served up annoying sermons.

Although almost universally panned, the movies of the summer of 1984 kicked the "breakdance" fad into high gear. The New York City Breakers, now managed by Michael Holman, donned bodysuits to spin at the Summer Olympics in Los Angeles, peddled how-to-break books, high-fived Gene Kelly at the Lincoln Center, and earned an ovation from Ronald and Nancy Reagan at his second inauguration. Rock Steady Crew, now managed by Kool Lady Blue, signed a recording contract with Malcolm McLaren's British label, Charisma, and were immediately forced to take singing lessons. The Dynamic Breakers commanded performance fees that started at $10,000 and lent their name to a line of "Breakdance Fever" toys, including branded plastic jewelry, wristbands and headbands, and sunglass/visor sets. Toy stores sold thousands of "breakdancing" linoleum mats. Thom McAnn ordered 17,000 shell-toed "Wild Style" brand shoes that, despite their name, were not a movie tie-in. McDonald's finally did a hip-hop-themed commercial, but not with the Rock Steady.[6]

Melle Mel's rap in *Beat Street* had climaxed with the chant, "If you believe that you're the future scream it out and say, 'Oh yeah!' " Then the rap gave way to a slickly produced musical number, fronted by a gospel-styled singer and anchored by the same *mbaqanga* baseline Malcolm McLaren had lifted for "Double Dutch." Dozens of dancers took the Roxy dressed in a glitter-glam history of American pop fashion shook, swung and spun simultaneously.

Hip-hop had been reduced to a kid-friendly Broadway production, scrubbed clean for prime-time, force-fitted into one-size-fits-all. But the style tribes of the Harajuku would have scoffed at this stuff. Hollywood had broadcast hip-hop onto tiny islands in the Pacific and into teeming working-class ethnic suburbs in Europe, but the spitshined thing only increased the craving for the *real* thing.

All for a Tag

Michael Stewart was slim, Black, about six feet and 140 pounds, a handsome twenty-five-year-old with ambitions as an artist and model. He wrote graffiti. His name would capture more fame in death than in life.

In the early morning of September 15, 1983, he left the Pyramid Club in the East Village and headed into the subway station at First Avenue and 14th Street to catch the L train back home to Clinton Hill in Brooklyn. He was alone but feeling good. He'd had a six-pack's worth of beers, it was warm out. No one else seemed to be on the platform. Perfect time to tag. He pulled out a marker and scrawled "ROS" when a white Transit Authority policeman walked up to arrest him. At this point, it was about ten minutes to three in the morning.

At twenty minutes after three, Michael Stewart was prone facedown on a gurney in the Bellevue Hospital emergency room. He had bruises all over his body. His face and hands were turning blue. His neck was scarred below his Adam's apple. There was swelling around his eyes, back to his temples and behind his ears. He was still hogtied—the cops had handcuffed him, secured his ankles with tape and then tied his wrists to his ankles with cord. He had no heartbeat, no pulse, no blood pressure. He was not breathing.

The medics were yelling for assistance. They could not remove Stewart's clothes because he was still handcuffed and bound. The head nurse tried to turn him sideways in hopes of helping him to breathe. She would later testify that the transit police had fumbled around for nearly five minutes trying to find the key to the cuffs. Finally, the medics were able to get Stewart breathing again. But he lay comatose.

The news of Stewart's condition came just as a group of ministers and Black community activists—including Minister Benjamin Chavis and the Reverend Calvin Butts—that called itself the Committee Against Racially Motivated Police Violence was announcing a congressional hearing to examine police brutality against communities of color. MTA spokesperson Edward Silberfarb hastened to let the press know that Stewart had become violent and had to be subdued. Stewart had been charged with criminal possession of cocaine and marijuana, and resisting arrest.

Thirteen days later, never having regained consciousness, Stewart died in his hospital bed. A spokesman for the MTA told the press, "We deny that he was beaten, but we are cooperating with the investigation." What had happened during that half-hour would bring down the city coroner's office, put the MTA and the policemen's union on the defensive, rattle the district attorney, the mayor and the governor and set off a new grass-roots Black power movement.

The public would learn that eleven transit cops had been involved with Stewart's arrest. But it was a mystery why so many were needed to subdue a 140-pound man. Stewart did have a half-smoked joint, and what looked to be cocaine paraphernalia—a straw, a mirror, and an empty baggie—in his pockets. Yet hospital tests on Stewart revealed not even a trace of drugs in his body. The MTA quietly dropped the cocaine charge.

The swelling around Michael's eyes and the mark on his neck were evidence that he had been choked by a nightstick. Other bruises indicated he had suffered serious blows to the head. Stewart's family suspected foul play, and immediately demanded that a doctor of their choosing examine him. "I removed the sheets," Dr. Robert Wolf said, "and it was obvious that he had incurred trauma to all major portions of his body, without exception. I determined that the most likely source of the wounds was a beating."

When the city's chief medical examiner, Dr. Elliot Gross released his autopsy the Stewart family was shocked. He hadn't been strangled, Gross said, Stewart died of a heart attack. Moreover, he said, "There is no evidence of physical injury resulting in or contributing to death."

The Stewarts' lawyer, Louis Clayton Jones, accused Gross of working in "some sort of collusion" with the transit police. The New York Times issued a four-part investigative report alleging that Gross had "produced a series of misleading or inaccurate autopsy reports on people who died in custody of the police."[7] According to the Times, Gross had mishandled the autopsy report in the controversial case of Eleanor Bumpurs, an elderly Black woman shot dead by police during an eviction proceeding in the Bronx. Before the Stewart case was over, Gross would change his opinion of the cause for Stewart's death at least three more times.

In 1982, police misconduct complaints in New York City had hit a new high. The gap between police and communities of color was growing. In response to the congressional inquiry, the police department found that an overwhelming number of cases of police brutality involved white officers and citizens of color. More worrisome was the fact that nearly half of those cases had resulted in death.[8]

Yet it still took District Attorney Robert Morgenthau seven months to go through a grand jury hearing process that would result in the indictments of only three of the transit officers for second-degree manslaughter charges. "If this had been a white boy who had been beaten by eleven Black officers, you would have had murder indictments within two days," Jones said.[9] At least now, the Stewarts thought, the truth would come out. And the prosecutors' account, based on interviews with some forty eyewitnesses, was indeed shocking.

Officer John Kostick had arrested and cuffed Stewart for tagging the subway station wall. Stewart suddenly made a dash for the stairs leading to the street and Kostick tackled him. Four other officers hastened to help Kostick pin Stewart, facedown on the ground. One of the cops pulled Stewart's head up and punched him. Then they put him in their van and drove him to the precinct headquarters at Union Square station.

Stewart again tried to escape. But he was caught by the officers and thrown to the ground. They beat him and choked him with their nightsticks. Witnesses said they saw Stewart facedown on the ground, screaming. They said the cops kicked him until he became silent. He was then hogtied, picked up and tossed into the back of the van like a bag of seed, and driven to Bellevue Hospital about thirteen blocks away for "psychiatric examination." In the van, he apparently struggled again, and one of the officers beat him until he stopped. His body was dangled partly over the back seat when the van pulled up to Bellevue's emergency entrance. Only after Stewart was on the gurney did the officers realize he was not breathing.

But before the case went to trial, a judge dismissed the indictments against the three transit police officers on the grounds that one of the grand jurors had been tainted. One juror, Ronald Fields, became convinced that the prosecutors were not going far enough in making their case and was moved to launch his own investigation. After the mistrial, Fields remained so disturbed by the prosecutors' conduct that he presented his version of the case to Governor Mario Cuomo's office.

In February 1985, District Attorney Morgenthau tried again, indicting transit police officers—six this time—in the killing of Michael Stewart. But his case rested on an untested, highly risky legal theory—that Stewart's death constituted "criminally negligent homicide" on the part of the police. Jones was convinced Morgenthau had no chance of winning the case, and indeed did not seriously want to win. Many seemed to agree. A day later, an early-morning bomb went off in the bathroom of the Patrolman's Benevolent Association, seriously damaging the bathroom and the offices. A group calling itself Red Guerilla Defense said in their messages to news organizations, "Tonight we bombed the offices of the PBA, which promotes racist murder and killer cops. The 10,000 racists are not worth one hair on the heads of Eleanor Bumpurs, Michael Stewart."

The trial began almost two years after Stewart's death and riveted New York City. Prosecutors mustered dozens of witnesses before the all-white jury—students from a nearby dorm who had witnessed the beating at Union Square, nurses and doctors from Bellevue, even Dr. Gross. On the stand, Gross agreed that the injuries contradicted the transit cops' testimony that Stewart had not been beaten. But he now had no official opinion on what had caused Stewart's death.

After three months of testimony, the defense rested without calling a single witness. "You quit while you're ahead," a defense attorney told the press. "As far as we're concerned, there is reasonable doubt in this case."[10] His hunch was solid. On November 24, 1985, the six officers were acquitted of all charges.

"What we have witnessed has been a farce," Jones said. "And all the players happened to be white. The six defendants, the six defense lawyers, the two prosecutors, the twelve jurors, the judge, and even every court officer in the well of the courtroom was white. The only Black person there was the victim, and he was unable to testify."[11]

The Stewart case—in which truth and justice both proved elusive—pointed toward the division to come.

Closing Time

Less than three months after Michael Stewart wrote his fatal tag, the renowned Sidney Janis Gallery opened its "Post-Graffiti" show. Janis had vaulted Pop Art into notoriety two decades before. Now, as the art market grew comfortable in its long boom, it was placing a big bet on graffiti. Could graffiti be rescued from the subway? The curator, Dolores Neumann, an idealistic art-lover who had married into one of the world's most famous art-collecting families, thought that it could.

For months, Neumann had opened her home to the writers and closely advised them on how to make their work presentable to the gallery crowd. In the introduction to the catalogue, she wrote: "In many ways the Post-Graffiti artist depicts tragedy and joy at the very source. Springing from a youthful conscience, its optimism addresses itself to a hope for future mankind."[12] *Voice* critic and subway art advocate Richard Goldstein wasn't sure this I-believe-that-children-are-the-future thing was going to work. But he did his part, writing, "The work is beginning to live up to its hype."[13]

That work included thirty-six entries from art-gallery favorites Jean-Michel Basquiat, Kenny Scharf and Keith Haring, as well as subway painters Lee

Quiñones, FUTURA, CRASH, DAZE, BEAR, KOOR, TOXIC, RAMMELLZEE and A-ONE. Marc Brasz, who said he was influenced by the "South Bronx Graffiti tradition" which expressed "a cartoonization of everyday life," did an acrylic of a Latino waiting for a subway train, wincing as if there were a fly on his nose. LADY PINK went aerosol O'Keefe with a full-bloomed rose. Her artist statement read, "My paintings are usually about the dying culture of the underground teenage art movement."[14]

On the chic stretch of West 57th Street, fur-coated and business-suited patrons rubbed elbows with the artists they referred to as "the kids." LADY PINK and CRASH smiled and shook hands with the patrons. Upper Manhattanites and lowdown taggers stood shoulder to shoulder, waiting for something to happen. The scheduled b-boying and rapping demonstration got started late because the kids were quarrelling, so old Sidney himself got up to break the ice, doing the fox trot to a warm round of applause.[15]

When the reviews came in during the following weeks, some might have wondered what drugs were in the punch bowl. *New York Times* critic Grace Glueck declared graffiti "a scourge," and the "Post-Graffiti" show a condescending gesture at best. "Apart from its illegality, the very idea of enshrining graffiti—an art of the streets impulsive and spontaneous by nature—in the traditional, time-honored medium of canvas, is ridiculous," she wrote. "By and large, their products are as much an eyesore on canvas as they are on the trains."[16]

The Janis Gallery show was the beginning of the end of the graffiti writers one-sided affair with the rich and famous. Sidney Janis himself would later disavow the writers, saying, "They were young, unreliable, and always broke no matter how much money they made."[17] Elizabeth Hess, who had been to the Fashion Moda's "Graffiti Art For Success" show at the beginning and was there at the end, summed up the era:

> It appeared at graffiti's high tide, that the art world was integrated for the first time. . . . But this was illusory. In retrospect, many artists think that they were used. "We provided the atmosphere," says Futura, "and that's it."[18]

The romance was over. The locks were changed.

Several years later, Hess found Quiñones repairing wheelchairs and FUTURA delivering messages by bike. Done with the subways, sustained only by the occasional patronage of European collectors and American universities, art for them had become a more solitary process than it had ever been. Meanwhile, their friends Jean-Michel Basquiat and Keith Haring had become stars.

Mugging the Liberals

Crown-happy Basquiat seemed to be on a mission to king himself in the art-world. Inside, he spiraled.

On canvas, he displayed a Bambaataa-sized appetite for signifiers, harnessing and redeploying them in Twombly-meets-PINK assaults of texture, repetition and color, and negating them like Lee "Scratch" Perry in the last days of the Black Ark.[19] He constantly toyed with names and classifications, exploring how science defined and ranked difference, how capital affixed weight and value. But his life was a high-wire act. As the biggest Black visual artist of the twentieth century, he spent his career in the minefield between white and Black expectations.

The white art world treated him as an exotic, a cipher onto whom they could project their fantasies. Basquiat had fun with the idea—posing alongside the pale aging Warhol as a hungry young boxer, mocking his patrons' God complex with paintings like the "Undiscovered Genius of the Mississippi Delta" series. Even his dark, laughing figures seemed to be having a grand time with the white art-world's perennial "return of representation" crisis.

Yet Basquiat also felt alienated from "Tartown," his own name—part nostalgic, part dismissive—for the African-American, Haitian and Puerto Rican Brooklyn neighborhoods of his childhood. Like FAB 5 FREDDY, he had been liberated by the graffiti movement and hip-hop culture, and looked to the careers of the be-bop pioneers—Max Roach, Charlie Parker, Miles Davis—as metaphor and roadmap.

Basquiat's only attempt at a record—called "Beat Bop," featuring rappers RAMMELLZEE and K-Rob, with music by Al Diaz, released on his Tartown label—was, in the words of music critic Jeff Mao, "the grand-daddy opus of hip-hop experimentalism." Indeed, these ten minutes of funk brought the aesthetic tensions of graffiti into rap: representation versus abstraction, roots-rocking versus avant-vanguardism. The same dialectics had played out between "The Message" and "Planet Rock," and would continue with Chuck D and Rakim, Marley Marl and the Bomb Squad, NWA and De La Soul, Mary J. Blige and Erykah Badu, and in Outkast, Black Star and Quannum.

The tensions were real. FAB 5 FREDDY had brought Basquiat, RAMMELLZEE and K-Rob together in an "interrogation," RAMMELLZEE shared many writers' opinions that because Basquiat had never hit a train, he was a fake. Mao writes:

> During the course of the 'interrogation,' a battle of one-upsmanship developed between Rammel and Jean-Michel that eventually extended from challenges within one discipline of hip hop culture, graffiti, to another—rhyming. Initially, "Beat Bop" was to be Basquiat's attempt to prove that he could conquer the art of emceeing. But after he submitted his lyrics to Rammel and his Bronx cohort K-Rob at the recording session, Rammel discarded them brusquely . . . Basquiat was never allowed to rhyme on the record. Rammellzee doesn't credit Basquiat with actually producing the song either—only putting up the money to finish it.[20]

The fraught exchange would lead to one of Basquiat's most pointed works, "Hollywood Africans," painted during a wild trip they later took to Los Angeles, name-checking "Zee" and graf writer TOXIC near the center of the canvas. While he was between art dealers, Basquiat exhibited at Patti Astor's Fun Gallery and kept RAMMELLZEE and other train writers in his party circle. But Basquiat dumped them as he moved closer to Warhol and the powerful art dealers Bruno Bischofberger and Mary Boone. RAMMELLZEE would later say, "Jean-Michel is the one they told, 'You must draw it this way and call it Black man folk art,' when it was really white man folk art that he was doing."[21]

Yet even as Basquiat's career soared, his demons would not rest. Suzanne Mallouk, one of Basquiat's lovers, noted that while on cocaine binges Basquiat became paranoid. "He thought the CIA was going to kill him because he was a famous Black man," she says.[22] When Michael Stewart was killed, he was inconsolable, repeating to Mallouk over and over, "It could have been me, it could have been me."[23] His heroin addiction could no longer cynically be dismissed as an homage to Bird and Diz; it was serious.

Haring grew up in Kutztown, Pennsylvania, the opposite of Tartown, and had come to New York to seek his artistic destiny. He made his reputation as a chalk artist in the subways, with an idiosyncratic visual vocabulary—the barking dog, the glowing pyramid, the radiant child rising from the two-dimensional wasteland of the Radiant City. He surged on the graffiti wave into art-stardom. Soon he opened the Pop Shop to mass-market his art-as-product, and branded his radiant children across consumer goods, billboards, theaters, nightclubs, public and corporate sponsored murals, and high fashion and design.

At the same time, Haring maintained a highly visible profile as an activist. In an anguished 1985 painting entitled "Michael Stewart—USA For Africa," he pictured Stewart's death as a symbol of racial violence that linked New York City with Johannesburg, literally drowning the world in blood. The sick green hand of big money loomed behind, ready to squeeze the corpse dry once the killing was done.

When Basquiat suffered a fatal heroin overdose in 1988 and Haring succumbed to AIDS complications in 1990, these two artists—for whom innocence and encounter, desire and celebrity, cartoon and property, childhood and commodity had been obsessive themes—vaulted into lasting art-world respectability. Shortly after their deaths, the values of their paintings escalated into the hundreds of thousands of dollars.[24] Haring's 1988 tribute to Basquiat seemed prophetic: one black crown alone sits precariously atop a pyramid-shaped heap of tossed and overturned crowns, a graveyard of kings.

By then something had changed. On a cold December day in 1985 in a crowded subway car, Bernhard Goetz shot four Black boys—two in the back—after one had asked him for five dollars. Then he disappeared into the downtown station, a face in the crowd. When he emerged two weeks later he was welcomed as a hero, the silent majority's avenger. Thousands of dollars poured in for his bail and defense. Without a trace of irony and perhaps more than a little delight, Harvard criminologist James Q. Wilson said, "In New York City there are no liberals anymore on the crime and the law-and-order issues. All the liberals have been mugged."

To a hip-hop head, recent history looked a lot different. Neglect had become seduction had turned to fear. Rescuing graffiti artists from the subway was the folly of rich liberals, an act of temporary insanity. But when the subway was rescued from graffiti, it was celebrated as an all-American victory.

On May 12, 1989, the MTA declared that it had achieved the ultimate buff, the final solution—a graffiti-free subway system. 6,200 clean cars were a powerful symbol. "When you're sitting in a graffiti-covered car, you don't feel safe. There was a sense that the system was out of control," said David L. Gunn, the Transit Authority president echoing the logic of Nathan Glazer and Bernhard Goetz.[25]

Pundits greeted the MTA announcement as if it were a Martin Luther King Jr.–sized achievement. "Free at last!" read one editorial headline.[26] Lee Quiñones had a different opinion. "I think if you buff history," he said, "you get violence."[27]

The Twilight of the Old School

After *Beat Street*, every kid across the country wanted to breakdance and every city council and shopping mall official wanted to ban it. But the only thing that put a stop to the dance was its marketing overkill. Within a year, the Bronx Rock had gone the way of Pet Rocks.

Rap continued to explode, but its center had forever shifted away from uptown. By 1984, the biggest rap crew was a trio from Queens. When Run DMC were getting started, they had to take long trips to perform in the Bronx and Manhattan. Managed by an energetic ex-Seven Immortals gangbanger named Russell Simmons, they dressed like Busy Bee and rapped like the Furious Five. But as they became more confident, their look and sound became a reaction to the old school. Using booming drum machines, their echoing raps contrasted sharply with the house-band disco rhythms that had fueled most of the early records and the crisp electro polyrhythms that replaced it. Their plaid suits gave way to a black-on-black presentation. Everything about them was stripped down, as if all the color of the old school was reduced back to its basic elements.

Run DMC had signed to a single deal with Profile Records for two thousand dollars. That single, "It's Like That"/"Sucker MCs," sold 250,000 copies. The subsequent albums established the crew as rap's hardest, and through the tag-team genius of Simmons and a Jewish NYU student from Long Island named

Rick Rubin, they would become the most successful. Simmons and Rubin went on to start their own label, Def Jam. The pair had their eye on the big crossover, and in a short period of time, they signed a million-dollar deal with Columbia, the first time a rap indie had gone major. They signed a cocky teen idol from Queens named LL Cool J and a trio of privileged young white ex-punkers who embraced the downtown hip-hop clubs as religion and called themselves the Beastie Boys.

But the uptown b-boys who had set downtown on fire in the first place found themselves becoming men. They had taken a roller-coaster ride beyond all their wildest dreams, and given the expectation—unreasonable, perhaps—of making a career from their teenage thrills. Just as quickly, it was all gone. Hip-hop had taken over the world, and left them behind. Crazy Legs was angry. "I didn't even want to bother looking at rap videos," he says. "I felt people had no respect for us. We helped you come up into the rap game."

After the gigs and the money dried up, FABEL retreated to *El Barrio*. "I was just going with the flow," he says. "Had I a long term plan it's a possibility that I could have spared myself a lot of pain and misery from hitting rock-bottom." With his twin brother, he latched onto the hardcore punk scene. "I was into politically conscious stuff, even though I was destroying my body and my mind. It was a strange trade-off. I'd listen to great rhymes about all of the injustices but wait, while I'm doing that let me take five hits of mescaline and down a fifth of Jack Daniels, smoke up an ounce of weed," he says.

DOZE had graduated from cocaine to freebase. "My check started going there, and then all the money I made from the tours started to going into the habit. My so-called friends who were down with me started turning their back, they're trying to sell me it," he says. He became homeless.

Many of the hip-hop heads who had come downtown were now nomads cut loose from the clubs and the entertainment industry. Drugs gave them back some structure. They could loop back to the drug spot like it was the only cipher they remembered how to close. Smoke, get money, score some more, smoke. As they fell deeper into the grip of a new kind of rock, drugs also seemed the only viable financial option, a way to chase the status they once had just like they were now chasing the high.

"See, this is what happened. A lot of us didn't want to be drug dealers. A lot of us did it by necessity," says DOZE. "But then a lot of them *did* want to be drug dealers. A lot of them said, 'You know what? Fuck this b-boying shit. We're all bummy and shit.' It went from camaraderie to like, 'Yo, I gotta get mines.' It just turned. The pulse shifted. I didn't want to fucking destroy anybody's life, if I was gonna destroy anybody's life it would be my own. That was my attitude. So I said, 'Fuck it, I'm not going to be a drug dealer.' I'm just going to live as a hermit. I'll live as an artist down in the Village. I had big illusions."

Crazy Legs, FABEL and DOZE survived. Others—Buck 4 and Kuriaki of Rock Steady, Cowboy of the Furious Five and so many others—did not.

The Blow-Up

Here was the other Planet Rock, born of a much different kind of worldview.

At the beginning of the century, heroin and cocaine were both off-the-shelf pharmaceuticals, manufactured and marketed as cure-alls. Heroin was sold as a cough suppressant and a stronger form of aspirin. Cocaine was available in soft-drinks like Coca Cola. Before long, both were recognized as deadly. In 1913, the *New York Times* reported a rash of heroin addictions in the South Bronx, the neighborhood's first known epidemic.[28] A decade later, both substances had been banned. Production shifted overseas, and distribution moved to the criminal syndicates. During the last half of the twentieth century, an ugly, illicit nexus between war and drugs developed.

When World War II raged, Alfred McCoy recounts in his epic history *The Politics of Heroin*, heroin importation dropped dramatically, the number of smack addicts plunged from 200,000 to 20,000, and the heroin problem was disappearing.[29] But in the all-or-nothing logic of the Cold War that followed, opium and coca products became the perfect commodities to advance coups or counterrevolution. The new Central Intelligence Agency often aligned itself with local movements that supported themselves through drug smuggling syndicates. Such was the case with the French Corsican and Italian Sicilian anticommunist fronts, who, through a combination of strategic CIA neglect and support and the enterprising wiles of American mobland deportees like Salvatore "Lucky Luciano" Luciana, soon reopened heroin trading lanes into the American ghettos.

By 1968, the battle against Communist China and Vietnam had led to the creation of what would become known as "the Golden Triangle"—the lawless zones of Burma, Thailand and Laos that came to fill a third of the global market for heroin. The yield of this extraordinary boom in heroin production was often pushed through air and sea transports run by the CIA and its foreign assets. Heroin addiction exploded amongst American troops—some reports claimed one in seven GIs were hooked—and in American ghettos.[30] In turn, the profits reverted back to anticommunist military operations in Southeast Asia. Wars halfway around the globe were helping create the world of pushers and junkies that the Bronx gangs walked through, the world against which Bambaataa would imagine his Planet Rock.

A decade later, cocaine was moving through routes that had sometimes been facilitated by U.S. right-wing interests in Latin America. It was a different kind of drug for a different kind of era. Heroin drove you inward and secluded you in the depths of your dreaming. Cocaine strengthened the shakiest of your convictions and made you feel powerful before the world.

Postwar cocaine trafficking began with wealthy Cuban counterrevolutionaries fleeing Castro.[31] As they plotted the removal of Castro and financed military attacks on the island with cocaine profits, U.S. intelligence agents looked the other way. By the late sixties, another group of favored anticommunists, the Corsicans, had set up in the southern hemisphere and were working with smugglers in Chile, Paraguay and Colombia to establish French connections north for illegal goods, including coca and marijuana. Entrepreneurs, like the American hippie George Jung and his Colombian partner Carlos Rivas Lehder, plugged in from the other end, marketing coke as a hip, aspirational drug to white American baby boomers.

At the same time, criminal syndicates consolidated coca farming and cocaine production in Latin America, particularly in Colombia, Peru and Bolivia. In the case of Bolivia's "narcocracy," an anti-leftist government put in place by what would come to be known as "the Cocaine Coup," syndicates ran the country.[32] In Colombia, the cartels shifted from working with the military to exterminating leftist guerillas who threatened their trade, or killing crusading government officials.

By 1976, Jamaican DJ Dillinger's song "Cokane In My Brain"—an unlikely smash hit in Kingston, New York and London—announced that the white-line pipelines out of the Andean "snowfields" through the remote Caribbean cays into the First World's leisure centers were open. In a 1981 cover story featuring a martini glass filled with cocaine, *Time* magazine toasted the "all-American drug," the powder that made you "alert, witty and with it."[33]

Best of all, this "emblem of wealth and status" was now available to millions of ordinary middle class Americans. During the early 1970s, rich New Yorkers paid one thousand dollars per ounce for the pleasure.[34] But a decade later, cocaine production and distribution became so efficient that the price of a gram had dropped to as little as one hundred dollars, or roughly three dollars per ounce.[35] The time was right for a chemical innovation to take care of the glut and increase cocaine's demand and profitability again.

Don't Ever Come Down

For years, Andean farmers had smoked coca paste, which they called *basuco*, or *basé*. The high one got from smoking the paste was much more intense than snorting it. In 1974, a San Francisco Bay Area coke-powder smuggler and his chemist friend tried to replicate the smokable coke. They converted the powder by mixing it with ether and heating it, creating not a paste, but little crystals. When they smoked them, they couldn't believe what they had done. This product got the name "freebase," because the process that made the rocks had literally, in chemist's terms, "freed" the "base." Their mistranslation—Spanish "basé" to English "base"—had led them to something entirely new.[36]

Freebase was marketed as even safer than the powder itself. Journalist Dominic Streatfield writes, "One 1979 manual I found in the Drugscope library in London, called *Attention Coke Lovers! Freebase = the best thing since sex!* . . . [concluded] that freebase is 'considerably less harmful, physically, than regular cocaine in any quantity.' "[37] At that point, cocaine's price was still too high for many to experiment with freebase, so for a time, cocaine smokers remained among the most elite of clientele.

But indications that smokable cocaine might not be so benign began to bubble up along the cocaine pipelines. In the early 1970s, doctors began to notice paste-smokers in Peru, Bolivia and Colombia turned to walking ghosts. And when the glut of cocaine hit the Bahamas—the key Caribbean transshipment point—cocaine smoking took off amongst the sufferers. Since the high was also shorter, it was chemically more addicting. Addicts spent all of their time chasing the next high. All that needed to happen was for the right entrepreneur to figure this all out.

That man, the Kid Charlemagne of cocaine, was Los Angeles legend Ricky "Freeway Rick" Ross, an illiterate ex-tennis champ who got his first fifty-dollar bag of coke for Christmas in 1979, flipped it and never looked back. Freeway Rick came onto the market at the right time. Cocaine production had never been higher and distribution was about to get much easier.

He began by selling powder to wealthy Black clients. As he expanded his market, he got cheaper prices from his suppliers. Then Rick systematically absorbed his competition, making them his own retailers by offering them better prices. Pushers of PCP—known on the streets as "sherm" or "water"—traded in their stuff in to get with him. He even began training Crips to be salesmen.

Freeway Rick's clients knew about freebase. Richard Pryor's 1980 explosive episode with a home-making kit—leaving him with third-degree burns—had been a great advertisement. But they didn't want to risk or bother cooking it up, so Rick learned how to make a simpler version of it by cutting it with baking soda and heating it. He called the result "Ready Rock" and took orders for their weekend parties in powder or rock.

By the end of 1982, as Freeway Rick's prices continued to drop, his clientele shifted down the economic ladder, and Ready Rock had completely replaced powder. Freeway Rick was not mad. Ready Rock was made for the masses. Once he figured out how to standardize production and prices, Ready Rock offered a potentially larger market at double or more the profits of powder.[38] Anyone could afford a deuce or a nickel rock. And who, after hitting it, didn't want more? Now the streets started getting really ugly.

Aqeela Sherrills, then a teenage Grape Street Crip, watched his Watts neighborhood change. "Once an individual got hooked on it that was their only pursuit. They was robbing, stealing, jacking, everything. Then you think about some of the neighborhood killers. When they was strung out on the shit, they was robbing a dice game, getting into it with some cats, shootouts would happen. Cats who was like big-time drug dealers in the neighborhood, all of a sudden they were strung out, with nothing."

He says, "The whole quality of life in the neighborhood just changed. I mean all of the girls that we were just crazy about when we were kids, that we all looked up to, became strawberries. The neighborhood was already tough, but people literally lost their families to drugs and the violence that came out of people utilizing drugs and making money off drugs. Folks went to jail for the rest of their life. People got murdered. It just totally devastated the neighborhood."

In Nicaragua, Reaganite hawks were concerned about the new leftist Sandinista government that had overthrown their dictator-of-choice Anastasio Somoza, the most stunning development since Fidel Castro had taken Cuba. But their zealous military interventions on behalf of the Contra counterrevolutionaries were not popular with the American public. By 1985, Congress voted to cut off funding the Contras. So intelligence and military operatives turned to covert illegal means of supporting their dirty war—selling guns to Iran, and assisting Contra supporters who were trafficking cocaine to fill the exploding demands in the north. At the other end of the pipeline, the illiterate, jobless and hopeless Ricky Ross and many others like him turned into vulture capitalists to feed their ghetto clienteles the illicit spoils of war.

When the *Wild Style* crew had stepped into the Harajuku, Freeway Rick's Ready Rock—this new, less pure, more popular cousin of freebase that the media would name "crack"—was flooding Los Angeles, Miami and New York City. Another Planet Rock was taking shape—a world defined by the constants of destabilization and collapse.

Raising Hell

Run DMC had hollowed out the music and killed the old school. Their *Raising Hell* album was bolting to platinum as they headed out of New York City with the Beastie Boys, LL Cool J and Whodini on a sixty-four-date tour. But even as they reigned as kings of the new school, the world was changing.

This new world could be heard one hundred miles from New York City in Philadelphia. Around the time the city's first Black mayor, W. Wilson Goode, authorized police to drop the bomb on the Black radical organization, MOVE, burning down sixty-one homes in a working-class Black neighborhood, a North Philly rapper named Schoolly D used a cheap drum machine, his partner DJ Code Money's scratch and a reverb knob to create menacing tracks like "Gucci Time" and "P.S.K."—the initials for his crew, the Park Side Killers—songs about beating down style-biters and screwing cheap whores.

Across the country, the hottest mixtape in Los Angeles was a homemade cassette made by Compton DJ Toddy Tee in his home-studio. On the tape, Toddy Tee rapped about the new cracked-out world over instrumentals of east coast hits. Whodini's "Freaks Come Out at Night" became "The Clucks Come Out at Night"; UTFO's "Roxanne Roxanne" became "Rockman, Rockman." Most famously, Rappin' Duke's "Rappin' Duke" became "Batterram," at tale about the military-armored personnel vehicle L.A. Police Chief Daryl Gates used to bust down the doors of rock-houses.

L.A. rap pioneer Tracey "Ice T" Marrow and his Chicano friend, Arturo "Kid Frost" Molina Jr., had cut a handful of tracks in the early '80s to no great consequence. Instead Ice T had parlayed his street rep into a starring role in *Breaking and Entering*, a 1982 cult movie about the L.A. dance scene that inspired *Breakin'*, and led to his casting in a role for that movie. He had started rapping as a teenage Crip with lines inspired by the Crips' poetry books and Iceberg Slim pulps, like:

Strollin' through the city in the middle of the night
Niggas on my left and niggas on my right
Yo I Cr-Cr-Cr-Cripped every nigga I see
If you bad enough come fuck with me.[39]

"Batterram" and "P.S.K." gave him the juice to revisit his old gang rhymes. In 1986, Ice T dropped "Six in the Morning" on the b-side of his single, "Dog N' The Wax." "That song," he told journalist and photographer Brian Cross, "turned out to be my identity."[40]

The tale of a "self-made monster of the city streets, remotely controlled by hard hip-hop beats," "Six in the Morning" was a revisionist rap history told from the hard streets of Los Angeles. The tale begins in 1979, the same year as "Rapper's Delight," with an early morning escape from the cops—no comic book superheroes here, just a ghetto *noir* anti-hero on the run. "Didn't know what the cops wanted, didn't have time to ask," he sneers.

As he runs, he stops on the corner to roll some dice, ends an argument with a woman by beating her down, and finally gets arrested and thrown in jail, where he causes a riot. When he emerges from prison seven years later, it's 1986, the old school is over, the action has moved west and the whole world has changed. "The Batterram's rolling, rocks are the thing," he raps. "Life has no meaning and money is king."

At the end of the summer of "Six in the Morning" and "P.S.K.," as the *Raising Hell* tour was heading into its final stretch, Run DMC's limo pulled up to the Long Beach Arena in Southern California. They anticipated fourteen thousand fans anxiously awaiting them inside. Instead they found a full-scale melee in progress. Los Angeles's gangs had turned the concert in the arena into their own private battlefield, with thousands of innocents caught in the middle.

Local radio personality Greg Mack was MCing the show. He told Brian Cross:

> [T]his guy threw this other guy right over the balcony on to the stage while Whodini was peforming, so they got up on the stage trying to talk to the guy, next thing you know a whole section was running, gangs were hittin' people, grabbing gold chains, beating people . . . I got the girls, ran to the car, there was a Crip standing next to me getting his shotgun, getting ready to do God knows what.[41]

This was a new breed of renegades. The hip-hop generation had reached childhood's end, and was coming into an era of rebellion.

"WHO AM I ?"

Hip-hop was not just a 'Fuck you' to white society, it was a 'Fuck you' to the previous Black generation as well.

—Bill Stephney

LOOP 3

The Message
1984–1992

The search for identity. Harlem, 1992.
Photo © John Van Hasselt/Corbis Sygma

In response to the killing of Michael Griffith, the "Day of Outrage" demonstration comes to Howard Beach, 1986.

© Eli Reed/Magnum Photos

11

Things Fall Apart

The Rise of the Post–Civil Rights Era

Not only there but right here's an apartheid.

—Rakim

If there was a single moral struggle that gripped the 1980s in the same way that desegregation had the 1960s, it was the global fight against apartheid, the racist South African apparatus of law and ideology that allowed the white minority, outnumbered five to one, to maintain political and economic power over the native Black majority. The anti-apartheid movement represented the climax of a century of anticolonial and antiracist resistance, the light piercing the last darkness before the dawn of a new global century.

Pedro Noguera, a student leader at U.C. Berkeley during the mid-'80s, says, "Apartheid was such a stark situation. It was so clear. How repressive the regime was, how unjust apartheid was—in some ways it was easier to see the issues there than it was to see the issues here."

The Black struggle in the American south for desegregation had inspired millions around the world to throw off the shackles of white rule, and the children of civil rights, the young Americans who came of age during the late seventies and early eighties, were never allowed to forget it. The elders spend a lot of time talking about the glories of the civil rights movement, while dismissing the hip-hop generation as apathetic and narcissistic.

Angela Brown, the daughter of a family of civil rights activists, was one youth organizer who wearied of her elders' criticism. "Most young people who have grown up in the South have really gone through hell with our elders," she says. "They have constantly challenged us, that we haven't done what they've done as far as moving the movement forward." But in the fight against apartheid, the post–civil rights children found a desegregation battle to call their own, something in which to find their own voice and stake their own claim to history.

The Divestment Strategy

The roots of the contemporary American anti-apartheid movement date to 1963, the peak of the civil rights movement, a year after the CIA aided South Africa's white-minority regime in their capture of freedom fighter Nelson Mandela.[1] That year, the United Church of Christ called for economic sanctions against the apartheid government, whose rule was being buttressed by highly profitable gold and diamond mining industries. By the end of the decade, the American Committee on Africa, the American Friends Service Committee, radical workers groups and others had launched educational campaigns in African-American communities.

In 1971, the National Council of Churches called upon General Motors to divest of all its direct investments in the South African economy. By pulling money out of South Africa, activists felt they could make a moral statement and weaken the apartheid regime. They then formed the Interfaith Center on Corporate Responsibility, which helped organize shareholder resolutions against ITT, AT&T, Union Carbide, Ford, Exxon, Polaroid, Sears, Xerox, IBM and Mobil.[2] The following year, African-American student Randall Robinson and others turned Harvard Yard into a cemetery of five hundred black coffins, representing the victims of the university's investments, and set off years of student protests against their universities' "complicity in apartheid." The movement would come to call for cultural and consumer boycotts, government sanctions, and divestment of public-sector and corporate funds.

In the beginning, the movement faced long odds. After arresting Mandela and banning his organization, the African National Congress, the South African government brutally quashed Black resistance and rapidly expanded its security, surveillance, and policing complex. The repression had the intended effect; foreign corporate investment skyrocketed. In 1973, U.S. direct investments in South Africa totaled over $1 billion a year.[3] The Nixon administration's so-called "tar baby option" further sealed North American participation in the regime, making it official U.S. policy to accommodate the white minority, and support South Africa as a strategic anticommunist beachhead in the region.

By the mid-1970s, South African youths had reshaped the growing Black Consciousness movement, and their protests took a more militant turn. The apartheid regime stepped up their repression. On June 6, 1976, South African troops fired on demonstrators in the townships of Soweto, leaving hundreds of youths dead. In the crackdown that followed, over a thousand were killed. In 1977, Stephen Biko, the father of Black Consciousness, died of injuries sustained in prison beatings. Dozens more Black and multiracial organizations were banned, newspapers were closed and hundreds more remained in jail. President Jimmy Carter recalled his South African ambassador and urged a tightening of the arms embargo. U.S. campus protests—from Princeton and Brown to Michigan State and Morgan State—took on a new urgency.

When Ronald Reagan took office in 1980, foreign policy swung back toward Nixon-style normalization, articulated as "constructive engagement." Reagan's United Nations ambassador, Jeanne Kirkpatrick, summed up the position by stating flatly that a racist dictatorship was not nearly as bad as a Marxist one.[4] In 1985, Reagan called the white-minority regime "a reformist administration," and stirred global uproar by saying, "They have eliminated the segregation that we once had in our own country—the type of thing where hotels and restaurants and places of entertainment and so forth were segregated. That has all been eliminated."[5]

But while Reagan was prematurely hailing the end of South African segregation, the apartheid regime had declared a state of emergency, the equivalent of martial law, in an attempt to crush the rising Black movement. Between 1984 and 1986, the regime detained 30,000 protestors and killed 2,500 more.[6]

The Rise of the Anti-Racism Movement

In 1984, the American anti-apartheid movement began to peak. Jesse Jackson made South African divestment a presidential campaign issue. States like Michigan, Connecticut, Maryland, Nebraska and Massachusetts, cities like New York City; Boston; Philadelphia; San Francisco; Gary, Indiana; Wilmington, Delaware; and Washington, D.C.; and universities like the City University of New York divested.

On November 26, Randall Robinson, now the national coordinator of the Free South Africa Movement, led a small group of protestors to the South

African embassy in Washington, D.C., and launched one of the starkest protests since the height of the civil rights struggle. For months, whether in bitter cold or blazing heat, celebrities, citizens, congresspersons, congregations, youth and elderly sat in at the Embassy doors, and were arrested in a quiet daily ritual. In under a year, over three thousand were arrested there demonstrating against apartheid.

U.S. campus protests swung into high gear. In March 1985, Columbia University students launched a three-week takeover of Hamilton Hall, renaming it Mandela Hall—the biggest campus protest there since 1968. Run DMC came down to perform and show its support. During the divestment springs of 1985 and 1986, hundreds of campuses exploded in demonstrations. On the quads or in front of administration buildings, the shantytown replaced the cemetery as the symbol of disruption.

In one important respect, the student movement of the 1980s was very different from that of the '60s—students of color played a central organizing and demand-making role. During the 1960s, organizations led by young people of color, like the Student Nonviolent Coordinating Committee, the Black Panthers and the Third World Studies coalitions at San Francisco State and U.C. Berkeley, had lent moral weight to the New Left. But white males had always dominated the student movement's leadership. Even the student anti-apartheid movement, at the beginning, had been led mainly by white students.

By the mid-1980s, students of color were no longer marginal. Students of color led the protests at pivotal campuses like Yale, Rutgers, Stanford and U.C. Berkeley. Columbia University's Coalition for a Free South Africa had emerged in 1981 out of the campus Black student organization. On many other campuses where whites led the anti-apartheid movement, a process of painful self-critique—often initiated by students of color—began to emerge.

"Most white radical or liberal types came [to the anti-apartheid movement] out of empathy abroad and a feeling they'd like to do something to support," says Pedro Noguera. "We had people from the Black fraternities and sororities, a real cross-section of students. We were trying to make links between issues facing people of color in United States and on the campus and the struggle in Africa. The white students didn't see those connections so clearly. With students of color, we made that connection real clear."

Apartheid gave the young students of color a frame to understand the power of whiteness—not only in South Africa, but in the institution and in the movement. They also began to critique the failures of the baby boomer generation. While desegregation had given the new activists a place on the university campus, they still found few professors and administrators of color, under-resourced ethnic studies programs, and inhospitable campus environments. The civil rights and Black power movements had left many promises unfulfilled.

For the student activists of color, the anti-apartheid movement unlocked the connections between their campus struggles and those in their communities, and the South African shantytowns revealed the links between the global and the local. By the late 1980s, the activists had transformed the anti-apartheid movement into a broad antiracist movement, calling for ethnic studies departments and course requirements, culturally sensitive student programming and faculty, staff and graduate student diversity. The cry was for greater, truer representation that would remove the invisibility of nonwhites and counterbalance the Eurocentric bias of the university.

By 1988, Yale student organizer Matthew Countryman could say, "I don't think we will ever be in a situation again where divestment will be the sole focus, rather it will be part of a range of activities dealing with the university's involvement with racism."[7]

Reaction and Victory

The anti-apartheid movement provoked particularly violent reactions from the right. At Dartmouth, conservative students cheered a nighttime sledgehammer attack on the shanties and the shanty-dwellers. Stanford's shantytown was similarly destroyed, and at University of Utah and Johns Hopkins University, they were set ablaze.[8] In April 1986, shantytown protests at Yale and Berkeley ended with police destroying the camps and beating peaceful demonstrators bloody. In an odd way, American university administrators, police and right-wingers were re-enacting the daily violence of the townships and strengthening public sympathy for the protestors.

But the tide of protests in South Africa, the United States and around the world were having an effect. Months after the "Mandela Hall" takeover, Columbia University trustees divested. On July 18, the University of California divested its $3.1-billion South African portfolio, an amount more than portfolios of all the other 130-plus divested universities combined.[9] In August, the state of California voted to divest $11 billion of stock, perhaps the single largest one-time global disinvestment ever. Emboldened, Congress passed the Comprehensive Anti-Apartheid Act of 1986, which banned any new investment in South Africa, except to Black-owned firms, and ended arms sales and military aid. When an angered Reagan vetoed the bill, Congress successfully voted to override his veto. It was a stunning rebuke to Reagan and the apartheid-tolerant Cold War right.

In 1990, after nearly three decades behind bars, Nelson Mandela, the man that the Reaganites and right-wingers had once called a racial terrorist, was released from jail. Four years later, he stood as the first elected Black president of the country, and he paid tribute to American anti-apartheid activists by consciously evoking the memory of Dr. King: "Free at last! Free at last!"

But in America all the energy—young and old, white, Black, brown, yellow and red—that had been mustered over three decades to fight segregation would slowly disperse. The end of apartheid would be remembered as one of the century's last great victories in the American struggle for desegregation. Nothing would be so stark or clear after this.

Enraged and Disengaged

During the last two decades of the millennium, neoconservatives—with the acquiescence of "moderates" in both parties—turned back a half-century of liberalism. Worker safety and environmental protections were undermined. The size and clout of labor unions atrophied to their weakest since the outbreak of World War II.[10] Hundreds of billions were shifted from battling poverty into building the military. Responsibility was no longer preceded by the word "social," but by the word "individual."

It was not just about survival of the fittest, but *gratification* of the fittest. Republican Kevin Phillips opened his landmark critique of Reagan's '80s, *The Politics of the Rich and Poor*, with these lines: "The 1980s were the triumph of upper America—an ostentatious celebration of wealth, the political ascendancy of the richest third of the population and a glorification of capitalism, free markets and finance."[11]

Reaganomists latched onto supply-side economics, better known as trickle-down theory—the dubious idea that tax cuts for the wealthy and for big businesses would stimulate the economy. The corporate share of federal taxes plunged to a mere 15 percent, half of what it had been during the 1950s, a drop of $250 billion in annual tax revenues.[12] Some American multinational corporations swelled bigger than most nations.

At the same time, Reagan and Bush asked for, and received from Congress, huge increases in the military budget to support Cold War adventurism around the globe. Despite coming into office vowing to rid the government of deficits and deliver "balanced budgets," the deficit ballooned to its highest levels in history, leaving the big payback to the next generation. Most of the tax burden shifted to middle-class and working-class taxpayers, while low-inflation monetary policies kept unemployment rates high.

The gap between rich and poor was higher than at any time since the eve of the Great Depression. Between 1983 and 1989, the top 1 percent of households saw their net worth increase by 66 percent, while four of five households saw their net worth decline. Families of color were hit even harder. In 1983, the median white family owned eleven times the amount of wealth as a median family of color. By 1989, the gap had nearly doubled.[13]

The 1980s began a massive redistribution of wealth back to the wealthy. Everyone else could tune into Robin Leach's *Lifestyles of the Rich and Famous*, which from 1983 on, displayed the overripe fruits of Reagan's tax cuts. On October 19, 1987, the speculative bubble finally burst in a stunning stock market crash.

Small wonder that American faith in democracy soured into cynicism. Election turnout plunged. The center could not hold. Idealism fled from politics. A downward spiral of disillusionment accelerated.

People turned inward, giving up on the possibility of larger unity.

The Splintering of the Civil Rights Coalition

Even that historical wellspring of hope and faith in unity, the civil rights movement, was foundering. Nowhere was this more evident than in the collapse of the Black-Jewish coalition.

The story of the Civil Rights Movement often begins in 1909 when Black and Jewish lawyers come together to found the NAACP in an effort to end racist lynchings. It moves through Black singer and activist Paul Robeson's denunciations of anti-Semitism, Nazism and racism, which prompts FBI chief J. Edgar Hoover to list him as a subversive. And it climaxes in 1964, as Bob Dylan's "The Times They Are A-Changin' " sets the scene for the discovery of three murdered Freedom Summer activists—two Jewish, one Black—at Old Jolly Farm in Mississippi.

To be sure, questions of racial interest had always plagued the NAACP. During the early 1960s, as young Jewish activists went south to become the targets of white racists, Jewish shopkeepers and slumlords in the northern ghettos were becoming targets of Black leaders. Malcolm X famously extended this local dissatisfaction to a critique of Zionism, especially Israel's treatment of Palestinians.

New York, the city where Malcolm X, Marcus Garvey and Louis Farrakhan had found their voices, never experienced the civil rights movement the same way the south did. Just two weeks after President Lyndon B. Johnson signed the 1964 Civil Rights Act, protests in Harlem and Bed-Stuy, spawned by a police killing of a Black teen, turned to days of rioting, catalyzing similar uprisings from Philadelphia to Rochester. Jewish businesses were often the first to burn. There was an almost physical militancy to the northern front, a kind that seemed to preclude - coalition-building.

This kind of militancy crested in 1968 in Brooklyn's Ocean Hill/Brownsville school district, a conflict that Black and Jewish activists, leaders and writers still bitterly bemoan today, and which, in retrospect, looks like one of the inaugurating events of America's post–civil rights era.

At its root, the battle in Ocean Hill/Brownsville pitted a poor, 95 percent African-American and Puerto Rican community against a mostly Jewish-American, liberal teachers union. In 1967, under the cry of "community control," a newly elected, mainly Black activist school board installed a new superintendent and five new principals, all Black. Separately, the United Federation of Teachers, whose citywide contract was up, began the school year by going on strike. The board moved to replace the union teachers with teachers of color from the community, and the conditions were set for a massive confrontation.

Over the next two years, the school district was in constant disruption as Black community activists and Jewish teachers union leaders clashed. In the end, the teachers union won, the board was dismantled, the black superintendent was forced to report to a state trustee and UFT teachers were reinstated. The "community control" movement disintegrated, and Black-Jewish relations in the city would never be the same again.

A World of Danger

With each going its own way, efforts turned to securing more narrow forms of power. The northern Black civil rights leadership came together to vault a number of Blacks into elected office but steadily lost ground with their urban youth constituencies. They abandoned popular base-building and leaned increasingly on electoral politics and media advocacy. Youths of color, considered marginal to the elections process and invisible in the pop culture mainstream, were abandoned. By the mid-1980s, there was barely any continuity between youth organizers and activists, who were emerging of necessity to address their own issues, and the civil rights establishment, who had long given up on developing young leaders.

And yet Reagan's America had become perilous to youths of color in ways that had never been seen before. The well-organized and well-financed right-wing backlash foreclosed opportunities for urban youths of color. Trickle-down economics and local taxpayer revolts starved local governments and encouraged suburban sprawl, which in turn speeded white flight and racial *resegregation*. These trends were occurring as demographers projected the most racially diverse generation of youths the United States had ever seen.

In northern cities such as Detroit, Chicago, Cleveland, and New York, almost all African Americans lived under conditions of increasing racial and economic isolation.[14] Sociologists, following William Julius Wilson, now spoke of an "underclass", a segment of communities of color permanently locked into poverty and joblessness. Yet even in the suburbs, more than 60 percent of Black and Latino students attended predominantly minority schools.[15] Two decades of progress in integration suddenly and dramatically reversed course. Young whites remained the most segregated group of all. The average white student attended schools that were well over 80 percent white.[16] Nationally, hate incidents spiked.

A New Black Moses

While Black politicians and civil rights organizations seemed to move slowly and ineffectually amidst these new conditions, the Nation of Islam's minister

Louis Farrakhan fired the imaginations of enraged and disengaged Black youths. He stood on the podium and waved his fist, shouting, "I stand boldly in America without an army, with no guns, and I speak against the wickedness of the United States Government."[17]

At a time when the right-wing and its coterie of well-funded Black conservatives had absorbed the language of civil rights to claim that Blacks were no longer oppressed, Farrakhan would say, "We don't have to waste time discussing whether racism exists. Racism is so pervasive it has corrupted religion, politics, education, science and economics, and every vital function of life."[18] Yet Farrakhan was not beholden to liberal pieties either. He called for slavery reparations, exhorted Black men to save the race, and constantly reminded his followers what Elijah Muhammad had preached: "Separation is the solution."

Where police corruption or incompetence left the streets to drugs and violence, the Nation of Islam's ministries moved in to forcibly close crack houses and take control of drug-torn blocks. The brio of the Nation's "Islamic patrols" and its Dopebusters programs impressed besieged ghetto residents. At the same time, Farrakhan's message of self-reliance and self-improvement as the foundation for community development struck a chord with the relatively privileged middle-class sons and daughters of civil rights and Black power.

When the hip-hop generation began to come of age, the Black left was a shadow of its former self. Instead, Black leadership was returning to an era of what progressive scholar Manning Marable once termed "the messiah complex." In African-American history, time and again, Marable argued, people turned to male religious figures to deliver them. Social movements were left in the hands of a Moses.[19] Minister Louis Farrakhan was the latest in this mold. The Black left took Farrakhan's emergence as a troubling sign of their own weakness and a serious threat to the advancement of the freedom struggle.

But to younger heads, who had been denied so much, told in so many ways to "just say 'No,'" they heard in Farrakhan a resounding, "Yes." Bill Stephney, who would become a founder of Public Enemy, says, "He was the only Black leader who said, 'You, Black man, can pick yourself up. You can have strong families. You can build your own businesses. You *can do.* He was the only affirming leader."

Farrakhan was despised by liberals and conservatives, whites and mainstream

Blacks. He had been unanimously censured by the U.S. Senate, was hounded by accusations of anti-Semitism and was treated as a pariah by the media. But all of these factors helped legitimize him as the rare man of an older generation whom young people might respond to.

Better than any Black leader, Farrakhan seemed to understand the crisis of the generation left to be abandoned or forcibly contained. As Black-on-Black violence climbed during the summer of 1989, he began to avidly court them. He went first to those furthest from the mainstream, holding an unprecedented peace summit for gang members in Chicago. Then he visited the Cook County Jail, where he was received as a hero.

His major theme for the next several years became "Stop the Killing." In his speeches, Farrakhan said the fact that Black men were killing Black men in unprecedented numbers was not an accident, it was by design. "We believe that the government . . . is frightened by the rise in population of our people," he told *Los Angeles Times* reporter Andrea Ford. "We believe (the government) sees in Black people a useless population that is considered by sociologists a permanent underclass. And when you have something that is useless, you attempt to get rid of it if you cannot make it serviceable."[20]

On June 25, he took his message to over a thousand gang leaders and members. "The government of the United States of America is planning an assault on the Black community, specifically aimed at our youth," he told them.[21] "Brothers, you are playing into the hand of your enemy and he is using you to set up your destruction."[22] If young Black men did not unite to defend themselves, they would certainly be crushed.

White liberals despaired at the deepening schisms, bemoaning "identity politics" and "Black paranoia." Others felt as if the clock had been turned back two decades. One white political scientist, an expert in urban riots, said, "We have produced in the Black underclass a revolutionary consciousness."[23]

Howard Beach

Only eleven weeks after the 1986 Congressional anti-apartheid victory, a twenty-three-year old Trinidadian American named Michael Griffith was run over by a car and killed in Queens after being beaten and chased by a mob of whites shouting, "Nigger, you're in the wrong neighborhood!"

The incident began the Friday afternoon before Christmas. Griffith, his friend, Timothy Grimes, his stepfather, Cedric Sandiford and his cousin, Curtis Sylvester, had gone to Far Rockaway to collect a paycheck for some construction work Griffith had done. When they were returning back across Jamaica Bay on a lonely stretch of the Cross Bay Boulevard, Sylvester's 1976 Buick overheated. Griffith, Sandiford and Grimes left Sylvester with his car and hiked three miles into the nearest town, Howard Beach, in the gathering darkness.

Nestled in the inner Jamaica Bay amidst soft salt marshes, Howard Beach had once been a resort area. By the mid-1980s, it was a whites-only enclave, situated between the Belt Parkway, garbage landfills and John F. Kennedy Airport. New York City's population was almost half people of color, yet there remained pockets in Queens and Brooklyn from which whites had never taken flight. Reaganomics had devastated many of these enclaves, like Bensonhurst—where whites attacked three African-American Veterans Administration workers in 1983—and Gravesend—where in 1982, a group of thugs chased three African-American transit workers and beat one of them to death.[24] Not so with Howard Beach, which was solidly middle-class and had registered solid economic gains through the decade.[25] Yet the area was now best known as the home of John Gotti and the prevailing view among residents seemed to be that Blacks or Hispanics mainly came into their neighborhood to rob or rape them.[26]

Griffith, Sandiford and Grimes were walking up the road into Howard Beach when a group of white youths drove by screaming racial epithets at them. The three continued on, then stopped at the New Park Pizzeria and asked for directions to the nearest subway station.[27] They sat to rest and eat. By the time they had got up to leave, the white boys in the car had returned. They had a dozen others with them.

It was going to be one of those nights. Two hours before, in another part of town, cops had received a call about a gang of whites who had beaten and chased two young Hispanics. And while Griffith, Sandiford and Grimes were eating, someone had called the police to report "three suspicious Black males." Police had come, seen only the three young men eating quietly, and left.

Now it was after midnight. This crowd was drunk, some had baseball bats, others had tree switches. The whites yelled at them, "Niggers, you don't belong here." When they stepped forward to leave, the mob surged forward and began beating them. Sandiford covered himself and yelled, "God, don't kill us!" Grimes suffered a blow but ran north into the cold night. Griffith and Sandiford ran west, with the mob in pursuit in car and on foot.

Eight blocks away, the mob caught up with them. In a field of bushes and weeds next to the Belt Parkway, they beat the young Black men mercilessly. Sandiford played dead as Griffith slipped through a hole in the fence onto the six-lane parkway. When Griffith tried to cross the parkway—perhaps confused, certainly in pain and terror—he was struck by a car. His body crushed the hood and he bounced off the windshield out toward the dividing barriers. Police later found Sandiford, badly injured and dazed, stumbling blindly through the streets.

Mayor Ed Koch compared the incident to a lynching in the Old South, called it "the most horrendous incident" of his term and went to Howard Beach to call for the formation of a new Kerner Commission. He told the media that the nation was still divided in two societies—one Black and one white. Howard Beach residents booed him. Some of them told reporters that if they had been walking in Bed-Stuy late at night, surely they would have expected to be visited with the same kind of violence.

Bishop Emerson J. Moore, New York City's only black Roman Catholic bishop, declared, "I have lived in New York all my life, and the racial polarization now is as bad as it's ever been. Things are very bad now, and I fear for a hot summer."[28]

In New York City's Black community, the message of the Michael Griffith's death, coming on top of the Stewart killing and the Goetz shooting and all the others, was clear. Northern racism was alive and well, and it was time for action. Rage was the dominant chord, an emotion that seemed to catch the Black civil rights leadership by surprise. Following the incident, some had even invited graying southern civil rights icons to come north to give them advice.[29] But many favored a more militant, nationalist line, and hoped that new leaders would step forward. They did not want someone who had marched with Martin in the misty past. They wanted a latter-day Malcolm who spoke to their fearful, tense present.

Sandiford's and Grimes's lawyers, Alton Maddox and C. Vernon Mason, took a confrontational approach. Sandiford himself was still angry that, after he was beaten, he had been harassed by police and treated as a suspect. And thirty-one-year-old Reverend Al Sharpton, whose résumé already included boy preacher, teen community organizer and tour promoter for James Brown and Michael Jackson, led a series of marches into Howard Beach, often ending at the New Park Pizzeria. Separated by thin blue police lines, the marchers faced off with angry white residents.

Young anti-apartheid activists also emerged, such as Rutgers' Lisa Williamson, the leader of the newly formed National African Youth and Student Alliance. Williamson, Sharpton and Ocean-Hill/Brownsville vet Sonny Carson called for a "Day of Mourning and Outrage" and a symbolic boycott of white businesses. On January 21, ten thousand marchers led police all over the city, before they stopped at Mayor Koch's residence. "Mayor Koch, have you heard? Howard Beach is Johannesburg," they chanted below his window. "Black power! African power!"[30]

Hip-Hop in a New Era

These were the currents that swirled during the mid-1980s. The culture that had poured out from the streets of the Bronx was transitioning into a new era.

Graffiti, pushed off the subways, poured onto the streets and highways and freight trains, initiating a new wave of police crackdowns and internecine fights. Style wars dispersed to thousands of distant cities, where fervent new movements opened new frontlines with local authorities.

B-boying, a dance style that had already died once in New York, disappeared again, to be replaced by a succession of fad dances. Steps like the Whop, the Reebok, the Cabbage Patch and countless others got everyone back on the dancefloor. But each one disappeared faster than b-boying ever had. Third-generation breaking adherents continued the artform as Rock Steady's disciples covered the globe.

Rap proved to be the ideal form to commodify hip-hop culture. It was endlessly novel, reproducible, malleable, perfectible. Records got shorter, raps more concise and tailored to pop-song structures. Rap groups shrank, from the Furious Five and the Funky 4 + 1 More down to the Treacherous Three, and now, to duos like Cash Money and Marvelous or Eric B. and Rakim.

DJs were still often billed first, and after Grandmaster Flash's epochal "Adventures on the Wheels of Steel," they enjoyed a brief artistic surge with singles like Herbie Hancock's "Rockit," Grandmixer DST's "Crazy Cuts," and the B-Boys' "2,3 Break." But DJs no longer enjoyed the eminence or the central musical role their billing implied. When drum-machine and sampling technology were turned into hip-hop tools, the record producer filled that space. Early rap labels had already marginalized the DJ, and the new technology effectively mimicked and extended the DJ's musical capabilities. The rise of the rap producer, the arrival of some extraordinary rappers, and the increasing flow of capital propelled hip-hop music into a period of remarkable stylistic development.

By 1986, rap eclipsed all the other movements. It had expanded to incorporate many more pop perspectives—satirical rap, teenybopper rap, X-rated rap, Roxanne rap, Reagan rap, John Wayne rap. But in the new crisis time, as it had been for Jamaica's embattled roots generation, rappers were increasingly being recognized as "the voices of their generation." The center of the rap world swung decidedly in a Black nationalist direction. Hip-hop culture realigned itself and reimagined its roots, representing itself now as a rap thing, a serious thing, a Black thing.

The unlikely hotbed of the new energy was in the Black Belt of Long Island.

The making of the Enemy, 1988.
Photo © Michael Benabib/Retna LTD.

12.

What We Got to Say

Black Suburbia, Segregation and Utopia in the Late 1980s

Ay uh we didn't get our forty acres and a mule but we did get you, C.C.
—George Clinton

Long Island, where I got 'em wild and
That's the reason they're claiming that I'm violent

—Chuck D

"Def Jam is the ultimate suburban record label," wrote music critic Frank Owen in one of the earliest articles on Public Enemy. He argued that Russell Simmons and Rick Rubin were creating "the first Black music that hasn't had to dress itself up in showbiz glamour and upwardly mobile mores in order to succeed." They were leading the battle "against the gentrification of black music."[1] Significantly, Simmons, Run DMC and LL Cool J were from home-owning Queens, and Rubin, Original Concept and Public Enemy were from "the well-to-do beach communities of Long Island."

Owen quoted Public Enemy's lead rapper, Chuck D, an intimidatingly articulate guy whose eyes always seemed hidden beneath the brim of his baseball cap. "Raps from the suburbs are a little more broad," Chuck said. "They don't have the closed-in focus like inner-city raps. In the suburbs you can rap about regular everyday life like going to the park and taking a swim. The rest of America can relate to that."

But Public Enemy's art would always belie easy sociology. Public Enemy's second single, "You're Gonna Get Yours," was Chuck's ode to his 98 Olds, "the ultimate homeboy car!"—a theme as American as The Beach Boys' "Little Deuce

231

Coupe." Yet the song was also about facing down racial profiling with Black posse power, an act of defiance set within the historical context of Robert Moses's expressway-fueled segregation and Levittown's racial covenants. Chuck himself would never rap about going to the park or taking a swim. The suburbs that birthed Def Jam's cultural vanguard were no white-bread New Frontier futurama.

The Black Belt and the Resegregation of Long Island

After World War II, African Americans began moving to the suburbs of Queens. Soon what would become known as "the Black Belt" spilled past Queens's eastern borders into Long Island's Nassau and Suffolk Counties. By the 1970s, it stretched from Merrick and Freeport through Roosevelt to Hempstead.

"Long Island represented an outpost for many New Yorkers trying to escape what had become the ravages of urban America in the '60s," says Bill Stephney. "White ethnics—Italians, European Jews, Irish—were all moving out from their various sectors of New York City to escape Blacks and Latinos. The thing is the working to middle-class Black generation living in the Bed-Stuys and the Parkchesters, the Bronx and Harlem, also wanted the same thing. Raise their kids with backyards and birds. The quote unquote American dream."

The core of what would become Public Enemy—Carlton "Chuck D" Ridenhour, Bill Stephney, Hank "Shocklee" Boxley, William "Flavor Flav" Drayton, Richard "Professor Griff" Griffin and Harry "Allen" McGregor—were all born between 1958 to 1961, and had moved to the Black Belt by the early '70s. 1980 census data showed that over 40 percent of white New Yorkers lived in the suburbs, but only 8 percent of Black New Yorkers did.[2] In other words, they were part of the race's "talented tenth," the very embodiment of the brightest hopes of integrationists.

Bill's father, Ted Stephney, had been a Jackie Robinson of sorts, joining the staff of *Sports Illustrated* magazine in 1954 and eventually rising to become the magazine's first Black editor. In 1965, he moved his family from Harlem to Hempstead. The Stephneys were pioneers on their block, one of three Black families among about forty whites. More Black families moved in, but in practice, integration never worked the way that civil rights activists had hoped.

In 1966, integration orders were issued by New York State education officials for Freeport, Glen Cove, Roosevelt and Amityville. These communities suddenly looked more attractive to Black homebuyers. White real estate agents descended on white homeowners to encourage them to sell their homes and "upgrade" to new developments to the north and east. By skillfully exploiting fears, real-estate agents could double their sales in a practice known as "blockbusting." For all practical purposes, racism and the market ensured that these neighborhoods were "integrated" only in passing.

When Chuck's family moved from the Queensbridge projects to Roosevelt in 1969, buying their piece of the dream for the relatively affordable price of $20,000, the number of Blacks in the neighborhood had long passed the tipping point—that unspoken ratio somewhere between 10 and 20 percent that triggered white flight. "Two years prior it was about maybe 90 percent white. When we moved in it was about 50 percent. Two years later, about 90 percent Black," he says. The oldest of three children, Chuck grew up in virtually an all-Black suburb.

Although the 1968 Fair Housing Act had banned discrimination in selling and renting homes, Stephney says, "Black folks were shown Hempstead and Roosevelt and parts of Freeport, also New Cassel." Other Long Island towns, like Wyandanch, Brentwood and Amityville—homes to the rappers Rakim Allah, EPMD and De La Soul, respectively—also became largely Black. In between, places like East Meadow, Baldwin, Rockville Centre, the fading *überburb* of Levittown and the sparkling "edge cities" or exurbs encircling the Black Belt to the north and east remained mostly white.

By the early 1970s, Long Island's Black Belt was firmly established. Two decades later, *Newsday* would find that illegal steering practices were still commonplace and called Long Island housing patterns "apartheid-like."[3] While the victories of the civil rights and Black power movements had expanded the Black middle-class, that middle-class was now just as segregated as its "underclass" counterparts were.

Always Between: The Black Middle Class

So yes, they had made it to Long Island. But no, this wasn't the promised land. Black suburbia was a safe island in a sea of whiteness, and incontrovertible evidence of white resistance to King's dream.

Newsday found that while many of Long Island's white students attended some of the best schools in the country,

> [m]ore than half of the Island's 40,000 Black public school children attend 11 districts where academic programs and resources are measurably inferior to those in white schools: They are poorly equipped, their teachers are less experienced and underpaid. Test scores are low, the dropout rate is high, few students go on to college.[4]

In a *Newsday* poll, most Blacks rated race relations as "fair" or "poor."[5] Three-quarters wanted to live in integrated communities. By contrast, fully 55 percent of white Long Islanders preferred to live in mostly white neighborhoods, a rate high above the national average.

Some white youths apparently shared their parents' feelings. In 1985, a cineplex in Franklin Square, a white town edging against Hempstead, opened the Run DMC vehicle, *Krush Groove*, next to the Freddy Krueger bloody-white-picket-fence flick, *Nightmare on Elm Street*, and fights between Black and white youths broke out. One white teenager complained that *Krush Groove* was "attracting a Black crowd to a white town. That means trouble, especially because they come out of the movie all psyched up."[6] The movie was a comedy. Critics hated the movie, but no one else had ever accused it of being provocative.

White cops seemed to treat the Black suburbs as an advancing border. Although Blacks made up only 9 percent of Long Island's population, they made up over 30 percent of the arrests in Nassau and Suffolk counties, and 43 percent of suspects shot at by police. Only 2 percent of the police force was Black.[7] The poll found that Blacks were four times more likely than whites to distrust police.

Sociologists had begun calling places like the Black Belt "inner-ring suburbs." The housing stock was aging, housing values had leveled off, education and social services were declining and crack dealers were beginning to appear. These suburban Blacks were caught between Black poverty and white flight. They were buffers between inner-city ghettos of color and the *new* New Frontier of white wealth in the exurbs.

To neoconservative and neoliberal pundits, the end of integration meant it was time for the Black race's talented tenth to take responsibility to save the race. But as journalist Ellis Cose wrote in his book *The Rage of a Privileged Class*, "The irony in such arguments is that the 'decent Black people' who will save America from the underclass, those paragons of middle-class virtue who will rescue the ghetto from violence, are themselves in a state of either silent resentment or deeply repressed rage. Taken as a group, they are at least as disaffected and pessimistic as those struggling at society's periphery."[8]

Living in this borderland, where everything mixed and clashed, one might be freighted with a feeling of being in-between all the time—a Duboisian double-consciousness complicated by the burden of class. But being Black and middle class could also be liberating. The *Newsday* poll noted what it thought to be a conundrum: "[M]ost Blacks were optimistic about the future even while believing that segregation will stay the same or increase."[9]

A sacred tenet of the civil rights movement had been that allowing Black families into white neighborhoods or Black students into white classrooms would lift their expectations, eliminate their alleged pathologies, and brighten their life chances. Integration was presumed to be the economic and cultural ideal for Blacks, just as assimilation was for immigrants. But while most Long Island Blacks liked the idea of integration—indeed, much more than their white counterparts—they certainly did not feel that they *needed* integration to succeed.

To them, the Black Belt was also an idyll, the sort of place in which Marcus Garvey's son, a doctor named Julius, could open his heart surgery practice. Whites often came to Dr. Garvey's office, took one look at him, and never returned. But this Black-owned business was not suffering, nor were many others.[10]

The Black Belt was culturally rich. Chuck's mother, Judy Ridenhour, formed the Roosevelt Community Theater and ran it from 1971 to 1985, mentoring a number of young actors and actresses, such as Chuck's childhood buddy, Eddie Murphy. Chuck, Hank, Eddie and Richard Griffin, were sent to study blackness on white campuses. Between 1970 and 1972, they attended a summer program at Hofstra and Adelphi universities organized and taught by Black Panthers, Black Muslims and university students, called "The Afro-American Experience," the local manifestation of the national movement for ethnic studies and Afro-American studies. The program proved instrumental in convincing Chuck and Hank to attend those still largely white universities years later.

And the Black Belt never felt far from the city. "Every weekend my family and most of our families would come back from Long Island and visit our grandparents, aunts, uncles, and cousins on the weekend in Harlem and in the Bronx," says Stephney. That's where the kids discovered the future culture.

"My grandmother lived in the projects in the northern Bronx where DJ Breakout basically was doing his thing in the Quadrangle," says Stephney. "I'm thirteen, fourteen. The noise that we heard my parents thought was *crime*," he laughs. Stephney was aware of the class gulf. These weekend trips offered a constant reminder of the way things *really were*, and even suggested an opportunity to be grabbed.

Stephney says, "We could sort of vicariously live out the life that our cousins were living. It was sort of like we were slumming. But then we could go back to Long Island and go to school and maybe get a couple of extra dollars from our parents to buy turntables, take some of the advantages that our cousins in Bronx River and Soundview Houses didn't have economic advantage to do."

They were products of the failure of the civil rights dream of integration, but the Black Belt youths also had access to different realities, and they had the time and space to think through and map out how to take their place in the new world.

The Big Street Beat Comes to Black Suburbia

When Schoolly D's "P.S.K." hit the Black suburbs of Long Island, Harold McGregor and Hank Boxley were two clerks in dead-end entry-level jobs at a fading department store called TSS. They were bored, unhappy and underemployed. They stole time to discuss the hottest new rap single and dream of the future.

By night, Boxley was a famous DJ, the Afrika Bambaataa of Long Island. In 1974, he had started doing shows as a teenager at the Roosevelt Youth Center. Now his mobile DJ unit, Spectrum City, was the one of the best-known sound systems in the Black Belt. But he had doubts about how far it could all go.

At one point, Spectrum City had been in the right place at the right time. In the mid-1970s, the teenagers of Queens's Black middle-class were building the biggest sound systems yet seen in the boroughs, putting scads of funk cover bands out of work. Long Island DJ crews followed soon after. Spectrum City and its rivals, Pleasure, King Charles, and the Infinity Machine, rocked community centers, roller rinks, Elks Club and hotel ballrooms, and then moved to a bigger, more attractive base, the area's universities, including Adelphi, C. W. Post and Boxley's alma mater, Hofstra. Soon, folks came from as far away as the Queens neighborhoods of Jamaica and Hollis to check out the campus parties.

Carlton Ridenhour began writing rhymes after the blackout of 1977, inspired by cassettes he had encountered while working summer jobs in Manhattan. He and Hank both came of age just as the nascent Long Island scene hit a transition point in 1978 and 1979. While the hip-hop core in the city was growing up and moving away from the big street beat, a young Long Island hip-hop constituency was forming. Spectrum City was at the center of a new energy.

But their flyers were wack. Ridenhour was at Adelphi studying graphic design. He stepped up to Hank to offer to redesign their flyers. "Hank looked at me like I was crazy," he says, and nothing came of the request.

By September 1979, Boxley was convinced he needed a permanent MC to front Spectrum City. One night at the end of an open mic session at Adelphi's Thursday Night Throwdown, a booming voice turned Shocklee's head. Ridenhour, it seemed, had other talents.

In fact he had the kind of voice that cut through brick walls. He had patterned himself after DJ Hollywood, DJ Smalls and Eddie Cheeba, disco rap DJs whose greatest skill lay in moving their crowds. "To get the party crowd amped, to get them hyped?" says Stephney, "Chuck D was one of the greatest party MCs of all time."

"When they got to 'Love Is the Message' or especially when they got to 'Good Times,' you had people lining up on the mic trying to get down. And me, I would just get on the mic just to shut people up, because I just didn't want to hear nine million people on the mic," Ridenhour recalls. "And when he found it was me, the same guy with the flyers, he was like, 'What the fuck! You from Roosevelt! Why don't you get down with me?'"

As Ridenhour pondered the decision, "Rapper's Delight" came out. The decision was sealed. He took over flyer design duties and became the rapper "Chuckie D." He began wearing his Spectrum City jacket around campus. He landed a daily cartoon in the school paper and called the Pedro Bell–styled strip, "Tales of the Skind." In it, Spectrum City became a crew of superheroes who regularly saved the world from Reagan the "King of the 666," and a host of lesser villains.

Harold McGregor wasn't much of a party-goer. His Jamaican parents were strivers who had moved to Costa Rica, then Brooklyn, and finally to Freeport. He had grown up a devout Seventh-Day Adventist and gone to a boarding school in upper Pennsylvania. At Adelphi, he came upon his future by accident. On the first day in an animation class, he sat next to a guy who was doodling. Struck dumb, he leaned over to tell Chuck he was a big fan of his work. ("I still am," he chuckles.) They teamed up to do an animated video set to Malcolm McLaren's "She's Looking Like a Hobo." In a few years, McGregor would be calling himself Harry Allen, Hip-Hop Activist and Media Assassin.

Bill Stephney came to Adelphi on an Urban League–sponsored communications scholarship that he had won by writing an essay on why more Blacks were needed in the media industry. Stephney had gone to Spectrum City parties as a youngster and now had a Monday night hip-hop show at the campus radio station, WBAU. The small Garden City liberal arts college was a predominantly white commuter campus. Most of the 10 percent of the student body that was African-American came from outside the area. So when Stephney spotted Chuck D sporting his Spectrum City jacket in the school cafeteria, he couldn't believe it. Stephney soon asked Chuck and Hank to join his radio show.

Stephney's scholarship had included a coveted internship at the trend-setting rock station, WLIR-FM. Armed with a wealth of radio tricks from WLIR and the famous Spectrum City crew, he began transforming a 300-watt station into a contender for rap-hungry ears on Strong Island. He became program director in 1982, and gave Chuck and Hank a Saturday night rap show, the "Super Spectrum Mix Hour." Harry was a frequent visitor.

It was the beginning of a long, some say fated, friendship. They did not fit in with the Black fraternity and sorority scene, full of bougie wannabes who looked down their noses on hip-hop. They mixed more easily with the white, mullet-haired Long Island freaks that hung around the radio station.

"We were the rebels," says Stephney, "and hip-hop was everything to us. Everything, all culture, all western civilization flowed through Bam, Herc, and Flash. We weren't trying to hear anything."

Many people remember their old homies by the adventures they shared. Chuck, Bill, Hank, and Harry talk about the intense debates they had. Every topic—the aesthetics of Schoolly D, the comparative emotional qualities of various basslines, the taste of White Castle cheeseburgers, the Mets and the Yankees and Jets and the Giants and the Knicks, Vanessa Williams's Miss America fiasco, Jesse Jackson's presidential campaign—was up for grabs.

To Allen, hanging with the crew was an advanced rap seminar. To Stephney, it was a salon reminiscent of the Harlem Renaissance. To the authorities, it was something else. One late night after a gig as they partied and argued in the parking lot of a White Castle, a police helicopter and a fleet of Nassau County cop cars swooped down and surrounded them. There were reports that a riot was going on.

Harder Intellect

Rap crews popped up all over the area, and many found their way into the WBAU-Spectrum City nexus. Stephney added Adelphi classmate Andre "Dr. Dre" Brown and his man, T-Money, who had a crew called Original Concept, to the BAU roster. Dre later took over Stephney's show and his program director duties, and gave a show to a bizarre, classical piano-playing, jheri-curled, all-black-wearing character from Freeport named William "Rico" Drayton who called himself the MC DJ Flavor.

A friend from Roosevelt, Richard Griffin, director of a martial arts school and a Nation of Islam devotee, came in to handle Spectrum City's security with a team he called Unity Force. Chuck's 98 Posse, a group of hard-rocks and hustlers from around the way, rolled to the parties in their tricked-out Oldsmobiles. The two crews—one representing form and discipline, the other street wildness—had that Zulu/Gestapo dynamic going on. They didn't always get along, but they came together under Spectrum City.

Chuck and Hank's radio drops topped WBAU's request lists. Run DMC came down from Hollis to do their first New York radio interview and left huge fans of the Spectrum City crew. Tapes of the shows spread into New York City, and they compared favorably with Mr. Magic's Rap Attack on WBLS, Eddie Cheeba's WFUV show and the World Famous Supreme Team's show on WHBI. The Spectrum City empire expanded to TV when Bill hooked up a UHF show. Hank, placing a bet on the future, rented out a space on 510 South Franklin Street in Hempstead and set up a recording studio.

They had the crew, they had the skills, they certainly had the desire. But could a hip-hop crew break out from Long Island? There was no road map. Then the rap-loving rebels found a mentor in a young African-American studies professor and jazz drummer named Andrei Strobert.

Born in 1950, Strobert grew up in Crown Heights and Bedford-Stuyvesant and become a drumming prodigy. By the time he was in his teens, Strobert was supporting himself with music gigs through Mayor Lindsay-funded youth programs like the Harlem Youth Opportunities Unlimited, "Har-You" for short, where he recorded his first record with fourteen other teens, the great Latin jazz album, *Har-You Percussion Group*. At eighteen, he left to tour North America. He later played with jazz mavericks Makanda Ken McIntyre and South African exile Abdullah "Dollar Brand" Ibrahim, and finally devoted himself to teaching.

The Black Arts movement had creatively and literally fed Strobert. But after the riot season of 1968, the network that sustained him began to dry up. Radio marginalized jazz. Clubs and theaters closed. Many school music programs and nonprofit youth organizations ended when government money dried up. Strobert recognized that hip-hop had come out of a traumatic break between generations, and he was now in a position to take the rap rebels back to their roots.

For two semesters, Strobert offered a class called "Black Music and Musicians." African music, he taught, was the source. It had come first; it was *first* world music, not *third* world music. Unlike many of his age, Strobert was respectful of rap music. Fats Waller, he told them, was a rapper. Louis Armstrong was a rapper. The only thing different with your rap, he told them, was that it went over a different rhythm. But even the beat wasn't new; it came from Ibo rhythms, through the pulse of the New Orleans second-line. Recognize the source, he said, return to the source. Bill, Harry, Andre, and Chuck—usually back-of-the-class kind of guys—were in the front row for all of Strobert's lectures.

After class, they peppered him with questions. Strobert gave them impromptu seminars. Control your image by developing your theme, he said. All the great artists—Mahalia Jackson, Dizzy Gillespie, James Brown—had a theme, and when the theme was over, they moved to a new one. Tell a story, he said. A rap means nothing if it tells no story. The students worried that critics were calling rap a passing fad and record companies might lose interest. Strobert laughed sagely.

"Don't believe the hype," he told them. Strobert now says, "I did *not* think they were really listening to me. I really didn't."

Understanding how they fit into the historical continuum gave Chuck, Harry, and Bill confidence, and reinforced their impatience with the state of hip-hop. Crack had ushered in an era of conspicuous wealth and raw violence, and even the slang reflected the change. It was all about getting ill, cold getting dumb. Chuck complained, "It's like being content with being stupid."[11]

When the media excoriated Run DMC for the gang violence at the 1986 Long Beach concert, Chuck got really angry. "Shit, if they ever come to me with that bullshit," he said, "I'll have some shit to say that they won't want to fuck with. I'll give them the exact reasons that bullshit like that happens."[12]

The times indeed called for someone new to flip "It's Like That" and "Proud to Be Black" the way those records had flipped "The Message" and "Planet Rock." But even more, the times required a harder kind of intellect.

Bill Stephney challenged Chuck, "Why don't you be the one?" Chuck wasn't so sure. But then he was writing as if he already had the freedom to say what folks couldn't: "I'm a MC protector, US defector, South African government wrecker. Panther power—you can feel it in my arm. Look out y'all, cause I'm a timebomb tickin'!"

False Start

The tempos were slowing down, the style changing. Run DMC's "It's Like That" and "Sucker MCs" shifted the game again—harder beats with harder rhymes that gave no quarter to anyone not already down. Hollis, Queens, was in the house, and the Spectrum City crew hoped Long Island could be next.

Chuck and Hank had always wanted to make a record. When the World's Famous Supreme Team broke out of WHBI in 1982, they began thinking it was possible. Two years later, Chuck and Hank landed a single deal with the dance indie, Vanguard. Harry Allen says he was convinced that "as soon as the rest of the world heard this music, we were just gonna take over."

The Spectrum City single duplicated the split of "It's Like That"/"Sucker MCs." On the A-side, "Lies." Chuck and fellow Spectrum City rapper Butch Cassidy went topical. Opening with the notes of "Hail to the Chief," the song seemed to promise a vivid deconstruction of Reagan. Instead it was a generic dis record, delivered over a beat derived from Arthur Baker, James Brown, and Larry Smith. Chuck's voice thundered like Melle Mel's second coming, but lyrically this was no "Message."

Instead, the B-side won. "Check Out the Radio" was based on one of Chuck's famous radio drops. Hank and his brother Keith assembled a beat based on a b-boy perennial, Juicy's "Catch a Groove," and took a risk by pitching it down. If the trend was to decrease the tempo and pump up the bass, the Shocklees wanted it slower and lower. In a year, as if tipping their baseball caps to them, Def Jam would drop two more B-side trunk crushers—Original Concept's "Pump That Bass/Live (Get a Little Stupid . . . HO!)" and the Beastie Boys' "Slow and Low."

The track hinted at Chuck's talent for deep signifying. He introduced Hank Boxley as Hank Shocklee, a very smart dis of the early-twentieth-century physicist and eugenicist William Shockley. But the crew still had not harnessed its strengths—Chuck's wordplay and presence, Hank and Keith's experimentalist drive, the crew's restless, race-conscious, collective intelligence. In December of that year, they found the prototype in a buzzsaw radio drop set to a loop of the intro to The JB's "Blow Your Head" and called, after James Brown's anti-heroin lament, "Public Enemy #1." But by then the single had stiffed. Chastened by the experience, the crew retreated to lick their wounds.

So now in the break room in the bowels of a dying department store in the middle of Still Nowhere, Hip-Hop America, Hank and Harry talked Schoolly D's "P.S.K."—repping Philly—with a mix of awe, envy and discouragement. "I think there was a lot of disappointment," says Harry. "It was like, we could be doing this the rest of our lives—working at TSS, handing out our fliers, having people come to our club, nothing really happening. And it would all just be a minor footnote somewhere."

Chuck graduated and helped land Flavor a job delivering furniture for his father's business. Then he moved on to work as a messenger for a photo company, scribbling raps on notepads on long drives into the city, letting WLIB's mix of Black-talk radio and booming beats fire his imagination.

The bills at their Spectrum City office in Hempstead were piling up. Their club and party audiences were maturing and moving on. The "Super Spectrum Mix Hour" was coming to an end.

In 1985, Original Concept signed to Def Jam. The label president Rick Rubin was calling Chuck's house to see if he would agree to be their rapper. "Mom!" Chuck would yell from his room, "Tell him I'm not home. Tell him I don't wanna make no stupid goddamn records!"[13] Once bitten, twice shy was the way he and Hank felt about record labels. They had already built a local empire by themselves. What next? At the end of long wearying days, they talked about starting their own indie record label.

Bill Stephney graduated and began working in the radio world, establishing a reputation in the record industry. Harry left for Brooklyn to finish his degree. Both of them were surrounded by the music, which seemed to be undergoing tectonic stylistic shifts every few weeks. The city seemed charged with importance—so many ideas, so much ferment. People were talking about things that mattered. Change was in the air. Something had to happen.

The Biggest Crossover

At Def Jam and Rush Artists Management, Russell Simmons and Rick Rubin's crew had big dreams.

Bill Adler was one of Russell's first hires. When he signed on to work at Rush Management and Def Jam in 1984 at thirty-two years of age, he was older than everyone on the tiny staff, twice as old as LL Cool J. A third-generation Jewish American from the Detroit suburb of Southfield, Adler had arrived at the University of Michigan in the feverish fall of 1969 and met a local hero, a self-described "cultural radical" named John Sinclair.

Sinclair was part of a generation of post–World War II whites, including Allen Ginsberg, Norman Mailer and Bob Dylan, who wanted to root themselves in what they thought was the special authenticity of African-American culture. To Sinclair, Black musicians like James Brown, John Coltrane, and Sun Ra offered a model of liberation for young whites. After Black Panther cofounder Bobby Seale told Sinclair whites could not do anything for Black people but to fix their square parents, he was inspired to form the White Panthers and draft their ten-point program. The first point was a full endorsement of the Black Panthers' program. The second read, "Total assault on the culture by any means necessary, including rock 'n' roll, dope and fucking in the streets." For Adler, who had spent his teen nights under the covers listening to blues, Motown, and "freedom jazz" on local radio, joining Sinclair's funkdafied guitar army of white radicals made perfect sense.

After Sinclair left Ann Arbor, so did Adler, moving first to Boston. Fired from his DJ job at WBCN for playing Joe Tex, bored with his pop music critic job at the *Boston Herald*, Adler left for New York City in 1980 with a box of brand new rap records under his arm. He met Russell Simmons while doing a story on rap for *People* magazine and they became fast friends. When Adler approached Simmons to try to sell him an anti-Reagan rap intended for Kurtis Blow, Simmons demurred but hired Adler to do publicity for his acts. Adler immediately understood what set Simmons apart from the Black-owned indie pioneers like Enjoy and Sugar Hill. "He was never gonna just be a guy who operated within the confines of Black cultural institutions," Adler says. "He was gonna take this Black culture and promote it everywhere."

Simmons was twenty-six, an extroverted, infectious son of civil rights activists, less concerned with political parties than with being the center of the party. Even during his brief stint as warlord of a Queens chapter of the Seven Immortals, his thing had been bumrushing school dances and concerts. No social crowd ever gathered that Simmons could not work his way into the middle of. He had a sixth sense for the popular.

When Simmons met Rick Rubin, a twenty-one-year-old, gnomic Jewish longhair with Bambaataa-sized tastes in music and a Sinclairian talent for fomenting white teen cultural rebellion, he found the perfect partner. Rubin had grown up on Long Island playing metal and punk, and became a rap devotee through the WBAU shows and Mr. Magic. When he moved to Manhattan to attend New York University, regular trips to Blue's "Wheels of Steel" night at Negril and The Roxy sealed his love for hip-hop.

Rubin had a hardcore aesthetic. "I think Rick helped radicalize Russell's rhetoric," says Adler. "He used to say, 'We're gonna pull the mainstream in our direction simply on the basis of the integrity of the records themselves. We are going to win with no compromise.' "

Radio had long calcified into racialized formats—Album-Oriented Rock for whites, Urban Contemporary for Blacks. Rap was the most exciting new music to come along in years, but there was no room for it in either. MTV had burst onto the scene by championing rock and new wave, and all but excluding Black artists. Only after Columbia reportedly threatened to boycott the young network in 1983 did MTV begin airing Michael Jackson videos. Winning meant desegregating radio and music video.

Not long after the ink dried on Def Jam's contract with Columbia in 1985, Rubin hired Bill Stephney as the label's first full-time staffer. Rubin was a Spectrum City fan. But perhaps more important was the fact that Stephney played guitar, was from Long Island, and dug AC/DC the way Rubin did Schoolly D. After graduating from Adelphi, Bill Stephney had done a short, influential stint at the College Music Journal, launching its "Beat Box" urban chart and mapping what would become a powerful network of rap radio shows. Stephney had also maintained his old white rock radio contacts, which later proved crucial to Def Jam's success.

Russell was a Black executive able to bridge Black and white tastes like no one since Berry Gordy. He hired Adler. Rick was a Jewish music producer who understood how profoundly Herc, Bam, and Flash's insights could reshape all of pop music. He hired Stephney. The staff for Rush and Def Jam was uniquely suited and highly motivated to pull off a racial crossover of historic proportions.

Bill Stephney convinced his friends at rock radio to stay on Run DMC's cover of Aerosmith's "Walk This Way," even when the call-out research showed racist, "get the niggers off the air" feedback. He then succeeded in propelling the Beastie Boys onto rap radio, a feat no less difficult. By the end of 1986, their strategy had been perfectly executed. The Black group crossed over to white audiences with *Raising Hell*, then the white group crossed over to Black audiences with *Licensed to Ill*.

Forget busing, Adler thought. Hip-hop was offering a much more radical, much more successful voluntary desegregation plan. It was bleeding-edge music with vast social implications. "Rap reintegrated American culture," Adler declared. Not only was hip-hop *not* a passing novelty, the ex-Sinclairite told journalists, it was culturally monumental, and Run DMC and the Beastie Boys were the new revolutionaries. "Young, smart, fast, hard," he called them. "Lean and winning."

Def Jam's epochal feat of pop integration unleashed a rap signing blitz. Majors realized that rap music was not a fad, and they were far behind the curve. Their Black music departments had become calcified, geared toward promoting expensive R&B acts that appealed to an upwardly mobile audience quickly losing its trend-setting power. By the end of 1986, and continuing for the better part of a decade, majors moved in the other direction, trying to sign every rap act they could. It was one of those rare moments in pop music history where major-label disorientation left the door open for any visionary to walk through and do something radical.

At the same time, the teens weaned on Herc and Bam and Flash were growing up, and they felt they had something to say. They simply needed to figure out what that something was.

Becoming the Enemy

When Stephney left CMJ, he had written in his last column that he hoped to develop a group that was equal parts Run DMC and The Clash. He wanted to be a part of making the rap *Sandinista!* Back in Hempstead, at 510 South Franklin, he, Hank, and Chuck were at a crossroads. If they were going to do something, Hank says, "We had to create our own myth for ourselves."

But while their homies from Hollis were taking over the world, Spectrum City had run out of steam. Chuck was about to turn twenty-six and had little intention of remaining a rapper. Rick Rubin was still pestering Chuck's mother with phone calls. Chuck was thinking, "Yo I need to make some radical moves. And that's not radical enough." He wanted to get a job as a commercial radio personality.

Rubin joked that if Stephney couldn't get his best friend signed to Def Jam, he would have to be fired. So Bill offered Chuck and Hank a meeting with Rubin. The two brought in a four-song demo which included "Public Enemy #1," "The Return of Public Enemy" (which would become "Miuzi Weighs a Ton"), "Sophisticated Bitch," and "You're Gonna Get Yours." Rubin immediately offered Chuck an album deal. "I was like, well I'm not going to go in there by myself," Chuck says. After he negotiated to include Flavor Flav and Hank, the deal was done, and he set about finding a place for the entire crew.

As he had done with "Tales of the Skind," he created alter-egos for each of them. Richard Griffin took the name "Professor Griff" and the title that Eldridge Cleaver had held in the Black Panthers, "Minister of Information." Unity Force, the Spectrum City's security team run by Griffin, were renamed the Security of the First World (S1Ws). Hank assembled the musical team, starting with his brother Keith, also known as "Wizard K-Jee." Army fatigue-wearing Eric "Vietnam" Sadler—like Stephney and Flavor Flav—was a veteran of the Long Island funk cover-band scene and was learning to program drums and synthesizers. Spectrum City DJ Norman Rogers became "Terminator X." Paul Shabazz and the DJ for the Kings of Pressure, Johnny "Juice" Rosado, also made key contributions. Hank's team became known as the Bomb Squad.

Most important, Chuck, Hank and Bill had to come up with a concept for the crew. Spectrum City was done. But they had yet to come up with a new name and concept.

Bill's dream was for the group to make the cover of the *Rolling Stone*. "Let's make every track political," he said. "Statements, manifestoes, the whole nine." Hank worried that kind of approach might lose them credibility with their core audience. He says, "Everyone making Hip-Hop wasn't a thug, everybody wasn't about being stupid." But, he adds, "we found that people were really against the political aspects of the music. That wasn't a slam dunk."

Characteristically, Chuck was somewhere in between. He wanted to write rhymes that were more explicit, but he says, "It was impossible to put that type of shit in your rhymes. It was like, you better rock the fucking crowd. You could throw in one line or two, like 'Reagan is bullshit.' Motherfuckers be like, 'Yeah, okay.'"

Then there was the crazy DJ MC Flavor, whom Hank had renamed Flavor Flav. Both Hank and Chuck wanted Flav to round out the crew, be the MC yin to Chuck's yang. Bill objected. "I wanted the group to be so serious, I didn't want Flavor in the group. Flavor was like a comic cut-up, so my thing was, 'Here we are trying to do some serious shit, how are we gonna fit this guy in?'" he says. "They were completely right. With Chuck being serious, with the stentorian tones, you needed a break, you needed someone to balance that or else it would have been too much."

One night while they were recording *Yo! Bum Rush the Show,* Bill returned from the Def Jam offices to 510 South Franklin. On a bulletin board, Hank had written the crew's new name: "Public Enemy." Stephney smiled. The name perfectly fit their underdog love and their developing politics. He recalls thinking, "Okay, I can spin this. We're all public enemies. Howard Beach. Bernhard Goetz. Michael Stewart. The Black man is definitely the public enemy."

Representing New Black Militancy

A generation after COINTELPRO, Black radicalism had gone underground. Chuck's striking logo for Public Enemy—a silhouette of a young black man in a gunsight—suggested exactly why. But Public Enemy and the other crew that most represented the bumrush aesthetic, Boogie Down Productions, used their album covers to depict the return of the black radical.

P.E.'s cover for *Yo! Bum Rush the Show* and B.D.P.'s cover for *Criminal Minded* depicted the crews in dim-palled basements, readying themselves to bring black militancy back into the high noon of the Reagan day. Scott La Rock and KRS-1 were bunkered down in the Bronx with handguns, ammo belt, grenade, and brick cell phone. Whether or not they intended to, they recalled southern revolutionary Robert F. Williams's bracing 1962 Black power manifesto, *Negroes with Guns*.

In 1959, Williams, an integrationist who supported armed self-defense, was thrown out of the NAACP. But his ideas helped theorize the shift from Civil Rights nonviolence to Black Power confrontation. In 1967, Huey Newton set Williams's concept in motion, using a California law that allowed individuals to carry loaded firearms in public. His Black Panther Party began brandishing rifles at rallies in the parks and streets of Oakland. When a white legislator tried to overturn the law, the Panthers stormed into the California State Capitol and national consciousness.

Those days had been long since eclipsed by counterrevolution and crack. But Public Enemy tapped back into that urgent theatricality when they called themselves "the Black Panthers of rap." On the shadowy basement shot for the cover of *Yo! Bum rush The Show*, Chuck D was the rightstarter/"riot starter," the only one bathed in Muslim white. Professor Griff looked in from the right in a red beret. Flavor Flav leaned his hand forward as if out of DONDI's *Children of the Grave* burner to consecrate the wax. Another black hand reached down from the corner to press the turntable's Start button to begin the revolution. Across the bottom ran the punchline, perfectly pitched and in repetition: THE GOVERNMENT'S RESPONSIBLE . . . THE GOVERNMENT'S RESPONSIBLE . . . THE GOVERNMENT'S RESPONSIBLE . . .

Old school rappers—and most of the new schoolers, for that matter—invited comparison with entertainers like Cab Calloway, Pigmeat Markham, Rufus

Thomas, Slim Gaillard. But Public Enemy and Boogie Down Productions pointed back to the voices of Black radicalism, heard on the albums of the Watts Prophets, the Last Poets, H. Rap Brown, and Gil Scott-Heron. While the new political radicals were out in the streets and on the campuses fighting apartheid and racism, Public Enemy and Boogie Down Productions repped the new cultural radical vanguard. Preparing to emerge from the darkness, they demanded to be heard as the expression of a new generation's definition of blackness.

The New Vanguard

The key issue of the '80s was representation. The political radicals saw overwhelming whiteness in institutions of power and fought for multiculturalism and diversity. The cultural radicals saw an ocean of negative images and tried to reverse the tide with their own visions.

From Fort Greene, a filmmaker named Spike Lee crashed through the gates of the movie industry with independently produced box-office hits, *She's Gotta Have It* and *School Daze*, unapologetic slices of Black life that refused to cater to *Superfly* blaxploitation cliches or Eddie Murphy crossover expectations. During the '70s, after the success of Melvin Van Peebles's breakthrough, *Sweet Sweetback's Baadasssss Song*, Hollywood had co-opted and finally crushed Black indie filmmaking sensibilities. In the '80s, communities of color boycotted Hollywood for the "cultural insensitivity" of films like *Fort Apache: The Bronx* and *Year of the Dragon*. But with Lee's success, Black filmmakers—including Robert Townsend, Keenen Ivory Wayans, Charles Burnett, John Singleton, Warrington and Reginald Hudlin and Allen and Albert Hughes—again received cautious studio backing.

Like Spike Lee, Chuck and his crew were ready to storm the citadel. He says, "We were all gonna bumrush the business from a bunch of different angles, be it radio, journalism, records." Chuck and Harry Allen, who had begun writing for the *Brooklyn City Sun* and *The Village Voice*, regarded mass media as inherently hostile to Black people. Allen, the "media assassin," coined the term "hip-hop activism" to describe how they could turn their culture into a weapon of resistance.

For the hip-hop generation, popular culture became the new frontline of the struggle. While the political radicals fought a rear-guard defense against right-wing attacks on the victories of the Civil Rights and Black Power movements, the cultural radicals stormed the machines of mythmaking. Their intention was not only to take their message into the media, but take over the media with their message. Pop music, rap radio, indie film, cultural journalism—these could all be staging areas for guerilla strikes.

Suckas Never Play Me

After Public Enemy finished *Yo! Bum Rush the Show*, Chuck came down to reconnect with Harry. Chuck was angry that, while white critics were excoriating him for his pro-Black nationalism, Black radio had remained indifferent to Public Enemy's music and message.

Black radio was a medium that survived on a paradox: integration had made it both obsolete and more necessary than ever. Before the '60s, Black radio had been a crucial space for marginalized Black voices. As the 1970s proceeded, it began to reflect the desires of a professional class trying to make good in the white world. The reactionary 1980s demanded an outlet for a resurgent rage against racism that united the middle class and the so-called underclass. But, caught up in the crossover, black radio was now afraid of being "too black." Chuck found this state of affairs maddening.

He and Harry sat down to plot an attack. The result was an article in the February 1988 issue of *Black Radio Exclusive*, an industry magazine targeted at Black music executives. In the interview, Chuck unleashed his 2,000-pound Uzi on the Black bourgeoisie. He said, "R&B *teaches* you to shuffle your feet, be laid back, don't be offensive, don't make no waves because, *look at us! We're fitting in as well as we can!*"[14]

Picking up a copy of *BRE*, he read it aloud: " '*Favorite Car*: Mercedes Sports. *Favorite vacation spot*: Brazil . . . Look at them! They're going for Mercedes, Audis and BMWs . . . And this is what all these boot-lickin', handkerchief-head, materialistic niggers want!"

Harry, playing the straight man, protested, "But Chuck, *BRE* is a music trade journal, not a mass circulation newspaper or magazine."

"But even so, Black radio has its responsibilities. The question they ought to be answering is, 'How we gonna make our listeners, the Black nation, rise?' " Chuck said, alluding to a never-aired rap classic by Brother D and The Collective Effort. "The juggernaut of white media never stops. We have to build a system that consistently combats and purifies that info that Black America gets through the media. Instead, Black radio is pushing a format that promises 'More Music, Less Talk,' which is the worst thing.

"The point is that there's no hard information in any of these formats. Where's the news about our lives in this country? Whether or not radio plays us, millions of people listen to rap because rap is America's TV station. Rap gives you the news on all phases of life, good and bad, pretty and ugly: drugs, sex, education, love, money, war, peace—you name it."[15]

In time, this idea would harden into Chuck's most famous soundbite, that rap was Black America's CNN, an alternative, youth-controlled media network that could pull a race fragmented by integration back together again. Here was the meaning of the media bumrush: to force media—Black or white—inimical to the interests of young Blacks to expose itself, and to break open a space for these voiceless to represent themselves more truthfully.

At the end of the article, in bold, read this disclaimer: "The interview with Chuck D in no way reflects the views of Columbia Records."

Never Walk Alone

And so the Trojan horse rolled through the gates. Bill Adler and indie publicist Leyla Turkkan pitched Chuck D to rock editors and writers as "the new Bob Dylan." In a year, Chuck D had probably done more interviews than any other rapper to that point. "Our interviews," Chuck says, "were better than most people's shows."

Chuck treated his mostly white interrogators as adversaries. He often mau-maued them, as if to extract a toll for every patronizing indignity and every highway robbery ever suffered by an old-schooler. He had never forgotten how the media treated Run DMC, and this antagonistic stance remained a constant for Public Enemy's first decade. When Harry Allen later became the crew's publicist, he added the additional honorific of "Director of Enemy Relations."

The British tabloid music press found this package irresistible, and with a strange mixture of fanboy irony, Frankfurt School skepticism and thinly disguised racial fear, they began calling Public Enemy the world's most dangerous band. Their music was so good it was scary. Their idea that rap should advance the radicalism of the Black Panthers and the Black Muslims—and that the white media's role was simply to transmit these messages—was even scarier.

In fact, Public Enemy was still trying to figure out what it was about. Stephney watched from the Def Jam offices as Chuck went out on the road and had an epiphany. Chuck told a reporter, "When kids have no father image, who fulfills that role? The drug dealer in the neighborhood? Motherfucking Michael Jordan? Rappers come along and say, 'This is everything you want to be. You want to be like me, I'm your peer, and I talk to you every day.' So the kid is being raised by LL Cool J, because LL Cool J is talking to the kid more directly than his parents ever did."[16]

Public Enemy's worldview began with a scathing generational critique of Black America. In a 1987 interview with Simon Reynolds, Chuck laid out his view of history:

> There was a complacency in the '70s after the civil rights victories of the '60s. Plus some of our leaders were killed off, others sold out or fled. There was propaganda by the state to make it seem like things had changed, a policy of tokenism elevating a few Blacks to positions of prominence, on TV shows and stuff, while the rest was held down. Blacks couldn't understand how they'd suddenly got these advantages, and so they forgot, they got lazy, they failed to teach their young what they had been taught in the sixties about our history and culture, about how *tight* we should be. And so there was a loss of *identity*—we began to think we were accepted as Americans, when in fact we *still* face a double-standard every minute of our lives.[17]

Public Enemy's theme was Black collectivity, the one thing that had been lost in the post–Civil Rights bourgeois individualist goldrush. Over the years, rap groups had shrunk down to duos, but Public Enemy brought the crew back. They rolled deep, because Black people always overcame through strength in numbers. The S1Ws epitomized the crew's values: strength, unity, self-defense and survival skills. They carried plastic Uzis as props to show that they were not slaves. They were in control because they were armed with knowledge. Violence became their primary, and most often misunderstood, metaphor.

Stephney says, "In dealing with the apparent day-to-day, minute-by-minute cultural power that Chuck saw Public Enemy wield, I think he truly and legitimately believed that you could create a generation of young people who had a drive and ambition to make serious change and reform within the community."

He adds, "Was it something that was mapped out by all of us at 510 South Franklin—a ten-point Panther-like plan on how we were going to take over the media? No." As the crew moved out into the world and encountered resistance from white journalists who took their symbolism on its face, they began freestyling their message. Stephney chuckles, "A good portion of Public Enemy was jazz improvisation."

Doing Contradiction Right

Like Bambaataa, Chuck had been raised within his mother's embrace of Black Panther—styled revolutionary nationalism and anticolonial Pan-Africanism. On his first presidential election ballot, he voted for Gus Hall and Angela Davis, the Communist Party ticket. In rhyme, he boasted that he was "rejected and accepted as a communist." He told a writer from the glossy teen zine *Right On!*: "We are talking about bringing back the Black Panther movement and Communism. That's dead serious. That's going a little too deep, but that's our edge."[18]

Yet he had also been raised on James Brown's "Say It Loud (I'm Black and I'm Proud)," and "I Don't Want Nobody to Give Me Nothing (Open the Door, I'll Get It Myself)," anthems that seemed not only to speak to the Black Panther's Sacramento takeover, but to the rise of the Booker T. Washington—like Black conservative movement that would push for economic self-sufficiency and the end of civil-rights programs like affirmative action. When Public Enemy was opening for the Beastie Boys, Professor Griff played cassettes of Farrakhan and Khallid Abdul Muhammad on the tour bus. Chuck listened closely. Here were the ultimate public enemies.

So Public Enemy's worldview did not adhere to traditional politics. Stephney, for instance, worked closely with civil rights organizations, and closely watched mainstream politics, but refused to join any political party. As Minister of Information, Griff told reporters Public Enemy was drawing on the thinking of Malcolm X, Mao Zedong, the Ayatollah Khomeini, Moammar Khaddafi, Winnie and Nelson Mandela and Minister Farrakhan.[19] As for Chuck, a self-declared communist captivated by Farrakhan, he says now, "I don't know what I was. I definitely wasn't a capitalist. And I definitely wasn't American."

In all of the crew's frequent discussions of politics, Stephney says, ideology had never come into question. Stephney admits, "In retrospect, I *wish* we had legitimate discourse about economic systems and what made sense and what didn't." In his autobiography, Chuck did not describe his core philosophy in terms of ideology but instead something close to fraternal responsibility.

What Flavor believes and what Griff believes may be two different things, but they were both a part of Public Enemy. What Drew believes and what James Allen believes may be two different things. It's my job to bring it to a center point and say what's true for all of us. "We're Black, we fight for our people and we respect our fellow human beings." Once you start getting into tit-for-tat rhetoric, then you fall into a sea full of contradiction.[20]

Stephney says, "Chuck sees much of what he does through the lens of sports. Teams. Teamwork. Working together as much as you possibly can until it may become too difficult on certain issues." The concept of the public enemy brought together Huey Newton and Elijah Muhammad, Assata Shakur and Sister Ava Muhammad. Teamwork—an NBA-era take on Black collectivity—was a manifestation of Black love.

But white and Black critics alike began to bait Chuck and Griff, especially on questions of racial separatism, homosexuality and militarism. Griff and Chuck often responded with lines straight from Farrakhan's and Khallid Abdul Muhammad's speeches. It was agit-prop, theater, call and response. It got the desired rise out of journalists.

They read the crew's militaristic symbolism, Chuck's aggressive approach, Griff's sometimes bizarre pronouncements and Public Enemy's encompassing embrace of Black Marxism and Black Islam as revealing of undercurrents of violent fascism. After interviewing Chuck and Griff, Simon Reynolds wrote:

Ahem. What *can* I say? Rectitude in the face of chaos. An admiration for Colonel Khadaffi ("Blacks in America didn't know who to side with"). Harmonious totality. No faggots. Uniform and drill. It all sounds quite logical and needed, the way they tell it. And it's all very very dodgy indeed.

If there's one thing more scary than a survivalist, it's a whole bunch of survivalists organised into a regiment . . . Fortunately, Public Enemy and Security of The First World are sufficiently powerless ("52 and growing") to remain fascinating to us pop swots, rather than disturbing . . . Let's hope it stays that way.[21]

Despite abhorring the crew's politics, the British music press took Public Enemy seriously enough to declare *Yo! Bum Rush the Show* one of the best albums of the year. Back home it was another story.

One key critic, John Leland, who wrote for *SPIN* and *The Village Voice*, set the tone early, ducking the group's politics entirely when he confessed that he found Chuck boring. "I like a good time," he wrote, "and when Flavor Flav says he's got girls on his jock like ants on candy, or threatens to scatter suckers' brains from here to White Plains . . . yo that's when I'm hooked."[22]

Stung by the criticism, Chuck told a British reporter he had gone looking for Leland at an industry reception to "fuck him up bad."[23] Later Chuck wrote "Don't Believe the Hype" and "Bring the Noise," dumping his critics in the same wastebin as racist cops, corrupt conservatives and Black radio programmers. It was the first shot in what would become an increasingly vituperative relationship with the American press.

But the group also agreed to play a National Writer's Union benefit with Sonic Youth to support the freelancers' bitter fight for recognition against *The Village Voice*'s management. "They do contradiction right," wrote *Voice* columnist R. J. Smith, "like publicly dissing music crits for what they've said about Public Enemy and then coming off by far the most militant in their solidarity with writers. Like quoting Malcolm X and saying Blacks deserve $250 billion in reparations *and* playing a benefit on the 18th for Jesse."[24]

The New School Rises

None of this press stuff would matter much if they didn't sell records. And at that point, the album had barely sold 100,000 copies. Against the Def Jam/Rush roster—with Run DMC, Whodini, LL Cool J and the Beastie Boys all pushing platinum-plus—it was a huge disappointment.

The record did decently in the south and the midwest, but New York City wasn't feeling the group. Melle Mel heckled the crew at their first show at the Latin Quarter. Mr. Magic played "Public Enemy #1" only once, making a point of saying that he hated it. And in Queens, Magic's DJ, Marlon "Marley Marl" Williams was making them look played-out with his sonic innovations.

Marley had been a studio apprentice to Arthur Baker, watching him struggle with the early, prohibitively expensive Fairlight sampler. In 1983, Marley launched his own producing career with a classic single, "Sucker DJs (I Will Survive)," featuring his smooth-rapping then-girlfriend, Dimples D. On his early dance records, like Aleem's 1984 club hit, "Release Yourself," he used a sampler to repeat and pitch up and down vocal snippets: "Release yourself! Re-re-rererere-rererere-release yourself! Yo-yo-yo-yourself!" While trying to sample a voice for another song on his affordable new E-mu Emulator, he caught a snare snap. Punching it a few times, he suddenly realized the machine's latent rhythmic capabilities.

On the 1986 hit "The Bridge" by MC Shan, he revealed the fruits of his discovery, with a booming loop of The Honeydrippers' "Impeach the President" drum break. No more tinny, programmed DMX or Linn drums, which stiffened the beat and reduced most rappers to sing-songy rhyming. On top, Marl kept his vocalists bathed in billowing Rubinesque arena echoes, but on the bottom, the groove suddenly felt slippery. Inevitably, his rappers responded with more intricate rhymes.

By contrast, Hank, Eric and Keith had made "Public Enemy #1" the old-fashioned way—with Eric banging out the drums in real time, and a long two-inch tape loop of "Blow Your Head" that stretched across the room and around a microphone stand. Marl's sampler breakthrough forever altered rap production techniques. It wasn't clear Public Enemy could stay competitive.

The Black Belt had bred a new school, and these artists—Biz Markie, De La Soul, JVC Force, Craig Mack (then known as MC EZ) and EPMD, even their homies, Son of Bazerk, Serious Lee Fine, True Mathematics and Kings of Pressure—were breathing down P.E.'s necks. And then there was Marley Marl's roommate, a DJ from the Black 'burbs of Queens named Eric Barrier, and his rapper, a Five Percenter from Wyandanch, Long Island, named William Griffin, Jr. (no relation to Professor Griff) who called himself Rakim Allah.

Can't Hold It Back

Rakim was about to graduate from high school, where he was the star quarterback, when a mutual friend introduced him to Eric B. The two hit it off, and Barrier asked Marl about recording something in their studio. They headed into Marl's studio and cut Rakim's demo, "Check Out My Melody." MC Shan sat in.

Rakim obviously had lyrics, battle rhymes funneled through Five Percenter millenarian poetics. He didn't just slay MCs, he took them out in three sets of seven. "My unusual style will confuse you a while," he rhymed. "If I was water, I'd flow in the Nile."

Shan and Marl weren't sure they understood this guy. At the time Shan's excitable high-pitched style ruled New York City. But Rakim refused to raise his voice. "Me and Marley would look at each other like, 'What kind of rap style is that? That shit is wack,'" Shan recalled.[25] "More energy, man!" he yelled at Rakim.[26]

Figuring "My Melody" was too sluggish, they gave Rakim another beat that was almost ten beats-per-minute faster. Based on Fonda Rae's "Over Like a Fat Rat" and James Brown's "Funky President" and alluding to Marl's by-now famous jacking of "Impeach the President," the concept became "Eric B. Is President," Marl and Shan listened to Rakim's intro in amazement:

I came in the door I said it before
I never let the mic magnetize me no more

In the lyric, Rakim described the act of rhyming as if it were a pit bull on a long leash, an undertow pulling into a deep ocean of words—above all, a dangerous habit from which there was no return:

But it's biting me, fighting me, inviting me to rhyme
I can't hold it back
I'm looking for the line

Rakim rocked a weird mix of braggadocio and self-consciousness, a metarhyme—encompassing the paralysis of stage-fright and the release of the moment of first utterance, all delivered with an uncanny sense of how to use silence and syncopation, lines spilling through bars, syllables catching off-beats, it made them believers. Rap had found its Coltrane.

Rakim came from a musical family. His mother was a jazz and opera singer. His aunt was R&B legend Ruth Brown. His brothers were session musicians who had worked on early rap records. He was a gifted saxophonist and had participated in statewide student competitions. He switched from tenor to baritone sax because he preferred the deeper tone.

The Griffins had left Brooklyn to come to Wyandanch, an unincorporated town of seven thousand, one of the oldest in the Black Belt and deteriorating into one of the most troubled. Blacks began moving there during the 1950s, expanding southward toward the wealthy white beach community of Babylon. By the end of the decade whites in Babylon rezoned its northern border from residential to industrial. From there, Wyandanch went downhill.

William was a smart student with a lean athleticism and a nose for trouble that kept him close to the streets. By his teens, he was a graffiti writer turned stick-up kid, getting high, staying paid, holding down corners in Wyandanch and spinning drunkenly out of the projects in Fort Greene, before he became righteous, took the name Ra King Islam Master Allah, recircled Strong Island and Brooklyn to build from cipher to cipher.

The graf burners on his bedroom wall were covered over by primer. Photos of Elijah Muhammad, Malcolm X and Minister Louis Farrakhan went up. He met Eric, Marl and Shan, cut the record, abandoned a football scholarship to the State University at Stony Brook, signed with Rush Management, and became a rap legend.

Rakim never smiled. Draped in African gold, inside Dapper-Dan customized *faux*-Gucci suits, he stood tall in a way that assured he was in supreme control of his body. He was, as he put it, "serious as cancer." He asked rhetorical questions like, "Who can keep the average dancer hyper as a heart attack?" Chuck D and Rakim had come from similar circumstances and had similar aspirations for themselves and the race, but they had different ways of seeking their utopias. As Greg Tate wrote, "Chuck D's forte is the overview, Rakim's is the innerview."

Rakim had joined the Nation of Gods and Earths, better known as the Five Percenters, in 1985, the year that Supreme Mathematics signified as: "*Build Power.*" Founded in Harlem (renamed Mecca) in 1963 by a charismatic former student minister of the Nation of Islam, Clarence 13X, their core belief was taken from Lost-Found Lesson Number 2. Eighty-five percent of the people were uncivilized, mentally deaf, dumb and blind slaves; 10 percent were bloodsuckers of the poor; and 5 percent were the poor righteous teachers with knowledge of self, enlightened teachers of freedom, justice and equality, destined to civilize the uncivilized.

Like Bambaataa, Rakim was now on a lifetime mission to lift the word from the street into the spiritual. Whether he could escape the social prisons represented by Fort Greene and Wyandanch was immaterial. Rakim told a journalist, "You're dealing with heaven while you're walking through hell. When I say heaven, I don't mean up in the clouds, because heaven is no higher than your head, and hell is no lower than your feet."[27]

"It's 120 degrees of lessons," he told Harry Allen, "and you gotta complete it by Knowledge, which is 120, Wisdom, another 120, and Understanding, which is 360 degrees. That's what I'm saying. 360 degrees I revolve. And 360 degrees is a complete circle—a cipher. So you must *complete* it."[28]

Closing the Circle

In rhyme, Chuck compared himself to Coltrane, but he had more in common with Miles Davis, whose earthy middle-class rage always boiled beneath the mask of blue minimalist cool. The streetwise mystic Rakim was closer to Coltrane, and "I Know You Got Soul" was Rakim's "Giant Steps," a marvel of rhythmic precision and indelible imagery, a masterful declaration of transcendent black identity and a certifiable crowd-pleaser.

Based on the Bobby Byrd song of the same name and featuring a monstrous Funkadelic drumroll by Ben Powers, Jr., "Soul" began with unusual flattery to its audience—an apology for keeping them waiting. It described writing as a difficult sacrament, but a necessary rite to uplift the race. In the end, the performance of the words—like a triumphant Ali title bout—became an act of deliverance.

"I Know You Got Soul" dropped only weeks after *Yo! Bum Rush the Show.* When Chuck and Hank heard it, they realized that hip-hop's aesthetic and political development had suddenly accelerated. Envious and yet confident that the game had somehow shifted decidedly in their direction, they retreated to 510 South Franklin to close the circle that Eric B. & Rakim had begun.

"We knew we had to make something that was aggressive," Hank says. "Chuck's voice is so powerful and his tone is so rich that you can't put him on smooth, silky, melodic music. It's only fitting to put a hailstorm around him, a tornado behind him, so that when his vocals come across, the two complement each other."

Unlike Marley Marl's method—which flowed with the possibilities of the new technology, privileging sampling and mixing over arranging—the Bomb Squad mapped out the samples in the song's key and structure, piled them atop each other, then played them by hand as if they were a band. A Bomb Squad composition mounted tension against all-too-brief release.

Their musical method mirrored their worldview. "We were timing freaks," Hank says. "[W]e might push the drum sample to make it a little bit out of time, to make you feel uneasy. We're used to a perfect world, to seeing everything revolve in a circle. When that circle is off by a little bit, that's weird . . . It's not predictable."[29] Public Enemy was never about elevating to perfect mathematics or merging with sleek machines, it was about wrestling with the messy contradictions of truth. "It's *tightrope* music," Chuck said, "in confrontation with itself."[60]

Hank and Chuck pulled out James Brown's "Funky Drummer," the not-yet-famous Clyde Stubblefield break, and the JBs' 1970 single, "The Grunt, Part 1," which had an elemental, squawking intro reminiscent of "Blow Your Head." On his Ensoniq Mirage sampler, they grabbed two seconds of Catfish Collins's guitar, Bobby Byrd's piano and, most important, Robert McCollough's sax squeal, sampled it at a low rate to grit it up, and then pounded it into ambulance claustrophobia. Underneath, Flavor Flav made the Akai drum machine boom and stutter. The only release came in a break that layered a live go-go groove, funky guitar, a horn-section blast and the drums from Jefferson Starship's "Rock Music." When Terminator X transformed Chubb Rock's shout, "Rock and roll!", "Rebel" staked a claim to more than soul. The effect was hypnotic and relentless.

From an intro as memorable as Rakim's through an ending that declared it was "my time," Chuck brought pure boxing-ring drama, with Rakim as muse and opponent. Chuck offered props where they were due—"I got soul too"—but reserved for himself the title of "the voice of power." Rakim had rapped, "It ain't where you're from, it's where you're at," an epigram not at all unlike "Who feels it, knows it." Chuck flipped that into an explicit call for Black solidarity: "No matter what the name, we're all the same—pieces in one big chess game." His lines encapsulated P.E.'s game-face competitiveness, anti-authoritarian howl and gleefully punning, polycultural, signifying trashing of Standard English:

> Impeach the president
> Pulling out the raygun (Reagan)
> Zap the next one
> I could be ya shogun!

"Man, you got to slow down," Flavor yelled over the break. "Man, you're losing 'em!"

Titled "Rebel Without a Pause," it was the perfect balance to "I Know You Got Soul." "Soul" moved the crowd in divine, timeless ritual. "Rebel" was a Black riot. Stephney took the record to club DJs at the Latin Quarter and the Rooftop, places that had dissed P.E., and watched from the booths as the fader slid over to "Rebel" and the room hit the boiling point like a kettle. It was John Brown playing "Soul Power," Kool Herc spinning Mandrill's "Fencewalk" or Grandmaster Flash dropping Baby Huey's "Listen to Me" all over again. "Just to see kids go crazy," Stephney remembers. "In many instances, fights started."

"Rebel," and its follow-up, "Bring the Noise"—in which Chuck ripped crack-peddling, Black incarceration and the death penalty, and then compared critics' condemnation of his support for Farrakhan to being shot by cops, all in just the first verse—captured the tensions of the time and externalized them. The records stormed the airwaves, boomboxes and car stereos that summer and fall. They became unavoidable. Public Enemy sounded like the new definition of black power—smarter, harder, faster, leaner and winning.

A Nation of Millions: A Las Vegas
Chicano goes home to beats and rhymes.

Photo © B+

13

Follow for Now

The Question of Post–Civil Rights Black Leadership

It's my sense that this is the summer it's all gonna come down.
—White American film critic to Spike Lee at Cannes Festival[1]

Oh 1989, man. I planned for it to be crazy. But shit.

—Chuck D

There would be no dead air on Public Enemy's second album, *It Takes a Nation of Millions to Hold Us Back,* not a second wasted. "Armageddon has been in effect," Professor Griff boomed on the live clip opening the album, "go get a late pass!"

Public Enemy's presentation had crystallized. They positioned themselves as heirs to James Brown's loud, Black and proud tradition, putting their black vinyl inside a re-creation of the soul-on-lockdown album cover of Brown's *Revolution of the Mind.* Chuck summed up how they had adapted JB's aesthetic: "Repetitive repetition, relentless—no escape. He took it to the bridge, we take it over the bridge. Over and over. Again and again."[2]

Across the bottom of the cover ran a quote lifted from the Bar-Kays at Wattstax: FREEDOM IS A ROAD SELDOM TRAVELED BY THE MULTITUDE. On the back, the crew glared upward, dressed for combat, their feet soiling an American flag on the prison floor. Flavor Flav's clock read somewhere round midnight. If you weren't getting yourself free in this hour of chaos, they seemed to say, your mind would always be behind bars.

Opening with an urgent speech by Nation of Islam "hip-hop minister" Dr. Khallid Abdul Muhammad, "Night of the Living Baseheads" was their sample-drenched *tour de force*—the emergency pulse of "Rebel Without a Pause" reversed, quickened, chopped up, disrupted and displaced to convey crack's poison attack. Bomb Squad alarms were more ironic than the Ohio Players' arson-era "Fire," more dramatic than the Clash's roots rebel rock, "White Riot." After *Nation of Millions,* the siren became a generational motif, a sign of provocation and reaction, not just through rap, but post-freestyle house (via the New York producer Todd Terry, whose best track was done under the pseudonym Black Riot), and the anarchic British rave scene.

Chuck and Flavor Flav described coming of age in a state of unending war. Even Flavor's showcase, "Cold Lampin," made dark humor of the ever-present danger of instant death. *Nation of Millions* represented organized reaction. "I never live alone, I never walk alone," Chuck rapped on "Louder than a Bomb." "My posse's always ready and they're waitin' in my zone." On the album's centerpiece, an Attica revenge tale called "Black Steel in the Hour of Chaos," he rapped, "I'm a Black man—and I could never be a veteran."

"Simply put," Harry Allen wrote in *The City Sun,* "this is the album that ends the '80s."[3]

But what were the '90s supposed to be about? That's where it got messy.

Over the Rainbow

On the campuses, the political and cultural rads of color who had once found common inspiration in the anti-apartheid struggle now seemed to be moving in different directions.

The political rads formed organizations like the Black Student Leadership Network, ran the United States Student Association, and formed the backbone of resurgent labor and community organizing movements. Their Third Worldist philosophy—drawn from the anticolonial writings of Franz Fanon and some of the last speeches of Malcolm X and Martin Luther King, Jr.—was summed up in the name of the powerful student coalition that had emerged at U.C. Berkeley during the anti-apartheid movement, United People of Color.

At the same time, cultural nationalists like Karenga and Molefi Kete Asante championed Afrocentricity as an intellectual program that would decenter Eurocentric educational bias, recover and reclaim the lost ancient roots of African glory, and recenter African thought and experience in the production of knowledge and self. They developed a curriculum based on an alternative canon of Chiekh Anta Diop, Chancellor Williams, John Henrik Clarke, Martin Bernal and their own writings. Their emphasis on self-esteem and self-actualization dovetailed with the street ministries of the Nation of Islam and the Five Percenters.

As the cultural rads spread the gospel of Afrocentricity from the Afro-American Studies programs to charter schools, black bookstores, and self-organized study groups, the political rads got out the vote for Jesse Jackson. His second presidential run in 1988 was pitched as a campaign of hope. At each whistle stop, he led rainbow crowds in chants of "Keep hope alive." It might have seemed strange, but after eight years of Reagan these white heartland farmers and Chicano farmworkers, Black factory workers and Asian seamstresses wanted to *believe*. The campaign would be a culmination of the '60s, a grand synthesis of the civil rights and Black power agendas, a united front of liberation movements saved from bullet nihilism by ballot-box optimism.

Jackson's campaign seemed to come out of nowhere. On Super Tuesday, Jackson took first or second in sixteen of the twenty-one Democratic primaries, and surged ahead of the field in total votes. In the next primary in Michigan, he crushed future presidential candidates Michael Dukakis and Al Gore, winning 55 percent of the vote. In Wisconsin, the next stop, his campaign was hitting new heights of fervor. Then Jackson ran headlong into an accusation he could never disprove.

The problem had begun during the 1984 campaign. While waiting for his plane one day in January, he beckoned to the Black reporters, "Let's talk Black talk."[4] During the course of his light rambling, he referred to Jewish people as "Hymies" and to New York City as "Hymietown." One of the reporters, Milton Coleman, reported the comments to another writer at his paper, the *Washington Post*, who ran them a month later in an article with the headline, PEACE WITH AMERICAN JEWS ELUDES JACKSON. Jackson was soon being called anti-Semitic.

Jackson's relationship to Minister Louis Farrakhan attracted close scrutiny. The two were old Chicago friends. When the Secret Service refused to protect Jackson, Farrakhan sent the Fruit of Islam. When Jackson traveled to Syria to secure the release of African-American fighter pilot Robert Goodman, he asked Farrakhan to join him. Now, at an assembly at his mosque, Farrakhan defended Jackson against the charges, pointing to him and saying, "If you harm this brother, I warn you in the name of Allah this will be the last one you harm."

Jewish critics were already incensed at Jackson for his position on Palestinian rights. They had widely circulated a 1979 photo of him embracing Palestinian Liberation Organization leader Yasir Arafat, taken during a meeting to dissuade Arafat from terrorism. Now they leaped to sandbag him. Nathan Perlmutter of the Anti-Defamation League later said, "There's an irony with 'Hymie.' On the scale of insults, 'Hymie' isn't a yellow star pinned to your sleeve. [But] it's what opened up [the chance] for somebody like myself to be heard on a dimension of Jesse Jackson's character. He could light candles every Friday night, and grow side curls, and it still wouldn't matter. He's still a whore."[5]

At the same time, the mainstream media combed Farrakhan's NOI addresses for evidence of anti-Semitism. In a March speech, Farrakhan seemed to threaten *Post* reporter Coleman and his wife, and was widely misquoted by the media as calling Hitler "great." Farrakhan's actual words had referred to "Hitler's evil toward Jewish people," and he later said that he meant Hitler was "wickedly great," but certainly he could not have been naive as to how such comments might play in the press.

In June, returning from a visit to Libya, Farrakhan condemned Israel by stating: "Now that nation called Israel never has had any peace in forty years and she will never have any peace because there can be no peace structured on injustice, thievery, lying and deceit and using the name of God to shield your dirty religion under his holy and righteous name."[6] Media reports held that he had called the Jewish faith a "gutter religion." Farrakhan biographer Arthur Magida would later note that Farrakhan had also used the term "dirty religion" to refer to incorrect interpretations of NOI theology.[7] But the damage was done. When the U.S. Senate voted unanimously to censure Farrakhan, Jackson quickly repudiated him.

And yet, to many in the Black community, the minister was speaking a deeper truth. While defending Jackson, Farrakhan had said, "We know that Blacks and Jews have had a good relationship in the past. We've gotten along well, because you're a suffering people and so are we. But my dear Jewish friends, you understand that everything comes of age. We cannot define our self-interest in terms of your self-interest."[8] In New York City, the national center of both African-American and Jewish-American power, the Black-Jewish coalition was in the final throes of its spectacular collapse.

In December 1987, the Palestinian *intifada* broke out in the West Bank and the Gaza Strip, instantly polarizing Jewish-American politics. The defense of Israel became a defense of Jewish-American identity itself. Now, just as some Black nationalists conflated Zionism with racism, Jewish-American nationalist groups like the Anti-Defamation League conflated anti-Zionism with anti-Semitism.

But as Black political commentator Adolph Reed pointed out, Israel and Farrakhan also provided symbolic cover for issues closer to home, ones that dated at least to Ocean Hill/Brownsville. Jackson's pro–affirmative action, pro-Black empowerment agenda could potentially upset Jewish privilege. At the same time, Jackson's "Black talk" revealed that upwardly mobile Blacks no longer perceived the Jewish middle-class as an ally but a threat. The result on both sides was, in Reed's words, "a meanness of spirit and small-mindedness."[9]

So the 1988 Wisconsin primary became crucial for Jackson and his opponents. On the eve of the primary, New York City mayor Ed Koch made his own Jewishness an issue and baited Jackson: "Would [Jackson] support any candidate who praised Botha in South Africa? I wouldn't. But on the other hand, he's praising Arafat, and he thinks maybe Jews and other supporters of Israel should vote for him." If Jews were to vote for him, Koch added, "they've got to be *crazy*—in the same way that they'd be crazy if they were Black and voted for someone who was praising Botha and the racist supporters of the South African administration."[10] With Koch's comments receiving extensive coverage, Jackson lost Wisconsin to Dukakis by twenty points.

The New York primary was to follow, and at almost every stop in New York City, Jackson had to answer to his "Hymietown" remarks and his relationship with Farrakhan. He continued his penitence—against the backdrop of the intensifying *intifada*—but it was like he had gone backward four years. Many Jews were angered anew, while many Blacks wondered what else Jackson could do to be forgiven. At one end of the unbridgeable gap was the Jewish Defense Organization, a tiny cadre of white-collar militiamen who showed up at

Jackson's appearances to call him a "Black Nazi." At the other, the Nation of Islam revived a passel of anti-Semitic tracts, including Henry Ford's *The International Jew*, and the long-discredited forgery, *The Protocols of the Elders of Zion*.

When the New York polls closed in 1988, Jackson had secured 94 percent of the Black vote, 17 percent of the white vote and a mere 8 percent of the Jewish vote. He lost to Dukakis by fourteen points. A former aide called it the most disheartening electoral defeat Jackson had ever faced.[11] The Rainbow dream had been dashed against the rocks of the Black-Jewish problem.

Despite collecting 1,200 delegates and 7 million actual votes and coming in second to Michael Dukakis, the closest any Black man had ever come to becoming president, Jackson felt that he was forced to beg to be Dukakis's running mate. In a final dis, he learned from a journalist that Dukakis had picked milquetoast Lloyd Bentsen as the vice presidential candidate. In the general election, the Dukakis-Bentsen ticket took Wisconsin and New York, but lost forty states to Bush and Quayle.

Perhaps Public Enemy had been prophetic in an unintended way. At the beginning of "Rebel Without a Pause," the Bomb Squad seemed to salute Jackson's decision to run again. But rather than using one of Jackson's signature affirmations, they sampled him introducing a protest song from The Soul Children at Wattstax. Divorced from context, Jackson now sounded uncertain and troubled: "Brothers and sisters, I don't know what this world is coming to."

After Jackson's candidacy was finished, Professor Griff said, "Not only didn't he win, he didn't even go out fighting."[12]

The Search for New Heroes

Perhaps the most vexing question of the post–civil rights generation—raised on *Sesame Street* and *Roots*, King's "I Have a Dream" speech and *The Autobiography of Malcolm X*, and living within the coils of an unsleeping, omnipresent, icon-hungry media—has been: "Who will be our leaders?"

"In our hunger for a charismatic, post-King/Malcolm figure, a vacuum existed," Bill Stephney says. "I don't think that the times of the eighties were any less politically volatile than at any other point in history. The difference was the vacuum of leadership."

In an influential article in 1996 in *Social Policy*, the late black activist Lisa Sullivan, cofounder of the Black Student Leadership Network and one of the first hip-hop intellectuals, laid out the politics—and the stakes—behind Stephney's claim:

> According to a wide range of critics, civil rights advocacy led by traditional civil rights leaders is unresponsive and impotent in this post–civil rights period, which is increasingly characterized by racial intolerance, the renewal of states rights and the dismantling of the federal government's protective domestic social policies and programs.
>
> This harsh critique of the civil rights movement is most pronounced amongst Black youth. . . . Many believe that traditional Black leaders lack the capacity, desire, and ingenuity to address the contemporary crises that destabilize Black working-class life and destroy Black neighborhoods and families.
>
> As a consequence, an entire generation is now profoundly disconnected from Black civic action and civil rights activism. And because traditional social and civic organizations in the Black community have failed to reach out and engage this new generation of post–civil rights citizens, the future of Black institutional and organizational leadership with the vision, capacity, and innovation necessary for the twenty-first century is bleak.[13]

Hip-hoppers embraced the ideas of the exiled and martyred icons of the past while rejecting the legitimacy of their living elders. After Scott La Rock was gunned down on a Bronx street, KRS-1 posed for Boogie Down Productions' second album cover alone, looking from behind a window curtain for enemies below, gripping an Uzi as Malcolm X had his rifle two decades before. In "Rebel Without a Pause," Chuck had declared himself a supporter of JoAnne Chesimard, the former Black Panther and Black Liberation Army member who was about to resurface in Cuba as an exile under a new name, Assata Shakur, and watched her autobiography became a Black bookstore best-seller.

He decided to work Minister Farrakhan's name into his next track, a B-side commissioned for the movie adaptation of Brett Easton Ellis's Gen-X novel, *Less*

Than Zero. That song, "Don't Believe the Hype"—with its line, "The follower of Farrakhan, don't tell me that you understand until you hear the man"—was rejected. But the next one they submitted, "Bring the Noise" was accepted and it was even more explicit: "Farrakhan's a prophet and I think you ought to listen to what he can say to you. What you ought to do is follow for now."

The kids had dumped their gold dookey ropes for African medallions. Some were reading George G. M. James's *Stolen Legacy* and Carter G. Woodson's *The Miseducation of the Negro*. Even the hustlers in Harlem had changed their style. Hip-hop journalist Reginald Dennis recalls, "Cats that were straight murderers were playing 'Self Destruction' on their new 10,000-watt Blaupunkt systems."

When Public Enemy came to Philadelphia, the city declared it "Public Enemy Day" and gave them a parade. "We're in open cars, coming down on Market Street, waving at folks and stuff," says Stephney. "But what struck me, we saw these guys who were at that point in their mid-forties. They had all run back, it seemed, into their apartments and homes and two-story brick houses in Philly and gotten all their old Panther shit out. Got the berets, got the black leather jackets, got their camouflages out and everything. You're seeing these graying forty-something Black men, tears in their eyes, throwing the Black power salute like the revolution has come back.

"I was just like, 'Shit. Okay,' " he sighs. "Yeah, we're the 'Black Panthers of rap." But when you're as young as we were doing all of this stuff—at that point, I was twenty-five—you don't have a clue as to the sort of impact you truly are generating."

Ready or not, leadership was being thrust on the hip-hop generation. The problem of how the new young Black elite would direct its rage and where it would take the race in the new century would be entirely their own.

Natty Cult-Nats vs. Rap Rebels

In a seminal 1989 essay, "The New Black Aesthetic," novelist Trey Ellis celebrated the sons and daughters of the Black middle class who were now at the cutting edge of American cultural and intellectual production. "All those Ezra Jack Keats Black children's books, *Roots* parties, *For Colored Girls* . . . theater excursions and the nationalist Christmastide holiday of Kwanzaa worked," he wrote. "Having scraped their way to relative wealth and, too often, crass materialism, our parents have freed (or compelled) us to bite those hands that fed us and sent us to college."[14]

Yet Ellis also saw a division developing in that rarified group, as plain as questions of style. At a birthday party for Andre Harrell, he noted, "Suzuki Samurai jeeps, Moet champagne, complete Gucci or Louis Vuitton leather outfits, Kangol hats, '[heavy] duty gold' rope necklaces, four-finger rings, and crotch-first machismo are all, for the moment rap *de rigueur*. Most all young, Black intellectuals, on the other hand, wear little, round glasses, Ghanaian, *kinte*-cloth scarves and, increasingly, tiny, neat dreadlocks."[15]

Bill Stephney straddled the line, trying to bridge the Black Belt with the East Village. He recalls, "I was called an 'art-nigger' because I insisted that we all go see *She's Gotta Have It*." Undaunted, he tried to get his homies to join the Black Rock Coalition. After one meeting they decided they weren't having it. "In the mid-eighties, young Black working-class males from Nassau County, Long Island, weren't the most broad-minded people in the world," he chuckles.

Also straddling the line was *Village Voice* critic Greg Tate, a cofounder of the Black Rock Coalition. Tate was a *kente*-cloth diaper baby. His parents were prominent cultural nationalists whose work with H. Rap Brown, Eldridge Cleaver and Amiri Baraka meant, he says, that "I kind of grew up with these Black superheroes around me."

As a teenager, Tate shared Chuck D.'s ambition to become a Black comic book artist. He invented a character, a trumpet player, and went to the library to learn everything he could about music. There he came upon Baraka's book, *Black Music*, which changed his life. He tuned in to Howard University's radio station, WHUR, and its groundbreaking "360 Degrees of the Black Experience" format, and heard the artists Baraka discussed—Coltrane, Coleman, Cherry, Shepp. He got his parents to take him to see Parliament-Funkadelic, War, Mandrill, and Graham Central Station. He attended Howard University during the late 1970s and became part of an avant-garde-in-training, working with jazz artists Geri Allen and Greg Osby, director Julie Dash, and cinematographers Ernest Dickerson and Arthur Jafa. He dropped out to become a father, moved to New York City and tried to make it as a writer.

Tate was raised on cultural nationalism, but had come to agree with the political rads about what he would call "the jiver parts of their program (like the sexist, anti-Semitic, Black supremacist, pseudo-African mumbo jumbo, paramilitary adventurist parts)."[16]

He says, "That movement had its own issues with sexism, homophobia, with multiculturalism. But at the same time, cultural nationalism really created a way to think about everything that people of African descent did as having a basis in a cultural experience, having a philosophical intent behind it. It was a way of responding to a racist environment." High on the possibilities of postmodernist and poststructuralist theory, he vowed to popularize an "anti-essentialist essentialism" and called himself, with a knowing smirk, a "reconstructed cultural nationalist."

When he came on staff in 1987, Tate helped turn *The Village Voice* into the central organ of a new Black public intellectualism, something like a post-integration *Crisis*. Boosted by editors like Thulani Davis and Robert Christgau, Tate and writers like Lisa Jones, Stanley Crouch, Harry Allen, Nelson George, Joan Morgan, Barry Michael Cooper, Carol Cooper, Ben Mapp, Lisa Kennedy and Donald Suggs aggressively complicated black politics and aesthetics from a dazzling diversity of positions—queer, feminist, progressive, conservative. *The Voice* became a spearhead of radical multiculturalism. If *Yo! Bum Rush the Show* was largely interpreted through white popcrit skepticism, *It Takes a Nation of Millions to Hold Us Back* came out amidst the blooming of yet another Black New York cultural renaissance.

Tate was one of the earliest and loudest supporters of Public Enemy. He played the advance cassette of *Nation of Millions* at his own house party in Harlem, and saw firsthand how it shocked a crowd of natty cult-nats into a hyperactive conscious party. He defended Chuck against those who called him a mere "bullshit artist," saying he had "as formidable a poetic mind as African-American literary tradition has ever produced."[17] "The thing about *Nation of Millions*," he says, "was that it dramatized Black identity in a way that it hadn't been since the sixties. It almost seemed like there was a mythic inevitability to it."

But as he listened closer, he also felt a shudder of ambivalence. By the end of "Party for Your Right to Fight," it was clear that Public Enemy's ideology was swinging from revolutionary nationalism to cultural nationalism, political radicalism to cultural radicalism. There was talk of masonry and hidden books of knowledge, "grafted devils" and "the original Asiatic Black man." The Black Panthers represented the past, the Black Muslims the future. By their next album, *Fear of a Black Planet*, the shift would be complete.

In a now-famous review, Tate used Griff quotes to skewer the crew:

> To know PE is to love the agitprop (and artful noise) and to worry over the whack retarded philosophy they espouse. Like: "The Black woman has always been kept up by the Black male because the white male has always wanted the Black woman." Like: "White people are actually monkey's uncles because that's who they made it with in the Caucasian hills." Like: "If the Palestinians took up arms, went into Israel and killed all the Jews it'd be alright." From this idiot blather, PE are obviously making it up as they go along. Since PE show sound reasoning when they focus on racism as a tool of the U.S. power structure, they should be intelligent enough to realize that dehumanizing gays, women and Jews isn't going to set Black people free.[18]

Tate's critique was different than John Leland's anti-political salvo. It hit a lot closer to home. The week that the review hit, Chuck was calling Tate a "porch nigger" from concert stages.

Black Artists As the New Black Leadership

Greg Tate and Chuck D were continuing in the tradition of Adam Clayton Powell Jr., Jackie Robinson and Malcolm X, talking the Black liberation struggle in scathingly personal terms. But there was a new sense of scale to the debate. The discourse was migrating from the realm of the political to the cultural, from the intimacy of street corners and race papers to the fishbowl of the global media.

Integration had begun to offer a new kind of power. Within two months of its release, *It Takes a Nation of Millions to Hold Us Back* had already sold a million copies and perhaps set off an equal number of debates. The rap rebels and the cult-nats might never leverage the lumbering political system that had begun rolling back over them, but they might figure out how to mobilize lightning-quick, idea-dumb capital for its uses.

So the question returned: what was the role and responsibility of artists to the liberation struggle? For the Panthers, and even for Karenga, artists were revolutionaries first. As "cultural workers"—a Marxist construct that meant to validate art-making as a form of labor—their job was merely to support the revolution, not to theorize, strategize, or steer it. But in the urgency of the moment, given the irreparable break in political leadership development, rappers were now being asked not just to be mirrors to the people, but to be their leaders.

The Stop the Violence Movement was an example of what rappers could do well. In 1987, gang fights broke out during a U.T.F.O. show in Los Angeles, a boy was stabbed to death at a Dana Dane show in New Haven, Connecticut, and two teenaged girls were trampled in an after-concert stampede at a show in Nashville, Tennessee, featuring Eric B. & Rakim, Public Enemy and NWA. Violence was also on the rise in rock concerts, but the media suddenly had a new reason to stigmatize youths of color, and calls for rap show bans spread.

On September 10, 1988, the violence came home to the Black Belt. One youth was killed and dozens others were hurt at a Saturday-night homecoming show for Eric B. & Rakim, Kool Moe Dee and Doug E. Fresh at the Nassau Veterans Memorial Coliseum in Uniondale. Frustrated with the sensationalist media coverage and worried about its effect on the emerging rap industry, journalist Nelson George, Jive A&R exec Ann Carli, publicist Leyla Turkkan and a number of execs met the following week. "It was time," Nelson George wrote, "for rappers to define the problem and defend themselves."[19]

They conceived a project that would include a benefit record, video, book and a rally around the theme "Stop the Violence," the title of KRS-One's ode to his fallen partner, Scott La Rock. Working quickly, the ad hoc committee assembled an all-star group of rappers and producers to become the "Stop the Violence Movement." They cut a record, "Self Destruction," shot a video and staged a march through Harlem. The song went gold and added $200,000 to the National Urban League's anti-violence programs. The well-executed marketing strategy significantly shifted the terms of the debate over rap concert bans.

But Stop the Violence was always less a movement than a media event. The project was never intended to be a political campaign against the Black-on-Black crime; that was for a civil rights organization like the Urban League to build. Stop the Violence meant to counterspin the mainstream media, reassure the entertainment business, show that rap artists could be responsible, and that hip-hop was a self-policing and stable industry. Nothing more should have been expected.

Many compared rappers to *griots*—the mythmakers, genealogists, praise singers, oral historians and social critics of Senegambian society. "One would expect the griots to be valued members of their societies," wrote Robert Palmer in *Deep Blues*, "but in fact they are both admired, for they often attain considerable reputations and amass wealth, and despised, for they are thought to consort with evil spirits, and their praise songs, when not properly rewarded, can become venomous songs of insult."[20] By definition, griots were not leaders, much less messiahs. They were a separate caste, an outcast class.

But many elders insisted that rappers, who clearly had the ability to move the media like no one since the Panthers, take their place in the community as leaders. At Howard University in 1987, Bill Stephney found himself on a panel discussion with Amiri Baraka, dub poet Mutabaruka, and musician James Mtume. The three asserted that rappers should be held to revolutionary standards of leadership. Stephney was aghast.

He argued, "Woe be it unto a community that has to rely on rappers for political leadership. Because that doesn't signify progress, that signifies default. Now that our community leaders cannot take up their responsibility, you're gonna leave it up to an eighteen-year-old kid who has mad flow? What is the criteria by which he has risen to his leadership? He can flow? That's the extent of it? If our leadership is to be determined by an eighteen-year-old without a plan, then we're in trouble. We're *fucked*."

The elders protested, wondered if he wasn't just trying to duck responsibility. A young woman stood up in the audience to defend Stephney. She was Lisa Williamson, the anti-apartheid and anti-racist activist who was one of the most visible student leaders of the day. In three years, she would transform herself into Sister Souljah and join the Public Enemy camp as a self-described "raptivist." In this generation, it was no longer about being a cultural *worker*, but being a political *rapper*. Stephney muses, "It was a reversal of the process."

Chuck had begun to recognize his role, and with it, his limits. In a generation, George Clinton's "Chocolate City" talk about painting the White House black and filling it with cultural icons like Muhammad Ali, Richard Pryor and Aretha Franklin was no longer a joke—it was what folks actually seemed to be asking for. But to call yourself a Black Panther of rap was one thing, to replace the Party was another.

"I'm not a politician, I'm a dispatcher of information," Chuck D complained to John Leland. "People are always looking to catch me in fucking doubletalk and loopholes. They're looking to say, 'Damn, in this interview he said that, and in this interview he said that.' They treat me like *I'm* Jesse Jackson."[21]

Chuck fashioned a new soundbite, describing a role he felt more capable of fulfilling. "In five years," he would say, "we intend to have cultivated five thousand Black leaders. Maybe another Marley or a Jesse Jackson, a Marcus Garvey or another Louis Farrakhan."[22] And if that seemed to some to be a political retreat, it still ranked as one of the most ambitious claims ever advanced on behalf of art.

Do the Right Thing

In the summer of 1988, thirty-one-year-old Spike Lee began filming *Do the Right Thing* in Bed-Stuy. Lee wrote and directed the movie, and it had been already rejected by one studio that found the ending too controversial. Angered at the white liberal platitudes of Steven Spielberg's *The Color Purple* and Alan Parker's *Mississippi Burning*, inspired by the Howard Beach incident and buoyed by the rising tide of cultural activism, Lee wanted to capture life on one racially tense Brooklyn block on the hottest day of the year. The movie would become a polarizing force in an already us-or-them kind of time.

He inserted himself in the lead as Mookie, an around-the-way Brooklyn guy in a Jackie Robinson jersey delivering pizzas for Sal's Famous Pizzeria. Mookie was, in film critic Ed Guerrero's words, a "b-boy survivalist," less aquaboogie-ing than treading water, committed to nothing but making ends.[23] His employers were an Italian-American family that drove daily from their Bensonhurst home to their commercial establishment in Bed-Stuy. Sal embodied nostalgia for the good old days of the Dodgers, when Black meant underdog, not majority. His eldest son, Pino, was hardened before his time, struggling with the fact that his father chose not to sell the pizzeria even as Bed-Stuy became unrecognizable. The youngest, Vito, was sweet, liberal and, in Pino's mind, hopelessly naive.

Their chief antagonist, Buggin' Out, played by half-Italian, half-Black actor Giancarlo Esposito, was a beetle-eyed political rad with attitude, issuing demands for Black faces on the Pizzeria's Wall of Fame—a comic play on Lee's own battle for representation. Radio Raheem was the strong, silent cultural rad, his face flickering minutely between menace and mask, letting his heroes, Public Enemy, project his anger from his omnipresent boombox. In his worldview, self-hatred and self-love were at constant war beneath his skin.

When Sal refused Buggin' Out's demands and forced Raheem to turn off his radio, the two teamed for an impromptu protest in the pizzeria. The result was a battered, silenced boombox, a do-or-die struggle between Sal and Raheem and a chain of events that would lead to Raheem's death, Michael Stewart-style, at the hands of NYPD. Only then would Mookie finally take a stand, tossing a garbage can through his employer's window. A riot ensued, culminating with Smiley, the neighborhood idiot who never smiled, striking the match as the block chanted, "Howard Beach! Howard Beach!" In this climax, Lee brought together newsreel images of the northern Black power riots of Harlem and Newark and the southern civil rights demonstrations of Birmingham and Montgomery in the context of the fraught new era of brutality and reaction.

Stuttering Smiley, whose very speech seemed paralyzed by the grandiloquent inquiries of Martin and Malcolm ("The ballot or the bullet?" "Where do we go from here?"), stepped through the flames to pin a postcard of them on the Wall of Fame, depicting the two unredeemed martyrs laughing and shaking hands in their only historic meeting. Then he allowed himself a private, inscrutable Sly Stone smile. The movie closed with opposing quotes from King and X on the question of violence as protest. Lee had offered no solutions. The power of Lee's statement lay in its dead-end generational rage and confusion.

Through no fault of Lee's, the movie opened on June 30, just two months after the sensational Central Park rape case, in which a group of Black male teenagers from Harlem were accused of a "wilding" rampage through the park culminating in a gang rape of a white female investment banker. (Years later, DNA evidence led a judge to overturn the five convictions, after each of the boys had become men, serving between seven and thirteen years in prison.) *Do the Right Thing* was greeted by a spasm of panic. Jack Kroll wrote in

Newsweek, "To put it bluntly: in this long hot summer, how will young urban audiences—Black and white—react to the film's climactic explosion of interracial violence?"[24]

Lee's film turned mild-mannered film critics into political prognosticators. *New York* magazine's David Denby wrote, "[I]f Spike Lee is a commercial opportunist, he's also playing with dynamite in an urban playground. The response to the movie could get away from him."[25] Political pundits turned film critics, too. In a famous column, *New York* magazine political writer Joe Klein argued, "His film . . . is more trendoid than tragic, reflecting the latest riffs in hip Black separatism rather than taking an intellectually honest look at the problems he's nibbling around."[26]

Klein wrote that white liberals would passionately debate what Lee meant to say. "Black kids," he wrote, "won't find it so hard, though. For them, the message is clear from the opening credits, which roll to the tune of "Fight the Power," performed by Public Enemy, a virulently anti-Semitic rap group: *The police are your enemy . . . White people are your enemy . . .*"[27]

But objections to Lee's film were not just racial, they were generational, too. In *The Village Voice*, Stanley Crouch compared Lee to Nazi propagandist Leni Riefenstahl, and wrote, "*Do the Right Thing*, for all its wit, is the sort of rancid fairy tale one expects of the racist, whether or not Lee actually is one."[28] If Chuck D had pointed the finger at Crouch's generation for selling the race down the river, Crouch pointed the finger back. He wrote:

> Intellectual cowardice, opportunism and the itch for riches by almost any means necessary define the demons within the Black community. The demons are presently symbolized by those Black college teachers so intimidated by career threats that they don't protest students bringing Louis Farrakhan on campus, by men like Vernon Mason who sold out a good reputation in a cynical bid for political power by pimping real victims of racism in order to smoke-screen Tawana Brawley's lies, by the crack dealers who have wrought unprecedented horrors and by Afro-fascist race baiters like Public Enemy who perform on the soundtrack to *Do the Right Thing*.[29]

The further critics got from the theater, the more the question hardened: come on, Spike, just exactly what *is* the right thing? In these upside-down times, political pundits and cultural critics wanted what they had little right to expect. Pundits snorted at platforms and proposals; instead, they turned politicians like Jesse Jackson into tragedies, and forced them to beg for redemption. Critics wanted from Spike Lee and Public Enemy the bland precision of diplomacy; instead, they got messy, plexus-pounding, fire-starting art.

Lee himself presented a strange mix of unblinking sincerity and brusque impenetrability that made him a seductive mainstream media subject. Suddenly Lee seemed more in demand as a race man than even Congressional Black Caucus head Ron Dellums. Once again, the questions haunted: Who speaks for young Black America? Were Black artists the new Black leaders? If they were, what did they really have to say?

Representing New Black Militancy (1989 Version)

Lee had commissioned Public Enemy to do the title track, for which Chuck, Keith and Eric put together "Fight the Power." His idea for the video was to stage a "Young People's March to End Racial Violence." Ads went out on urban radio to drum up turnout for the event.

On the day of the march, "Fight the Power" T-shirts were handed out to the youths, as well as placards featuring images of Angela Davis, Jesse Jackson, Paul Robeson, Frederick Douglass, Medgar Evers, Thurgood Marshall, Marcus Garvey, Muhammad Ali and the Public Enemy logo. Pickets reading "Brooklyn," "Montgomery," "Selma," "Philadelphia," "Wash. D.C.," "Miami" and "Watts," as well as "S1Ws," "Flavor Flav" and "Terminator X," were distributed into the crowd. Then they marched a mile up from the Eastern Parkway to the block where the movie had been shot.

There the group performed the song on a red, black and green stage framed by a large photo of Malcolm X, as the crowd danced and mugged for the cameras. The presentation was street demonstration, Black pride march and rap concert, as if the 1972 National Black Political Assembly had been transformed into a millennial Brooklyn block party.

Lee opened the video with historic footage of the 1963 March on Washington. Chuck broke in, "Young Black America, we rolling up with seminars, press conferences and straight-up rallies. Am I right? We gonna get what we got to get coming to us. We ain't going out like that '63 nonsense." Then it began with Chuck proclaiming, "1989! The number, another summer," marking the moment for history.

It was just a seven-minute short to promote a record, a group, a brand. But the video also seemed to firmly establish Chuck's cultural authority. Public Enemy's first video, for "Night of the Living Baseheads," was amateurish, almost a parody of Chuck's rap-as-CNN idea. But on "Fight the Power," Lee placed Chuck in the streets amidst the likenesses of Black power fighters, one new Black icon anointing another.

Chuck was reluctant to be seen as his generation's Malcolm X or Paul Robeson. He wanted to provoke, not to lead. But after this video, the question would be out of his hands. Public Enemy had gone, as Bill Stephney says, "from a rap group playing the Latin Quarter with Biz and Shan and Run and Whodini to now being the saviors of the Black community." Soon they would be forced to confront a crisis that would test both Chuck's leadership of the group and the group's leadership within the community.

The Enemy Implodes

As the summer of 1989 opened, Chuck was ready for controversy. He says, "I remember specifically when I did 'Fuck him and John Wayne.' I was totally prepared to handle all that shit." Then Professor Griff gave an interview to David Mills of the *Washington Times*.

Chuck recalls, "It was almost like I'm going in to make a tackle and I get cross-body-blocked by a 500-pounder like out of nowhere, man, knocking me entirely out of the play. I was ready to go after John Wayne and Elvis with a vengeance, and then all of a sudden—blaaaau! Now I'm fucking getting chased. I'm scrambling in the pocket, man. I'm like, what the fuck? I can't throw this shit out of bounds!"

In fact, by the time they shot the "Fight the Power" video, Public Enemy was beginning to unravel. *It Takes a Nation of Millions to Hold Us Back* had gone platinum and raised the industry's expectations for the group. But the original decision-making core of Chuck, Hank and Bill was coming apart.

Hank was in demand because of a run of number-one singles through his

Bomb Squad production work for Vanessa Williams and Bell Biv Devoe. Bill was consumed by his duties as vice president of Def Jam, which itself was melting down. Rick and Russell were in the process of splitting, the Beastie Boys were suing the label for unpaid royalties (while trying to hire Stephney away) and the label's artists were accusing Stephney of playing favorites with Public Enemy. The solution was for Hank, Bill and Chuck to set up their own label.

When word got out that they were plotting to leave Def Jam a number of offers came in, the most serious a multimillion-dollar proposal from MCA Records, a company that had just purchased Motown—Chuck's personal ideal of Black business. In the late spring of 1989, Bill quit Def Jam, and he and Hank formalized the deal. Then they worked on setting up the new label, called "SOUL: The Sound of Urban Listeners," and waited for Chuck to return from tour. These new label duties took them further from the daily activities of the group. As Public Enemy fulfilled a heavy schedule of touring and appearances, Chuck had become the de facto leader of the crew.

Public Enemy was carefully balanced on a set of dualities, with Chuck at the center of each. Chuck and Hank constituted the musical axis. Chuck and Flav were the focal sonic and visual points of the group. Chuck and Griff confronted the media. In 1988, Chuck had described his role in the group to *New Music Express*:

> I'm like the mediator in all this. Flavor is what America would like to see in a Black man—sad to say, but true—whereas Griff is very much what America would not like to see. And there's no acting here—sometimes I can't put Flavor and Griff in the same room.
>
> I'm in the middle. When Griff says something too much, I come to the rescue of white people; when Flavor does something, I come to the defense of Black people. I do constrain them, but not much, because Public Enemy are the only Black group making noises *outside* of their records.[30]

In their Hempstead studio, these tensions worked together to create magnificent art. But the day-in, day-out stresses of the road made these same tensions crippling.

The disciplined, temperamental Griff had been given the role as road manager, and he began resenting the elusive, disorganized Flavor for ignoring group rules. Flavor's problems seemed complicated by his addictions. He was prone to disappearing for hours. When Flav showed up late for one show, Griff blew up and kicked him in the chest. Flav quickly got lost.

Griff's abrasiveness had even alienated the S1Ws, jeopardizing his road manager responsibilities. He wanted more involvement with the Bomb Squad, but the production team was already self-contained and Griff was always away on tour. He wanted a larger role as Minister of Information, and resented Chuck's role as chief spokesperson. He was becoming increasingly isolated from the crew.

On the other hand Chuck would ignore the problems until they became unbearable, frozen by loyalty to each of his old friends. In decision-making, he was reluctant to dictate terms. He preferred a democratic process of consensus-making. In any case, he figured, everyone was supposed to play his position. They knew their role. He sighs, "I thought that men could fix their problems amongst themselves, and I kinda like would be the guy in charge. But see, how the fuck can a *man* be in charge of men?"

A crew of old friends had suddenly been thrown into the spotlight of massive success. Amidst incessant touring and fishbowl scrutiny, the personal and the political quickly became intertwined and threatened to blow.

Over the Edge

Def Jam/Rush publicist Bill Adler had tutored Chuck in how to become adept at playing a kind of brinksmanship with the media. When reporters tried to pin him down, Chuck flipped the question into a big-picture statement or a personal story. Griff thought Chuck was becoming soft. The more distanced Griff was from the crew, the harder the line he wanted to take.

From the earliest tours, Chuck had included Griff in Public Enemy interviews. After some disastrous early British interviews, Chuck took up the primary press role again.[31] But as Public Enemy took off, Chuck's leadership responsibilities, which included handling tour scheduling and details Griff's refusal to continue as road manager, and the extraordinary media demands caused Chuck to delegate some media duties back to Griff. When Public Enemy toured through

Europe and America in the summer of *Nation of Millions*, Griff's rhetoric began to overheat. "No more of this media darling this and darling that," he told British reporters, "let's turn it up a notch."[32]

In Switzerland during May to promote the record, Griff led the discussion like a wild goose chase, jumping from apartheid in South Africa to the origins of the diamond and slave trades to the ethics of the *intifada* to whites mating with monkeys. Some of Griff's opinions were confrontational, lots of them were just weird, but none of them would be as explosive as this one reported by *Melody Maker* in its May 28, 1988, issue: "If the Palestinians took up arms, went into Israel and killed all the Jews, it'd be alright."[33] To this day, Chuck traces the beginnings of 1989's meltdown to this very moment.

First Fallout

Three weeks after the *Melody Maker* article ran, Chuck showed up at the New Music Seminar in New York City to find the crowd holding flyers that read "Don't Believe the HATE," and listing some of Griff's more outrageous quotes. John Leland, whom Chuck had threatened in *NME* some months before, sat with Chuck for an interview:

> Q: Chuck, what's your reaction to the handbill distributed at the New Music Seminar?
> A: They're making a whole lot of shit about nothing. A lot of paranoia going on. People think I got the ability to fucking turn a country around.
> Q: Do you back the statements that Griff made?
> A: I back Griff. Whatever he says, he can prove.
> Q: You mean he can prove that white people mated with monkeys? That it wouldn't be such a bad idea if Palestinians were to kill all Jews in Israel?
> A: Now that was taken out of context. I was there. He said, by Western civilization's standards it wouldn't be bad for the Palestinians to come into Palestine and kill all the Jews, because that's what's been done right throughout Western civilization: invasion, conquering and killing. That wasn't mentioned.[34]

Bill Adler was concerned. He says, "I had no trouble repeating what Chuck said vis-a-vis the criticism that Public Enemy was anti-white. They'd say, 'No, we're pro-Black.' Fine. Their racial politics I had no problem with. The problem for me was when Griff began giving anti-Semitic interviews.

"Griff is sober, disciplined, clean and well spoken—soft spoken, too. Not a screamer, not a ranter. He's got every appearance of rationality, sobriety and thoughtfulness and yet, in this very calm voice, he's going to say the goofiest shit in the world about how the Jews are in a conspiracy, and have been in a conspiracy forever, to destroy the Black man."

Adler confronted Griff about his quotes to *Melody Maker*. He was worried these kinds of statements could become a serious flashpoint for the group. But rather than deny that he'd said them, Adler says, Griff dug in his heels. "I said to him, I said 'Griff, where did you hear these things?' And he said, *'The International Jew.'* I said, *'The International Jew,* the book by Henry Ford, right?' He said 'Yeah.' I said, 'Griff, you know about Henry Ford. Henry Ford is a guy who established two cities for his workers on the outskirts of Detroit. One was for white folks only and it was called Dearborn and the other was for his Black workers only and it was called Inkster. Understand, he would as gladly have upholstered the seats of his Model T with your Black hide as with my Jewish hide.' And Griff shrugged. He was absolutely unmoved. He said, 'I'm sorry, Bill. It's in the book.' "

The Interview

When the band came to Washington, D.C., a year later, on May 9, 1989, tensions within the group had only increased. The band had been on the road for months, and the personal issues were taking their toll. "The split in the ranks, I just kind of left alone. Like, oh it will handle itself. And it never did," Chuck says. When he needed to attend a meeting about tour scheduling, he sent Griff to meet with Black reporter David Mills from the conservative, Reverend Sun Myung Moon-funded *Washington Times* newspaper. By this point, Chuck says, "I guess Griff really felt like, 'Hey, I'm not getting no love out of this group.' And now Chuck is telling me to do this damn interview."

Griff had just given a TV interview in which he stated he did not wear gold chains because of Jewish support for apartheid.[35] Mills pressed Griff on this point and Griff, citing the Nation of Islam's recently published book, *The Secret Relationship Between Blacks and Jews,* became more insistent:

> *Professor Griff:* . . . Is it a coincidence that the Jews run the jewelry business, and it's named *jew-elry*? No coincidence. Is it a coincidence to you that probably the gold from this ring was brought up out of South Africa, and that the Jews have a tight grip on our brothers in South Africa?
>
> *David Mills:* What do you mean "the Jews"? Are the Jews in America responsible for that? Are Jews as a totality responsible for that?
>
> *Professor Griff:* No, because there are some Jews that are righteous, that are following the Torah given to them by Moses . . . I'm not saying all of them. The majority of them (laughter), the majority of them, yes.
>
> *David Mills:* Are what? Are responsible for—
>
> *Professor Griff:* The majority of wickedness that goes on across the globe? Yes. Jews. Yes.

Spin Cycles

On May 11, in an effort at damage control, the crew invited Mills to meet them in Hempstead. Mills accepted. "We're not hung up on Jews. We've got no time to get hung up on Jewish people," S1W James Norman told Mills. "We're battling to try to regain a Black consciousness for our people."[36]

But Chuck, despite Hank's pleading, refused to dignify the proceeding by showing up. He eventually spoke to Mills over the phone, trying to dial back Griff's comments. Mills wasn't buying it. The article ran on May 22, included a transcript of parts of the interview with Griff, and closed with this kicker:

> Chuck D doesn't know how Def Jam Records will react to this story. "A lot of people are not ready for the truth," he said. "[Record companies] never dealt with anything like this before in their lives. They're used to dealing with sending groups out there, talking about girls, anything," he says. "It's all right to even be derogatory to Blacks. Just don't be derogatory to most of the people in the business. Ninety percent of the business is operated by Jews, who started it.[37]

The story went unnoticed until Mills began faxing it nationally to newspapers and music magazines like *Rolling Stone* and *SPIN* with the help of the *Washington Times* publicist. It was republished on the front page of the *New York Tribune,* the Moonie paper in New York City, on May 29.

But controversy didn't erupt until *The Village Voice* hit the streets three Tuesdays later, on June 13. In his "Swing Shift" column, R. J. Smith ran excerpts of the Mills-Griff dialogue verbatim. "What I read in that interview made little sense to me and I felt a sense of betrayal," Smith says. "It was depressing as hell."

In the column, Smith tried to pin Chuck on Griff's views. "Although I don't agree with everything he said, Griff has a right to speak as an artist," Chuck answered. Smith countered, "[T]he leaders of 1963 would never quote Henry Ford, believer in *The Protocols of the Elders of Zion.*" Chuck called *The International Jew* "bullshit," but said Griff had done his research and "is looking for someone to debate him." He called the efforts to have him renounce Griff "divide and conquer."[38]

Up until this point, Bill Stephney says, no one in the crew took Mills, his article and the claims it made very seriously. The charge of anti-Semitism especially, Stephney says, "seemed ridiculous on its face, just by virtue of who Public Enemy was in business with. They had been signed by Rick Rubin. Bill Adler was their publicist. They were managed by Lyor Cohen, Ron Skoler and Ed Chalpin. Their photographer and art director was Glen Friedman. As Bill Adler once put it, they were not anti-Semites, they were philo-Semites.

The Crisis

But behind the scenes, the pressure mounted. Spike Lee was preparing to release *Do the Right Thing* with "Fight the Power" as the lead-in single. But movie distributors were questioning Lee over Public Enemy's involvement with the film. None of the top brass at Columbia moved to formally censure Def Jam, but Russell, Lyor Cohen and Bill Adler all heard earfuls from Jewish industry leaders. Privately, Russell responded that he felt it was a free-speech issue, and Lyor vowed to work with the group. Adler was less sure, and soon removed himself as Public Enemy's publicist.

Before doing so, he, Hank and Bill Stephney met with Chuck to try to sound him out. "Everything was in jeopardy," Hank later told *Rolling Stone.* "The people we worked with were receiving lots of threats. My studio, Griff's mother . . . Chuck's mother. It got really nasty."[39]

Chuck listened to Hank and Bill Stephney discuss the impact the incident was having on their deal with MCA, and to Bill Adler remind him his closest working relationships were with Jewish people. The three pressured Chuck to distance himself from Griff. He appeared unmoved.

There appeared to be a sense of ennui within the Public Enemy camp. They had returned home to get their first rest in months and to resolve their personal issues. The band was in crisis, and they looked like they were sleepwalking through it. In reality, they were gasping for air, hoping for Chuck to take control.

They convened to try to work out a consensus, but the energy around these meetings was low. Chuck says, "Somebody would show up not on point. Either Griff would come late, I would be present or not present or somebody else would be present or not present. So therefore the meeting grew into meetings and there was different ideas and philosophies on how to handle it.

"I said no matter how we deal with this, chances are we should deal with this as together as we can, even if motherfuckers ain't feeling each other. Regardless of whatever the fuck we gonna do, we all gonna be looking at each other in Roosevelt one day or another so let's handle this right. And it just wasn't handled totally right."

Chuck was reluctant to lead. He felt he should defer to Bill Stephney and Hank Shocklee, especially Hank, who was two years his senior and had been the leader since their Spectrum City days. At the same time, he says, "I didn't want anybody handling me, telling me what I should do."

By now Griff's statements had hit the network newscasts and Hank and Bill were convinced something needed to be done. Chuck wanted a compromise that would save him and the touring crew some face. He felt Hank and Bill were forcing him into a difficult choice, to choose between Public Enemy as an idea dreamed up at 510 South Franklin and the actual group that it had become, a choice between "the creation and the creators."

"The only thing that would have made everything fit is if I actually assumed leadership and jacked everybody and said, 'This is how it is and fuck y'all!' " he says. But that was the last thing he was going to do.

At the same time, Chuck was pissed at Griff. He felt Griff knew the line not to cross with interviewers, but he had taken it there by himself. In one of the crew meetings at 510 South Franklin, Hank and Bill had played a taped copy of the taped interview with Mills, and questioned Griff about it. Stephney says, "Griff, at that meeting, basically said he was having difficulties with the group. He had had a bad day that day, that apparently some dissension had been building that [Hank and I] were unaware of. That perhaps these comments were a cry for help. But then again, later, Griff said they weren't a cry for help, that it was what he believed."

The crew was torn. Some believed Griff had tried to sabotage the group. They could either demand Griff's ouster or publicly affirm that the crew stand by him. They would do neither. They were paralyzed.

The Case for Public Enemy

Yet Smith's column had created a firestorm that demanded a resolution. First Chuck called Smith and yelled at him, "Listen to me, R.J., any shit comes down on me, it's coming down on you! And that's a goddamned threat! Write this down! I ain't gonna write no white-boy liberal letter to the editor, no article either."[40]

But Chuck did write a letter, dated Monday, June 19, 1989. Addressed TO ALL OFFENDED, CONCERNED AND UNCONCERNED, it read as much like a manifesto of Public Enemy's cultural radicalism as a condemnation of Griff:

Public Enemy stands for the rebuilding and the preservation of the Black mind, be it young, old or unborn. Our sole purpose is to make our people and all people recognize and repair the true state that we are in . . .

Professor Griff's timing, choice of words or attitude reflected in his statements is not representative of the program of Public Enemy or reflective of the position of Minister of Information for the group. . . . In that this is the first Black music group whose goal it is to raise the consciousness level of Black people and let them know that the real enemy is a system, not a people, this form of information (music) breaks down barriers quicker than any previous methods . . .

This is a *Black* and I repeat *Black* family matter. This decision had to be made in a Black disciplined manner, since this industry has a large vested interest in the Black community, as well as a history of unfair compensation to our Black artists, producers and talented people involved. We feel that our decision should be acknowledged and respected. The outside points of view and feelings to oust our brother are that of an emotional lynch mob. We can understand the mentality behind that. Also understand that Public Enemy is the official voice of the rap world, Black youth, oppressed youth and yes, many white youth in the western world . . .

This is an important summer for Black youth and white youth as well; never have they shared so much in common. The once reluctant MTV brass seemingly cannot handle the mix of Black culture and white youth in a way that previous corporate structures have exploited this combination in the past. At the same time, it is "make it" or "break it" in 1989, the line between acceptance and exploitation is very vague and if the true word is not there, magnify Central Park times one hundred in the 1990s, that's how serious these crossroads are. This unnecessary noise in the quest for Black Power has halted progress for the future of the Black mindset here. Why Black Power? And what is it? Black Power is only a self-defense movement that counterattacks the system of white world supremacy, not white people or the religious sects that they choose. It does not mean anti-white, it means anti-a-system that has been designed by the European elite for the wrong purpose of benefiting off of people of color or at Black people's expense . . . [41]

In this letter, Chuck announced that Griff had been removed from the Minister of Information position, to be replaced by Brother James "Bomb" Allen of the S1Ws. He would remain in the group but be relieved of spokesperson duties. Chuck alone would handle all interviews.

"Peace to all who are right," Chuck's letter concluded. "Peace to all offended."

The Moment of Indecision

Although David Mills reported on the letter in the *Washington Times*, it was never officially released. But by Tuesday evening, after Smith's account of his phone call with Chuck had hit the newsstands, a suspension seemed inadequate.

Adler, in particular, was encouraging Chuck to do more than suspend Griff. The two of them and Bill Stephney convened to write a press statement and called a press conference for the very next day.

Chuck says now, "Of course, people look back, 'Oh Chuck was waffling.' Well, goddamn right I was waffling! What the fuck. How could you not waffle? And at the same time I would have to assume leadership in order to make that decision, knowing that one side or the other would be gone.

"It happened that both of them disappeared. Hank and Bill went off to do their thing, and Griff was out." For Chuck, it was the worst of all possible worlds. And yet Public Enemy had still not hit bottom.

On Wednesday, June 21, flanked by Stephney and Rush Communications president Carmen Ashhurst-Watson in a midtown hotel room, before nearly three dozen reporters and cameramen, the unflappable Chuck was uncharacteristically stiff and formal, cap pulled low over his eyes, as he read the prepared statement:

> The Black community, both here and abroad, is in the midst of a terrible crisis. Our plan has been, first, to define the problems then to suggest solutions. Offensive remarks by Professor Griff over the past, I should say, year, in a couple of interviews, are not in line with Public Enemy's program at all. We are not anti-Jewish. We are not anti-anyone. We are pro-Black, pro-Black culture and pro–human race, and that's been said before many times. You see, Griff's responsibility as Minister of Information was to faithfully transmit these values to everybody. In practice, he sabotaged those values.
>
> In the interest of keeping the group together, we tried to deal with Griff's problems internally, but we were unsuccessful. Consequently, as of today. Professor Griff is no longer a member of Public Enemy.

This was the first anyone in the group besides Hank and Bill had heard of Chuck's decision. Now he departed from the text.

> It is my obligation to discipline my brother if he's offended anybody. We apologize to anybody who might have been offended by Griff's remarks and we're kind of offended, too. Cause our policy is not to offend anyone,

it's to offend the system that works against us 24 hours a day, 365 days a year.[42]

Praise from Jewish leaders and the mainstream media, including *New York Newsday*, was immediate.

But in the Black community, there were different words. Some felt Chuck's statement was proof that Jews *were* running things. Others wondered if Griff were a counterintelligence agent. At the press conference, Armond White, one of the only Blacks in the room, asked Chuck point-blank if he wasn't caving to white pressure. In an essay in the *Brooklyn City Sun*, White dismissed the event as a "rap show" meant to smooth whites' ruffled feathers."

White believed Chuck's stance, especially on Black-Jewish relations, was a crucial test. Was he really the organic intellectual he claimed to be? Could he engage the race and show them the way forward? Could a rapper be a Black leader? Chuck was found lacking.

"Here's the sad part: the fiery beauty of Public Enemy was that it refused to pander to 'brotherhood' sentimentalists. PE made the uplifting of Black people seem connected to all human struggle," he wrote. "Now, in apology, Chuck says that the specific discussion of race and Black-Jewish relations is a 'conversation that's so detailed and so intense and so wrapped up, it goes outside the area of music and dealing with the masses. 'Cause the masses of our people are not even at the level to understand something like that.'

"With this attitude, Chuck D isn't good for anything except recording mindless, pointless confections," White angrily wrote. "This is the first tough fight Public Enemy has had to face and they've crumbled like chalk."[43]

Chuck left the room as the press dispersed, stepped into an adjacent room and angrily began kicking over chairs. That night, he drafted another statement to the Black community. But even this statement wouldn't change the three most upsetting facts: Griff had never apologized to the crew; many Black fans felt Chuck had sold Griff down the river; and some youths might be learning the wrong lesson from the whole episode: that taking any kind of stand was futile. This letter, too, went in the wastebasket.

Chuck felt he was treading water: "You try to swim to the edge, wherever that edge was, and the edge was miles away." With no good solution, he resorted to elusiveness, rhetorical bobbing and weaving. The next day, in interviews with Kurt Loder for MTV News and on WLIB, Chuck announced, "We got sand-bagged. And being that we got sandbagged, the group is over today."[44] Chuck spun it as a political statement: they were going out by boycotting a music industry that had robbed them of self-determination.

Behind the scenes, the group was still roiling. Chuck, Hank and a close associate Aliyah Mubarak drafted a final statement called "The Real Story." While supporting Griff "as a brother," the letter pointed the blame back at him. But this statement also ended up in the trash. Chuck says, "I didn't think the real story was anybody's business."

Long ago, when Public Enemy was still on the drawing board at 510 South Franklin, Hank had concocted a plan and taken it to Chuck. "I wanted PE to have a born date and a death date," Hank says. "The beauty of that would be to have an album called 'The Day PE Died.'" Chuck brushed it aside, and they had forgotten about it. Now that Hank, Bill and Griff were gone, that day seemed to have come.

In Chicago, Chuck led Public Enemy through a final gig, then the crew retreated to meet privately with Minister Farrakhan. He told them they were in for a trying time, that they needed to watch their words. For the time being, Farrakhan said, they should be to be silent and hope to ride the situation out. Humbled, they returned to Long Island to sort out the implosion.

Bensonhurst: The Rise and Fall of Black Power

At the end of 1989's riotous summer, two months after *Do the Right Thing* opened and Public Enemy collapsed, Bensonhurst happened. On the evening of August 23, sixteen-year-old Bed-Stuy resident Yusuf Hawkins was on the subway with three friends to see a used Pontiac G2000 in the primarily Italian Brooklyn neighborhood. There were eerie parallels to the Howard Beach incident.

Hawkins and his friends stepped into a bodega to ask directions and get some drinks and candy bars. They walked a few blocks up the street past a schoolyard where a mob of more than twenty young white males was gathering. A neighborhood girl had taunted them all day, telling them her Black and Latino boys were coming around to party with her, the local equivalent of nuclear aggression. Armed with bats and golf clubs, the young whites were preparing to chase the outsiders out of their hood.

When Hawkins and his friends passed, the mob left the yard and followed them up the street. As Hawkins neared the address of the car owner, the mob stopped them. "What are you niggers doing here?" one yelled. Then Joey Fama stepped out of the mob and said, "To hell with beating them up. I'm gonna shoot the nigger!"[45] Hawkins received four bullets in the chest, and died shortly thereafter.

In the following weeks, the Reverend Al Sharpton marched into Bensonhurst chanting, "No justice, no peace!" He was met by angry young whites holding up watermelons and screaming, "Niggers go home!"[46] On September 1, in another Day of Outrage protest, Sonny Carson and his son's hip-hop crew, X-Clan and the Blackwatch Movement, led ten thousand demonstrators through downtown Brooklyn toward the Brooklyn Bridge, where they engaged in a bottle-throwing, baton-swinging standoff with the police that left forty-four cops injured. Perhaps, after years of racist killings and street reactions, the Black power activists were hitting a rhetorical and tactical standoff.

Where Jackson's presidential run had failed, demographics kept the Rainbow dream alive. The city was now more than half nonwhite, suggesting that a progressive coalition of nonmajority groups could win. Black Manhattan Borough President David Dinkins emerged as a popular mayoral favorite to reduce tensions and heal divisions. A Tribe Called Quest's Phife Dawg pleaded on "Can I Kick It?": "Mr. Dinkins, will you please be my mayor? You'd be doing us a really big favor."

Dinkins trounced Koch in the Democratic primary. Then, handily defeating Republican candidate Rudy Giuliani, he was elected the city's first Black mayor. But the "gorgeous mosaic" he had described in his campaign speeches was never to be. Just two and a half weeks into office, Dinkins saw it smashed.

After an afternoon encounter in the Red Apple Grocery between Korean shopkeeper Bong Ok Jang and Haitian customer Ghiselaine Felissaint—some say Jang beat her, others say he didn't—an angry crowd of Black Caribbeans formed outside the grocery. One fearful Korean worker bolted across the street to another Korean-owned store, Church Fruits. Two days later, a formal boycott of both stores began.

To the boycott spokesperson Sonny Carson and others, Korean Americans were the new Jews. Carson told Professor Claire Jean Kim, "The boycotts weren't aimed at the Koreans themselves. The boycotts were aimed at the attitude of people coming into our community and taking advantage of what the system allowed to have, to provide them a place to continue to rip us off, that the crackers had done before they got here."[47]

The truth was much more complicated. In many cases, Korean Americans had bought or rented from Jewish or Italian Americans, who then became their wholesale suppliers. Korean Americans often complained that these whites gave them discriminatory prices and treated them in a racist manner. These arguments sometimes rose to the level of physical confrontation, and Koreans had launched their own boycotts against white wholesalers.[48]

But from winter cold through summer heat, the Flatbush boycott continued for eight months, leaving Korean Americans and African Americans tense and the progressive coalition in ruins. In Crown Heights the following August, relations between Blacks and Jews reached a horrific new low in two days of rioting following the hit-and-run killing of a Black boy by a Lubavitcher Jewish driver, and the subsequent murder of a Hasidic scholar by a group of black teens.

Mayor David Dinkins's one-and-done term was in for three long lame-duck years. The Rainbow dream and the 1960s idealism that birthed it had suffered a death blow.

The Enemy Strikes Black

But Public Enemy was staging a comeback. After several weeks of media silence, Chuck issued a press release on August 1—both his and Griff's birthday—announcing that the group was back in effect, that James Norman was now the Minister of Information and that Griff had taken on the title of Supreme Allied Chief of Community Relations.

"The show must go on. Brace yourselves for 1990," the press release read. "We're still pro-Black, pro–Black culture and pro–human race. Please direct any further questions to Axl Rose."

Hank and Bill were preparing to launch SOUL. By the fall, Griff, still a source of tension, had landed a record deal with Luther Campbell's Luke Records and left the group. Chuck, Flavor, Keith and Eric holed up to start work on the new Public Enemy album.

But the controversy would not die. Chuck's words were now under close scrutiny. His next single, "Welcome to the Terrordome," did not disappoint. "Terrordome" was the sound of 1989, not as Chuck had imagined it for "Fight the Power," but as it actually went down. It was full of indirection and blind rage.

Two lines in particular—"Told the rab to get off the rag" and "Crucifixion ain't no fiction, so-called chosen frozen, apologies made to whoever please, still they got me like Jesus"—caused the JDO and ADL to renew calls for boycotts. Even Rabbi Abraham Cooper of the Simon Wiesenthal Center, who had taken Chuck on a tour of the Holocaust Museum, was wondering what had gotten into him.

The *New York Post* devoted a lead editorial to the boycott: "Jews should make their attitude toward this ugly development clear and unmistakable—by boycotting Public Enemy. Blacks and other foes of racism who fail to join the boycott effort should not continue to expect the sympathy and financial support from Jews they have come to rely on."[49] Public Enemy, it seemed, had now become important enough to compel mainstream tabloids to pronounce judgment. In an odd way, it was a measure of how far the cultural radicals had moved in just a few years.

Chuck called his detractors "paranoid" and defended his lyrics in the *Washington Post*, " 'Apology made to whoever pleases'—I came out and made the apology but 'still they got me like Jesus,' which doesn't imply that the Jewish community is crucifying me, but that I got crucified by the media and the media hype coming afterwards. I'm not comparing myself to Jesus."[50]

The controversy overshadowed the fact that "Terrordome" included some of the most personal lines Chuck had ever penned. It began with the group's formation and implosion, then moved on in the second and third verse to confront his accusers. The allegedly anti-Semitic middle verses had garnered all the attention. But much of the first verse seemed to be directed at his own crew, perhaps even Griff, Hank and Bill Stephney:

Now I can't protect a paid-off defect
Check the record

And reckon an intentional wreck
Played off as some intellect

Made the call, took the fall
Broke the laws
Not my fault that they're falling off
Known as fair square throughout my years

At the top of the last verse, he rapped, "It's weak to speak and blame some-body else, when you destroy yourself." Then he closed the song by returning to the big picture: the murder of Yusuf Hawkins; the Labor Day anti-police riots at the annual Black Greek festival in Virginia Beach where thousands had defi-antly chanted "Fight the power!" He reaffirmed his ideal: that rap had the power to unify and confront through a revolution of the mind. "Move as a team, never move alone," he concluded, "but welcome to the Terrordome."

Perhaps because he has worked so hard in the intervening years to reconcile with all of his old friends, Chuck will not confirm that some of lines in "Terror-dome" were aimed toward his own crew. Instead he says, "It was directed to-ward everybody. It was my 'Leave Me the Fuck Alone' song! It was with that song that I assumed leadership of everything. For real. This is what it's going to be whether you like it or not."

One Last Punch

Harry Allen stepped in as the group's publicist. Armed with an arched brow, a Macintosh fax program and stacks of files and books, Harry immediately got to work. Taking a page from the conservative Heritage Foundation, he used weekly faxes to strike back at the group's attackers and to force the discussion of Public Enemy back into the context of race and racism.

Harry shocked white critics by enclosing with the advance cassettes of the new album photocopies of author Frances Cress-Welsing's "Cress Theory of Color Confrontation and Racism"—a two-decade-old Afrocentric tract that was enjoying popular revival in Black communities. Cress-Welsing believed the roots of white world supremacy lay in the white race's melanin deficiency. Their neu-rosis over being a shrinking numerical minority, she argued, led them to establish a system of racial oppression.

White critics were mystified. Did these guys really believe this claptrap? Were they spoiling for another Griff-type fight? Harry and Chuck played it coy. "Does the word *oversimplification* mean anything to you?" Harry joked in a letter to them.[51]

The album was entitled *Fear of a Black Planet*. For better or worse, it was going to be a hip-hop world now.

Eazy E: Aiming straight at your arteries.

Photo © B⁺

14

The Culture Assassins

Geography, Generation and Gangsta Rap

We want "poems that kill."
Assassin poems, Poems that shoot
guns. Poems that wrestle cops into alleys
and take their weapons leaving them dead

—Amiri Baraka

They shot bullets that brought streams of blood and death. Death. From the age of seven on, Jonathan saw George only during prison visits. He saw his brother living with the reality of death, every day, every hour, every moment.
—Angela Davis

When nineteen-year-old O'Shea Jackson returned to South Central Los Angeles in the summer of 1988, he was hopeful. All he had ever wanted to do in life was rap, and now it looked like he might be able to make something of it. Arizona had been hell—hot, dry and boring. Still, his architectural drafting degree from the Phoenix Institute of Technology might get moms and pops off his back for a few months, and within that time perhaps he could write some rhymes, make some records, cash some checks and soon move out of his folks' house.

Just two years before, he had been a junior at Taft High School, bused from his home in South Central to the suburbs of San Fernando Valley, slipping out on the weekend to grab the microphone at Eve's After Dark nightclub in Compton as the rapper named Ice Cube. He and his partners Tony "Sir Jinx" Wheatob and Darrell "K-Dee" Johnson had a group named C.I.A. (Criminals In Action). They dropped sex rhymes to shocked, delighted crowds over the hits of the day.

It was a silly act—Dolemite karaoke over UTFO beats—but it was getting atten-tion. Eve's was owned by Alonzo Williams, and because of Alonzo, Eve's was the place to be. A smooth-talking type who had secured a contract from CBS Records for his recording project, the World Class Wreckin Cru, Lonzo used the money to build a studio in back of the club to lure producing and rapping talent.

Eric Wright was in the crowd every weekend, prowling for talent. Wright had seen the South Central hip-hop scene mature around him in the early eighties. Now the diminutive twenty-three-year-old drug dealer hoped to make some quick cash on rap, a way to go legit after years of hustling. At Eve's, Wright would catch Antoine "DJ Yella" Carraby and Andre "Dr. Dre" Young spinning records. They were members of the Cru, had a mixtape side-hustle going and were learning to make beats in Lonzo's studio. They were also two of the first DJs on KDAY's AM hip-hop radio station to join the taste-making Mixmasters Crew. New tracks that they played on the weekends often became Monday's hottest sellers.

Dre, his cousin Tony and O'Shea had been neighbors in the South Central neighborhood near Washington High School, and Dre had taken a liking to the C.I.A. boys, especially Jackson, with whom he formed a side group called Stereo Crew. He got them a gig at Skateland where he was DJing. He told them how and what to rap—filthy, dirty-down X-rated rhymes. After they stole the show and got invited back, he helped them make mixtapes to get their name out, got them a shot a Eve's, and eventually, a deal to do a single for Lonzo's Kru-Cut Records.

Dre kicked in the bass for C.I.A.'s three cuts. "My Posse" and "Ill-Legal" were Beastie Boys' bites that replaced references to White Castle with lines about cruising down Crenshaw. On the third track, "Just 4 the Cash," Cube rapped, "It's all about making those dollars and cents." Now they were indemnified to Lonzo, who gave them all tiny weekly stipends instead of royalty checks.[1]

Wright had begun talking to Dre, Yella and Jackson individually. Wright told Jackson he would put them all together and form a South Central supergroup. Why not? Jackson figured. "Eazy had a partner named Ron-De-Vu, Dre was in the World Class Wreckin Cru, I was in C.I.A.," recalls Jackson. "We all kinda was committed to these groups so we figured we'd make an all-star group and just do dirty records on the side."

So one night early in 1987, Young and Wright were in Lonzo's studio with a stack of rhymes that Jackson had penned. Wright had bought some time for an East Coast duo called HBO that Dre had found. The idea was that the duo's slower New York–styled cadences and accents would be more marketable than the uptempo techno-pop rhymes that sold everywhere else—Seattle, San Francisco, Miami, Los Angeles. New York, after all, was supposed to represent the epitome of authenticity. But this notion would soon be obsolete.

Dancing to Banging

In the early 1980s, one prominent node on the Los Angeles hip-hop map was a downtown club called Radio. It was modeled on the Roxy's "Wheels of Steel" night, and presided over by local rap kingpin Ice T and jet-setting Zulu Nation DJ Afrika Islam.

New York–style b-boying went off there, but West Coast styles dominated the dancefloor. There was locking, a funk style dance started by the Watts crew, the Campbellockers, in the early '70s; popping, a surging, stuttering elaboration of The Robot, pioneered by Fresno dancer Boogaloo Sam, that would later show up in New York as the Electric Boogaloo; and strutting, a style that had come down from San Francisco's African-American and Filipino 'hoods to take hold with L.A.'s Samoan gangs.[2]

Radio made the Roxy's diversity look like a Benetton ad. Kid Frost and his *cholos* rolled down to the club in their low-riders, sporting their Pendletons and khakis. There were slumming Hollywood whites and South Central Korean-American one-point-fivers escaping long hours at the family business. Everyone but the hardest brothers left the menacing Blue City Strutters—a Samoan Blood set from Carson that would become the Boo-Yaa Tribe—alone.

When Radio faded, live hip-hop parties spread through the efforts of a popular sound system called Uncle Jam's Army, led by Rodger "Uncle Jam" Clayton who had begun throwing house parties in 1973 in South Central. A decade later, the Army was regularly filling the Los Angeles Convention Center and the Sports Arena. At their wild dances, the Army showed up in army fatigues and bright Egyptian costumes. They stacked thirty-two booming Cerwin-Vega speakers in the shape of pyramids.

Then shit turned real bad real quick.

Dance crews like the Carson Freakateers, Group Sex and the Hot Coochie Mamaz gave way to the Rolling 60s Crips and the Grape Street Boys. Playlists featuring frenetic sensual funk like Prince's "Head" and the Army's own "Yes Yes Yes" slowed down for a new audience that wanted Roger's "So Ruff So Tuff" and George Clinton's "Atomic Dog." The Freak was replaced by the Crip Walk. American-made .22's were replaced by Israeli-made Uzis. Chains got snatched, folks got robbed. One night a woman pulled a gun out of her purse and shot a guy in the jaw.

The New Style

Although they had come up in 111 Neighborhood Crip territory, Cube and Dre were not active gang members. Perhaps it was because Cube was being bused out of his 'hood or maybe it was because he was a jock. As far as Dre was concerned, banging didn't pay.[3]

But it wasn't hard for them to notice that the streets were changing. The effects of Reagan's southern hemisphere foreign policy were coming home, making millionaires of Contra entrepreneurs, illegal arms dealers, and Freeway Rick. There was a lot of firepower out there now. Since 1982, the number of gang homicides had doubled.[4] Forget knowing the ledge. Lots of these West Coast ghetto stars had already leapt screaming over it.

Yet the music on the West Coast wasn't changing. It was still about Prince-style expensive purple leather suits and slick drum machines. The World Class Wreckin Cru was a perfect example. Dre thought Lonzo was corny, but he owed him lots of money. Lonzo not only owned the studio Dre used, he had handed out loans to Dre, sometimes bailed him out of jail for not paying his parking tickets, and even let Dre take his old car.

While Lonzo was still paying off the note, the car got stolen and ended up impounded. At the same time, Dre landed himself in jail once again, just as Lonzo was coming up short and ready to cut him off anyway. Wright saw his chance, and offered the nine hundred dollars to bail him out.[5] But Dre had to agree to produce tracks for Wright's new record label, Ruthless.

What the hell, Dre figured. That's why he was now in Lonzo's studio on Wright's dime. He was working off the bond and the fees for getting the car back. Lonzo was out of a car and a DJ. Dre's mercenary willingness to sell his creativity in exchange for security would prove his downfall over and again.

One of the records in heavy rotation on KDAY was by Russ Parr's local comedy rap act Bobby Jimmy and the Critters, a track called "New York Rapper" in which Parr covered Run DMC, LL Cool J, the Beastie Boys, Eric B. & Rakim, UTFO, Roxanne Shante and Kurtis Blow in a goofy country accent. "New York rappers made the street-hard sounds. L.A. rappers? Buncha plagiarizing clowns," he rapped, with emphasis on the word "clowns." By 1987, that shit wasn't so funny anymore.

L.A. rap had hit an artistic dead end; it could carry on its raunchy, cartoonish sound or imitate serious-as-cancer New York. Lonzo was milking a four-year-old cow that was going dry. Meanwhile, Dre working with HBO seemed like an admission of defeat. Cube was tired of being a follower. He had done sex rhymes, he'd done East Coast. Maybe he wanted to show these no-name New Yorkers what Los Angeles was really about. The rap he penned for them was packed with local detail, violent in the extreme.

On hearing the lyrics, HBO refused to do it, saying the track was "some West Coast shit," and walked out. Dre, Laylaw, and Wright looked at each other—now what? Dre suggested that Wright to take a turn with the track. Wright was reluctant. He was supposed to be a manager, not a rapper. Dre pressed, not wanting to see a great beat and precious studio time going to waste. When Wright reluctantly agreed, Eazy E was born, and they began recording "Boyz-N-The Hood."

The record hit the streets in September of 1987, but Jackson had already left for Phoenix. The single he cut for Lonzo had not done anything. Who knew what this single would do? "The rap game wasn't looking too solid at that time, so I decided to go ahead and go to school," he says. "I went to a technical school just to make sure that I did what I wanted to do for a living, no matter what."

But now that Jackson was returning to Los Angeles, it was becoming clear that something had changed. While Jackson was working with T-squares, Wright's hustle and Dre and Yella's radio pull was getting the record off the ground. By the end of 1987, it was the most requested record on KDAY. Wright went from selling the record out of the trunk to swap meet vendors and retailers to a distribution deal with indie vanity label Macola. He had even paid Lonzo $750 to introduce him to a white Jewish manager in the Valley, a guy named

Jerry Heller who had once promoted Creedence Clearwater Revival, Pink Floyd, Elton John and REO Speedwagon.[6] A year after they had cut "Boyz," the single was taking hold on the streets, selling thousands of copies every week.

A Dub History of "Boyz-N-The Hood"

Jackson was proud of his rhyme. In it, Eazy cruises through town, "bored as hell" and wanting "to get ill." First he spots his car-thief friend Kilo G cruising around looking for autos to jack. Then he catches his crackhead friend JD trying to steal his car stereo. After having words, JD walks off. When Eazy follows him to make peace, JD pulls his .22 automatic. In an instant, Eazy kills him.

Like nothing has happened, he decides to see his girl for a sexual interlude. But she pisses him off, so he "reach(es) back like a pimp and slap(s) the hoe," then does the same to her angry father. Later, he witnesses Kilo G getting arrested. Kilo won't be given bail, so he sets off a prison riot.

In "Boyz-N-The Hood," girls serviced the boys, fathers were suckers and crackheads were marks. It was a seemingly irredeemable sub–Donald Goines pulp world. But then there was the unexpected finale.

Kilo makes his trial appearance and there his girlfriend, Suzy, takes up guns against the state. In the gunfight, Suzy seems bulletproof. The deputies can't stop her. Instead she goes out on her feet, not on her knees, getting sent up for a bid just like her man, barbed-wire love. By introducing this twist, a sly interpolation of Jonathan Jackson's real-life drama, "Boyz-N-The Hood" rose to the level of generational myth.

Perhaps O'Shea had heard the story as a youngster of another seventeen-year-old brother named Jackson, killed by sheriffs and prison guards in a 1970 Marin County courthouse shootout.

As Angela Davis would later remind jurors in her own trial, Jonathan Jackson lost his brother, the writer George Jackson, to the prison system at the age of seven, serving a one-to-life sentence for second-degree robbery. In early 1970, some white and black prisoners at Soledad had a minor fistfight. White prison guard O. G. Miller swiftly ended the fight by firing at three black inmates—all of whom had been known as political activists. Two died almost instantly. Guards refused to allow medical aid, and the third was left in the yard to die. Later that winter, after an announcement that a grand jury investigation had cleared Miller, prisoners attacked another guard and threw him off a third-floor balcony. George and two others, Fleeta Drumgo and John Clutchette, the ones considered the political leaders of the prison, were framed for the murder. The crime could automatically bring George the death penalty.

George's letters to Jonathan, later collected in *Soledad Brother,* revealed the depth of their relationship. In the letters, he taught the younger sibling about communism, sex, resistance, being a man. But the letters remained much of what Jonathan would know of his brother, and words only hinted at the loss Jonathan was feeling. Davis wrote, "[B]ecause it had been cramped into prison visitors' cubicles, into two-page, censored letters, the whole relationship revolved around a single aim—how to get George out here, on this side of the walls." In turn, George noticed a change in his brother. In a letter to Angela Davis in May of 1970, he wrote of Jonathan, "[He] is at that dangerous age where confusion sets in and sends brothers either to the undertaker or to prison."

On August 3, in what many took to be an ominous sign, George was transferred from Soledad Prison to San Quentin Prison, in whose gas chamber he might be executed. Four days later, Jonathan strode into the Marin County Courthouse where a prisoner named John McClain was defending himself against charges he had stabbed a prison guard. Two other prisoners, Ruchell Magee and William Christmas, were also present to testify on McClain's behalf. Jackson marched into the trial chambers with an assault rifle and a cache of weapons, and sat down. When he rose, it was to calmly say, "All right, gentleman, I'm taking over now."

Jackson taped a gun to the judge's head, took several jurors and the district attorney as hostages, then walked with the three prisoners out to a van in the parking lot. Soon enough, a San Quentin guard shot at the van, and other guards and sheriffs joined in with a hail of gunfire. The bullets wounded the district attorney and a juror. The judge, Christmas, McClain and Jackson were killed.

Deputies immediately began a nationwide search for Angela Davis, who was accused of supplying Jackson with one of the guns. She was captured and sent to prison on trumped-up charges of murder, kidnapping and conspiracy. During Davis's trial, George was killed by prison guards in a deadly prison-break attempt. Davis, Drumgo and Clutchette were later acquitted of all charges.

Jonathan Jackson's rebellion had been fearless, inarticulate and fatal. George mourned his brother by writing, "I want people to wonder at what forces created him, terrible, vindictive, cold, calm man-child, courage in one hand, machine gun in the other, scourge of the unrighteous."[7] He considered Jonathan "a soldier of the people," an image that would find a different resonance in the Los Angeles street wars of the '80s.

Whether Cube had intended to or not, "Boyz-N-The Hood" recovered the painful memory. Tracking the lives of Compton hardrocks "knowing nothing in life but to be legit," "Boyz-N-The Hood" became an anthem for the fatherless, brotherless, state-assaulted, heavily armed West Coast urban youth, a generation of Jonathan Jacksons. The impact of "Boyz" had to do with its affirmation, its boast: "We're taking over now."

And even as these boys unloaded both barrels into their authority symbols, Eazy E revealed their vulnerability. He delivered the rap in a deadpan singsong, a voice perhaps as much a result of self-conscious nervousness as hardcore fronting. Dre mirrored Eazy's ambivalence in the jumpy robotic tics of the tiny drum machine bell. And as if to cover E's studio anxiety, Dre added a pounding set of bass drum kicks to help drive home the chorus:

Now the boys in the hood are always hard
You come talking that trash we'll pull your card
Knowing nothing in life but to be legit
Don't quote me boy, 'cause I ain't said shit

The kids knew Eazy's mask instantly. They might have quoted his lines in their own adrenalin-infused, heart-poundingly defiant stances against their parents, teachers, the principal, the police, the probation officer.

So Eazy E's mask stayed. The mercenary b-boys were suddenly a group, perhaps even the "supergroup" Wright had talked about. He named it Niggaz With Attitude, a ridiculous tag that set impossibly high stakes. Now they had an image to uphold.

Los Angeles Black

Gangsta rap and postindustrial gangs did not begin in Compton, but a short distance north in Watts. Just like the Bronx gangs, they rose out of, as the ex-Crip warrior Sanyika Shakur would put it, "the ashes and ruins of the sixties."[8]

Watts was a desolate, treeless area located in a gully of sand and mud, the flood catchment for all the other neighborhoods springing up around downtown. In the 1920s Blacks had nowhere else to go.

They had been present at the very first settling of Los Angeles in the late eighteenth century, and established their first community one hundred years later. Starting at First and Los Angeles streets in downtown, they spread east and south along San Pedro and Central Avenues, where they began developing businesses.[9]

While the UNIA and the Urban League had established offices in the city by the 1920s, Los Angeles's Blacks were different—less idealistic, more pragmatic, even a little mercenary. They joined together to break into all-white neighborhoods by sending a light-skinned buyer or a sympathetic white real estate agent to make the down payment. When Blacks moved in, whites moved out. In this way, they won blocks one by one. Sociologists had a term for this process of reverse block-busting: "Negro invasion."

One Black entrepreneur had even figured out how to hustle racial fear. He told the scholar J. Max Bond:

> One of my white friends would tip me off, and I would give him the money to buy a choice lot in a white community. The next day I would go out to look over my property. Whenever a white person seemed curious, I would inform him that I was planning to build soon. On the next day the whites would be after me to sell. I would buy the property sometimes for $200 and sell it for $800 or $900. The white people would pay any price to keep the colored folks out of their communities.[10]

But during the 1920s, the Ku Klux Klan burnt crosses at 109th Street and Central Avenue, and whites erected racial covenants and block restrictions that prevented blacks from moving into their neighborhoods under legal threat of eviction. Watts, literally the bottom, called "Mud Town" even by its own residents, was the only place left to go. Because so many Blacks were moving into the city, and a Black mayor was certain to be the result, Los Angeles hastened to annex Watts in the mid-1920s.

When World War II broke out, southern migrants poured into Los Angeles to fill the need for over half a million new workers in the shipyards, aircraft and rubber industries.[11] Now African-American neighborhoods, especially Watts—which had become the center of Black Los Angeles—were overwhelmed with demands for health care, schooling, transportation and most of all, housing. Racial discrimination kept rents artificially high, and led to overcrowding as slumlords exploited poor families, who often joined together to split a monthly bill. Historian Keith Collins writes, "Single-dwelling units suddenly became four-unit dwellings; four-unit dwellings became small apartment dwellings; garages and attics, heretofore neglected, were suddenly deemed fit for human habitation."[12]

These conditions were barely eased when racial covenants were ruled unconstitutional in 1948 and huge public housing projects—the largest of which were Nickerson Gardens, Jordan Downs, Imperial Courts and Hacienda Village—began opening in the mid-1940s.[13] Watts soon had the highest concentration of public housing west of the Mississippi. But after the end of the World War II, a deep recession set in, and much of Black Los Angeles never recovered.

To the south, Compton looked like a promised land.[14] The bungalow houses were clean and pleasant; the lots had lawns and space to grow gardens. At one time, the Pacific Electric Railroad station had hung a sign: NEGROES! BE OUT OF COMPTON BY NIGHTFALL.[15] But after desegregation, Blacks filled the Central Avenue corridor from downtown all the way through Compton—the area that would come to be known as South Central.

Black Los Angeles now had a rough dividing line down Vermont Street, separating the striving "Westside" from the suffering "Eastside."[16] East of Watts, in towns like Southgate and Huntington Park, white gangs like the Spook Hunters enforced a border at Alameda Avenue.[17] And when whites began to leave the area in the 1950s, they were replaced by an aggressive, zero-tolerance police department under the leadership of Police Chief William Parker, a John Wayne–type character that made no secret of his racism.[18] Black youth clubs became protective gangs.

Los Angeles was a new kind of city, one in which most of the high-wage job growth would occur far from the inner-city outside a ring ten miles north and west of City Hall.[19] When these suburban communities proliferated after the war, people of color were effectively excluded from the job and housing bonanza. Indeed, from nearly the beginning of the city's history, Blacks and other people of color in Los Angeles had been confined to living in The Bottoms—the job-scarce, mass-transit deprived, densely populated urban core.

These were the conditions that underlined the city's first race riots, 1943's Zoot Suit riots, in which white sailors, marines and soldiers brutalized Chicanos and then Blacks from Venice Beach to East Los Angeles to Watts. And these conditions had only worsened by the time a late summer heatwave hit Watts in 1965.

Remember Watts

On the night of August 11, a routine drunk driving arrest on Avalon Boulevard and 116th Street escalated into a night of rioting. White police had stopped a pair of young Black brothers, Marquette and Ronald Frye, returning from a party only a few blocks from their home for driving erratically. As a crowd formed in the summer dusk and their mother, Rena Frye, came out to scold the boys, dozens of police units rumbled onto Avalon. In an instant, the scene began to deteriorate.

Marquette, perhaps embarrassed by the appearance of his mother, began resisting the officer's attempts to handcuff him. Soon the cops were beating him with a baton. Seeing this, Frye's brother and mother tussled with other cops and were arrested as well. Another woman, a hairdresser from down the street who had come to see what was going on, was beaten and arrested after spitting on a cop's shirt. Chanting "Burn, baby, burn!" the crowd erupted.

Over the next two nights, the police lost control of the streets. They were ambushed by rock-throwing youths. They were attacked by women who seized their guns. Their helicopters came under sniper fire. Systematic looting and burning began. Among the first things to go up in smoke were the files of credit records in the department stores.[20] Groceries, furniture stores and gun and surplus outlets were hit next. After these places were ransacked, they were set ablaze. One expert attributed the riot's blueprint to the local gangs—the Slausons, the Gladiators and the mainly Chicano set, Watts Gang V—who had temporarily dropped their rivalries.[21]

"This situation is very much like fighting the Viet Cong," Police Chief William Parker told the press on Friday the 13th. "We haven't the slightest idea when this can be brought under control."[22] Later he called the rioters "monkeys in a zoo."[23] By the evening, the LAPD and the Sheriff's Office had begun firing on looters and unarmed citizens, leaving at least six dead. Two angry whites reportedly drove into Jordan Downs and began shooting at Black residents.[24] Newspaper headlines read ANARCHY U.S.A.[25]

The National Guard arrived the next day. The death toll peaked sharply in the last two days of civil unrest. Rioting lasted five days and resulted in $40 million in damages and thirty-four dead. Until 1992, they were the worst urban riots ever recorded.

After the riots, Watts became a hotbed of political and cultural activity. Author Odie Hawkins wrote, "Watts, post outrage, was in a heavy state of fermentation. Everybody was a poet, a philosopher, an artist or simply something exotic. Even people who weren't any of those things thought they were."[26] It was a time of new beginnings: A week after the riots, the Nation of Islam's downtown mosque had been shot up and nearly destroyed by LAPD officers who claimed to be searching for a nonexistent cache of looted weapons. But the mosque survived and thrived. Soon the Nation would welcome Marquette Frye as its most prominent new member.

The gangs, as Mike Davis wrote, "joined the Revolution."[27] Maulana Ron Karenga put together the US Organization by recruiting the Gladiators and the Businessmen.[28] Members of the Slausons and the Orientals formed the Sons of Watts, another cultural nationalist organization. The powerful Slauson leader Alprentice "Bunchy" Carter led many more ex-Slausons and other gang members to reject Karenga and the cultural nationalists and affiliate with the revolutionary nationalist Black Panthers.[29]

On 103rd Street, the Black Panthers set up an office next to the Watts Happening Coffee House, which housed Mafundi, a cultural performance space. In 1966, the screenwriter and poet Bud Schulberg opened the Watts Writers Workshop there. It quickly became a cultural haven for some of the most promising artistic voices in the area, including Hawkins, author Quincy Troupe, poet Kamau Daa'ood, and three young poets that would call themselves the Watts Prophets.

Anthony "Amde" Hamilton, a Watts native, was an ex-convict and an activist when he found the Workshop through Hawkins. Soon he was working at Mafundi and serving as the Assistant Director of the Workshop. In 1969, Hawkins and Hamilton assembled a group of poets from the Workshop to record *The Black Voices: On the Streets in Watts*. In a bulldog voice—one that Eazy E would later evoke, and that would be sampled by dozens of gangsta rap producers— Hamilton growled, "The meek ain't gon' inherit *shit*, 'cause I'll take it!"

Through the happenings on 103rd Street, Hamilton met Richard Dedeaux, a Louisiana transplant, and Otis O'Solomon (then Otis Smith) from Alabama. They began performing poetry with a female pianist Dee Dee O'Neal, and conga accompaniment. In 1971, they recorded *Rapping Black in a White World*, a prophetic rap document. On the cover a child of the Revolution—a boy who would come of age in the eighties—wrapped himself in a soldier's oversized uniform and embraced a shotgun.

During the Watts riots, they had seen a racial apocalypse outlined in the "freedom flames" blackening the structures they did not own and could not control. Their poems were decidedly edgy, imbued with righteous rage, full of wordly pessimism. On "A Pimp," Otis O'Solomon rapped,

> Growing up in world of dog eat dog I learned
> the dirtiest dog got the bone
> meaning not the dog with the loudest bark
> but the coldest heart.

They chronicled tragic pimps, recounted drug-addled and bullet-riddled deaths, and called for the rise of ghetto warriors in the mold of Nat Turner. It was Black Art, as Baraka had called for, that drew blood. But this ferment could not last forever.

Panthers to Crips

The Prophets were close to the young Bunchy Carter. Once a feared leader of the Slausons, as well as its roughneck inner-core army, the Slauson Renegades, he met Eldridge Cleaver while doing time for armed robbery, and was now the Southern California leader of the Black Panther Party. He was formidable—an organic intellectual, community organizer, corner rapper, and "street nigga" all at the same time—"considered," Elaine Brown wrote, "the most dangerous Black man in Los Angeles."[30] The Slausons had started at Fremont High in Watts, but Carter now commanded the love of Black teens of the high schools in South Central.[31] His bodyguard was a Vietnam veteran named Elmer Pratt, whom he renamed Geronimo ji Jaga. The two were enrolled at UCLA, where they studied and planned the Revolution.

The Panthers and Karenga's US Organization were fighting for control of UCLA's Black Studies department, as FBI and LAPD provocateurs secretly and systematically raised the personal and ideological tensions between the two. On the morning of January 17, 1969, a Black Student Union meeting ended with the organizations firing on each other in Campbell Hall. Carter and Panther John Huggins were shot dead. Coming after a year of bloody confrontations with authorities across the country that had left dozens of Party leaders dead, the Panthers called Carter's and Huggins's deaths assassinations.

A year later, after the beef between the two organizations had been squashed, L.A. police arrested Pratt, the new Panther leader, on false charges, found an informant to pin a murder to him, and had him sent away for life. Even the Watts Writers Workshop was destroyed through the efforts of a FBI double agent who had been employed as the Workshop's publicist.

Filling the void of leadership was Raymond Washington, a charismatic teen at Watts's Fremont High School who had been a follower of Bunchy Carter. By the time Washington turned fifteen, the Slausons and the Panthers had both died with Bunchy. In 1969, Washington formed the Baby Avenues, carrying on the legacy of a fading local gang, the Avenues.[32] Over the next two years, he walked across the eastside with a gangsta limp and an intimidating walking cane, kicked his rap to impressed youths, and built the gang.

The Baby Avenues wore black leather jackets in a display of solidarity with the Panthers' style and credo of self-defense. But somewhere along the line, the goal changed to simply beating down other Black youths for their jackets.[33] Godfather Jimel Barnes, who had joined in the early days when Washington came to the Avalon Gardens projects, says Washington had summed up his vision in this way: "Chitty chitty bang bang, nothing but a Crip thang, Eastside Cuz. This is going to be the most notorious gang in the world. It's going to go from generation to generation."[34]

The origins of the name are now shrouded in legend. It may have been a corruption of "Cribs" or "Crypts." It may have stood for "C-RIP," all words that represented the gang's emerging "cradle to grave" gang-banging credo. Or it may have come from an Asian-American victim's description of her attacker, a " 'crip' with a stick."[35] In any case, as O. G. Crip Danifu told L.A. gang historian Alejandro Alonso, " 'Crippin' meant robbing and stealing, and then it developed into a way of life."[36]

For years, Mexican *pachuco* gangs had been the most organized and most feared in town. Now the Crips would transform young Black Los Angeles. Spreading through the Black corridor south to Compton and west to South Central, the Crips became, in Davis's words, "a hybrid of teen cult and proto-Mafia" and "the power source of last resort for thousands of abandoned youth."[37]

During the Nixon years, Crip sets proliferated and gang rivalries intensified. When Washington was kicked out of Fremont and sent to Washington High on the westside, he recruited Stanley "Tookie" Williams, and Crip sets expanded into South Central Los Angeles. By 1972, where there had recently been none, there were eighteen new Black gangs.[38]

Youths on Compton's Piru Street organized themselves into groups they called Pirus or Bloods. Other Crip rivals also emerged. In 1973, the beefs turned bloody. Through the efforts of Bobby Lavender, Sylvester "Puddin' " Scott and others, Brims, Bloods and Pirus formed a Bloods confederation.[39] Gang fashion had shifted from Black power dress to an appropriation of *cholo* style—Pendletons, white tees, khakis—and when Crips began flagging blue, Bloods flagged red.

Like a national map on the night of a presidential election, the Los Angeles grid was now being tallied into columns of red and blue. In the unbreachable logic of turf warfare, sets proliferated in the Black corridor, stretching through the colored suburbs west to the beach at Venice, south to Long Beach, and north to Altadena. Soon there were so many Crip sets they even went to war with each other.

"During the late seventies it slowed down," Athens Park Bloods member Cle "Bone" Sloan says, "because niggas started working in the factories. When they took the jobs away, shit started back up. Then cocaine hit the streets and niggas were in it for real."[40] As the 1980s dawned, Raymond Washington was dead in prison, killed by a rival, and 155 gangs claimed 30,000 members across the city.[41]

The Bottoms

Firestone, Goodyear and General Motors closed their manufacturing plants in South Central. In all, 131 plants shuttered during the 1980s, eliminating unionized manufacturing jobs in the rubber, steel, and auto industries and leaving 124,000 people unemployed in the center city. Job growth shifted to service and information industries located beyond the rim of the ten-mile ring. Bobby Lavender saw the effects: "Thousands of parents lost their jobs. Homes and cars were repossessed. People who had just started to become middle-class were losing everything and sinking down."[42]

In 1978, California voters, spurred by the same right-wing strategists who would soon lift Reagan from his former governorship into the presidency, passed Proposition 13, an initiative that capped property taxes and dramatically altered state and local government financing, launching a national tax revolt and permanently plunging the state into the cruelest cycle of state budget crises in the country. Passage of Proposition 13 had the kind of effect on California's cities that turning off the water might have had on its farm belt. Three decades of investment had made the state's primary and secondary education, college and university systems the envy of the nation—a model of access and quality. After Proposition 13, the state's K–12 system tumbled down all national educational indices, and as fees exploded, its colleges and universities became increasingly inaccessible to the working-class and the poor. Now that the postwar generation had gotten what it needed for itself and its children, it was pulling up the ladder.

In Los Angeles, the signs of the new mood of the state's aging white electorate read, "Armed Response." Around the downtown and at the edges of the ten-mile ring, in what Mike Davis called "post-liberal Los Angeles," security fences and security forces sprung up in commercial buildings and around gated communities. Meanwhile, Chief Darryl Gates's army locked down the interior—the vast area running south of the Santa Monica Freeway, along both sides of the Harbor Freeway and back west with the Century Freeway that had been swallowed up into the construct called "South Central," a heaving barbarian space behind the walls, the Everywhere Else at the bottom of the ten-mile ring, viewed mainly through the nightly news or from behind the surveillance camera.

During the Reagan recession of 1983, Los Angeles's official unemployment rate hit 11 percent.[43] But in South Central, it was much higher, at least 50 percent for youths.[44] The median household income there was just half the state median. While white poverty rates in Los Angeles County actually declined to 7 percent, a quarter of Blacks and Latinos and 14 percent of Asians lived below the poverty line. In South Central, the rate was higher than 30 percent. Almost half of South Central's children lived below the poverty level.[45] Infant mortality in Watts was triple the rate in Santa Monica, only twenty miles away.[46] By any index, conditions had deteriorated for the generation born after the Watts Uprising.

What the South Bronx had been to the 1970s, South Central would be for the 1980s. It was the epitome of a growing number of inner-city nexuses where deindustrialization, devolution, Cold War adventurism, the drug trade, gang structures and rivalries, arms profiteering, and police brutality were combining to destabilize poor communities and alienate massive numbers of youths.

The Sound of the Batterram

Chaos was settling in for a long stay. Even an otherwise innocuous knock on one's door could bring the threat of fathomless violence. The chief symbol of the new repression was the Batterram—a V-100 armored military vehicle equipped with a massive battering ram that police used to barge into suspected crackhouses. With the drug war in full swing, the Batterram was getting a lot of action.

By the summer of 1985, nineteen-year-old rapper Toddy Tee's "Batterram" tape was the most popular cassette on the streets. Telling a story of a working-class family man whose life is interrupted by cluckheads and the Batterram, the tape was one of the first to describe the changing streets. Toddy had written and recorded the rap in his bedroom as he watched the Batterram crash through a crackhouse live on television, then duplicated the initial copies on a cheap dubbing deck, and gone out in the streets to hawk them. To his surprise, the song became a sensation, a top request on KDAY. By the end of the year, he was recutting the track in an expensive studio with a major-label budget over music produced by big-name funk musician Leon Haywood (whose 1975 hit, "I Want' a Do Something Freaky to You" would later be used on Dr. Dre's "Nuthin' But a 'G' Thing").

Toddy Tee was one of several teenagers who had hung out in the garage of a local rap legend named Mixmaster Spade. If Lonzo's empire was one center where South Central rap talent gathered, Spade's was the other major one. Spade was an older cat who had come up on '70s funk, and had developed a singing style of rap that made him a mixtape and house party legend from Watts to Long Beach. Although he never became more than a local rap hero, his style was carried on by artists like Snoop Dogg, Nate Dogg, Warren G and DJ Quik.

At Spade's house on 156th and Wilmington, right under the flight path of the two-strip Compton Airport, he held court with a kind of advanced rap school, teaching the finer points of rapping, mixing and scratching to a burgeoning crew of kids that called themselves the Compton Posse—Toddy, King Tee, Coolio, DJ Pooh, DJ Alladin, J-Ro (later of the Alkaholiks) and others. But classes ended for good one afternoon in late 1987 when L.A. county sheriffs tried to raid the house, and Spade and seven associates engaged the sheriffs in a shootout. During the fracas, one of the sheriffs plugged another in the back and sent him to King-Drew hospital. When the smoke cleared and Spade and his crew had surrendered, sheriffs confiscated $3,000 in cash, a MAC-10 and twenty-five gallons of PCP—better known in the 'hood as "sherm" or "water."[47] The local rap school had been doubling as the neighborhood narcotics factory.

These South Central rap songs were like the new blues. But the Mississippi blues culture had developed under the conditions of back-breakingly oppressive work, the toil of building a modern nation. Hip-hop culture, whether in the South Bronx or South Central, had developed under alienated play, as solid jobs evaporated into the airy buzz and flow of a network society. As Greg Brown, a resident of Nickerson Gardens, put it, "In the sixties, General Motors in neighboring Southgate was the future. In the seventies, King Hospital was the future. Now the future in Watts and South Central is jail. You see that new Seventy-seventh Street LAPD station? It's beautiful. You see anything else in the community that looks better than that jail?"[48]

Hip-hop was close to the underground economy because, more often than not, it was being made by youths who were not exploitable, but expendable. The flatland ghettos of South Central had more in common with the distant hill-side *favelas* of Rio De Janeiro, 'hoods switched off from the global network, than with the walled estates of Beverly Hills just miles away. The main difference, though, was the proximity of the L.A. 'hoods to the heart of the most advanced culture industry in the world. So from homemade cassettes, grandiose dreams were swelling.

These new blues captured the feel of the serpentine twists of daily inner-city life on the hair-trigger margin. With their urban-canyon echoing drums and casual descriptions of explosive violence, the new myths of crack, guns, and gangs sounded a lot larger than life. On *Straight Outta Compton*, they reached their apotheosis.

The Alternative to Black Power

Bryan Turner was a young white SoCal transplant from Winnipeg. In 1981, he had set out to make a living in the Los Angeles music industry, going to work at Capitol Records' Special Markets department where he put together cheap anthologies for niche markets. He left to start his own label, Priority Records, and turned a profit from novelty records like The California Raisins. After selling two million units of the Raisins, Turner's staff swelled to ten and was securing annual sales of $5 million. Now he needed a real artist.

Eazy E's manager Jerry Heller had his offices in the same building. Despite the fact that "Boyz-N-The Hood" had begun moving thousands of copies, Heller was receiving rejection after rejection from major labels for Eazy's "super-group." The stuff was too violent, he was told, too street. Heller walked down to Turner's office one day and told him of his new rap project. He played Turner "Boyz-N-The Hood" and a rough demo of "Fuck Tha Police." Turner could not believe his ears, and immediately scheduled a meeting with Heller, Eric Wright and the group.

As they discussed the group and the music, Wright impressed Turner as a man with a plan. Turner says, "Almost instinctively, without a lot of experience, I wanted to be in business with these kids." He signed NWA as Priority's first act, and quickly sold over 300,000 copies of "Boyz-N-The Hood."

When Jackson returned from Phoenix, he jumped back into the fold. He,

Wright's neighbor from Compton, Lorenzo Patterson, who called himself MC Ren, and an associate of Dre and Wright, Tracy "The DOC" Curry, penned the lyrics for Eazy E's debut, *Eazy Duz It*. Their diminutive character inflated stereotypes to their breaking point—equal parts urban threat, hypersexed Black male, and class clown. The album was not half as compelling as "Boyz-N-The Hood," but when it came out in 1988, it went gold.

Then they turned their attention to the NWA album. Confident that they were on to something, they decided to go as far out as they could. Dr. Dre bragged to Brian Cross, "I wanted to make people go: 'Oh shit, I can't believe he's saying that shit.' I wanted to go all the way left. Everybody trying to do this Black power and shit, so I was like, let's give 'em an alternative. Nigger niggernigger niggernigger fuck this fuck that bitch bitch bitch bitch suck my dick, all this kind of shit, you know what I'm saying?"[49]

If the thing was protest, they would toss the ideology and go straight to the riot. If the thing was sex, they would chuck the seduction and go straight to the fuck. Forget knowledge of self or empowering the race. This was about, as Eazy would put it, the strength of street knowledge.

The Aesthetics of Excess

For the album's opener, the title track, Dre looped up the drum break from D.C. funk band, the Winstons' "Amen Brother," a frenetic horn-driven instrumental funk take on the joyous hymn, "Amen," that had been revived by Curtis Mayfield and was now played with Sunday-morning abandon. The raucous and herky-jerky breakdown—which later formed the backbone for the equally frenetic drum 'n' bass sound a decade later—was the most stable element of the track.

These were not going to be the old Negro spirituals. Under Dre's hand, the "Amen" break took on a brutal, menacing efficiency. Although Dre's production was not as minimalist as Marley Marl's, it shared the desire for streamlining. He bassed up the kick drum, cued an insistent double-time hi-hat, and added a "Yeah! Huh!" affirmation and a scratched snare to propel the beat futureward. Then he inserted an sustaining horn line and a staccato guitar riff to increase the pre-millennial tension. It sounded like the drums of death.

Dre was creating a hybrid production style, adding studio player Stan "the

Guitar Man" Jones's vamps and Yella's turntable-cuts to sampled funk fragments and concrete-destroying Roland 808 bass drops. He slowed the tempo from technopop/electrodance speeds to more aggrandizing bpm's. High-pitched horn stabs lit up the tracks like rocket launchers.

Hip hop's braggadocio, too, was about to enter a new era. Jackson was exploring the contours of his new identity, Ice Cube. In "Straight Outta Compton," "Fuck Tha Police," "Gangsta Gangsta" and "I Ain't Tha 1," he portrayed himself as an untouchable rebel without a cause. Police, girls, rivals—none of them could get in Cube's game.

Reaganism had eliminated youth programs while bombarding youths with messages to desist and abstain; it was all about tough love and denial and getting used to having nothing. Even the East Coast utopians like Rakim and Chuck talked control and discipline. By contrast, excess was the essence of NWA's appeal. These poems celebrated pushers, played bitches, killed enemies, and assassinated police. Fuck delayed gratification, they said, take it all now. "Gangsta Gangsta" was the first single released from these sessions. On it, Ice Cube hollered,

> And then you realize we don't care
> We don't "Just say no"
> We're too busy saying, "Yeah!"

Oddly enough, the album ended with a techno-pop groove produced by an uncredited Arabian Prince, "Something 2 Dance 2," more G-rated than G'ed down. It was as if the crew had hedged their bets. When the song was released as a B-side to "Gangsta Gangsta," it became a mixshow and club staple and one of the biggest urban hits of 1988 in the West and the South. In fact, "Something 2 Dance 2" pointed sideways to the dance-floor-fillers Dre and Arabian Prince were doing for pop crossover acts like J.J. Fad, Cli-N-Tel, the Sleeze Boyz, and Dre's then-girlfriend Michel'le. J.J. Fad's *Supersonic: The Album* had easily outsold *Eazy Duz It*. But all these songs were like echoes of Eve's After Dark or an Uncle Jam's party, relics of an age of innocence that the rest of *Straight Outta Compton* was about to slam the door on forever. Nobody would be dancing anymore.

The Return of The Local

After the album was officially released on January 25, 1989, it went gold in six weeks. It had been recorded for under $10,000. Radio would not dare go near it, so Priority did almost nothing to promote it. The album's runaway success signaled the beginning of a sea-change in pop-culture tastes.

Because the sound was so powerful that it had to be named, someone called NWA's music "gangsta rap" after Cube's indomitable anthem, despite the fact that he would have preferred they had paid more attention to the next line of the chorus—KRS-One's pronouncement: "It's not about a salary, it's all about reality." But the moniker stuck, naming the theatrics and the threat, the liberating wordsound power and the internalized oppression, the coolest rebellion and the latest pathology, the new Black poetry and the "new punk rock."

As young populations browned, youths were increasingly uninterested in whitewashed hand-me-downs. The surprising success of Ted Demme and Fab 5 Freddy's *Yo! MTV Raps* in 1988 made African-American, Chicano and Latino urban style instantly accessible to millions of youths. With its claims to street authenticity, its teen rebellion, its extension of urban stereotype, and its individualist "get mine" credo, gangsta rap fit hand-in-glove with a multiculti youth demographic weaned on racism and Reaganism, the first generation in a half century to face downward mobility.

"That's how we sold two million," Turner says. "The white kids in the Valley picked it up and they decided they wanted to live vicariously through this music. Kids were just waiting for it." Although MTV banned the video for the title track two months after the record's release, the album became a cultural phenomenon. Fab 5 Freddy bucked upper management and brought his *Yo! MTV Raps* crew to tour with the crew through the streets of Compton.

Like a hurricane that had gathered energy over hot open waters before heading inland, *Straight Outta Compton* hit American popular culture with the same force as the Sex Pistols' *Never Mind the Bollocks* had in the U.K. eleven years earlier. Hip-hop critic Billy Jam says, "Like the Sex Pistols, NWA made it look easy, inspiring a Do-It-Yourself movement for anyone from the streets to crank out gangsta rap tapes." All one had to have was a pen and a pad of paper, a mic, a mixer, and a sampler. Thousands of kids labored over their raps in their dark bedrooms, then stepped onto the streets to learn first-hand the vagaries of hustling and distribution—all just so that people could hear their stories.

NWA's *Straight Outta Compton* democratized rap and allowed the world to rush in. It was as if NWA overturned transnational pop culture like a police car, gleefully set the offending thing on fire, then popped open some forties, and danced to their own murder rap.

As capital fled deindustrialized inner cities and inner-ring suburbs for Third World countries and tax-sheltered exurban "edge cities," the idea of the Local returned with a vengeance. Big thinkers like Chuck D and Rakim had broadened hip-hop's appeal with revolutionary programs and universalist messages. But two years after Rakim's open invitation to join the hip-hop nation—"It ain't where you're from, it's where you're at"—gangsta rap revoked it.

"We're born and raised in Compton!" NWA bellowed, decentering hip-hop from New York forever. NWA dropped hip-hop like a '64 Chevy right down to street-corner level, lowered it from the mountaintop view of Public Enemy's recombinant nationalism and Rakim's streetwise spiritualism, and made hip-hop narratives specific, more coded in local symbol and slang than ever before.

After *Straight Outta Compton*, it really was all about where you were from. NWA conflated myth and place, made the narratives root themselves on the corner of every 'hood. And now every 'hood could be Compton, everyone had a story to tell. Even Bill Clinton's sepia-toned videobio, aired at the 1992 Democratic Convention, could have been titled *Straight Outta Hope*.

That a hood-centric aesthetic might rise with the Reagan right's attack on big government seemed appropriate. To combat their defense-bloated deficits, Republicans had introduced a strategy of devolution, shifting much of the burden of health, education and social services from federal government back to the states and cities. By the 1990s, under President Clinton, Democrats moved to the so-called center, joining Republicans in the slashing and burning of their own legacy.

Federal government would no longer be a place to seek remedies, as it had been during the civil rights and Black power era. Politics in the Beltway was becoming increasingly symbolic, just sound and fury. Nor could the courts, stuffed with Reagan appointees, be a source of relief. Many major political struggles had already shifted to the level of state and city governments, and were being waged amidst declining resources. States with older, less urban, more homogenous populations and low social service needs—usually the "red-column" Republican-dominated states—made it through this transition just fine. States with younger, browning, urban populations and expanding social service needs—usually "blue-column" Democratic-dominated states—fell into a brutal cycle of crisis and cleanup, each more severe than the last.

The gangsta rappers were more right than they ever knew. Where you were from was exactly the story.

The War on Gangs

If the new national consensus around federal government was less-is-more, the new urban consensus around local government was more-is-more, particularly when it came to attacking crime and those old social pariahs, gang members. But the War on Gangs soon soured into something else entirely. And once again, Los Angeles was the bellwether.

The shot that launched the War on Gangs was not fired in Compton, East Los Angeles, or the central city neighborhoods of the Bottoms, but in Westwood Village, amidst hip clothing boutiques, theaters and eateries a short distance from UCLA's Fraternity Row.

There on January 30, 1988, in the teeming Saturday night crowd of students, wealthy westsiders, and youths who had come from throughout the city to cruise the Village, a Rolling 60s Crip named Durrell DeWitt "Baby Rock" Collins spotted an enemy from the Mansfield Hustler Crips walking up Broxton Avenue. Two young Asian Americans, Karen Toshima and her boyfriend, Eddie Poon, were out celebrating Toshima's promotion to senior art director at a local ad agency. They unwittingly walked into the crossfire. Even as Poon tried to pull Toshima to the ground, one of two bullets intended for Collins's rival struck her in the head.[50] She died at UCLA Medical Center the next day.

City Hall leaders reacted with outrage. To many Asian Americans' dismay, Toshima became a symbol of the city's racial divide. For whites, Toshima's death was a sign that gang violence was drawing uncomfortably close. To Blacks and Latinos, one death in Westwood was apparently more important to City Hall than hundreds in East and South Central Los Angeles.

Police Chief Darryl Gates had been itching for a war. Now he would get it. In weeks, City Hall leaders voted to add 650 officers to LAPD, bringing the department to its largest size in history. LAPD held an emergency summit on gang violence and pushed for millions in emergency funds for a new military-style operation on the gangs. City Hall gave its blessing to Gates's Operation Hammer, a program of heavy-handed sweeps in Black and brown communities touted as a national model in the War on Gangs.

On August 1, in what was supposed to be Operation Hammer's crowning moment, Gates brought the War on Gangs to South Central. That evening, eighty-eight LAPD officers, supported by thundering helicopters overhead, trained their firepower on two apartment buildings at the corner of 39th Street and Dalton Avenue in South Central Los Angeles. Cops stormed through the two buildings, taking axes to furniture and walls, overturning washing machines and stoves, smashing mirrors, toilets and stereos, rounding up residents and beating dozens of them. They spray-painted LAPD RULES and ROLLIN 30S DIE on apartment walls. One resident was forced wet and naked out of the shower and forced to watch her two toddlers taken away while cops destroyed her apartment with sledgehammers.[51] "We weren't just searching for drugs. We were delivering a message that there was a price to pay for selling drugs and being a gang member," said one policeman who participated in the raid. "I looked at it as something of a Normandy Beach, a D-Day."[52]

Residents in the area had indeed complained to police of the drug dealing by Crips on the block. But none of those dealers lived in these two buildings. The raid yielded only trace amounts of crack and less than six ounces of marijuana. The Red Cross was forced to house nearly two dozen of the buildings' tenants, who had been effectively rendered homeless. One relief official termed it "a total disaster, a shocking disaster."[53]

In fact, Operation Hammer had been a massive failure from the start. In the year following Toshima's death, Gates's operation netted 25,000 arrests, mainly of youths that appeared to fit the department's gang profile. 1,500 youths could be swept up into jail in a day; 90 percent of them might be released without charge, after their information was entered into the gang database, now teeming with the names of thousands of innocents.[54] Meanwhile, hardcore bangers often tipped each other off in advance of the sweeps and escaped the LAPD dragnet.[55] The math of the Hammer did not add up. By 1992, the city was paying out $11 million annually in brutality settlements while allocating less than $2 million to gang intervention programs, and almost half of all young Black males living in South Central were in the gang database.[56]

Twilight Bey, a former Cirkle City Piru, described to hip-hop journalist and DJ David "Davey D" Cook a typically harrowing day in the life of a young male in South Central.

> One of the things that would always happen is [the police] would stop you and ask you "What gang are you from?" . . . In some cases, if you had a snappy answer and by that I mean, if you were quick and to the point and had one word answers they would get up in your face and grab your collar, push you up against the police car and choke you. Or they would call us over and tell us to put our hands up and place them on the hood of the police car. Now usually the car had been running all day, which meant that the engine was hot. So the car is burning our hands which meant that we would have to remove our hands from the car. When that happened, the police would accuse of us of not cooperating. Next thing you know you would get pushed in the back or knocked over . . .
>
> You have to remember most of us at that time were between the ages of twelve and sixteen. Just a year ago we were ten and eleven and playing in the sheriff's basketball league where they would treat us like little kids. A year later when we are close to being teenagers we are suddenly being treated with all this abuse.
>
> In a lot of cases you had kids who had chosen never to be a gang member. . . . If you told them you weren't in a gang, they would look at whatever graffiti was written on the wall and put you on record as being part of that gang.
>
> DAVEY D: . . . It seems like it was some sort of sick rites of passage so that by the time you became a grown man you knew to never cross that line with the police.
>
> TWILIGHT: Yes, that's exactly what it was. It was some sort of social conditioning. Instilling fear is the strongest motivation that this world has to use. It's also the most negative. . . . What I mean by that is, if you are constantly being pushed into a corner where you are afraid, you're going to get to a point where you one day won't be. Eventually one day you will

fight back. Eventually one day you will push back. When you push back what is going to be the end result? How far will this go?

The Backlash

By June 1989, a right-wing backlash against NWA was in full effect. That month, the newsletter *Focus On the Family Citizen* bore the headline RAP GROUP NWA SAYS "KILL POLICE." Police departments across the South and Midwest faxed each other the song's lyrics. Tour dates were abruptly cancelled. Cops refused to provide security for NWA shows in Toledo and Milwaukee. In Cincinnati, federal agents subjected the crew to drug searches, asking if they were L.A. gang members using their tour as a front to expand their crack-selling operations. Nothing was ever found.[57]

In August, FBI assistant director Milt Ahlerich fired off a letter bluntly warning Priority Records on "Fuck Tha Police." It read:

A song recorded by the rap group N.W.A. on their album entitled *Straight Outta Compton* encourages violence against and disrespect for the law enforcement officer and has been brought to my attention. I understand your company recorded and distributed this album and I am writing to share my thoughts and concerns with you.

Advocating violence and assault is wrong, and we in the law enforcement community take exception to such action. Violent crime, a major problem in our country, reached an unprecedented high in 1988. Seventy-eight law enforcement officers were feloniously slain in the line of duty during 1988, four more than in 1987. Law enforcement officers dedicate their lives to the protection of our citizens, and recordings such as the one from N.W.A. are both discouraging and degrading to these brave, dedicated officers.

Music plays a significant role in society, and I wanted you to be aware of the FBI's position relative to this song and its message. I believe my views reflect the opinion of the entire law enforcement community.[58]

The letter came as NWA was touring, and had the effect of further mobilizing police along the tour route. NWA's tour promoters tried to secure an agreement from the band not to perform the song. The national 200,000-member Fraternal Order of Police voted to boycott groups that advocated assaults on officers of the law. But in Detroit, where local police showed in intimidatingly large numbers, the crowd chanted "Fuck the police" all night, and the crew decided to try anyway. As Cube began the song, the cops rushed the stage. The group fled.

Music critic David Marsh and publicist Phyllis Pollack broke the Ahlerich story in a cover article in *The Village Voice*, and through their organization Music In Action, mobilized the ACLU and industry leaders to formally protest. Turner forwarded the letter to sympathetic congresspersons and the FBI backed off.

Choosing Sides

But NWA's scattershot test of the limits of free speech provoked outrage even in sympathetic quarters.

"I thought NWA was Satan's spawn. I was like, fuck these Negroes for real," says hip-hop journalist Sheena Lester, then the youth and culture editor for the Black-owned, South Central–based *Los Angeles Sentinel,* later an editor at *Rap Pages and Vibe*. "I was reading about them—who are these motherfuckers? What do you mean, 'bitch' this and 'ho' that? Fuck them. If I'm a bitch, kiss my ass. I just felt like dealing with NWA was counterproductive."

She was not alone. The political and cultural rads had become hip-hop progressives, deeply influenced by their elders' Third World liberation politics but drawn to the rapidly transforming landscape of pop culture's present. The media dam holding back representations of youths of color was near to bursting, and hip-hop gave them confidence the flood would soon come. They took over college and community radio stations, started up magazines, cafes and clubs, and created art, design and poetry with the same kind of energy they took to storming administration buildings.

NWA presented them with a thorny dilemma. There was the I-am-somebody rap rewrite of Charles Wright's Watts 103rd Street Band's "Express Yourself" and the lumpenprole rebellion of "Fuck Tha Police." But they certainly couldn't ignore the allure of lines like, "To a kid looking up to me, life ain't nothing but bitches and money," not least when the rhyme was being delivered boldly over thrilling beats that made a heart race.

The first boycotts against NWA came from community radio DJs and hip-hop writers, who were publicly outraged at the crew's belligerent ignorance, and privately ambivalent about the music's visceral heart-pounding power. Bay Area hip-hop DJs Davey D and Kevin "Kevvy Kev" Montague led a boycott of NWA and Eazy E on their nationally influential college radio shows, believing it would be contradictory to play such music while they were trying to create an Afrocentric space on the air. Both devoted hours of call-in radio to the debate, and their listeners finally supported the ban. The boycott spread to other hip-hop shows across the nation.

To the hip-hop progressives, the true believers who embraced rap as the voice of their generation, NWA sounded militantly incoherent. Their music drew new lines over issues of misogyny, homophobia, and violence. NWA had stepped up rap's dialogics; reaction was the point. They anticipated the criticisms, but silenced them by shouting them down. Defiant and confident, Yella even disclosed the in-joke, scratching in a female voice, "Hoping all you sophisticated motherfuckers hear what I have to say."

The hip-hop progressives were hearing it and were conflicted. Three decades after Baraka's call for "poems that kill," radical chic had become gangsta chic. Just as the blues had for a generation of white baby boomers, these tall tales populated with drunken, high, rowdy, irresponsible, criminal, murderous niggas with attitude seemed to be just what the masses of their generation wanted. Even more disconcerting, they lined up all the right enemies: the Christian right, the FBI, baby boomer demagogues. NWA was going to force every hip-hop progressive to confront her or his relationship to the music and choose sides.

When *Straight Outta Compton* crossed over to white audiences, things became very unpleasant. Gangsta rap was proving more than just "the new punk rock"; it became a more formidable lightning rod for the suppression of youth culture than white rock music ever had been. Yet the music was undoubtedly difficult to defend. To the hip-hop progressives, it sometimes seemed less than a cultural effect of material realities, a catalyst for progressive discussion, or objective street reportage of social despair, than the start of further reversal. Yet the music was undoubtedly difficult to defend. It sometimes seemed less than a cultural effect of material realities, a catalyst for progressive discussion, or objective street reportage of social despair, than the start of further reversal.

In the photo for a 1990 *Source* cover story, Eazy E aimed his 9mm at the reader, over the cover line, THE GANGSTA RAPPER: VIOLENT HERO OR NEGATIVE ROLE MODEL? Inside, a fierce debate raged over gangsta rap. David Mills asked, "[Y]ou wonder whether things have gotten out of control, and whether, like radiation exposure, it'll be years before we can really know the consequences of our nasty little entertainments."[59]

Worse yet, the culture wars seemed to stoke the political wars—the War on Gangs, the War on Drugs, the War on Youth. As Rob Marriott, James Bernard and Allen Gordon would write in *The Source,* "The saddest thing is that these attacks on rap have helped set the stage for the most oppressive and wrongheaded crime legislation. Three strikes out? Mandatory sentences? More cops? More prisons? Utter bullshit."[60]

But the hip-hop progressives had always argued that the media needed to be opened to unheard voices. By calling themselves journalists, Ice Cube and NWA outmaneuvered the hip-hop progressives, positioning themselves between the mainstream and those voices. No one else, they claimed, was speaking for the brother on the corner but them—loudly, defiantly and unapologetically. So *Straight Outta Compton* also marked the beginning of hip-hop's obsession with "The Real." From now on, rappers had to *represent*—to scream for the unheard and otherwise speak the unspeakable. Life on the hair-trigger margin—with all of its unpredictability, contradiction, instability, menace, tragedy and irony, with its daily death and resistance—needed to be described in its passionate complexity, painted in bold strokes, framed in wide angles, targeted with laser precision. A generation needed to assassinate its demons.

Many young hip-hop progressives would thus come to have their "NWA moment," that moment of surprise and surrender when outrage turned to empathy, rejection became recognition and intolerance gave way to embrace. "I was going to a club called 'Funky Reggae,' and I remember being in the middle of the dance floor, hearing 'Dopeman' for the first time and stopping," says Lester. "And going over to the side of the dance floor and just concentrating on what they were saying—which was tough to do because the beat was so bananas. The lyrics just struck me so tough I had to step to the side and really concentrate on what they were talking about. And that's when I fell in love with NWA. There's been moments in my life when I've thought certain things or put up with certain things and felt a certain way about things and then, with the snap of a finger, clarity came. And this was one of those moments."

Suddenly the ghosts of 1965 seemed not only prescient, but present. They were gazing over Ice Cube's shoulder. They were pushing hip-hop progressives to give up the certainty of the past, to embrace their generation and its future, even if that meant coming closer to apocalypse and decay. A millennial impulse was brewing.

Richard Dedeaux's words from Watts seemed prophetic:

Ever since they passed them civil rights
Those fires have been lighting up the nights
And they say they ain't gon' stop til we all have equal rights
Looks to me like dem niggas ain't playing.

Ice Cube's Amerikkkan colors, 1993.

15.

The Real Enemy

The Cultural Riot of Ice Cube's *Death Certificate*

Rap is really funny, man. But if you don't see that it's funny, it will scare the shit out of you.

—Ice T

Sometime in the middle of 1991, two icons of Black power—past and present, female and male, progressive and nationalist—sat down to break bread. It would be an eye-opening afternoon for Angela Y. Davis and O'Shea "Ice Cube" Jackson.

Ice Cube had just been through two years of turmoil. After coming off a tour that had ended with something close to a police riot, he returned home to the same bed he had slept in as a teenager. His mom had him washing the dishes and taking out the trash.[1] The house got fired upon, mistakenly, in a gang drive-by.[2] What was he still doing here, he wondered, and what was up with his money?

Together, *Straight Outta Compton* and *Eazy Duz It* had sold three million copies. The tour grossed $650,000. Cube went to ask Jerry Heller about his cut. He received $23,000 for the tour, $32,700 for the album, and was told to leave it alone. "Jerry Heller lives in a half-million-dollar house in Westlake and I'm still living at home with my mother. Jerry's driving a Corvette and a Mercedes-Benz and I've got a Suzuki Sidekick," he told Frank Owen. "Jerry's making all the money and I'm not."[3] He got his own lawyer and accountant, and took off for the east coast.

The magnet was the Bomb Squad. "I just thought, at the time, there was two producers that was even worth fucking with—Dr. Dre and the Bomb Squad. If I couldn't get Dre, I was going to the Bomb Squad. To me it was simple," he says.

Creatively and philosophically, Cube felt he had taken the idea of Black teen rebellion to its logical end. He was ready to grow up, and in Chuck and the S1Ws, he found willing mentors. They gave him books to read, introduced him into the Nation of Islam, and he soaked it all up with the wide-eyed hunger of a younger brother. "Up to this point, I was just rolling through life trying to get money. That was my life before," Cube says. "This kind of opened me up to a whole new world. It gave me my freedom mentally to deal with this world."

The Politics of Getting Mine

Amerikkka's Most Wanted was completed in February 1990 just after the Bomb Squad had wrapped up *Fear of a Black Planet*. If *Black Planet* had seemed tightly wound, the result of a need to regain control, *Most Wanted* was the opposite, like Cube had been waiting to exhale. Eager to flaunt his skills and his knowledge, he made every track a hot blast.

From police and street rivals, Cube moved to new targets, like naïve pan-Africanists and jock-riding fans. But, reflecting his newfound interest in Farrakhan-style nationalism, he reserved most of his venom for the pathologically dependent.

On "Once Upon a Time in the Projects," Cube's middle-class narrator pays his girl a visit in her public housing apartment. Her neglectful mom has abandoned one of her brothers to the gangs and left the other to run around in a dirty diaper while she cooks up crack in the kitchen. The detail may have come off as *In Living Color*–funny, but it barely hid his outrage: here was how government handouts degraded the weak-minded Black poor.

"You Can't Fade Me" leapt headlong into controversy with feminists. The narrator imagines "kick(ing) the bitch in the tummy" and going "in the closet looking for the hanger" to end the pregnancy of a girl with whom he had a one-night stand. The woman is "the neighborhood hussy," looking to pin a man for child support. The song may have seemed equally merciless to its narrator—a jobless drunk trying to look good to his homies, more concerned about taking care of his dick than taking care of a kid—except that in the end the man crows when it turns out the baby is not his. Taking care of yourself was the only way to maintain self-respect. It was Darwinian politics, survival of the fittest. Weakness was feminized.

At the same time, Cube brought depth to the male characters he played—on record or on screen. Tapped to play Doughboy in John Singleton's film *Boyz N The Hood*, Cube became a post-industrial Cain suffering from a mother's derision and a father's absence. Both Singleton and Ice Cube had strong, loving relationships with their fathers, but fatherlessness would always loom large in their work, the ghosts of Malcolm, Martin, Bunchy, and George appearing as absent fathers to a wayward generation gone nihilistic.

Cube now saw his experience being bused to the Valley as formative. He realized, "I was mad at everything. When I went to the schools in the Valley, going through those neighborhoods, seeing how different they were from mine, that angered me. The injustice of it, that's what always got me—the injustice."[4] Cube was moving toward a racial and generational view, his gangsta aesthetic evolving into a proto-nationalism.

On the title track, Cube's criminal antihero is literally breaking out of South Central, heading into the suburbs, seventy years after Blacks spilled south out of downtown, to launch a "nigga invasion, point blank, on the Caucasian." This is payback. Jacking, he muses, is "the American way, 'cause I'm the G-A-N-G-S-T-A." Suddenly the police crack down on him. "I said it before and I still taunt it," he concludes. "Every motherfucker with a color is most wanted." The ambiguity of "color"—did he mean blue and red or Black and brown?—summed up Cube's move from repping his streets to something bigger.

When he returned to South Central to film the movie, he met Craig "Kam" Miller, a rapper and a former gang member who was in the process of becoming Craig X at the Compton Mosque #54. Cube was soon meeting with Khallid Abdul Muhammad, the charismatic firebrand who had organized Muhammad Mosque #27. The bald-domed Muhammad called himself a "truth terrorist and knowledge gangsta, a Black history hit man and an urban guerilla," and his mosque expanded its ministry into the broadening gang peace movement, becoming a national model for Farrakhan's gang outreach work.[5] Cube shaved off his jheri-curl and took refuge in the Nation of Islam. Full of new ideas, he was confident his next album, *Death Certificate*, would be his masterpiece.

The Image of Revolution

Angela Y. Davis had grown up in the South in an activist household, and proved an intellectual prodigy. At Brandeis University, where she was one of a handful of African-American students, she was enthralled by a speech given by Malcolm X. Later, while studying in Germany with Theodor Adorno, she had come upon a picture of the Black Panthers in the Sacramento Assembly chambers. She returned to South Central Los Angeles to join the Revolution. After checking out the various political organizations, she rejected Karenga's US Organization as anti-feminist, and joined both SNCC and the Black Panther Party. Soon after, she would note, the Panthers published an essay by Huey Newton in its newspaper that called for solidarity with the emerging gay liberation movement.

After George and Jonathan Jackson were killed and her trial ended in acquittal, she had emerged as an international hero and a leading light in the anti-prisons movement. She became a professor in women's studies and African-American Studies, finally landing at the University of California at Santa Cruz.

As the 1990s opened, she had become painfully aware of how images of her youthful life-and-death struggles were being revived to signify an all-too-vague oppositional style. In a speech she mused, "On the one hand it is inspiring to discover a measure of historical awareness that, in our youth, my generation often lacked. But it is also unsettling. Because I know that almost inevitably my image is associated with a certain representation of Black nationalism that privileges those particular nationalisms with which some of us were locked in constant struggle."[6]

She said, "The image of an armed Black man is considered the 'essence' of revolutionary commitment today. As dismayed as I may feel about this simplistic, phallocentric image, I remember my own responses to romanticized images of brothers (and sometimes sisters) with guns. And, in actuality, it was empowering to go to target practice and shoot—or break down a weapon—as well, or better, than a man. I can relate to the young people who passionately want to do something today, but are misdirected . . ."[7]

These youths still saw Angela Y. Davis's afro and her Black fist frozen in time. But she had moved on, and she hoped to engage them as an elder would.

The Gangsta Meets the Revolutionary

It had been publicist Leyla Turkkan's idea to sit Angela Davis and Ice Cube together. Turkkan had grown up on New York's Upper East Side, a bohemian "parkie" hanging out with graffiti writers like ZEPHYR and REVOLT. In college, she became a promoter for Black Uhuru on their breakthrough *Red* tour, then moved into publicity, always looking for ways to bring together her P.R. skills, her extensive industry contacts and her progressive politics. Like Bill Adler, she was particularly ready for the rise of Black radical rap. But after the success of the Stop the Violence Movement, she had felt sideswiped by Public Enemy's Griff debacle. At one point, David Mills forced her to deny that she and Adler had ever tried to build up Public Enemy as politicians or social activists. Turkkan felt she had another chance with Ice Cube. By sitting Cube with Davis, he could be presented as an inheritor of the Black radical tradition.

The interview was a provocative idea—one that both Davis and Cube welcomed. But none of them had any idea how the conversation would turn when they got together in Cube's Street Knowledge business offices.

To begin with, Davis only heard a few tracks from the still unfinished album, including "My Summer Vacation," "Us" and a track called "Lord Have Mercy," which never made it to the album. She did not hear the song that would become most controversial—a rap entitled "Black Korea." In another way, she was at a more fundamental disadvantage in the conversation.

Like Davis, Cube's mother had grown up in the South. After moving to Watts, she had come of age as a participant in the 1965 riots. While Cube and his mother were close, they often argued about politics and his lyrics. Now it was like Cube was sitting down to talk with his mother. Davis was at a loss the way any parent is with her child at the moment he is in the fullest agitation of his becoming.

Cube sat back behind his glass desk in a black leather chair, the walls covered with framed gold records and posters for *Boyz N The Hood* and his albums. Copies of *URB, The Source* and *The Final Call* were laid out in front of him. Davis asked Cube how he felt about the older generation.

"When I look at older people, I don't think they feel that they can learn from the younger generation. I try and tell my mother things that she just doesn't want to hear sometimes," he answered.

"We're at a point where I hear people like Darryl Gates saying, 'We've got to have a war on gangs.' And I see a lot of Black parents clapping and saying: 'Oh yes, we have to have a war on gangs.' But when young men with baseball caps and T-shirts are considered gangs, what you doing is clapping for a war against your children."[8]

When the conversation swung from generation to gender, Cube's discomfort was palpable:

ICE CUBE: What you have is Black people wanting to be like white people, not realizing that white people want to be like Black people. So the best thing to do is to eliminate that type of thinking. You need Black men who are not looking up to the white man, who are not trying to be like the white man.

ANGELA: What about the women. You keep talking about Black men. I'd like to hear you say Black men and Black women.

ICE CUBE: Black people.

ANGELA: I think that you often exclude your sisters from your thought process. We're never going to get anywhere if we're not together.

ICE CUBE: Of course. But the Black man is down.

ANGELA: Well, the Black woman's down, too.

ICE CUBE: But the Black woman can't look up to the Black man until we get up.

ANGELA: Well why should the Black woman look *up* to the Black man? Why can't we look at each other as equals?

ICE CUBE: If we look at each other on an equal level, what you're going to have is a divide. It's going to be divided.

ANGELA: As I told you, I teach at the San Francisco County Jail. Many of the women there have been arrested in connection with drugs. But they are invisible to most people. People talk about the drug problem without mentioning the fact that the majority of crack users in our community are women. So when we talk about progress in the community, we have to talk about progress in the community, we have to talk about the sisters as well as the brothers.

ICE CUBE: The sisters have held up the community.

ANGELA: When you refer to "the Black man," I would like to hear something explicit about Black women. That will convince me that you are thinking about your sisters as well as your brothers.

ICE CUBE: I think about everybody.[9]

When Davis tried to suggest the power of building alliances with women, Latinos, Native Americans, and others, Cube was dismissive. He said, "You have people who fight for integration, but I'd say we need to fight for equal rights. In the schools, they want equal books, they don't want no torn books. That was more important than fighting to sit at the same counter and eat. I think it's more healthy if we sit over there, just as long as we have good food."

Davis replied, "Suppose we say we want to sit in the same place or wherever we want to sit, but we also want to eat food of our own choosing. You understand what I'm saying? We want to be respected as equals, but also for our differences. I don't want to be invisible as a Black woman."

Cube answered, "It's all about teaching our kids about the nature of the slave master. Teaching them about his nature, and how he is always going to beat you no matter how many books you push in front of him, no matter how many leaders you send to talk to him. He's always going to be the same way. We've got to understand that everything has natural energies."

Then he cited Farrakhan's analogy: "There's the chicken and the chicken hawk. The ant and the anteater. They are enemies by nature. That's what we've got to instill in our kids."[10]

Two Videotapes

In May 1963, news footage of Black civil rights protestors being attacked by police and dogs and firehoses in Birmingham, Alabama, had a powerful effect in mobilizing public opinion during debates over the Civil Rights Act. In March 1991, there was no remotely comparable legislation on the table when two videotapes—one from an amateur's camcorder, the other from a store surveillance camera—surfaced. Public horror and outrage would have no channel to find. Tension filled the moment to its bursting point.

After midnight on Sunday, March 3, Rodney King was beaten by five police officers at the entrance to Hansen Dam Park in Lakeview Terrace. He had led police on a chase in his battered old Hyundai before stopping there.

King had just done less than a year in prison for trying to rob a Korean American–owned store with a tire iron. He had been such an ineffectual thief that the store-owner had seized the weapon from King and sent him running for his Hyundai as the store-owner took down the license plate number. King got out early for good behavior, and found work as a construction laborer.

After a hard week of work, he had been unwinding that Sunday, drinking 8-Ball and watching a basketball game with friends. By midnight, he was drunk and behind the wheel, pushing the limits of what his Hyundai could take, terrified of being sent back to prison. His carmates were yelling at him to pull over.

In the video, King is a shadow in the middle of a uniformed cipher lit by sirens, headlamps, and a ghetto-bird searchlight, a dark mass tossed and rolled by flashing batons for a minute and a half. By the time he whimpered, "Please stop," and was hog-tied, he had suffered fifty-six baton blows and shoe stomps and kicks to the head and body. Within twenty-four hours, the video was being broadcast nationwide.

Two weekends later, on the morning of March 16, Latasha Harlins was shot dead by Korean-American storekeeper Soon Ja Du at the Empire Liquor Market Deli at 9127 South Figueroa in South Central Los Angeles. Harlins had been orphaned when her mother was shot to death when she was nine. When her mother's killer got off with a light sentence, she decided she wanted to become a lawyer. She had sprouted to a slender five foot five, and though she was now having difficulties fighting with other girls in her ninth-grade year, her aunt and grandmother doted on her.

Harlins had spent the evening at a friend's place, and as she walked back home, she decided to purchase a bottle of orange juice for breakfast. She put it in her backpack and went to the counter to pay for it. Du grabbed Harlins' sweater and screamed, "You bitch, you are trying to steal my orange juice! That's my orange juice!" Harlins yelled back, "Bitch, let me go! I'm trying to pay for it."

In the video, the two are pulling on the bottle of orange juice. Harlins swings at Du a few times and then backs away. The bottle falls to the floor. Du picks up a stool and throws it over the counter at Harlins. The girl ducks and reaches down to pick up the bottle. She places the bottle on the counter. Du swipes it away. She has unholstered the gun. Harlins pivots and prepares to step away. Du has raised the gun. Harlins shudders and falls out of the frame. All of this happens in under a minute.

Du was fragile, plagued by ill health, finding comfort only in her Korean-American Presbyterian church. The hours in the liquor store were long, and she suffered from migraine headaches. Recently their son, Joseph, had been harassed by more than ten Main Street Crips, and now some of them were in police custody. The store was briefly closed for fear of Crip retaliation. It had been held up more than thirty times, including the previous Saturday. But Du's husband, a former Korean army colonel, had worked fourteen hours the day before and that's why Soon Ja Du was behind the counter when Latasha Harlins walked in.

To many African Americans, the Dus were the symbol of Asian carpetbaggers. In fact, many of the liquor stores that Asian Americans bought in the area had been sold to them by African Americans, who had purchased them from Jewish owners after the Watts Uprising. This trend accelerated in 1978, when liquor prices were deregulated and profit margins plunged. Many Black owners were happy to get out of the business, even happier to sell to Korean immigrants at more than double their investment. "Seven days a week, twenty hours a day, no vacations, people stealing. That's slave labor," said one African-American store seller. "I wouldn't buy another liquor store."[11]

The bigger problem was that liquor stores were poor substitutes for grocery stores. Since 1965, very few supermarkets had reopened, and even fewer were built in the area. Vons had three hundred stores in the region, but only two in South Central.[12] Worse, study after study found that supermarkets in South Central were the most expensive in the county, with grocery prices up to 20 percent to 30 percent higher than those in the suburbs and exurbs.[13] Politicians would not do anything about it. It was as if they figured liquor was more important to inner-city residents than food. Immigrant liquor-store entrepreneurs did not provide what people really needed, but they still filled a void that no one else was willing to.

Unwanted, they became easy prey for local thugs. In 1986, African-American and Korean-American civil rights leaders formed the Black-Korean Alliance after four Korean merchants were killed in one bloody month. The group wanted to increase dialogue in the community through programs like youth and cultural exchanges between Black and Korean churches. Yet they were unable to stop a 1989 boycott of the Korean American–owned Slauson Swap Meet. And as the Bush recession hit Los Angeles hard in 1991, eliminating 300,000 more jobs, eleven Korean-American merchants in Los Angeles County were killed in robberies. Another fourteen were seriously wounded.

The mainstream media largely ignored these killings, and the Harlins-Du video foreclosed any further discussion. Black and Korean-American civil rights leaders pleaded for their communities not to overreact. But before too long, events had slipped far beyond their grasp.

Pointing Fingers

Who was the real enemy? Everyone had a different answer. Aubry wrote in the *Los Angeles Sentinel,* "The so-called Black-Korean problem reflects the pent-up frustration of both communities. And it is a problem that goes well beyond Blacks and Koreans per se; its genesis is the racist history and structure of the country which fosters social and economic inequality and leaves it to the victims to fashion solutions."[14]

On the other hand, Danny Bakewell, leader of the South Central–based organization, the Brotherhood Crusade, told the press that Blacks were tired of Koreans who would not hire community members, and who took money out of the community. He hastened to add that he was against all merchants—not just Korean ones—who were disrespectful to Blacks.

But Latino and Asian community leaders were not so sure of Bakewell's intentions. Bakewell was leading Black protests against construction sites that largely employed Latino workers. And when a Korean-American store owner at Chung's Liquor Store shot and killed an African American who allegedly was attempting to rob the shop, Bakewell led a 110-day boycott. The picketers often shouted into the empty store, "Go back to Korea!"[15]

The boycott soon expanded to other stores where incidents between Korean-American proprietors and Black customers had been reported. In August, Chung's, Empire and other Korean-owned markets became targets of firebombing. In early October, Bakewell finally succeeded in brokering a deal forcing the owner of Chung's to sell the store to an unnamed Black investor.

Most pundits cast the crisis in terms of race—a clash of two incompatible cultures—or class—Korean entrepreneurs versus Black welfare dependents. These were flimsy interpretations based on hollow stereotypes. To K. W. Lee, the pioneering Asian-American journalist and the publisher of the *Korea Times*, the mainstream media—which by now was broadcasting the Harlins videotape as often as the King videotape—was manufacturing a "race war in which Korean-American newcomers were singled out for destruction as a convenient scapegoat for the structural and racial injustices that had long afflicted the inner city of Los Angeles."

He wrote, "In L.A.'s huge cutthroat media market, a racial incident was tailormade for TV ratings, especially when it involved Koreans. Every time the 'Black-Korean conflict' barked in headlines and sound bites, the Korean merchants caught deadly gunfire and firebombs." Years of dogged efforts to improve African- and Korean-American relations had been crushed under the wheels of a news cycle that Lee said found a "win-win-win formula of race, crime and violence."[16]

In a press conference called to denounce violence against store owners, Korean-American civil rights and business leaders refused to be baited into pointing fingers at African Americans. "Cultural differences do exist. But at the very heart of the so-called racial conflict is a devastating economic struggle," said Gary Kim, the president of the Korean American Coalition. "We are not here today to compare or to say that Korean Americans suffer the same oppression as African Americans. However, we do face many of the same problems."[17]

Instead, they pleaded to African Americans for some equanimity. "When Koreans and Blacks are involved in a crime, and we have a Black victim, it's almost automatically shown as a racially motivated incident," Kim said. "When there's a Korean victim involved, they're quick to say that it's not a racially motivated incident. And I don't think we're playing the game fair here."[18]

Two weeks later, *Death Certificate* hit the streets.

The Limits of Gangstacentrism

The album marked a pregnant pause before the April 29, 1992, explosion. It came when headlines were unrevealing, names and dates were loaded symbols, and questions overwhelmed the possibility of answers. The moment swirled with confusion, waiting for a rowdy, foul-mouthed twenty-two-year-old to try to sort it all out.

If *Nation of Millions* had signaled the end of the civil rights era, *Death Certifi-*

cate's primary impulse was to dance on the grave. Cube still took a coarse anarchic joy in exploding propriety. But having played a central role in defining the gangsta aesthetic, he was also trying to find a politics of gangstacentricism, perhaps the most impassioned attempt to speak to the young guns of South Central since Bunchy Carter had left the Slausons for the Panthers. On the cover of the album, he stood next to a white body on a coroner's gurney, covered with a flag, a tag reading UNCLE SAM hanging from its toe. The Death Side would be "a mirror image of where we are today." The Life Side would be "a vision of where we need to go."

Confident now in his understanding of both the "street nigga" and the conscious Black, he positioned himself in the middle. On the record sleeve, he stood between his Lench Mob—loose, unformed, staring in all directions defensively— and the Fruit of Islam—aligned in crisp formation ready for war—reading a copy of *The Final Call,* whose headline read UNITE OR PERISH.

Except for the Lench Mob and the Nation of Islam, everyone—whites, bourgeois Blacks, women, gays, gang-bangers, dope pushers, Korean shopkeepers, Japanese capitalists, the American army, President Bush, Darryl Gates, Jesse Jackson, Jerry Heller, MC Ren, Dr. Dre, Eazy E, the list went on—seemed to be enemies. It was as if Cube had taken Public Enemy's gunsight off the young Black male, and was waving the weapon from target to target, at each and all of those lined up around and against him.

On the Death Side, the same rapper who once condemned Pan-Africanists with the line, "Put 'em overseas they'll be begging to come back," became a polemicist. Tales of corner-hustling were now set within a context of national politics. On "A Bird in the Hand," Cube's crack-dealer raged over a moody loop from B. B. King's meditation on slavery, "Chains and Things": "Do I gotta sell me a whole lotta crack for decent shelter and clothes on my back? Or should I just wait for help from Bush or Jesse Jackson and Operation PUSH?" Fuck keeping hope alive. On these streets, "Man's Best Friend" was a gat.

In gripping, often funny moral parables, Cube pushed the characters of *Amerikkka's Most Wanted* toward their grim ends. On "My Summer Vacation," the narrator of "Amerikkka's Most Wanted" exported his gang-banging, crack-slanging business to a new frontier, St. Louis. "Some of them are even looking up to us, wearing our colors and talking that gang fuss, giving up much love, dying for a street that they ain't even heard of," Cube's character mused.

But by the end, his friend was dead at the hands of local bangers and he was heading to prison for life. "It's illegal business, niggas still can't stick together," Cube rapped as if it were the character's epitaph. The song closed with cops launching a bloody crackdown on the streets. Cube was inverting the real-life FBI accusations he had encountered on tour with NWA, and slyly commenting on gangsta chic's move into the mainstream. There was also a lesson here: unite or perish.

The horny narrator of "Once Upon a Time in the Projects" returned to visit a suburban girl in "Givin' Up the Nappy Dugout." When he encountered her bougie father, he delighted in graphically describing all the things he and his crew were doing to his daughter. By "Look Who's Burnin' " he was paying the price at the free clinic. But when he spots an around-the-way girl who dissed him for a college boy, he has a laugh at her wannabe expense. Cube's enemies now included race traitors, especially those who had forsaken their ghetto roots.

He further refined his take on the Dopeman, replacing glamour with grit and layering the inevitable bloody end with telling details. On "Alive on Arrival," the low-level pusher of "A Bird in the Hand" is shot on a street corner while trying to make a sale. At King-Drew Hospital, the emergency ward is as crowded as the county jail dayroom, and although the pusher is bleeding buckets, he attracts more attention from LAPD than the MDs. "I don't bang I rock the good rhymes," he protests once again, before adding ironically, "and I'm a victim of neighborhood crime." The character dies while waiting for treatment. The song indicted both butcher-shop health care and drug-dealing nihilism.

Dr. Khallid Abdul Muhammad closed the Death Side. "Look the goddamn white man in his cold blue eyes. Devil, don't even try. Bebe's kids, we don't die, we multiply," Muhammad said, flipping the Crip slogan into a call for solidarity. "You've heard the Death Side, open your Black eyes for the rebirth, resurrection and rise."

On the Life Side, Cube revisited the themes of the Death Side in explicitly nationalist critiques. "I Wanna Kill Sam," written in the context of the Persian Gulf War, ripped into military recruiting by comparing the United States to a rapacious slave-master. "True to the Game" condemned sellout Blacks: "Trying to be a white or a Jew, but ask yourself, who are they to be equal to?" "Doin' Dumb Shit" and "Us" were Cube's most personal tracks, handing listeners the proper way to interpret the stories of the Death Side. "Us" was the closest he would ever come to a manifesto, chastising the Black community for its disunity, materialism, violence, indolence and indulgence.

For "Colorblind," a song about gang-banging, Cube brought in a crew of rappers who had lived the life. DJ Pooh and the Boogiemen hooked up an appropriately N'awlins-fried track—the Meters' "Pungee"—for these sons of once-hopeful Southern migrants now walking through the graveyard of their future. Cube stayed on message, delivering a verse in which he backs down from a stoplight confrontation. But he looked like Jesse Jackson next to the other rappers—WC, Coolio, Kam, Threat, and King Tee.

"Niggas in the 'hood ain't changed," King Tee rapped, "and I finally figured out that we're not in the same gang." Threat was even more pessimistic. "Killa Cali, the state where they kill over colors, 'cause brothers don't know the deal," he rapped. "But every nigga on my block *can't* stop and he *won't* stop and he *don't* stop." Here was the famous Crip motto, and its get-mine-while-I-still-can cynicism overwhelmed Cube's idealism.

Cube's gangstacentricity proceeded from the assumption that one had to be tougher than tough, that life itself was a front. But of all of its problems—its dismissal of history, its victimization of women and gays and its we-against-the-world enemy-making—none would be more fatal than its inability to imagine an alternative that felt harder, more compelling than that single tragic slice of Crip wisdom.

Fear of a Non-Black Planet

Angela Davis asked Cube to clarify whom he thought was his audience: "Many people assume that when you are rapping, your words reflect your own beliefs and values. For example when you talk about 'bitches' and 'ho's' the assumption is that you believe women are bitches and ho's. Are you saying that this is the accepted language in some circles in the community?"

"Of course," Cube answered, "People who say Ice Cube thinks all women are bitches and ho's are not listening to the lyrics. They ain't listening to the situations. They really are not. I don't think they really get past the profanity. Parents say, 'Oh, oh, I can't hear this.' But we learned it from our parents, from TV. This isn't something new that just popped up."

"What do you think about all the efforts over the years to transform the language we use to refer to ourselves as Black people and specifically as Black women?" Davis asked. "How do you think progressive African Americans of my generation [feel] when we hear all over again—especially in hip-hop culture—'nigger nigger nigger' . . . How do you think Black feminists like myself and younger women as well respond to the word 'bitch'?"

Ice Cube avoided a direct answer: "Since the sixties, and even before that, we've moved. But we still ain't gained. We are still in the same situation as before, as far as getting a piece of the rock is concerned. The language of the streets is the only language I can use to communicate with the streets."[19]

The conversation between Davis and Cube not only pointed to fissures around gender and generation, but class and education. Davis's formative years in California had been the late 1960s, when the Black Panthers were calling for a united front of all oppressed peoples and the Third World Liberation Front was launching the movement for ethnic studies programs at San Francisco State and U.C. Berkeley. Back then, students of color were still rare, and so it was natural for them to find racial solidarity across class lines.

Two decades later, affirmative action had turned the state's public universities into the nation's most diverse campuses, reflecting the massive demographic change the state itself had undergone. But Black, Latino and American Indian enrollments were still largely economically segregated, with mainly middle-class students attending the highly selective University of California system and working-class students going to the California State Universities and Community College. Retention rates for students of color were also troubling, with less than half of Blacks and Latinos matriculating at some University of California campuses. And with the steep fee increases prompted by the state's budget crisis and a gathering affirmative action backlash led by Black neocon Ward Connerly, a golden era of access was drawing to a close.

As prominent leaders like L.A. mayor Tom Bradley and assembly speaker Willie Brown were at the apex of their political power, many of California's African Americans felt that they were losing economic, political and social ground to the emerging Chicano, Latino and Asian-American communities. In strictly representational terms, they were correct. Seventy-five thousand middle-class Blacks had left South Central and Compton for San Bernardino and Riverside during the 1980s, and reverse migration to the New South, particularly the shining Mecca of Atlanta, was under way. Waves of new immigrants replaced them in the inner city. In 1965, the area was 81 percent Black. By 1991, one in three living in South Central were foreign born, and Latinos were about to surpass Blacks as the numerical majority.

Whites, of course, had long abandoned the Bottoms—physically, economically and emotionally. When communities of color battled for jobs, education, and representation, it was like crumb-snatching. That these fights would flare into interracial violence was as predictable as it was tragic.

For the college-educated, middle-class, rainbow-embracing African-American elite, there was a painful ambivalence. This was not the world they had fought for. For the rest, there was a growing sense of a loss of control that fed into a siege mentality.

The title of one of Chuck D's favorite books, a collection of essays by Black-power generation poet and writer Haki Madhubuti, had posed a provocative question: *Black Men: Obsolete, Single, Dangerous?* With Chuck's assistance, Cube had begun to respond with *Amerikkka's Most Wanted's* "Endangered Species." *Death Certificate* was the fully elaborated answer. Underneath it all was the acute fear of being overwhelmed by change, a deep-seated fear of erasure.

Black Korea

For Ice Cube, these fears took the form of older Asian-American immigrant entrepreneurs. Here the lines of race and class and generation and difference all came together. In a gangstacentric view, South Central was becoming Black Korea.

Tension between African Americans and Asian Americans was a major subtext running through *Death Certificate*. On "Us," he called for racial solidarity to respond to "Japs grabbing every vacant lot in my 'hood to build a store and sell they goods"—a sonic analogue to John Singleton's "Seoul to Seoul Realty" billboard in *Boyz N The Hood*. On "Horny Lil' Devil," a track about Black male emasculation, he metaphorically wiped out the "devils"—white sexual harassers of black women, racists and "fags"—and finished up at the corner store beating down the "Jap" owner. "Black Korea" was the fiery climax.

In Spike Lee's *Do the Right Thing*, Korean-American shopkeeper Sonny saves his store from being burned by arguing he, too, is Black. Cube's "Black Korea" focuses instead on the beginning of that confrontation, creating a parallel between Radio Raheem attempting to purchase twenty batteries for his boombox ("D, motherfucker, D!"), and Cube attempting to purchase a forty-ounce bottle of malt liquor. As the music bursts forth, Ice Cube confronts two prejudiced, "Oriental, one penny counting" proprietors who hawk him as he walks through their store. Cube turns and leers at the woman storekeeper, "Bitch, I got a job!" At the song's bridge, the shop erupts into argument when his friends raise their voices in his support.

By now, the original Spike Lee scene has been stripped of its humor, leaving only the raw racial conflict. Then the bass surges back and the song rushes to its conclusion. Cube issues a threat, "Don't follow me up and down your crazy little market, or your little chop-suey ass will be the target of a nationwide boycott." In a final defiant gesture, he raises the prospect of a racially vengeful conflagration. "Pay respect to the Black fist," he yells, "or we'll burn your store right down to a crisp! And then we'll see ya, 'cause you can't turn the ghetto into Black Korea." The store owner, Sonny, has the last word: "Mother fuck you!"

All of this happens in under a minute.

The Real Stakes

No rap album had ever been as controversial as *Death Certificate*. High-brow magazines that rarely felt compelled to comment on "low" culture seized on the album as an example of rap's depravity. An editorial in *The Economist* invoked Adorno's criticism of jazz as neo-fascistic, evoking "rhythmically obedient" hip-hoppers. "In rap as in rock, rebellion sells," the editorial read. "Sadly, too few fans distinguish between the rebellious and the reactionary."[20] In *The New Republic*, David Samuels took this pretzel logic beyond all sense, confusing album-listening with murder. "This kind of consumption—of racist stereotypes, of brutality toward women or even of uplifting tributes to Dr. Martin Luther King—is of a particularly corrupting kind. The values it instills find their ultimate expression in the ease in which we watch young Black men killing each other: in movies, on records and on streets of cities and towns across the country."[21]

Three weeks after the album's release, the debate suddenly went supernova. In *Billboard* magazine, editor Timothy White called for record-store chains to boycott the record, writing, "His unabashed espousal of violence against Koreans, Jews and other whites crosses the line that divides art from the advocacy of crime."[22] In a trade magazine that normally avoided controversies over artistic merit or lyrical content, the editorial was extraordinary. *Death Certificate* remains the only album ever singled out for such condemnation in *Billboard* history.

James Bernard, senior editor of *The Source,* defended Ice Cube against calls for boycotts, "Yes, Ice Cube is very angry, and he expresses that anger in harsh, blunt and unmistakable terms. But the source of his rage is very real. Many in the Black community, particularly Los Angeles, Cube's home, feel as if it's open season on Blacks with the Rodney King assault and the recent murder of a young Black girl by a Korean merchant."[23] Bernard and other African-American fans understood the fiery conclusion of "Black Korea" as a mythical resolution.

Ice Cube remarked that the song was

inspired by everyday life in the Black community with the Koreans. Blacks don't like them and it's vice versa. The Koreans have a lot of businesses in the Black community. The [Harlins] shooting is just proof of the problem, just another example of their disrespect for Black people. You go in their stores and they think you're going to steal something. They follow you around the store like you're a criminal. They say, "Buy something or get out." If it hasn't happened to you, you can't know how bad it feels for somebody to make you feel like a criminal when you're in their store and you haven't done anything.[24]

He would also say, " 'Black Korea' holds the tone of the neighborhood and the feelings of the people."[25] A UCLA survey of racial attitudes in Los Angeles conducted before and just after the April uprising supported his contention: more than 41 percent of Blacks and 48 percent of Asians felt that it was difficult to get along with the other group. Blacks felt *worse* about Asians after the riots. Asians, too, saw Blacks more negatively.[26]

In all the ink spilled over "Black Korea" and *Death Certificate,* none was more measured and poignant than those of young Dong Suh, a hip-hop generation son of a Korean-American store owner. In an editorial for *Asian Week,* he said he was writing to "move away from the issue of censorship and the stereotyping of rap as violent and move toward addressing the core problem."

Several years ago, a prominent radio personality in Philadelphia, where my family operates a small corner store in a predominantly African-American neighborhood, expressed a similar sentiment. I clearly remember his warning that if Koreans did not respect Blacks, firebombings were likely. . . . When compared to Korean Americans, African Americans are a numerical and political majority. Ice Cube does not realize that as a member of the majority, he wields real power against Koreans.[27]

The Target of a Nationwide Boycott

Upon its release on October 31, 1991, *Death Certificate* had advance orders of more than a million copies, making it an instant hit. It was immediately greeted with boycotts.

On November 1, the Simon Wiesenthal Center called upon four major retail record chains to boycott the album, calling it a "a cultural Molotov cocktail" and "a real threat."[28] In particular, the center took three lines in "No Vaseline" directed specifically at Jerry Heller—"You let a Jew break up my crew," "You can't be the Niggaz 4 Life crew with a white Jew telling you what to do" and "Get rid of that Devil real simple, put a bullet in his temple"—to be anti-Semitic.

Two days later, the Korean American Coalition (KAC) held its own press conference, issuing a statement jointly signed by a rainbow coalition of civil rights organizations: the Japanese American Citizens League, the Los Angeles Urban League, the NAACP, the Mexican American Legal Defense and Educational Fund and the Southern Christian Leadership Conference. Guardian Angels began pickets in New York and Los Angeles at record stores carrying the album. Korean swap-meet vendors and the Camelot Music chain also joined the boycott.[29]

"In the minds of Korean Americans, this is all part of the oppression or unfairness we face. We're constantly trampled on, nobody listens to us, we're constantly seen through distorted images in the media," said executive director Jerry Yu. "We're not really battling against Ice Cube, all we're trying to do is get him to understand our concerns, get him to respond to our issues."

But the record went on to sell well over a million and a half records. Perhaps, as Ice Cube had bragged, he was the "wrong nigga to fuck with." A month before, Soon Ja Du had been convicted of voluntary manslaughter in the killing of

Latasha Harlins. As they awaited the Du sentencing, Korean-American leaders worried about the firebombings and the racial tensions. They decided that they needed to take a stand against "Black Korea." Yumi Jhang-Park, the executive director of the Korean American Grocers' Association (KAGRO), said, "This is a life-and-death situation. What if someone listened to the song and set fire to a store?"[30]

But Korean-American activists were unable to reach the mainstream press with their message. When *Entertainment Tonight* interviewed Yu regarding the boycott, they videotaped him for over thirty minutes, yet the story only featured him briefly, reading lyric excerpts from "Black Korea." Instead, Rabbi Abraham Cooper of the Simon Wiesenthal Center was shown explaining the boycott for most of the segment. It was clear to Korean-American leaders that they would have to try a different tack. KAGRO decided to hit Cube where it hurt him the most.

Do You Wanna Go to the Liquor Store?

In 1987, McKenzie River Corporation of San Francisco had introduced a new forty-ounce malt liquor product that it called St. Ides to compete with Pabst's Olde English 800 brand, better known as "8 Ball." Soon McKenzie River and Pabst were scrumming like Coca-Cola and Pepsi, with the urban communities of Los Angeles as the key battleground.

No one had ever cared what malt liquor tasted like, just how fast they could get trashed after drinking it. St. Ides's main selling point was its 8 percent alcohol content, compared to 6 percent in a bottle of 8 Ball and 3.5 percent in an average can of beer. But how to get this message out?

In 1988, McKenzie River went to KDAY Music Director Greg Mack and DJ Pooh to recruit rappers to record sixty-second music commercials. For one of the first spots, Pooh called King Tee and they revived Mixmaster Spade's old street classic, "Do You Want to Go to the Liquor Store?" Rakim, EPMD, Yo-Yo, the Geto Boys and many others recorded "Crooked I" commercials. It was good money; King Tee says he made $50,000, and got all the St. Ides he wanted delivered right to his apartment door. When excited listeners began requesting the spots more than songs in KDAY's regular playlist, McKenzie River knew it had a winning marketing plan. In 1990, they landed pro–Black Muslim Ice Cube as their primary endorser. By the time *Death Certificate* was released, St. Ides was the 'hood's malt liquor of choice.

KAGRO alone represented 3,500 stores in Southern California alone, had over 20,000 members who generated $2 billion in annual sales, and controlled roughly 7 percent of the national market. They demanded that McKenzie River withdraw all promotional materials and commercials featuring Ice Cube and to sever its relationship with him. On November 7, they reached an impasse in negotiations. McKenzie River declined KAGRO's demands, saying it would financially damage their small company. KAGRO ordered its stores to return deliveries and cease orders. Yang Il Kim, the national president of KAGRO, expressed sympathy in the *Korea Times* for McKenzie River's business worries, but pointedly mentioned that the company had chosen the wrong rapper to work with.[31]

At its peak, between five thousand and six thousand stores in Los Angeles, San Francisco, Oakland, San Jose, Seattle, Tacoma, Portland, Philadelphia, Baltimore, Richmond and Washington, D.C., honored the boycott.[32] On November 16, McKenzie River finally conceded to KAGRO's demands, ending the use of all ads that featured Ice Cube and agreeing not to use him for new promotions until the issue was resolved to KAGRO's satisfaction. They also agreed to create a scholarship fund and a jobs program for Blacks with profits from the sales of St. Ides. KAGRO officially ended its boycott on November 20, three weeks after the release of *Death Certificate*.[33]

Conciliation took place three months later. In early February, McKenzie River organized a joint meeting between Ice Cube and the KAGRO leadership. Ice Cube apologized to the merchants and pledged to discourage violence against store owners and to continue "working to bring our communities closer together." In a follow-up letter to Kim, he wrote of the meeting:

> I explained some of the feelings and attitudes of Black people today, and the problems and frustrations that we confront. And I clarified the intent of my album *Death Certificate*. It was not intended to offend anyone or to incite violence of any kind. It was not directed at all Korean Americans or at all Korean American store owners. I respect Korean Americans. It was directed at a few stores where my friends and I have had actual problems.

Working together we can help solve these problems and build a bridge between our communities.[34]

Many Blacks debated passionately whether Cube had sold out, and at what point. Was it when he apologized to the Korean-American store owners? Was it when he let McKenzie River punk him after he had generated so much business for them? Was it when he endorsed a malt liquor beer while studying with the Nation of Islam?

But Ice Cube was moving on; he was no utopian hard-liner. Lessons learned, points made, back to business. He resumed his St. Ides sponsorship deal, and donated all of the proceeds to charity, including a large monetary gift to the King-Drew Hospital, the same place he had indicted on "Alive on Arrival." He pored over the movie scripts being offered to him.

Within KAGRO, as in many other Korean- and Asian-American organizations, there had also been soul-searching. In January, KAGRO had adopted a ten-point code of behavior for its 3,200 store owners, an event that African-American and Asian-American activists hailed as a breakthrough. After their meeting, KAGRO conceded that Ice Cube had legitimate complaints and expressed hope that Blacks and Koreans would "help each other and learn to understand each other's cultures."[35]

On November 15, Judge Joyce Karlin sentenced Soon Ja Du to just five years of probation. As she read her judgment, she seemed to go out of her way to lecture the African-American community. "This is not a time for revenge," she said, "and it is not my job as a sentencing court to seek revenge for those who demand it."[36] The African-American community reacted with horror. Many Asian-American leaders, too, were shocked. Nobody had been asking for revenge.

In South Central—where there were already three times the number of liquor stores as in the entire state of Rhode Island—community activists began to talk about a campaign to close liquor stores. African-American, Latino and Asian-American community leaders met behind closed doors to find common ground. But the trial of the four police officers who had beaten Rodney King was about to get underway in the 80 percent white community of Simi Valley, more than sixty miles to the north and there was now a gnawing sense that some kind of a disaster lay ahead.

A picture of Ice Cube shaking hands with David Kim, the Southern California president of KAGRO, appeared on the cover of the *Korea Times* under the headline, ICE CUBE THE PEACEMAKER. Although the meeting had happened in February, the picture and story were appearing in the May 4, 1992, issue. It seemed, all at once, a tragic irony and a bittersweet celebration of a moment that now seemed so far away.

The arc of history is that every generation has to fight the liberation struggle. And the time you're on that historical stage is short.

—Richie Perez

LOOP 4

Stakes Is High

1992–2001

Disposable futures. From the
"Hip-Hop Poster Series."
Photo © Beuford Smith/Césaire

The National Guard comes to Crenshaw Square. May 1, 1992.

Photo © Ben Higa

16.

Gonna Work It Out

Peace and Rebellion in Los Angeles

> REPORTER: Does Mr. King feel guilty about all the rioting that has taken place . . . Does Mr. King feel the guilt all upon his shoulders?
>
> STEVE LERMAN, ATTORNEY FOR RODNEY KING: Mr. King is proud to be an African-American man living in Los Angeles in 1992 and was proud to be so in 1991. The sense of violation and shame that these offi-cers visited upon him is what he has distress in. He is not guilty for anything. The officers that beat Rodney King are the ones to concern themselves with guilt. Mr. King is innocent of wrongdoing.
>
> REPORTER: He doesn't feel apologetic for anything?
>
> —Exchange at May 1 press conference

By the time the Simi Valley jury delivered its verdict on April 29, 1992, in the trial of the four white officers who had beaten Rodney King, a gang truce had already been secured fifty miles away in the housing projects of Watts.

Since the 1970s, gang peace workers had struggled to establish peace agreements between gangs in various neighborhoods and had been hobbled by the enormity of the problem. Gangs were growing and beefs were escalating much faster than the ability of any shoestring agency to keep up. Even if gang peace workers could get two gangs to agree to a peace, it did not automatically mean others would follow. Indeed, other gangs might figure that the peacemak-ing sets had given up their neighborhoods and that they were ripe for conquest.

Los Angeles's demographics also made peace work complicated. Inner-city gangs once largely fought along racial lines. Mexicans against Mexicans, Blacks against Blacks, Asians against Asians. But by the 1980s, the ethnic math had become trickier. Samoan gangs formed from Carson to Compton, often af-filiating with Black Blood or Crip sets. Cambodians and Latinos turned bloody rivals in Long Beach. Salvadorans clashed with Mexicans from MacArthur Park to the Valley. Blacks and Latinos warred on the beach in Venice.

In 1980, a gang peace conference at California State University at Northridge drew 1,500 Latino gang members, and ended with a treaty that lasted a year and a half. In 1984, a treaty in Hawthorne brought together a number of *Sureño* sets. But both these peaces were doomed by the quickly changing conditions on the streets. The crack trade was spreading. Giving up one's 'hood was no longer an option.

After the Long Beach Arena riots in 1986, KDAY sponsored an anti-gang radio show with Run DMC and Barry White, a former member of the pre-riot Watts gang, the Businessmen, that received over 1,500 calls. The station decided to hold a "Day of Peace" concert and rally in November. These events supported the efforts of the Community Youth Gang Services (CYGS) to organize a holiday truce from Thanksgiving through New Year's Day.

CYGS was successful in lining up dozens of gangs, including a number of eastside Latino gangs and the mostly Black Bounty Hunters (Blood) set of Watts's Nickerson Gardens projects, to sign temporary truces. By 1988, black churches, civil rights and nonprofit organizations mounted competing efforts to forge a broader, permanent truce. Bickering between community leaders ended these initiatives, but the idea took root among key gang leaders and activists. The breakthrough moment came at a peace summit later that year, when a Cirkle City Piru named Twilight Bey stood before flashing cameras and shook the hand of Danifu, one of the founding Crips.

Brothers weren't ready for this yet. The media had incorrectly described Bey as a shot-caller. He had never made that claim, but soon his own Blood comrades were coming to his house to threaten his life. Bey stood his ground. He told them he was ready to die for peace, and then he demonstrated with his fists, and slowly won the respect of his homies. He was one of a new breed of street soldiers.

The Deadly Geography of Watts

Bey was from the Watts projects of Hacienda Village. During the 1950s, Simon Rodia's gift of beauty-from-rubble, the Watts Towers, marked the physical and psychological center of the city. After the '65 Uprising, the action shifted to the revolutionary motion and light on 103rd Street. As the long decline began in the 1970s, the four major public housing developments—Jordan Downs to the northeast, Imperial Courts to the southeast, Nickerson Gardens to the southwest and Hacienda Village to the northwest—became Watts's irregular heartbeat and tortured soul.

Down the middle of the city ran the old railroad tracks. The train line that had once delivered big-dreaming southern Blacks to Watts was now the dividing line between the Bloods on the west and the Crips on the east. At Hacienda Village, there were the Cirkle City Pirus, and at Nickerson Gardens, the Bounty Hunter Bloods. On the other side, there were the Jordan Crips and at Imperial Courts, the PJ Watts Crips. Edwin Markham Intermediate School, located directly across the tracks from the three major spires of the Watts Towers, was literally in the troubled heart of the city.

Administrators at Markham figured that 10 percent of the students banged. The 1,600 seventh-to-ninth graders knew the number was closer to a third.[1] They called it "Gladiator School." It was where youths underwent their rites of passage into ganghood.

"All of the factions went to that school," says Aqeela Sherrills, who grew up with his older brother, Daude, in the Jordan Downs projects. "In '78, one of the brothers from my neighborhood got killed up there by a brother from Nickerson Gardens. And that started the war. So when I got there in '81, it was scary."

The older guys in the neighborhood, Sherrills says, "told us when somebody asks you where you from, you fire on him. That was like a sign to say you about to get jumped. Somebody asked me where I was from, I was like, okay, those are the words. So I stole on this cat, we got into a fight, and then eventually I was associated with the crew that I ran with." Whether he liked it or not, he was representing for the Jordan Downs Crips.

In 1984, when Aqeela was in the ninth grade, he and his homies got into a fight with kids from Nickerson Gardens. Later that afternoon, as they sat on the track-field bleachers, their rivals came back with guns and shot his best friend in the head. Boys who played with each other in athletic leagues just a few years before were now deadly enemies, handed a cold destiny by history and geography.

New Black Nation

By 1986, the gang leadership at Jordan Downs was changing. The Jordan Downs Crips were fading, and a new generation of Crips grew from the ground up. In the sprawling projects they cliqued up in different factions like the Playboy

Hoo-Rides, the JDC, Eastside Kids, the Sunset Ave. Boys, the Young Hustlas and the Watts Baby Locs. In time the Baby Locs took over, and began "courting in" all the shorties from the cliques into a set of sets, the Grape Street Crips. " 'Courtin' in'," says Daude Sherrills, "is when everybody got to fight each other. That was a part of your initiation process." The new Grape Streets positioned themselves outside the traditional Crip/Blood axis. Instead of red or blue, Daude says, "The whole 'hood started banging purple."

In high school, Aqeela distanced himself from gang life, got a job after school selling candy in the shiny exurbs of Orange County, and was accepted to Cal State Northridge in 1988. Daude had a more difficult time. He was determined to make up for getting kicked out of junior high and being held back a grade. He attended night school to graduate with his class in 1986. But as just another eighteen-year-old in Watts, he had no job prospects, and returned to his old ways.

"I was crackin', selling weed, beefing with rivals, escaping raids and escaping shootouts, the whole nine, just trying to survive. I didn't care if I lived or died. It was no role models, no teachers, no preachers, no *imams*, none of that was around," he says. Instead he saw his friends heading off to prison or into early graves. On his twentieth birthday, with the news that his girlfriend was expecting his first son, Daude finally decided to save himself.

Both the Sherrills, who had grown up with the Nation of Islam, noticed that Minister Farrakhan had launched the "Stop the Killing" campaign. Across town, Imam Mujahid Abdul-Karim from the local Masjid al-Rasul was working to end the violence with Nickerson Gardens O.G.'s—an effort which included Loaf, one of the Bloods who had set off the war with Jordan Downs at Markham in the late '70s. At the gym in Nickerson Gardens, the peacemakers put up a new mural, entitled "Crossfire (The First Word on Peace)," a memorial to the dozens of residents who had been killed in gang warfare. The words on the wall read, KEEP THE FUTURE ALIVE, and NOBODY CAN STOP THIS WAR BUT US.[2]

At Northridge, Aqeela soaked up the music of KRS-One, X-Clan and Public Enemy, read *The Evidence of Things Not Seen*, James Baldwin's account of the Atlanta child murders, and was stirred. He joined the Black Student Union, and embarked on a journey into knowledge of self. He became a fundamentalist Shi'ite, and studied Egyptology, the Supreme Mathematics and esoterica. He was searching for a life mission, and staring at a map of Watts one day, he found it.

"One of the things I came to is that three of the four major housing projects—the

Jordan Downs, Imperial Courts and the Nickerson Gardens—fell in a perfect ninety-degree angle. And the hypotenuse runs from the Nickerson Gardens to the Jordan Downs, which in my studies, was the Line of God, the infinite line," says Sherrills. "My epiphany was if we connected the Jordan Downs and the Nickerson Gardens, if we brought those two neighborhoods together, we would create a domino effect for peace all across the country." Geography had been destiny, but history did not have to keep them shackled. Here was the evidence of a higher creative power, a master plan.

Aqeela took this insight back to Daude, who had already thrown away his purple Grape Street gear for African garb and begun organizing peace efforts in Jordan Downs. First they organized the African Brothers Collective, recruiting Black student activists from UCLA, Cal State Northridge and USC to join brothers from the projects in Watts. They held study group sessions and demonstrations. Then they started speaking to their Grape Street comrades, framing peace in the new language and imagery of the streets.

Aqeela says, "I had to convince the brothers in the neighborhood that we had to be the ones to initiate the process. The way that I was explaining it is that when you take the colors red and blue, which are both represented by the Nickersons and the PJs, you get purple, you get the Jordan Downs. And the whole concept of grapes, they're all on the vine, but they're all connected."

At Jordan Downs and Nickerson Gardens, the collective broke up dice games, and gave speeches under a red, black, and green flag. They chanted, "I don't know but I've been told, African people on a mighty road. Let's destroy the old plantation, now we're gonna build a new Black nation." They were updating the spirit of '66 with the unique outsider knowledge of the gang-ridden '80s.

"Because of this transition that was taking place, law enforcement was struggling to keep things the way they were. We were job security," says Aqeela. "So we started standing up to the police."

They distributed information about citizens' rights. They put up anticop messages on the walls. They intervened to stop police beatings. In the projects, fascination slowly replaced fear. The group of voices calling for peace grew.

Father Figures

At the same time, Jim Brown, the football and movie hero, was looking for the next generation of leaders. After his storied NFL career and big-screen stardom,

Brown had devoted his life to Black nationalist causes. He had developed a life management skills curriculum that he was teaching in prisons, but he felt he had a bigger calling. When he saw Chuck D on a TV interview, he was inspired. "It's a whole new culture out there, new music, a new language," he said. "The NAACP has been good in courts, the Urban League helps with jobs. They're all above these guys on the street and the guys coming out of prison. They can't relate to them."[3] With fascination and concern, Brown watched his old friend Minister Farrakhan expand his work with the gangs.

From its mosques in Compton and South Central, the Nation of Islam was sending "God Squads" into the neighborhoods to convert gang members and talk peace. But the squads suddenly seemed to be drawing unwanted attention from the authorities. Just before sunrise on January 3, 1990, a car of two L.A. police officers tailed a God Squad caravan of three cars of thirteen Black Muslims leaving for a morning workout at a Crenshaw gym. The police pulled one of the cars over a traffic violation. One of the Muslims stepped forward to question why they were being ticketed, while the others surrounded the officers. The cops radioed for backup, and a fight broke out. By the end, twenty-four officers, four of whom were later treated for injuries, had used a stun gun and batons to subdue the thirteen Muslims.

Representatives of the Nation of Islam met with the LAPD a few weeks later to ease tensions. But the day after the meeting, on January 23, L.A. sheriff's deputies wounded one Black Muslim and shot Oliver X. Beasley in the head, after a confrontation that had begun with another traffic-stop gone awry. Elders were reminded of the authorities' vicious attacks on Nation mosques and the Black Panthers. Youths—whether gangbangers or not—were looking for someone to defend and protect them, something like a father figure.

Minister Farrakhan hastily returned to Los Angeles. At Beasley's funeral, Farrakhan praised him as a man working for an end to gang violence and crack slanging. "Drug dealers deal on the corner and they let it happen," he said. "The moment someone puts on a suit and bow tie to clean up the problem, here come the police to shoot them dead."[4]

The following week, Farrakhan delivered another public address, this time to a massive crowd of twenty thousand at the Sports Arena. He warned the police and sheriffs that the city was on the verge of erupting. "If we reach a point where we can tolerate this abuse no longer, we will rise up against your authority," he said. "And we would rather die than live like dogs under your roof."[5]

Thousands of Crips and Bloods were in the audience, and Farrakhan directed the rest of his speech to them. "Stop the killing," he said, standing beneath a fifteen-foot picture of Beasley. "Why can we take the trigger and pull it at each other? We are killing ourselves."[6]

As he spoke, another message rippled through the crowd: The Minister and Jim Brown would be hosting a meeting that weekend to discuss a ceasefire. It would be held at Brown's mansion in the Hollywood hills, on neutral ground high above the city.

Learning to Speak

From Brown's deck, the city grid sprawled far to the south, from the hills westward to the coast. Even the city's violent, smog-altered sunsets would look a lot different up there.

More than two hundred Crips and Bloods from neighborhoods across the city came to Brown's house, including the Sherrills, Twilight Bey and an O. G. Blood from the neighborhood of Inglewood known as "The Jungle" named T. Rodgers. Minister Farrakhan said a prayer for peace. Brown took the floor to say that the meeting would not have an agenda, it was a safe space for them to get things off their chests and discuss starting a peace movement. Then Minister Farrakhan, his son, Mustapha, and Brown sat down to listen. And slowly, putting years of bloodshed behind them, the gang members, one after another, stood up to speak.

After this gathering, the peace work intensified. Brown opened his house to the gang members, first throwing parties, then holding regular Wednesday night meetings. Members of the Rolling 60s, the Rolling 40s, the Harlem 30s Crips, the Venice Shoreline Crips and the Van Ness Gangster Bloods—sets engaged in some of the city's bloodiest wars—came to participate.

"Young men expressed their anger and pain but also expressed that they would try to communicate," Twilight Bey said. "We were asked questions that weren't ever asked before: What are we going to do to change our situation? Do we have the power? . . . Do we have any say on what happens in political arena? What does it take to change things?"[7]

The Sherrills, Bey, Rodgers and several others became the core of Brown's new organization, Amer-I-Can. They revamped Brown's curriculum, which, Aqeela says, "became the foundation for the peace being able to happen. It created a common language for us to be able to communicate with. And also it required individuals to take responsibility for their own lives and not blame people for where they were."

Twilight Bey and his comrades began organizing peace among the Bloods in Hacienda Village. Imam Mujahid, Big Hank, Donny, Brother Bobby and others did the same at Nickerson Gardens. The Sherrills brothers opened a storefront across the street from Jordan Downs to sell incense and thrift clothes, to feed the homeless and to hold peace meetings. Brown picked up the rent. When Amer-I-Can got its first contract at Nickerson Gardens, all of them came together to teach classes to the next generation of young bangers from Markham.

Uprisings

But even as the peace work intensified, gang wars had left 690 dead by the end of 1990, yet another tragic record. The new year brought a new sense of urgency. In March, Rodney King was beaten and Latasha Harlins killed. In June, three cops in the Dalton Avenue raids were acquitted of misdemeanor vandalism counts.

At Nickerson Gardens, Hacienda Village and Jordan Downs, the leadership was almost in place to broker a truce. But Imperial Courts remained a major question mark. The PJ Watts set at Imperial Courts was run by an O.G. named Tony Bogard, who had recently been arrested for shooting at a sister of a Grape Street Crip. The war between the PJs and Grape Street had been running for at least two years, and it seemed to many that Bogard was in no mood for peace.[8]

The day after Thanksgiving, two weeks after Soon Ja Du was sentenced to probation, police were called to Imperial Courts during a temporary blackout. They heard gunfire and feared they had walked into an ambush, so they began blasting rounds into the playground. When the shooting ended, Henry Peco was dead, hit by five police bullets, one between the eyes, lying in a sandbox. Residents poured out of the projects to stone and bottle the cops. Before the cops retreated, they took into custody one of Peco's cousins who had been cradling his bleeding body and trying to resuscitate him. They questioned whether she had tampered with evidence.[9]

Peco was a former resident of Imperial Courts who had moved to Sacramento after serving a two-year bid in the early '80s. He had taken in a younger cousin, Dewayne "Sniper" Holmes, an ex–PJ Watts Crip trying to escape the life. The two had returned that weekend from Sacramento to Imperial Courts for Thanksgiving dinner with the family. When Peco was shot, residents said, he was leading children out of the playground to the safety of their apartments. Police claimed that Peco had fired on them with an AK-47. No rifle was ever found.

Community activists organized anti-police brutality protests and picked up the support to Congresswoman Maxine Waters and Jesse Jackson. Three weeks after the incident, cops destroyed a memorial to Peco in the housing developments' courtyard. Now residents greeted every police patrol with bottles.

Police responded by initiating regular sweeps of residents. Then on New Year's Eve, under the pretext of stopping holiday gunfire celebrations, police staged their largest raid, confiscating no weapons but arresting forty-four residents. Tension in the city over the King trial and the Harlins shooting was already thick, and now Imperial Courts threatened to become a third flashpoint. Before long, FBI investigators and a U.S. Justice Department mediator were en route to the housing development. When they arrived, the walls read, LAPD KILLA.

Cease-Fire

Peco's cousin, Dewayne Holmes, watched the tensions rising, and tried to persuade the PJs not to go to war with the cops. At a meeting of the Henry Peco Justice Committee, Imam Mujahid approached Holmes and persuaded him that a permanent truce might come out of Peco's murder. Holmes decided to put his body on the line. In a life-risking journey, he walked first into Jordan Downs to ask the Grape Street Crips for a truce until Peco could be buried. He turned and walked down the Line of God, crossing the tracks into Nickerson Gardens to ask the same of the Bounty Hunter Bloods.

So on a Sunday in March, the delicate peace meetings, facilitated by Daude Sherrills and Imam Mujahid at his Masjid al-Rasul on 112th and Central, began. At the first meeting, there were less than ten people in attendance, including Holmes and his mother, and Twilight Bey. "A lot of brothers didn't trust the situation," says Daude Sherrills. "They wanted to make sure that nobody was going to get ambushed."

But the meetings grew, expanded exponentially and organically. "Instead of eight brothers in there, it was damn near fifty brothers, then a hundred brothers in there," he says. There was a feeling of destiny to the talks. By April, Daude says, "It was time."

He dispatched another staffer of Amer-I-Can, Anthony Perry, to find a document that could codify the peace. In the library of USC's Von Kleinsmid Center for International and Public Affairs, Perry dug out a 1949 United Nations cease-fire agreement that had temporarily ended hostilities between Egypt and Israel. Struck by the historical weight of the document, he copied it by hand, and then attempted to translate it into terms that could hold in Watts.

He and Daude finished the drafting together, altering the armistice agreement to refer to drive-bys and random shootings, and to take into account the loose structure of gang leadership, with its shot-callers and soldiers. Now called the Multi-Peace Treaty, the document called for "the return to permanent peace in Watts, California," and "the return of Black businesses, economic development and advancement of educational programs.

"The establishment of a cease-fire between the community representatives of all parties is accepted as a necessary step toward the renewal of peace in Watts, California," it read. "The right of each party to its security and freedom from fear of attack by each other shall be fully respected."[10]

Daude Sherrills added a United Black Community Code, a code of conduct for gang members. It began, "I accept the duty to honor, uphold and defend the spirit of the red, blue and purple, to teach the black family its legacy and protracted struggle for freedom and justice."[11] It warned against alcohol and drug abuse and use of the "N-word and B-word," and even laid down rules of etiquette for flagging and sign-throwing.[12] It called for literacy, school attendance, voter registration programs and for community investment.

Sherrills and Perry presented it to the truce leaders at the Masjid. All agreed to endorse it and to take a message back to their respective neighborhoods. On April 26, 1992, three days before the Rodney King verdict, the truce was officially in effect.

Making It Real

And yet, as Aqeela says, "Nobody had went into anybody's territory yet." By the afternoon of April 26, he was sitting at Jordan Downs with other Grape Street Crips. Twenty years of bloodshed, and four years of peace work had come to this moment. The Sherrills and Grape Street peacemakers piled into a van and headed south.

"We all drove into the PJs, got out," Aqeela says. "When all the brothers from the PJs saw us, they all came out and they was like, 'Man, come on in the gym, we need to talk.' So we all went in the gym and Tony Bogard was there [saying,] 'Man, this shit can't just happen like this, homeboy. It's gon' take years, man.' But a whole group of our OGs was there, older brothers from the Jordan Downs, so they argued back and forth.

"A lot of the youngsters, we went outside and was like, 'Shit, y'all with it?' 'We with it! Y'all with it?' 'We with it!' " he laughs. "So while they in the gym still talking, we all celebrating outside. Whooooo! Watts! Watts!

"After that it was just on. Like, phone calls—'The peace treaty on!' I mean, everybody, that night in the PJs, it was probably two or three thousand people over there. Everybody outside. Mamas crying, dudes coming over to see the girl that they been sneaking to see for the past couple of years. Oh man, it was wild. Peace Treaty babies!"

Two days later, the party moved to Nickerson Gardens. Blue, red and purple rags were tied together. Generations celebrated. It was like a family reunion. The war was over.

Sets came from all over town to the parties, often expressing disbelief that a peace was actually on. "All the neighborhoods started saying, man, if Watts can do it, we can do it," says Daude. "You had brothers from Compton, brothers from South Central. We had rivals coming in, we was negotiating cease-fires with *their* rivals, right inside the housing project developments."

The stakes were much higher now. Against all odds, they had built an infrastructure of communication for peace. But for the peace to last, it would take more than talk. There would need to be jobs, services, and support. So on April 28, as the party went down at Nickerson Gardens, the peacemakers marched with 250 Crips and Bloods from seven different neighborhoods to City Hall to announce the truce at a Los Angeles City Council meeting.

"We made a presentation to the City Council, telling them that we was coming together to bring an end to all the violence in the 'hood," says Aqeela. "We told them we would like to have access to funding."

But Council members didn't exactly jump out of their chairs. One suggested applying for a $500 grant, Aqeela recalls, "And they were like, 'Thank you very much,' and ushered us out of there as quickly as they possibly could."

The next afternoon, the peace party came back to Jordan Downs, the final point on the triangle. The courtyard was full and the music was bumping when the verdicts came down.

Show Them How We Feel

At 1 P.M. on Wednesday, April 29, 1992, the jury in Simi Valley sent out word that it had reached a decision in the ten verdicts against the four cops, but were intractably deadlocked on the last. They had been deliberating for a week, leaving the city agitated and breathless. Judge Stanley Weisberg announced that the verdicts would be read at 3 P.M., giving authorities time to prepare for any potential unrest.

At about 3:15 P.M., the ten "not guilty" verdicts were read. The last charge—one count of assault under the color of authority against Lawrence Powell—had fallen in favor of acquittal 8–4.

Thirty miles to the southeast, near the intersection of Florence and Normandie in South Central, the young men debated what to do. This was Eight Tray Gangster Crip turf, the territory of the set made famous by prison memoirist Sanyika Shakur in his previous life as Kody "Monster" Scott.

While Shakur served out his sentence, his brother, Kershaun, had gone to college like Aqeela Sherrills, and become a peacemaker. But his position was clear. "There were homies who said, 'Let's get some signs and have a peaceful protest'," Kershaun told reporter Jeffrey Anderson years later. "I said, 'Let's rip shit up, let's show the powers that be how we feel."[13]

At 4 P.M., five young associates hit Pay-Less Liquor and Deli on Florence and Dalton, and grabbed bottles of 8-Ball. When the Korean-American owner's son, David Lee, blocked the entrance, one of the kids smashed him on the head with a bottle. "This is for Rodney King!" they shouted, and ran into the street.

Down the block on Florence and Normandie, guys were drinking and carousing. Some starting taking baseball bats to passing car windows. As cop cruisers screeched into the intersection, their cars were pelted with rocks. Two policemen chased a sixteen-year-old rock-thrower down an alley, pulled him down off a chain-link fence and hog-tied him as he screamed, "I can't breathe!" More than two dozen cops arrived, and they made two more arrests.

But the mass at Florence and Normandie Streets had lost its fear. In the 1970s the chant had been, "It's Nation time!" Now the streets filled with the cry: "It's Uzi time! Cops gonna die tonight!"[14] At a quarter to six, on orders of Lieutenant Mike Moulin, the police unit retreated with the three arrestees to a command post assembling at a bus depot further north, at 54th and Arlington.

First Blood

Anyone not Black and unlucky enough to enter the intersection was attacked. Driving his big rig through an hour later, Reginald Denny would become the riots' most celebrated victim. But most of the victims were Asian or Latino immigrants. In almost every instance, African Americans came to their aid, a fact that would later be lost in the rush to declare it a "race riot."

Community and civic leaders were gathering for a peace service at the symbolic heart of Los Angeles' civil rights movement, the First African Methodist Episcopal Church, seven miles north. Two South Central activists, Karen Bass and Sylvia Castillo, the director and assistant director of the Community Coalition for Substance Abuse Prevention and Treatment, were heading toward the Church west down Florence after another day of counting and mapping liquor stores in South Central. They had been conducting research for a campaign they launched in January to close fifteen particularly noxious, crime-inducing liquor stores in the area.

Castillo followed Bass as she slowed down at Normandie. The crowd had broken down the riot gates to Tom Suzuki's liquor store and hauled the alcohol back into the streets. They had grabbed tires from the gas station and set them on fire, the beginnings of a roadblock. When Bass, an African American, signaled to turn right, they let her car pass. But they rained rocks, concrete and malt liquor bottles on Castillo's car, shattering the passenger-side windows and the windshield. Suddenly a guy was in Castillo's car, trying to open her door. "Bitch, you're gonna die," he yelled. Castillo hit the accelerator and sped south down Normandie, her face bleeding.

Twice police tried to take back Florence and Normandie; twice they gave up. So the crowd moved north on Normandie. By now, disturbances were breaking out across the inner city. At Western and Slauson, three fires burned. Near U.S.C., another crowd was throwing rocks at passing cars.[15]

Downtown, at the police headquarters called Parker Center, political protestors gathered to denounce the verdicts. Michael Zinzun, one of the city's leading anti-police brutality activists, told a reporter, "This community has got to realize that an unstable Black community means an unstable L.A."[16]

When night fell, the activists were replaced by young men who set American flags and a parking kiosk afire and tried to storm the glass entrance before being repelled by riot police. They moved into downtown, overturning police cars and setting them on fire. They threw rocks at the *Los Angeles Times* building.

Cold and Hot

Despite the growing reports of unrest, and the apparent inability of LAPD to do anything about them, Chief Darryl Gates left his command post and headed out to the posh Westside. He was a lame duck. The Christopher Commission, created by Mayor Tom Bradley a month after the King beating, had already passed judgment on Gates's tenure, finding a pattern of racism in the police department and proposing broad reforms of the department's leadership, operations and accountability. His successor had already been chosen.

So instead of reacting to the riots, Gates was being driven to a right-wing fundraiser against a Commission-initiated police reform measure on the June ballot, Charter Amendment F. His motorcade sped down the Santa Monica Highway past the First African Methodist Episcopal Church.

Thousands were jammed into the church. On the dais, Mayor Tom Bradley, City Council members, church and community leaders and Rodney King's mother exhorted people to keep calm, to express their anger through the political system. Pastor Cecil Murray prayed for peace, and the gospel choir sang. "Operation Cool Response" was underway. But outside, angry young men and women from the neighborhood weren't having it. "We ain't gon' turn another cheek so they can come and kick us in the ass," one told filmmaker Matthew McDaniels.[17] "We gotta do *shit*!" The crowd outside the First A.M.E. started doing shit—destroying cars, looting stores.

Soon the streets were jammed: boys slow-rolling in their rides as if it were a Crenshaw night blasting "Fuck Tha Police," flash mobs of young girls protesting, "No more Simi Valley!" In West Hollywood, lesbian and gay activists marched toward Sunset Boulevard. Near U.C.L.A., students poured down Westwood

Boulevard. From the site of the Rodney King beating, hundreds marched to the LAPD Foothill Division headquarters, all echoing the same cry across the city: "No justice no peace."

At 8 P.M., fifteen fires raged. Two hours later, there were nearly fifty.[18] Rioting had spread to Long Beach, Baldwin Hills, Inglewood, Pasadena and Hollywood. Gates returned from the fundraiser to a police force hamstrung by indecision and incompetence. Rather than take control, Gates immediately demanded a helicopter tour of the city. "He took something like an hour-and-a-half ride and never issued any instructions as far as I could determine," said William Webster, the former FBI director who would be appointed to lead an investigation into LAPD's response to the riots. "So he is just up there watching Rome burn."[19]

At 11 P.M., near Nickerson Gardens, a liquor store was ablaze and the streets were full of looters. When cops and firefighters pulled up, snipers opened fire on them. For hours, the shootout continued, with police expending hundreds of rounds. When it was all over, three Black men were dead, and three more were wounded.[20]

By midnight on April 29, the riots had taken fourteen lives. Three new fires were being reported every minute. Governor Pete Wilson had declared a state of emergency and Mayor Bradley established a dusk-to-dawn curfew. Eighteen hundred officers had reached the command post. But most were still standing around awaiting instructions. The few deployments in the field were mostly placed at the edge of the inner city.[21] The urban core was once again abandoned to looting and war.

Paying the Price

At dawn on Thursday, the writing on the wall read: MEXICANS & CRIPS & BLOODS TOGETHER TONITE 4–30–92.

Seeing evidence that authorities had no interest in maintaining order in the urban core, and hearing reports that the National Guard was on its way, some figured it was last call. Rusty, junk-ready cars filled the streets, the mini-malls, and supermarket parking lots.

People got their essentials—diapers, canned goods, milk, butter and guns. After all, these were wartime conditions. "I felt some shame," said one Salvadoran refugee. "But I thought, if we don't take the food now, what will we give our children to eat? When will we be able to buy food again?"[22]

Some got a lot more—shoes, clothes, toys, tires, videos, stereos, beds. For many it was payback time. "The cops can do anything they want and nothing happens," said one young Latino, whose take included a goat, two sides of beef and thirty-seven cases of beer, and whose plan was to invite friends over for a riot-feast. "Well, we got away with our stuff. Daryl Gates can kiss my ass. It was fun, lots of fun."[23]

When they were done, the arsonists moved in. They burned ice-cream shops and fast-food franchises, glassmakers and camera vendors, flea markets and hair salons, one-hour photos and next-day dry cleaners, check cashers, churches and cultural centers; businesses that sold sheepskins, pagers and lingerie; the offices of dentists, chiropractors and acupuncturists. They torched Mobil, Union, Arco, the Bank of America, The Boys' Supermarkets and the Slauson Swap Meet.

All night, Radio Korea's announcers had broadcast street-by-street reports of Korean-owned businesses that had were being looted or burned. 911 was a joke. The police or the fire department would not come to save the day. The calls went out. Bring all your guns. The looters and arsonists are coming to Koreatown.

The young men called into the ranks of Koreatown's makeshift militia identified themselves with white headbands. One of them was Cal State Fullerton's student body president Joseph Ahn. The first-born son of a once high-ranking Korean diplomat, Ahn's family had come upon hard times, immigrated to San Pedro and moved into the housing projects. Coming to America meant beatdowns at first, football next, and then all-night popping battles with Ice T at Radio.

Joe was pushing his gray Civic to join his dad, rifles and ammo in the back seat. A long line of cars streamed south out of the city. But no one was on the road ahead of him. As he speeded up the 10, he could see billows of black smoke filling the sky over Koreatown. He wondered if he would see old friends on the other side of the gunsight.

On the roof of their bakery in Koreatown below the arc of street-fired bullets, he and his friends kept one ear on Radio Korea, their only lifeline to the world beyond the block, another to potential danger—the distant roar of the crowd, the crackle of flaming buildings, bottles shattering, rocks hitting metal, rounds of gunfire. Much less frequently, they heard a police bullhorn from a barricaded van: "What you are doing is illegal. Disperse immediately."

By nightfall, the air was acrid and smoky, and there was no electricity. The only light came from the fires in the building across the street. "Fuck the police," Joe thought, bitterly. "Koreans and Blacks pay taxes into the system and ain't nobody getting shit back from nobody."

When it was all over, the young volunteer security forces had saved most of Koreatown from being burned to the ground. Damages to Korean-American businesses in Koreatown were less than half as much as damages to Korean-American businesses in South Central.[24] A shift began to take place within the community, as leadership and power pushed toward the "1.5ers"—the generation born in Korea but raised mostly in America. They had come of age, but not without paying a dear price.

Two miles away from the Ahns' bakery, eighteen-year-old Edward Song Lee, James Kang and two other close friends headed up to Koreatown. All day, they had fired warning shots at looters who drove into the neighborhood to scope the pickings. After dark, they heard a call on Radio Korea about looters on the roof of a restaurant on Third Street. They got into their cars and headed up there.

As it turned out, the call was false. Radio Korea was being flooded with calls by stay-at-home store owners who hoped the young men would protect their businesses. As they reached the restaurant, Lee's friend in the lead car fired a warning shot in the air. The men on the roof loosed a barrage of bullets. They were, in fact, also young Korean Americans who had come to protect the businesses.

When the shooting ended, Kang was wounded. Another friend, Sam Lee, came and pulled them out of the car. Eddie Lee lay on the pavement, his white shirt stained red shoulder to shoulder, neck to stomach, and died: "I still can't forgive for this," Kang said later of the incident. "It didn't need to happen this way."[25]

Attacking "The Aliens"

The twelve hours between noon and midnight on Thursday were the most intense of the riots. The fire department received nearly 5,000 calls, five times the norm.[26] Hospitals reported over 750 injuries, 10 percent of them critical.[27]

Thursday was crucial in another way. The media had portrayed the riots as a Black thing, an echo of Watts. But this frame was obsolete; it rendered the flood of satellite images incomprehensible. Here were shots of children wheeling shopping carts of diapers and food. Most of them were not Black, but Latino.

The "race riot"—with Blacks centrally cast as Blacks and Korean Americans in the role of the long-gone whites—had suddenly become what Mike Davis termed a "postmodern bread riot," and the images seemed as if they were coming from a Central America country, not from within U.S. borders.[28] Newscasters were confused.

Most of these Latinos were recent working-class immigrants or refugees. For years, they had quietly transformed the inner city. Jordan Downs was nearing 40 percent Latino. Koreatown was overwhelmingly Latino. Southgate, the town on Watts's east border, where the Spook Hunters had once patrolled, was now the home of a trio of rappers—Italian, Cuban and Cuban-Mexican—named for an imaginary piece of real estate they called Cypress Hill.

That crew's 1991 debut opened on Pico Boulevard west of downtown, in the heart of the growing Central American and Mexican neighborhoods of West-lake and Pico-Union, with the hot hum of a police dispatch and a seething anti-pig rant over a steamy Albert King blues beat. *Cypress Hill* described yet another hole in the network society where English was broken, jobs were en-dangered, paranoia was palpable and the most advanced technology was in the killing hands of the cops. It was as accurate and specific a predictor of the ri-ots as any record from Compton, South Central or Watts.

On KABC-TV Channel 7, white reporter Linda Mour had tried vainly to find looters who would agree to be interviewed. When she returned to the studio, she was asked by the studio anchor Harold Greene, "Did you get the impres-sion that a lot of those people were illegal aliens?" Mour answered, "Yes."[29] Her botched assignment seemed to give assignment editors and Daryl Gates a new target: "illegal aliens." By May 2, images of burning buildings had been re-placed by images of Latinos facedown on the pavement in mass arrests—including plastic-tied pregnant women and mothers with confused toddlers at their sides. A thousand INS and Border Patrol agents set up command posts in Pico-Union and MacArthur Park.[30]

Gates's new sweeps were supplemented by federal agents. In open violation of Special Order 40, a city order limiting local police intervention in federal im-migration cases, agents rode shotgun with police as they swept through the 'hoods looking for stolen merchandise. When stupefied residents could not pro-duce receipts for anything in their apartment that looked new, the object—a bed, a television, a bicycle—was confiscated. One activist called it "reverse looting."[31]

Cops and agents swept up anyone who happened be in the wrong place at the wrong time—day laborers on the corner, security guards trying to get to work, families at bus stops. Many were taken in for curfew violations. Many were never charged with any crimes. All now faced deportation without due process.

Between April 29 and May 4, 37 percent of the nearly 10,000 arrestees were Latino, more than any other racial group.[32] The LAPD and the Sheriff's office turned over 1,500 to the INS for deportation proceedings. Detainees were forced to sign voluntary deportation forms or face long prison terms and up to $20,000 in fines. At least seven hundred were deported. One desperate mother was certain her mentally retarded fourteen-year-old girl had been picked up by the INS and bused to Mexico.[33]

City Councilmember Mike Hernandez, who represented Pico-Union and Koreatown, was livid. "The response to me when I needed the National Guard to protect the people of this area and I needed to protect the businesses, protect the homes, is they gave me the Border Patrol. It was totally an insult," he said. "To arrest people and put them into custody or to turn them over directly to INS for deportation and to do it simply because they look Latino does not make sense. That's not what this country is about."[34]

Yet right-wing race-baiters like Congressman Dana Rohrabacher and Pat Buchanan had already picked up on Mour and Gates's message and were using it to batter President George Bush and moderate Republicans, whom they accused of tolerating "illegal aliens." On May 12, Bush belatedly claimed credit for the deportations, and claimed that a third of the first six thousand arrested were "illegal aliens," a number that has never been substantiated. The backlash against immigrants culminated two years later in the passage of California's appropriately-named Proposition 187, an initiative that banned all state services, including health care and education, to undocumented immigrants.

Two Speeches

By Friday, May 1, the National Guard had posted tanks at the entrances to Westwood Village. At the same time, all but two supermarkets and dozens of Black businesses in Compton had been burned to the ground, and Korean American-owned businesses had suffered nearly $400 million of the estimated

$800 million to $1 billion in total property damages.[35] When it was all over, 2,383 had been wounded and 53 were dead, most by gunfire.

Rodney King believed he should make some public statement. After the verdicts were read on April 29, Rodney King had returned home, and as the images of fires and the smiling faces of acquitted cops repeated in an endless loop, King had locked himself in his bedroom and raged at his television. "Why? Why? Why? Why?" he screamed. "Why are they beating me again?"[36]

On May 1, Lerman finally agreed to let King speak. King was still badly bruised, looked bewildered and broken and unbearably sad, once again a tragic symbol of a broken city. King's voice was shaky and unstable, as if he could not close all the thoughts chasing around in his head.

> I just um
> I just want to say
> you know can we can we all get along
> can we can we get along
> um
> can we stop making it
> making it horrible for
> for the for the older people and and the and the kids?

Yet, fleetingly—perhaps when he thought of how he had been demonized in the trials or when his mind's eye fixed on the blood spreading across the white shirt of Edward Song Lee—he rose toward the clarity of an unfathomable fury.

> I love
> you know I I'm neutral I love people every I love people of color
> you know I I'm not uh I'm not like they
> *making me out*
> *making me out to be*
>
> um we we've gotta we've gotta quit
> we've got to quit
>
> you know after all I mean

I can understand the
the first upsets of the first two hours after the verdict
but uh to go on to keep going on like like this and to
see the security guard shot on
on the ground
it uh-huh-hum

it's it's uh
it's just not right
it's just not right
because those people will will never go home to to their families again
and uh
I mean
please we can
we can get along here
we we all can get along
we just gotta
just gotta you know
I mean we're all stuck here for a while

let's
you know let's
let's let's try to work it out
let's try to be you
you know
Let's try and work it out.

Later that evening, in a national address, President Bush told L.A. residents what they already knew, that American firepower was on the ground in their city—including FBI SWAT teams, U.S. Marshal riot control units and the Border Patrol. He said:

What we saw last night and the night before in Los Angeles is not about civil rights. It's not about the great cause of equality that all Americans must uphold. It's not a message of protest. It's been the brutality of a mob, pure and simple. And let me assure you, I will use whatever force is necessary to restore order . . .

Television has become a medium that often brings us together. But its vivid display of Rodney King's beating shocked us. And the America it has shown us on our screens these last forty-eight hours has appalled us . . .

Let me say to the people saddened by the spectacle of the past few days, to the good people of Los Angeles, caught at the center of this senseless suffering: the violence will end, justice will be served, hope will return.

Thank you and may God bless the United States of America.

History's Loop

The next day, L.A.'s Korean-American community marched thirty thousand strong—elderly, children, immigrants who no longer had livelihoods. They wore the white headbands of the young men of April 30. They banged Korean drums and chanted "No justice, no peace." Their signs read JUSTICE FOR ALL PEOPLE, BLACK PEOPLE ARE NOT OUR ENEMIES, and WHERE IS THE GOVERNMENT WHEN WE REALLY NEED THEM? In the intervening years, some would become homeless, some would commit suicide, families would fall apart, many would lose their worldly possessions, but at that moment, they were taking a stand, showing what side they were on.

From the streets to the halls of power across the country, a loud chorus began calling for renewed investment in the inner cities. So, over the weekend, the right-wing went on the offensive. An executive memorandum by Heritage Foundation Vice President Stuart Butler was distributed to key Republicans and to the media. It praised Bush for being "wise and forceful" and set out the new terms of the debate over the nation's urban crisis:

> Bush next must address the anger and hopelessness that created the environment for the violence. In doing so he must first reject the phoney [sic] argument that what is needed is a "Marshall Plan" for urban America. Vast new public housing projects, even more generous welfare benefits for single mothers and another army of social welfare administrators will do nothing to improve America's cities. Indeed it is such programs, which underpinned the Great Society and continue to be the basis of today's "anti-poverty" strategy, that are the root cause of the problem.[37]

On cue, Republicans like Bush press secretary Marlin Fitzwater, presidential candidate Pat Buchanan and Housing Secretary Jack Kemp called the riots the result of failed liberal policies of President Lyndon B. Johnson's Great Society programs, the final repudiation of the progressive urban agenda. When Congress opened its most important debate on urban policy since Carter set foot in the Bronx, the Heritage Foundation's message dominated the discussion.

In fact, the Great Society programs that conservatives were blaming had long been gutted. During the Reagan-Bush era, federal spending on subsidized housing had been slashed by 82 percent, job training and employment by 63 percent, and community service and development program by 40 percent.[38] Because Bush faced a difficult reelection battle, he agreed to sign an emergency $1 billion aid bill for the cities, largely in the form of disaster relief and summer jobs, an amount the nation's mayors agreed would make little long-term difference. In fact, Bush had forced Congress to cut another $1 billion from the bill before agreeing to sign it. But after losing the election in November, he vetoed a much broader $30 billion bipartisan urban aid and tax bill. The politics of abandonment tied the Bronx of 1977 to the Los Angeles of 1992.

Some had called it an Uprising, others a Rebellion. The official term was "civil disturbance." Korean Americans simply called it by the date it had begun, 4-2-9, *Sa-I-Gu*. Whatever the name, these days would mark the hip-hop generation's passage through fire. After this, there would be the backlash.

In the park after the truce. Eazy E video shoot, 1993.

Photo © B+

17

All in the Same Gang

The War on Youth and the Quest for Unity

And so our brief subject today is taken from the American Constitution and these words, "Toward a more perfect union." Toward a more perfect union.

—Minister Louis Farrakhan

We are facing a potential bloodbath of teenage violence in years ahead that will be so bad, we'll look back at the 1990s and say those were the good old days.

—Criminologist James Alan Fox

First there were the parties. With calm restored to the streets, spontaneous celebrations broke out across from Lynwood to Watts, South Central to Compton, Willowbrook to Inglewood, as rival gang sets tied their colors together, fired up the barbecues and broke bread. Parks that had once been exclusive turf were thrown open. Public spaces were public once again. The rapper Kam summed up the vibe in his epochal single, "Peace Treaty," its hydraulic "Atomic Dog" bassline pumping a giddy joy:

I'ma always remember this
Because my niggas made the history books
And now the mystery looks a lot clearer
The man in the mirror's got power
It's now or never

More than ever
Black people got to stick together

For Los Angeles's war-weary youths, the gang truce and the Uprising un-leashed a burst of creative energy. Rappers like DJ Quik, Compton's Most Wanted and Above The Law were making noise on the national charts. From the fiercely competitive freestyle ciphers at the Good Life Café on the westside to the intergenerational ferment of spoken word, free jazz and hip-hop in Leimert Park to the free floating parties at the Pharcyde Manor in Hancock Park, an un-derground was taking shape. At the Hip-Hop Shop on Melrose, b-boys and b-girls gathered to advance the elements. Graffiti writers like HEX and SLICK were engaged in a new age of style wars. Some were joining the surge of en-ergy that was transforming street fashion and graphic design. A number of grass-roots magazines, led by *URB* and *Rap Sheet*, captured the local scene and articulated a new West Coast aesthetic.

In the streets, gang members turned their attention to creating a future for themselves and their city.

Give Us the Hammer and Nails

Everyone seemed to agree that economic development was the key to saving Los Angeles. On May 2, Mayor Bradley named Peter Ueberroth, the head of the city's 1984 Olympics, to be the head of a private-sector organization that would be called "Rebuild L.A.," charged with mobilizing business, government, and community investment. It began assembling a board of directors of nearly one hundred city, corporate, Hollywood and community players, including the likes of Jim Brown, Danny Bakewell, Johnnie Cochran, Michael Ovitz and Ed-ward James Olmos.

Ueberroth predicted that Rebuild L.A. would convince five hundred corpo-rations from three continents to invest more than $1 billion in the city.[1] Eco-nomic consultants told them that to begin to turn around the inner-city, they would need to raise $6 billion and create more than 90,000 jobs.[2] But by any measure, the organization was a complete failure. Ueberroth stepped down from the leadership after only a year, leaving the organization in disar-ray. Over the next four years, Rebuild L.A. raised less than $300 million. Only half of the thirty-two supermarkets that the organization had been promised were actually built. Vons Corporation had pledged to build two stores but opened only one, in the supermarket-starved city of Compton, and sold it as soon as it could. Rebuild L.A. was, in Mike Davis's words, "the cruelest joke of all."[3]

At the same time Rebuild L.A. was announced in May of 1992, an alternative proposal to rebuild Los Angeles, purported to come from the Bloods and Crips, circulated through the streets, the media and upper levels of government. Its provenance was in question, particularly because of the document's closing words—"Meet these demands and the targeting of police officers will stop!"—a threat that clearly had not been sanctioned by the peacemakers and that seemed inimical to common sense. But the proposal's details drew interest and support from many gang leaders.

Among other things, the $3.7 billion plan for inner-city investment called for three new hospitals and forty additional health care centers to be built and the replacement of welfare programs with manufacturing plants. It demanded increased lighting of city streets, $20 million in business loans and community job creation, new books and accelerated learning programs in inner-city schools, and community policing that incorporated former gang members. "Give us the hammer and the nails," the document read, "and we will rebuild the city."

For a brief period before and after their 1971 truce, the Bronx gangs had turned to the government for relief as they sought to turn themselves around. But two decades later, this generation of gangs would have no Great Society and no Mayor Lindsay. The infrastructure of aid and rehabilitation had been replaced by Bush's "thousand points of light," which usually took the form of do-for-self, faith-based grass-roots nationalism or the trickle-down charities of the anything-goes, everything-is-for-sale marketplace.

To be sure, the new generation was not interested in government promises. Kam put it in the Nation of Islam's terms: "Less government relief checks, more labor." They readily admitted that they would need to do their part to make peace work. "We've got to show people that this eye-for-an-eye stuff is out the door," Charles "Q-Bone" Rachal of the Five-Duce Broadway Crips said. "But we have to do it ourselves. All that hand-out stuff from the '60s was messed up, and those people who did it messed up. We're the generation of the '90s, and we've got to show action."[4]

So gang members met with the Korean American Grocers Organization, who immediately got the point but could only promise a handful of jobs. That was a path Ice T had already known to be useless. "They aimed at Korean people because they felt Koreans were one step above them, so that's the closest step to the system," he wrote of the burners and looters in *The Ice Opinion*. "They didn't know the Koreans are just as broke as them."[5] In time, many more Black and brown faces appeared behind the counter of these stores, but most of the 2,000 destroyed Korean-American businesses would never be rebuilt, and tiny markets and laundromats could never replace the hundreds of thousands of jobs that corporate flight had spirited away.

Gang peacemakers seized on Minister Farrakhan's up-from-the-bootstraps optimism and leapt into entrepreneurship. Two men from Jordan Downs secured a contract from the Eurostar shoe company to sell a "Truce" brand sneaker. With funds from Congresswoman Maxine Waters, they opened a storefront they called the Playground, where they sponsored basketball games, created a community hangout, and sold the shoes. In a year, the venture was over. The burden of economic and community development, one of the shoe company's representatives later said, was "more of a job for the president of the United States than for a shoe salesman."[6]

The most audacious idea came from Daude Sherrills, who had come to the first peace meeting at the Masjid with a proposal for a nonprofit organization that he called "Hands Across Watts," a government-funded group that would create jobs for former gang-members and sponsor job training, child care and recreational programs. A week after the Uprising, when the Crips and Bloods publicly announced their truce at a press conference at Jordan Downs, Sherrills and Tony Bogard presented the plan, announcing $100,000 as their fundraising goal. When corporate money did not rush in, they took to the streets to sell car-washing solution, soft drinks, and peace treaty T-shirts. The organization secured federal, city and private grants and job-training contracts, but Sherrills left after disagreements with Bogard over its direction.

Soon after, Bogard was shot dead by another PJ Watts Crip, allegedly as the result of a dispute over cocaine profits. The deal had nothing to do with Hands Across Watts, but grants, contracts, and donations evaporated, and the organization crumbled. "Economics plays a major role in maintaining the peace," Bogard had once told a reporter. "If we had industry and venture capital, we wouldn't have all the drug selling and robbing that's going on. Economics is the key to everything."[7] It was a tragic epitaph.

At the corner of Florence and Normandie, three of the four corners remained burned down. Tom's Liquors was the only building that remained. Behind it, one billboard advertised the television talent show, "Star Search." The other read: "Looking for a new career? Join your LAPD. Earn $34,000 to $43,000."[8]

"A lot of things was promised," Daude Sherrills says. "They didn't put a billion dollars in the truce movement. So this is where we're at today."

Pressure Drop (Yet Another Version)

But against all odds, the gang truce held in Watts and spread. In the weeks after the uprising, gang homicide tallies plunged, and stayed there.

Police were skeptical. "I'm concerned as to the true motives of the gang members as to why they would make peace," one policeman said. "Is it so they can better fight with us, so they can better deal dope or so they can better be constructive in their neighborhoods? That would be the last item I would choose because gang members have a thug mentality."[9]

Peacemakers came to believe that police were actively trying to undermine the truce. Hours after the National Guard had left town, newspapers reported the appearance of a crude flyer that read: *To all Crips and Bloods: Let's unit [sic] and dont [sic] gangbang and let it be a black thing for the little black girl and the homie Rodney King. An eye for an eye, a tooth for a tooth. If LAPD hurt a black we'll kill two. Pow. Pow. Pow.* From there, the anti-gang rhetoric accelerated. The sheriff's office issued a gang intelligence briefing which stated Black Muslims had organized the gangs to loot and burn, and warned that Crips and Bloods were preparing to attack police stations. Mike Davis scoffed, "This is right off that movie *Assault on Precinct 13*."[10]

Was there a disinformation campaign afoot? On May 22, the CBS Evening News reported a bizarre story alleging gang members were trading drugs for military weapons from local U.S. Army bases.[11] No one was ever arrested in connection with the alleged transaction, and the story sunk like a rock. But the next day, the *Washington Post* reported that four thousand weapons had been stolen and were probably in the hands of gang members. By May 27, outgoing Chief Daryl Gates was spinning on Larry King's CNN show, "You know, I'd love to see peace in the city, peace among gangs," he said. "But I just don't think it's going to happen. These people simply don't have it in them, I don't believe, to create peace among the gangs or in any other way."[12]

Gates was contradicting at least one of his own officers on the ground. Deputy Chief Matthew Hunt, the police commander of the South Los Angeles area, admitted to the Police Commission, "There's no question the amount of violent crime has decreased. People in the community say they haven't heard a shot fired in weeks. They are elated."[13]

But it had become clear to peacemakers that LAPD was out to disrupt and harass peace meetings and parties. At some events, cops appeared in large numbers without provoking an incident. At others, they forcibly broke up the meetings. In Compton, Congresswoman Waters and City Councilman Mark Ridley-Thomas came in person to intervene with police who were harassing gang members leaving a peace meeting.

At Imperial Courts, police helicopters and riot squadrons swooped in to break up truce barbecues. When they did the same thing at Jordan Downs, residents and gang members sent thirty police officers to the hospital. With this clash as a pretext, LAPD created a special "crime suppression task force," transferring forty police officers from the San Fernando Valley and the Westside to the South Bureau.[14] Then, in what feds touted as their largest anti-gang effort ever, the FBI beefed up its Los Angeles office with twenty-six additional agents and the ATF added ten. They announced they would use racketeering laws to sweep up the gang leadership.

In August an important peacemaker was taken off the streets. Dewayne Holmes, the cousin of Henry Peco who became one of key architects of the peace, was convicted and sentenced to seven years for a ten-dollar robbery that community organizers and politicians like former Governor Jerry Brown insisted he had not committed. Community leaders wondered if he and others had been targeted for political reasons, not criminal ones.

Author Luis Rodriguez and peacemakers Cle "Bone" Sloan, from the Athens Park Bloods, and Kershaun "Lil Monster" Scott, from the Eight-Tray Gangster Crips, wrote in the *Los Angeles Times*, "The Los Angeles Police Department told the media that the gangs were going to turn on police officers, even ambush them. Yet no police officer in South-Central has been killed or severely hurt since April 29, the day the King-beating verdict came down."[15]

"Now that we're chilling, they want to attack us," Scott said in an interview. "Isn't that ironic?"

Farrakhan put it more bluntly, "Why is there an apparent conspiracy to destroy the youth? In 1992, our fearless Black youth are ready to move for liberation."[16]

The Politics of Containment

After the riots, a generation raised on the politics of abandonment saw that it now also faced a sharply evolving politics of containment.

From the beginnings of the juvenile justice system in America, a central doctrine had been that youthful indiscretion could be corrected through proper rehabilitation. The juvenile justice system was there to save as much as it was to punish. This was a benevolent and essentially paternalistic view of how the state should treat youth. With the arrival of the boomers, a more liberalized, permissive view emerged.

But by the late 1980s, a reversal began, and after the riots, the trend accelerated. Forty-eight states made their juvenile crime statutes more punitive. Forty-one states made it easier for prosecutors to try juveniles as young as twelve as adults. A number of states began to consider the death penalty for juveniles as young as thirteen. Teens were too young to hang out, but too old to save.

Social ecologist Mike Males explained the source of the reaction:

> The Census Bureau reports that 80 percent of America's adults over age forty are whites of European origin (Euro-white). Thirty-five percent of children and youths under age eighteen are nonwhite or of Hispanic (Latino) origin, a proportion that has doubled since 1970. In most of America's big cities, white elders govern nonwhite kids. In California, two-thirds of the elders are Euro-white; three-fifths of the youths are nonwhite or Latino.[17]

The Los Angeles Uprising had clarified these abstractions in a dramatic, unavoidable way, fanning fears of a browning nation, and unleashing a political and cultural backlash of massive proportions. The War on Gangs expanded into what young activists came to call "the War on Youth."

The 1988 killing of Karen Toshima had precipitated the War on Gangs. That year, California Governor George Deukmejian signed the Street Terrorism Enforcement and Prevention Act (STEP), the broadest legal criminalization of street gangs in history. Gang-related offenses received enhanced punishments, and new categories of gang crimes were created. Under STEP, gang membership itself was punishable by up to three years in state prison. By the end of the century, most major cities and at least nineteen states had laws similar to STEP, and anti-gang units to enforce them.

One of the most profound implications of STEP was its attempt to write into law a process of determining who was a gang member, a move that helped fuel the growth of gang databases. In 1987, the Law Enforcement Communication Network and the Los Angeles County Sheriff's Department had begun developing a large database—the Gang Reporting, Evaluation, and Tracking System (GREAT)—to collect, store, and analyze personal information about suspected gang members. Its creation, and the spread of STEP-type laws across the country, spurred the Justice Department and the FBI to fund national databases.

But these databases could be indiscriminate, often identifying "suspects" before any crime had been committed. There were no universal standards for entry. Many youths were added by virtue of an arrest, whether or not the arrestee was charged. Others merely fit a "gang profile." STEP's attempt to define this profile fostered a multitude of local variations. By 1999, wearing baggy jeans and being related to a gang suspect was enough to meet the definition of being a "gang member" in at least five states. Abuses were rampant.

In 1992, a Denver community organization, Actions for a Better Community (ABC), protested that the city's gang database had unfairly captured thousands of innocent youths of color. A year later, investigations revealed that eight of every ten young people of color in the entire city were listed in the database. Appearing in the database was no neutral thing. Gloria Yellowhorse, an ABC organizer, says, "Employers could call the gang list to see if a young person was on the list." Police met with ABC and quietly changed their protocols.

But minutes from downtown Denver in suburban Aurora, any two of the following could still constitute gang membership to the local police: "slang," "clothing of a particular color," "pagers," "hairstyles" or "jewelry." Nearly 80 percent of Aurora's list was African-American. One activist said, "They might as well call it a Black list."

In California's Orange County, where less than half of young people were of color, 92 percent of those listed in the gang database were of color, primarily Latino and Asian. "The 'gang label' has everything to do with race," says John Crew of the California ACLU. "Frankly, we do not believe that this tactic would have spread so widely, and come to be accepted within law enforcement generally, if it was not being applied almost exclusively to people of color."

The rapid growth of the databases coincided with the rise of sweep laws—anti-loitering laws, anti-cruising laws, and curfews—that proliferated as local municipalities searched for methods to limit the movement of young people in public spaces.

Cruising bans came after a decade of street scenes—boulevards and neighborhoods where young people's cruising and partying overtook local traffic on Friday and Saturday nights. In Los Angeles, cruising bans ended the scenes in East Los Angles, Westwood, downtown and Crenshaw Boulevard. In Atlanta, outcry from white homeowners over the city's annual Freaknik event in 1996 resulted in a cruising ban that ended one of the nation's biggest Black collegiate gatherings.

Between 1988 and 1997, curfew arrests doubled nationwide. In California, they quadrupled. Washington, D.C.'s law, which punished parents along with their children, went so far in abridging civil liberties that it was declared unconstitutional. Curfew enforcement was not color blind. In Ventura County, California, Latino and Black youths were arrested at more than seven times the rate of whites. In New Orleans, Blacks were arrested at nineteen times the rate of whites. But these laws, such as the stringent weekday curfews in Detroit, did nothing to stop increases in crime. They did fatten gang databases with false data.

During the mid-1980s there had been scattered anti-breakdancing ordinances and outbreaks of boombox citations. But what united the sweep laws of the '90s was a new logic of erasing youths—particularly youths of color—from public space. Not only were there to be no more boomboxes, sagging jeans, street dancing, or public displays of affection, there were to be *no more young people*. Youth itself was being criminalized. The most extreme forms of this logic emerged in Los Angeles and Chicago.

In Los Angeles, City Attorney James K. Hahn pioneered the gang injunction strategy when he won a court order against the Playboy Gangster Crips of

West Los Angeles. The injunction named dozens of alleged members of the set, and, within a twenty-six-block area, prevented them from hanging out together, talking on the street, or being seen in public for more than five minutes. In effect, the gang injunctions removed alleged gang member's freedoms in their own neighborhood without actually sending them to jail. This tactic proved so politically popular that it attracted millions in state and city funds. But in a study of the effects of this strategy, the ACLU concluded that the injunction did not suppress violent crime in the area and may, in fact, have forced gang members simply to shift their activities outside of the area covered by the injunction.[18] Still, the strategy spread to other cities with the blessing of tough-on-crime, tough-on-youth politicians.

In Chicago, anti-youth-of-color hysteria had begun to mount in the late '80s. An anti-cruising ordinance was passed in the southwest portion of the city, and similar measures soon spread across the city's suburbs and exurbs. By 1992, the sweep solution came to the city in the form of the nation's broadest anti-loitering law, which sponsors had drafted with Los Angeles's gang injunctions in mind.

Although it was pitched as an anti-gang initiative, legal experts likened it to Jim Crow laws that were established to restrict Southern Blacks in their leisure time. The law made it illegal just to stand on the street with any person whom a cop "reasonably believed" to be in a gang. Under the ordinance, 45,000 young Chicagoans—mostly Black and Latino—were arrested in just two years. Only a small fraction of them were actually charged with a crime. The Cook County gang database quickly became more than two-thirds black.

"They were arresting lots of innocent people," said Jeremy Lahoud, a youth organizer with Chicago's Southwest Youth Collaborative, who noted that the ordinance distorted police priorities. "It takes police away from the real work, and pushes them to simply sweeping youth off the street." The law was so broadly dismissive of basic liberties that it was declared unconstitutional by a conservative U.S. Supreme Court in 1999.

The racial effects of all of these sweep laws were lopsided. While white youths made up 79 percent of national juvenile arrests, 62 percent of youths in juvenile detention facilities were of color. Even when charged with the same offense, Latinos and Native Americans were 2.5 times more likely to end up in custody than whites. Black youths were five times more likely to be detained.[19]

Fear and the Ballot Box

The politics of containment moved next to the ballot box.

In 1993, the state of Washington passed the first "three strikes" initiative in the country, establishing life without parole for convicts with three violent felony offenses. The following year, although crime rates were lower than in 1980, California voters passed Proposition 184, a much harsher three-strikes law.[20] The effect was to imprison thousands in life sentences for nonviolent crimes.[21]

Right-wing anti-immigration ideologues also pressed Proposition 187, an initiative to ban all government services to undocumented immigrants, like health care, social services and education. Playing up the image of young Latino looters, they claimed the "Save Our State" initiative would end incentives for "illegal aliens" to immigrate. Instead, the initiative would have denied basic human services to thousands and bounced many children from the public schools. Although the measure passed, it was never implemented, and was finally ruled unconstitutional.

In 1994, University of California regent and Black Republican Ward Connerly began pushing to overturn affirmative action in the nine-campus system. The University, a recurring right-wing target, was one of the most diverse elite public systems in the country. On July 20, 1995, Connerly and Governor Pete Wilson combined to force a proposal through the Board of Regents to end affirmative action in hiring and admissions. The following year, Connerly's Proposition 209, ending affirmative action throughout California state government, was passed by the electorate. Nineteen ninety-six also marked the first year in the state's history that spending on prisons and corrections exceeded spending on higher education.

When the ban took effect in 1998, the number of Black and Latino freshmen admitted to the system dropped by 10 percent. At U.C. Berkeley alone, the numbers plunged by over 50 percent. By the end of the decade, the Justice Policy Institute estimated that nearly 50,000 black males were in a California prison, while 60,000 were in a California university. Across the country, 800,000 black males were in prison, while 600,000 were in college.[22]

Sentencing Project assistant director Marc Mauer tells this story: shortly after President Clinton took office, he proposed a $30 billion aid package for job creation and economic development for urban America. Congress reduced the proposal into a $5 billion allocation, primarily for unemployment insurance. The following year, Congress pushed through its own $30 billion proposal—for crime prevention. The bill included sixty new death penalty offenses, $8 billion in prison construction and federal "three strikes" sentencing.[23] Clinton, of course, signed it.

Harvard criminologist James Q. Wilson, the father of the "Broken Windows" theory, had begun telling another story:

> Meanwhile, just beyond the horizon, there lurks a cloud that the winds will soon bring over us. The population will start getting younger again. By the end of this decade there will be a million more people between the ages of fourteen and seventeen than there are now. . . . This extra million will be half male. Six percent of them will become high rate, repeat offenders—30,000 more young muggers, killers and thieves than we have now. Get ready.[24]

Here were the naked post-riot fears of imminent racial and generational change codified into more crackpot conservative pseudo-theory, into an ideology that could preserve the War on Youth.

The truth was that juvenile violence had already peaked. National homicide arrest rates dropped by forty percent between 1993 and 1997. In 1998, California reported its lowest juvenile felony arrest rate since 1966. National crime rates were at their lowest since the mid-'70s. But fears outweighed facts. It was as if the generation that had coined the aphorism, "Never trust anyone over thirty," was now unable to trust anyone *under* thirty.

Sister Souljah's declaration no longer seemed hyperbole: "We are at war!"

Rap and the Culture War

During the 1980s, cultural conservatives had launched attacks on everything from government funding of transgressive art to campus initiatives toward multiculturalism and inclusion. But in rap music, race, generation and pop culture all came together. By attacking hip-hop, conservatives could move their culture-war agenda out of obscure Congressional debates and campus Academic Senates into the twenty-four-hour media spin cycle.

In 1985, Tipper Gore, the wife of Tennessee Democratic senator and future presidential candidate Al Gore, and three other Washington wives launched the Parents Music Resource Center to combat sexually explicit lyrics. Gore's eureka moment had come when she heard her daughter, Karenna, enjoying Prince's "Darling Nikki" in her bedroom. Citing songs by Twisted Sister, Cyndi Lauper, David Lee Roth and Madonna, the PMRC successfully pressured the record industry began placing "Parental Adivsory" stickers on potentially explicit records.

At first, "satanic" heavy metal artists drew most of the cultural conservatives' ire. But after NWA's brush with the FBI, Gore and the cultural conservatives turned their attention to rap music. In 1990, she wrote an editorial in the *Washington Post* ripping Ice T for a rap from an album ironically subtitled *Freedom of Speech . . . Just Watch What You Say*: 'Do we want [our kids] describing themselves or each other as 'niggers'? Do we want our daughters to think of themselves as 'bitches' to be abused? Do we want our sons to measure success in gold guns hanging from thick neck chains?"[25]

A network of Christian fundamentalist groups sprung up to fight rap, pressing the Bush Administration and state and local politicians to ban rap groups like the 2 Live Crew. The campaign was led by Florida lawyer and failed political candidate Jack Thompson, who sent letters to hundreds of sheriff's departments and politicians urging them join the fight to ban rap records. "I think there is a cultural civil war going on," Thompson said. "I'm kind of the foot-soldier type."[26]

In 1990, Thompson's campaign against the 2 Live Crew's *As Nasty As They Wanna Be* got the album banned from Broward County, Florida, to Ontario, Canada. Dozens more record-store employees were fined or arrested for selling the album to minors. Conservative Florida governor Bob Martinez, in a difficult reelection race, denounced the album. Apparently, rappers in gold chains presented a better target than rockers with headless pigeons. Frank Zappa, an early opponent of the PMRC, told *The Source*, "The whole racist aroma swinging from the metal aspect to the rap aspect is a bit suspicious. The devil stuff didn't work. The devil business only played in certain parts of the country."[27]

A Florida judge later ruled 2 Live Crew's album obscene, effectively banning the record. But on May 7, 1992, a Federal Court of Appeals in Atlanta over-turned the decision, a decision the Supreme Court let stand. "It's gonna go over to the majors next," Campbell had predicted at the height of the controversy. "The censors will come after them when they finish with us."

Clinton Vs. Souljah

When the 1992 presidential election season rolled around, Campbell's comments proved prophetic. While Democrat Bill Clinton and President George Bush moved toward their formal nominations, Texas billionaire H. Ross Perot threatened to upset the usual political calculus with a third-party run. Perot was particularly attractive to middle-aged, upper-middle class, suburban and exurban "swing" voters, the so-called center that both parties so desperately coveted. Skillful exploitation of racial and generational fears might prove the key to the election. A month after 2 Live Crew's victory, rappers Sister Souljah and Ice T were both in the gunsights.

Young Black activist Lisa Williamson had become Sister Souljah when she joined Public Enemy in 1990. During the late '80s, she had worked with the crew when she served as organizer for the National African Youth/Student Alliance. After Professor Griff left the group, she became "Sister of Instruction/Director of Attitude." "Rap is a vehicle for mass marketing Black consciousness," she now said. "You cannot fight fire with a flyer."[28]

After appearing on the Terminator X and Public Enemy albums, she worked with Eric "Vietnam" Sadler on her own album, called *360 Degrees of Power*. Released in March, it had not been a big seller. Souljah was a better polemicist than a rapper, and she settled into a heavy schedule of interviews and lectures. Days after the uprising, she sat down for an interview with David Mills, who had now moved downtown to the *Washington Post*.

Mills baited Souljah on the riots, asking her if she thought the violence against Reginald Denny was "wise, reasoned action." Here, he writes, "Souljah's empathy for the rioters reached a chilling extreme." He quoted her answering:

"I mean, if Black people kill Black people every day, why not have a week and kill white people? You understand what I'm saying? In other words, white people, this government, and that mayor were well aware of the fact that Black people were dying every day in Los Angeles under gang violence. So if you're a gang member and you would normally be killing somebody, why not kill a white person? Do you think that somebody thinks that white people are better, or above dying, when they would kill their own kind?"

As she said on "Sunday Today": "Unfortunately for white people, they think it's all right for our children to die, for our men to be in prison, and not theirs."[29]

On June 13, as a guest of Jesse Jackson at the Rainbow Coalition's political convention, Bill Clinton read an edited version of Souljah's words in disgust. The night before, Souljah had participated in the convention's youth panel, and Clinton's advisors believed he had been handed the perfect opportunity to distance himself from Jackson's constituencies and ingratiate himself with Perot voters. Clinton said to the stunned crowd:

Just listen to this, what she said: She told the *Washington Post* about a month ago, and I quote, "If Black people kill Black people every day, why not have a week and kill white people? So if you're a gang member and you would normally be killing somebody, why not kill a white person?"

I know she is a young person, but she has a big influence on a lot of people, and when people say that—if you took the words white and Black and you reversed them, you might think David Duke was giving that speech.[30]

Souljah blasted Clinton for taking her statements out of context. She had never personally advocated violence against whites, she said. She was trying to describe the mindset of those who had committed such actions. Clinton, she said, was trying to make her "a Willie Horton, a campaign issue, a Black monster that would scare the white population."[31] Jackson and other Black leaders seethed at Clinton's well-placed, high-profile 10 percent dis. "She represents the feelings and hopes of a whole generation of people," Jackson said after Clinton's speech. "She should receive an apology."[32]

None was forthcoming. Instead, political pundits heaped praise on Clinton.

New York Times writer Gwen Ifill wrote, "There is no question that the Clinton campaign is quite satisfied with the outcome of the Sister Souljah episode, and that it may become a blueprint for future risky missions to rescue the campaign's flagging fortunes."[33]

Ice T Vs. the Police

The same week, the National Rifle Association and police organizations presented Republicans with an opportunity to resuscitate their own plunging poll numbers. On June 10 and 11, in press conferences from Maryland to Texas, they called for a boycott of Time Warner businesses because of a song called "Cop Killer," released on their Sire Records label by Ice T's Black heavy metal band Body Count.

In Austin, the law enforcement group pushed to close the Time Warner–owned Six Flags Over Texas theme park. In Houston, the Police Officers Association pressed the City Council to block renewal of its Time Warner Cable contract. Within a week, the national Fraternal Order of Police, the National Association of Chiefs of Police and the governor of Alabama had joined the call for a boycott and a ban.

"People who ride around all night and use crack cocaine and listen to rap music that talks about killing cops—it's bound to pump them up," Paul Taylor, the Fraternal Order's president, said. "No matter what anybody tells you, this kind of music is dangerous."[34]

Vice President Dan Quayle attacked Time Warner's execs as a "cultural elite" that cared less about family values than about making a buck. At a National Association of Radio Talk Show Hosts convention, he asked to thunderous applause, "So where is the corporate responsibility here?"[35] The line worked so well it became a permanent part of Quayle's limited repertoire. In one stump speech, Quayle even stated he felt his Democratic opponent Clinton had been correct to criticize Sister Souljah.[36] Not to be left out, Oliver North hired Jack Thompson to take on Time Warner on behalf of his Freedom Alliance organization and President Bush let reporters know he felt "Cop Killer" was "sick." No one could muster the same passion to protest Republican Arnold Schwarzenegger's cop-killing movie, *The Terminator*.

Lost in the noise was a statement from the National Black Police Association, which represented 35,000 Black cops, condemning the ban and the Time-Warner boycott. "This song is not a call for murder. It's a rap of protest. Ice T isn't just making this stuff up," said Ronald Hampton, the Association's director. "There are no statistics to support the argument that a song can incite someone to violence."[37]

The cultural conservatives' position on "Cop Killer" was not even consistent with their stance on campus hate speech codes, which they huffed would restrict the free flow of ideas and bend discourse to the forces of "political correctness." But the battle over "Cop Killer" indicated that conservatives were willing to be intellectually dishonest if it helped advance their agenda. In late June, at the request of a Florida sheriff, John McDougall, the state's attorney general began investigating whether Ice T could be charged under the Florida hate crime laws for speech that "dehumanized" police officers.

Why were law enforcement organizations and right-wingers so passionately committed to banning one song from a rapper's heavy metal side-project? A clue came in a report by Amnesty International on police brutality in Los Angeles released in the middle of the "Cop Killer" controversy. Investigators from the human rights organization had come to the city after the beating of Rodney King to look at police practices. In a year-long inquiry, they found that police and sheriffs' treatment of harmless suspects sometimes "amounted to torture or cruel, inhuman or degrading treatment." Police brutality, Amnesty International Secretary General Ian Martin said, was "one of a number of current human rights scandals in the U.S. that undermine its credibility in promoting rights internationally."[38]

Calls for police reform across the country had reached deafening pitch since the March 1991 beating of Rodney King. The Amnesty report reflected the fact that Los Angeles had become a global symbol of American law enforcement's systemic breakdown over issues of race and youth. Embattled police associations, it seemed, saw "Cop Killer" as an opportunity to reverse unwanted scrutiny. Here was the culture war as a strategic diversion.

Charlton Heston stepped into the Time Warner shareholders meeting on July 16 and gave a masterful performance. With the voice of Moses, he condemned Time Warner executives for choosing greed over responsibility, and proceeded to dramatically read the lyrics to Body Count's "KKK Bitch"—a song in which ice-T's character imagines rough sex with the daughter of a Grand Wizard and Tipper Gore's two twelve-year-old nieces. Then he turned to "Cop Killer." Heston asked a rhetorical question, "If that song were titled 'Fag Killer' or the lyrics went, 'Die, die, die, Kike, die,' would you still sell it?"[39] Outside, police carried picket signs that read, TIME WARNER PUTS PROFITS OVER POLICE LIVES and MEDIA MOGULS OF MURDER. They chanted, "Ban rap! It's all crap!"

Thousands of record stores pulled Body Count's album, many at the request of California state attorney general Dan Lungren. The city of Philadelphia's pension fund voted to divest millions of dollars in Time Warner stock. Republican party officials made an issue of Clinton receiving political contributions from Time Warner. When Body Count played a show in Hollywood, one fan mused, "There are more cops out here than at Florence and Normandie."[40]

Ice T called a press conference for July 28. Before he spoke, he showed a half-hour clip about the Black Panther Party. "One of the main problems with the press is that they don't have the slightest idea of what I'm talking about," he said. Then he announced he was pulling the song off the album so that he could offer it free at his concerts. It was never about money, he said, "This song is about anger and the community and how people get that way. It is not a call to murder police.[41]

"The police are sending out a message to all the other record companies," he added, admitting that he and Time Warner execs had received death threats. "I predict they will try to shut down rap music in the next three years."[42]

Working for the Clampdown

Major labels immediately began to re-evaluate their investments in hip-hop, scrutinizing their rosters for artists whose works might prove politically provocative. By the end of 1992, the witch-hunt had affected dozens of major-label rappers. Kool G Rap and DJ Polo's *Live and Let Die* album was withheld. Tragedy was forced to drop a song called "Bullet," about a revenge hit on a killer cop. Almighty RSO saw their single "One in the Chamba" lose its promotion budget after protests from the Boston Police Patrolman's Association. The centerpiece of a Boo-Yaa Tribe EP, a song called "Shoot 'Em Down" that condemned the acquittal of a Compton policeman who had killed two Samoan brothers with nineteen shots, was shelved.

Bay Area rapper Paris was signed to Tom Silverman's Tommy Boy Records, who had a distribution deal with Time Warner. The political rapper had not only recorded two songs for his new album *Sleeping with the Enemy*—"Coffee Donuts and Death" and "Bush Killa"—which assassinated corrupt cops and President Bush, but he had turned in cover artwork which depicted him laying in wait with a gun near the White House. Paris admitted it was all agit-prop. "In the real world, particularly Black and Latino communities, the problem isn't cop killers, much less records about cop killers," he said. "The problem is killer cops."

After President Bush joined the debate around "Cop Killer," the album's cover art was leaked to the New York Sheriffs Association, and hit the tabloids. In September, Time Warner execs forced Silverman to drop him from Tommy Boy. His next deal with 4th and Broadway, an imprint of the multinational Polygram, was thwarted by high-level execs who, he says, were concerned that his record might visit the same kind of political attacks on the parent company that Time Warner had suffered.

By October, Paris had signed with Rick Rubin, who was also distributed by Time Warner. To avoid being hamstrung by Time Warner, Rubin formed an indie label, Sex Records, and hurriedly geared up to release the record before the election. But before the elections, Time Warner stopped Rubin from releasing the record and gave Paris $100,000 as a settlement. With the money Paris finally released the album on his own Scarface label three weeks after Clinton and Gore had defeated Bush and Quayle.

Ice T spent the last months of 1992 in bitter negotiations with Time Warner over the release of his next album, *Home Invasion*. He came to the realization, he later wrote, "that Warner Brothers cannot afford to be in the business of Black rage. They can be in the business of white rage, but Black rage is much more sensitive. The angry Black person is liable to say anything. The angry Black person might just want to kill everybody. You just don't know. So, they can't be in the business of Black anger while being in the business of Black control, which is another part of the system."[43] He left Time Warner and signed a deal with Byran Turner's indie, Priority Records.

In just a decade, major labels had gone from playing catch-up in a musical genre they had once pegged as a passing novelty to signing every rap act they could to shaking out large numbers of rappers because of their political beliefs. It was that old familiar cycle: neglect, seduction, fear.

A Call to Atone

Amidst all the political and cultural attacks, the young burned for something that would give them a renewed sense of purpose and move them out of a defensive posture. The hip-hop generation waited for a call.

The gang peacemakers worked with a special urgency. Their truce movement literally meant the difference between life and death. And the victories came. From Orange County to the San Fernando Valley, Latino gangs began peace meetings. Fifty Latino gangs in Santa Ana signed a truce in 1992. Months later, an edict from prison leadership in the Mexican Mafia declared an end to drive-bys. On Halloween in 1993, hundreds of Latino gang members declared a massive truce in the Valley. By 1994, the Rollin' 60s, Eight-Tray Gangsters, Hoover Crips and the Black P-Stones—four of the most intensely warring Black sets—gathered to announce a truce in the Los Angeles' Harbor area.

From Los Angeles, the movement expanded nationwide. On April 29, 1993, Carl Upchurch and the Council for Urban Peace and Justice, with support from Reverend Benjamin Chavis and the NAACP, convened the first national gang summit in Kansas City with representatives from twenty-six cities. Summits were soon organized in Chicago, Cleveland, Minneapolis, Pittsburgh and San Antonio, and truces followed in each of those cities. The energy unleashed by the gang peace movement helped to catalyze Minister Louis Farrakhan's call for the Million Man March.

Beginning in the summer of 1994, Farrakhan began to shift the tone of his "Stop the Killing" speeches toward a new idea that might climax the street peace ministry he had begun five years before. He would gather a million Black men on the steps of the Capitol in Washington, D.C., in a display of unity and peace. It would show to the world, he said, "The image that you have of Black men is not the image of who and what we really are."[44] He called it a holy day of atonement and reconciliation.

For several years, the Nation of Islam had been moving into closer relations with traditional civil rights organizations and the Congressional Black Caucus. By December, he had tapped the ex-NAACP head Reverend Benjamin Chavis to serve as the national organizer for the March. Chavis had recently been dismissed from the organization amidst charges of sexual and fiscal misconduct, but Farrakhan welcomed him into the Nation, telling followers that Chavis had been run out because he had been too closely courting youth and the poor. Chavis began a massive organizing effort, working outside of the Nation to recruit Christian churches and college student, community, youth and gang peace organizations.

The Quest for Unity

The effort would be surrounded with controversy. In speeches, Farrakhan had told his followers that the day was to be for men only, that women should stay home and support the March from there. "If not for the woman in the home there could be no strong family or strong community," Farrakhan said. "We are saying to our Black women you have always been by our sides. In fact you have been leading us. So now that we have made up our minds to stand up for you and our families, we want you to help us in this march by staying at home and teaching to our children what their fathers, uncles or brothers have decided to do."[45]

This line closely echoed the ministry of the Promise Keepers, a Christian evangelical organization that had made inroads into working-class and middle-class communities of color. Society was falling apart, they said, because the men were not fulfilling their traditional roles as patriarchs and providers. But to Black feminists, this was retrograde politics. Marcia A. Gillespie, editor-in-chief of Ms. magazine said, "They are stepping up to a patriarchal vision that automatically says Black men are the leaders, and that women's place and role is with the children, frying the chicken, providing medical assistance when needed and writing a poem. I don't think so."[46]

Gillespie, Angela Davis, Jewell Jackson McCabe, the founder of the National Coalition of 100 Black Women, and Barbara Arnwine of the Lawyers Committee for Civil Rights formed an organization called African-American Agenda 2000 to oppose the March. Others, like Julianne Malveaux, Kimberle Crenshaw and Michelle Wallace, also raised their voices against the March. It was no less, bell hooks said, than a "celebration of fascist patriarchy."[47] For their criticism, the women became targets of personal attacks, called race traitors and worse.

Black gay men debated how best to engage the Million Man March. Some boycotted it, convinced the March's definition of masculinity was not inclusive.

Their fears were confirmed when the March organizers declined a call to include a Black gay speaker and an HIV-positive speaker on the March platform. The National Black Gay and Lesbian Leadership Forum voted not to endorse the rally because of Farrakhan's "sexist and patriarchal tone and the homophobic comments made by some march organizers."[48] But many chose to attend the March anyway. Gregory Adams decided the March was not about Farrakhan. "I think we belong right next to our straight brothers," he said. "We experience the same racism. I'm a Black gay man who still can't get a cab in D.C."[49]

As the March neared and it became clear that hundreds of thousands had been inspired by the call for the March, African Americans argued over how much credit Farrakhan himself should get. In the end, Reverend Chavis sought to establish the March as a big-tent event. "Minister Farrakhan will tell you himself that this is not a Farrakhan march. This is a Black people's march," Chavis told the *Washington Post*. "We have never said that we are requiring people to agree with a particular philosophy or particular ideology."[50]

Morning in a Perfect World

At dawn on Monday, October 16, 1995, the highways into Washington, D.C., were jammed with carpools and 15,000 buses. Hundreds of thousands of Black men had already gathered on the Mall. The mood was upbeat. The usual tourist-oriented kiosks had been replaced by vendors of jerk chicken and fruit juices, African trinkets and Afrocentric books, Million Man March T-shirts and baseball caps. D.C. activist Al-Malik Farrakhan's gang peace organization was doing a brisk business selling its DON'T SMOKE THE BROTHERS T-shirts. Husbands brought their wives and children. Behind the desks of dozens of voter registration booths were women volunteers.

And as the sun rose in the clear sky, they streamed into the National Mall—senators and city councilpersons, country preachers and urban ministers, gang members and college fraternity brothers, pro-Black militants and Vietnam veterans, desk jockeys and blue-collar workers, elderly and teenagers. They wore buttons that said, 1 IN A MILLION and carried signs that read, THIS IS HISTORY.[51]

On Ninth Street, a contingent of 150 Black gay men gathered. The night before, they had quietly and seriously discussed what they would do if they faced violence. Now they marched toward the Mall, chanting, "Gay men of African descent!" They carried signs that read, I AM A BLACK, GAY MAN. I AM A BLACK MAN. I AM A MAN.

"People were honking their horns and some of them would put their fists up in support. And when we got to the Mall it was just overwhelming," Maurice Franklin, one of the marchers, told Michelangelo Signorile. "I'm not trying to dismiss the issue of homophobia in our community, because clearly it exists. But on that day, on that Mall, I felt like I knew what it was like to be in the promised land. I felt safe, as if I was in a perfect world for one day."[52]

On the platform, Rosa Parks, Kweisi Mfume, Tynetta Muhammad, Maulana Karenga, Queen Mother Moore, Carol Moseley Braun, Cornel West, Stevie Wonder and Jesse Jackson came to the podium. Maya Angelou read a poem: "And so we rise, and so we rise again."

In the afternoon, Minister Louis Farrakhan rose before the crowd. He spoke of the slaves that had once been sold on the ground they were standing on. "George Washington said he feared that before too many years passed over his head, this slave would prove to become a most troublesome species of property," he said. "And so we stand here today at this historic moment." Then, for two-and-a-half hours, with poetry, history, numerology, esoterica and wordplay, he gave a quintessentially American speech on his chosen topic: "Toward a more perfect union."

"Freedom can't come from white folks. Freedom can't come from staying here and petitioning this great government. We're here to make a statement to the great government, but not to beg them," Farrakhan said. "Freedom cannot come from no one but the God who can liberate the soul from the burden of sin."

Through personal atonement could come reconciliation, and then unity. Through unity, brothers could bring an end to white supremacy, which Farrakhan said was the ultimate source of America's and the world's sickness. But it all started with the redemption of one's self.

He ended by asking the gathering to join him in a pledge:

Say with me please, I, say your name, pledge that from this day forward I will strive to love my brother as I love myself. I, say your name, from this day forward will strive to improve myself spiritually, morally, mentally, socially, politically and economically for the benefit of myself, my family and my people.

I, say your name, pledge that I will strive to build business, build houses, build hospitals, build factories and then to enter international trade for the good of myself, my family and my people. I, say your name, pledge that from this day forward I will never raise my hand with a knife or a gun to beat, cut or shoot any member of my family or any human being, except in self-defense.

I, say your name, pledge from this day forward I will never abuse my wife by striking her, disrespecting her, for she is the mother of my children and the producer of my future. I, say your name, pledge that from this day forward I will never engage in the abuse of children, little boys, or little girls for sexual gratification. But I will let them grow in peace to be strong men and women for the future of our people. I, say your name, will never again use the B-word to describe my female, but particularly my own Black sister.

I, say your name, pledge from this day forward that I will not poison my body with drugs or that which is destructive to my health and my well being. I, say your name, pledge from this day forward, I will support Black newspapers, Black radio, Black television. I will support Black artists, who clean up their acts to show respect for themselves and respect for their people, and respect for the ears of the human family.

I, say your name, will do all of this, so help me God.

As they left that evening, a generation seemed to have been moved.

The Nature of Transformation

Angela Davis would ask the hard question, "All of us have reasons to atone. But is that going to bring about jobs or halt the rising punishment industry? This march may have been the first demonstration in history where Black people were mobilized, not around any goals or political agenda, but simply because they were Black men."[53]

In 1963, the March on Washington had been a watershed event, a moment pregnant with the possibility of transformation. By the hundreds of thousands, a generation had come to make change. They were a tide that would force the leaders in the Capitol on the opposite side of the Mall to become agents of that transformation, to pass the most important civil rights legislation in the nation's history.

Thirty-two years later, the Million Man March was no less a pivotal cultural moment. But times were different. When another generation came to face the Capitol, one million strong, the white edifice was a hollow symbol and the leaders in it were mainly agents of reversal, chasing each other round in a politics of symbolism, stopping every once in a while to pass legislation that only seemed to further the devastation. This generation had no reason to expect change to come from inside the Capitol.

For weeks before the march, they had quarreled about the march's substance and meaning. But as a million men left the Mall that bright Monday, there was a new clarity. Surrounded by the symbols of American power, they contemplated their own redemption. For now, change would have to be measured in single lives.

Angela Davis felt she understood why the march had been so powerful to so many. "I think that the way the Million Man March captured the imagination of so many people had to do with this desire to feel a part of the larger Black struggle. Many people have not felt that connection for quite some time," she said.[54] "Now perhaps we can use that."[55]

A generation went home with themselves, back to the business of becoming.

Bentleys and bling at twilight: David Mays (left) and Raymond "Benzino" Scott (right), 2001. Photo © Christian Lantry

18.

Becoming the Hip-Hop Generation

The Source, the Industry and the Big Crossover

In the home of the brave, land of the free
I don't want to be mistreated by no bourgeoisie
—Leadbelly, "The Bourgeois Blues"

. . . to fuss about the exploitation of hip hop is quite often to take sides against the hip hoppers themselves—even though in the end that exploitation is certain to prove a juggernaut that the hip hoppers (and even the exploiters) can't control. To counsel purity isn't impermissible, but it's certainly complicated, with ramifications that stretch far beyond the scope of this review, or indeed of any piece of writing of any length on any similar subject that has ever come to my attention.

—Robert Christgau, 1986

Hip-hop may have turned the world into Planet Rock, and may have had a lot to do with a million men gathering on the National Mall, but it never conquered Washington, D.C.'s Chocolate City. In the Black neighborhoods encircling the white structures of global power, the people embraced the music and culture they called go-go.

In D.C., bands had never lost their hold on the nightclub scene. Flesh-and-blood musicians still ruled. Dancers moved to two-hour suites of covers and originals yoked together with steaming fatback breaks of drums, percussion and bass pulls. DJs filled the set breaks and cursed the day they had refused to take trumpet lessons.

The godfather of go-go was an amiable gentleman named Chuck Brown. He had spent the first half of the sixties in Lorton prison for shooting a man in self-defense, but learned to play blues guitar there. He emerged into a city where the passage of civil rights legislation in the halls of power downtown had done little to change the race and class realities that had angered Leadbelly enough to write "The Bourgeois Blues." Nightclubs were still segregated: whites went to the big clubs downtown, Blacks went to "go-gos" in cabarets, churches and community halls.

Brown found work in the go-gos with a top-40 dance band named Los Latinos, whose Afro-Cubanized backbeat enthralled him. When he formed the first Soul Searchers band in 1966, he brought together a little Latin and a little sanctified church and created a rhythm to glue together medleys that could last for hours. His beat drove the dancers crazy.

He had figured out what bandleaders in other cities would not until it was too late. Instead of the songs, he realized the transitions between the songs—the hypersyncopated breaks, hyped-up shout-outs, and church-style call-and-response—were the band's main draw. What Kool Herc was doing for Bronx partyers at the same time, Chuck Brown was doing for D.C.'s go-go patrons. Brown short-circuited the rise of the disco DJ by reinventing the dance band format with go-go music.

At the beginning of the 1980s, go-go and hip-hop music were both outsider genres, inner-city musical cousins. Go-go bands lifted rap hooks for their jams and DJs like Charlie Chase and Cash Money rocked doubles of Trouble Funk and E.U. singles. Kurtis Blow, Doug E. Fresh, Teddy Riley and Salt-N-Pepa jacked go-go beats, while Big Tony, Jas. Funk, Lil' Benny and D.C. Scorpio moved from singing to rapping.

When Run DMC was changing the rap game, Chris Blackwell, then the owner of Island Records and Island Pictures, arrived in D.C. with a plan to launch go-go like he had reggae—via a movie vehicle, backed up with a host of band signings. Unfortunately the movie, *Good to Go*, was no *Harder They Come*. After it flopped, Charles Stephenson, then E.U.'s manager, says, "It was almost like the bottom dropped out."

Despite the best efforts of Chuck, E.U., Trouble Funk and Rare Essence, go-go never crossed over. When the '90s came, New York execs rushed to sign hip-hop acts and stopped returning D.C. artists' phone calls. Go-go survived as one of the last independent, indigenous Black youth cultures.

For its devotees in the Beltway, the Black suburbs of Maryland and Virginia, and southern Black colleges, that fact remained a point of pride. The most popular go-go bands could play to 20,000 fans every week. Clothing companies and concert bootleg ("P.A. tape") purveyors sprung up. Rare Essence and Backyard Band recorded some of the most compelling dance music of the decade. Go-go evolved without the pressure of mainstream expectations, but it also remained a largely segregated world in a culturally desegregating era, a fiercely local scene in a globalizing era.

It was also an industrial-era music for a postindustrial era. Just as it was when Chuck Brown walked out of Lorton, bands' fierce competition to remain atop the club scene remained the primary engine of go-go music. Making records and three-minute hit singles, the thing the music industry was most concerned with, was an afterthought. Economics partly explains why, after the 1980s, hip-hop went global and go-go remained local.

But there was also something else, something which producer Reo Edwards put like this: "I was talking to a go-go songwriter one time. I said, 'Man, you need a verse here.' The guy said, 'The rototom's talking! Hear the rototom?' Swear to god, he said the rototom was telling the story. 'Can't put no verse there, the rototom telling the story.' Okay. Alright. You know what the rototom is saying. Maybe the people in the *audience* know what the rototom saying. But the people in Baltimore don't know what the hell that dang rototom is saying!"

He shakes his head. "Go-go's got the same problem today as it did back then. You don't have no good storylines. Hip-hop," he paused for emphasis, "*tells stories.*"

Hip-Hop Nation

If go-go was a rhythm machine, hip-hop was also an idea machine. It provided a bottomless well of stories. The culture was the call and hip-hop journalism was the response. Out of this, a generation's sense of itself would begin to cohere.

When hip-hop burst into downtown consciousness in the early '80s, there were journalists ready to catch it, like Nelson George at *Billboard* and David Toop at *The Face* in London. Most of the pioneering writers worked for underground papers and alternative weeklies—Steven Hager at the *East Village Eye*, David Hershkovits at the *Soho News*, and Sally Banes, Robert Christgau and Vince Aletti at *The Village Voice*. Scenester entrepreneurs like Tim Carr, Michael Holman, and Aaron Fuchs also wrote about the young scene. By the mid-1980s, British zines like *Black Echoes, Black Music and Jazz Review* and *Soul Underground* were offering features, breakbeat charts and playlists, and American rock music tabloids *Spin* and *Rolling Stone* were covering hip-hop artists.

In January 1988, *The Village Voice*, under the aegis of Doug Simmons, Greg Tate, R. J. Smith, and Harry Allen, devoted a special issue to hip-hop entitled "Hip-Hop Nation." Wrapped behind a cover featuring a who's-who of the rap scene, the issue's point was simple: this culture could make you *believe*. In Tate's words, it was "the only avant-garde around, still delivering the shock of the new (over recycled James Brown compost modernism like a bitch), and it's got a shockable bourgeoisie, to boot." Most prophetically, he wrote, "Hip-hop might be bought and sold like gold, but the miners of its rich ore still represent a sleeping-giant constituency. Hip-hop locates their market potential and their potential militancy."

Outside of New York City, the hip-hop nation was not yet born. It was a unorganized mass of true believers—dancers anxiously waiting for the DJ to drop a beat that would open a cipher; aerosolists in their bedrooms tearing open parcels of graf photos from towns they had never heard of; soon-to-be-turntablists scouring the bins in tiny specialty shops in Black or gay neighborhoods for twelve-inch records that had the word "rap" on their candy-colored labels. If there was to be a hip-hop nation, hip-hop journalism might provide a hip-hop nationalism to bring them together.

In August 1988, two white Jewish Harvard juniors named David Mays and Jon Shecter pooled two hundred dollars to put together a one-page hip-hop music tipsheet which they grandly named *The Source*. Both had been raised in upper middle-class liberal Jewish families—Mays in northwest Washington, D.C., Shecter in Philadelphia—and fallen in love with black style and culture. Upon arriving at Harvard in 1986, they realized, as Maximillian Potter wrote, that they were "probably the only two white guys wearing Fila suits."[1]

Mays was an aficionado of Chuck Brown's beat and was known as "Go-Go Dave." Shecter, who called himself "J The Sultan MC," had cut a twelve-inch single for his crimson-baseball capped crew called B.M.O.C. (Big Men On Campus), rapping over Wild Cherry's "Play That Funky Music." Shecter converted Mays to the gospel of hip-hop and they landed a weekend radio show they called "Streetbeats" on their campus station WHRB. Soon after, they launched *The Source* from their Cabot House dorm room. The tipsheet's main attraction was the radio show's "Hot Picks," a rap singles shopping list for their listeners. In order to finance the newsletter, Mays sold ads to retailers. They netted $25 on their first issue.

This modest offering was not the first of its kind. Bay Area DJ David "Davey D" Cook, for instance, had launched a similar kind of newsletter for listeners to his KALX show on the University of California, Berkeley, campus about a year earlier. But Mays and Shecter were quick to grasp the size and the opportunity in the burgeoning national audience. Mays built *The Source*'s readership from a mailing list of listeners and industry folks he kept on his tiny Mac. As his industry contacts expanded, so did the mailing list. Major labels were still figuring out how to reach rap-friendly radio DJs, promoters, and retailers. *The Source* did the work of assembling just such a national network.

In under a year, with aggressive business acumen and a swaggering editorial voice, they had moved from a black-and-white Xerox format to a full-color covered, staple-bound magazine. Soon two other Harvard students, both Black—undergrad H. Edward Young and first-year law student James Bernard—came on board and become part owners. Bernard joined Shecter in shaping editorial content. Young helped Mays sell ads and publish the magazine.

Two years later, Mays, Shecter and Young graduated and moved *The Source*'s operations to New York City. Bernard moved to Berkeley to finish up law school and open a west-coast office. The staff expanded to include columnists like Dave "Funken" Klein, contributors like Chris Wilder, Matt Capoluongo, Rob "Reef" Tewlow, Bobbito Garcia and a host of passionate, big-dreaming heads. By now, the magazine claimed fifteen thousand readers, two thousand of whom were record and radio industry insiders in the rapidly professionalizing genre.

Harlem-raised Rutgers grad Reginald Dennis joined the staff as an intern, and inputted ten thousand subscribers into the Mac. "I knew that these ten thousand people, you could build an empire around," he says. "These were the tastemakers." In their press kit, *The Source* boasted of being "the most widely-read, well-respected rap music publication in existence."[2] They backed it up by filling 30 percent of the pages with advertising. Then they declared themselves "the voice of the rap music industry."

The Source's tenth issue, which arrived at the beginning of 1990, boldly canonized "The Rap Music Decade: 1980 to 1990"—who else had the knowledge and confidence to champion the Crash Crew or the Ultramagnetic MCs?—and immediately established themselves as *the* rap insiders. Jon Shecter, now editor-in-chief of the magazine, crowed, "The magazine you are holding your hands is, easily, the best thing ever published concerning hip-hop."

There was better criticism to be had in *The Village Voice*, better industry coverage in *Billboard*, better reporting and actual copy-editing in *Spin*, but *The Source* had the authority of young heads on a mission. Hip-hop wasn't kid stuff; it was the kind of tidal wave that rolls through once in a generation and takes everyone with it. Up to that point, Dennis says, "Hip-hop writing was done by people who were looking at it from the outside. It wasn't life or death. They weren't gonna die if they didn't write about the stuff. Whereas we probably would have."

In a media where urban youths were most often seen in handcuffs or police drawings, *The Source* would speak to its audience in their own voice, reflect their concerns and controversies, and feed their needs. It would epitomize hip-hop's *attitude*—that b-boy stance, with its brimming streetwise confidence, scowling generational defiance, the barely secret joy of having something no army of parents, baby-boomer cultural critics, or grizzled rock journalists could ever really understand—and put it into words.

Nearing the Crossroads

As *The Source* grew, the tension that hip-hop's downtown patrons had seen taking shape in the early '80s, and that Tate had named by the late '80s, became its central dialectic. The magazine was caught between wanting to exploit its generation's market potential and representing its potential militancy.

In the beginning, *The Source* looked and read like Mays had originally planned it to be: a rap industry trade magazine. In an effort to rationalize the national market, *The Source* reached out to local DJs and promoters and gave them "regional scene" columns in exchange for street promotion. This advertorial content-for-promotion swap had long been a tradition of magazines in emerging music scenes. For years, Tom Silverman had done the same with his *Disco News* and *Dance Music Report* magazines. The insider-intelligence gave the magazine a backbone of legitimacy, while industry execs used the regional columns and the radio, retail and video charts as a roadmap through the music and as a vehicle to promote their new high-risk signings.

But as *The Source* developed its readership, its mission changed. By 1992, the regional columns and charts had become a casualty of the increased emphasis on full-length features, reviews, and issue-advocacy journalism. For a time, local heads angrily denounced the magazine for selling out, but *The Source* had a larger destiny to fulfill. No longer just "the voice of the rap music industry," it was now "the magazine of hip-hop music, culture and politics."

The editorial staff, who flamboyantly dubbed itself the "Mind Squad," took that idea seriously. They created the template for hip-hop magazines, including sections like record release dates, Hip-Hop Quotables, and the controversial five-mic record ratings guides. At the back of the book, they often featured hip-hop fashion and models. Fashion editors Julia Chance and Sonya Magett featured Sean "Puffy" Combs and Tyson Beckford in their first photo shoots. Matty C and Reef's "Unsigned Hype" column, a demo showcase, became an A&R's wet dream, discovering artists like Notorious B.I.G., DMX, Common, Mobb Deep and DJ Shadow. Dave "Funken" Klein's "Gangsta Limpin' " was an irreverent stream-of-consciousness freestyle of witty disses, reluctant props, and gratuitous shout-outs. James Bernard's "Doin' the Knowledge" column became the stylistic blueprint for a generation's tough, opinionated political writing, putting a hip-hop gen spin on the issues of the day—crime, incarceration, AIDS, Islam, electoral politics, the Persian Gulf War.

Above all, the Mind Squad was committed. They had daylong debates about what belonged in the magazine. Did rapper X deserve a 200-word blurb? Was TLC really hip-hop? Was Too Short's record really worth four mics or just three and half? Every month, that passion was reflected back by its readers. Fans complained they were too critical or not critical enough, too West Coast or too East Coast. Rappers and promoters angrily stepped to staffers in the clubs about perceived slights. Mays began to hear complaints from his advertisers.

But the wall between the business staff and editorial staff was sacred, and anyway, the editorial side would never back down. From the tenth issue on, the "Publisher's Credo" at the bottom of the masthead read:

> We at *The Source* take very seriously the challenge of being the only independent voice for the rap music industry. . . . With respect to any of our business relationships, we feel it is our responsibility always to strictly police the integrity of our editorial content. Only in this way can we continue to bring to you the clear and unbiased coverage which we hope has won the respect of our readers.

When James Bernard returned from the west coast in 1991, he took up most of the staff management duties, and eventually became coeditor-in-chief. Chris Wilder became senior editor and Reginald Dennis became music editor. New staffers like Kierna Mayo and dream hampton added strong female voices to the magazine, forcing gender issues onto the table. Together they formed one of the most integrated staffs in the history of magazine publishing. Content-wise the magazine had become decidedly blacker. In their March 1990 issue, they put a picture of Malcolm X in Egypt on the cover. "I think it was a natural evolution," says Bernard. "Jon and Dave knew that the magazine needed to be perceived as real."

In their 1991 year-end wrap-up, after Rodney King and Latasha Harlins and Crown Heights, they convened for what would become a heated staff discussion, using Ice Cube's *Death Certificate* as a starting point. Shecter asked a question about anti-Semitism on "No Vaseline": "By pointing out that Jerry Heller is Jewish—why did he bother to say that he was a Jew?" Chris Wilder retorted, "Because it rhymes with 'to do'."[3] And then it was on. The conversation swerved for another three hundred words through Black-Jewish and Black-Korean relations, Black diversity, misogyny and homophobia. A feisty, fractious, principled bunch, the Mind Squad were going to represent where they had come from, to say what could not be said anywhere else, even if that meant arguing all day to get to consensus on an album, or splashing their personal and ideological tensions all over their pages. With increasing probity and passion, the Mind Squad tackled the question: what does it mean to be a member of the hip-hop generation?

The Source gave youths a sense of a hip-hop nation beyond their lunch-table rap ciphers, community center break-battles, bedroom studios, and graffiti yards, one that was populated by others exactly like them. Hip-hop journalism had the opportunity to center plain-speaking from the margins, insist on the added value of free speech and the entertainment value of shit-talking, argue an aesthetics of boom-bap, celebrate different kinds of beauty, and take the money, all at once.

"We all knew that there was a slight chance that, if everyone played their cards right, it could possibly diverge from *all* historical precedent," Dennis says. "Maybe the business could be right, maybe the journalism could be correct, maybe the point-of-view could be correct."

On the other hand, Dave Mays had begun to invoke the name of Jann Wenner, the baby-boomer counterculturalist-turned-magazine-mogul, as he boasted to the *Wall Street Journal* that his magazine could become "the *Rolling Stone* of the next generation."[4] His slow, painful process of estrangement from the Mind Squad had begun.

In 1991, a year after their move to New York, *The Source* had a circulation of 40,000, captured 286 ad pages at between $2,000 to $3,000 per page, and was clocking nearly a million in total revenues.[5] That success seemed mind-boggling. But by the end of the decade *The Source* had increased its circulation to 500,000, and its $30 million brand name was being leveraged across a website, a TV show, record albums and a televised gala annual awards show. On the newsstands, it even outsold *Rolling Stone*. What happened in between is an archetypal story of the hip-hop generation.

Broadcast to Niche

When *The Source* came on the scene, the entertainment and media industries were undergoing a once-in-a-lifetime paradigm shift, moving from a broadcast model to a niche model.

From World War II through the peak of the broadcast era in the 1970s, large companies like television networks and the film and music conglomerates, created and pushed their programming to mass audiences. It was a one-size-fits-all popular culture, where centralized decision-makers filtered through "subcultures" and repackaged them for the mainstream. The broadcast model favored high capital investments, massive economies of scale, and vast infrastructures of production and promotion. The late '70s, after all, were the era of the sitcom, the blockbuster film and soft rock.

But by the mid-1980s, the broadcast model came under fire. In TV, cable began to segment audiences that were formerly the sole province of the Big Three networks. In 1991, a new data-tracking system called Soundscan transformed the music industry when *Billboard* magazine switched its weekly record charts to the new program.

Before then, the magazine's charts were based on a network of retail reporters. "Nobody knew what criteria they used for their top twenty," says Tommy Boy owner Tom Silverman, an early advocate of Soundscan. "Someone sent them a check, free records or a refrigerator that week—you could've had number one." Silverman's indie label was hit hard by the reporting system. "Planet Rock" sold 15,000 copies a week at its peak and went gold, but it never charted higher than number forty-seven. Soundscan's innovation was to install a bar-code-reading, point-of-purchase system to tally actual sales.

When the first *Billboard* chart based on Soundscan was released on May 25, 1991, the results shocked the music industry. Within weeks, country singer Garth Brooks and hair-metal band Skid Row had hit number one. Independently distributed N.W.A.'s *Efil4zaggin* debuted at number two. At the same time, dozens of big-bank pop and rock acts tumbled off the charts. What the industry thought were mere niche markets—country, metal, and rap—were in fact the biggest things going. And while the country industry was well established and the heavy metal market had peaked, the rap industry, because of years of major label prejudice, remained sorely underdeveloped. Suddenly rap appeared to have boundless crossover potential. Apparently lots of suburbanites and whites were down with a "Niggaz 4 Life" program.

Soundscan told the music industry what the kids had been trying to tell them for years. Broadcast culture was too limiting. They weren't interested in being "programmed" or hard-sold into the mainstream. They wanted control over their pop choices; they wanted to define their own identities. The emerging niche model favored fluid, proliferating, self-organizing grass-roots undergrounds with their tiny economies of scale and their passionate, defensive audiences that always seemed caught between discovery and preservation, boosterism and insularity.

The center had given way, and the pop field looked like a jumble of frag-ments. With the rise of the niche model, the singular underdog idea that the Bronx b-boys and b-girls had advanced—like politics, all cool is local—could be triumphant. Hip-hop's fractal spread in the new decade felt inevitable.

Hip-Hop As Urban Lifestyle

At the same time, mass marketers were scrambling to re-establish brand pre-eminence. Advertising budgets were plunging, as aging white baby boomers opted for value over brand. Low-cost big-box retailers made a comeback, their shelves teeming with generic products, and ad agencies were in a panic. But as companies like Nike, Adidas, and Pepsi searched for new markets, they discov-ered that urban youth of color—until then an ignored niche—were a more brand-conscious, indeed brand-leading, demographic than they had ever realized.

In 1986, Run DMC had turned Adidas into a hip-hop brand with a song. Two years later, Spike Lee and Michael Jordan took hip-hop branding to the next level. Nike, then the number-two company in the shoe business, was in a bruising but losing battle with Reebok. They started by refocusing small manage-ment teams on developing or revamping their shoe lines in narrow niche mar-kets.[6] Then, in 1986, they fired their ad agency and hired Wieden and Kennedy and put $40 million into brand marketing.[7]

One night, two W&K admen saw *She's Gotta Have It*, in which Spike Lee's oddball character Mars Blackmon stomped around in Air Jordans. A light bulb went off. They called Lee and told him they wanted to pair him with Jordan. In 1988, when Spike and Mike began filming a series of spots that would shock the advertising world, Reebok was a $1.8 billion company, and Nike trailed at $1.2 billion. A year later, Spike and Mike's ads helped propel Nike past Reebok, and the company never looked back. Not only did Nike's success con-firm that niches were the future, it also confirmed that a massive shift in tastes was occurring—from baby boomer to youth, from suburb to city, from whiteness to Blackness.

Black advertising agencies were also being forced to retool. Noticing that Black-targeted advertising budgets had begun to decline, industry leaders like the $60-million Mingo Group began to push for "urban marketing." The idea had come from Black radio, which, during the '80s, had shifted to describing itself as "urban radio," a transparent ploy, Nelson George writes, "aimed as much at Madison Avenue as at Black listeners."[8] "Urban" still signified "crossing over," but in the '90s, the process reversed. Back then, Lionel Richie and Michael Jackson sold a softened "urban," moving up and out from the ghetto, from afro-picks to Alfa Romeos. Now hip-hop sold a hardened "urban," drawing back in to the ghetto, from Sperry Topsiders to Nike Dunks.

What was a concession to white corporate interests in the suites during the 1980s was a recognition of the new racial dynamics in the streets of the '90s. Now the word "urban" described how cultural change was emerging from cities like New York, Philadelphia and Chicago, where young Blacks seemed to initiate style shifts and a cohort of hip, multiracial youth spread them. Or perhaps the process was reversed. "You go to a city like Philadelphia, which is largely Black, or Washington, or New York for that matter, and wonder who's driving social changes," said Mingo Group head Samuel J. Chisholm.[9]

The emerging leaders of the rap industry were often whites comfortable and conversant with a nonwhite world. Monica Lynch, who ran Tommy Boy's operations, was a feminist ex-go-go dancer with a canny eye for urban style and a golden ear for leftfield acts. Dave "Funken" Klein, *The Source* columnist, left Def Jam to start the first globally minded hip-hop label, Hollywood/BASIC, where he plucked artists from Zimbabwe and England, and signed seminal acts like Organized Konfusion, Peanut Butter Wolf, and DJ Shadow. Dante Ross was a Lower East Side red-diaper-baby-turned-skate-punk who had grown up with the Bad Brains and the Beastie Boys. Ross was the first hip-hop A&R to leave the indies for a major, jumping from Def Jam and Tommy Boy to join rock-oriented Elektra Records. There, he championed Afrocentric rappers like Brand Nubian, KMD, Leaders of The New School, and Pete Rock and CL Smooth, against hostile Black R&B execs still caught in an '80s idea of what it meant to be "urban."

Five years after Michael Jackson, then the still unreconstructed King of Pop, broke the color line at MTV, white production assistant Ted Demme brought a concept for a rap video show to MTV heads. Dozens of local shows, led by Ralph McDaniels and Lionel Martin's Video Music Box in New York City, had attracted strong followings, and the cable, pay-request Video Jukebox (later "The Box") channel had expanded its rap videos on offer. Demme thought the time was right for a national show. The *Yo! MTV Raps* pilot debuted on August

6, 1988, with Fab 5 Freddy as host. Within months it was the network's most-watched show.

MTV added former WBAU DJ and Original Concept leader Andre "Dr. Dre" Brown and radio host Ed "Ed Lover" Roberts as additional hosts, and gave *Yo! MTV Raps* daily airings. Within a year, MTV had gone from almost no rap videos to twelve hours of rap programming.[10] Urban style no longer trickled up from multiracial networks of cool, but was instantly available via remote control to vanilla exurbs where teens were adjusting to lowered life expectations. Fab 5 Freddy understood what those kids liked about it. "People identify with rap," he told a *Time* reporter. "You feel that you can look like that, that you can be a part of it immediately."[11]

At Tommy Boy Records, Lynch and her boss, Silverman, realized that they were not in the record business anymore, they were in the "lifestyle" business. They diversified into clothing, designing brand-name gear and partnering with lines like Carhart and Stussy that hip-hoppers had already made popular on the street. A decade before, hip-hop sold Absolut vodka, Williwear clothing, Swatch watches, even Honda automobiles. But few then thought hip-hop was anything but a passing youth fad. Now it was clear that hip-hop was not only selling $400 million dollars worth of records a year, but hundreds of millions of dollars worth of other products—shoes, jeans, *haute couture*, soda, beer, liquor, videogames, movies and more. In marketing terms, hip-hop had become the urban lifestyle.

The Post-Gangsta Crossover

At the end of 1992, as Los Angeles still recovered from the riots, ex-NWA producer Andre "Dr. Dre" Young dropped *The Chronic*. Television had brought middle America closer to a generation's rage than ever before, and Ice T had brought media multinational Time Warner closer to the establishment's rage than ever before. *The Chronic* seemed a heaven-sent balm.

Dre and Snoop's videos for "Nuthin' But a 'G' Thang" and "Let Me Ride" drove the album beyond triple platinum. Dre was finally moving on up—out of Compton and into the Valley, not far from Eazy E's and Jerry Heller's mansions—closer to the growing fanbase. In a strange, somewhat disquieting way, Dre and Snoop had become reassuring, as if their presence now signified that the difference between the ghetto and the exurbs needed not be measured in social indicators but in degrees of cool.

The formula for *The Chronic* had not been all that different from the formula for *Efil4zaggin*. But the riots had changed mainstream reception. Before then, "Lil' Ghetto Boy" and "The Day the Niggas Took Over" might have garnered most of the critical attention, while the third single, "Dre Day"—a brutal dis of Dre's former partners, Eazy E and Ice Cube, but interestingly, not Jerry Heller—may have stirred outcry.[12] Instead, Dre's songcraft, rather than his sociology, was now the focus. He was hailed as Spectorian in his pop majesty, and " 'G' Thang" and "Let Me Ride" were celebrated as all-American music, compared to the endless summer vibes of the Beach Boys an The Mamas and The Papas.

The irony was that these songs clearly spoke to the outbreak of gang peace and the truce parties, the ecstatic sense of freedom of being able to drive down the street without worrying about cops or enemies. Just as the gang peace movement desired to mainstream hardcore bangers into civic society, *The Chronic* wanted to drive hardcore rap into the popstream. It could be heard as as guiltless, gentrified gangsta—no Peace Treaties, rebuilding demands, or calls for reparations, just the party and the bullshit. The video for " 'G' Thang" seemed to ask: didn't all boys everywhere just want to bounce in hot cars to hotter beats, hang out with their crew, party all night, and spray conceited bitches with malt-liquor?

In 1993, the popularity of *Yo! MTV Raps* was fading, and majors were clearing their rosters of potential political liabilities. But "Nuthin' But a 'G' Thang" and "Let Me Ride" propelled the post-gangsta aesthetic into heavy rotation. Later, on *Doggy Style*, Dre and Snoop largely ditched the inner-city blues for more smoothed-out roughness and gangsta parties, and sold even more records.

Artistically, *The Chronic* and *Doggy Style* were remarkable achievements because they synthesized contradictory vectors—inner-city and suburbs, street and tech, First World and Fourth, like a Gehry building covered in graffiti. But these albums also distilled a shift in corporate thinking, a growing conviction that these massive paradigm shifts—demographic change, broadcast to niche, whiteness to post-whiteness, the rise of the "urban"—were not such a bad thing after all. Hip-hop offered a way this elusive generation could be assimilated, categorized, made profitable.

The disposable could become indispensable. The Black thing you once couldn't understand had now become the G thang you could buy into—the chronic, the crip walk, condoms, ConArt, Chevrolet, Pendleton, Zig-Zag, Seagram, Remy, Hennessey, Tanqueray, Desert Eagle, Dogg Pound, Death Row. Here was the short-lived post-truce freedom recast as the sweet sound of rapsploitation and a new corporate multiculturalism:

> Rollin down the street smokin indo
> Sippin on gin and juice
> Laaaid back
> With my mind on my money
> And my money on my mind

Polyculturalism and Post-Whiteness

Now that corporations were climbing aboard the urban, multicultural gravy train, what would happen to cultural desegregation? Historian Robin D.G. Kelley and scholar Vijay Prashad believed that the idea of "multiculturalism" had been co-opted by the state and capitalism. During the '80s, multiculturalists had pushed for inclusion and representation. But post-*Chronic* corporate multiculturalism reinforced backward notions of identity. Kelley coined the term "polyculturalism" to try to revive a radical vision of integration.

Polyculturalism built on the idea that civil society did not need Eurocentrism or whiteness at its core to function. In the real world, cultures layered, blended, and sounded together like the polyrhythms of a jazz song or a DJ riding the cross-fader. In its truest sense, this kind of integration could lift everyone. But urban marketing threatened to confer the trappings of integration while preserving the realities of segregation and inequality. So rap's big crossover set off paroxysms of self-examination in the hip-hop nation.

In a much-discussed essay in *The Source* called "We Use Words Like Mackadocious", white Chicago graffiti writer William "UPSKI" Wimsatt ripped on the sudden influx of what he called "wiggers" into hip-hop culture that the success of *The Source* and *Yo! MTV Raps* had made possible. "One day the rap audience may be as white as tables in a jazz club, and rap will become just another platform for every white ethnic group—not only the Irish—to express their suddenly funky selves," he wrote.

Wimsatt followed the article with a book entitled *Bomb the Suburbs*, and, in its perceptive rage over race and generation, it became an instant classic. "The suburbs is more than just an unfortunate geographical location, it is an unfortunate state-of-mind," he began. "It's the American state-of-mind, founded on fear, conformity, shallowness of character and dullness of imagination.[13]

"I say bomb the suburbs because the suburbs have been bombing us for at least the last forty years. They have waged an economic, political and cultural war on life in the city," he wrote. "*Bomb the Suburbs* means let's celebrate the city. Let's celebrate the ghetto and the few people who aren't running away from it."[14]

Here was the idea of the "urban" addressed with a thorough-going optimism. Hip-hop separated from marketing imperatives was still something his generation could control and define. Suburbanites could unite with ghetto-dwellers. Whites could learn to respect Blackness, not merely consume it. Wimsatt, the militant dreamer, wanted a world that was not just polycultural, but postwhite.

Strictly Underground

Wimsatt appealed to the highest aspirations of the hip-hop generation: intellectual honesty, independent-mindedness, principled realness. Wimsatt self published *Bomb The Suburbs* and hawked it by hand to Blacks, whites, Latinos and Asians on subways and in the streets as he criss-crossed the country, selling 23,000 copies. To him, hip-hop nationalism was about staying true to yourself and your peers, backing up your words with your life.

If the city street was hip-hop nationalism's mythical wellspring, the college campus was its hothouse, the hub of the local underground. In the '60s, during the long economic boom, the youths had marched. In the '90s, with the bleakest prospects since the Depression, the youths got creative.

Around nearly every college radio station, a hip-hop underground popped up—supporting energetic enterprising networks of radio shows, b-boy, MC and DJ battles, poetry slams, cafés, clothing stores, indie record labels, and hip-hop zines. By the mid-'90s, these networks were vibrant and thriving. At national conferences like the Gavin Convention, Jack the Rapper, or How Can I Be Down, mixshow and college radio DJs, street promoters, and hip-hop journalists got organized. Grass-roots groups like the Bay Area Hip-Hop Coalition became a model for underground radio DJs, influencing national radio playlists and press coverage, and propelling grassroots artists into the mainstream. Independent music distribution networks, particularly in the South, generated million-dollar-grossing artists and labels.

Inspired by the do-for-self energy, hip-hop journalism exploded. Some zines, like *The Bomb, Flavor, Straight From the Lip, Divine Styler, 4080, Stress, On The Go,* or *One Nut Network,* were basically bedroom projects handed out to industry insiders or sold in specialty record, graffiti, skateboard and clothing stores. Others, like *Rap Sheet, URB, The Kronick,* and *Ego Trip* began as free newsprint offerings. Some featured high-end design and edgy content, but all offered low-cost ads that attracted the new pool of major-label promo capital and, more important, local, independent start-ups, including clothing lines, record labels and club and rave promotions. Especially after *The Source* dumped its regional reports, these local magazines proliferated. Some, like *URB, Rap Sheet,* and *Rap Pages* works become newsstand sellers. Through their content and their commerce, they helped to consolidate the local scenes.

So while hip-hop's crossover had created new problems, there was also a sense that bigger opportunities than anyone could imagine awaited. Hip-hop had reached the point where it was ready to flow out of its niche into the mainstream. The only question left was whether reaching market potential and fanning potential militancy could remain consonant goals.

Vibe and the Triumph of the Urban

In 1993, *The Source*'s advertisers expanded beyond record labels to include Nike, Reebok, Sega and Bugle Boy. Its circulation was up to 90,000 readers; the average reader was a twenty-one-year-old male. Over half were Black, over a quarter were white.[15] "This isn't a niche market, or just an ethnic market," Mays told magazine industry people. "Hip-hop is like rock and roll was twenty-five years ago. It's a music-driven lifestyle being lived by an entire generation of young people now."

He added, "This market is dying to be marketed to."[16]

Quincy Jones, Russell Simmons and Time Warner agreed. In 1991, they had entered into discussions with Mays, Shecter and Bernard to buy *The Source.* "Their thing was we were too narrow," says Bernard. "I think the Time Warner people didn't think that there was going to be a big enough magazine for a hardcore hip-hop magazine, which they were wrong about. They also thought that there was a market for a mainstream Black music magazine that came out of hip-hop, which they were right about." Bernard says the negotiations ended after Time Warner lowballed them.

Instead, Jones and Simmons took a $1-million investment from Time Warner and began developing an upmarket hip-hop magazine. How upmarket was a key question: Simmons liked *The Source*'s raw edginess, Jones wanted a slick *Rolling Stone*–styled glossy. Jones installed Carol Smith as the publisher, a white forty-three-year-old founder of *Parenting* magazine who admitted she had never seen *Do the Right Thing* or *Boyz N The Hood*. Jonathan Van Meter, a white, gay twenty-nine-year-old, was hired as editor-in-chief. Simmons quit, famously complaining, "They didn't hire one straight Black man to work on that magazine.

"I don't think anybody who knows me would accuse me of homophobia," he added. "The idea that [this]'ll be the bible for the hip-hop community is dead."[17]

With Simmons gone before *Vibe*'s September 1992 test launch, all of the principals admitted they had no idea what to expect, or even who would buy the magazine. They just figured their "Black music *Rolling Stone*" would be huge. On the advertising side, they had picked up The Gap, Swatch and Nintendo, but they also landed Benetton, Armani Exchange, Gianni Versace, four pages of Levi's and five pages of Nike. Ad pages sold for between $5,000 and $6,000.[18] Their 144-page tester had fifty-four ad pages and hit the stands with 200,000 copies, twice the circulation of *The Source*. The response was strong enough for Time-Warner to make the full plunge.

Vibe began as a high-brow experiment, mixing celebrity and investigative journalism with minimalist high-concept photography and disorienting Madison Avenue-goes-Uptown fashion spreads. The writing was often superb: Joan Morgan challenging Ice Cube on his nationalism, Kevin Powell confronting Death Row Records at its peak, Danyel Smith both documenting and mourning Tupac's tragic career. *Vibe*'s elegant photography and design now looks groundbreaking, pointing forward to the pre-millennial rush of hip-hop culture-as-post white *haute couture*, 1982 eternal. The Avedon-influenced photographs presented their subjects against blank, decontextualized backgrounds, emphasizing their many shades of nonwhiteness. No gritty street-scene backgrounds here, *Vibe* was all icon-making foreground. At the time, *Vibe* left many heads cold. To them, the magazine seemed to be turning hip-hop into a museum piece—cool but cerebral, artful but funkless, gorgeous but bourgeois.

Yet *Vibe* did not just survive, it thrived. The demand for hip-hop was larger than anyone had imagined. When, at the end of 1993, advertising execs realized that *The Source* and *Vibe*, and a host of smaller competitors like *Rap Pages* and *URB*, had not killed each other off, they turned on the tap. Brands that hip-hop heads had long embraced—like Tommy Hilfiger and Timberland—belatedly returned the attention. Other brands—The Gap, Sprite—jumped in, hoping to re-brand themselves by generating tremors from the inner city out to the exurbs. Sony, AT&T, even the U.S. Army began pouring money into hip-hop magazines, which suddenly became consumer catalogs to the hip-hop lifestyle.

Hip-hop lifestyling offered, to use an advertising term, a complicated kind of *aspirational* quality. In one sense, hip-hop had triumphed over America in a way the civil rights movement never had. No matter the race, class, or geography, the kids wore the same clothes, spoke the same language, listened to the same music. Ice T and Chuck D saw this development as an unmitigated triumph of cultural desegregation. That was why, they said, white parents were so afraid of rap.

Here again, the reality was complicated. As Upski had pointed out, what kind of desegregation allowed white kids to get away without questioning their whiteness? Tommy Hilfiger's mid-1990s makeover from Ralph Lauren pretender to avatar of urban cool, Naomi Klein wrote, "feeds off the alienation at the heart of America's race relations: selling white youth on their fetishization of black style, and black youth on their fetishization of white wealth."[19]

Hip-hop journalists bemoaned the popular success of artists like Vanilla Ice, whom they dismissed as a white poseur, and M.C. Hammer, whom they derided as a black sellout, and accepted A Tribe Called Quest's "Industry Rule No. 4080"—"Record company people are shady"—as a truism. But at the same time, hip-hop relentlessly pushed toward the mainstream. "Strictly underground," EPMD rapped on MTV. "Keep the crossover." Perhaps this new confusion—about race and class, underground and mainstream, keeping it real and making it big—was the ultimate price of the media bumrush.

Editors like Jon Shecter and James Bernard, Dane Webb, Darryl James,

Sheena Lester and, later, Danyel Smith and Selwyn Seyfu Hinds were constructing a hip-hop nationalist worldview that was hard *and* complicated. Hip-hop nationalism was about defending a generation that loved its contradictions. Being down with hip-hop was, in Smith's words, "about the intense kind of aspiration that comes from having little. It's about the ambivalence of having a lot but knowing others don't.

"[M]ost of the time, feminists chant sexist rhymes, reformers boogie to money lust," she wrote. "White people sing along to songs that curse their existence on this planet. Black people memorize joints that exist only to extol self-destruction. Are we close to hip-hop? Yes. Where else to be but close to the truth?"[20]

The Moment of Truth

By the end of 1994, Dre and Snoop had dominated video and radio for two years, hundreds of "cool hunter" marketing agencies had sprung up in the gap between the broadcasters and the niches to teach confused corporations how to re-brand themselves for an elusive new generation, and the rap industry, now commanding more than 10 percent of the music market and driving massive change in the sound of pop radio, was flush with money. *The Source* had a circulation of 140,000, landed five hundred advertising pages at more than $5,000 a page, and clocked nearly $4 million in total revenues.[21] Stakes were higher than ever.

The flipside of the post-riot creative explosion was that hip-hop had become a fiercely competitive field. Majors signed hundreds of acts, indies were popping up everywhere, and the rap market was crowded with product. Radio DJs were drowning in records, magazine editors in interview and review requests.

Journalists from *The Source* and other hip-hop magazines had become targets. Angry over negative coverage or reviews, sometimes even angry over positive coverage, rappers and their handlers issued threats that sometimes became physical attacks. Bernard, Dennis and Shecter strengthened the magazine's code of ethics. Dennis says, "The rule was if someone cornered you, you handled the situation right then. You had to defend the shit. If anyone stepped to anyone on staff, when you saw them you stepped to them. Just to keep everybody honest."

He adds, "This was when people was, everyday, 'We're gonna come up there and shoot all you motherfuckers. Man, I'm gonna kill you. I know where you live.' And I'm a little concerned because niggas did know where I lived. I lived in the city and I seen these motherfuckers every day, getting irrational over this rap music. 'Why you gonna fuck with my money like that?' Soon as motherfuckers start talking money, the guns is next."

Shecter and Dennis vowed that any group that had threatened a staffer or a freelancer would not receive any coverage. Wu-Tang Clan, whose Master Killa had punched freelancer Cheo Coker because he didn't like the cartoons that accompanied *Coker's Rap Pages* article, artwork for which Coker was not even responsible, was one of the first groups to get on the list. "We didn't cover a lot of people just because they crossed that line," says Dennis. "You've got to be fair to these guys and make an example out of someone so they respect you."

Relations between the editorial and business halves of *The Source* had become strained. With the editorial side enforcing its code of ethics, complaints from rappers, managers, promoters and label execs about editorial decisions spilled over to the business side. David Mays got earfuls. He had not written an article for *The Source* since 1989, or interfered with the editorial side. Now he began complaining to the editors about certain reviews. The editors brushed him off.

Bernard says, "Especially in the beginning, when we were kind of barely hanging on, people said, 'We're looking out for you and you're not reviewing our records.' And of course, everybody, whatever records they put out, they all think it's a five. They all think we're not being fair. That's why we had the division between editorial and business. Because the people selling ads need to be able to say, 'Look, I have nothing to do with it.'

"I think that people didn't really have respect for those rules," he adds. "I don't think people were calling up Jann Wenner at *Rolling Stone* and threatening things."

At the same time, the entry of *Vibe* into the market cast light on *The Source's* shortcomings. "After a while, me and Jon and Reggie got really frustrated with Dave because we were putting out a dope magazine that people read every month and Dave would sort of get on us because sometimes we were late. We were like, 'What are you doing? You're still selling ads, and Ed is still doing circulation,'" says Bernard. "We realized that the publisher should not just be selling ads, particularly since the ads at that point were like fishing in a bucket. We were questioning what was going on, like, 'How come you're not launching new businesses, breaking into new ads? What are you doing that's growing this thing?' " Mays responded, in part, by launching The Source Music Awards, an event that he billed as "the rap Grammys." He wanted to move *The Source* from grass-roots to the glamorous life.

"In the midst of this stuff going on," Dennis says, "Dave had the Almighty RSO which is everything we all hated, everything people accused us of, and ultimately if you take this seriously, ethically, everything you can't be a part of."

The RSO and the Mind Squad

The Almighty Roxbury Street Organization was a rap crew and street clique that Mays and Shecter had met at a rap show in Boston during their Harvard days. Mays and Raymond "Ray Dog" Scott, the leader of Almighty RSO, became close friends. RSO DJ Deff Jeff joined Mays and Shecter on their WHRB show. Mays eventually moved in with Scott and began managing the RSO. Soon Mays and Shecter lost their show, and rumors spread that Scott and his friends may have been responsible. The story, however apocryphal, had the DJs before Mays and Shecter going past their allotted time by five minutes and getting beat down for their error.

Shecter was aware of Scott's rep. It was a matter of public record that at least two RSO associates had been murdered. Word was that the names of crew members were turning up in drug and murder investigations. Friends say that Shecter never thought it was a good idea for Mays to manage Scott. But even as *The Source* took off, and Mays's relationship with the crew clearly violated his own "Publisher's Credo," he remained Scott's manager.

In 1991, Mays secured a deal for Almighty RSO through Tommy Boy. The crew cut "One in the Chamba," a protest song against the police killing of two young Black men that was released into the height of "Cop Killer" hysteria. Claiming the song advocated cop killing, the Boston Police Patrolman's Association and Oliver North's Freedom Alliance threatened to file a lawsuit against the group. Tommy Boy dropped the group, saying the record had generated no interest at radio or retail. Another deal for RSO with Flavor Unit ended in 1993. Scott pressed Mays to get them another deal, while Mays tried to avoid Scott's calls. When Mays secured an EP deal for RSO with RCA in May of 1994, the calls finally stopped. The crew finished a five-song EP, entitled *Revenge of Da Badd Boyz*, scheduled for a September release.

The Mind Squad had covered the "One in the Chamba" controversy sympathetically and included Scott in their "gangsta rap summit," but the editorial staff did not consider the EP worth wasting any ink, especially once the squabbling began.

Scott seemed to have concluded that most of the new staffers, particularly associate editors Rob Marriott and Carter Harris, were not showing him enough respect. Staffers complained that the RSO crew would come to the magazine, go into their offices to snatch their records and get into shouting matches with them. Bernard recalls taking Scott and the RSO members aside to cool them out. "It wasn't like we were cowering on the editorial side. In fact my main problem was that there were a lot of people who were armed at *The Source*," Bernard says. "My fear was that things could get really out of hand."

Staffers say that Mays asked them for coverage on RSO, and for the right of final edits. "We knew he was under pressure and Dave was damn near pleading to help with RSO," says Dennis. "But by the time they got the deal with RCA, Ray had already dug his grave with us. His music, while average at best, wasn't the worst thing that had ever appeared in the magazine, but it certainly wasn't worth our integrity as a group to go along with the program. It was a situation Dave had to deal with by himself."

In June and July, Scott specifically threatened associate editors Carter Harris and Rob Marriott. According to Bernard, when Scott still believed he was getting a review he told staffers, "If I don't get at least a four, I'm putting niggas in bodybags."[22] He was threatening Mays again, too. Bernard told Mays they should call the cops, but he says that Mays refused to do anything. Then the threats suddenly ceased. "And I didn't think about it at that point that it was strange," says Bernard. "I'd see them and it wasn't like it used to be, but it was fine."

As the staff began to prepare for the November issue, which would hit the stands in October, Bernard penned a lead editorial decrying rapper violence and defining the values he felt that the hip-hop generation should uphold. "First, if artists are too thin-skinned to take fair (or even unfair) criticism, then don't put your music in record stores, on music video shows or on the radio where it's up for public discussion and consumption," he wrote. "Our responsibility—whether you're an artist, a writer, a fan or all of the above—is to build hip-hop. And hip-hop cannot be built unless we hold each other up to the highest standards imaginable.

"I don't equate building hip-hop with propping up the careers of individual artists when they put out weak shit," he continued. "Ask anybody who has successfully built up any thriving sports team, business, grassroots revolutionary organization, or, fuck it, a Crip or Blood set, and they'll tell you. Your friends ain't those who soup you on the regular, holding their tongues. Your true homeboys are the ones who care enough to take you aside to let you know when you're slippin'. It's best for you and it's best for the whole crew.

"Anybody who hasn't learned this yet had better grow the fuck up."[23]

The Edits

In September, the editorial staff closed the November issue and sent it off to the printer. The RSO fiasco seemed to be behind them.

Bernard and Mays's relationship had completely deteriorated. The militant and the marketer were barely speaking to each other. Mirroring their split, *The Source*'s editorial and business sides had become divided camps. Mays proposed the two go to lunch at the end of the week. It was Friday, September 23.

Mays asked Bernard what he needed to do to make things right. Bernard and Shecter had been working without proper ownership papers, so Bernard asked Mays to take care of their stock certificates. Mays agreed. Bernard said he had to meet Dennis for a previous engagement. Mays nodded and said that he had one more thing to tell him. When they returned to the office building, Mays explained to Bernard that before the magazine went to the printer, he had exercised his right as publisher to insert a three-page feature into the November issue on the Almighty RSO.

Bernard was dumbstruck. This wasn't keeping it real. This was gunpoint ethics and crony capitalism. He asked Mays for a copy of the article, and went to meet Dennis. "The first thing Reggie said," Bernard recalls, "was 'I guess that's it.'"

The next day a copy of the article—a virtual press release entitled "Boston

Bigshots" that Bernard realized was ghost-written by Mays himself—was under his door. He read it, composed a resignation letter, then called each of the editorial staffers to an emergency Sunday night meeting. When they convened, Bernard passed out copies of the letter he had written.

The staff agreed with all of Bernard's points but one: Bernard did not need to resign, Mays did. They decided that Bernard would leave later in the week, and fax his resignation letter out. The following week, the rest of the staff would resign in solidarity. First, Shecter and Bernard would meet with Mays to get him to admit what he had done, and they would tape the conversation. The next day, the two confronted Mays.

Although Shecter was supposed to let Mays confess, he instead began debating with Mays, using arguments from Bernard's still unreleased resignation letter. Mays realized that the staff was planning to expose his RSO gambit. When Shecter and Bernard left the office, he called Scott. By the afternoon, Scott had escalated the tension to the breaking point with a threatening voice-mail message for Shecter:

Yo, you fuckin' bitch. You better keep your fuckin' mouth shut. A-ight . . . You can't help niggas out? You fuckin' faggot. You let me hear one more fuckin' word out of you, Jon, I'ma fuckin drag you up out of there. A-ight? You better keep your fuckin' mouth shut. You fuckin' sellout white boy bitch. Don't fuckin' play us, man, we fuckin' knew you before, before there was any *Source*. Don't fuckin' play us.

Bernard, Dennis and Shecter took the tape to the police.

The detective told the three that they could make an arrest, but that Scott would be likely be back on the street in a day and an arrest might escalate the situation. Instead, they were offered the option of using a voluntary writ that would begin a conflict-resolution process. The next day was a RSO press day at RCA. The three agreed to deliver the writ then.

Shecter never showed up. So Bernard and Dennis walked it up to the press suite. When they entered, Scott and three others from the crew were surprised. "Ray literally looked like he had seen a ghost," says Dennis. "He was visibly shook and stammered, 'Yo, I didn't know *The Source* was coming down.'"

Bernard handed the summons to Scott and told him, "Look, you can't be threatening our people like that."

Scott's mood turned sour. "You trying to embarrass niggas on our press day?" he shouted. The four rushed Bernard and Dennis, and they all exchanged blows. Bernard and Dennis made it to the doorway, caught the elevators down, and headed back to the office. By then, Scott had called Mays, who immediately headed up to RCA. As Mays and Scott discussed what to do, Bernard's resignation letter came through on the label's fax machine.

Bernard had written, "You have made a mockery of my efforts to protect our staff from physical assault as well as the magazine's efforts to take a stand against the rising tide of violence in the Hip-Hop Nation. And in the process, you have destroyed every bit of the magazine's integrity.

"Dave, it is a tenet of journalism that there is a wall between the editorial ventures and the business ventures," Bernard's letter continued. "But it seems as if you are willing to push me to shape the editorial vision so that we don't step on too many toes in order for you to build your entertainment empire. This is simply unacceptable."

Overnight, a remote automatic fax machine would deposit the letter in 750 industry offices. When Mays and RSO rushed back to the offices, the staff was gone.

The Rewrites

Later that week, Bernard told the press, "This is a fight for a precious thing, a magazine that speaks directly to a hip-hop generation from people who are part of that."[24] But he and his staffers knew the battle had already been lost; the conviction to storm the mainstream on their own generation's terms, the standards and codes that they had upheld against the threat of corruption—all of that seemed to be crumbling. Hip-hop seemed free for the taking. On the other side of this moment lay empires and ruins.

Bernard and Dennis had found an investor willing to put up $3 million for a buy-out, but without Ed Young, they did not have the controlling interest to force Mays to sell. They considered other options, including "further violence and retaliation," Dennis says. "But it was clear that there was nothing that could be done to salvage the situation. Our time at *The Source* was over, and outside of a time machine there was no way to repair the damage." Soon after, Bernard and Shecter received their stock certificates from Mays, a move that was part pre-emptive strike and part pimp-slap.

Mays was forced to rebuild an editorial staff from scratch. He told anyone who would listen, "The Almighty RSO—whether they were my partner or not—merited some kind of coverage in the magazine, the way any other group that had an album on a major label that was making some kind of noise deserved coverage. Because of their problems with me, [the former editorial staff] refused to cover the group in any way."[25] The crew's EP stiffed.

Almighty RSO was renamed Made Men, and Ray Dog became Benzino. None of their records became big hits, but with Mays as their manager, they always seemed to land another major label deal and some new fans. Each time a new Made Men or Benzino record was about to be released, it seemed, a struggle broke out between Mays and his editorial staff, people walked out in protest, and Mays was forced to rebuild again.

But his entertainment empire grew. He began the nationally syndicated *The Source Magazine* Radio Network, *The Source Magazine All Hip-Hop Hour* television program, a series of hits compilation CDs, the annual *Source Hip-Hop Music Awards* syndicated television special, thesource.com, and The Source Youth Foundation. He bought back Bernard's and Shecter's shares.

In 1997, as Bernard and Dennis launched *XXL Magazine* to compete directly with *The Source*, Mays entered into partnership negotiations with *Rolling Stone's* Jann Wenner. But Wenner reportedly refused to pony up $15 million for only a quarter ownership of the company.[26] Now Mays had a new goal. "I want to build the Time-Warner of this generation," he told anyone who asked.[27]

The law continued to hawk Scott and his crew. An FBI investigation into Scott's murky past commenced. Two Made Men associates were convicted of stabbing Boston Celtics star Paul Pierce.

"I'm not going to stand here and pretend that myself or the guys grew up as angels, but the wreckage of our past should not be used to judge the path of our future," Scott angrily told the press in 2000, after serving a thirty-day bid stemming from a shopping-mall confrontation with police. "For years the media has been slandering our name and it's time for this vicious attack to stop."[28]

In 2003, as Scott prepared for the release of another record and *The Source* continued under yet another editorial staff lineup he suddenly appeared on the masthead as a "cofounder." Scott revealed that he and Mays were coowners of *The Source*. "I didn't buy in," he said. "I didn't give Dave a dollar." Instead of cash, he said, "I gave him my love, my loyalty, my honor and my vision."[29]

Coda

Just months after the meltdown, at the second annual Source Music Awards in the spring of 1995, Suge Knight stepped up to the podium and called out Puffy and Bad Boy. The rap industry had become the fastest-growing sector of the music industry. By then it was also out of control.

The Source's collapse seemed to prophesy a new kind of predatory, mercenary, get-it-while-you-can impulse in the hip-hop nation. Beef—Death Row and Bad Boy, Tupac and Biggie—rose to a high-stakes spectacle. Competition inspired paranoia. Greed led to violence. A bloody climax from the deadly end of warm guns felt inevitable.

Four years later, DJ Kool Herc stepped onto the same stage, to finally receive his due recognition, and to make things right. Flanked by Grandmaster Flash to his right and Jam Master Jay to his left, Herc received a long standing ovation. He said:

I want to thank God for me being here, alive, drug free, to live to see this day . . .

Let me set the record straight, it's been twenty-nine years. Got stabbed, nearly got killed in a party, but I didn't give up because the youth was having fun. They said, "Herc when is the next party?" and that's what kept me going.

1520 Sedgwick Avenue. My sister was behind me. In the Bronx y'all, in the Bronx right here is where it started. But it went worldwide. And we give the kids a culture. That's what came up out of it. . . . Because kids could have been doing something else, but now people living good, having good jobs, an economy . . .

There's a lot of heroes that's not here, that died for this here. Ain't no sense for us to be killing each other over this music. We got to love each other for this, man.

Because I'll tell you one thing, what happened was the gangs back in the days killed it at the Puzzle, the Tunnel, and I'm the one that started to play, and all I asked for was respect. . . . It wasn't about me being big and brawn, I never used that over nobody.

I gave respect to get respect and that's how I keep my life flowing.

Branding everything: P-Diddy at play in the New World Order.

Photo © Kevin Winter/Getty Images

19.

New World Order

Globalization, Containment and Counterculture at the End of the Century

Every truth ain't evident
Every slave story present tense
Every uprise a consequence

—Boots Riley, The Coup

Pre-millennium tension came early to the hip-hop generation.

In the mid-1990s, the talk in Five Percent street ciphers and Zulu Nation study sessions was of the New World Order. The time of Revelations seemed imminent. The sound—Wu-Tang Clan, Mobb Deep, Outkast, Company Flow—fit the mood, claustrophobic and swarming. Youths trooped through the cities in camouflage jumpsuits and combat boots and called each other "souljahs." Streetside book vendors from Harlem to Atlanta to Oakland did brisk business with alt-histories like Howard Zinn's *People's History of the United States* and Ward Churchill's *The COINTELPRO Papers*, and mysterious tracts like *The Illuminati 666*, *Secrets of Freemasonry*, and *The Unseen Hand*.

This particular miasma of dread had been unleashed by President George Herbert Walker Bush's peculiar phrase, "new world order," used in speeches meant to justify U.S. military action against Saddam Hussein in the Persian Gulf. The Berlin Wall had fallen, the Communist threat was fading and the president was mobilizing against new enemies. In January 1991, as fighters screamed toward Baghdad and police forces drew down on American ghettoes, Bush said, "We have before us the opportunity to forge for ourselves and for future generations a new world order, a world where the rule of law, not the law of the jungle, governs the conduct of nations."

To the street soldiers, that future presented itself, as Atlanta's Goodie Mob would put it, as one of "cell therapy," a lockdown nation. On their skin-crawling

1995 single, Bush's one-world "rule of law" was connected with resistance-destroying addictions and military-trained assassins, social conformity numbers and computer chip implants, nighttime paratroopers and black helicopters, gated projects and concentration camps.

Conspiracies were a shorthand for grasping the astonishing pace of change: school closures and skyrocketing university tuitions, the rise of youth curfews and sweeps and urban zero-tolerance campaigns, Big Brother technology and racial profiling, a prison-building boom and soaring incarceration rates. The Goodie Mob looked at these developments and concluded Bush's enemy really was *them*. "Time is getting shorter," Cee-Lo warned. "People, if we don't get prepared it's gon' be a slaughter."

Every street soldier carried a copy of M. William Cooper's *Behold a Pale Horse*, the survivalist's bible. It was a strange match. Cooper was a white radio broadcaster and a hero of the right-wing Patriot movement. When his end came, he did not die on his knees. One of the two Apache County sheriffs who came to his mobile home to arrest him on November 5, 2001, received a bullet in the head. The other shot Cooper dead on the desolate stretch of Arizona desert where he lived with his shortwave radio, two dogs, a rooster and a chicken. Cooper may have written his book for high-plains tax protestors and free-land patriots, but the book found a willing readership on the streets.

What made Cooper so compelling to rural white militiamen and ghetto youths of color alike? His worldview grafted post-COINTELPRO conspiracy onto New World Order paranoia. *Behold a Pale Horse*, which reportedly sold hundreds of thousands of copies, was like an overstuffed folder—five hundred pages of autobiography, news clippings, photos, Congressional legislation and allegedly top secret transcripts and memoranda meant to document the creation of a malign, shadowy one-world government and its efforts to enslave the masses. Armageddon was already here, Cooper was saying. *Behold a Pale Horse* was your late pass *and* your lesson plan.

Large portions of Cooper's "proof" were just the same old thing. Cooper offered up the old saw, *The Protocols of the Elders of Zion*, with strange instructions that "any reference to Jews should be replaced with the word 'Illuminati'; and the word 'goyim' should be replaced with the word 'cattle.'"[1] But for the street soldiers, *Behold a Pale Horse* affirmed their realities like no other media would.

When Cooper argued that drug-war legislation and the Federal Emergency

Management Agency Act was laying the foundation for the suspension of the constitution and the permanent establishment of a police state, it was just a different version of Farrakhan's message. In the 'hood, state pressure certainly could feel a short step away from martial law.

Cooper spoke of CIA ops that smuggled drugs into the ghetto to finance covert political operations. In 1996, newspaper reporter Gary Webb uncovered evidence of a crack pipeline from Nicaragua to Los Angeles opened by U.S. government-backed supporters of the Contras in his infamous "Dark Alliance" series in the *San Jose Mercury News*. Webb was hounded by official denial and concerted media blackballing, but his basic facts were later confirmed in investigations by both Congress and the CIA.

Cooper's strange worldview insinuated into the mainstream like a virus, seeping out into hundreds of rap songs, then suddenly exploding into social consciousness on September 10, 1993, when *The X-Files*—with its motto, "The Truth Is Out There"—debuted. Fox Mulder's Cooper-esque rantings about one-world government, master-race plotters, alien abductees, secret torture chambers and Tuskegee-style bioterror experiments felt realer than reality, a speculative history of the Cold War in which the actual struggle had always actually been between the leaders and the people, the Illuminati and the cattle, the one-worlders and the sheeple. Against end-of-history crowing and worldwide web ecstasy, the passionate pessimism of *The X-Files* matched that of the street soldiers.

"Hip-hop," Russell Simmons said, "moves as an army." But exactly who and what they were going to move against seemed still as spectral as Mulder's enemies. Nobody knew how to define the attacks, or where the next attack might be coming from. "Who's that peekin' in my windows?" Goodie Mob had said. "*Pow!* Nobody now." Here was the defensive b-boy stance recast as complete social alienation.

Planet Rock had entered the new order: a world in which the War on Youth was being driven to new heights of hysteria and repression, and government-deregulated, globalized media monopolies were colonizing and branding hip-hop's countercultural spirit.

The Case of Hip-Hop Radio

Once, there had been a creative tension between hip-hop's role as a commodity in the global media industry and as the lifeblood of a vast vibrant network of local undergrounds. But during the mid-'90s, the power shifted decisively in the direction of the media monopolies. And when corporations began to understand the global demand for postwhite pop culture, hip-hop became the primary content for the new globally consolidated media, the equivalent of gold dust in the millennial monopoly rush. The tensions between the culture's true believers and the captains of industry intermittently flared into open, polarizing conflict. Such was the case of hip-hop radio at the end of the century.

At the beginning of the 1990s, San Francisco's KMEL-FM was one of the country's leading urban stations. Calling itself "the people's station," it produced on-air personalities that seemed as of the streets as hip-hop itself. Through its innovative community-affairs programming, it engaged the social issues of the hip-hop generation.

To be sure, KMEL had not become "the people's station" because of enlightened corporate philosophy. It happened to be located in an area blessed with one of the strongest campus and community radio networks in the country, as well as one of the mostly fiercely competitive commercial markets in the country. Its makeover, however, became a win-win situation for its owners and the community.

During the early '80s, Bay Area urban radio was a stagnating format dominated by slick, disposable R&B. But college and community stations like KPOO, KZSU, KUSF and KALX were championing hip-hop. Author and former *Vibe* editor Danyel Smith grew up with the frequencies on the left-of-the-dial.

"You had to know where Billy Jam was gonna be playing, where Davey D was gonna be playing. To the rest of the world they were very little radio stations that came in staticky and the show was on in the middle of the night, but you were in the know and things were really exciting," she says. "And as much as I think we all liked being part of our little secret thing, we all thought, 'Wow this music needs to be heard by everyone. Someone needs to take it and blow it up, give it the respect that it deserves.' And for the Bay Area, that station was KMEL."

In the mid-1980s KMEL changed from a rock format to a "contemporary hits" format and became one of the first crossover pop stations in the nation to target young multiracial audiences with hip-hop, house, and dancehall music. To make it work, KMEL desperately needed street credibility. College and community radio jocks, such as KALX's David "Davey D" Cook, Sadiki Nia, Tamu du Ewa, and KZSU's Kevin "Kevvy Kev" Montague, and local artists like Sway and King Tech, were recruited to the station. "They took what we were doing at community radio and brought it to the station," says KPOO radio personality KK Baby, who joined the station in 1991. "They would use us to attract the rest of the pop music audience."

Most of the jocks were never offered full-time positions, but they brought their listeners with them, and pushed KMEL to play cutting-edge music and offer community-oriented programming. The station's ratings soared. KMEL's approach fit the Bay Area well—progressive, edgy, multicultural, inclusive—and listeners embraced "the people's station" with open arms.

KMEL's music shows, community-affairs talk-show programming, and its pioneering Summer Jam concerts were soon imitated throughout the country. The station helped launch the rap careers of Tupac Shakur, Hammer, Digital Underground, Too Short and E-40, and introduced local slang like "fa sheezy" into the hip-hop nation's lexicon. Although much smaller than Chicago, Miami and Los Angeles, the Bay Area became the number-two hip-hop market in the country.

In 1992, an upstart station, KYLD, emerged to challenge KMEL. Michael Martin, then the KYLD Program Director, says, "We felt KMEL was a little lazy, so we came in with a vengeance." In the cauldron of this fierce competition, nationally influential shows like Sway and Tech's "Wake-Up Show," Joe Marshall's "Street Soldiers," and Davey D's "Street Knowledge" were forged. At the same time, the dueling stations often deferred to the mixshow DJs to break new artists, resulting in national hits for local artists. The result was a massive growth in the local urban radio audience.

Then Congress passed the 1996 Telecommunications Act, a landmark of deregulation, the legal codification of the pro-media monopoly stance. At the time of its passage, the act was barely debated.

The Telecom Act profoundly affected the radio business, removing station ownership caps, and unleashing an unprecedented wave of consolidation. Radio deregulation left the public airwaves dominated by less than a handful of companies—Clear Channel, Cumulus, Citadel and Viacom—who laid off hundreds, decimated community programming and all but standardized playlists across the country. Average listening time plunged. FCC Chair Reed Hundt had justified the legislation by arguing, "We are fostering innovation and competition in radio." But by all accounts, KMEL's innovative years were over, and competition, the driving force of that innovation, was about to end.

Before the ink on the act was dry, KMEL's parent company Evergreen Media ended a ratings war by purchasing KMEL's competitor, KYLD, and the stations found themselves literally under the same roof. It didn't end there. A series of ever-larger mergers culminated in 1999 with a whopping $24 billion deal in which KMEL and KYLD were two of the hundreds of stations that passed from AMFM, Inc. into the hands of Clear Channel Communications. That's when, critics say, everything that was once so right began to go so wrong.

Waves of layoffs left all the Clear Channel radio stations with one sales force, fewer music programmers, a smaller promotions staff and no community affairs department. Individual staff responsibilities often doubled. Employees complained that they were being worked harder than ever. No other firm had benefited from the Telecom Act as much as Clear Channel. It went from owning forty stations in 1996 to 1,240 in 2003, commanding a whopping 28 percent share of all radio revenues and 27 percent of all radio listeners. Its closest competitor, Cumulus, owned 248 stations. But many industry insiders speculated that Clear Channel was eager to slash its payrolls because it had overpaid for its radio properties.

Technology replaced engineers, and sometimes even DJs. From the beginning of the radio industry, one of its most cherished tenets was that all radio was local. But in a process known as "voice tracking," Clear Channel jocks might pre-record vocal drops and listener calls to send out to other Clear Channel stations. Conglomerates had no commitment to the idea of the local. The future of their profits was in global monopolies.

To the average listener, the effect of consolidation was most apparent in the radio's sound. KMEL and KYLD's playlists now looked so similar that, on any given weeknight, more than half of each station's "Hot 7 at 7" countdowns might be the exact same songs. The same executive, Michael Martin, now Clear Channel's regional vice president of programming, was programming both stations.

The national trend, Martin said, was toward fewer songs. "When I first signed on at KYLD, I signed it on with eighty-six records," he said. "Around the country the stations that play less have bigger ratings. Power 106 in LA, who has huge ratings, their most spun record in a day can go up to sixteen times in a day. My most-played will hit eleven maybe twelve, that's it. Because at the end of the day, the hits are the hits. And the audience comes to you for a reason—to hear the hits."

But with narrowing playlists, local, new, and independent artists—the kinds of folks unable to compete with six-figure major label marketing budgets—inevitably got squeezed out. Even mixshow DJs—once hired to be the tastemakers and to break records—increasingly found their mixes subject to executive approval. As one local rapper put it, "What good is a request line?"

Specialty shows were quietly eliminated. Local personalities got fired. And KMEL's community affairs programming was severely reduced. Shortly after September 11, 2001, on-air personality and hip-hop activist Davey D was fired. The station blamed economic woes. Some critics saw a company that had overpaid for its market share and was now desperate to reduce costs. Others saw the sinister silencing of a key activist voice. Soon youths of color—KMEL's target audience—began to launch protests against the station. The people's station had become a target of the people's anger.

The New Corporate Order

By then, just ten companies controlled most of the U.S. media landscape—down from fifty in 1983—including music, movies, magazines, television, video games and the Internet.[2] At the beginning of the new millennium, five of these companies— Vivendi Universal, Sony, AOL Time Warner, Bertelsmann and EMI—controlled 80 percent of the music industry. Another, Viacom, owned both MTV and BET.

To Chuck D, the forces that controlled hip-hop looked like this: "You got five corporations that control retail. You got four who are the dominant record labels. Then you got three radio outlets who own all the stations. You got two television networks and you got one video outlet. I call it 5-4-3-2-1. Boom!"

The impulse of any monopoly is to absorb all profit potential. Local hip-hop undergrounds suddenly appeared to be veins of gold waiting to be exploited. During the mid-1990s, indies were bought up, squeezed out or rolled right over.

Take the experience of the indie distributors and the indie labels. During the

'80s, a thriving network of independent regional distributors could take independent label records gold, sometimes even platinum. The proof was in artists like Grandmaster Flash and the Furious Five, The Geto Boys and Magic Mike, and labels like Sugar Hill, Rap-A-Lot and Cheetah.

But by 1995, the two remaining national independent distributors, INDI and Alliance, faced serious financial difficulties and merged. Before long, Alliance closed its INDI operations, laid off its two hundred employees and filed for bankruptcy. In three years, it had gone from a $500-million company to one that owed $500 million. Soon there would be no national independently owned distributor. The next dominoes to fall were the regional "one-stops" like Valley Record Distributors, M. S. Distribution and Select-O-Hits. Smaller local distributors and niche distributors struggled to hang on in the new environment.

The trigger was the massive shakeout in music retailing. Major distributors, the end of the media monopoly's pipeline, were partly to blame. Major distributors squeezed indie distributors by offering chain stores deep discounts and incentives at the expense of indie retailers. As hundreds of stores and dozens of chains closed, indie distributors were stuck with millions in unpaid invoices and forced to fold. The effect on indie labels was immediate.

In 1996, indie record label market share had peaked. For the first time, and probably the last, indies together had actually outsold all the major labels. The indie leader was Ruthless Records, the label Eazy E had formed to put himself and NWA out in 1987.[3] But as soon as that happened, media monopolies went on a buying binge. Armed with the substantial capital their parent companies gave them, they snapped up indie labels like Master P's No Limit Records, E-40's Sick Wid It Records and Tony Draper's Texas-based Suave House label. Indies had three choices to survive in the new market: cut deals with major label distributors if they could, get comfortable with reaching a niche market through a crazy-quilt of much smaller distributors, or go under. When the millennium arrived, indie label market share had plunged. There was a notable historical equivalent: during the late '50s, rhythm-and-blues and rock indies owned up to half the market share. By the end of the sixties, the number of record label-owning firms had dropped from forty to twenty, as majors absorbed the indies to capitalize on the rise of the baby boomers.[4]

Once major labels made these big investments they had to make them pay off. Artist marketing budgets routinely pushed northward of six figures; break-even points sometimes climbed above gold sales. A decade before, rap music and Black film had surprised corporate execs by showing huge profits on tiny investments. Now the music industry had adopted the big Hollywood studios' blockbuster-or-bust mentality. They placed bigger bets on fewer projects in the hopes of bigger payoffs. The more that Soundscan-hawking execs spent on an album, the more units they forced through their distributors into retail chains, searching for that first-week score.

On the one hand, some hip-hop artists—not to mention executives, entrepreneurs, promoters, managers, and others—cashed in and built bigger empires than black artists of previous generations might have ever imagined possible. On the other, there was a steady narrowing of voices available through the majors' channels, a decrease in the diversity of sounds, opinions, ideas, news, and art available to mass audiences.

The New Exploitation

Hip hop had blown out of its niche into the mainstream. It suddenly seemed difficult to remember a time when youths of color had not been represented in the media, whether as consumers or producers. But just as hip-hop was now crucial content for the consolidated media, media consolidation also affected hip-hop's content. Women in hip-hop lost the most.

During the late 1980s, videos had been a boon to women rappers. Queen Latifah, for instance, presented herself in the Fab 5 Freddy–directed video for "Ladies First" as a matriarch, military strategist and militant. Others—Salt-N-Pepa, MC Lyte, Roxanne Shante—established their own personalities, equals alongside their male peers. A decade later, successful female artists like Missy Elliott and Lauryn Hill were the exceptions rather than the rule. Scantily-clad dancers seemed in endless supply, while women rappers were scarce. Big money clearly had a distorting effect.

At the same time, hip-hop feminism emerged in the work of writers and poets like Joan Morgan, Toni Blackman, Rha Goddess and dream hampton, offering a loyal but vocal opposition to hip-hop's übermasculinity. Hip-hop feminism's musical counterpart was not in rap but in the so-called "neo-soul" movement, a genre opened up by Elliott and Hill, Mary J. Blige, Meshell Ndegeocello, Jill

Scott, and Erykah Badu, that put the groove back into the music and the love back into lyrics. Emblematic of the shift was Angie Stone, who had been a female rap pioneer in The Sequence, and now returned to the limelight as a singer.

In one sense, "neo-soul" was a clever marketing strategy, invented by Motown exec Kedar Massenburg to package R&B artists that he had discovered, including Badu, India.Arie and D'Angelo. In time, the artists themselves would disavow the term, a reflection of their sensitivity to the fickleness of the market and the cycle of cool. But neo-soul also created space for voices to dissect the masculinist attitudes and ideals projected in the hip-hop mainstream. Badu sang, "The world is mine. When I wake up I don't need nobody telling me the time."

There was an unstable mix of Million Woman March–styled self-empowerment and AIDS- and gangsta-rap-era self-defense in the music, perhaps best epitomized by Hill's hit "Doo Wop (That Thing)." In these songs, critiques of hip-hop and patriarchy came together. Jill Scott imagined reconciliation, no longer having to love hip-hop from a distance. On "Love Rain," she sang of meeting a new man: "Talked about Moses and Mumia, reparations, blue colors, memories of shell top Adidas, he was fresh like summer peaches." But the relationship ended badly: "All you did was make a mockery of somethin' so incredible beautiful. I honestly did love you so." If hip-hop had dominated discussion of the crisis of gender relations with a boys' locker-room point of view, neo-soul responded with the sista-cipher.

Neo-soul's hip-hop feminist critique came into sharp relief in 2001. After years of flying high, rap sales crashed by 15 percent, leading a music industry-wide plunge. But newcomers Alicia Keys and India.Arie were honored with a bevy of Grammy nominations, and embraced by millions of fans. Keys and Arie celebrated "a woman's worth" and were frankly critical of male irresponsibility. India.Arie's breakout hit "Video"—in which she sang, "I'm not the average girl from your video"—took joy in flipping the music that had once been sampled for Akinyele's deez-nuts ode, "Put It in Your Mouth." On "Fallin," Alicia Keys wove the chords of James Brown's "It's a Man's World" into a complicated examination of a relationship. In her video, it became a symbol-laden examination of Black love—the man caught in the prison-industrial complex, the woman torn between loyalty and leaving.

The questions raised resonated far beyond the fraught issues of gender: what did it mean to "keep it real" anymore? What did it mean to be true to something when that something had changed? Could one preserve any kind of individual agency or did one have to ride with the new flow of exploitation?

Identity was on sale. Brands had become sophisticated. During the 2001 holiday season, the Modernista!-designed Gap ads sold a single line of clothes by using different artists as stand-ins for different niches: Sheryl Crow for the VH1 lifestyle, Seal for the SUV lifestyle, Liz Phair for aging indie-rockers, Robbie Robertson for aged arena-rockers, India.Arie for urban hipsters, Shaggy for urban players.

Media monopolies favored artists who did not merely produce hits, but synergies of goods. In this new corporate order, a song could become a movie could could become a book could become a soundtrack could become a music video could become a videogame. Here was the media monopolies' appropriation of dub logic, profits stacking up with each new version.

The biggest artists were brands themselves, generating lifestyles based on their own ineffable beings. Sean "P-Diddy" Combs leveraged himself across music, film, television and high fashion. Jay-Z peddled movies, clothing, shoes and vodka. Once the journey of cool had made the complete circuit from the artist to the mall, the artists had to reject what they had created, and reinvent themselves. In Jay-Z's case, the ultimate reinvention would be retirement, as if to recognize that excessive branding and positioning had prematurely exhausted the possibilities of art.

The cycle of cool was the oldest hip-hop story ever told. Busy Bee had influenced his followers, like a young Run DMC, to wear bugged-out, geek-chic, plaid-striped suits. Run DMC then commanded their black-on-black sporting audiences to throw their white Adidas shelltoes in the air, branding-on-top-of-branding. The difference was in scale. At the turn of the century the hip-hop generation was now at the center of a global capitalist process generating billions in revenues. "We're survivalists turned to consumers," rapped Talib Kweli.

Just as brands developed their niches, each niche, in turn, came with its own set of brands. "Political rap" was defanged as "conscious rap," and retooled as an *alternative* hip-hop lifestyle. Instead of drinking Alizé, you drank Sprite. Instead of Versace, you wore Ecko. Instead of Jay-Z, you dug the Roots. Teen rap, party rap, gangsta rap, political rap—at the dawn of hip-hop journalism these tags were just a music critic's game. Now they had literally become serious business.

What materially separated Jay-Z from a rapper like Talib Kweli? The answer was in the marketing. Media monopolies saw Jay-Z as an artist with universal appeal, Kweli as a "conscious rapper." A matter of taste, perhaps, except that the niche of "conscious rap" might be industry shorthand for reaching a certain kind of market—say, college-educated, iPod-rocking, Northface backpacking, vegan, hip-hop fans. In this late-capitalist logic, it was not the rappers' message that brought the audience together, it was the things that the audience bought that brought the rappers together.

So Talib Kweli faced the uniquely thorny problem of the "conscious rapper." "Once you put a prefix on an MC's name, that's a death trap," he said. When he unveiled a song called "Gun Music"—a complicated critique of street-arms fetishism—his fans grumbled he wasn't being conscious enough. At the same time, Kweli worried that being pigeonholed as "political" would prevent him from being promoted to the kids who loved Jay-Z. In fact, Jay-Z had cut anti-war and anti-police brutality raps. But by the turn of the century, to be labeled a "conscious" or "political" rapper by the music industry was to be condemned to preach to a very small choir.

Christgau's old-school observation—that hip-hop exploitation had layers of complication—had boomeranged back.

The End of the American Century

The further one got from North America, the greater the dissonance became.

For two decades, Bambaataa had been a hip-hop ambassador, seeding cities around the world with Universal Zulu Nation chapters and the basic elements. By the end of the century, many of these cities—from Sarajevo to Sydney, Amsterdam to Zanzibar—had been through two generations of hip-hop heads with their own defiant youth countercultures. The cultural revolution had been won.

So it was in a spirit of triumph that the Black August tour—with an entourage of the cream of "conscious rappers" including Talib Kweli, Black Thought of The Roots, Boots Riley of The Coup, Jeru The Damaja, and dead prez—arrived in 2001 to play a concert at the World Conference Against Racism in Durban and a series of dates in South Africa. Black August had begun in Brooklyn as part of the Malcolm X Grassroots Movement's project to educate rappers and hip-hop audiences on the plight of Black political prisoners. It had taken rappers and activists—including Common, Tony Touch and Mos Def—to Cuba in successful exchanges that participants described as profoundly moving. South Africa would prove profound, too, but for much different reasons.

The moment seemed perfect to define a hip-hop generation moving toward global solidarity. U.S. Secretary of State Colin Powell had refused to attend the conference, an action many took as reflective of George W. Bush's administration's disinterest in addressing racism. The Black August crew was well aware that their very presence in South Africa was a protest against their government's unilateralist silence.

South Africa's hip-hop movement had taken root during apartheid in cities like Cape Town and Johannesburg (Gauteng) during the early '80s, and helped fuel some of the most dangerous forms of cultural protest of the era. Rappers that decried the government received death threats from right-wing extremists. Graffiti writers piecing political slogans after dark amidst curfews risked being shot by government soldiers.[5]

When the Black August crew came to South Africa, local heads hoped for an exchange of ideas and a sharing of stories of struggle. Instead they came away feeling snubbed. Some of South African rap's leading stars offered to take the Americans around; they thought it was a mutual opportunity to get to know each other better. But they found themselves treated like hired drivers.

Onstage, it began to look to them as if some of the American rappers had developed a Moses complex, dispensing vague pieties about loving the motherland, and stamping across the stage to lecture the crowd about racism and reparations in the United States. "The idea behind Black August is to facilitate the international cultural exchange between youth across the globe while supporting and promoting social consciousness and positive self-expression," wrote South African journalist Niren Tolsi. "What we got were a bunch of Yanks jerking off on the tits of Mother Africa."[6]

At a press conference in Durban the growing tensions—exacerbated by the fact that the South African promoters had failed to secure the shows promised the Black August collective—finally exploded. African youth activists demanded to know from the Black August rappers: Who were they to come off a plane, stay in expensive hotels and then whine onstage about how bad racism was in America? Some decried their rap as a new form of American cultural imperialism. "They came here either to conquer Africa with their rhymes," South African rapper Emile of Black Noise told journalist Cristina Verán, "or thinking, 'Here we are, ready to save you.' "[7]

The irony was that the Black August rappers were among the most politically educated and committed of commercially successful North American artists. "People expect a lot from MCs who are considered 'conscious rappers.' If the people detect any kind of 'studio activist' vibe, then they are harder on those MCs than the 'studio gangstas,' " explained Capetonian hip-hop pioneer activist, producer and radio personality Shaheen Ariefdien. "I don't equate them with MTV or Nike, but this was just disrespectful."

To frustrated Black August organizer Baye Adofo, who had the thankless task of piecing together the rest of the tour and making it pay for itself after being abandoned by the local promoters, the complaints spoke to complicated issues of privilege.

"I felt that what people didn't want to hear about was American racism," he says. "But I do feel that we had a right to protest U.S. Racism at the World Conference Against Racism where Colin Powell and the U.S. wanted to deny that it existed. The issue became: Given how poor and racist other countries are, especially South Africa, was racism in the United States worthy of international attention?" With the agreement of the artists, Adofo organized free dates in the townships of Cape Town and Soweto.

"I don't know if these American MCs realize the impact they make on, say, a kid living in a shack in Khayelitsha [township] who's listening to what they say and trying to apply it to his own life," said another South African hip-hop activist, Marlon Burgess. "It would be quite interesting to know what life is like on that side of cultural imperialism."[8]

The Great Divide

If the arc of hip-hop generation's cultural revolution was bowing toward difficult issues of engagement and exploitation, its political revolution was just taking flight.

Born in 1965 to prominent civil rights organizers in North Carolina, Angela

Brown had been a child activist, leading campaigns to free Black women political prisoners. But her life changed in 1982, when the state of North Carolina decided to put a toxic waste landfill in the middle of a nearby working-class Black community. Brown and other teenage girls lay down on the road to prevent trucks from bringing in PCB-tainted soil for the landfill. That battle in Warren County became known as the opening shot in the environmental justice movement, a struggle that combined anti-racist and environmental activism.

A decade later, Brown was on the staff of the Atlanta-based civil rights stalwart, the Southern Organizing Committee, where she formed the Youth Task Force to organize youths from ten states and eighty-five universities into the environmental justice movement. She began to realize that a sharp, traumatic generational divide was emerging. Elders called her generation apathetic, but Brown saw a fundamentally different politics.

"The way in which they built their movement was around the 'lunch counter'—SNCC and others coming down to the South to challenge segregation on the lunch counter," she says. "We didn't have a single 'lunch counter.' We have had *many* 'lunch counters.' Our fight has been a constant barrage of struggles." No longer was there a single Movement, but dozens of movements—civil rights, education, environmental justice, AIDS, prisons, the list went on. But Brown noticed that where the dialogue really collapsed, where the generation gap was deepest, was over the question of hip-hop culture and rap music.

It was a divide that a fading Black Pennsylvania politician named C. Delores Tucker tried to exploit. Born in 1929 and raised in northern Philadelphia, Tucker inherited twenty-four tenement buildings from her parents and by 1966 had been singled out by the local newspaper as one of the city's worst slumlords. Her buildings were all soon boarded up, taken over by the city, given to charities or simply abandoned.[8]

Tucker's failures as a property manager did not stop her from seeking the civil rights limelight. She marched arm-in-arm with Martin Luther King Jr. in Selma and became a close ally of Jesse Jackson. She became a rainmaker for the Democratic Party and was appointed Pennsylvania's secretary of state in 1971, the highest-ranking Black woman official in the state's history. Six years later, she was fired by the Democratic governor for allegedly using state employees to write personal speeches and collecting kickbacks from charities.

In 1984, Tucker formed a lobby group called the National Political Congress of Black Women. Two years later, she became the chairwoman of the Democratic National Committee's Black Caucus. She then embarked on a series of unsuccessful runs for lieutenant governor and Congress before fading back into obscurity. In 1993, her friends Dionne Warwick and Melba Moore gave Tucker an opportunity to climb back into the spotlight when they approached her about having the NPCBW take up the fight against gangsta rap. Reverend Calvin Butts had already been steamrolling rap CDs in Harlem. They wanted in on the action.

Tucker repeated the same critique that hip-hop feminists had been leveling at media monopolies and rap misogynists for years. Corporations were not taking responsibility for the images they were distributing, and ducking serious discussion by hiding behind the First Amendment. But there was something disingenuous and opportunistic about her attacks.

Tucker won over both the liberal and conservative wings of her party by courting Senators Carol Moseley Braun and Joe Lieberman. Yet she also avidly welcomed the support of cultural conservatives like prominent Reagan/Bush cabinet member Bill Bennett. As the presidential election season rolled around, she joined with Republican candidate Bob Dole. Together, Bennett, Dole and Tucker made Suge Knight, Death Row Records and Snoop Dogg into clay pigeons for their culture war.

Tucker was enormously helpful to white cultural conservatives. In interviews, she compared herself to Martin Luther King and Rosa Parks and made an explicitly racial appeal that insulated white cult-cons from criticism. Tucker was also mouthing the most extreme fears of many disillusioned, middle-class, middle-aged people of color, the very same civil rights generation elders who felt they had given everything in struggle for their kids, only to see them turn out to be spoiled, anarchic, value-free ingrates. She attracted Blacks who supported police crackdowns and strengthening juvenile-crime laws, the very same elders with whom Angela Brown was having anguishing arguments. To the cult-cons, Tucker was mobilizing fresh troops for further attacks on youths of color.

In early 1994, Tucker prevailed upon Moseley Braun to convene an unprecedented Senate Judiciary Committee hearing on gangsta rap, an inquiry into "the effects of violent and demeaning imagery in popular music on American youth." Tucker was the star witness. Echoing right-wing backlash architects like

James Q. Wilson, John Dilulio and James Alan Fox, she called for a broadening of the War on Youth:

> As we have seen in the last thirty years, increasing law enforcement and correctional facilities have not reduced crime. These short-term fixes will do nothing to improve the lives of children like the nineteen that [sic] were recently removed from a home in Chicago because of parental neglect and abuse. Because of the lack of positive influences, their minds will be fertile and receptive ground for internalizing the violence glorified in gangster rap. Children such as these, our most neglected population, will become a social time bomb in our midst. Being coaxed by gangster rap, they will trigger a crime wave of epidemic proportions that we have never seen the likes of. Regardless of the number of jails built, it will not be enough. Neither will there be enough police or government programs to contain the explosion of crime. We as a Nation must act now and we must act decisively.[9]

The Return of Hip-Hop Activism

Brown and the Youth Task Force had heard enough. Not only had Tucker committed the political equivalent of taking a family argument public, she seemed to be calling down the wrath of the government on the hip-hop generation by arguing that sweep laws, new prisons, and profiling were *inadequate*, that youth culture also needed to be regulated. Not just bodies, but ideas needed to be contained. By articulating a broader basis for the politics of containment, Tucker had turned the debate over hip-hop culture misogyny and violence into something much worse—she had mobilized the elders to turn on their children, to join their enemies in a broad political and cultural attack on youth of color.

The Task Force reacted by organizing the Atlanta hip-hop community. They initiated a series of forums to defend hip-hop and constructively critique it. The forums brought artists like the Goodie Mob, Tupac and Afeni Shakur, and Lil' Jon and the Eastside Boyz together with elders, lawyers, scholars, activists, and poets. The Task Force catalyzed an active response in activism, the arts, and the record industry. Many now credit their work as laying the foundation for Atlanta's leap to the cutting edge of both the rap industry and hip-hop activism by the end of the decade.

Around the country, hip-hop heads took similar stands. These activists were not trying to stifle or chastise the artists Tucker-style, they were trying to create a sense of community and responsibility, and to define a new praxis of politics and culture. The aim was, as Maxine Waters had put it during the gangsta rap hearings, to "embrace and transform rather than to confront, isolate, and marginalize."[10] They were dealing with a unique paradox—a generation that had greater access to the media and culture than any other in history remained as politically scapegoated and marginalized as any in history. They called themselves "hip-hop activists" because the term spoke to the way culture and politics came together for them, and because it was a way to reclaim and define their generational identity.

In fact, the hip-hop generation was at least as, if not more, politically active than the civil rights generation. In 2001, the UCLA Freshman Survey—the definitive documentation of college-age youth attitudes since 1966—found that nearly half of all freshman said they had participated in an organized demonstration during the past year. That number was three times greater than in the inaugural survey, conducted at the peak of the civil rights movement.

Civil rights may have fixed an image of "The Movement" as picket-waving masses on the National Mall listening to Dr. King. If the youths weren't there in D.C., elders figured, nothing must be happening. But hip-hop activism largely took place below the national radar. Capitol Hill's diminished powers, big-money lobbying and campaign financing, and symbolic politics made it a less likely place than ever to go to get a problem solved. From Watergate to Monicagate, national politics often seemed just a lesser form of entertainment. Why bother marching on Washington?

The life-and-death struggles were happening at the local level, where hip-hop activists were busy fighting in the streets, neighborhoods, school boards, city halls, state legislatures and corporate offices. This time, the whole world would *not* be watching; global media monopolies could make sure of that. But the hip-hop generation was pushing forward in a complicated world, in more sophisticated ways than previous generations ever had.

Most visibly, Russell Simmons was assembling his hip-hop army, forming the Hip Hop Summit Action Network to bring together rappers, academics, music industry leaders, civil rights leaders, and politicians to push for social change. But the most compelling work was happening at the local level, outside of the traditional institutions. In Chicago, Brooklyn and Oakland, hip-hop activists used graffiti, b-boying, and DJing to educate and organize around education, gentrification, and juvenile justice issues. In Louisville, they fought book bans and youth curfews. In the Bay Area and the Bronx, they organized to stop the expansion of the juvenile detention facilities. In Albuquerque, they tossed out city council members who supported the building of a highway through sacred Native lands. On campuses across the country, they fought for labor unions, living wages, and against sweatshops and companies that invested in the prison industry.

In introducing *The Future 500*, a ground-breaking study of five hundred U.S. hip-hop activist and youth organizations, William "UPSKI" Wimsatt wrote, "Young people are noticing that the only thing that can't be bought sold, co-opted or marketed anymore is substantive political organizing and dissent."[11]

More War

The millennium would not open with a Y2K apocalypse or the fulfillment of an obscure prophecy, but with a very real explosion of rage against a decade of an expanding War on Youth.

In the streets of New York City, hip-hop activists took to the streets to protest Giuliani Time. Mayor Rudy Giuliani had implemented a zero-tolerance campaign focused on rooting out low-level "quality-of-life" crimes—the culmination of the Broken Windows theory—aimed at youths, the poor, the homeless and people of color. This zero-tolerance model would spread to urban centers across the country. It empowered a certain kind of lawless cop. In the summer of 1997, an innocent Haitian immigrant named Abner Louima was swept up and arrested when police broke up a fight outside an Afro-Caribbean nightclub in Brooklyn, then sodomized with a broom handle in the bathroom of the 70th precinct by outlaw cops.

The shock troops of the campaign were NYPD's Street Crime Units, mobilized into the poor neighborhoods at the borders of business districts. In 1997 and 1998, they stopped and frisked 45,000 people, mostly young, male and Black or brown. They were supposed to be stopping nuisance crimes, but their presence itself was a nuisance: fewer than nine thousand arrests were made.

In February 1999, a report of a rape led four Street Crime Unit cops to a Soundview apartment building two blocks from Bronx River Houses where they found a slim, Senegalese immigrant looking at them quizzically from the vestibule. When Amadou Diallo reached into his pocket to pull out his wallet, the cops fired forty-one shots, killing him with nineteen bullets. There were many more victims: Yong Xin Huang, a sixteen-year-old Chinese American; Gidone Busch, a thirty-one-year-old Hasidic Jew; Patrick Bailey, a twenty-year-old Jamaican immigrant; Anthony Baez, a twenty-nine-year-old Puerto Rican.

Three weeks after Diallo's killer cops were acquitted, an undercover cop approached Haitian-American Patrick Dorismond to ask where he could buy drugs. Dorismond refused to answer. He was trying to turn his life around and didn't need trouble. But the cop persisted and a scuffle broke out. Dorismond was shot dead in the chest. At his funeral in Brooklyn, policemen provoked funeral marchers by arriving in riot gear, then moved in with batons to make arrests. Rocks and bottles rained down on them from apartment windows. Hip-hop activists began angry street protests the following month.

In Los Angeles, the biggest police scandal in American history broke out in the Rampart Division, the same Westlake/Pico-Union neighborhood hit hard by the police and the INS after the riots. At Rampart, the rogue CRASH (Community Resources Against Street Hoodlums) anti-gang unit "jumped in" new members gang-style, kept a "CRASH pad" where they brought prostitutes to screw and get high, stole and resold confiscated cocaine, planted guns and drugs on gang members, and left many of them paralyzed or dead.

Just as the brutality and murders of New York City's Street Crimes Unit had been tolerated, Rampart CRASH's lawlessness was overlooked. Politicians demanded numbers that would support their tough-on-crime, tough-on-youth bonafides—arrests, confiscations, prosecutions, anything at all. The means to these ends were less important. Zero-tolerance only worked in one direction.

This attitude culminated in a March 2000 ballot initiative in California, numbered Proposition 21. The so-called Gang Violence and Juvenile Crime Prevention Act made it easier to unseal confidential juvenile records, to try juveniles as young as fourteen as adults or to send them to adult prisons, severely increased punishment for a number of juvenile crimes and expanded juvenile sentencing under Three-Strikes. Youths faced three years for just $400 of vandalism, or the death penalty for a "gang-related" homicide. Cops could wiretap young people they identified as gang members, and force them to be registered like sex offenders. Proposition 21 was counterintuitive. Juvenile crime rates were at their lowest levels since the mid-1960s. But on March 7, 2000, Proposition 21 passed with 62 percent of the vote.

If there was an upside, it was that six years of ballot attacks in Propositions 184, 187, 209 and 227 had fueled a widespread politicization of youth. In 1994, hundreds of thousands of Latino student activists had staged a statewide school walkout to protest Proposition 187, the largest Latino student protests since the 1970 Chicano Moratorium. Under constant attack, the youth movement built a strong infrastructure for protest. By the end of the century, some of the young hip-hop activists began making connections to other emerging movements.

In late November 1999, Jasmine De La Rosa, an organizer with the Bay Area's Third Eye Movement, and a contingent of hip-hop activists attended the biggest North American demonstrations in decades, the protests in Seattle at the meeting of World Trade Organization. "There were only a small number of hip-hop activists in Seattle because the World Trade Organization wasn't characterized in the words that we would understand. If motherfuckers heard, 'The leaders of the New World Order are trying to meet in Seattle,' I think that it might have brought more people," she said.

But Proposition 21 seemed to paint the New World Order in bold, vivid strokes. A month after the initiative passed, a bigger contingent of Californians joined hip-hop activists from Seattle, Boston and New York City at April 16, 2000, anti-corporate globalization protests at the World Bank and International Monetary Fund meetings in Washington, D.C. They began to see connections. After returning, De La Rosa said, "Worldwide, there's a militarization of the police forces. Governments are increasingly using them to push agendas that are intimately connected to the corporations."

Hoping to draw the links between the local and the global, hip-hop activists set their sights on the 2000 presidential election season. They had not forgotten that in the previous two elections their generation had been targeted and scapegoated. This time they would take a stand.

A Different Kind of Globalization

Few stories could illustrate the stakes for the hip-hop generation better than that of a Salvadoran ex-gangbanger in Los Angeles named Alex Sanchez.

The stocky, charismatic program director of a peace organization called Homies Unidos was a legend on the streets, working tirelessly to calm the violence between the warring Latino gangs that dominated the Pico-Union and Westlake neighborhoods, a role that won him the respect of gang members as well as some of California's leading politicians.

Nothing in life had ever come easy for Sanchez. He was working for peace in the most corrupt police precinct in the nation—LAPD's Rampart Division. And the U.S. government was trying to deport him to El Salvador, where he was certain to face execution.

Alex Sanchez was born in San Salvador in 1979. He fled with his family at the age of six to Los Angeles, a refugee of a brutal civil war which came to global attention after the Reagan-backed right-wing government assassinated six leftist opposition leaders. "When they got here, they'd already been through violence, they'd seen their fathers shot," says Tom Hayden, the 1960s activist who, as a state senator, became close to Sanchez. "And they get here and there's Mexican gangs and Black gangs, so they form gangs to claim a space."

During the late 1980s, Sanchez's family obtained green cards, but Sanchez had run away from home by that time. He was rolling with Mara Salvatrucha (MS-13), a gang swelling with disaffected immigrant and second-generation Salvadoran youths. "It was a complete liberation, it was complete independence. I wanted to rebel against everybody," Sanchez says.

Emerging during the mid-1980s, the quickly expanding gang was soon bumping heads on the Pico-Union streets with the largely Chicano 18th Street Gang. Sanchez became known to other gang members and to police, and spent much of his teens shuttling in and out of juvenile detention facilities. When he became an adult, he went to prison for grand theft auto. After his bid was up in 1994, prison officials discovered he had never secured his citizenship papers and handed him over to the INS for deportation.

By then, Sanchez was trying to find a way out of the gangs. He had no desire to go back to San Salvador, but hoped he might at least get a chance at a new start. But when he stepped off the plane, he stared up at a nearby hillside and saw stenciled into it four chilling letters: MS-13.

The INS was literally exporting the American gang problem. The streets of San Salvador were now divided into warring turfs the same way they had been in Los Angeles. That was not the only source of violence and instability. After the Salvadoran civil war, shadowy right-wing vigilante squads had reorganized to launch a covert terrorist 'social cleansing' program. Mayra Gomez, El Salvador country specialist with Amnesty International USA, says the targets were "alleged criminals, prostitutes, street children and transvestites." Now, like many others throughout the southern hemisphere, San Salvador was suddenly not only rife with highly armed, CIA-trained, right-wing-driven death squads, but highly armed, U.S. street-trained, criminal-minded street gangs.

Deciding there was no future for him there and determined to get back to his newborn son, Sanchez again embarked on the long trek through Guatemala and Mexico back to *El Norte*. Near starvation, Sanchez crossed back across the border into Texas and made his way back to his old Los Angeles 'hood.

He reconciled with his family and tried to avoid his old gang hangouts, and he met Magdaleno Rose-Avila, the founder of Homies Unidos, who steered him toward peace work. Inspired by Rose-Avila's mentoring and hoping to do better for his newborn son, Sanchez joined Homies as a volunteer, removed many of his old gang tattoos, and began to turn his life around. He was a natural leader, and people knew he was no snitch. He won youths' respect. At one point, he prevented a bloody war with a simple three-way phone call.

"He took the kids out of the street, and took them to a church and showed them the different kinds of opportunities they could have. They went camping, they went to parks, they did theater," says Oscar Sanchez, Alex's brother. "They were getting an alternative to the traditional gang life of violence."

Alex also began to politicize the youths. In workshops and meetings he held at the Immanuel Presbyterian church, he brought in civil rights attorneys to educate the youths on their rights with police stops. Homies Unidos' efforts were bearing fruit in moving gang members off the streets. They partnered with a powerful new network of gang peacemakers across the city that included many veterans of the post-rebellion peace work.

So in 1999, Rampart CRASH cops began regularly harrassing Sanchez and his youths. Police called Homies' peace efforts a front for the creation of a "supergang," and increased their surveillance. "They would target everyone who came to the meetings," says Silvia Beltran, then a legislative aide to Tom Hayden. They followed Homies members and beat them. "At one point they came and asked the church leaders if they could come and spy on the meetings that the group had," Beltran says. "The pastor said no."

The cops tried to falsely pin an MS drive-by murder of an 18th Streeter on a fourteen-year-old who had been at a Homies meeting, and Sanchez agreed to testify on behalf of the teen. "At that point," Oscar says, "the cops really started targeting him, telling him that they were gonna arrest him, that they were gonna finish Homies Unidos one by one."

When Hayden came to the Immanuel Presbyterian to chair a State Senate investigation into police harassment and brutality, with Sanchez as the star witness, CRASH cops stormed in and searched the crowd for Sanchez. As it happened, Alex was late, walking in after Hayden had dispensed with the cops. He stepped forward to give his testimony to a shocked panel and audience. "I told them that they saw firsthand what we go through every day," Alex says. Before long, he understood how high the stakes were. The cops put a message on the street for him: Homies Unidos had six months to die.

There was also the threat of INS deportation hanging over him. Special Order 40, a Los Angeles executive order, had forbidden police intervention in immigration cases. But as the riots had demonstrated, police suspended the law at will. Police and immigration officials knew that if Homies leaders were deported, they would certainly end up dead in San Salvador, either at the hands of the right-wing death squads or the gang leadership. The death squads were known to eliminate criminal deportees, peacemaker or not, and the transnational gangs were directly threatened by Homies Unidos' peace efforts in Los Angeles and San Salvador. Five members of Homies Unidos had been deported to El Salvador—and all five were murdered, under mysterious circumstances.

Hayden brought Homies Unidos leaders to meet with INS officials and Salvadoran government officials, including San Salvador's mayor and police chief, to seek permanent visas, so that they could organize without fear of being deported. "[The INS] gives visas to undocumented people who are informants and spies for the police, so why not a peacemaker?" says Hayden. The San Salvador police chief confirmed that Sanchez's life would be in grave danger if he was deported. But the INS refused.

In January 2000, CRASH officers arrested Sanchez and turned him over to the INS, in blatant disregard of Special Order 40. Sanchez says that the police had no charges; he was arrested, simply to be handed to the INS. "I still have the pink slip [given to him at the police station] that says, 'Deportation proceedings,' " Sanchez says.

When hip-hop activists came to Los Angeles to demonstrate at the Democratic Party Convention in the middle of August 2000, Sanchez—who had spent so much of his life behind bars and was now trying now to do something positive with his life for the sake of so many others—was locked in an acrid, overheated, filthy INS Detention Facility at Terminal Island, awaiting his deportation hearing.

Our Streets

Two weeks before, in Philadelphia, hip-hop activists joined the network of protestors to shut down the business district on the first day of the Republican Convention. Dozens of tightly organized groups roamed through downtown intersections, waving pickets that described their causes—workers' rights, immigrants' rights, environment, corporate globalization, prisons, racial profiling. "Whose streets?" they chanted. "Our streets!"

On one highway offramp near the INS offices, three hundred hip-hop activists—half of them of color—faced down rows of riot cops and INS police. As the protestors and the cops stared across the divide at each other, the chant became: "This is what democracy looks like!" In the afternoon, the scene turned uglier, with horsebacked cops beating and arresting hundreds. By twilight, on the deserted Ben Franklin Parkway, a few abandoned cop cruisers sat in the middle of the street—tires deflated, paint-bomb-splattered, with FUCK THE POLICE tagged across them.

In Los Angeles, the activists moved into an unused former swap meet building across the street from MacArthur Park, at the edge of the Rampart Division, to prepare for the Democratic National Convention and set up a "Convergence Center." Ten cops stopped in for an impromptu warrantless search. Then they retreated to a rented apartment behind the Center, set up their surveillance equipment, and every once in a while, sent a ghetto bird to hover over the building. Although MacArthur Park was known as one of the city's hottest drug trafficking centers, it had taken the arrival of tens of thousands of DNC protestors for the LAPD to beef up patrols in the neighborhood.

Cops handed out jaywalking tickets. They wrote down license plate numbers of the cars in the parking lot. When a young activist posted her address on a website offering help to out-of-towners looking for housing, the cops raided her house. On Monday night, police pulled the plug in the middle of a Rage Against The Machine and Ozomatli concert outside the Staples Convention Center, setting off a mini-riot. Police fired tear gas and gave orders to disperse as kids screamed, "Fuck you, I won't do what you tell me!"

A few days later, marchers passed through the heart of the Pico-Union barrio. Dominique Nisperos, a Filipina who had just turned seventeen, was there with her crew of seven from the Central Valley town of Stockton. They were white, Black, Mexican and Chinese, all sporting black T-shirts and baggy pants, with black bandannas to cover their faces. A little wide-eyed and a little nervous, she said, "I hope I can do a good job here."

Moonshine was marching also, a tall, striking, dreadlocked sixteen-year-old Black girl from New York who had hitchhiked across the country to be there. After the demonstrations she would hitchhike back north. "I want to go up to the redwoods and live there for a while," she said. "I don't really have any plans, that's my only plan." On her T-shirt, she had scrawled, "Chant Down Babylon." A button of a bereted Huey Newton, shotgun in hand, adorned her beat-up grey backpack.

Silvia Beltran and Oscar Sanchez were there too, holding pickets adorned with a photo of a charismatic Latino and words that read, FREE ALEX SANCHEZ. Beltran and Sanchez were marching with thousands to demonstrate at the doorstep of the Rampart Division.

Earlier, Tom Hayden, the veteran of the 1968 Democratic Convention riots in Chicago, stood on the back of a flatbed truck in MacArthur Park, and told the crowd Alex Sanchez's story. He said that Alex had begun a hunger strike to protest the prison conditions at Terminal Island, and had organized a hundred others to join him. The crowd roared. "This is a dangerous place," he said. "Have good heart, have no fear."

By now, the CRASH units had been dismantled by LAPD. But part of the Democratic platform being touted a couple of miles away at the Staples Convention Center was a proposal to hire 10,000 new prosecutors and 50,000 new police to match the 100,000 added during the Clinton-Gore administration. Even as the Street Crime Units and CRASH squads had come under fire, there was no discussion of community-based solutions. But the problem, community leaders were saying, was not that the elite police units had been taken off the streets, it was that the peacemakers like Alex Sanchez had been had off the streets.

A month later, Sanchez was released by a federal judge. Under pressure from Hayden's office, the U.S. Attorney dropped its illegal reentry case. The INS continued to press its bid for deportation, and in 2002, a federal judge finally granted Sanchez political asylum in 2002, allowing him to apply for citizenship status. "Now I don't have to run anymore," Alex said.[12]

But he also was aware that while he had been locked down at Terminal Island, gang homicides had again begun to skyrocket on the streets of Los Angeles, ending ten years of steep decline. The jobs were not there. The guns and the beefs still were. A new breed of gang members was coming up. The cycle was turning again.

No Words

The hip-hop activists who gathered at the most poignant protest that summer week in Los Angeles were not seeking a confrontation with police. Instead they had come to peacefully dramatize their causes: women's issues, immigrant rights, sweatshop labor, transportation policy, educational access.

They were organized like an army. At 9 A.M, on August 15, the sun already burning hard and clear, a thousand of them, almost all of color, gathered to march at the Belmont Learning Center, a new school in the largely Latino and Filipino neighborhood just west of downtown.

The Belmont Learning Center had become a powerful symbol in the city. Located at the eastern edge of the Rampart Division at the midpoint between Echo Park, MacArthur Park, and downtown, in an impoverished inner city area, it was a desperately needed school. Kirti Baranwal, a twenty-five-year-old sixth-grade art teacher, said, "This is a high school that was built to reduce overcrowding. The reality is we do need new schools. Since 1978, L.A. Unified built eight new schools while enrollments increased by 10,000 people per year."

It had become the most expensive high school ever built in the nation, at a price tag of $200 million. But Belmont had hardly been an enlightened investment into an underserved community. Millions were blown on a bizarre plan to create retail commercial development on school property. Then parents and students were horrified to learn the new school had been built over abandoned oil wells. Soil testing showed high levels of toxicity, and experts warned of methane leaks. The site might literally blow up. So tens of millions more were spent on elaborate environmental mitigation. Outraged parents and students fought to have the school closed. Now the sparkling new three-story edifice was sitting completed but unused, a monument, they said, to corporate pollution and municipal profligacy.

"The thing is," Baranwal said, "people of color and working class people don't need to be given choices that aren't really choices. If the choice is between a school on a toxic site and no school, that's not a very good choice. Our kids deserve real options."

So now the youths gathered to march toward downtown to make a statement. Some wore red-shirts emblazoned with the words: "Justice For Youth." Some sported T-shirts and banners that proclaim their affiliations: African Student Union, MEChA, Samahang Pilipino, Asian Left Forum. Others proclaimed their passions: "The Ummah," "Freestyle Fellowship," "Chicana Nation."

A flatbed truck travelling in the outer lane kept the group out of the westbound lanes and moving up the hill. It was outfitted with graffiti murals, a turntable rig, a drum and conga set, and a bass amplifier. The rappers and musicians on the truck fed a steady stream of hip-hop beats, flipping DMX's "Ruff Ryders Anthem" into a chant that went, "Who-ooa no-ooo. Toxic schools got to go-ooo!"

The march had been organized by a collective of Latino student organizers, environmental justice activists, teachers, parents and students. The older youths were veterans of the Proposition 187 blowouts, the younger ones were moved by Proposition 21. They were asking for schools not jails, a return of affirmative action and an end to standardized testing.

As in Chicago 1968, the battle lines were drawn between an aging white establishment and young radicals. On Monday night at the Staples Convention Center, outgoing two-term President Bill Clinton had drawn long ovations by trumpeting the longest economic expansion since the Kennedy and Johnson administrations. The bloody convention protests of 1968 had also come at the end of a seven-year economic expansion during an eight-year Democratic rule.

And again as in 1968, only one who was young or poor or of color could quarrel with Clinton's triumphalism. Before Clinton's speech, failed presidential candidate Bill Bradley seemed to recognize as much. "You don't have to give up your idealism to be successful in America. You don't have to become complacent. To the contrary, you should be outraged over the undermining of our democracy, the poverty of so many American children, the absence of health care, the shame of racism," he said. "To all these young people who believe that America can be just, I say never give up and never never sell out."

As the march proceeded toward the Ronald Reagan State Building, twenty cop cars drew up behind them, and black vans disgorged black-clad riot cops, armed with a rubber bullet guns, a baker's dozen of silver tear-gas cannisters hanging from their shoulder vests. They ran alongside the march, stopped in baton-ready formation, and as the marchers continued down the street, they would break and jog ahead to the next block to reassemble.

The march moved forward, passing in front of a war memorial. The rappers on the flatbed truck were freestyling over a fat bass line and drum snap, tumbling sheets of words throwing off history's weight. Four young women began to dance, and spontaneous movement rippled up and down the march line. Now the chant was a joyous, middle-finger salute to the cops: "This is how we protest—nonviolent!" When they arrived in front of the State Building, these daughters and sons of the revolution—to whom so much had been given, from whom so much had been stolen—stopped and turned to face the offices above.

They united in a single defiant gesture. They stopped the march. They stopped the music. They bowed their heads, and against a granite sky in the filling silence of the midday city, a thousand proud fists rose into the air.

Tomorrow is the question.
Democratic Convention,
2000.

Photo © Peter Holderness

Appendix

Words, Images and Sounds: A Selected Resource Guide

LOOP 1. Babylon Is Burning: 1968–1977.

1. Necropolis: The Bronx and the Politics of Abandonment.

Word

Berman, Marshall. *All That Is Solid Melts into Air: The Experience of Modernity*. New York: Simon & Schuster, 1982.

Caro, Robert. *The Power Broker*. New York: Knopf, 1974.

Cowan, Paul. "On a Very Tense Frontier: Street-Fighting in the Bronx." In *The Village* Voice, June 22, 1972.

DeLillo, Don. *Underworld*. New York: Scribner, 1997.

Devastation/Resurrection: The South Bronx. Robert Jensen, project curator. New York: Bronx Museum of the Arts, 1980.

Jackson, Reggie, with Mike Lupica. *Reggie: The Autobiography*. New York: Villard, 1984.

Jonnes, Jill. *"We're Still Here": The Rise, Fall, and Resurrection of the South Bronx*. New York: Atlantic Monthly Press, 1986. Reprinted in 2003 as *South Bronx Rising: The Rise, Fall, and Resurrection of an American City*. New York City: Fordham University Press, 2002.

Plunz, Richard. *A History of Housing in New York City: Dwelling Type and Social Change in the American Metropolis*. New York: Columbia University Press, 1990.

Rampersad, Arnold. *Jackie Robinson: A Biography*. New York: Knopf, 1997.

The South Bronx: A Plan for Revitalization. Report prepared by the Office of the Mayor, Office of the Bronx Borough President, Department of City Planning, Office of Economic Development, Office of Management and Budget, Department of Housing Preservation and Development. December 1977.

Wallace, Deborah and Rodrick. *A Plague on Your Houses*. New York: Verso Books, 1998.

Vergara, Camilo José. *The New American Ghetto*. New Brunswick, N.J.: Rutgers University Press, 1995.

Image

CBS Reports: The Fire Next Door. Aired March 22, 1977. Viewable at the Museum of Television and Radio.

The Jeffersons. "Blackout." Jack Shea, director, Richard B. Eckhaus, writer. Aired January 21, 1978. Viewable at the Museum of Television and Radio.

Appendix

2. Sipple Out Deh: Jamaica's Roots Generation and the Cultural Turn.

Word

Barrett, Sr. Leonard. *The Rastafarians*. Boston: Beacon Press, 1988.

Barrow, Steve and Peter Dalton. *Reggae: The Rough Guide*. London & New York: Rough Guides/Penguin, 1997. Revised edition, 2001.

Bradley, Lloyd. *This Is Reggae Music: The Story of Jamaica's Music*. New York: Grove Press, 2000.

Chang, Kevin O'Brien and Wayne Chen. *Reggae Routes: The Story of Jamaican Music*. Philadelphia: Temple University Press, 1998.

Chanting Down Babylon. Nathaniel Samuel Murrell, William David Spencer and Adrian Anthony McFarlane, eds. Philadelphia: Temple University Press, 1998.

Chevannes, Barry. *Rastafari: Roots and Ideology*. Syracuse, N.Y.: Syracuse University Press, 1994.

Gunst, Laurie. *Born Fi Dead*. New York: Henry Holt, 1995.

Hopkinson, Nalo. *Midnight Robber*. New York: Warner Aspect, 2000.

Katz, David. *People Funny Boy: The Genius of Lee "Scratch" Perry*. London: Payback Press, 2000.

Katz, David. *Solid Foundation: An Oral History of Reggae*. New York: Bloomsbury, 2003.

Manley, Michael. *Struggle in the Periphery*. London: Third World Media Limited, 1982.

Nettleford, Rex, ed. *Jamaica in Independence: Essays on the Early Years*. Kingston: Heinemann Caribbean, 1989.

Stephens, Evelyne Huber and John D. Stephens. *Democratic Socialism in Jamaica*. London: Macmillan, 1986:

Stolzoff, Norman. *Wake the Town and Tell the People*. Durham: Duke University Press, 2000.

Image

Classic Albums: Catch a Fire. Jeremy Marre, director. Rhino Image, 2000.

Enter the Dragon. Robert Clouse, director. 1973, reissued on DVD, 1998.

The Harder They Come. Perry Henzell, director. 1973, reissued on Criterion DVD, 2000.

Heartland Reggae. James P. Lewis, director. 1978, reissued on DVD, 2001.

Life and Debt. DVD. Stephanie Black, director. Originally released 2001.

Rebel Music: The Bob Marley Story. Jeremy Marre, director. Island/Tuff Gong, 2001.

Rockers. Theodorus Bafaloukos, director. 1977, reissued on DVD, 2000.

Sound

The Abyssinians and Friends, *Tree of Satta, Volume 1*. Blood and Fire Records, 2004.

Augustus Pablo. *Classic Rockers*. CD. Island Jamaica, 1995. Includes Jacob Miller's "Baby I Love You So."

——. *King Tubbys Meets Rockers Uptown Deluxe Edition*. LP. Clocktower, 1976. CD. Shanachie, 2003.

——. *Original Rockers*. CD. Greensleeves, 2001. Originally released 1979.

Bob Marley and The Wailers. *Catch a Fire: Deluxe Edition*. 2-CD. Tuff Gong/Island, 2001. Originally released 1973.

——. "Chances Are." 45 rpm single. Cotillion, 1981.

——. *Confrontation*. CD. Tuff Gong/Island, 1983.

——. *Exodus: Deluxe Edition*. 2-CD. Tuff Gong/Island, 2001. Originally released 1977.

——. *Rastaman Vibration*. CD. Tuff Gong/Island. Originally released 1976.

——. *Trenchtown Rock Anthology '69–'78*. 2-CD. Trojan, 2002. Features 1971 Lee "Scratch" Perry productions of "Small Axe" and "Dreamland."

Bunny Wailer. *Blackheart Man*. LP. Mango, 1976.

The Congos. *The Heart of the Congos*. 2-CD. Blood and Fire, 1996. Originally released 1977.

Count Ossie & The Mystic Revelation of Rastafari. *Grounation*. 3-LP. MRR Records, 1973.

Culture. *Two Sevens Clash*. LP. Shanachie, 1987. Originally released 1976.

Dennis Brown. *Brown Sugar*. LP. Dynamic Sounds, 1986.

Duke Reid. *Duke Reid's Treasure Chest*. 2-CD. Heartbeat, 1992.

Harry Mudie. *Meet King Tubby's In Dub Conference, Vol. 1–Vol. 3*. LP. Moodisc, 1975–1977.

The Harder They Come: Deluxe Edition. 2-CD. Island, 2003. Originally released 1973.

The Heptones. *Party Time*. LP. Mango, 1977.

Jacob Miller. *Songbook: Chapter a Day*. 2-CD. VP, 1999.

Joe Gibbs and The Professionals. *State of Emergency*. LP. Rocky One, 1999. Originally released 1976.

——. *African Dub All-Mighty Chapters 1–3*. LP. Rocky One, 1994–95. Originally released 1975–78.

Keith Hudson. *Brand*. Also known as *The Joint*. LP. Pressure Sounds, 1995. Originally released 1977.

——. *Rasta Communication*. CD. Greensleeves, 2002. Originally released 1978.

Lee Scratch Perry. *Arkology*. 3-CD. Island, 1997.

——. *Super Ape*. LP. Mango, 1976.

Let's Do Rocksteady: The Story of Rocksteady, 1964–1968. 2-CD. Trojan, 2002.

Little Roy. *Tafari Earth Uprising*. CD. Pressure Sounds, 1996.

Max Romeo. *War In a Babylon*. LP. Mango, 1976.

Appendix

Mighty Diamonds. *Right Time*. LP. Virgin, 1976. Also available as *I Need A Roof*. Hitbound.

Niney the Observer. *Sledgehammer Dub*. CD. Motion, 2002. Originally released 1977.

Peter Tosh. *Equal Rights*. LP. CBS, 1977.

Prince Far I. *Under Heavy Manners*. LP. Joe Gibbs, 1977.

The Reggae Box. 4-CD. Hip-O, 2001.

Respect to Studio One. 2-CD. Heartbeat, 1994.

Rockers Soundtrack. LP Mango, 1979.

Studio One Story. 2-LP +DVD. Soul Jazz, 2002

Tapper Zukie. *MPLA*. CD. Caroline, 2001. Originally released 1976.

——. *Tappa Zukie in Dub*. CD. Blood and Fire, 1995. Originally released 1976.

This Is Reggae Music: The Golden Age 1960–1975. 4-CD. Trojan, 2004.

Tougher Than Tough: The Story of Reggae Music. 4-CD. Mango, 1993. Curated by Steve Barrow.

3. Blood and Fire, with Occasional Music: The Gangs of the Bronx

Word

The Black Panthers Speak. Philip S. Foner, ed. Philadelphia: J.B. Lippincott and Company, 1970.

Churchill, Ward, and Jim Vander Wall. *The COINTELPRO Papers: Documents from the FBI's Secret Wars Against Dissent in the United States*. Boston: South End Press, 1990.

Gale, William. *The Compound*. New York: Ballantine, 1977.

Hager, Steven. *Hip Hop: The Illustrated History of Break Dancing, Rap Music and Graffiti*. New York: St. Martin's Press, 1984. Reprinted in *Adventures in the Counterculture: From Hip Hop to High Times*. New York: High Times Press, 2002.

Levitt, Leonard. "The Rebirth of the Gangs." In *New York Sunday News Magazine Daily News*. August 20, 1972.

Roberts, John Storm. *The Latin Tinge: The Impact of Latin American Music on the United States*, second edition. New York: Oxford University Press, 1999.

Schneider, Eric C. *Vampires, Dragons, and Egyptian Kings: Youth Gangs in Post-War New York*. Princeton, N.J.: Princeton University Press, 1999.

Tolchin, Martin. "Gangs Spread Terror in the South Bronx." In the *New York Times*. January 16, 1973.

Weingarten, Gene. "East Bronx Story: Return of the Street Gangs." In *New York Magazine*. March 27. 1972.

More Word

The history of Bronx gangs is still a story waiting to be told in full. Gang histories—not just in the Bronx—remain largely oral. So I am full of gratitude to the following, all of whom were extraordinarily gracious with their recollections and time:

Afrika Bambaataa

Martine Barrat

BOM 5

Michael "Lucky Strike" Corral

Danny DeJesus

Henry Chalfant

Mike, Savage Skulls

Benjamin and Wanda Melendez

Felipe "Blackie" Mercado

Richie Perez

Carlos Suarez

Gabriel Torres

I am in special debt to the late Rita Fecher, who opened her library and her life to me, and to Richie Perez, the great organizer who has been a profound influence on the hip-hop generation. Both are greatly missed.

Image

Ain't Gonna Eat My Mind. Tony Batten, director. 1972. Viewable at Museum of Television and Radio.

80 Blocks From Tiffany's. VHS. Gary Weis, director. 1979.

The 51st State: Bronx Gangs. Patrick Watson, host. 1972. Viewable at Museum of Television and Radio.

Flyin' Cut Sleeves. Rita Fecher and Henry Chalfant, co-producers. Henry Chalfant, director. 1993.

New York Illustrated: The Savage Skulls with Piri Thomas. Abigail Child, producer and writer. Aired WNBC, November 18, 1973. Viewable at Museum of Television and Radio.

You Do the Crime, You Do the Time. Martine Barrat, director. 1976.

Appendix

Sound

Eddie Palmieri. *Justicia*. CD. Sonida. Originally released 1970.

Ghetto Brothers. *Power–Fuerza!* LP. Mary Lou/Salsa International, 1972.

Grand Funk Railroad. *Closer to Home*. LP. Capitol, 1970.

Joe Bataan. *Best of Joe Bataan*. CD. Charly, 1997.

Joe Cuba. *The Best of Joe Cuba/Lo Mejor De Joe Cuba*. LP. Tico, 1972.

Ray Barretto. *Acid/Hard Hands*. CD. Nascente, 2001. Originally released 1968.

The Salsa All-Stars. *The Salsa All-Stars*. CD. Salsa International. Originally released 1968.

Santana. *Abraxas*. LP. CBS, 1970.

Willie Colon. *Asalto Navideño, Volumes 1 & 2*. CD. Fania. Originally released 1972–1973.

——. *El Malo*. LP. Fania, 1968.

4. Making a Name: How DJ Kool Herc Lost His Accent and Started Hip-Hop

Word

Hager, Steven. "The Herculords at the Hevalo." In *Record Magazine*. February 1985.

Kohl, Herbert. *Golden Boy as Anthony Cool: A Photo Essay on Naming and Graffiti*. New York: The Dial Press, 1972.

Mailer, Norman. *The Faith of Graffiti*. New York: Praeger, 1974.

Powers, Stephen ESPO. *The Art of Getting Over: Graffiti at the Millennium*. New York: St. Martin's Press, 1999.

Stewart, Jack. *Subway Graffiti: An Aesthetic Study of Graffiti on the Subway System of New York City*. Dissertation for Doctor of Philosophy. School of Education, Health, Nursing, and Arts Professions. New York University, 1989.

Style: Writing from the UnderGround, Revolutions of Aerosol Linguistics. Italy: Stampa Alternativa and IGTimes, 1996.

Sound

Big Youth. *Natty Universal Dread: 1973–1979*. 3-CD. Blood and Fire, 2000.

Dennis Coffey. *Evolution*. LP. Sussex, 1971.

James Brown. *Star Time*. 4-CD. Polygram, 1991.

Mandrill. *Fencewalk: The Anthology*. 2-CD. Polygram, 1997.

Michael Viner's Incredible Bongo Band. *Bongo Rock: The Story of the Incredible Bongo Band*. 2-LP. Strut, 2001.

Rare Earth. *Get Ready*. LP. Motown, 1969.

Shaft in Africa Soundtrack. LP. ABC, 1973.

LOOP 2. Planet Rock: 1975–1986.

5. Soul Salvation: The Mystery and Faith of Afrika Bambaataa.

Word

Hager, Steven. "Afrika Bambaataa's Hip Hop." In *The Village Voice*. September 21, 1982. Also available in *And It Don't Stop: The Best American Hip-Hop Journalism of the Last 25 Years*, edited by Raquel Cepeda. New York: Faber & Faber, 2004.

Jardim, Gary. "The Great Facilitator." In *The Village Voice*. October 2, 1984.

Rivera, Raquel Z. *New York Ricans from the Hip Hop Zone*. New York: Palgrave, 2003.

Toop, David. *The Rap Attack: African Jive to New York Hip-Hop*. New York: South End Press, 1984.

"Two shot dead in Bronx duel." In *Amsterdam News*. January 11, 1975.

Universal Zulu Nation. "Infinity Lessons." No date listed.

Universal Zulu Nation website. "Afrika Bambaataa biography." http://www.zulunation.com/afrika.html.

Vincent, Rickey. *Funk: The Music, the People, and the Rhythm of the One*. New York: St. Martin's Press, 1996.

Image

Assault on Precinct 13. DVD. Originally released 1976.

Fort Apache: The Bronx. DVD. Originally released 1981.

The Warriors. DVD. Originally released 1979.

Zulu. DVD. Originally released 1964.

Sound

Afrika Bambaataa and Family. "Bambaataa's Theme." b/w "Tension." 12-inch single. Tommy Boy, 1986.

Death Mix: The Best of Paul Winley Records. 2-LP. Landspeed, 2001. Includes "Zulu Nation Throwdown, Parts 1 and 2" and "Death Mix, Parts 1 and 2."

P Brothers. "Zulu Beat Mixtape." CD. 2004.

Parliament. *Mothership Connection*. LP. Casablanca, 1976.

Sly and The Family Stone. *Stand!* LP. CBS, 1969.

——. *There's a Riot Goin' On*. LP. CBS, 1971.

Ultimate Breaks and Beats, SB-501. LP. Street Beat Records, 1986.

Ultimate Breaks and Beats, SB-505. LP. Street Beat Records, 1986.

Zulu Nation. *Bronx River Center*. Mixtape. 1980.

6. Furious Styles: The Evolution of Style in the Seven-Mile World.

Word

Brewster, Bill, and Frank Broughton, *Last Night a DJ Saved My Life: The History of the Disc Jockey.* New York: Grove Press, 2000.

Chalfant, Henry, and Martha Cooper. *Subway Art.* London: Thames and Hudson, 1984.

Fernando, S. H. *The New Beats: Exploring the Music, Culture and Attitudes of Hip-Hop.* New York: Anchor, 1994.

Goldstein, Richard. "This Thing Has Gotten Completely Out of Hand." In *New York Magazine.* March 26, 1973.

Hazzard-Gordon, Katrina. *Jookin': The Rise of Social Dance Formations in African-American Culture.* Philadelphia: Temple University Press, 1992.

Hurston, Zora Neale. *Folklore, Memoirs, and Other Writings.* New York: Library of America, 1995.

Miller, Ivor. *Aerosol Kingdom: Subway Painters of New York City.* Jackson, Miss.: University Press of Mississippi, 2002.

Rap Pages. "Don't Stop The Body Rock: The Dance Special." Guest editors, Cristina Verán and Ben Higa. September 1996.

——. "Play That Beat: The DJ Special." Guest editors Chairman Mao. (Jeff Mao) and DJ Zen (Jeff Chang). April 1996.

——. "Out for Fame: Graf Pages Special." Guest editors, Rock A. Party (Sacha Jenkins) and Ben Higa. February 1996.

Rose, Tricia. *Black Noise: Rap Music and Black Culture in Contemporary America.* Hanover: Wesleyan University Press, 1994.

Stearns, Marshall and Jean. *Jazz Dance: The Story of American Vernacular Dance.* Cambridge, Mass.: DaCapo Press, 1994.

Image

The Freshest Kids: A History of the B-Boy From The Boogie Down Bronx and Beyond. DVD. Israel, director. 2002.

DMC B-Boy Foundations. Hosted by Popmaster Fabel. Featuring Trac-2, Mr. Freeze and B-Boy Fever One. VHS. Jorge FABEL Pabon, director. 1999.

Scratch. 2-DVD. Doug Pray, director. 2002. Originally released 2001.

Stations of the Elevated. VHS. Manny Kirchheimer, director. 1980.

Sound

Grandmaster Flash and the Furious Five. "The Adventures of Grandmaster Flash on the Wheels of Steel." 12-inch single. Sugar Hill, 1981.

——. "Flash It to the Beat," b/w "Fusion Beats, Volume 2." 12-inch single. Bozo Meko, 1982.

Mandalit Del Barco. "Origins of Breakdancing." Aired on National Public Radio, October 14, 2002. http://www.npr.org/programs/morning/features/patc/breakdancing/

7. The World Is Ours: The Survival and Transformation of Bronx Style.

Word

Austin, Joe. *Taking the Train: How Graffiti Art Became an Urban Crisis in New York City*. New York: Columbia University Press, 2001.

Castleman, Craig. *Getting Up: Subway Graffiti in New York*. Cambridge, Mass.: The MIT Press, 1982.

Chalfant, Henry, and Jim Prigoff. *Spraycan Art*. London: Thames and Hudson, 1987.

Fricke, Jim and Charlie Ahearn, eds. *Yes Yes Y'all: The Experience Music Project Oral History of Hip-Hop's First Decade*. Cambridge, Mass.: Da Capo Press, 2002.

Glazer, Nathan. "On Subway Graffiti in New York." In *Public Interest*. Winter 1979.

Wilson, James Q. and George Kelling. "Broken Window: The Police and Neighborhood Safety." In *Atlantic Monthly*. March 1982. http://www.theatlantic.com/politics/crime/windows.htm

Image

Roots of Rap: Sugar Hill Records. VHS. Rhino, 1998.

Sound

The Best of Enjoy! Records. 2-LP. Hot Productions, 1990.

Chic. "Good Times." 12-inch single. Atlantic, 1979.

Fatback Band. "You're My Candy Sweet" b/w "King Tim III Personality Jock." 12-inch single. Spring, 1979.

Grandmaster Flash and The Furious Five. "Superappin'." 12-inch single. Enjoy, 1979.

Jimmy Castor. "It's Just Begun." 12-inch single. Salsoul, 1983.

The Jimmy Castor Bunch. *It's Just Begun*. LP. RCA, 1972.

Kurtis Blow. *Kurtis Blow*. LP. Phonogram, 1980.

MFSB. *TSOP*. LP. CBS, 1975.

The Sugar Hill Gang. "Rapper's Delight." 12-inch single. Sugar Hill, 1979.

The Sugar Hill Records Story. 5-CD. Rhino, 1997.

Ultimate Breaks and Beats, SB-506. LP. Street Beat Records, 1986.

Ultimate Breaks and Beats, SB-524. LP. Street Beat Records, 1990.

8. Zulus on a Time Bomb. Hip-Hop Meets the Rockers Downtown.

Word

Banes, Sally. "To the Beat Y'all: Breaking Is Hard to Do." In *The Village Voice*. April 22–28, 1981. Also available in *And It Don't Stop: The Best American Hip-Hop Journalism of the Last 25 Years*, edited by Raquel Cepeda. New York: Faber & Faber, 2004.

——. "Breakdancing: A Reporter's Story." In *Folklife Annual*. 1986. Includes photos by Martha Cooper.

Bromberg, Craig. *The Wicked Ways of Malcolm McLaren*. New York: HarperCollins, 1989.

Coming from the Subway: New York Graffiti Art. France: VBI, 1992.

Cooper, Martha, with interviews by Akim Walta. *The Hip-Hop Files: Photographs 1979–1984*. Germany: From Here to Fame, 2004.

Goldstein, Richard. "The Fire Down Below." In *The Village Voice*. December 24–28, 1980.

Hess, Elizabeth. "Graffiti R.I.P.: How The Art World Loved 'Em and Left 'Em." In *The Village Voice*. December 22, 1987.

New York Graffiti @ 149 St. website http://www.at149st.com

Witten, Andrew ZEPHYR, and Michael White. *Dondi White Style Master General*. New York: Regan Books, 2001.

Zephyr Graffiti website. http://www.zephyrgraffiti.com

Image

Downtown 81. DVD. Edo Bertoglio, director. Patrick Montgomery and Glen O'Brien, co-producers. Originally released 1981.

Duck Rock. VHS. Malcolm McLaren, producer and director, 1983.

Style Wars. Tony Silver, director. Tony Silver and Henry Chalfant, producers. 1983.

Westway to the World. DVD. Don Lefts, director. 2001. Includes "Clash on Broadway" filmed in 1981.

Sound

The Clash. *The Clash*. LP. U.S. Version. Epic, 1979.

——. *Sandinista!* 3-LP. Epic, 1981.

ESG. *A South Bronx Story*. 2-LP. Soul Jazz, 2000.

"Live Convention '81." 12-inch single. Disco Wax, 1981.

"Live Convention '82." 12-inch single. Disco Wax, 1982.

Malcolm McLaren. *Duck Rock*. LP. Island, 1983.

Soweto Never Sleeps. LP. Shanachie, 1986.

9. 1982: Rapture in Reagan's America.

Word

Futura 2000. *Futura*. London: Booth-Clibborn Editions, 2000.

George, Nelson, Sally Banes, Susan Flinker, and Patty Romanowski. *Fresh: Hip Hop Don't Stop*. New York: Random House/Sarah Lazin, 1985.

Hershkovits, David. "London Rocks, Pans Bums, and the B-Boys Break a Leg." In *And It Don't Stop: The Best American Hip-Hop Journalism of the Last 25 Years*, edited by Raquel Cepeda. New York: Faber & Faber, 2004. Originally published in *Sunday News Magazine,* April 3, 1983.

Jenkins, Sacha, Elliott Wilson, Chairman Mao, Gabriel Alvarez, and Brent Rollins. *Ego Trip's Book of Rap Lists*. New York: St. Martin's Griffin, 1999.

Shabazz, Jamel. *Back in the Days*. New York: powerHouse, 2001.

Image

Graffiti Rock and Other Hip-Hop Delights. DVD. 2002. Originally aired 1984.

Wild Style. DVD. Charlie Ahearn, director. 2002. Originally released 1982.

Sounds

Black Uhuru. *Red*. LP. Island, 1981.

Blondie. "Rapture." 12-inch single. Chrysalis, 1981.

DJ Charlie Chase. *DJ Charlie Chase Presents Cold Crush Brothers Vs. Fantastic Romantic 5 From Harlem World 1981*. 2-LP. Charlie Chase Entertainment/Slammin' Records, 1998.

Fab 5 Freddy and B-Side. "Change the Beat." 12-inch single. Celluloid, 1982.

Grandmaster Flash. *The Message*. LP. Sugar Hill, 1982.

Kurtis Blow. *I'm Tough*. EP. Mercury. 1982.

The Perfect Beats, Volumes 1–4. CD. Tommy Boy/Timber!, 1998.

Phase 2. "The Roxy." 12-inch single. Celluloid, 1982.

Steinski. *Beg, Borrow, & Steal: A Steinski Archive*. CD. Unreleased CD-R, 2002.

Timezone. "The Wildstyle." 12-inch single. Celluloid, 1983.

Tommy Boy Greatest Beats. 2-LP. Tommy Boy, 1985. This is the original all electro set.

Tom Tom Club. "Genius of Love." 12-inch single. Sire, 1981.

Trouble Funk. *Drop the Bomb*. LP. Sugar Hill, 1982.

Wild Style Soundtrack. CD. Rhino, 1997, with bonus tracks. Originally released 1983.

Appendix

10. End of Innocence: The Fall of the Old School

Word

Banes, Sally. "Breaking Changing." In *The Village Voice*. June 12, 1984.

Cockburn, Alexander, and Jeffrey St. Clair. *White Out: The CIA, Drugs, and The Press*. New York: Verso, 1998.

Dawson, Alexander, "Art and Soul: FUTURA 2000." In *Wax Poetics*. Issue 6, Fall 2003.

Glueck, Grace. "Gallery View: On Canvas, Yes, But Still Eyesores," In the *New York Times*. December 25, 1983.

Goldstein, Richard. "The Future of Graffiti." In *The Village Voice*. December 13, 1983.

Hargreaves, Clare. *Snowfields*. New York: Holmes & Meier Publishers, 1992.

Jonnes, Jill, Hep Cats, Narcs, and Pipe Dreams: *A History of America's Romance with Illegal Drugs*. New York: Scribner, 1996.

Lusane, Clarence. *Pipe Dream Blues*. Boston: South End Press, 1991.

McCoy, Alfred. *The Politics of Heroin: CIA Complicity in the Global Drug Trade*. Chicago: Lawrence Hill Books, 1991.

Marshall, Richard, et al. *Jean-Michel Basquiat*. New York: Harry Abrams, 1993.

Scott, Peter Dale, and Jonathan Marshall. *Cocaine Politics: Drugs, Armies, and the CIA in Central America*. Berkeley: University of California Press, 1991.

Sidney Janis Gallery. *Post-Graffiti*. New York, 1983.

Sussman, Elizabeth, et al. *Keith Haring*. New York: Whitney Museum of American Art, 1997.

Streatfield, Dominic, Cocaine: *An Unauthorized Biography*. New York: Thomas Dunne Books, 2001.

Watkins, S. Craig. *Representing: Hip Hop Culture and the Production of Black Cinema*. Chicago: University of Chicago Press, 1998

Webb, Gary. *Dark Alliance: The CIA, the Contras, and the Crack Cocaine Explosion*. New York: Seven Stories Press, 1998.

Image

Beat Street. VHS. Stan Lathan, director. Harry Belafonte, producer. 1984.

Breakin'. VHS. Joel Silberg, director. 1984.

Flashdance. VHS. Adrian Lyne, director. 1983.

Run-DMC: The Video. VHS. 1987.

Sounds

Afrika Bambaataa. *Looking for the Perfect Beat 1980–1985*. CD. Tommy Boy, 2001.

Afrika Bambaataa and Soulsonic Force. "Renegades of Funk" b/w "Renegades Chant." 12-inch single. Tommy Boy, 1983.

Dillinger. "Cokane in My Brain" b/w "Buckingham Palace/Ragnampiza." 12-inch single. Mango, 1977.

Ego Trip's The Big Playback. CD. Rawkus, 2000.

Ice T. "Dog N' The Wax Ya Don't Quit Part II" b/w "6 in the Morning." 12-inch single. Techno-Hop, 1986.

Manu Dibango. *Makossa Man*. LP. Atlantic, 1974. Originally released 1973.

Run DMC. *Raising Hell*. LP. Profile, 1986.

——. *Run DMC*. LP. Profile, 1983.

Schoolly D. *Schoolly*. LP. Schoolly-D Records, 1985. Reissued as *The Adventures of Schoolly D*, Rykodisc.

Willie Colon. *The Big Break/La Gran Fuga*. LP. Fania, 1976.

LOOP 3. The Message: 1984–1992.

11. Things Fall Apart: The Rise of the Post–Civil Rights Era

Word

Alexander, Amy, ed. *The Farrakhan Factor*. New York: Grove, 1998.

Baker, Pauline. *The United States and South Africa: The Reagan Years*. New York: Ford Foundation and the Foreign Policy Association, 1989.

Barlett, Donald L., and James B. Steele. *America: Who Really Pays Taxes?* New York: Touchstone, 1994.

Clegg III, Claude A. *An Original Man: The Life and Times of Elijah Muhammad*. New York: St. Martin's Press, 2000.

Collins, Chuck, and Felice Yeskel, with United for a Fair Economy. *Economic Apartheid in America*. New York: The New Press, 2000.

Culbertson, Donald. *Contesting Apartheid US Activism, 1967–1980*. Boulder, Colo.: Westview Press, 1999.

Evanzz, Karl. *The Messenger: The Rise and Fall of Elijah Muhammad*. New York: Random House, 1999.

Gardell, Mattias. *In the Name of Elijah Muhammad: Louis Farrakhan and the Nation of Islam*. Durham, N.C.: Duke University Press, 1996.

Lincoln, C. Eric. *The Black Muslims in America*, third edition. Grand Rapids, Mich.: William B. Eerdmans and Africa World Press, 1994.

Appendix

Magida, Arthur. *Prophet of Rage: A Life of Louis Farrakhan and His Nation.* New York: Harper-Collins, 1996.

Marable, Manning. *Beyond Black and White: Transforming African American Politics.* New York: Verso, 1995.

Massey, Douglas, and Nancy A. Denton. *American Apartheid. Segregation and the Making of the Underclass.* Cambridge, Mass.: Harvard University Press, 1993.

Mollenkopf, John H. *New, York City in the 1980s: A Social Economic and Political Atlas.* New York: Simon and Schuster, 1993.

Muhammad, Toure. *Chronology of Nation of Islam History: Highlights of the Honorable Minister Louis Farrakhan and the Nation of Islam, 1977–1996.* Chicago: Steal Away Productions, 1996.

Orfield, Gary, with Sara Schley, Diane Glass, and Sean Reardon. "The Growth of Segregation in American Schools: Changing Patterns of Separation and Poverty Since 1968." A Report of the Harvard Project on School Desegregation to the National School Boards Association. December 1993.

Phillips, Kevin. *The Politics of Rich and Poor: Wealth and the American Electorate in the Reagan Aftermath.* New York: Harper Perennial, 1990.

Wolff, Edward N. *Top Heavy: A Study of The Increasing Inequality of Wealth in America.* New York: The Twentieth Century Fund Press, 1995.

Image

Amandia! A Revolution In Four-Part Harmony. DVD. Lee Hirsch, director. 2003. Originally released 2002.

Rhythm of Resistance: Black South African Music. DVD. Jeremy Marre, director. Originally released 1979.

Sun City: Artists United Against Apartheid. VHS. 1985.

Sound

Artists United Against Apartheid. *Sun City.* EP. Manhattan, 1985.

B-Boys. "2,3 Break." 12-inch single. Vintertainment, 1983.

——. "Rock the House" b/w "Cuttin' Herbie." 12-inch single. Vintertainment, 1983.

Herbie Hancock. "Rockit." 12-inch single. Columbia, 1982.

"Hip-Hop on Wax, Volumes 1 and 2." 12-inch singles. Vintertainment, 1984.

Grandmixer DSt. "Crazy Cuts." 12-inch single. Celluloid, 1983.

Pumpkin and the Profile All-Stars. "Here Comes That Beat!" 12-inch single. Profile, 1984.

UTFO. "Roxanne Roxanne." 12-inch single. Select, 1984.

12. What We Got to Say: Black Suburbia, Segregation and Utopia in the Late 1980s.

Word

"A World Apart: Segregation on Long Island." In *Newsday*. 10-part series ran in September 1990.

Adler, Bill. "The South Bronx was getting a bad rap until a club called Disco Fever came along." In *People*. May 16, 1983. Also available in *And It Don't Stop: The Best American Hip-Hop Journalism of the Last 25 Years*, edited by Raquel Cepeda. New York: Faber & Faber, 2004.

Allen, Harry. "Public Enemy: Leading a Radio Rebellion." In *Black Radio Exclusive*. February 26, 1988.

——. "Soul Power." In *SPIN*. December 1987.

Chuck D, with Yusuf Jah. *Fight The Power: Rap Race and Reality*. New York: Delacorte Press, 1997.

Cose, Ellis. *The Rage of a Privileged Class*. New York: HarperCollins, 1993.

Frazier, E. Franklin. *Black Bourgeoise*. 2nd edition. New York: Free Press, 1962.

Leland, John. "Noise Annoys." In *The Village Voice*. April 21, 1987.

Mao, Chairman (Jefferson Mao). "The Microphone God." In *Vibe*. 1997.

Marriott, Rob. "Allah's on Me." In *XXL Magazine*. Issue #1, 1997. Also available in *And It Don't Stop: The Best American Hip-Hop Journalism of the Last 25 Years*, edited by Raquel Cepeda. New York: Faber & Faber, 2004.

Owen, Frank. "Def Not Dumb." In *Melody Maker*. March 21, 1987.

Pattillo-McCoy, Mary. *Black Picket Fences: Privilege and Peril Among the Black Middle Class*. Chicago: University of Chicago Press, 1999.

Pearson, Hugh. *The Shadow of the Panther: Huey Newton and the Price of Black Power in America*. Reading, Mass.: Addison-Wesley, 1994.

Reeves, Marcus. "Allah's Messenger." In *The Source*. December 1997.

Reynolds, Simon. "Strength to Strength." In *Melody Maker*. October 17, 1987.

Richards, Clay F. "Poll: Prejudice a Fact of Life." In *Newsday*. September 17, 1990.

Sinclair, John. *Guitar Army: Street Writings/Prison Writings*. New York: Douglas, 1971.

Tyson, Timothy B. *Radio Free Dixie: Robert F. Williams and the Roots of Black Power*. Chapel Hill: University of North Carolina Press, 1999.

Williams, Robert F. *Negroes with Guns*. Detroit: Wayne State University Press, 1998. Originally published 1962.

Image

Krush Groove. VHS. Michael Schultz, director. 1985.

School Daze. VHS. Spike Lee, director. 1988.

She's Gotta Have It. VHS. Spike Lee, director. 1986.

Sweet Sweetback's Baadasssss Song. DVD. Melvin Van Peebles, director. 1971.

Sound

Aleem. "Release Yourself." 12-inch single. Nia, 1984.

Beastie Boys. *Licensed to Ill*. LP. Def Jam, 1986.

Biz Markie. *Goin' Off*. LP. Cold Chillin', 1988.

Boogie Down Productions. *Criminal Minded*. LP. B-Boy, 1986.

De La Soul. *Three Feet High and Rising*. LP. Tommy Boy, 1988.

Dimples D. "Sucker DJs I Will Survive." 12-inch single. Party Time, 1983.

EPMD. *Strictly Business*. LP. Sleeping Bag, 1988.

Eric B. & Rakim. *Paid in Full: The Platinum Edition*. 2-CD. Island, 1998. Originally released 1987.

Har-You Percussion Group. *Har-You Percussion Group*. LP. Cubop Records, 1996. Originally released 1969.

The JB's. *Pass the Peas: The Best of The JB's*. CD. Polygram, 2000.

——. *Funky Good Time: The Anthology*. 2-CD. Polygram, 1995.

JVC Force. "Strong Island" b/w "Nu Skool" 12-inch single. B-Boy, 1987.

Kings Of Pressure. *Slang Teacher*. LP. Next Plateau, 1989.

MC Shan. "The Bridge" b/w "Beat Biter." 12-inch single. Bridge, 1986.

The Meters. *Funkify Your Life: The Meters Anthology*. 2-CD. Rhino, 1995.

Original Concept. *Straight From the Basement of Kooley High!* LP. Def Jam, 1988.

Parliament. *Chocolate City*. LP. Casablanca, 1975.

Public Enemy. *Yo! Bum Rush the Show*. LP. Def Jam, 1987.

Spectrum City. "Lies" b/w "Check Out the Radio." 12-inch single. Vanguard, 1984.

True Mathematics. *Greatest Hits*. LP. Select, 1988.

13. Follow for Now: The Question of Post–Civil Rights Black Leadership.

Word

Cole, Lewis. "Def or Dumb?" In *Rolling Stone*. October 19, 1989.

DeSantis, John. *For the Color of His Skin: The Murder of Yusuf Hawkins and the Trial of Bensonhurst*. New York: Pharos, 1991.

Ellis, Trey. "The New Black Aesthetic." In *Callaloo* 12, no. 1. Winter 1989.

Eure, Joseph D. and James G. Spady. *Nation Conscious Rap*. New York: PC International Press, 1991.

Frady, Marshall. *Jesse: The Life and Pilgrimage of Jesse Jackson*. New York: Random House, 1996.

Guerrero, Ed. *Do the Right Thing*. London: British Film Institute, 2001.

Howe, Stephen. *Afrocentrism: Mythical Pasts and Imagined Homes*. London: Verso, 1998.

Karenga, Maulana. *Introduction to Black Studies*, second edition. Los Angeles: University of Sankore Press, 1993.

Kim, Claire Jean. *Bitter Fruit: The Politics of Black-Korean Conflict in New York City*. New Haven Conn.: Yale University Press, 2000.

Lee, Spike, with Lisa Jones. *Do the Right Thing*. New York: Fireside, 1989.

Leland, John. "Armageddon In Effect." In *SPIN,* September 1988.

———. "Do the Right Thing." In *SPIN*. September 1989.

Mills, David. "Professor Griff: 'the Jews are wicked.' " In the *Washington Times*. May 22, 1989.

National Urban League. *Stop the Violence: Overcoming Self-Destruction, Rap Speaks Out*. Edited by Nelson George. New York: Pantheon, 1990.

Neal, Mark Anthony. *Soul Babies: Black Popular Culture and the Post-Soul Aesthetic*. New York: Routledge, 2002.

O'Hagan, Sean. "Rebels with a Cause." In *New Musical Express*. October 10, 1987.

Reed, Adolph. *The Jesse Jackson Phenomenon: The Crisis of Purpose in Afro-American Politics*. New Haven Conn.: Yale University Press, 1986.

Shakur, Assata. *Assata: An Autobiography*. London: Zed Books, 1987.

Smith, R. J. "The Enemy Within." In *The Village Voice*. June 20, 1989.

———. "Bring the Goys." In *The Village Voice*. June 27, 1989.

The Stud Brothers. "Black Power." In *Melody Maker*. May 28, 1988.

———. "Prophets of Rage." In *Melody Maker*. July 9, 1988.

Sullivan, Lisa Y. "The Demise of Black Civil Society: Once Upon A Time When We Were Colored Meets the Hip-Hop Generation." In *Social Policy*. Winter 1996.

Tate, Greg. *Flyboy in the Buttermilk: Essays on Contemporary America*. New York: Fireside, 1992.

Welsing, Frances Cress. *The Isis Papers: Keys to the Colors*. Third World Press, 1990.

White, Armond. "Bought. Can We Get a Witness?" In *The City Sun*. June 28–July 4, 1989.

Image

Do the Right Thing. 2-DVD. Criterion Collection, 2001. Includes "Fight the Power Video." Originally released 1989.

Public Enemy. *Fight the Power Live*. VHS. 1989.

——. *Tour of a Black Planet*. VHS. 1991.

Sound

A Tribe Called Quest. *People's Instinctive Travels and The Paths of Rhythm*. LP. Jive, 1990.

Black Riot. "A Day in the Life" b/w "Warlock." 12-inch single. Fourth Floor, 1988.

Boogie Down Productions. *By All Means Necessary*. LP. Jive, 1987.

Fishbone. *In Your Face*. LP. Columbia, 1986.

Living Colour. *Vivid*. LP. Epic, 1988.

Public Enemy. *It Takes a Nation of Millions to Hold Us Back*. LP. Def Jam, 1988.

——. "Fight the Power." 12-inch single. Motown, 1989.

——. "Welcome to the Terrordome." 12-inch single. Def Jam, 1989.

Stop the Violence Movement. *Self Destruction*. EP. Jive, 1989.

X-Clan. *To the East Blackwards*. LP. 4th and Broadway, 1990.

14. The Culture Assassins: Geography, Generation and Gangsta Rap.

Word

Alonso, Alejandro A. "Territoriality Among African American Street Gangs." M.A. thesis, University of Southern California, Department of Geography. May 1999.

Bakeer, Donald. *Crips: The Story of The L.A. Street Gang From 1971–1985*. Los Angeles: Precocious Publishing, 1987, 1992.

Bing, Leon. *Do or Die*. New York: HarperCollins, 1991.

Bond, J. Max. *The Negro in Los Angeles*. Ph.D. dissertation, University of Southern California. June 1936.

Brown, Elaine. *A Taste of Power: A Black Woman's Story*. New York: Pantheon, 1992.

Cohen, Jerry, and William S. Murphy. *Burn, Baby, Burn! The Watts Riot*. New York: Avon, 1966.

Collins, Keith E. *Black Los Angeles: The Maturing of the Ghetto, 1940–1950*. Saratoga, Calif.: Century Twenty One Publishing, 1980.

Conot, Robert. *Rivers of Blood, Years of Darkness*. New York: Bantam, 1967.

Cross, Brian. *Its Not About a Salary: Rap, Race and Resistance in Los Angeles*. New York: Verso, 1993.

Davis, Angela Y. *With My Mind on Freedom: An Autobiography*. New York: Random House, 1974.

Davis, Mike. *City of Quartz: Excavating the Future in Los Angeles*. New York: Verso, 1990.

Gold, Jonathan. "N.W.A.: Hard Rap and Hype from the Streets of Compton." In *Los Angeles Weekly*. May 5–May 11, 1989.

Hawkins, Odie. *Scars and Memories: The Story of a Life.* Los Angeles: Holloway House, 1987.

Horne, Gerald. *Fire This Time: The Watts Uprisings and the 1960s.* New York: DaCapo Press, 1997.

Jackson, George. *Soledad Brother: The Prison Letters of George Jackson.* New York: Bantam, 1970.

Jah, Yusuf, and Sister Shah'Keyah. *Uprising: Crips and Bloods Tell the Story of America's Youth in the Crossfire.* New York: Touchstone, 1997.

Kelley, Robin D. G. *Race Rebels: Culture, Politics, and the Black Working Class.* New York: The Free Press, 1994.

Marriott, Rob, James Bernard, and Allen S. Gordon. "Reality Check," In *The Source.* June 1994.

Marsh, Dave, and Phyllis Pollack. "Wanted for Attitude." In *The Village Voice.* October 10, 1989.

McDermott, Terry. "Parental Advisory: Explicit Lyrics." In *Los Angeles Times Magazine.* April 14, 2002.

Olsen, Jack. *Last Man Standing: The Tragedy and Triumph of Geronimo Pratt.* New York: Doubleday, 2000.

Owen, Frank. "Hanging Tough." In *SPIN.* April 1990.

Palmer, Robert. *Deep Blues.* New York: Penguin, 1981.

Ro, Ronin. *Have Gun Will Travel.* New York: Doubleday, 1998.

Tackwood, Louis and Citizen's Research and Investigation Committee. *The Glass House Tapes.* New York: Avon, 1973.

Vigil, James. *A Rainbow of Gangs.* Austin, Tex.: University of Texas Press, 2002.

Watts Prophets. *Poetic Reflections.* Los Angeles: W. P. Publishing Company, 1993. Originally published 1976.

——. *The Rising Sons.* Los Angeles: W. P. Publishing Company, 1993. Originally published 1973.

Image

Colors. VHS. Dennis Hooper, director. 1988.

The Fire This Time. VHS. Randy Holland, director. Blacktop Films, 1993.

Sound

The Black Voices. *The Black Voices: On the Streets of Watts.* CD. FFRR, 1996. Originally released 1969.

C.I.A. Criminals In Action. "My Posse" b/w "Ill-Legal"/"Just 4 The Cash." 12-inch single. Kru-Cut, 1987.

Central Avenue Sounds: Jazz in Los Angeles, 1921–1956. 4-CD. Rhino, 1999.

Eazy E. "Boyz-N-The Hood" b/w "L.A. Is The Place"/"Fat Girl." 12-inch single. Macola, 1987.

Eazy E. *Eazy Duz It.* LP. Ruthless/Priority, 1988.

Mixmaster Spade and the Compton Posse. "Genius Is Back." 12-inch single. L.A. Posse, 1988.

NWA and the Posse. LP. Macola, 1987. Re-released by Priority in 1989.

The NWA Legacy, Volume 1: 1988–1998. 2-CD. Priority, 1999.

NWA. *Straight Outta Compton.* LP. Ruthless/Priority, 1988. Note: Cover bears a 1988 copy-right and copies were undoubtedly on the street in December 1988, but the official release date was January 25, 1989.

Street Kuts, Volume 1. LP. Instant, 1990. This import comp includes a number of KDAY hits from 1986 and 1987, like King Yee's "Payback's a Mutha," King Tee and Mixmaster Spade's "Ya Better Bring a Gun," Toddy Tee and Mixmaster Spade's "Do You Want to Go to the Liquor Store," Bobby Jimmy's "New York Rapper," and C.I.A.'s "My Posse."

Toddy Tee. "Batterram." 12-inch single. Epic, 1986.

Uncle Jam's Army. "Yes Yes Yes" b/w "Dial a Freak." 12-inch single. Freak Beat, 1984.

Watts Prophets. *Rapping Black in a White World.* CD. FFRR, 1996. Originally released 1971.

———. *When the 90s Came.* CD. FFRR, 1996.

World Class Wreckin Cru. *World Class.* LP. Kru-Cut, 1985.

Zapp & Roger. *We Can Make You Dance: The Zapp & Roger Anthology.* 2-CD. Rhino, 2002.

15. The Real Enemy: The Cultural Riot of Ice Cube's *Death Certificate.*

Word

Bobo, Lawrence, with James Johnson, Melvin Oliver, James Sidanius, and Camille Zubrinsky. "Public Opinion Before and After a Spring of Discontent." UCLA Center for the Study of Ur-ban Poverty, Occasional Working Paper Series, 3. Los Angeles: UCLA Center for the Study of Urban Poverty, September 1992.

Davis, Angela Y. "Black Nationalism: The Sixties and The Nineties." In *Black Popular Culture,* edited by Gina Dent. Seattle: Bay Press, 1992.

———. *Women, Culture, and Politics.* New York: Random House, 1989.

Dawsey, Darrell. "No Sympathy for the Devil." In *XXL Magazine.* 1997.

Ice Cube and Angela Y. Davis. "Nappy Happy." In *Transition.* Issue 58 1992.

Kim, Elaine H. "Home Is Where the Han Is." In *Reading Rodney King, Reading Urban Uprising.* New York: Routledge, 1993.

Kim, Sophia Kyung. "Ice Cube the Peacemaker." In *Korea Times.* May 4, 1992.

Madhubuti, Haki. *Black Men: Obsolete, Single, Dangerous?* Chicago: Third World Press, 1990.

Noel, Peter. "Unholy War: Khallid Muhammad and the Battle for The Nation of Islam." In *The Village Voice*. August 2, 1994.

Samuels, David. "The Rap on Rap." In the *New Republic*. November 11, 1991.

Suh, Dong. "The Source of Korean and African American Tensions." In *Asian Week*. February 21, 1992.

Image

"A Conversation with Angela Davis and Ice Cube." Priority Records Promotional video, 1991.

Boyz N The Hood. 2-DVD. John Singleton, director. 2003. Originally released 1993.

Sound

DJ Dank. *Greatest Malt Liquor Hits*. CD. Hip Hop History Series, 2003.

Ice Cube. *Amerikkka's Most Wanted*. LP. Priority, 1990.

——. *Death Certificate*. LP. Priority, 1991.

——. Promotional interview tape. Priority Records, Los Angeles, 1991.

Public Enemy. *Fear of a Black Planet*. 2-LP. Def Jam, 1990.

LOOP 4. Stakes Is High: 1992–2001.

16. Gonna Work It Out: Peace and Rebellion in Los Angeles.

Word

Baldwin, James. *The Evidence of Things Not Seen*. New York: Henry Holt, 1986.

Butler, Stuart. "The Urban Policy America Needs." In the Heritage Foundation Reports. Executive Memorandum No. 330. May 5. 1992.

Cannon, Lou. *Official Negligence*. New York: Times Books, 1997.

Davis, Mike. "In L.A., Burning All Illusions." In *The Nation*. June 1, 1992.

Gooding-Williams, Robert. *Reading Rodney King, Reading Urban Uprising*. New York: Routledge, 1993.

Hayden, Tom. *Street Wars: Gangs and the Future of Violence*. New York: The New Press, 2004.

Hazen, Don, ed. *Inside The L.A. Riots: What Really Happened and Why It Will Happen Again*. San Francisco: Institute for Alternative Journalism, 1992.

Kelly, Raegan. "Watts Love: The Truce Is ON!" In *URB Magazine*. Vol. 3, No. 6, Issue 30. 1993.

Krikorian, Michael, and Greg Kirikorian. "Watts Truce Holds Even As Hopes Fade." In the *Los Angeles Times*. May 18, 1997.

KoreAm Journal. "The Messengers: The L.A. Riots Ten Years Later" special issue. Volume 13, No. 4, April 2002.

Ong, Paul, and Suzanne Hee. *Losses in the Los Angeles Civil Unrest.* Los Angeles: Center for Pacific Rim Studies, University of California, Los Angeles, 1993.

Research Group on the Los Angeles Economy. *The Widening Divide: Income Inequallity and Poverty in Los Angeles.* Los Angeles: UCLA Urban Planning Program, 1989.

Shakur, Sanyika (Kody Scott). *Monster.* New York: Atlantic Monthly Press, 1993.

Senate Office of Research. *The South-Central Los Angeles and Koreatown Riots: A Study of Civil Unrest.* Sacramento, Calif.: State Senate Office of Research. June 17, 1992.

Staff of the *Los Angeles Times. Understanding the Riots: Los Angeles Before and After the Rodney King Case.* Los Angeles: *Los Angeles Times,* July 1992.

State of California Emergency Medical Services Authority. *Medical Care for the Injured: The Emergency Medical Response to the April 1992 Civil Disturbance.* March 1993. EMSA #393-01.

Image

Birth of a Nation: 4×29×92. Matthew McDaniel, director. 1994.

Menace II Society. DVD. Allen and Albert Hughes, directors. 1997. Originally released 1993.

Sa-i-gu. Dai Sil Kim-Gibson, Christine Choy, co-directors. 1993.

Straight from the Streets. VHS. Keith O'Derek and Robert Corsini, co-directors. 1999.

Sound

Cypress Hill. *Cypress Hill.* LP. Ruffhouse, 1991.

Da Lench Mob. *Guerillas in the Mist.* CD. Street Knowledge/East West, 1992.

WC and the MAAD Circle. *Ain't a Damn Thing Changed.* LP. Priority, 1991.

17. All in the Same Gang: The War on Youth and the Quest for Unity.

Word

Abramsky, Sasha. *Hard Time Blues: How Politics Built a Prison Nation.* New York: St. Martin's Press, 2002.

Building Blocks for Youth. *And Justice For Some.* 2000.
http://www.buildingblocksforyouth.org/justiceforsome/jfs.html.

Feld, Barry C. *Bad Kids: Race and the Transformation of the Juvenile Court.* New York: Oxford University Press, 1999.

Gore, Tipper. "Hate, Rape and Rap." In the *Washington Post.* January 8, 1990.

Ice T, as told to Heidi Siegmund. *The Ice Opinion.* New York: St. Martin's Press, 1994.

"Interview with Angela Davis." Conducted 1997. From PBS Web site, "The Two Nations of Black America." http://www.pbs.org/wgbh/pages/frontline/shows/race/interviews/davis.html.

Males, Mike. *Framing Youth: Ten Myths About the Next Generation*. Monroe, Maine: Common Courage Press, 1999.

Mauer, Marc, and The Sentencing Project. *Race to Incarcerate*. New York: The New Press 1999.

Rodriguez, Luis. *Hearts and Hands: Creating Community in Violent Times*. New York: Seven Stories Press, 2001.

Rodriguez, Luis, Cle "Bone" Sloan, and Kershaun "Lil Monster" Scott. "Gangs: The New Political Force in Los Angeles." In the *Los Angeles Times*. September 13, 1992.

Signorile, Michelangelo. "Queer in a Million." In *OUT Magazine*. February 1996. http://www.signorile.com/articles/outqiam.html.

Wilson, James Q. "Crime and Public Policy." In *Crime*. Editors, James Q. Wilson and Joan Petersilia. San Francisco: Institute for Contemporary Studies Press, 1995.

Zeidenburg, Jason, and Vince Schiraldi. *Cellblocks or Classrooms?: The Funding of Higher Education and Corrections and Its Impact on African American Men*. Washington, D.C.: Justice Policy Institute, 2002.

Zimring, Franklin. *American Youth Violence*. New York: Oxford University Press, 1998.

Sound

Above The Law. *Livin' Like Hustlers*. LP. Ruthless, 1990.

Body Count. *Body Count*. CD. Sire, 1992.

Compton's Most Wanted. *Straight Check'N Em*. LP. Orpheus, 1991.

DJ Quik. *Quik Is the Name*. LP. Profile, 1991.

Freestyle Fellowship. *To Whom It May Concern*. LP. Sun Music, 1991.

——. *Inner City Griots*. CD. Island, 1993.

Ice T. *The Iceberg. Freedom of Speech . . . Just Watch What You Say*. LP. Sire, 1989.

Kam. *Neva Again*. CD. Street Knowledge/East West, 1993.

Kool G Rap and DJ Polo. *Live and Let Die*. Cold Chillin', 1993.

MC Ren. *Shock of the Hour*. CD. Ruthless, 1993.

Paris. *Sleeping with the Enemy*. CD. Scarface, 1992.

The Pharcyde. *Bizarre Ride II the Pharcyde*. 2-LP. Delicious Vinyl, 1992.

Sister Souljah. *360 Degrees of Power*. LP. Epic, 1992.

2 Live Crew. *As Nasty As They Wanna Be*. LP. Luke, 1990.

OFTB (Watts OFTB). *Straight Up Watts*. LP. Big Beat, 1992.

18. Becoming the Hip-Hop Generation: *The Source*, the Industry and the Big Crossover.

Word

Bernard, James. Letter to David Mays. September 28, 1994.

Chang, Jeff. "Word Power: A Brief, Highly Opinionated History of Hip-Hop Journalism." In *Pop Music and the Press*, edited by Steve Jones. Philadelphia: Temple University Press, 2002.

Editors of *The Source*. "An Open Letter from the Editors of *The Source Magazine*." October 6, 1994.

George, Nelson. *The Death of Rhythm and Blues*. New York: Pantheon, 1988.

Hinds, Selwyn Seyfu. *Gunshots in My Cook-Up: Bits and Bits from a Hip-Hop Caribbean Life*. New York: Atria, 2002.

Kelley, Robin D. G. "The People in Me." in *Colorlines*. Winter 1999.

Klein, Naomi. *No Logo*. New York: Picador, 1999.

Light, Alan, ed. *The Vibe History of Hip-Hop*. New York: Three Rivers Press, 1999.

Lornell, Kip, and Charles Stephenson Jr. *The Beat: Go-Go's Fusion of Funk and Hip-Hop*. New York: Billboard Books, 2001.

Mcleod, Kembrew. "The Politics and History of Hip-Hop Journalism." In *Pop Music and the Press*, edited by Steve Jones. Philadelphia: Temple University Press, 2002.

Potter, Maximillian. "Getting to the Source." In GQ. December 2001.

Prashad, Vijay. *Everybody Was Kung Fu Fighting: Afro-Asian Connections and the Myth of Cultural Purity*. Boston: Beacon Press, 2001.

"The Rap Music Decade: 1980 to 1990." Special issue. In *The Source*. January/February 1990.

Rothenberg, Randall. "Shift Sought from 'Black' to 'Urban'." In the *New York Times*. November 30, 1989.

Sokol, Brett. "He Ain't Guilty, He's My Partner." In *Miami New Times*. September 6. 2001.

——. "It's a Hip-Hop World." In *Miami New Times*. July 5, 2001.

——. "Still in the Hood?" In *Miami New Times*. May 22, 2003.

Wimsatt, William Upski. *Bomb the Suburbs*. New York: Subway and Elevated, 1994.

Wynter, Leon. *American Skin: Pop Culture, Big Business, and the End of White America*. New York: Crown, 2002.

Image

Biggie and Tupac. DVD. Nick Broomfield, director. 2002.

Dr. Dre. "Let Me Ride." Video. 1993.

——. "Nuthin' But a 'G' Thang." Video. 1993.

Put Your Hands Up! The Tribute Concert to Chuck Brown. DVD. J. Kevin Swain, director. 2002.

Welcome to Death Row. DVD. Leigh Savidge, director. 2001.

Sound

Backyard Band. *Skillet.* CD. Future, 1999. One of the best unsung albums of the '90s.

Basic Beats Sampler. CD. Hollywood/BASIC, 1992. Includes Organized Konfusion, Lifers Group, Raw Fusion, Ziimbabwe Legit and a 12-minute DJ Shadow megamix.

The Beat. Go-Go's *Fusion of Funk and Hip-Hop.* 2-CD, Liaison. 2001.

Brand Nubian. *One for All.* LP. Elektra, 1990.

Chuck Brown. *Your Game . . . Live at the 9:30 Club.* CD. Liaison/Raw Venture, 2001.

Dr. Dre. *The Chronic.* CD. Death Row, 1992.

Dr. Funkenstein and DJ Cash Money. "Scratchin to the Funk." 12-inch single. Sound Makers, 1985.

EPMD. *Business Never Personal.* LP. Def Jam, 1992.

KMD. *Mr. Hood.* LP. Elektra, 1991.

Leaders of the New School. *Future Without A Past.* LP. Elektra, 1991.

NWA. *Efil4zaggin.* LP. Ruthless/Priority, 1991.

Organized Konfusion. *Organized Konfusion.* LP. Hollywood/BASIC, 1991.

Pete Rock and CL Smooth. *Mecca and the Soul Brother.* 2-LP. Elektra, 1992.

Rare Essence. *Doin It Old School Style Live At Club* U. CD+CD-ROM. Rare One, 2001.

Snoop Doggy Dogg. *Doggystyle.* CD. Death Row, 1993.

Tommy Boy Greatest Beats, Volumes 1–4. LP. Tommy Boy, 1998. This is a label retrospective that covers largely the hip-hop era, post-electro.

Trouble Funk. *Live.* CD. Infinite Zero, 1996. Originally released as *Straight Up Funk* Go-Go *Style.* 2-LP. Jamtu, 1981.

19. New World Order: Globalization, Containment and Counterculture at the End of the Century.

Word

Bagdikian, Ben. *The Media Monopoly.* Boston: Beacon Press, 1997.

"Belmont in *The L.A. Weekly.*" In *Los Angeles Weekly.* May 4–10, 2001. http://www.laweekly.com/ink/01/24/belmont-archive.php.

Appendix

Blackman, Toni. *Inner-course: A Plea for Real Love.* New York: Villard, 2003.

Cooper, M. William. *Behold a Pale Horse.* Flagstaff, Ariz.: Light Technology Publishing, 1991.

Future 500: Youth Organizing and Activism in the United States. Jee Kim, Mathilda de Rios, Pablo Caraballo, Manuela Arciniegas, Ibrahim Abdul-Martin, Kofi Taha, compilers. New Orleans: Subway and Elevated, 2002.

Higher Education Research Institute, University of California at Los Angeles. "The American Freshman: 2001." http://www.gseis.ucla.edu/heri/norms_pr_01.html

Kelley, Norman, ed. *R&B: Rhythm and Business.* Brooklyn: Akashic Books, 2002.

Kitwana, Bakari. *The Hip Hop Generation: Young Blacks and the Crisis in African-American Culture.* New York: Basic Civitas, 2002.

Mayo, Kierna. "Caught Up in the Gangsta Rapture." In *The Source.* June 1994.

McArdle, Andrea and Tanya Erzen, eds. *Zero Tolerance: Quality of Life and the New Police Brutality in New York City.* New York: New York University Press, 2001.

McChesney, Robert, and John Nichols. *Our Media, Not Theirs: The Democratic Struggle Against Corporate Media.* New York: Seven Stories Press, 2002.

Morgan, Joan. *When Chickenheads Come Home to Roost.* New York: Touchstone, 1999.

Nelson, Jill, ed. *Police Brutality.* New York: Norton, 2000.

October 22nd Coalition to Stop Police Brutality, Anthony Baez Foundation and the National Lawyers Guild. *Stolen Lives: Killed by Law Enforcement,* second edition. New York: October 22nd Coalition, 1999. http://stolenlives.org/

"Shaping Our Responses to Violent and Demeaning Imagery in Popular Music." Hearing Before the Subcommittee on Juvenile Justice of the Committee of the Judiciary, United States Senate. February 23, 1994.

Verán, Cristina. "Soul by the Pound." In *One World.* December/January 2003.

Wimsatt, William Upski. *No More Prisons.* New York: Subway and Elevated/Soft Skull Press, 1999.

Image

Books Not Bars. Mark Landesman, director. 2002. http://www.witness.org

Frontline: LAPD Blues. Michael Kirk, producer and director. Aired May 15, 2001. http://www.pbs.org/wgbh/pages/frontline/shows/lapd/bare.html

Jails, Hospitals, and Hip-Hop. Mark Benjamin & Danny Hoch, directors. 2001.

Nobody Knows My Name. Rachel Raimist, director. 1999.

Straight Outta Hunters Point. Kevin Epps, director. 2001.

Sound

Africa Raps. CD. Trikont, 2002.

Alicia Keys. *Songs in A Minor*. CD. J, 2001.

Angie Stone. *Black Diamond*. CD. Arista, 1999.

Blackalicious. *Nia*. Quannum, 2000.

Black Star. *Mos Def and Talib Kweli Are Black Star*. CD. Rawkus, 1998.

The Coup. *Party Music*. CD. 75 Ark/Tommy Boy, 2001.

D'Angelo. *Voodoo*. CD. EMI, 2000.

Dead Prez. *Let's Get Free*. CD. Loud, 2000.

Erykah Badu. *Baduizm*. CD. Kedar/Motown, 1997.

Goodie Mob. *Soul Food*. 2-LP. LaFace, 1995.

Hip-Hop For Respect. *Hip-Hop For Respect*. EP. CD. Rawkus, 2000.

India Arie. *Acoustic Soul*. CD. Motown, 2001.

Jill Scott. *Who Is Jill Scott?: Words and Sounds, Volume 1*. CD. Hidden Beach, 2000.

Latyrx. *Latyrx*. CD. Quannum, 2003. Originally released 1997.

Lauryn Hill. *The Miseducation of Lauryn Hill*. CD. Ruffhouse, 1998.

Mary J. Blige. *Share My World*. CD. MCA, 1997.

Meshell Ndegeocello. *Bitter*. CD. Maverick, 1999.

Missy Elliott. *Supa Dupa Fly*. CD. East West, 1997.

Mr. Lif. *I Phantom*. CD. Definitive Jux, 2002.

Outkast. *Aquemini*. CD. LaFace, 1998.

No More Prisons. CD. Raptivism, 1999.

The Roots. *Things Fall Apart*. CD. MCA, 1999.

Shame the Devil. CD. Freedom Fighter Music, 2002.

SoleSides' Greatest Bumps. 2-CD. Quannum, 2001.

Talib Kweli. *Quality*. CD. Rawkus, 2002.

For more articles and research resources, visit the Can't Stop Won't Stop Web site at http//www.cantstopwontstop.com.

Notes

Author's note: Quotations not cited in the text are from personal interviews.

LOOP 1. Babylon Is Burning: 1968–1977.

1. Necropolis: The Bronx and the Politics of Abandonment.

1. Reggie Jackson with Mike Lupica, *Reggie: The Autobiography* (New York: Villard, 1984), 170–171. Ed Linn, *The Great Rivalry: The Yankees and the Red Sox, 1901–1990* (New York: Tickner and Fields, 1991), 287. Roger Kahn, *October Men* (Orlando: Harcourt, Inc., 2003), 158–159.

2. Maury Allen, *Damn Yankee: The Billy Martin Story* (New York: Times Books, 1980), 200.

3. Jackie Robinson and Malcolm X in "An Exchange of Letters," *The Jackie Robinson Reader,* ed. Jules Tygiel (New York: Dutton, 1997), 236–247.

4. Arnold Rampersad, *Jackie Robinson: A Biography* (New York: Knopf, 1997), 391–392.

5. Phil Pepe, *Talkin' Baseball: An Oral History of Baseball in the 1970s* (New York: Ballantine Books, 1998), 290.

6. Robert Caro, *The Power Broker* (New York: Knopf, 1974), 860.

7. Ibid., 840–841.

8. Camilo José Vergara, *The New American Ghetto* (New Brunswick, N.J.: Rutgers University Press, 1995), 49.

9. Richard Plunz, *A History of Housing in New York City: Dwelling Type and Social Change in the American Metropolis* (New York: Columbia University Press, 1990), 257, 267–273.

10. Marshall Berman, *All That Is Solid Melts into Air: The Experience of Modernity* (New York: Simon & Schuster, 1982), 291.

11. Paul Cowan, "On a Very Tense Frontier: Street-Fighting in the Bronx," *Village Voice* (June 22, 1972), 1, 16, 18, 20, 22.

12. Policeman Anthony Bouza, "The Fire Next Door," *CBS Reports,* broadcast March 22, 1977.

13. Jill Jonnes, *"We're Still Here": The Rise, Fall and Resurrection of the South Bronx* (New York: Atlantic Monthly Press, 1986), 125–126.

14. Amalia Batanzos, Youth Services Agency Commissioner, said, "In the South Bronx, the young male Puerto Rican unemployment rate is 80 percent. He sees that there's no way out and if there's no way out, it really does not matter if you're violent." "New York

Illustrated: The Savage Skulls with Piri Thomas," produced and directed by Abigail Child, WNBC Community Affairs Program (New York), aired November 18, 1973.

15. Joseph B. Treaster, "20% Rise in Fires Is Adding to Decline of South Bronx," *New York Times* (May 18, 1975), 1, 50.

16. *CBS Reports*, "The Fire Next Door."

17. Joe Conason and Jack Newfield, "The Men Who Are Burning New York," *Village Voice* (June 2, 1980), 1, 15–19. Jack Newfield, "A Budget for Bankers and Arsonists," *Village Voice* (June 2, 1980), 13.

18. H. Rainie, "U.S. Housing Program in South Bronx Called a Waste by Moynihan," *New York Daily News* (December 20, 1978), 3.

19. Geoffrey Hodgson, *The Gentleman from New York: Daniel Patrick Moynihan* (New York: Houghton Mifflin, 2000), 157–158.

20. Deborah and Rodrick Wallace, *A Plague on Your Houses* (New York: Verso Books, 1998), 22–77.

21. Lessie Sanders, quoted in *Devastation/Resurrection: The South Bronx* (New York: Bronx Museum of the Arts, 1980), 64. Robert Jensen, project curator.

22. Ivor L. Miller, *Aerosol Kingdom: Subway Painters of New York City* (Jackson: University Press of Mississippi, 2002), 187–188.

23. Martin Tolchin, "South Bronx: A Jungle Stalked by Fear, Seized by Rage," *New York Times* (January 15, 1973), sec. A1, 19.

24. Ibid.

25. Robert Jensen, "Introduction" in *Devastation/Resurrection: The South Bronx* (New York: Bronx Museum of the Arts, 1980), 13.

26. *The South Bronx: A Plan for Revitalization* (December 1977), 8. Report prepared by the Office of the Mayor, Office of the Bronx Borough President, Department of City Planning, Office of Economic Development, Office of Management and Budget, Department of Housing Preservation and Development .

27. "The Ups and Downs of the South Bronx," *National Journal* (October 6, 1979), 1648.

28. Martin Tolchin, "Future Looks Bleak for South Bronx," *New York Times* (January 18, 1973), sec. A1, A50.

29. Robert Fitch, *The Assassination of New York* (London: Verso, 1993), vii–viii. Wallace and Wallace, *A Plague on Your Houses*, 24–26. A decade later, Starr would apply the same logic to welfare and lead the neoconservative push toward "welfare reform" into the 90s.

30. Gerald Eskenazi, "Delirious Fans Run Wild As Some Violence Erupts," and "Police: 'We Won Battle, But Lost War,'" *New York Times* (October 19, 1977), B6, B19–B20.

31. Murray Cass, "Jackson, the Player of the Series, Is Controversial and Charismatic," *New York Times* (October 19, 1977), sec. A1, B6.

32. Dave Anderson, "The Two Seasons of Reggie Jackson," *New York Times* (October 20, 1977), 19.

2. Sipple Out Deh: Jamaica's Roots Generation and The Cultural Turn.

1. Verena Reckord, "From Burru Drums to Reggae Ridims," *Chanting Down Babylon*, ed. Nathaniel Samuel Murrell, William David Spencer and Adrian Anthony McFarlane (Philadelphia: Temple University Press, 1998), 245.

2. Laurie Gunst, *Born Fi Dead* (New York: Henry Holt, 1995), 84. Darrell Levi notes that the political violence lasted into 1967 and that for a time a state of emergency was imposed. He also cites a 1980 *Jamaica Gleaner* article by PNP Secretary D. K. Duncan that portrays Seaga as violent, saying, "It will be blood for blood, fire for fire, thunder for thunder." Darrell Levi, *Michael Manley: The Making of a Leader* (Athens, Ga.: University of Georgia Press, 1989), 117–118, 221, 319n.

3. Leonard Barrett Sr., *The Rastafarians* (Boston: Beacon Press, 1988), 156.

4. Laurie Gunst, *Born Fi Dead*, 79–80.

5. *Classic Albums: Catch a Fire Documentary*, directed by Jeremy Marre (Rhino Video videotape, 2000).

6. Norman Stolzoff, *Wake the Town and Tell the People* (Durham: Duke University Press, 2000), 41–43.

7. David Katz, *People Funny Boy: The Genius of Lee "Scratch" Perry* (London: Payback Press, 2000), 11–24.

8. The best discussion of the development of the Jamaican sound system is to be found in Norman Stolzoff, *Wake the Town and Tell the People*.

9. This section relies on interviews with Steve Barrow. Steve Barrow and Peter Dalton, *Reggae: The Rough Guide* (London & New York: Rough Guides/Penguin, 1997).

10. Lloyd Bradley, *This Is Reggae Music: The Story of Jamaica's Music* (New York: Grove Press, 2000), 270.

11. Gunst, *Born Fi Dead*, xvii.

12. Evelyne Huber Stephens and John D. Stephens, *Democratic Socialism in Jamaica* (London: Macmillan, 1986), Table A-20, 397.

13. Omar Davies and Michael Witter, "The Development of the Jamaican Economy Since Independence," *Jamaica in Independence: Essays on the Early Years*, ed. Rex Nettleford (Kingston: Heinemann Caribbean, 1989), Table 4b, 85. Director Stephanie Black contrasts Michael Manley's views with those of IMF official Stanley Fischer while documenting the effects of IMF, Inter-American Development Bank and World Trade Organization policies on the island's dairy farming, beef, carrot and banana industries. She also covers the disastrous "free trade zone" experiment, where sweatshops producing

Tommy Hilfiger and Brooks Brothers clothes are closed after workers begin demanding better working conditions. *Life and Debt,* directed by Stephanie Black (Tuff Gong Pictures, 2001).

14. Melville Cooke, "A Killer Interview," *Jamaica Gleaner* (August 23, 2001).

15. Stephens and Stephens, *Democratic Socialism in Jamaica,* 132–135.

16. Michael Manley, *Struggle in the Periphery* (London: Third World Media Limited, 1982), 140.

17. Katz, *People Funny Boy,* 246.

18. Steve Barrow, liner notes from The Abyssinians and Friends, *Tree of Satta, Volume 1* (Blood and Fire Records compact disc BAFCD 045, January 2004).

19. Laurie Gunst, *Born Fi Dead,* 96–106.

20. Ibid., 105.

21. Katz, *People Funny Boy,* 305–307.

22. "When Johnny Comes Marching Home" was reportedly adapted by Union Army bandleader Patrick S. Gilmore from an African-American spiritual.

23. Gunst, *Born Fi Dead,* 106–108.

24. Katz, *People Funny Boy,* 411.

3. Blood and Fire, With Occasional Music: The Gangs of The Bronx.

1. Grady-Willis, Winston A., "The Black Panther Party: State Repression and Political Prisoners," in *The Black Panther Party Reconsidered,* ed. Charles E. Jones (Baltimore: Black Classic Press, 1998), 370–372. Ward Churchill and Jim Vander Wall, *The COINTELPRO Papers: Documents from the FBI's Secret Wars Against Dissent in the United States* (Boston: South End Press, 1990), 138–139.

2. Hoover in Churchill and Vander Wall, *The COINTELPRO Papers,* 111.

3. Afeni Shakur, "We Will Win: Letter from Prison by Afeni Shakur," in *The Black Panthers Speak,* ed. Philip S. Foner (Philadelphia: J. B. Lippincott and Company, 1970), 161, 163.

4. "New York Illustrated: The Savage Skulls with Piri Thomas," produced and directed by Abigail Child, WNBC Community Affairs Program (New York), aired November 18, 1973.

5. Pete Hamill, "The Gangs," *New York Post* (circa May 1972); from the papers of Rita Fecher.

6. "Execution in the Bronx," *New York Times* (June 17, 1973).

7. In 2004, Eddie Perez, a former Ghetto Brother from Hartford, Connecticut, became mayor of the city.

8. *Ain't Gonna Eat My Mind*, directed by Tony Batten (1972).

9. Gene Weingarten, "East Bronx Story: Return of the Street Gangs," *New York* (March 27, 1972), 35.

10. Ibid., 34.

11. Jose Torres, "Ghetto Brothers," *New York Post* (November 6, 1971).

12. Jerry Schmetterer, "Trouble Was His Scene," New York *Daily News* (December 3, 1971), 3.

13. See "Ain't Gonna Eat My Mind" in Eric C. Schneider, *Vampires, Dragons and Egyptian Kings: Youth Gangs in Post-War New York* (Princeton, N.J.: Princeton University Press, 1999), 243–245.

14. Edward Kirkman, "Gangs Hold Rap Session on Cops," New York *Daily News* (December 17, 1971).

15. See "Ain't Gonna Eat My Mind" in Schneider, *Vampires, Dragons and Egyptian Kings*.

16. Aida Alvarez, "Savage Skulls Feared As Worst Bronx Gang," *New York Post* (September 15, 1975), 28.

17. "Execution in the Bronx," *New York Times* (June 17, 1973).

18. *The 51st State: Bronx Gangs,* hosted by Patrick Watson, WNYC (New York), broadcast in 1972.

4. Making a Name: How DJ Kool Herc Lost His Accent And Started Hip-Hop.

1. Jack Stewart, *Subway Graffiti; An Aesthetic Study of Graffiti on the Subway System of New York City* (Ph.D. diss., New York University, 1989), 148–190.

2. "TAKI 183 Spawns Pen Pals," *New York Times* (July 21, 1971), 37.

3. Greg Tate, "Graf Rulers/Graf UnTrained," *One Planet Under a Groove: Hip Hop and Contemporary Art* (New York: Bronx Museum of Arts, 2001), 38.

4. Herbert Kohl and James Hinton, *Golden Boy As Anthony Cool: A Photo Essay on Naming and Graffiti* (New York: The Dial Press, 1972), 120. This great little book offers insight on how far Herc had now moved from the gangs: "On gang rosters we sometimes see inscriptions such as 'Clarence as Lefty.' However, they are not common; the 'as' phenomenon is more often found on lists of names of people from the same block or of boys and girls that 'hang out' together. It is more likely that 'Lefty' would stand alone on the gang roster. The name Clarence, identifying 'Lefty' as the son of his parents, is more thoroughly renounced through gang membership than through becoming part of a more loosely structured and less demanding peer group."

5. Steven Hager, "The Herculords at the Hevalo," *Record Magazine* (February 1985), 34.

6. Davey D, interview by Afrika Bambaataa for Hard Knock Radio, recorded at KPFA-FM, Berkeley (November 29, 2002).

7. It's interesting that these beats shared the element of cinema or theater. While David Toop believed the Incredible Bongo Band was a Jamaican disco band, they were in fact a band put together by sometime film composer Michael Viner, featuring another soundtrack composer, Perry Botkin Jr., and the formidable bongo playing of King Errisson, a Jamaican immigrant. Dennis Coffey was a studio musician whose career was furthered by his work for blaxploitation soundtracks. James Brown's "live" record was actually recorded in a studio and given live audience overdubs. It was later marketed as a performance in his hometown of Augusta, Georgia.

8. The Rock Steady Crew's Jorge "Popmaster Fabel" Pabon, a respected hip-hop historian, said in 2001, "The most respected b-boy crews was the Zulu Kings, the Twins formerly known as the Nigger Twins. There was a group that the Twins told me about called 'The B-Boys.' They have a very interesting claim. They say that the word 'b-boys' was really referring to those guys. Like for instance, the Lockers. There was a similar argument that came up where one of the Lockers recently [was asked], 'What do you do?' And he said he's a Locker. And then some young kid said, 'I'm a Locker,' and he looked at him and he said, 'No you're not, I'm a Locker.' In other words, it gets into semantics like you know how to lock, okay, but I'm the Locker, I'm one of the original Lockers. And that same argument I heard pop up with b-boying. Where the Twins said, 'Well I don't know why everyone's calling himself a b-boy. Those guys were the B-Boys!' Hey, I have an open mind and it's an interesting concept. I'm not gonna debate it, I don't have any artillery to debate it with!" (Interview with the author, November 20, 2001.)

LOOP 2. Planet Rock: 1975–1986.

5. Soul Salvation: The Mystery and Faith of Afrika Bambaataa.

1. Steven Hager, "Afrika Bambaataa's Hip Hop," *Village Voice* (September 21, 1982), 73. Kevin Donovan is credited as the "Arranger" on the label of Bambaataa and Cosmic Force's first record, *Zulu Nation Throwdown, Volume 1*. Bambaataa had no love lost for Paul Winley or his house band. This from Hager's *Village Voice* article:

   Finally, in 1980, he succeeded in obtaining a deal with Paul Winley's struggling label. In November, he recorded two 12-inch versions of "Zulu Nation Throwdown," one with the Cosmic Force and the other with the Soul Sonic Force. When the first single was released, however, Bambaataa discovered Winley had added instruments without even consulting him. "It was crazy," says Bambaataa. "I recorded the songs to just drums. When the record came out, Winley added a bass and some crazy guitar music. Then, when it came time to get paid, he started jivin' us."

2. Jens Peter de Pedro and TBL, "The Godfather of Hip Hop," *Underground Productions* (Stockholm, Sweden, August 1997). Special shout-out to Joe Austin for the article.

3. Gary Jardim, "The Great Facilitator," *Village Voice* (October 2, 1984), 63.

4. Steven Hager, *Hip Hop: The Illustrated History of Break Dancing, Rap Music and Graffiti* (New York: St. Martin's Press, 1984), 6.

5. Ibid., 9–10.

6. The Universal Zulu Nation actually dates its anniversary to November 12, 1973, which is likely the date The Organization came into being. Its Infinity Lesson #3 reads: "The Universal Zulu Nation was founded in the year 1973 but started to come into power in the year 1975 A.D. by a young student at Adlai Stevenson High School named Afrika Bambaataa. . . . He also ran the group called The Organization for 2 years and the street gang called the Black Spades for 5 years."

7. "Two Shot Dead in Bronx Duel," New York *Amsterdam News* (January 11, 1975), B-9.

8. Stewart, *Subway Graffiti*, 260 (see chap. 4, n. 1).

6. Furious Styles: The Evolution of Style in the Seven Mile World.

1. Luis Angel Matteo, "Origins of Breakdancing," interview by Mandalit Del Barco, National Public Radio (October 14, 2002). Available online at http://www.npr.org/programs/morning/features/patc/breakdancing/.

2. Zora Neale Hurston, "Characteristics of Negro Expression," in *Folklore, Memoirs and Other Writings* (New York: Library of America, 1995), 835. The article was originally published in 1934.

3. Ibid.

4. Cristina Verán, "(Puerto) Rock of Ages," *Rap Pages* (September 1996), 47

5. Stewart, *Subway Graffiti*, 229 (see chap. 4, n. 1).

6. Richard Goldstein, "This Thing Has Gotten Completely Out of Hand," *New York* (March 26, 1973), 36, 39.

7. Lee Quiñones wrote this in a famous 1978 piece done with BILLY 167, but Henry Chalfant has documented other instances and Jack Stewart dates the slogan to 1974, before Lee was on the trains. Ibid., 475. Another Lee mural, called "Roaring Thunder," has this: "Graffiti is Art, and if Art is a crime, let God forgive all."

8. Ivor Miller, *Aerosol Kingdom: Subway Painters of New York City* (Jackson, Miss.: University Press of Misssissippi, 2002), 109.

9. Richard Goldstein, "The Fire Down Below," *Village Voice* (December 24–28, 1980), 55.

10. Stewart, *Subway Graffiti*, 382–387 (see chap. 4, n. 1).

11. Ibid., 457–458

12. Phoebe Hoban, *Basquiat: A Quick Killing in Art* (New York: Viking, 1998), 36.

13. *Style Wars,* directed by Tony Silver, produced by Tony Silver and Henry Chalfant (1983).

7. The World Is Ours: The Survival and Transformation of Bronx Style.

1. For a recording of the Flash and the Furious Five's live beatbox routine in its context, including Flash rocking the beatbox, find the version of "Flash It to the Beat" on the Bozo Meko label, an apparently bootlegged tape from the Bronx River Community Center in 1979 or 1980. Bonus: the Furious Five get the crowd going in a frenzied "Zulu! Gestapo!" chant! The flip-side features Jazzy Jay cutting up breakbeats on a track entitled "Fusion Beats," an early classic of the instrumental hip-hop record genre. There is a studio version on Sugar Hill of "Flash It to the Beat," also a great listen, but the house band sounds almost anemic, stripped down to a bass, drums and percussion.

2. Craig Castleman, *Getting Up: Subway Graffiti in New York* (Cambridge: The MIT Press, 1982), 137.

3. Ibid., 142.

4. Joe Austin, *Taking the Train: How Graffiti Art Became an Urban Crisis in New York City* (New York: Columbia University Press, 2001), 130.

5. Reproduced in Stewart, *Subway Graffiti,* 203–204 (see chap. 4, n. 1).

6. Nathan Glazer, "On Subway Graffiti in New York," *Public Interest* (Winter 1979), 207.

8. Zulus on a Time Bomb: Hip-Hop Meets The Rockers Downtown.

1. "Henry Chalfant: Photographer to the Cars," *East Village Eye* (August 1982), 24.

2. Goldstein, "The Fire Down Below," 58 (see chap. 6, n. 9).

3. Michael A. Steargman, *The Dynamics of Rental Housing in New York City* (Piscataway, N.J.: Rutgers University Center for Urban Policy Research, 1982), 51, 54, 147.

4. Richie Perez, "Committee Against Fort Apache: The Bronx Mobilizes Against Multinational Media," in *Cultures in Contention,* ed. Douglas Kahn and Diane Neumaier (Seattle: Real Comet Press, 1985), 195. Photo by Jerry Kearns.

5. See the cover of her 1985 *Island Life* compilation for an idea of what her bowling form might have looked like!

6. Elizabeth Hess, "Graffiti R.I.P.: How The Art World Loved 'Em and Left 'Em," *Village Voice* (December 22, 1987), 41.

7. Michael Small, "When Graffiti Paintings Sell for Thousands, the Art World Sees the Writing on the Wall," *People* (August 22, 1983), 50.

8. Ibid., 52.

9. Michael Hill, "The Clash at the Clampdown," *Village Voice* (June 10–16, 1981), 74.

10. Robert Christgau, "Magnificent Seven," *Village Voice* (November 2, 1982), 59.

11. Sally Banes, "To the Beat Y'all: Breaking Is Hard to Do," *Village Voice* (April 22–28, 1981), 31.

12. Ibid.

13. From the notes of Martha Cooper.

14. This is the battle scene featured in *Style Wars*.

15. From an article proposal by Sally Banes and Martha Cooper, "Breaking: From the Bronx to Shinjuku" (undated, probably 1983); from the files of Martha Cooper. (Note: They eventually did get a piece in *Folklife Annual* [1986], 8–21.)

16. From a book proposal by Sally Banes and Martha Cooper, "Rapping, Writing and Rocking: Street Style in New York" (undated, probably 1983); from the files of Martha Cooper.

17. Henry Chalfant, "Making Style Wars," *SVA Newsletter* (Spring 1987), 16.

18. Lloyd Sachs. "A Hard Sell; Malcolm McLaren's Square Dancing Music," *Playboy* (October 1983), 24.

19. Susan Orlean, "Profiles: Living Large," *New Yorker* (June 17, 1991), 44.

9. 1982: Rapture In Reagan's America.

1. Mel Rosenthal, *In the South Bronx of America* (Willimantic, Conn.: Curbstone, 2000), 49.

2. Gary Jardim, "The Great Facilitator," *Village Voice* (October 2, 1984), 63.

3. The other point it would share with "Rapper's Delight" was that it, too, became the target of litigation for publishing royalties.

4. Robert Elms, "Nightclubbing," *The Face One Hundred* (date unknown), 37; from the files of Kool Lady Blue.

5. Chi Chi Valenti, "Out of the Blue," *Village Voice* (date unknown, probably late 1980s); from the files of Kool Lady Blue. Bill Brewster and Frank Broughton, *Last Night a DJ Saved My Life: The History of the Disc Jockey* (New York: Grove Press, 2000), 250.

6. Howard Zinn, *A People's History of the United States, 1492–Present* (New York: HarperPerennial, 1995), 565–566.

7. The National Urban League's "State of Black America," cited in Nelson George, "The Complete History of Post-Soul Culture," *Village Voice* (March 17, 1992).

8. Rick Hampson, "City's Chronic Teen-Age Jobless Called a Lost Generation by Labor Officials," *Staten Island Advance* (August 1, 1983), as cited in Joe Austin, *Taking the Train*, 212 (see chap. 7, n. 4).

9. Vince Aletti, "Furious," *Village Voice* (July 20, 1982), 64.

10. "Getting Up," *Village Voice* (May 4, 1999), 39. Andrew Witten and Michael White, *Dondi White: Style Master General* (New York: Regan Books, 2001).

11. Tom Matthews, "Sons of Spray," *Harper and Queen* (UK) (October 1984), 270.

12. Hoban, *Basquiat,* 158 (see chap. 6, n. 12).

13. Hess, "Graffiti R.I.P.," 38 (see chap. 8, n. 6).

14. Witten and White, *Dondi White: Style Master General,* 113.

10. End of Innocence: The Fall of The Old School.

1. Malu Halasa, "Visions of the Future," *Black Music and Jazz Review* (UK) (date unknown, probably 1983), 19; from the archives of Bill Adler.

2. Interview by Davey D for Hard Knock Radio, recorded at KPFA-FM, Berkeley (November 29, 2002).

3. Kelefa Sanneh, "After the Beginning Again: The Afrocentric Ordeal," *Transition 87* (1999), 73.

4. S. Craig Watkins, *Representing: Hip Hop Culture and the Production of Black Cinema* (Chicago: University of Chicago Press, 1998), 93–96.

5. Richard Grabel, "The South Bronx Is Up," *Village Voice* (November 22, 1983), 86.

6. Sally Banes, "Breaking Changing," *Village Voice* (June 12, 1984), 82.

7. After four investigations following the *New York Times* series found no criminal wrongdoing or professional misconduct on Gross's part, he filed a libel lawsuit against the *Times,* which was eventually dismissed by the New York State Supreme Court.

8. Sam Roberts, "One Year After Hearings on Police Brutality, Critics Report Some Progress," *New York Times* (July 25, 1984), B1+.

9. "Three Transit Police Officers Indicted in Beating Death," Associated Press wire report (June 2, 1984).

10. Isabel Wilkerson, "Defense Lawyers in Stewart Trial Say They Will Call No Witnesses," *New York Times* (October 31,1984), B8.

11. Isabel Wilkerson, "Jury Acquits All Transit Officers in 1983 Death of Michael Stewart," *New York Times* (November 25, 1985), A1.

12. Sidney Janis Gallery. *Post-Graffiti* (New York: self-published, 1983).

13. Richard Goldstein, "The Future of Graffiti," *Village Voice* (December 13, 1983).

14. Gallery, *Post-Graffiti.*

15. Kim Levin, "The 57th Street Stop," *Village Voice* (December 20, 1983), 119. Goldstein, "The Future of Graffiti."

16. Grace Glueck. "Gallery View: On Canvas, Yes, But Still Eyesores." *New York Times* (December 25. 1983), sec. 2, 20.

17. Hess, "Graffiti R.I.P.," 38, 41 (see chap. 8, n. 6).

18. Ibid., 41.

19. This from FUTURA's insight told to Alexander Dawson: "Jean-Michel was not really do-
    ing original things upon further inspection. He was looking at Twombly and PINK and
    other artists who were scribbling and doing that thing, but totally a genius guy and
    made a lot of fucking work." Alexander Dawson, "Art and Soul: FUTURA 2000," *Wax
    Poetics* 6 (Fall 2003), 97.

20. Chairman Jefferson Mao. Liner notes from Ego Trip, *The Big Playback* (Rawkus Records
    compact disc, February 2000).

21. Greg Tate, *Flyboy in the Buttermilk: Essays on Contemporary America* (New York: Si-
    mon & Schuster, 1992), 236.

22. Hoban, *Basquiat,* 100 (see chap. 6, n. 12).

23. M. Franklin Sirmans, "Chronology," in Richard Marshall, *Jean-Michel Basquiat* (New
    York: Harry Abrams, 1993), 243

24. Art Sales Index. *Auction Prices of American Artists, 1990–1992* (Surrey, England: Art
    Sales Index, 1992), 16–17, 145–146.

25. "Free at Last," *The Record* (May 12, 1989), B10.

26. Ibid.

27. "Buffed Out," *New Yorker* (February 26, 1990), 37–38.

28. Jill Jonnes, *Hep Cats, Narcs and Pipe Dreams: A History of America's Romance With Il-
    legal Drugs* (New York: Scribner, 1996), 38.

29. Alfred McCoy, *The Politics of Heroin: CIA Complicity in the Global Drug Trade*
    (Chicago: Lawrence Hill Books, 1991), 18–19.

30. Clarence Lusane, *Pipe Dream Blues* (Boston: South End Press, 1991), 119.

31. Jonnes, *Hep Cats,* 371, citing Gordon Witkin, "The Men Who Created Crack," *U.S.
    News and World Report* (August 19, 1991), 47.

32. For more information, read Claire Hargreaves, *Snowfields* (New York: Holmes and
    Meier Publishers), 1992.

33. "Cocaine: Middle Class High," *Time* (July 6, 1981).

34. Ann Crittenden and Michael Ruby, "The Champagne of Drugs," *New York Times Mag-
    azine* (September 1 1974), 14.

35. Jonnes, *Hep Cats,* 376, citing James A. Inciardi, *The War on Drugs II: The Continuing
    Epic of Heroin, Cocaine, Crack, Crime, AIDS and Public Policy* (Mountain View, Calif.:
    Mayfield Pub. Co., 1992), 113.

36. Gary Webb, *Dark Alliance: The CIA, the Contras and the Crack Cocaine Explosion*
    (New York: Seven Stories Press, 1998), 33–34.

37. Dominic Streatfield, *Cocaine: An Unauthorized Biography* (New York: Thomas Dunne Books, 2001), 275.

38. Webb, *Dark Alliance*, 144. Jonnes, *Hep Cats*, 376.

39. Brian Cross, *It's Not About a Salary: Rap, Race and Resistance in Los Angeles* (New York: Verso, 1993), 180–181.

40. Ibid., 184.

41. Ibid., 156–157. Also, Rodger "Uncle Jam" Clayton, who says he promoted the show, told me this story during an interview:

Raising Hell—that wasn't gangs in Long Beach. It was a race riot. Let me tell you what happened. The Long Beach Insanes had stole a Mexican girl's purse and some Mexican dudes went upstairs, broke in the broom closet and hit up the Long Beach Insanes. They broke some brooms and mops and sticks with sharp edges on 'em. Then all the black gangs got together that was out there and they just start whooping every Mexican or white boy, throwing 'em off the second level, whooping they ass and everything. But no one's ever brought that to light. I was right there on the stage trying to calm the crowd down like I always did. They had 100 T-shirt security guards. End of the night you supposed to turn your T-shirt in. End of the night there was only about 30 of them left. They had took off and left and ran. That shit was never brought to light on TV, media or nothing. That was a fucking race riot. It wasn't about gangs. All the black gangs had combined and started whooping ass.

LOOP 3. The Message: 1984–1992.

11. Things Fall Apart: The Rise of the Post–Civil Rights Era.

1. Joseph Albright and Marcia Kunstel, "CIA Tip Led to '62 Arrest of Mandela: Ex-Official Tells of U.S. Coup to Aid South Africa," *Atlanta Constitution* (June 10, 1990).

2. Donald Culbertson, *Contesting Apartheid U.S. Activism, 1967–1980* (Boulder, Co: Westview Press, 1999), 65.

3. Ibid., 57, citing U.S. Department of Commerce, *Statistical Abstract of the United States* (Washington, D.C.: 1968–1976).

4. "Africa: Certainly Not Neglected," *The Economist* 278, no. 7178 (March 28, 1981), 24.

5. George de Lama, "Reagan: South Africa Reforming, President Says Segregation Over," *Chicago Tribune* (August 27, 1985), C1. Norman D. Sandler, "Washington Window; Reagan on Apartheid: A Potential Problem," United Press International wire report (August 28, 1985).

6. Pauline Baker, *The United States and South Africa: The Reagan Years* (New York: Ford Foundation and the Foreign Policy Association, 1989), 34.

7. Ken Brown, "Anti-Apartheid Protests Waning, Students Fight Racism," United Press International wire report (May 23, 1988).

8. Jon Wiener, "Divestment Report Card," *The Nation* (October 11, 1986), 337.

9. Joseph Berger, "Campus Turmoil over South Africa Ties Fades," *New York Times* (December 30, 1987), B8.

10. Chuck Collins and Felice Yeskel, with United for a Fair Economy, *Economic Apartheid in America* (New York: The New Press, 2000), 80–84.

11. Kevin Phillips, *The Politics of Rich and Poor: Wealth and the American Electorate in the Reagan Aftermath* (New York: Harper Perennial, 1990), xvii.

12. Donald L. Barlett and James B. Steele, *America: Who Really Pays Taxes?* (New York: Touchstone, 1994), 140.

13. Edward Wolff. *Top Heavy: A Study of the Increasing Inequality of Wealth in America* (New York: The Twentieth Century Fund Press, 1995), 2, 17–18.

14. Scott Minerbrook, "Blacks Locked Out of the American Dream; Real Estate Discrimination," *Business and Society Review* (September 22, 1993), 23. Douglas Massey and Nancy A. Denton. *American Apartheid: Segregation and the Making of the Underclass* (Cambridge: Harvard University Press, 1993), 160–162.

15. Gary Orfield, with Sara Schley, Diane Glass and Sean Reardon, "The Growth of Segregation in American Schools: Changing Patterns of Separation and Poverty Since 1968," A Report of the Harvard Project on School Desegregation to the National School Boards Association (December 1993), 20, 29.

16. Ibid., 21.

17. Toure Muhammad, *Chronology of Nation of Islam History: Highlights of the Honorable Minister Louis Farrakhan and the Nation of Islam, 1977–1996* (Chicago: Steal Away Productions, 1996), 40.

18. Ibid., 55.

19. Manning Marable, *Beyond Black and White: Transforming African American Politics* (New York: Verso, 1995), 223–224.

20. Andrea Ford, "Farrakhan Says U.S. Should View Nation of Islam As Friend," *Los Angeles Times* (February 4, 1990), B1.

21. Muhammad, *Chronology of Nation of Islam History,* 45–46.

22. Howard Kurtz, "Drug Plague a Racist Conspiracy?" *Washington Post* (January 2, 1990), E1. Muhammad, *Chronology of Nation of Islam History,* 45–46.

23. Michael Powell, "Fear of Race Violence Rising in New York City," *The Record* (June 21, 1987).

24. Robert McFadden, "Black Man Dies After Beating by Whites in Queens," *New York Times* (December 21, 1986).

25. Michael Oreskes, "Why Howard Beach?" *New York Times* (January 15, 1987). See also John H. Mollenkopf, *New York City in the 1980s: A Social, Economic and Political Atlas* (New York: Simon and Schuster, 1993), 42–43.

26. Richard Stengel, "Black vs. White in Howard Beach," *Time* (January 5, 1984), 48.

27. Robert McFadden, "The Howard Beach Inquiry: Many Key Questions Persist," *New York Times* (December 28, 1986).

28. Powell, "Fear of Race Violence."

29. Esther Pessin, United Press International wire report (December 23, 1986).

30. Jeffrey Page and Victor E. Sasson, "New York Blacks Stage Day of Protest," *The Record* (January 22, 1987).

12. What We Got to Say: Black Suburbia, Segregation and Utopia in the Late 1980s.

1. Frank Owen, "Def Not Dumb," *Melody Maker* (March 21, 1987).

2. Minerbrook, "Blacks Locked Out" (see chap. 11, n. 14).

3. "Viewpoints: The Walls Between Us," *Newsday* (October 15, 1990), 40.

4. "A World Apart: How Long Island's School Districts Can Be Desegregated," *Newsday* (January 13, 1991).

5. Clay F. Richards, "Poll: Prejudice a Fact of Life," *Newsday* (September 17, 1990).

6. Clifford May, "On Long Island, Fights Follow a Film on Rap Music," *New York Times* (November 6, 1985), B1.

7. Bill Mason and Richard C. Firstman, "Police Relations with Black Communities Still Strained," *Newsday* (September 17, 1990).

8. Ellis Cose, *The Rage of a Privileged Class* (New York: Harper Collins, 1993), 38.

9. Richards, "Poll: Prejudice a Fact of Life."

10. Ibid.

11. Owen, "Def Not Dumb."

12. Ibid.

13. Danny Kelly, "Rhyme and Reason," *New Musical Express* (October 8, 1988), 54.

14. Harry Allen, "Public Enemy: Leading a Radio Rebellion," *Black Radio Exclusive* (February 26, 1988), 9–10.

15. Ibid.

16. Jonathan Gold, "Enemy of the People," *LA Weekly* (January 6–12, 1989), 18.

17. Simon Reynolds, "Strength to Strength," *Melody Maker* (October 17, 1987), 14.

18. Cynthia Horner, "Meet Public Enemy!" *Right On!* (October 1987).

19. Paul Cruikshank, "Public Enemy: The Complete Rap," *Valley Regional* (November 1988). John Leland, "Do the Right Thing," *Spin* (September 1989), 72.

20. Chuck D with Yusef Jah, *Fight the Power: Rap, Race and Reality* (New York: Delacorte Press, 1997), 216–217.

21. Reynolds, "Strength to Strength," 15.

22. John Leland, "Noise Annoys," *Village Voice* (April 21, 1987).

23. Sean O'Hagan, "Rebels with a Cause," *New Musical Express* (October 10, 1987), 52.

24. R. J. Smith, "Swing Shift: Living Room," *Village Voice* (April 26, 1988).

25. Marcus Reeves, "Allah's Messenger," *The Source* (December 1997), 98.

26. Jefferson Mao (Chairman Mao), "The Microphone God," *Vibe* (December 1997), 134.

27. Nick Smash, "The Dollar Sign," *Echoes* (November 21, 1987), 14.

28. Harry Allen, "Soul Power," *Spin* (December 1987), 61.

29. Robert L. Doerschuk, "Hank Shocklee: Bomb Squad Leader Declares War on Music," *Keyboard* (September 1990), 96.

30. O'Hagan, "Rebels with a Cause," 15.

13. Follow for Now: The Question of Post–Civil Rights Black Leadership.

1. Christopher Dickey, "That's the Truth Ruth," *Newsweek* (July 3, 1989), 66.

2. O'Hagan, "Rebels with a Cause," 52 (see chap. 12, n. 23).

3. Harry Allen, "Grandmaster Flash Takes Aim at Public Enemy," *The City Sun* (January 1988).

4. Marshall Frady, *Jesse: The Life and Pilgrimage of Jesse Jackson* (New York: Random House, 1996), 343.

5. Ibid., 348.

6. Muhammad, *Chronology of Nation of Islam History*, 27 (see chap. 11, n. 17). "Farrakhan Says He Called Judaism 'Dirty Religion,' Not 'Gutter,'" Associated Press wire report (June 29, 1984).

7. Arthur Magida, *Prophet of Rage: A Life of Louis Farrakhan and His History* (New York: Basic Books, 1996), 149.

8. Muhammad, *Chronology of Nation of Islam History*, 25–26 (see chap. 11, n. 17).

9. Adolph Reed, *The Jesse Jackson Phenomenon: The Crisis of Purpose in Afro-American Politics* (New Haven: Yale University Press, 1986), 101

10. Warren Weaver Jr., "Warning from Koch," *New York Times* (April 2, 1988).

11. Elizabeth Colton, *The Jackson Phenomenon* (New York: Doubleday, 1989), 215.

12. Cruikshank, "Public Enemy: The Complete Rap," 11 (see chap. 12, n. 19).

13. Lisa Y. Sullivan, "The Demise of Black Civil Society: Once Upon A Time When We Were Colored Meets the Hip-Hop Generation," *Social Policy* (Winter 1996), 7.

14. Trey Ellis, "The New Black Aesthetic," *Callaloo* (12)1 (Winter 1989), 236, 237.

15. Ibid., 240.

16. Tate, *Flyboy,* 199 (see chap. 10, n. 21).

17. Ibid., 127,129.

18. Ibid., 125.

19. National Urban League, *Stop the Violence: Overcoming Self Destruction,* ed. Nelson George (New York: Pantheon Books, 1990), 12.

20. Robert Palmer, *Deep Blues* (New York and London: Penguin Books, 1981), 27.

21. Chuck D, interview by John Leland, unpublished transcript (July 17, 1988); from Bill Adler's Hip-Hop Archives.

22. "Public Enemy—Rebels on Fast Forward," *Caribbean Times* (UK) (November 27, 1987), 17. Julian Rake, "Behind Enemy Lines, *Sounds* (November 7, 1987), 40.

23. Ed Guerrero, *Do the Right Thing* (London: British Film Institute, 2001), 33, 84.

24. Jack Kroll, "How Hot Is Too Hot?: The Fuse Has Been Lit," *Newsweek* (July 3, 1989), 64.

25. David Denby, "He's Gotta Have It," *New York* (June 26, 1989), 53.

26. Joe Klein, "Spiked?" *New York* (June 26, 1989), 14–15.

27. Ibid. Emphasis in original text.

28. Stanley Crouch, "Do the Race Thing," *Village Voice* (June 20, 1989), 74.

29. Ibid., 74–76.

30. Kelly, "Rhyme and Reason," 63 (see chap. 12, n. 13).

31. Leland, "Do the Right Thing," 72 (see chap. 12, n. 19).

32. The Stud Brothers, "Prophets of Rage," *Melody Maker* (July 9, 1988).

33. The Stud Brothers, "Black Power," *Melody Maker* (May 28, 1988).

34. John Leland, "Armageddon in Effect," *Spin* (September 1988), 48.

35. David Mills, "Professor Griff: 'The Jews Are Wicked,' " *Washington Times* (May 22, 1989), E1.

36. Ibid., E1–E2.

37. Ibid., E2.

38. R. J. Smith, "The Enemy Within," *Village Voice* (June 20, 1989).

39. Lewis Cole, "Def or Dumb?" *Rolling Stone* (October 19, 1989), 96.

40. R. J. Smith, "Bring the Goys," *Village Voice* (June 27, 1989).

41. Chuck D, letter dated June 19, 1989; from the files of Bill Adler.

42. Armond White, "Bought. Can We Get a Witness?" *City Sun* (June 28–July 4, 1989), 15.

43. Ibid.

44. Leland, "Do the Right Thing," 100 (see chap. 12, n. 19).

45. John DeSantis, *For The Color of His Skin: The Murder of Yusuf Hawkins and the Trial of Bensonhurst* (New York: Pharos, 1991), 76.

46. Ibid., 117.

47. Claire Jean Kim, *Bitter Fruit: The Politics of Black-Korean Conflict in New York City* (New Haven: Yale University Press, 2000), 128–129.

48. Pyong Gap Min, *Caught in the Middle: Korean Communities in New York and Los Angeles* (Berkeley: University of California Press, 1996), 170–172.

49. "Boycott Public Enemy," *New York Post* (August 20, 1989).

50. Richard Harrington, "Public Enemy's Rap Record Stirs Jewish Protests," *Washington Post* (December 27, 1989), D4.

51. Harry Allen, "Why Are The Media Getting Crazed over the Cress Theory?" draft press release (May 9, 1990); from the files of Bill Adler.

14. The Culture Assassins: Geography, Generation and Gangsta Rap.

1. Cross, *It's Not About a Salary,* 201–202 (see chap. 10, n. 39).

2. Rennie Harris, interview by Rudy Corpuz (September 16, 2003).

3. Cross, *It's Not About a Salary,* 102, 143 (see chap. 10, n. 39).

4. Alejandro A. Alonso, "Territoriality Among African American Street Gangs" (master's thesis, University of Southern California, May 1999), 8.

5. Cross, *It's Not About a Salary,* 143 (see chap. 10, n. 39).

6. Terry McDermott, "Parental Advisory: Explicit Lyrics," *Los Angeles Times Magazine* (April 14, 2002). Jonathan Gold, "N.W.A.: Hard Rap and Hype from the Streets of Compton," *Los Angeles Weekly* (May 5–May 11, 1989), 17. Frank Owen, "Hanging Tough," *Spin* (April 1990), 34.

7. George Jackson, *Soledad Brother: The Prison Letters of George Jackson* (New York: Bantam, 1970), 250.

8. Alexander Cockburn, "What Goes Around, Comes Around," *The Nation* (June 1, 1992), 739.

9. J. Max Bond, "The Negro in Los Angeles" (Ph.D. diss., University of Southern California, June 1936), 12, 33. Keith E. Collins, *Black Los Angeles: The Maturing of the Ghetto, 1940–1950* (Saratoga, Calif.: Century Twenty One Publishing, 1980), 13.

10. Bond, "The Negro in Los Angeles," 12, 33. This man would find an ironic counterpart seventy years later in John Singleton's *Boyz N The Hood*, in the fictional character of Furious Styles, a Black real estate agent struggling to keep his area from being gentrified by whites and overseas Asians.

11. Collins, *Black Los Angeles,* 20–22.

12. Ibid., 70.

13. Gerald Horne, *Fire This Time: The Watts Uprisings and the 1960s* (New York: Da Capo Press, 1997), 35.

14. This is according to the Athens Park Blood O.G. named Bone, quoted in the cover story, *F.E.D.S. Magazine* (no date), 78.

15. James Vigil, *A Rainbow of Gangs* (Austin, Tex.: University of Texas Press, 2002), 67.

16. This is according to the Crip O.G. named Red, in *Uprising: Crips and Bloods Tell The Story of America's Youth in the Crossfire,* ed. Yusuf Jah and Sister Shah'Keyah (New York: Touchstone, 1997).

17. Alonso, "Territoriality Among African American Street Gangs," 74–75.

18. Richard Serrano, "Dreams of LAPD Class Become Tarnished," *Los Angeles Times* (January 21, 1992), B1.

19. This argument has been advanced most forcefully by the scholar Greg Hise. Greg Hise, *Magnetic Los Angeles* (Baltimore: Johns Hopkins University Press, 1997).

20. Horne, *Fire This Time,* 65.

21. Mike Davis, *City of Quartz* (New York: Verso, 1990), 297–298. Horne, *Fire This Time,* 99.

22. Horne, *Fire This Time,* 64–69.

23. Richard Serrano. "Dreams of LAPD Class Become Tarnished."

24. Horne, *Fire This Time,* 91.

25. *Daily Chronicle* newspaper seen in *The Fire This Time* (Blacktop Films, 1993).

26. Odie Hawkins, *Scars and Memories: The Story of a Life* (Los Angeles: Holloway House, 1987), 125.

27. Davis, *City of Quartz,* 297.

28. *F.E.D.S. Magazine,* 79.

29. Ibid.

30. Elaine Brown, *A Taste of Power: A Black Woman's Story* (New York: Pantheon, 1992), 118, 165. Jack Olsen, *Last Man Standing: The Tragedy and Triumph of Geronimo Pratt* (New York: Doubleday, 2000), 38.

31. Donald Bakeer, *Crips: The Story of the L.A. Street Gang from 1971–1985* (Los Angeles: Precocious Publishing, 1987, 1992), 116.

32. Alonso, "Territoriality Among African American Street Gangs," 90.

33. Ibid., 90–93.

34. Godfather Jimel Barnes in *Uprising,* 152.

35. Bone in *F.E.D.S. Magazine.* Leon Bing, *Do or Die* (New York: Harper Collins, 1991), 149–150. Godfather Jimel Barnes in *Uprising,* 151–152.

36. Alonso, "Territoriality Among African American Street Gangs," 91.

37. Davis, *City of Quartz,* 300.

38. Alonso, "Territoriality Among African American Street Gangs," 7, 97.

39. Ibid., 95.

40. Bone in *F.E.D.S. Magazine,* 82.

41. Alonso, "Territoriality Among African American Street Gangs," 98.

42. Bettijane Levine, "An OG Tries to Make Things Right," *Los Angeles Times* (November 24, 1991), E2.

43. Research Group on the Los Angeles Economy, *The Widening Divide: Income Inequallity and Poverty in Los Angeles* (Los Angeles: UCLA Urban Planning Program, 1989), 1.

44. Robin D. G. Kelley, *Race Rebels: Culture, Politics and the Black Working Class* (New York: The Free Press, 1994), 192.

45. California Legislature, Senate, Office of Research, *The South-Central Los Angeles and Koreatown Riots: A Study of Civil Unrest* (Sacramento: State Senate Office of Research, June 17, 1992), 3.

46. Sandy Banks, "Health Center A Vital Aid in Distressed Community," *Los Angeles Times* (January 27, 1985), Metro sect., 1.

47. "Metro Digest: Local News in Brief," *Los Angeles Times* (November 17, 1987), 2.

48. Michael Krikorian and Greg Krikorian, "Watts Truce Holds Even As Hopes Fade," *Los Angeles Times* (May 18, 1997), B1.

49. Cross, *It's Not About a Salary,* 197 (see chap. 10, n. 39).

50. John Glionna, "A Murder That Woke Up L.A.," *Los Angeles Times* (January 30, 1998), A1. Sandy Banks, "Fate Leads Witnesses to Focal Point of Gang Strife," *Los Angeles Times* (October 1, 1989).

51. Kenneth J. Garcia, "Residents Still Coping with Raid's Effects. Police Gang Sweep Left Families Homeless," *Los Angeles Times* (January 6, 1989), Metro sect., 1.

52. John L. Mitchell, "The Raid That Still Haunts L.A.," *Los Angeles Times* (March 14, 2001), A1.

53. John A. Oswald, "LAPD to Investigate Raid Damage," *Los Angeles Times* (August 5, 1988), Metro sect., 1.

54. Marc Cooper, "L.A.'s State of Siege: City of Angeles, Cops From Hell," in *Inside The*

L.A. Riots: What Really Happened and Why It Will Happen Again, ed. Don Hazen (San Francisco: Institute For Alternative Journalism, 1992), 15.

55. Bob Baker, "A Year After Westwood Killing, L.A. Outrage Makes Little Impact on Gang Epidemic," *Los Angeles Times* (January 30, 1989), 1.

56. Cooper, "L.A.'s State of Siege," 14. Bill Martinez, interview (September 18, 2003). (Martinez is a gang intervention trainer and former community youth gang services staffer.) Wendy E. Lane, "DA's Report: Almost Half of L.A. County's Young Black Males in Gangs," Associated Press wire report (May 21, 1992).

57. Gregory Sandow, "What's NWA All About? Anger, Yes. Violence, No," *Los Angeles Herald Examiner* (July 16, 1989), E-1, E-10.

58. Dave Marsh and Phyllis Pollack, "Wanted for Attitude," *Village Voice* (October 10. 1989), 33.

59. David Mills, "The Gangsta Rapper: Violent Hero or Negative Role Model?" *The Source* (December 1990).

60. Rob Marriott, James Bernard and Allen S. Gordon, "Reality Check," *The Source* (June 1994), 64–65.

15. The Real Enemy: The Cultural Riot of Ice Cube's *Death Certificate*.

1. Cheo Hodari Coker, "Down for Whatever," *The Source* (February 1994).

2. Owen, "Hanging Tough," 34 (see chap. 14, n. 6).

3. Ibid., 32, 34.

4. Terry McDermott. "Parental Advisory: Explicit Lyrics" (see chap. 14, n. 6).

5. Eric Ture Muhammad, "An Elegy for Khallid Abdul Muhammad" (March 2001). Available online at 360hiphop.com.

6. Angela Y. Davis, "Black Nationalism: The Sixties and the Nineties," in *Black Popular Culture*, ed. Gina Dent (Seattle: Bay Press, 1992), 322.

7. Ibid., 327.

8. "A Conversation with Angela Davis and Ice Cube" (Priority Records promotional video, 1991). The original transcript for this 20-minute video (incorrectly dated July 29, 1992; the actual date is likely July 29, 1991) is from the archives of Bill Adler.

9. "A Conversation with Angela Davis and Ice Cube," original transcript. (This exchange was also published in an abridged version in "Nappy Happy," *Transition* 58 [1992], 181–182.)

10. Ibid., 30–31.

11. Elaine H. Kim, "Home Is Where the Han Is," in *Reading Rodney King, Reading Urban Uprising* (New York: Routledge, 1993), 217, 255.

12. Paul Ong and Suzanne Hee, *Losses in the Los Angeles Civil Unrest* (Los Angeles: Center for Pacific Rim Studies, University of California, 1993).

13. Jube Shiver, "Poor Penalized as Food Chains Exit Inner City," *Los Angeles Times* (January 2, 1989).

14. Larry Aubry, "Death and Violence: Unfortunate Equalizers," *Los Angeles Sentinel* (October 17, 1991), 6A.

15. Seth Mydans, "Shooting Puts Focus on Korean-Black Frictions in Los Angeles," *Los Angeles Times* (October 6, 1991), 20.

16. K. W. Lee, "The Haunting Prelude," *KoreAm Journal* (April 2002), 27.

17. "Koreans Say Conflict is Economic, Not Racial," *Los Angeles Sentinel* (October 17, 1991), 17A.

18. Ibid.

19. "A Conversation with Angela Davis and Ice Cube," original transcript, 7–9.

20. "Cracked Ice," *The Economist* 321, no. 7735 (November 30, 1991).

21. David Samuels, "The Rap on Rap," *New Republic* (November 11, 1991), 29.

22. Editorial, *Billboard* (November 23, 1991).

23. James Bernard, " 'Death Certificate' Gives Birth to Debate," *Billboard* (December 7, 1991).

24. Quoted in Dennis Hunt, "Outrageous As He Wants to Be," *Los Angeles Times* (November 3, 1991).

25. Ice Cube, promotional interview tape (Priority Records, 1991).

26. Lawrence Bobo, James Johnson, Melvin Oliver, James Sidanius and Camille Zubrinsky, "Public Opinion Before and After a Spring of Discontent," Occasional Working Paper Series, 3 (Los Angeles: UCLA Center for the Study of Urban Poverty, September 1992).

27. Dong Suh, "The Source of Korean and African American Tensions," *Asian Week* (February 21, 1992).

28. Chuck Phillips. "Wiesenthal Center Denounces Ice Cube's Album." *Los Angeles Times.* November 2, 1991.

29. Sophia Kyung Kim, "Chilling Fields: Ice Cube Rap," *Korea Times* (November 11, 1991).

30. John Leland, "Cube on Thin Ice," *Newsweek* (December 2, 1991), 69.

31. Richard Reyes Fruto, "KAGRO Puts Freeze on Ice Cube," *Korea Times* (November 18, 1991).

32. Lynne Duke, "Rapper's Number Chills Black-Korean Relations," *Washington Post* (December 1, 1991).

33. Richard Reyes Fruto, "St. Ide's Cans Ice Cube," *Korea Times* (November 11, 1991).

34. Sophia Kyung Kim, "Ice Cube the Peacemaker," *Korea Times* (May 4, 1992).

35. Ibid.

36. Lou Cannon, *Official Negligence* (New York: Times Books, 1997), 166.

LOOP 4. Stakes Is High: 1992–2001.

16. Gonna Work It Out: Peace and Rebellion in Los Angeles.

1. Judy Pasternak, "In the Crossfire: L.A.'s Gang Crisis," *Los Angeles Times* (February 5, 1989), 1.

2. Raegan Kelly, "Watts Love: The Truce Is ON!" *URB Magazine* 3, no. 6 (1993), 42.

3. Jocelyn Stewart, "Civil Rights Groups out of Touch, Many Blacks Believe," *Los Angeles Times* (August 31, 1992), A1.

4. Dollie Ryan, "Farrakhan Eulogizes Slain Muslim," United Press International wire report (January 27, 1990).

5. "Nation of Islam Leader Tells Crowd: 'Stop the Killing,'" Associated Press wire report (February 3, 1990).

6. Andrea Ford and Charisse Jones, "Respect Life, Farrakhan Asks L.A. Crowd," *Los Angeles Times* (February 3, 1990), B1.

7. Beatriz Johnson Hernandez, "Searching for Inner-City Peace," *Third Force* (June 1996), 18.

8. Rich Connell, "Reaction Mixed in Boycott," *Los Angeles Times* (February 22, 1989), B1. Jesse Katz, "Corrupting Power of Life on the Streets," *Los Angeles Times* (May 15, 1994), A1.

9. Stephanie Chavez and Louis Sahagun, "Slaying by LAPD Becomes Rallying Point," *Los Angeles Times* (January 5, 1992), B1.

10. Multi-Peace Treaty, signed April 29, 1994. The treaty, Sherrills explains, was agreed upon verbally, but not signed until the second anniversary of the rebellion in a formal ceremony at Imperial Courts. The treaty was signed by ex-gang representatives from Hacienda, Imperial Courts, Jordan Downs and Nickerson Gardens. Also see Jesse Katz and Andrea Ford, "Ex-Gang Members Look to Mideast for a Peace Plan," *Los Angeles Times* (June 17, 1992), B1. Kelly, "Watts Love: The Truce Is ON!" 45.

11. Katz and Ford, "Ex-Gang Members Look to Mideast for a Peace Plan."

12. Ibid.

13. Jeffrey Anderson, "Dealing with a Monster," *Los Angeles Weekly* (January 30–February 5, 2004).

14. David Whitman, "The Untold Story of the L.A. Riot," *U.S. News and World Report* (May 31, 1993), 34.

15. Cannon, *Official Negligence,* 319–320 (see chap. 15, n. 36).

16. Jim Crogan, "Riot Chronology," in *Inside The L.A. Riots,* 35 (see chap. 14, n. 54).

17. *Birth of a Nation: 4x29x92,* directed by Matthew McDaniel (1994).

18. Cannon, *Official Negligence,* 322 (see chap. 15, n. 36).

19. Ibid., 324.

20. Ashley Dunn, "The Riots' Enduring Wounds," *Los Angeles Times* (August 18, 1992), A1. Robert Jablon, "51 Lives and Deaths in the City of Angels," Associated Press wire report (May 14, 1992).

21. Cannon, *Official Negligence,* 328 (see chap. 15, n. 36).

22. Paul Lieberman, "ACLU Lawsuit Charges Riot Curfew Was Illegal," *Los Angeles Times* (June 24, 1992), B1. Ashley Dunn, "Years of '2-Cent' Insults Added Up to Rampage," *Los Angeles Times* (May 7, 1992), A1.

23. Dunn, "Years of '2-Cent' Insults Added Up to Rampage."

24. Paul Ong and Suzanne Hee, *Losses in the Los Angeles Civil Unrest: April 29–May 1, 1992* (Los Angeles: UCLA Center for Pacific Rim Studies, 1993), 12.

25. Dunn, "The Riots' Enduring Wounds."

26. State of California Emergency Medical Services Authority. *Medical Care for the Injured: The Emergency Medical Response to the April 1992 Civil Disturbance* (March 1993). EMSA #393-01. http://www.usc.edu/isd/archives/cityinstress/medical/table11.html

27. Ibid., http://www.usc.edu/isd/archives/cityinstress/medical/table02.html

28. Mike Davis, "Uprising and Repression In L.A.," in *Reading Rodney King Reading Urban Uprising,* 142 (see chap. 15, n. 11).

29. Howard Rosenberg, "Medium's Influence Sometimes Warps Our Sense of Reality," *Los Angeles Times* (May 2, 1992), A8.

30. Davis, "Uprising and Repression In L.A.," 145.

31. Mike Davis, "In L.A., Burning All Illusions," *The Nation* (June 1, 1992), 743. "10 Years After the Riots: In Their Own Words," *Los Angeles Times Magazine* (April 28, 2002).

32. Melvin Oliver, James H. Johnson Jr. and Walter C. Farrell Jr., "Anatomy of a Rebellion: A Political-Economic Analysis," in *Reading Rodney King Reading Urban Uprising,* 121 (see chap. 15, n. 11).

33. Louis Sahagun and Patrick J. McDonnell, "Mother Prays, Burns Candles for Disabled Girl Missing in Riot," *Los Angeles Times* (May 7, 1992).

34. Isabel Alegria, "Hispanics Round Up During L.A. Riots," on *National Public Radio Morning Edition,* broadcast May 14, 1992.

35. Ong and Hee, 12 (see chap. 15, n. 12).

36. The Staff of the *Los Angeles Times, Understanding the Riots: Los Angeles Before and After the Rodney King Case* (Los Angeles: Los Angeles Times, July 1992), 65.

37. Stuart Butler, "The Urban Policy America Needs," Heritage Foundation Reports, Executive Memorandum No. 330 (May 5. 1992).

38. Martin Walker, "Less Welfare, More Warfare" *The Guardian* (London) (May 6, 1992), 21, citing a report by the Center on Budget and Policy Priorities.

17. All in the Same Gang: The War on Youth and the Quest for Unity.

1. Don Lee, "5 Years Later a Mixed Legacy of Rebuilding," *Los Angeles Times* (April 22, 1997), A1.

2. James Sterngold, "L.A. Story: What Is Made of Broken Promises," *New York Times* (October 13, 1996), 1.

3. Marcos Frommer, "An Interview with Mike Davis," *Chicago Review* 38, no. 4 (1992).

4. April Lynch, "L.A. Gangs Clinging to a Shaky Truce," *San Francisco Chronicle* (June 2, 1992), A1.

5. Ice T, as told to Heidi Siegmund, *The Ice Opinion* (New York: St. Martin's Press, 1994), 149–150.

6. Michael and Greg Krikorian, "Watts Truce Holds Even As Hopes Fade," *Los Angeles Times* (May 18, 1997), B1.

7. Syvester Monroe, "Trading Colors For A Future," *Emerge* (August 1993), 46.

8. Peter Leyden, "Can Gang Members Turn the Tide Toward Peace?" *Minneapolis Star-Tribune* (August 31, 1992), 1A.

9. Russell Ben-Ali, "Deadly Force Wish: Gang Pact: An Uneasy LA Truce," *Newsday* (May 10, 1992), 7.

10. Frommer, "An Interview with Mike Davis."

11. Ron Allen, *CBS Evening News,* broadcast May 22, 1992.

12. *Larry King Live,* CNN, broadcast May 27, 1992.

13. Jennifer Rowland, "L.A. Police Say Gang Truce Works," United Press International wire report (June 17, 1992).

14. Richard A. Serrano and Jesse Katz, "LAPD Gang Task Force Deployed Despite Truce," *Los Angeles Times* (June 26, 1992), A1.

15. Luis Rodriguez, Cle "Bone" Sloan and Kershaun "Lil Monster" Scott, "Gangs: The New Political Force in Los Angeles," *Los Angeles Times* (September 13, 1992), M1.

16. Muhammad, *Chronology of Nation of Islam History,* 58 (see chap. 11, n. 17).

17. Mike Males, *Framing Youth: Ten Myths About the Next Generation* (Monroe, Maine: Common Courage Press, 1999), 8.

18. ACLU Foundation of Southern California, *False Promises, False Premises: The Blythe Street Gang Injunction and Its Aftermath* (May 1997), 44.

19. Building Blocks for Youth, *And Justice for Some* (2000). http://www.buildingblocksforyouth.org/justiceforsome/jfs.html

20. Sasha Abramsky, *Hard Time Blues: How Politics Built a Prison Nation* (New York: St. Martin's Press, 2002), 63.

21. Ibid., 71–72.

22. Jason Zeidenburg and Vince Schiraldi, *Cellblocks or Classrooms?: The Funding of Higher Education and Corrections and Its Impact on African American Men* (Washington, D.C.: Justice Policy Institute), 2002.

23. Marc Mauer, *The Sentencing Project: Race To Incarcerate* (New York: The New Press, 1999), 169–170.

24. James Q. Wilson, "Crime and Public Policy," in *Crime,* ed. James Q. Wilson and Joan Petersilia (San Francisco: Institute for Contemporary Studies Press, 1995), 507.

25. Tipper Gore, "Hate, Rape and Rap," *Washington Post* (January 8, 1990), A15.

26. Mark Pankowski, "Seminole Sheriff Raps 2 Live Crew's Music," *Orlando Sentinel* (February 24, 1990), D1. Chuck Philips, "The 'Batman' Who Took on Rap," *Los Angeles Times* (June 18, 1990), F1.

27. Phyllis Pollack. "FBI Hit List Sa Prize Part II," *The Source.* (September 1990, 20.)

28. Nelson George, "She Has a Dream," *Village Voice* (circa October 1990; specific date unavailable); from the files of Bill Adler. Robert Knight, "Antihero," *Spin* (August 1992), 97.

29. David Mills, "Sister Souljah's Call to Arms," *Washington Post* (May 13, 1992), B1.

30. Thomas Edsall, "Clinton Stuns Rainbow Coalition," *Washington Post* (June 14, 1992), A1. *Crossfire,* CNN, transcript of June 15, 1992, broadcast.

31. Knight, "Antihero."

32. Edsall, "Clinton Stuns Rainbow Coalition."

33. Gwen Ifill, "Clinton Deftly Navigates Shoals of Racial Issues," *New York Times* (June 17, 1992), A22.

34. Chuck Philips, "Police Groups Urge Halt of Record's Sale," *Los Angeles Times* (June 16, 1992), F1.

35. Remarks made by Vice President Dan Quayle to the National Association of Radio Talk Show Hosts Fourth Annual Convention, at the Mayflower Hotel, Washington D.C. Transcript, June 19, 1992.

36. John Stehr, "Vice President Agrees With Clinton About Sister Souljah," *CBS Morning News,* transcript of June 23, 1992, broadcast.

37. Chuck Philips, "Cop Killer Controversy Spurs Ice-T Album Sales," *Los Angeles Times* (June 18, 1992), F1.

38. "Amnesty Decries L.A. 'Torture,' " Associated Press wire report (June 27, 1992).

39. Susan Spillman, "More Heat on Ice-T's 'Cop Killer,' " *USA Today* (July 17, 1992), D1.

40. Tracey Kaplan and Jim Zamora, "The Heat Turns Out for Ice-T Rap Concert," *Los Angeles Times* (July 25, 1992), B1.

41. "Warner Pulls 'Cop Killer' At Ice-T's Request," United Press International wire report (July 28, 1992).

42. Ibid.

43. Ice T, as told to Heidi Siegmund, *The Ice Opinion,* 183.

44. *Talk Back Live,* CNN, transcript of October 13, 1995, broadcast.

45. Tony White, "We're Ready to Take Our Place," *Richmond Afro-American* (August 23, 1995), 1.

46. Beth Harpaz, "Angela Davis Denounces Farrakhan March for Excluding Women," Associated Press wire report (October 14, 1995).

47. Salim Muwakkil, "Divided Loyalties," *In These Times* (February 17, 1997), 24.

48. Jeanne Dewey and Brian Blomquist, "Black Foes of March Schedule Visible Events in Opposition," *Washington Times* (October 15, 1995), A11.

49. Michelangelo Signorile, "Queer in a Million," *OUT Magazine* (February 1996). http://www.signorile.coom/articles/outqiam.html

50. Hamil R. Harris and John F. Harris, "March Called Endorsement of Farrakhan," *Washington Post* (October 13, 1995), A21.

51. Roderick Terry, *One Million Strong* (Edgewood, Md.: Duncan & Duncan, 1996), 52–53.

52. Signorile, "Queer in a Million."

53. Diane Weathers and Tara Roberts, "Kathleen Cleaver and Angela Davis: Rekindling The Flame," *Essence* (May 1996), 82.

54. Ibid.

55. "Interview: Angela Davis," from the Web page "*Frontline:* The Two Nations of Black America," available on the PBS Web site at http://www.pbs.org/wgbh/pages/frontline/shows/race/interviews/Davis.html. The interview was conducted in 1997.

18. Becoming the Hip-Hop Generation: *The Source,* The Industry and the Big Crossover.

1. Maximillian Potter. "Getting to The Source," *GQ* (December 2001), 149.

2. *The Source* Rate Kit (1991).

3. The Source Mind Squad, "Rap Session," *The Source* (January 1992), 40.

4. Meg Cox, "Little Rap-Music Magazine Has Big Aims," *Wall Street Journal* (September 25, 1991), B1–B2.

5. Ibid. See also Janice Kelly, "The Printed Word," *Advertising Age* (May 11, 1992), 45.

6. Douglas McGill, "Nike Is Bounding Past Reebok," *New York Times* (July 11, 1989), D3. "The Year's 25 Most Fascinating Business People," *Fortune* (January 1990), 62.

7. Randall Rothenberg, "Second Shoe Drops for Image Ads," *New York Times* (February 19, 1989), D1.

8. Nelson George, *The Death of Rhythm and Blues* (New York: Pantheon Books, 1988), 160.

9. Randall Rothenberg, "Shift Sought from 'Black' to 'Urban,'" *New York Times* (November 30, 1989), D19.

10. Paul Grein, "Pop Eye: Rappers Welcome MTV's Enthusiasm," *Los Angeles Times* (June 18, 1989), 64.

11. Janice Simpson, "Yo! Rap Gets On The Map," *Time* (February 5, 1990), 60.

12. Sources say that the advance promotion cassettes contained explicit references to Heller and his Jewishness.

13. William Upski Wimsatt, *Bomb the Suburbs* (Chicago: Subway and Elevated Press. 1994).

14. Ibid.

15. Anne Marie Kerwin and Melanie Warner, "Check It Out: 10 Independently Published Periodicals with Over 50,000 Circulation," *Inside Media* (May 25, 1994), 48.

16. Ibid.

17. David Mills, "Jonathan Van Meter: The Corporate Hip-Hop Hope," *Washington Post* (September 14, 1992), D1.

18. Scott Donaton, "New Hip-Hop Magazine Attracts Mainstream Ads," *Advertising Age* (September 14, 1992), 3.

19. Naomi Klein, *No Logo* (New York: Picador, 1999), 76.

20. Danyel Smith, "Preface," *The Vibe History of Hip Hop* (New York: Three Rivers Press, 1999), ix.

21. Alan Mirabella, "Rap Magazine Gets Busy, Trailblazer Diversifies, Gains Amid Turmoil," *Crain's New York Business* (January 9, 1995), 3.

22. Letter from James Bernard to David Mays, September 28, 1994.

23. James Bernard, "Negative Reviews," *The Source* (November 1994), 8.

24. Steve Hochman, "Pop Eye," *Los Angeles Times* (October 16, 1994).

25. Brett Sokol, "He Ain't Guilty, He's My Partner," *Miami New Times* (September 6. 2001).

26. Potter, "Getting to the Source."

27. Brett Sokol, "It's a Hip-Hop World," *Miami New Times* (July 5, 2001).

28. Jose Martinez, "Newly Freed Made Men Front Man Raps Press," *Boston Herald* (November 4, 2000), 5.

29. Brett Sokol, "Still in the Hood?" *Miami New Times* (May 22, 2003).

19. New World Order: Globalization, Containment and Counterculture at the End of the Century.

1. M. William Cooper, *Behold a Pale Horse* (Flagstaff, Ariz.: Light Technology Publishing, 1991), 267.

2. Ben Bagdikian, *The Media Monopoly* (Boston: Beacon Press, 1997), xiii.

3. Ed Chrisman, "Indies No. 1 In Total Album Market Share for First Time," *Billboard* (January 18, 1998).

4. Michael Roberts, "Papa's Got a Brand New Bag," in *Rhythm & Business: The Political Economy of Black Music*, ed. Norman Kelley (Brooklyn: Akashic Books, 2002), 36.

5. Cristina Verán, "Soul by the Pound," *One World* (December 2002/January 2003).

6. Niren Tolsi, "Preacher Men," *Rage: South African Street Culture Online*. http://www.rage.co.za/issue30/durbaug.htm.

7. Verán, "Soul by the Pound," 82.

8. Chuck Philips, "Anti-Rap Crusader Under Fire," *Los Angeles Times* (March 20, 1996), A1.

9. United States Senate, Committee of the Judiciary, Hearing Before the Subcommittee on Juvenile Justice, *Shaping Our Responses to Violent and Demeaning Imagery in Popular Music*, February 23, 1994, 14.

10. Ibid., 10.

11. William Upski Wimsatt, "State of The Movement," in *Future 500: Youth Organizing and Activism in the United States*, comp. Jee Kim, Mathilda de Rios, Pablo Caraballo, Manuela Arciniegas, Ibrahim Abdul-Martin and Kofi Taha (New Orleans, La.: Subway and Elevated, 2002), 4.

12. Nora Zamichow, "Ex-Gang Member Gets Political Asylum," *Los Angeles Times* (July 12, 2002).

Acknowledgments

It wouldn't be hip-hop without a ton of shout-outs. That's because no hip-hopper counts their success—however big or small—as individual. There are debts and reciprocations at every turn, and it's good that way.

This book began on a long trip back from Lake Tahoe in the cab of a tow truck in January 1998. We had just decided to end SoleSides, a project to which I had devoted the better part of five years. At that moment, change seemed in order. It wasn't until three and half years later that I had the distance to recognize that my next big project was already in motion.

So this first shout-out goes to Josh Davis, Xavier Mosley, Tom Shimura, Lateef Daumont, Joy Malig, Tim Parker and Lisa Haugen, who seemed to know what I was put here to do and set me off to do it. A deeply felt appreciation goes to Brian Cross, who applied the necessary verbal ass-whipping to get me moving. To those that gave their all to the old SoleSides—Winston Chiong, Gene Kim Whitney, David Maduli, Jason Malig, Omari Patterson, Rodney Sino-Cruz, Benjamin Davis (R.I.P) and all the others who were down—I ain't forgot you. To D-Sharp and Alicia, the Lifesavas fam, Isaac Bess and Lydia Popovich, the legacy continues.

To all those who generously opened up their lives to me: the Melendezes, the Suarezes, DJ Kool Herc and Cindy Campbell, Afrika Bambaataa, Lucky Strike, FABEL and Christie, Jazzy Jay, Kool Lady Blue, Grandmaster Flash, BOM 5, ZEPHYR, Joseph Ahn, King Tee and crew, Reginald Dennis, James Bernard, Alex Sanchez, Silvia Beltran, Aqeela and Daude Sherrills, Bakari Kitwana, Bill Stephney, Harry Allen, Felipe Mercado, Danny DeJesus, Charlie Ahearn, Chuck D, Hank Shocklee, Crazy Legs, Dante Ross, David Hershkovits, DJ AJ, DOZE, FAB 5 FREDDY, Greg Tate, Ice Cube, Kam, LADY PINK, Leyla Turkkan, Rennie Harris, Rudy Corpuz, Matthew Countryman, Pedro Noguera, R. J. Smith, Sadiki Nia, Tamu du Ewa, SPAR ONE, IZ THE WIZ, Steven Hager, Tom Silverman, Talib Kweli, Uncle Jam, Egyptian Lover, Iceberg, Andrei Strobert, Chuck Brown, Reo Edwards, Steve Barrow, Dave Katz, Jasmine De La Rosa, Roger Steffens, and the many more heads, players and creators whom I've spoken with through the years, I hope that I represented well.

Thank you to the libraries and librarians that fed my ravenous appetite—the Brooklyn Public Library, the Donnell Library, the Schomburg Center, the Lincoln

Acknowledgments

Center Library, the Museum of Television and Radio, the U.C. Berkeley libraries, the Berkeley Public Library, and especially, Bill Adler's Hip-Hop Archives. To the Ego Trip crew, thanks for the free advice, the magazine lending library, the job offer and the jokes. To Jacquie Juceam, Michelle Lin, Pat Meschino, Radcliffe Roye and family, Corey, Miss P and Jah Lou, Afflicted Yard, Ajamu Myrie, Dave Kelly, Jeremy Harding, Sean Paul, Italee, and Tullah Carter, thanks for the island hospitality.

To everyone involved in the UCLA Asian American Studies Center, the Applied Research Center, and the Center for Third World Organizing, thanks for letting me soak up game and always having my back. To the editors that always demanded more—Raymond Roker, Sue Cummings, Sheena Lester, Danyel Smith, J. H. Tompkins, Jon Dolan, Selwyn Seyfu Hinds, Chuck Eddy, Bob Christgau; to the homies who gave much and asked for little—Rickey Vincent, Davey D, Billy Jam, Adisa Banjoko, Tomas Palermo, Cheo Hodari Coker, Rob Kenner, Serena Kim, Todd Inoue, Cristina Verán, Joe Schloss and Ogbonna Ogbar, thank you for leaving me better than you found me.

To the entire crew from 360hiphop.com, every day was an honor, and thanks for never letting me sip wack juice. To the Soundings crew past and present—Jon Caramanica, Neil Drumming, Will Hermes, Charles Aaron, Windy Chien, Sia Michel, Sylvia Chan, Mark Anthony Neal, Ta-Nehisi Coates, Josh DuLac, Sasha Frere-Jones, Jessica Hopper, Julianne Shepherd, Josh Kun, Amanda Nowinski, Mosi Reeves, Peter Shapiro, Tony Green, Hua Hsu, Chris Ryan, R. J. Smith, Elizabeth Mendez Berry—we came, we saw, we got our bylines.

To the organizers and activists that keep the world moving forward: Billy UPSKI Wimsatt, Kofi Taha, Kate Rhee, Angela Brown, Malika Sanders, Favianna Rodriguez, Weyland Southon, Gita Drury, Tram Nguyen, Jee Kim, Van Jones and the EBC Crew, Taj James and the MSC Crew, Malkia Cyril and the YMC Crew, Harmony, Nicole, Omana and everyone at Mandela Arts Center, Bakari Kitwana, Baye Adofo-Wilson, Boots Riley, Dereca Blackmon, Troy Nkrumah, Angela Garretson, Jeff Johnson, Reverend Osagyefo Sekou, Hashim Shomari, Daryl Scipio, Angela Woodson, Jessica Tully, Jan Adams, Libero Della Piana, Mark Toney, Gabriel Torres, Black Artemis, Danny Hoch, Raquel Cepeda, the Hard Knock Radio crew, the Divine Forces Radio crew, Jeff Perlstein, Kristina Rizga and the Media Alliance crew, the PopandPolitics.com crew, the Alternet and Wiretap crew, Bill Martinez, Monifa Akinwole, Kali Akuno, and the Malcolm X Grassroots Movement, Marinieves Alba, Peter Chung, Kim McGillicuddy, Kevin Powell, Kimi Lee, David Muhammad, Jiaching Chen, Edget Betru, Jennifer "J-Love" Calderon, Robin Templeton, James Kass, Martha Diaz, Tricia Wang, Hekter Gonzalez, Jeremy Lahoud, Homies Unidos, the Community Self-Determination Institute, the Kensington Welfare Rights Union, Pacific News Service, Listen, Inc., CAAAV, the National Hip-Hop Political Convention, Bay-LOC, the LA LOC, San Jose Hip-Hop Coup, Future 500+, there are so many more to name—thank you all for your inspiration.

To all the folks who made great things happen: Russell Simmons, Robin D. G. Kelley, Joe Austin, Roberta Uno, San San Wong, the La Peña crew, Amanda Berger, Alvin Starks, Anna Lefer, Jolyn Matsumuro, Gerry Villareal, Jody Miller, Gabe Tesoriero, Nikkia Jackson, Mark Hines, Nikki Smith, Kris Ex, Ola Kudu, Nandi Dallen, Stephanie Reyes, Andrea Duncan, Yvette Russell, Kweli Wright, Sonya Maggett, Ryan Pintado-Vertner, Chris Veltri, Eothen Alapatt, Barbara Osborn, Eric Weisbard, Ann Powers, Raquel Cepeda, Joan Morgan, Eric Ture Muhammad, Nisa Muhammad, Adam Mansbach, Tanya Diaz, Margaret Rea, Martine Barrat, Karl Evanzz, Zen & Tanya Matsuura, Cedric Muhammad, Rebecca Deshpande, Vince Beiser, Monika Bauerlein, Tim Dickinson, Johnny Temple, Hillary Frey, William Jelani Cobb, Farai Chideya, Raymond Codrington, Mike Davis, Karen Dere, Tricia Rose, Simon Reynolds, Dawn-Elissa Fischer, Sandy Close, Adrian Gaskins, Ann-Marie Nicholson, Janet Francedese, Michael Jarrett, Theresa Park, Assata Wright, Akiba Solomon, King EMZ, Tom Goldfogle, Rha Goddess, Andy Hsiao, Tisha Hooks, Chisun Lee, Jehmu Greene, Darren Keast, Craig Smith, Lillian Matulic, Roberta Magrini, Adam Ma'anit, Lisa Lowe, Vijay Prashad, Thuylinh Tu, Tony Silver, Shelana DeSilva, Richie Monroe, Ed Park, Phyllis Pollack, Jim Prigoff, Devin Roberson, Luis Rodriguez, East Wind Books, Tresa Sanders, Trevor Schoonmaker, Paul Heck, Norman Stolzoff, Corey Takahashi, Julio Trejo, Mattie Weiss, Eric Arnold, David Paul, Peanut Butter Wolf, Shingo Annen, Spence Abbott, Jason Bentley, Elinor Tatum, Walter Leapheart, Lathan Hodge, Janice Suguitan, Richard Goldstein, Armond White, Sally Banes, Mimi Valdes, Shani Saxob-Parrish, Erik Parker, and the whole *Vibe* crew, Kathryn McGuire, Andre Torres, Joann Wypijewski, and especially everyone else I forgot, thank you.

Acknowledgments

To the indefatigable, incessantly intricate Dave Tompkins, still the best hip-hop writer ever born, thanks for the save. Thanks to Dan McCarthy and Sanjev De-Silva for transcriptions. Thanks to all the graphic designers whose visions have blessed this project: James Sinclair and the St. Martin's Press design department, Sharon Mizota, the Brent Rollins Design Explosion, Keith Tamashiro at Soap Design, EugeneKuo @ 226-design, and Mike Stern of Origin.

Big ups to the tireless and endlessly resourceful Monica Hernandez, who secured many of the photos in this book. Thanks to all the photographers and agencies: Ben Higa, Martha Cooper, Josh Cheuse, Ajamu, Brian Jahn, Mel Rosenthal, Daniel Hastings, Beuford Smith, Peter Holderness, Lisa Haun, Librado Romero, Matt Daly, Michael Benabib, Eli Reed, Alex Webb, Kevin Winter, John Van Hasselt, Michael Heller at 911 Pictures, Julie Grahame at Retna, Lisa Haun, Jonathan Hyams at the Michael Ochs Archive, Katie Shanks at Corbis, Phyllis Collazo at the New York Times Agency, Michael Shulman at Magnum, and Thomas Tinervin at Getty Images.

Much love to Gary Delgado, Don T. Nakanishi, Glenn Omatsu, Makani Themba-Nixon, Bob Wing, Davy D, Bill Adler, and Henry Chalfant, whom I adopted as mentors, and who all suffered me with great humor, and to Mike and Linette Nardone, Joseph Patel, Jungwon Kim and Sango Amoda, and Oliver Wang, whose boundless generosity sustained me.

To all my blood kin from the Pacific to the Atlantic and around the world, I have been informed that if I were to thank each and every one of you individually the price of the book would have to go up by several dollars. Business Affairs has asked me to thank you all for your consideration. I'll make you some fried rice.

Thanks to Benee and Diane. Thanks to the great staff at St. Martin's Press, especially John Cunningham, Elizabeth Bewley, Mark Steven Long, Barbara Gratch Cohen, Becki Heller and Stephen Lee. And to the folks who pulled me through from beginning to end: the Changs (Eugene and Eleanor, Spencer and May, Fletcher and Joanne) and Pagaduans (Nestor and Melinda, Agnes and Raul, Ryan, Brandon and Justin, Arnel and Heidi), my super-agent Victoria Sanders, my super-editor Monique Patterson, the incredible Imani Wilson, my boys, Jonathan and Solomon, and my boss, Lourdes. For all of your good vibes, hard work, timely rants and raves, and especially your patience, I am forever grateful and indebted.

And it's good that way.

Index

Index

Index

Index

Index

Index